READING
AUTOBIOGRAPHY NOW

READING AUTOBIOGRAPHY NOW

An Updated Guide for Interpreting Life Narratives

THIRD EDITION

Sidonie Smith and
Julia Watson

University of Minnesota Press
Minneapolis
London

Copyright 2024 by the Regents of the University of Minnesota

First edition published in 2001 and second edition in 2010 by the University of Minnesota Press

All rights reserved. No part of this publication may be reproduced, stored in a retrieval system, or transmitted, in any form or by any means, electronic, mechanical, photocopying, recording, or otherwise, without the prior written permission of the publisher.

Published by the University of Minnesota Press
111 Third Avenue South, Suite 290
Minneapolis, MN 55401–2520
http://www.upress.umn.edu

ISBN 978-1-5179-1687-9 (hc)
ISBN 978-1-5179-1688-6 (pb)

Library of Congress record available at https://lccn.loc.gov/2024002413

The University of Minnesota is an equal-opportunity educator and

employer.

For our colleagues in the International Auto/Biography Association

and for our departed and beloved family members
Gregory Grieco and Barbara Watson Hill

and our dear departed friends
Janet Braun-Reinitz, Gisela Brinker-Gabler, and Kay Schaffer

What eye can see itself?

—Stendhal, *The Life of Henry Brulard*

Contents

Preface xi

Part I. Theorizing Life Narrative

1–Defining and Discerning Life Narrative Forms 3

2–Autobiographical Subjects 39

3–Autobiographical Acts 103

4–What about Autobiographical Truth? 153

Part II. A Guide to Reading Life Narrative

5–Reading Life Narratives: A Tool Kit of Strategies 169

6–Kinds of Life Narratives: A Compendium of Key Concepts and Genres 193

Acknowledgments 319

Notes 325

Bibliography 333

Publication History 395

Index 397

Preface

Life narrative studies has become an expansive, transnational, multimedia field. This third edition, *Reading Autobiography Now: An Updated Guide for Interpreting Life Narratives*, offers a comprehensive critical exploration of its diverse features. We provide both an updated discussion of theorizing life narrative and an expanded, user-friendly compendium for engaging with it. Situating autobiographical texts and acts in relation to other genres, we consider not only the established ones of biography, history writing, and fiction but also the emergent ones of autotheory, autoethnography, and autofiction. We extend the theoretical exploration of autobiographical subjects by analyzing the concept of relationality. And we expand the exploration of kinds of autobiographical acts to include graphic, witnessing, online, and computational "I" variations. To address vexed questions of autobiographical truth claims, we take up selected narratives of Annie Ernaux, the 2022 Nobel Laureate in Literature, as well as other contemporary texts. Throughout, we incorporate discussions of online platforms and such automedial modes as graphic memoir and auto-photography. To allow for more extensive exploration of new material, we incorporated discussions from the two chapters on the history of autobiography criticism but deleted the chapters as such; they may be found in the 2010 edition of *Reading Autobiography*.

For instructors in departments of literature, history, American studies, African American and African studies, women's/gender/sexuality studies, ethnic and cultural studies, education, ethnography, and other fields that probe the autobiographical in texts, discourses, and visual and online practices, *Reading Autobiography Now* is an accessible guide and a spur to undertaking theoretical, thematic, sociopolitical, and historical analyses. For graduate students, *Reading Autobiography Now* is a primer on the field of autobiography studies, with capacious primary and secondary resources for undertaking theoretical work. For advanced undergraduates, this guide can usefully accompany reading lists in survey, period, or multicultural courses on life writing, memoir, and creative nonfiction, as well as literary history more broadly. The many questions in the expanded Tool Kit offer strategies for developing sophisticated reading practices with autobiographical texts and acts. And the dozens of mini essays in the Compendium on both key concepts and autobiographical genres make *Reading Autobiography Now* a helpful companion for navigating the field in this moment of Too Much Information. We hope that scholars in diverse areas of the social sciences and the arts, as well as general readers, will also find *Reading Autobiography Now* a helpful guide to negotiating the contemporary flood of memoirs, graphic life narratives, auto-photography, and self-presentation in performance, film and video, the plastic arts, and across online platforms.

It is our intent, and hope, that readers and users in all fields and at all levels will find resources in *Reading Autobiography Now* to whet their appetites for engaging intensively with this richly rewarding field to which we have devoted our professional lives.

I
THEORIZING LIFE NARRATIVE

1
Defining and Discerning Life Narrative Forms

Only autobiography is literature. . . . Novels are what we peel off, and come at last to the core, which is you and me.

—Virginia Woolf, "A Sketch of the Past"

My life is history, politics, geography. It is religion and metaphysics. It is music and language.

—Paula Gunn Allen, "The Autobiography of a Confluence"

THE TERMS OF LIFE NARRATIVE

What could be simpler to understand than the act of people representing what they know best, their own lives? Yet this act is anything but simple, for the tellers of stories become, in the act of narration, both the observing subject and the object of investigation, remembrance, and contemplation. We might best approach life narrative, then, as a moving target, a set of shifting self-referential practices that, in engaging past experience, shape identity in the present. We intend in this book to complicate ordinary understandings of the concept and practices of self-referential narrative. A first step is to define terms and draw distinctions between autobiographical self-representation and other closely related kinds of life writing.

In Greek, *autos* denotes "self," *bios* "life," and *graphe* "writing."[1] Taken together in this order, the words *self-life-writing* offer a brief definition of *autobiography*. British poet and critic Stephen Spender cited the dictionary definition of *autobiography* as "the story of one's life written by himself" but notes its inadequacy to the "world that each is to himself" (115). French theorist Philippe Lejeune expanded that definition in a pronouncement many would call definitive: "We call autobiography the retrospective narrative in prose that someone makes of his own existence

4 Defining and Discerning Life Narrative Forms

when he puts the principal accent upon his life, especially upon the story of his own personality."[2] But he and others also expand that definition to include *how* one has become what one is at a given moment in an interactive process of reflection and creation. Yet, even this expansion is inadequate to encompass the complexity of autobiographical narratives as a set of acts and practices that need contextualizing historically, geographically, and generically.

In English the term *autobiography* first appeared in the review of Isaac D'Israeli's *Miscellanies* by William Taylor of Norwich in the *Monthly Review* (1797). Its first use, however, is often ascribed to Robert Southey's anglicizing of the three Greek words in 1809.[3] In his extensive survey of the term *autobiography*, Robert Folkenflik specifies the exact dates of the word's emergence in the West: "The term *autobiography* and its synonym *self-biography*, having never been used in earlier periods, appeared in the late eighteenth century in several forms, in isolated instances in the seventies, eighties, and nineties in both England and Germany with no sign that one use influenced another" (5). Folkenflik also notes that until the twentieth century the word *memoirs* (in French *les mémoires*) was commonly used to designate "self-life-writing."

Autobiography, now the most commonly used term for life writing, thus describes writing being produced at a particular historical juncture, the period prior to the Enlightenment in the West. Central to that movement was the concept of the self-interested individual of property who was intent on assessing the status of the soul or the meaning of public achievement. By the eighteenth century, notions of self-interest, self-consciousness, and self-knowledge informed the figure of the "Enlightened individual" described by philosophers and social and political theorists. And "autobiographies" as studies in self-interest were sought by a growing reading public with access to affordable printed books (see Krailsheimer, Weintraub, and Sturrock).

But the relatively recent coinage of the term *autobiography* does not mean that the practice of self-referential writing began only in the later eighteenth century. The practice of writing autobiographically has a history extending back to, and perhaps before, the Greeks and Romans in antiquity and extending beyond Western culture. Georg Misch, an eminent early twentieth-century German scholar of autobiography, identified hundreds of texts and inscriptions in his multivolume history translated in part as *A History of Autobiography in Antiquity*. Misch

Defining and Discerning Life Narrative Forms

found evidence of an "I" commemorated in funerary inscriptions about feats of battle and in early texts such as funeral orations, familiar letters, and travel narratives that have both the autobiographical content and the structure of self-reference. Certainly the lyric poems of Sappho of Lesbos (circa 600 BCE) present the voices of a woman candidly exploring her emotions and the somatic designs of love and physical desire, often with self-mocking wit, as feminist scholars have recently argued.

Beyond the West, the oral performance of self-narrative has existed in many Indigenous cultures prior to literacy—in, for example, the naming songs of Native American cultures, the oral narratives of genealogy and descent among Africans, the communal self-locating of the "song lines" of Indigenous Australians, and others. In addition to the long-standing practices of oral tradition throughout the world, there are modes of written self-inscription in China as early as two thousand years ago, in Japan as early as a thousand years ago, in Islamic-Arabic literature as early as the twelfth century,[4] in India during the medieval period (the *bhakti* poetry of devotional engagement with the sacred), and in North Africa in the fourteenth century (Ibn Khaldûn's *Life*). This widespread use of self-representation in both preliterate and literate non-Western cultures contradicts the allegation of an earlier generation of literary critics that autobiography is a uniquely Western form and a specific achievement of Western culture at a moment of individuation in the wake of the Enlightenment.[5]

Moreover, across the centuries, the forms of the autobiographical have been numerous. The court diary and poetic memoir (Lady Murasaki of Heian Japan), the pillow book of observations and musings in Heian Japan (Sei Shōnagon), the book of travels (Ibn Battuta), the memoir (Madame de Staël, Glückel of Hameln), the *Life* (Teresa of Avila and Benvenuto Cellini) or *The Book of My Life* (Girolamo Cardano), or the *Confessions* (Augustine, Rousseau) or *Essays* (Montaigne) signaled the writer's focus on self-reflection through speculations about history, politics, religion, science, and culture, and often involved developing a method of and vocabulary for self-study. And since the end of the eighteenth century a host of terms, such as *testimonio* and *autoethnography,* have been coined to designate new kinds and contexts of self-referential writing. In this century, the explosion of online platforms and sites for narrating lives interactively and serially has generated a new repertoire of modes. This rich and diverse history of self-referential modes

requires that we make some crucial distinctions among key terms—
autobiography, biography, memoir, life writing, life narrative, autofiction—
that may seem to imply the same thing.

Autobiography, as we have seen, became the term for a particular generic practice that emerged in the Enlightenment and subsequently became definitive for life writing in the West. In the seventeenth century, René Descartes situated the contemplative, epistemological self in a new house of philosophy. The solitary "I" of his *Discourse on Method* subordinates body to mind, nature to intellect, and others to a sovereign philosophical self, the cogito. Isolated and individuated, the Enlightenment subject is born and, with it, a new world of Cartesian dualism created from its desires and certainties. It is this subject that is associated with the tradition of canonical autobiography in the West, typified by John Stuart Mill's *Autobiography* and Harriet Martineau's *Autobiography.* The term *autobiography* remains the most widely used and most generally understood term for life narrative. But because the term privileges the autonomous individual and the universalizing life story as the definitive achievement of life writing, it has been vigorously challenged in the wake of poststructuralist, postmodern, and postcolonial critiques of the Enlightenment subject. Early twentieth-century theorists acclaimed this master narrative of "the sovereign self" as an institution of literature and culture, and identified a canon of representative self-life-writings. Implicit in this canonization, however, was the assumption that many other kinds of life writings produced at the same time had lesser value and were not "true" autobiography—"slave" narrative, narratives of women's domestic lives, coming-of-age and travel narratives, among them.

Thus, many postmodern and postcolonial theorists contend that the term *autobiography* is inadequate to describe the extensive historical range and the diverse genres and practices of life writing around the globe. Indeed, these critics contend, the concept of autobiography, celebrated by an earlier generation of scholars such as Georges Gusdorf and Karl Joachim Weintraub as the highest achievement of individuality in Western civilization, has been defined against many coexistent forms of life writing. Thus, its politics has been exclusionary. Other critics, among them Julie Rak and Leigh Gilmore, address this troubling, exclusionary aspect of autobiography by shifting the term of reference to autobiographical discourse, that is, to discursive formations of truth-telling "sustained by the trappings of identification that have underwritten what

Defining and Discerning Life Narrative Forms

the self is and how it has been seen in much of the Western World" (Rak, *Negotiated Memory,* ix). Reformulating the term of reference as autobiographical discourse brings into focus differential power relations in autobiographical writing, circulation, and reception. Doing so also illuminates how those whose identities and experiences were obscured or marginalized have been engaged in contesting and altering normative or traditional formations of identity (Rak, *Negotiated Memory,* ix).

At this moment, another term has gained currency in popular and scholarly arenas. Predating the term *autobiography, memoir* is now the word used by publishing houses to describe various practices and genres of self-life-writing. Historically, memoir was understood as *mémoire (les mémoires),* recollections by the publicly prominent who chronicled their social accomplishments (see Quinby). These recollections often bracketed one moment or period of experience rather than an entire life span and offered reflections on its significance for the writer's previous status or self-understanding. Rak suggests that "memoir" has long been attached to popular forms of life writing and used as a nominal marker to distinguish stories about unacknowledged aspects of people's lives, sometimes considered scandalous or titillating, and often written by the socially marginal (*Negotiated Memory,* 316–20). In contemporary writing, the categorization of memoir often signals autobiographical works characterized by their density of language and self-reflexivity about the writing process, yoking the author's standing as a professional writer with the work's status as an aesthetic object. For Nancy K. Miller the term *memoir* captures a dynamic postmodernism in its movement between the "private and the public, subject and object" (*Bequest and Betrayal,* 2). The term *memoir,* then, seems more malleable than the term *autobiography,* foregrounding historical shifts and intersecting cultural formations; when a narrative emphasizes its mode as memoir, as in Maxine Hong Kingston's *The Woman Warrior: Memoirs of a Girlhood among Ghosts,* readers are invited to think about the significance of that choice and the kind of reading it invites.

In this book, we have chosen to use the term *autobiography* only to refer to the traditional Western mode of retrospective life narrative and not to use the more common term *memoir* to designate all self-reflexive writing. We often use the adjective *autobiographical* to signal self-referential writing. Throughout we use the terms *life writing* and *life narrative* to mark the heterogeneity of self-referential practices. We

8 Defining and Discerning Life Narrative Forms

understand *life writing* as a general term for writing that takes a life, one's own or another's, as its subject. Such writing can be biographical, novelistic, historical, or explicitly self-referential and therefore autobiographical. The autobiographical mode of life writing might more precisely be called *self-life-writing*, but because of its clumsiness, we employ this phrase only for occasional emphasis. Both memoir and autobiography are encompassed in the term *life writing*. We understand *life narrative*, by contrast, as a general term for acts of self-presentation of all kinds and in diverse media that take the producer's life as their subject, whether written, performed, visual, cinematic, or digital.[6] In other words, we employ the term *life writing* for written forms of the autobiographical, and *life narrative* to refer to autobiographical acts in any medium.[7] As G. Thomas Couser has noted, "the use of the terms 'life writing' and 'life narrative' does not deny generic distinctions but rather reflects an impulse toward catholicity and toward reconsideration of traditional definitions and distinctions" ("Genre Matters," 126). Furthermore, a shift from *autobiography* and *memoir* to *life writing* and *life narrative* signals that a more capacious and flexible set of frameworks is being articulated for mapping a global history of autobiographical acts and practices, as Craig Howes observes in extending the terms to both multiple media and research in other disciplines ("Life Writing").

Now let us turn to distinctions between autobiographical writing and the practices of related kinds of narrative, namely, history-writing, biography, and the novel. We then explore how the current coinages of *autotheory, autoethnography,* and *autofiction* inflect practices of life narrative now.

LIFE NARRATIVE AND HISTORY

Sometimes people read autobiographical narratives as historical documents, sources of evidence for the analysis of movements, events, or persons. From this perspective, autobiographical narrative and history-writing might seem to be synonymous. Although it can be read as a history of the writing/speaking subject, however, life narrative cannot be reduced to or understood only as historical record. While autobiographical narratives may contain information regarded as "facts," they are not factual history about a particular time, person, or event. Rather, they incorporate usable facts into subjective "truth," a concept we take up in later chapters.

Defining and Discerning Life Narrative Forms

When life narrators write to chronicle an event, to explore a certain time period, or to enshrine a community, they are making history in a sense. But they are also performing several rhetorical acts: justifying their own perceptions, upholding their reputations, disputing the accounts of others, settling scores, conveying cultural information, and inventing desirable futures, among others. The complexity of autobiographical texts requires reading practices that engage the narrative tropes, sociocultural contexts, rhetorical aims, and narrative shifts within the historical or chronological trajectory of the text. To reduce autobiographical narration to facticity is to strip it of its rhetorical, literary, ethical, political, and cultural dimensions.

Jeremy D. Popkin, a historian interested in both the parallels and the differences between autobiographical writing and history, points to a distinction between the modes of life narrative and history-writing in terms of temporality. Life writing, Popkin suggests, "privilege[s] a temporal framework based on the individual author's lifespan, whereas historical narrative takes place in collective time." The "arbitrary and concrete" personal time of experience in life writing does not have to engage the moments of shared experience that historians identify as significant in the collective time of an era, nation, or culture, or present the "big picture" expected of a historian ("Historians on the Autobiographical Frontier," 727).[8]

Historians, like life narrators, tell a story about the past, as Hayden White persuasively argues, proposing the "truth" of the past through a narrativization of events that "is always a figurative account" (48). Like life writing, history-writing is replete with literary tropes (metaphor and metonymy, for instance) and intelligible plots (a rise and fall, for instance). But historians, attentive to the norms of the discipline, place themselves outside or at the margin of the historical picture, even as they remain present in the discourses they mobilize, the very words they use, the shaping of the story they tell.[9] They preserve a professional norm of objectivity and the truthfulness it pledges by establishing distance from their material and typically removing or qualifying any reference to themselves in the narrative.

Autobiographical narrators, in contrast, place themselves at the center of the stories they assemble and are interested in the meaning of larger forces, or conditions, or events for their *own* stories. The power of William Apess's "A Son of the Forest" and "The Experience of Five

Christian Indians of the Pequot Tribe" derives from the way in which Apess situates himself as an agent of American history, negotiating his status as Native American in his relationships to a series of white people and to literacy in the new republic. In the details and the immediacy of the lived lives of such autobiographical narrators, the political and cultural contexts of the historical past become vivid and memorable. Autobiographical narrators claim agency through telling their experiential life story to supplement or reinterpret official narratives and offer alternative versions of historical accounts.

LIFE NARRATIVE AND BIOGRAPHY

While self-life-writing and biography are both modes of narrating a life, they are not interchangeable. To be sure, bookstores shelve both in the biography section, and people may think of autobiography as the biography someone writes about him- or herself, as Nigel Hamilton suggests in *Biography: A Brief History*. But there are crucial distinctions in *how* these forms narrate a life.[10] In biography, scholars of other people's lives document and interpret those lives from a point of view external to the subject. In self-life-writing, subjects write about their own lives predominantly, even if they write about themselves in the second or third person, or as a member of a community. And they write simultaneously from externalized and internal points of view, taking themselves as both subject and object, and may thematize that difference. Philippe Lejeune nicely sums up this distinction: "In biography resemblance grounds identity, while in autobiography identity grounds resemblance." This is the case because "identity is the real starting point of autobiography, resemblance the impossible horizon of biography" ("Autobiographical Pact," 24). Louis Menand observes a second crucial distinction concerning temporality: "All biographies are retrospective in the same sense. Though they read chronologically forward, they are composed essentially backward" (66). That is, the events for which the subject becomes renowned determine what the biographer selects to interpret as formative. By contrast, in self-life-writing the interpreters often recognize that their choices of what to narrate as formative are subjective and idiosyncratic.

What is the significance of differences between these kinds of life writing? Stephen Spender suggested that the life writer confronts not one life but two. One is the self that others see—the social, historical

Defining and Discerning Life Narrative Forms

person, with achievements, personal appearance, social relationships. These are "real" attributes of a person living in the world. But there is also the self experienced only by that person, the self felt from the inside that the writer can never get "outside of." The "inside," or personally experienced, self has a history. While it may not be meaningful as an objective "history of the times," it is a record of self-observation, not a history observed by others. Spender writes that "we are seen from the outside by our neighbors; but we remain always at the back of our eyes and our senses, situated in our bodies, like a driver in the front seat of a car seeing the other cars coming toward him. A single person . . . is one consciousness within one machine, confronting all the other traffic" (116). To continue Spender's metaphor of driving the automobile, biographers can circle the car with the driver in it to record the history, character, and motivations of the driver, the traffic, the vehicle, and the facts of transportation. But only life narrators know the experience of traffic rushing toward them and compose an interpretation of that situation, that is, write their subjectivity.

Matters of time and timing also differentiate biography and life writing. For a biographer the death of the subject is not definitive. A biography can be written either during the life or after the death of the person being written about. In fact, biographies offering different interpretations of particular historical figures may appear periodically over many centuries, as have biographies of Caesar, Galileo, Michelangelo, and Byron. For the life writer, on the other hand, death is the end of the matter. While self-life-writing can be serial, and often is written over a long span of time, as is the case with the multiple narratives of Edward Gibbon, Maya Angelou, and John Edgar Wideman, it must be written during the writer's life span—or be published posthumously "as is."

In writing a life, the self-life-narrator and the biographer also engage different kinds of evidence. Most biographers incorporate multiple forms of evidence, including historical documents, interviews, and family archives, which they evaluate for validity. Relatively few biographers use their personal memories of their subject as reliable evidence, unless they had a personal relationship to the subject of the biography (as a relative, child, friend, or colleague). For life narrators, by contrast, personal memories are a primary archival source. They may have recourse to other kinds of sources—letters, journals, photographs, conversations— and to their knowledge of a historical moment. But the usefulness of such evidence for their stories lies in the ways in which they employ that evidence to support, supplement, or offer commentary on their idiosyncratic acts of remembering. In autobiographical narratives, imaginative acts of remembering always intersect with such rhetorical acts as assertion, justification, judgment, conviction, and interrogation. That is, life narrators address readers whom they want to persuade of their version of experience. As we will see in chapter 2, memory is a subjective form of evidence that cannot be fully verified externally; rather, it is asserted on the subject's authority.

Biographers usually write about the object of their studies in the third person, while life narrators frequently employ the first person singular. Certainly, there are autobiographical narrators who present their subjects in the second and/or third person. In *The Education of Henry Adams: An Autobiography,* Henry Adams refers to himself as "Henry Adams," "he," and "him." But readers understand that this is Adams's convention for presenting himself and that the teller and protagonist of the narrative are one and the same. "Henry Adams" appears as both subject and author on the title page. Biographers, however, cannot present their subjects in the first person—except when quoting statements or letters or books written by that person.

Of course, there are texts that combine biographical and autobiographical modes of narration. As early as the second century BCE, Plutarch wove his own ethical observations and judgments into his parallel *Lives of the Noble Grecians and Romans.* In the seventeenth century, aristocratic women in England such as Anne, Lady Halkett, and Margaret Cavendish, Duchess of Newcastle, appended brief narratives of their lives to the adulatory biographies they wrote of their husbands. Contemporary life narrators have blurred the boundary separating autobiographical and biographical modes by embedding their versions of the life of a family member in what is called a relational narrative, for example, Kim Chernin in *In My Mother's House: A Daughter's Story,* John Edgar Wideman in *Brothers and Keepers,* and Drusilla Modjeska in *Poppy.* Or they may entwine the case history of a patient with the writer's own self-analysis, as did Kay Redfield Jamison in *An Unquiet Mind.* (See chapter 2 for an extended discussion of relationality.) As much as we have argued for distinguishing autobiographical writing and biography here, it is important to note that contemporary practices increasingly blend them into a hybrid.

Defining and Discerning Life Narrative Forms

Over the last century, forms of biographical writing have shuttled between the fictive and the biographically referential. Modernist biographer Lytton Strachey innovated on existing forms in his empathic and irreverent *Eminent Victorians*. And Virginia Woolf, herself the daughter of an editor of the British *Dictionary of National Biography*, suggested that her *Orlando* was an imaginative biography of her friend Vita Sackville-West. More recently, professional biographers, novelists, and literary critics have adapted biographical modes to embed the story of a historical subject into the exploration of larger social, intellectual, and political movements. Ramón Saldívar uses "the new biography" in *The Borderlands of Culture: Américo Paredes and the Transnational Imaginary* to entwine a study of the Mexican American author and scholar with the development and growth of Chicanx studies as a field attentive to border identities and transnational imaginaries and with his own identity formation as a scholar in this field.[11] Carolyn Steedman's *Landscape for a Good Woman* could also be considered a form of new biography. In it she considers her mother, the "good woman" of the title, as a working-class woman with middle-class aspirations and tells the story of frustrated ambition in a protofeminist moment rarely considered by historians of social class. That story is combined with the biography Steedman largely omits of a father who abandoned his family. And this case study of the Lancaster working class is joined to her obliquely autobiographical narrative of education and movement into the professional class where she achieves the status that eluded her mother.

Some experiments with forms of biographical telling may engage subjective narration to the extent that it becomes an indeterminate fictional form. In *The Emigrants*, W. G. Sebald exploits the form of biography to undermine its premises. Sebald's narrator presents apparently biographical vignettes of four German exiles in the aftermath of the Holocaust as melancholy stories interspersed with apparently documentary materials, including photos that are left unlabeled. The blend of historical reportage and deeply subjective detail undercuts biography's claim to objectivity and exposes readers' investment in its historicity and authenticity.

Most recently, the term *biofiction* has been used to characterize boldly hybrid generic forms plying the porous terrain between the biographical and fictive. Such biofictions are to be distinguished from works such as the Hillary Mantel trilogy on Thomas Cromwell, which are avowedly novelistic treatments of historical events. In introducing essays on "Locating and Defining the Bio in Biofiction," Michael Lackey observes that "most authors of biofiction explicitly claim that they are not doing biography" (5); instead, they "forgo the desire to get the biographical subject's life 'right' and, rather, use the biographical subject in order to project their own vision of life and the world" (7). In a later essay, Lackey asserts: "Central to my view of biofiction is that the literary form is more performative than representational—that instead of trying to represent a person's life and therewith the past accurately, authors fictionalize something of major symbolic significance from an actual life in order to project into existence a new, better, and more socially just way of thinking and being in the authorial present and for the indefinite future" ("Beyond Postmodern Blurring," 8). Biofiction, then, is an experimental form that, rather than making authoritative truth claims, proposes provisional versions of another's life to perform interpretations of authorial possibility. As such, while its inventions may be postmodern, the desire to innovate on existing biographical templates has a long history.

Biography is an enduringly popular form of life narrative in television, cinematic, and visual media. What scholars call the "biopic" has become an innovative and ubiquitous mode for telling a life.[12] Some biopics offer straightforward chronological narratives of their subjects as heroes, villains, or innovators; others offer complex explorations of a life and its moment, such as Raoul Peck's *Lumumba* and *I Am Not Your Negro* based on James Baldwin's writings, recent presentations of Vincent van Gogh's life in the animated film *Loving Vincent* by Dorota Kobiela and Hugh Welchman, and *At Eternity's Gate* (2018) by Julian Schnabel. Todd Haynes's biopic on Bob Dylan, *I'm Not There,* employs six actors less to impersonate Dylan than to stand in for aspects of his protean presence at various moments in his career. With each episode narrated through a different genre and visual style, the ensemble interrogates the notion that a "life," especially one so diverse and creative, can be told as a single story.

These experiments in new modes of biography, then, signal many kinds of practices that explore the boundaries drawn between biography and fiction and seek innovative templates adequate to the complexity of narrating a life at this moment of paradigm shift. This has led some theorists to combine the two words and insert a slash between "auto"

Defining and Discerning Life Narrative Forms

and "biography," implying that the two modes are always joined. We, however, find it useful to preserve the distinction while acknowledging hybrid practices.

LIFE NARRATIVE AND THE NOVEL

People often confuse autobiographical writing and the form of the novel. Typically, they call autobiographical texts "novels," though they rarely call novels "autobiographies." But autobiographical texts are not novels, and calling autobiographical writing "nonfiction" confuses, rather than resolves, the issue. Autobiographical writing and the novel share features we ascribe to fictional writing: plot, dialogue, setting, characterization, and so on. But they are distinguished by their relationship to and claims about a referential world and a lived history. We might helpfully think of what fiction represents as "*a* world," and what autobiographical writing refers to as "*the* world." Further, differences that have historically arisen between these forms are crucial to understanding the distinct practices, audiences, truth claims, and traditions of autobiographical writing.

In the nineteenth century many novels were presented as autobiographical narratives, the life stories of fictional characters. Think of Charles Dickens's *David Copperfield,* Charlotte Brontë's *Jane Eyre,* Johann Wolfgang von Goethe's *Wilhelm Meister's Apprenticeship,* and Fyodor Dostoyevsky's *Notes from Underground.* The narrators of these texts employ the intimate first person as protagonists confiding their personal histories and attempting to understand how their past experiences formed them as social subjects. Such narratives and the traditions from which they emerged are part of the development of the bildungsroman, or coming-of-age novel, a form that German scholar Wilhelm Dilthey defined as the story of an individual's struggle to become a social subject who "becomes aware of his purpose in the world" (cited in Burt, 105). The individual's potential, thwarted by circumstances of birth and repressive social convention, by constraints of class and gender, is discovered in the extended process of becoming educated; and that education involves encounters with mentors, apprenticeships, journeys, and reckonings with the costs of accommodating to social conventions and structures.

Many twentieth- and twenty-first-century novels are also narrated as first-person autobiographies, for example, Junot Diaz's *The Brief Wondrous Life of Oscar Wao,* J. D. Salinger's *Catcher in the Rye,* Ralph Ellison's *Invisible Man,* and Jamaica Kincaid's *Annie John.* But, as Raymond L.

Burt suggests, the teleology of the bildungsroman collapses throughout the twentieth century (105). The great modernists Thomas Mann, Marcel Proust, Virginia Woolf, James Joyce, and Robert Musil invoke its tropes of individuation to show the fragmentation of selfhood and the constructed nature of social relations. And readers of such narratives observe the biases and fantasies of young protagonists and discover discrepancies between how they view themselves at various moments and how we, as readers, regard the limitations or blind spots of their knowledge. The fractured selves and inhospitable sociality of the twentieth-century bildungsroman find a parallel in many autobiographical works, making distinctions between the two modes increasingly tenuous. Nonetheless, first-person novels continue to signal readers in various ways that they are reading a novel and not an autobiographical narrative. Most obviously, the author's name on the title page differs from the name of the character narrating the tale. That is, the named narrator on Diaz's cover is Oscar Wao, and Holden Caulfield is the named narrator of Salinger's *Catcher in the Rye*.

The identification of authorial signature with the narrator, by contrast, is a distinguishing mark of autobiography, as Philippe Lejeune argued in his influential essay "The Autobiographical Pact." Lejeune usefully defines the relationship between author and reader in autobiographical writing as a contract: "What defines autobiography for the one who is reading is above all a contract of identity that is sealed by the proper name. And this is true also for the one who is writing the text" (19).[13] For Lejeune, two things indisputably distinguish autobiography, and, by implication, a wide range of life narratives, from the novel: the "vital statistics" of the author, such as date and place of birth and education, are identical to those of the narrator; and an implicit contract exists between author and publisher attesting to the truth of the "signature" on the cover and title page (21). When we recognize the person who claims authorship of the narrative as its protagonist or central figure—that is, we believe them to be the same person—we read the text written by the author to whom it refers as self-reflexive or autobiographical. With this recognition of the autobiographical pact, Lejeune argues, we read differently and assess the narrative as making truth claims of a sort that are suspended in fictional forms such as the novel.

There is also a temporal distinction between a novel and an autobiographical text. Novelists are not bound by historical time. They can

Defining and Discerning Life Narrative Forms

situate their narratives at any time in the past, present, or future. This does not mean that life narrators only and simply offer a retrospective narrative in chronological order about the life lived to the point of its writing. They can return to the past, even the cultural past before the writer's birth, or offer an imaginative journey into a fantasized future. The narrator of Thomas De Quincey's *Confessions of an English Opium Eater*, for example, is stimulated by opium to transport his life to other centuries and continents; yet corporeally he remains located in nineteenth-century London, increasingly the victim of his addiction. Novelists, by contrast, are bound only by the reader's expectation of internal consistency in the world of verisimilitude created within the novel. They are not bound by rules of evidence that link the world of the narrative with a historical world outside the narrative. As Samuel Taylor Coleridge famously observed, we practice a "suspension of disbelief" when engaging fictional or poetic worlds. Unlike novelists, life narrators have to anchor their narratives in the world of their own temporal, geographical, and cultural milieu.

These key concepts anchor fundamental distinctions between the novel and life writing; yet we do not want to imply that the boundary between them can be persistently maintained. Some works deliberately trouble the boundary by repeatedly recrossing it, as does Georges Perec in his experimental memoir *W, Or the Memory of Childhood* (1975). In trying to assess his childhood during the Nazi occupation of France, he alternates autobiographical chapters with conspicuously fictional ones that signal the young narrated I's confusion and dread. Thus, boundaries are increasingly porous and have never been as firm or fixed as autobiography theorists once argued. Practitioners of life narrative blur those boundaries; and theorists of life narrative find themselves challenged to account for the heterogeneity, intensities, and effects of that blurring.

LIFE NARRATIVE AND AUTOTHEORY

In contemporary life narrative, distinctions between autobiographical and theoretical writing in the philosophical, literary, and aesthetics fields have become increasingly blurred. The practice of writing autotheory is, however, by no means a new phenomenon. The Augustinian mode of self-presentation rejected the embodied self of Greco-Roman antiquity as it became immersed in and transformed by Christian rebirth and self-transcendence. With the turn to vernacular languages in fifteenth-

and sixteenth-century Humanism, interest grew in presenting a secular, public self whose exteriority was distinct from the material signs of God's grace.

How to write and visualize a self through a different prism than the landscapes of interiority characterizing Christian spirituality became a central focus as both philosophical and literary thinkers responded vigorously and innovatively. For example, in *The Book of My Life*, considered the first psychological life narrative, Italian mathematician Girolamo Cardano minutely inventories aspects of his personal life in chapters with such titles as "A Meditation on the Perpetuation of My Name," "Those Things in Which I Take Pleasure," "My Manner of Walking and Thinking," and "Things in Which I Feel I Have Failed." His emphasis on self-evaluation, albeit written in Latin, remains open-ended, never coming to rest in a completed self-portrait. The great writer Montaigne turned to the French vernacular to compose a vast group of *Essays* investigating the conditions of knowledge and generating an idiosyncratic self-portrait in ever-shifting perspective. Not a retrospective chronicle of a lived life, the *Essays* are "self-tryouts" exploring Montaigne's motto, "What do I know?" ("Que sçay-je?"). His interlinear habit throughout his life of adding commentary to previous layers of text creates a reflexive network, as the narrating "I" of one moment engages in ongoing dialogue and critique with his past narrated "I"s, creating a dynamic, intersubjective self-portrait of a kind that few later writers other than Stendhal achieved.

The Humanist development of self-reflexive literature was a revolution in autocritical self-representation. Such nonfictional prose writers as Giambattista Vico in Italy, Desiderius Erasmus in Holland, Robert Burton and Thomas Browne in England and self-reflexive poets in the wake of Dante, such as Louise Labé, DuBellay, and Ronsard in France, focused on lyrically presenting their own interior worlds. While Descartes and Blaise Pascal, as well as later Enlightenment writers, would criticize this self-absorption as what Pascal called Montaigne's "stupid plan to paint himself" ("le sot projet de se peindre," *Pensées* VI, 33), the "I" had been inserted doubly, as both a subject and an object of literary and philosophical discourse.

In the nineteenth century, the narrator of Goethe's late, lengthy autobiography, *Truth and Poetry: From My Own Life,* looks back on Romantic idealism as a disease to be overcome by immersion in the Greco-Roman classical tradition and relentless self-critique. At the end

Defining and Discerning Life Narrative Forms

of the century Friedrich Nietzsche's *Ecce Homo* is both a culmination and a rejection of philosophical literature of the self. His autobiographical presentation critiques the metaphysics of self even while depending on it. Characterizing himself as a *"Doppelgänger,"* a dual-faced, even triple-faced, figure—"I have a second face in addition to the first. And perhaps also a third"—he describes himself in the contradictions of the Western metaphysical tradition; he is both Dionysus and Apollo, as well as their negation in the decadence of the West and his own dying body (Nietzsche, cited in Lionnet, *Autobiographical Voices,* 225). Detailing the history of his suffering, the narrating I challenges the foundational principles of Christianity and Western metaphysics of self; but, despite his antispiritualist critique, Nietzsche cannot fully extricate himself from his own subjectivity.

While this mini overview of autocriticism as a self-reflexive act in the Western philosophical, literary, and aesthetic tradition cannot do justice to the complex and shifting history of concepts of the self, it may suggest how deeply that tradition has been both embedded in and critical of a metaphysics of self. In the twenty-first century, the blurring of autobiographical and theoretical boundaries has led to coining the term *autotheory* (sometimes called *autocritique*) to denote the fluidity between writing or performing a life narrative and probing the theoretical and critical dynamics of the self, subjectivity, social relations, political forms of subjection, and tropes and modes of experiential history. Autotheory is variously defined. Katherine Baxter and Cat Auburn observe in their introduction to a special issue on "Autotheory in Contemporary Visual Arts Practice" that autotheory's "boundaries stretch to encompass literary genres, critical discourse, creative practice, and academic methodology" (1). Lauren Fournier succinctly defines autotheory as "a mode of theorizing that draws attention to itself as such" (30) and asserts that "entailed in the use of the self *(auto)* as material alongside theory comes a degree of self-analysis and criticality about one's own life as part of the practice" (35). She productively extends her discussion to what she calls "proto-post-modernist" women, "gender-nonconforming artists, writers, and filmmakers like Zora Neale Hurston, the Baroness Elsa von Freytag-Loringhoven, Claude Cahun, and Gertrude Stein marking ruptures in existing genre and media designations" as progenitors of practices that since 1998 have contributed to the emergence of contemporary autotheory (37–38). Other feminist scholars such as Robyn Wiegman regard

20 Defining and Discerning Life Narrative Forms

autotheory as a feminist practice because it presses against and contests the hold of traditional Western theories of the subject that undergird concepts of a universal self often inscribed in the Enlightenment mode of traditional autobiography. In the view of these theorists, autotheory critiques multiple systems of power, including masculinist modes and practices of theorizing. That is, they situate autotheory as a mode of engaging with writers' struggle to wrest meaning from their experiential histories.

Concepts central to autotheoretical acts and practices include verbal experimentation, hybridity, fractiousness, and the dispersal of authorship across edgy citations. Its texts are often multiply mediated through technologies and forms of embodiment, as well as engagement with the voices of others in ways that aim to be nonappropriative. Yet, although practitioners of autotheory optimistically intend to subvert traditional norms, they often encounter tensions in doing so. For instance, Baxter and Auburn caution: "Autotheory thus always risks co-opting the voice of the other, even as it purports to collaborate and 'speak with' these voices; this risk is due to, amongst other factors, curatorial processes" (4).

Self-proclaimed autotheory narratives engage in three distinct yet related practices: (1) theorizing the condition of the subject in telling one's story from the standpoint of a particular discipline, such as philosophy, sociology, or history; (2) theorizing the process of autobiographical writing as an aspect of telling one's story; and (3) theorizing the dynamics that have shaped the life being narrated, including social institutions, structural forms of disadvantage, systems of representation complicit in structural power arrangements, cultural formations, and public policy. Some autotheoretical acts and practices take up all these critiques and strive not to arrive at final formulations but to foreground their dialogical examinations.

There is, as noted above, a larger history of autotheoretical writing within which to situate the claims of autotheorists that will be familiar to readers of life writing. An example of the first practice are the personal narratives of German twentieth-century writer Walter Benjamin, which critique the condition of the subject from the standpoint of political philosophy. In *Moscow Diary, A Berlin Chronicle,* and *Berlin Childhood around 1900,* Benjamin employs autobiographical stories to ground his political analyses in the perspectives of, respectively, the body, the ear, and the eye, thereby resituating the subject's relation to history. Gerhard

Defining and Discerning Life Narrative Forms

Richter, characterizing Benjamin's life narratives as "archaeological montage" (47), notes that they "offer an experience of singularity and transgression in which the history of the self is inseparable from the history of its culture" (33).

The work of Roland Barthes also often contests a larger social or philosophical paradigm of the self, particularly in the field of semiotics. In sketching out theoretical positions on such topics as the death of the author and the dispersal of the "self" into a fragmented subject, Barthes wrote autobiographical essays as experiments with the media, the chronology, and the subjectivity of life writing. His putatively autobiographical *Roland Barthes by Roland Barthes*, with Barthes's epigraph urging readers to read it as a novel, is at once an autobiographical and an anti-autobiographical engagement with notions of selfhood. In it Barthes routes his provocative intervention into conventions of self-representation through personal photographs and quasi-alphabetical textual fragments that blur the contours of his personal life by using first-, second-, and third-person pronouns. Barthes's *Camera Lucida,* by contrast, nominally a book of critique, combines speculations on the effects of photography on the spectator with a meditation on his mother's death. He presents an elegiac portrait of her as an other whose loss is felt through the effects of the *punctum,* a photographic detail that in emotionally piercing the viewer, creates an intimate bond with the lost loved one. Despite his extensive use of personal reflection and interest in a new mode of writing, however, Barthes did not systematically lay out a theory of the autobiographical; rather, he problematized its assumed transparency in ways that continue to be provocative for scholars (see Sheringham, especially *Everyday Life*).

Only in recent decades have we begun to think of the second strand of autotheory—theorizing the process of life narration in telling one's story—as centrally implicated in its practice. In the United States, for instance, some writers have consistently defined their writing practice as a version of autocritique. In essays such as "Crows Written on the Poplars: Autocritical Autobiographies," Chippewa mixed-blood writer Gerald Vizenor composes a collage by interweaving citations from scholars of autobiography with his own critique of their limited understanding of hybridized identity and an extended narrative linking his coming of age to the memory of a violent act of killing a squirrel. Similarly, the narratives of Cherríe Moraga *(Loving in the War Years)* and Gloria Anzaldúa

(*Borderlands/La Frontera*) use autocritical writing as a practice of *mestiza* identity in which the poles of critical and creative writing, like those of the English and Spanish languages, formal speech and dialect, Mexican and American identities, and hetero- and homosexuality, are fractured to create a hybrid form of life writing. In many of her essays and her memoir, bell hooks makes autocritique an illuminating form for observations about contemporary culture as exemplified by episodes from her own life. In *Bone Black: Memories of Girlhood,* critical concepts about the implicit norms of writing autobiography frame hooks's coming-of-age narrative. Nancy K. Miller, as both critic and practitioner of life writing, incorporates a musing, reflective narrative voice into *Bequest and Betrayal* (on the deaths of her parents), which weaves conceptual insights drawn from analyses of the tropes and discourses of self-narration into a relationally autobiographical text.

The third strand of autotheory practice, theorizing the dynamics of social institutions and cultural formations that shape the life being narrated, is often linked to activist social and political movements centered on feminist, disability, LGBTQI, and/or antiracist protest. That is, narrators may entwine their experiential histories with a critique of systemic oppression and disadvantage, or of the blind spots of public policy, or of the politics of representation itself. This autotheoretical life writing has been fueled by earlier movements, including the second-wave feminism agenda of "the personal is political," the difference-feminism of women-of-color activists since the late twentieth century, and the Indigenous Rights, Latinx, LGBTQI, Black Lives Matter, Trans*, and #MeToo movements. For example, Stephanie D. Clare revives the feminist practice of standpoint epistemology to advance a theory of nonbinary "structures of feeling," which she defines as "a disidentification with the female sexed body, a desire for a form of embodiment that has not been differentiated for the purposes of reproduction, and identification with aspects of both traditional masculinity and femininity" (5.3). In exploring such structures of feeling, Clare narrates her experience of reading theoretical books and life narratives together, and offers a reading of the works of Simone de Beauvoir from the standpoint of her felt experience of nonbinary gender. Reflecting on her own transformation of consciousness, Clare asserts that "writing from my position allows for the continued investigation of how feminism, including queer feminism, changes (and ought to change) in its encounter with trans thought" (2).

Defining and Discerning Life Narrative Forms

Similarly, some narratives engaged with the disability rights movement deploy autocritical practice in powerfully personal ways. They respond in part to the work of some earlier disability life writers who portrayed themselves as victims and represented impairment as a personal illness or tragedy to be overcome by extraordinary effort, as does, for example, Helen Keller in *The Story of My Life* and other narratives. These autotheoretical disability rights activists argue that if cultural conditions were changed, impaired individuals could be accommodated in society; and they criticize the social discourses attached to those with disabilities as stigmatizing and degrading because they reproduce ableist norms that encode such differences as abnormative (Gerschick, 1264).

By experimenting with autobiographical genres that explicitly challenge their narrators' identities as differently-abled and the history of abnormative bodies as socially constructed, disability life writers "write back" to conventional victim narratives of wounded suffering in their call for social change. Several women's memoirs enact or perform alternative subjectivities that claim the possibility of a sexualized body distinct from representations of disabled women as either desexualized or hypersexualized. By positioning themselves as disabled subjects who address the history of their own marginalization, these differently-abled writers reframe their impairment by refusing the stigmatizing diagnosis of abnormality. For example, in *Blind Rage: Letters to Helen Keller,* Georgina Kleege reflects on her own loss of sight by staging an engagement with Keller as a disabled other that challenges the paradigm of silent, valiant, female suffering and sketches a countermodel of reading blind bodies. Similarly, Stephen Kuusisto in *Planet of the Blind* narrates his experience of passing as sighted throughout his childhood and indicts social practices that stigmatize and marginalize the "blind." In *Being Heumann: An Unrepentant Memoir of a Disability Rights Activist,* Judith Heumann explores her long struggle to change the conditions of everyday life that render her fit only for an institution and prevent her and others from becoming fully human. Anne Finger, in *Elegy for a Disease: A Personal and Cultural History of Polio,* takes issue with being socially positioned as "paralyzed" and examines the cultural conditions that have impeded the negotiation of her life.

In sum, using the term *autotheory* to signal texts that "fus[e] self-representation with philosophy and critical theory" in ways that "often exceed . . . disciplinary boundaries, genres, and forms" (Fournier, "Call for Papers") alludes to some current practices but occludes the long history from which they emerge. Nonetheless, this twenty-first-century moment is a prescient one for autotheory in extending its practice to new media and forms of embodiment. Alex Brostoff and Fournier point to the self-theorizing practice of a burgeoning groups of works such as Paul B. Preciado's *Testo Junkie*. Preciado narrates taking a topical testosterone as a political, performative act that he calls a "body-essay" in the "pharmacopornographic era" of late capitalism (33). They also observe that Claudia Rankine's *Citizen: An American Lyric* (2014), Moyra Davey's *Les Goddesses* (2011), and Maggie Nelson's *The Argonauts* (2015), as well as earlier narratives such as Clarice Lispector's *Água Viva* (1973) and Chris Kraus's *I Love Dick* (1997) call on critics to read contemporary texts of autotheory transmedially and transnationally as a way of "bring[ing] theory to life and life to theory" (490) across historical and geopolitical contexts. These extended acts of autotheoretical narration now stimulate and complicate our understanding of how life writing can circulate as both narrative and critique.

LIFE NARRATIVE AND AUTOETHNOGRAPHY

Another distinction to explore is the relationship of autobiographical to autoethnographic writing, a practice in the field of anthropological ethnography, which is generally understood as a method of qualitative research grounded in immersive fieldwork and participant-observation. Autoethnography often joins seemingly disparate kinds of lives in projecting an "I" who speaks its own story and a narrator who explores and conveys the specificity and feltness of life in a larger community and culture under duress.

Within literary studies, autoethnography emerged as a theoretical term around 1990 in studies by Françoise Lionnet and Mary Louise Pratt. Both scholars analyzed a range of colonial and postcolonial first-person narratives situated at multiple cultural boundaries between metropolitan and local languages, oral and written modes of storytelling, individual and collective modes of self-presentation, and national and indigenous identities. Pratt employs a revisionist method to historicize autoethnography in *Imperial Eyes: Travel Writing and Transculturation,* describing autoethnographic acts as "instances in which colonized subjects undertake to represent themselves in ways that engage with the colonizer's own terms" (7). In her view autoethnographic texts, as a

Defining and Discerning Life Narrative Forms

mode of counternarrative that engages and interrogates Western discourses of truth and identity, are situated in a "contact zone" that is at once geographic, linguistic, and cultural (6). There, indigenous subjects who take up writing both collaborate with and appropriate a colonizer's discursive modes by "transculturating" them into indigenous idioms, in texts that are heterogeneous for both writer and reader.

Similarly, Lionnet emphasizes the dialectical movement writers make between cultures in their *métissage* or braiding of disparate discourses, without privileging one over the other (*Postcolonial Representations,* 12 and n. 21). For her, autoethnography is a dynamic process of reciprocity in which subgroups perform operations on language in order to better represent their regional cultural realities as neither "other" nor only local. In this view, subjectivity is irreducibly pluralistic, transnational, and transactional, as it oscillates between voicing and writing autobiography.

While we earlier glossed autoethnography as "collectivized and situated life writing in which the *bios* of autobiography is replaced by *ethnos* or social group" (Smith and Watson, *Reading Autobiography,* 2nd ed., 258–59), recent critical studies have greatly expanded this notion. Within the qualitative social sciences, autoethnography is deployed by a range of theorists to differing ends. Over centuries Western anthropologists and ethnographers have collaborated with members of specific cultures and communities, especially communities "othered" and positioned as "strange," "primitive," "backward," or "vanishing," to produce the life stories of an "ethnos." In the wake of movements of decolonization around the globe and civil rights movements in the United States, anthropologists and ethnographers were persuaded by the critiques of Clifford Geertz, James Clifford, Michael M. J. Fischer, and others to situate themselves within their studies of other cultures and thereby make visible the subjective, messy, and partial nature of quests for knowledge of other people's lives and sociocultural world views. In this disciplinary context, critical ethnographic writing can be distinguished from autoethnographical acts and practices. Anthropologist Deborah Reed-Danahay has helpfully specified key terms and methods, noting that autoethnography can signal either "the ethnography of one's own group" or "autobiographical writing that has ethnographic interest" (2). She defines autoethnography as "a form of self-narrative that places the self within a social context. It is both a method and a text" that can be performed by anthropologists, nonethnographers, or life writers (9).

Other fields in qualitative social science, in expanding the concept of autoethnography to encompass the social settings of personal interactions, have diluted the term's geopolitical charge by downplaying the historical freight and transnational aspects of exchange in contexts of cultural displacement or exile and the contact zones critical to Pratt and Lionnet. Carolyn Ellis, Tony E. Adams, and Arthur P. Bochner, for example, define autoethnography as "an approach to research and writing that seeks to describe and systematically analyze *(graphy)* personal experience *(auto)* in order to understand cultural experience *(ethno)* . . . [that] challenges canonical ways of doing research and representing others" (273). The *Handbook of Autoethnography* emphasizes research methods, observing how autoethnography "uses . . . personal experience to describe and critique cultural beliefs, practices, and experiences" and "acknowledges and values a researcher's relationships with others," as well as using reflexivity, interrogating self–society intersections, and striving for social justice (Adams, Jones, and Ellis, 1–2). While life-narrative theorists would concur that the autoethnographic researcher is both an observing and an observed "I," methods of interrogating how "experience" and "authenticity" are constructed and how kinds of relationality are specified in particular cases are needed to tighten the categories of such discussions.

By contrast, both Lionnet and Pratt emphasize how new subject formations emerge in postcolonial contexts that do not simply reproduce the individualized "I" of Western autobiography, but critique its singularity and resituate it within explicitly sociopolitical contexts. For example, Julia Watson analyzes Esmeralda Santiago's *When I Was Puerto Rican* as a "strategic autoethnography" that, despite its use of metrics of authenticity, "tells a story of incomplete 'self-transculturation' about the incommensurability of different languages and cultures" after the family emigrates to New York and the narrative becomes an immigration story ("Strategic Autoethnography," 129). While the narrative strategies in such processes of dissident self-representation were at times subsumed in the trope of "talking back," the means and modes of autoethnography extend beyond that inverted mirroring, in what Homi Bhabha characterized as a kind of parodic mimicry, to new hybridized forms of subjectivity—and at times creolization—that ask readers and viewers to

Defining and Discerning Life Narrative Forms

revise their own practices for engaging the subjects of autobiographical discourse. Such analyses of literary narratives, attentive to the poetics of storytelling, clearly focus on debates about colonialism and citizenship. They employ a multiply relational form of autoethnography to engage dynamics among the narrating "I," the narrated "I" as an insider-outsider who experiences being positioned as a subordinate, and various individual and communal others. In such analyses, autoethnography is not so much a genre as a method of narrating personal experience as imbricated in social formations that enable the recall of, and intervention in, existing power relations where possible—if only vicariously and textually.

In his recent summation of theorizing autoethnography, German literary historian Christian Moser, who has written extensively on the form, attends to aspects of alienation and defamiliarization. He observes how identities are constructed in narratives that combine autobiographical and ethnographic elements to shape "socially constrained and culturally determined" subjects and link "the analysis of self to the description of culture" as a collective other—a society or an ethnic group—that can be one's own or within a plurality of cultures (232). Moser's examples suggest that acquiring self-knowledge through encounters with cultural otherness is linked to a "technique of controlled self-alienation" (234). His historical examples include Montaigne's *Essays,* Jean-Jacques Rousseau's *Confessions,* Walter Benjamin's *Berlin Childhood around 1900,* Michel Leiris's *The Rules of the Game,* Jean-Paul Sartre's *The Words,* and Zora Neale Hurston's *Dust Tracks on a Road,* texts that "stress the objectifying distance that separates the narrator from the protagonist and her or his cultural context" and rely on "the participant observer's ability to step out of culture and to effect a productive defamiliarization" (235). Moser notes, further, that writers of migrant narratives often resist the categorization of those narratives as autoethnographic because it seems to reduce them to "informants," in part a problem of how autoethnographic discourse is defined (237). In marshalling historical contexts and theoretical terms to formulate the differences of autoethnography, Moser moves the discussion beyond binary oppositions that have often vexed it.

Other literary examples of autoethnographically constructed narratives suggest how temporality is a key aspect of theorizing. The "biomythography" of Audre Lorde demonstrated, before the concept of intersectionality was theorized in feminism, that narrating stories of her multiple differences, as a Black lesbian feminist of Grenadan descent,

28   Defining and Discerning Life Narrative Forms

required a new mode of storytelling. She sought not just to intervene in the social inequities of 1960s New York, but to break through prevailing modes of self-presentation by proclaiming her autobiographical narrative as *Zami* (a version of "les amies," friends and lesbians) and subtitling it *A New Spelling of My Name,* a collectivized identity. In its mixed modes of storytelling and movement back and forth between New York City and her mother's birth island of Carriacou, Grenada, *Zami* is a "biomythography" of and for a collectivity of loving women friends seeking to create a new—as yet virtual—kind of home in futurity. As Lorde observes, "we came to realize that our place was the very house of difference rather than the security of any one particular difference" (*Zami*, 226) to shape a poetic autoethnographic story generative of new voices and visions.

Another kind of autoethnographic practice focused on temporality occurs in the ongoing series of narratives by French writer Annie Ernaux. Typically situating her personal experience in densely rendered micro- and macro-surrounds, Ernaux inscribes her subjective feelings within a social context and historicizes both the moments of an event and the set of relations to others within and against whom her narrating "I" defines herself. Above all in *The Years,* Ernaux crafts a sustained narrative of each year of her life that filters significant events through both the lens of a subjective "I," often rendered in the third person, and a kind of collective historical voice blending reportage and reflection to shape a collectivized generational "we" or "*je* collectif" (Strayer, "Translator's Note," 234).

Autoethnographic storytelling is also widely practiced in visual media by, for example, Manthia Diawara in two of his films and a memoir. His early *Rouch in Reverse* is an explicitly counterethnographic film—a rejoinder to the ethnographic filmmaking of French anthropologist Jean Rouch in West Africa—that rejects situating autoethnography as simply a reversal of investigator-informant positions. By contrast, his *In Search of Africa* is realized as both a memoir and a short film using autoethnographic methods to depict his navigations between complex worlds when he returns to West Africa after decades. He links his search for a childhood friend with the larger quest for a new Pan-African consciousness enriched by multiple past iterations of African-centered experience. *An Opera of the World,* Diawara's recent, multivocal documentary film, exceeds the contours and constraints of the autoethnographic in incorporating geographic and psychic/cultural migration between the historically polarized spheres of the global South and North.

Like Ernaux and Lorde, Diawara acutely registers shifts in what Raymond Williams defined as "structures of feeling" that resonate in individuals attuned to emergent processes and expresses them in a range of cultural formats and stories to narrate encounters with multiple social worlds over a lengthy timespan. All of these autoethnographers embed their "I"s in the larger ethnos of a "we" situated at vectors of change that implicate disparate and discordant worlds.

LIFE NARRATIVE AND AUTOFICTION

To discuss distinctions between life writing and other related forms we address in some detail a concept that has become widespread and influential in describing the terrain and status of autobiographical acts and practices. That term is *autofiction*, a concept that its proponents define in distinction to "autobiography," which they regard as a bounded genre of "faction." Over the last five decades, new modes of novelistic writing have troubled the assumed boundary between fictional and autobiographical narration in the Franco-Belgian-Quebecois tradition. Practitioners of the *nouvelle Roman* in France such as Marguerite Duras, Nathalie Sarraute, and Alain Robbe-Grillet re-formed the novel in works with a deliberate, often ironic, interplay between the fictional and the autobiographical. As *Roland Barthes by Roland Barthes* suggests, no definitive truth about past selves may be available. The referential "real" assumed to be "outside" a text cannot be written, and the subject is inescapably an unstable fiction.

Yet an autobiography-fiction boundary remained demarcated until French critic and writer Serge Doubrovsky, in 1977, began using the term *autofiction* to theorize an unstable boundary and to highlight his own literary forays. This was in part a challenge to Philippe Lejeune's foundational work on defining the autobiographical pact and Gerard Genette's genre-mapping narratological studies. While scholars commonly attribute the origin of the term to Doubrovsky, Max Saunders adds a historical corrective, noting that one early twentieth-century critic, Stephen Reynolds, elaborated schemas of autofictional modes that would later play out in the century's great Modernist texts by Marcel Proust, James Joyce, Virginia Woolf, and others. However the term originated, it has now gained traction in European contexts, as the three-volume *Handbook of Autobiography/Autofiction* edited by Martina Wagner-Egelhaaf signals, in employing a slash to mark a porous boundary between the two modes. In her view, "autofiction" denotes narratives distinct from traditional autobiography that work the boundary of "fact" and "fiction" by eliding distinctions between the authorial narrator and the fictional character, even as they document references to contemporaneous historical events and documentary materials.

But there is a conceptual problem here. In situating autofiction, in its various modes, as a radically boundary-crossing postmodernist practice, Doubrovsky and his followers simultaneously situate autobiography narrowly as autofiction's antithesis. For instance, Doubrovsky summarizes his theorizing about and practice of his coinage "autofiction" in these terms: "Fiction, of facts and events strictly real, if you prefer, is called *autofiction,* where the language of adventure has been entrusted to the adventure of language in its total freedom" (2, his translation). He goes on to assert that in distinction to "faction," "the '*reality*' of facts and events thus defined was . . . from my own personal life, in its most intimate details" (2). He argues that "the classical autobiography is a continuous, historical and logical narrative gathering the meaning of one's own life. Autofiction can seize on the same facts and events, but assembles them in a radically altered presentation, disorderly or in an order, which deconstructs and reconstructs the narrative account's own logic with a novelistic design of its own" (2–3). Calling autofiction "a postmodern version of autobiography" and a "self-novel," Doubrovsky thus both reduces the multifarious manifestations of life narrative into a static, chronological form called traditional autobiography—ignoring its many generic forms and templates since at least Augustine—and appropriates all temporal and narrative complexity to his coinage, autofiction.

Doubrovsky's schema is thus limited in at least three ways. First, it rests on an exclusionary corpus of texts, encompassing only the classic narratives of self-assured "great men" of the past who inscribed retrospective narratives of their lives in the masculinist canon of autobiography. Second, he assumes the autobiographical cannot be allusive, unruly, disruptive, or disunified; and he associates the concept of a deeper, intersubjective "truth" with the transgressive mode of autofiction: "Unlike autobiography, which explains and unifies . . . autofiction doesn't perceive someone's life to be a whole. It is only concerned with separate fragments, with broken-up chunks of existence, and a divided

Defining and Discerning Life Narrative Forms

subject who doesn't coincide with him- or herself" (Doubrovsky, cited in Jones, "Autofiction," 176). Third, Doubrovsky and his followers initially reserved the term *autofiction* for narratives that project the unknowability of the self in metadiscursive play and probe the impossibility of scripting it. They assert that "the referential self conceives of itself—in the fabric of the text—as part of a fiction because no author can claim to know the real meaning of his or her story" (Gronemann, 245). In these ways, Doubrovsky's concept of autofiction denies the dynamic, experimental, metacritical playfulness of much autobiographical writing. In our view, autofiction has been discussed less as a genre postulated by some elite, experimental writers than as a realignment of terms that reduces the generative field of life narrative to a narrow and static notion of "autobiography," and renders life narrative insufficiently "literary."

Before Doubrovsky claimed the term *autofiction,* theorists had observed that autobiographical forms employ, in Roy Pascal's term, "design" in their narration of "truth" and incorporate such fictional strategies as dialogue and point of view. Since Doubrovsky's use of the term, life writing critics have contested his distinction, most notably Lejeune in a series of exchanges. Acknowledging that "one does not escape one's self" ("Autobiographical Pact *(bis),*" 133), Lejeune proceeds to write autobiographically on how his study of the relationship of the author's name and the name of the main character led him to confront Doubrovsky's concept of "autofiction" and to acknowledge that the upsurge in novels using the author's name provokes the question, "under what conditions can the proper name of an author be perceived by a reader as 'fictitious' or ambiguous?" (cited in Watson, "Exquisite Ironies of Philippe Lejeune," 10). For Lejeune, that is, the notion of "lying truly" embedded in autofiction is an indeterminacy built into the structure of language. For us, too, as theorists of life writing, Doubrovsky's binary distinctions ignore the capacious heterogeneity of autobiographical acts and practices, historically and in the present. Finally, how does autofiction's "fictionality" differ from that in many genres of the autobiographical that engage with referentiality but do not claim to be identical with "fact"? Life narratives often emphasize their use of fictional techniques such as dialogue, characterization, and metaphor, for several reasons: to problematize the factual, thematize indeterminacy, or project self-fracturing and the failure of memory.

Max Saunders also questions Doubrovsky's influential ascription of a deeper intersubjective truth to autofictional, as opposed to autobiographical, texts, offering a genealogy and taxonomy of autofiction. Asserting that current definitions do not account for how works that are "autobiographical in *content*" differ from works that are "autobiographical in *form*" (764, 770), he proposes useful distinctions among four related terms: autofiction, autobiografiction, autofabrication, and auto-heteronymic fiction, all of which are at times subsumed under auto/fiction (771, 775). In autobiografiction, early critic Reynolds, cited by Saunders, suggests that "the words look like an autobiography, the narrator is fictional, and the events are also partly fictional, but draw on a core of real feelings experienced by the author" (770). Autofabrications, by contrast, are "fake or fraudulent autobiography" because they are "no longer deemed to contain significant autobiographical truth" and sometimes "the narrator's identity is revealed to be itself a fictional construct" (772), as in the case of Binjamin Wilkomirski's *Fragments* and James Frey's *A Million Little Pieces*. If both a narrator and his, her, or their experiences are fictionalized, yet the text is written in an autobiographical form—that is, "the utterance of a person not the author, describing experiences the author hasn't had"—another kind of fabricated identity arises that Saunders, employing a term from poet Fernando Pessoa, calls "heteronymic autobiography" (772). These works present "the self and the history of another" as "writing the words of the other, in the person of the other" (773).

As Saunders acknowledges, autobiographical works calling attention to their own partially fictional status can be thought of as hybrids oscillating across referential and fictive registers (774); they take liberties with novelistic form in order to negotiate struggles with the past and articulate complex identities in the present. As Arnaud Schmitt has observed, the concept of "autofiction" may become "an opportunity for the author to enter a fictional world while retaining her/his name, or her/his psychological/physical features; in other words, describing or even using oneself as an avatar" ("Avatars," 15). For example, some narratives respond to the seeming limitations of the autobiographical by employing pseudonymous characters to deepen the truth of experiential history, as in Tim O'Brien's *The Things They Carried* and the narratives of Paul Auster and Ruth Ozeki. Similarly, the practice of Dave Eggers suggests that the concept of autofiction is insufficient to characterize the encounters he stages among biographical fact, historical events, and

Defining and Discerning Life Narrative Forms   33

personal narratives in *What Is the What: The Autobiography of Valentino Achak Deng* and *A Heartbreaking Work of Staggering Genius*.[14] Eggers's works exemplify how life narratives are now engaging with the affordances of both fictional and autobiographical discourses to represent— and probe—the complexity of larger historical events.

But assuredly, scholars of life narrative are gravitating to the form, despite the conceptual baggage it brings and the decades of scholarship in theorizing the autobiographical it ignores. Alexandra Effe and Hannie Lawlor, in their introduction to a collection of essays, define the autofictional as "a combination of real and invented elements; onomastic correspondence between author and character or narrator; and stylistic or linguistic experimentation" and postulate the "autofictional" as a mode of telling and a technique that may occasionally become a genre (4). Narrative theorists, on the other hand, make various distinctions among kinds of nonfictional narrative, but only a few have attended to the differences of autobiographical discourse. One, Stefan Iverson, proposes a matrix of four kinds of autofictional practice, including texts that are either "pro- or anti-fiction/invention" and either "pro- or anti-auto/self" (561). These distinctions seem helpful with antiself texts, such as many of Jorge Luis Borges's short pieces, which move toward a deconstruction of the self; and with pro-self texts, such as Karl Ove Knausgaard's *My Struggle* sextet, discussed below.

Many narratives that explore subjectivities forged in the aftermath of colonial oppression have long worked the boundaries between the autobiographical and the novelistic to create hybrid modes tied to local histories of violence. But, in our view, regarding such narratives as autofictional metanarratives undercuts their political urgency. Such narratives as Michelle Cliff's *Abeng: A Novel* (Jamaica), Assia Djebar's *Fantasia, an Algerian Cavalcade* (Algeria), Tsitsi Dangarembga's *Nervous Conditions* (Zimbabwe), Maryse Condé's *Hérémakhonon: A Novel* (Guadeloupe), Myriam Warner-Vieyra's *Juletane* (Guadeloupe-Senegal), and Camara Laye's *The Dark Child* (Guinea) take up the bildungsroman form of the novel, even as they distance themselves from the alliance of autobiography with colonial regimes, in order to shape narratives that entwine local histories, languages, and customs.[15] As Lionnet notes of her decision to treat such narratives as self-referential texts, their fictionalizing serves to illuminate the processes of identity formation through a subjectively rendered consciousness ("Of Mangoes

34 Defining and Discerning Life Narrative Forms

and Maroons," 321–23). When these writers claim the agency to voice traumatic experiential histories of marginalization and oppression, categorizing their interventions in autobiographical norms and conventions as autofiction is politically undermining; it effectively erases the realities of violence and neocolonial afterlife. At this moment of ferment, many more examples could be discussed from Latin American, Anglo-American-Australian, and other canons that mix autobiographical detail with storytelling in taking some distance from the tradition of autobiography.

In European contexts, the term *autofiction* is an inadequate categorization for the six volumes of Norwegian Karl Ove Knausgaard's *My Struggle,* which he announces as a novel and narrates as a memoir. Astonishingly, its narrator seems to have total recall of details of the past as he enacts a sustained meditation on the meaning of events.[16] Stefan Kjerkegaard and Arnaud Schmitt presciently observe that Knausgaard is not narrating a life but a self, a process they term "identity-in-the-making" (555); they consider both "fiction" and "autobiography" inadequate designations for the "mirror effect" into which these self-narrations draw the reader, an experience of reciprocity. Their analysis suggests that literary theory has not yet caught up to the complexity of recent experiments in autobiographical writing, as writers move beyond the confines of a narrow concept of autofiction.

Examples of life narratives moving beyond a factual-fictional or autobiography-autofiction binary abound, perhaps nowhere more than in France. We have already discussed Annie Ernaux's challenges to the fictions of memory in the autoethnography section above. Here we would observe that her narratives, with their unnamed narrator, take pains to avoid slippage into fictional invention or approximation by tethering the subjective narration of memories and impressions to documentation by factual evidence. In *The Years,* Ernaux's narration of the span of her own and her family's life (from 1941 to 2006), a new kind of autobiographical discourse emerges, at once subjective and impersonal, private and collective, that traces an auto/biographical image of a generation while putting the intimate portrait of its narrator in the third person. She asserts that her combination of past and present impressions with scraps of documents of each year—photos, books, music, media advertising, and the like—juxtaposed to notes drawn from decades of diary-writing is not fictional, but an effort to approach "reality." (See

Defining and Discerning Life Narrative Forms

chapter 4, "What about Autobiographical Truth?," for further discussion of Ernaux's work.) Emmanuel Carrère is a different kind of boundary-crosser. His experimental texts, which he calls "nonfiction novels," test the limits of the autobiographical. After writing five novels, he composed five book-length nonfictional narratives that reconfigure the form and set up an ambivalent reader-text relationship along the lines of films by Werner Herzog, whose admixture of real and fictional stories he admires. In *My Life as a Russian Novel* (2007), Carrère combines narratives of his mother's father's conflicted political allegiances; the feature documentary he made in 2002; the woman he was involved with to whom he published a pornographic letter in *Le Monde*; his own subsequent maniacal unraveling; and an open letter to his mother, a famous Russian historian. As Wyatt Mason observed, in "combining elements that at first seem cumbersomely heterogeneous but that turn out to be meaningfully conjoined . . . Carrère's idea of nonfiction [is] to occupy your own position as fully as possible" ("How Emmanuel Carrère Reinvented Nonfiction"). Reviewing Carrère's most recent narrative, *Yoga*, Rob Doyle describes the work as "an amazing feat of 'self-cannibalisation'" in which Carrère's "trademark blend of extreme exhibitionism and digressive interest" combine as "all manner of insights, anecdotes and conjectures [are] stacked up like hoops around the long slender 'I'" ("*Yoga* by Emmanuel Carrère Review"). Here again, life narrative exceeds the prescriptive norms of "autofiction."

To those who try to firmly fix the boundaries of the autobiographical, we would caution that distinctions remain tentative; amid the hybrid modalities of nonfictionality, the autobiographical domain is an evolving one. Those who champion the concept of autofiction seem to hypostasize an autobiography-autofiction polarity that collapses autobiographical diversity into a binary, ignoring the complexity of life narrative and the productive theorizing of autobiography studies. Preserving such a polarity would create a hierarchy privileging the canonization of complexity and metanarrative. We prefer to reserve the term "autofiction" for a narrow range of works, such as Doubrovsky's own *Fils,* that foreground their experiments with self-writing in his terms.

Rather, we regard autobiographical acts as porous and theorize the autobiographical pact as a shifting set of author-subject-publisher/producer negotiations that change in response to emergent practices and

36 Defining and Discerning Life Narrative Forms

new insights. Despite the difficulty of fixing the boundary between the novelistic and the autobiographical, readers come to an autobiographical text with at least two expectations: that the protagonist is a person living in the experiential world, not a fictional character; and that the narrative will inscribe some kind of subjective truth earned by the struggle to tell or enact a story from a life. Responses to this struggle with autobiographical representation and its intersubjective and social truths both provoke controversies and elicit the fascinating boundary-crossing narratives that have emerged in recent decades.

Autobiographical narrators establish for their readers a different set of expectations from those established in either the verisimilitude and suspension of disbelief of the novel or the verifiable evidence and professional norms of biography and history-writing. Even this rudimentary set of distinctions among history, biography, fiction, autofiction, autotheory and autocritique, and autoethnography, however, is tentative. For example, *Summertime,* the third volume of Nobel laureate J. M. Coetzee's extended engagement with his past (here, his thirties), blurs any easy distinction between the fictional and the autobiographical. Confounding the norms of genre, Coetzee's work is a novel about a writer assembling the biography of the deceased writer "John Coetzee." The biographer, as part of his research, interviews characters who knew the young "Coetzee" and cites their critical points of view on him. The pseudo-archive mobilized by the biographer becomes a route of self-investigation for the novelist and life writer to examine the meanings of memory, obligation, and vulnerability. In an intriguing riff on the conventional relationship between the authorial signature and the narrator of the story, Coetzee appears on the cover as the author and in the narrative as the object of biographical representation. Here Lejeune's concept of the autobiographical pact as the negotiated relationship of author, reader, and publisher is fractured. Frank Kermode aptly reviewed Coetzee's narrative as "fictioneering," a metatextual reflection that situates writing as fundamentally self-reflexive, regardless of its declared genre.

In sum, our working definition of *self-life-writing* assumes that it is not the single unitary genre or form of "autobiography." Rather, the historically situated practices of self-representation adopt many forms as narrators selectively engage their lived experience and situate their social identities through personal storytelling. Located in specific

Defining and Discerning Life Narrative Forms

times and places, narrators are at the same time in dialogue with the processes and archives of memory and the expectations of disparate readers. As G. Thomas Couser observes, ever constrained by occasion and convention, and ever contingent, adaptable, fluid, and dynamic, autobiographical narratives manifestly share features with the novel, biography, and history ("Genre Matters," 125). They may employ the dialogue, plot, setting, and density of language of the novel. They may incorporate microbiographies of others in their representations of family, friends, and historical or religious figures. They may project multiple histories—of communities, families, nations, movements. They may adopt the inventions of fictionality to texture both the narrated I's experience and the narrating I's reflections while maintaining a relationship to the referential world in its historical contingencies. To those who try to firmly fix the boundaries of the autobiographical, we would caution that such distinctions are tentative and evolving. Paradoxically, self-life-writing is not a Procrustean bed but "a rumpled bed" distinguished by its dynamic variation and multiplicity (see Smith and Watson, "The Rumpled Bed of Autobiography" 2001).

The preliminary distinctions clarified here are developed throughout the book. Chapter 2 explores in detail the components of autobiographical subjects: memory, relationality, experience, identity, space, embodiment, and agency. Chapter 3 elaborates the narrative features of particular autobiographical acts in their multiple contexts. These two chapters suggest the processes, formal options, and rhetorical addresses that taken together, comprise the resources on which life narrators draw and the diverse contexts they negotiate and mobilize. Chapter 4 turns to the thorny question about the status of "truth" and "truth claims" in life narrative, always an occasion for fierce debate and analyses of intractable confusion, ambivalence, and desire.

2

Autobiographical Subjects

I occasionally experience myself as a cluster of flowing currents. I prefer this to the idea of a solid self, the identity to which so many attach so much significance.

—Edward Said, *Out of Place*

Memory: For lack of a natural memory, I make one of paper.

—Michel de Montaigne, *Essays*

In this chapter we explore a set of theoretical concepts helpful for understanding the dynamic processes of the subject and of autobiographical subjectivity.

MEMORY

A life narrator depends on access to memory to narrate the past in ways that situate an experiential history within the present. Memory is at once the source, authenticator, and destabilizer of autobiographical acts. But what is memory and how does it work?

Sensory Memory

Memory, apparently so immaterial, personal, and elusive, is always implicated in the materiality of sound, stone, text, garment, integrated circuits and circuit boards, or the materiality of our very bodies—the synapses and electrons of our brains and our nervous systems. Memory is evoked by the senses—smell, taste, touch, sight, sound—and encoded in objects or events with particular meaning for the narrator. In the *Confessions*, Augustine's memory of stealing pears from a tree is imbued with the sense-awakening qualities of the pears that momentarily overcome him in writing that moment. In the early twentieth century, the aroma of the madeleine stirs Marcel Proust's narrator as an olfactory conduit imaginatively returning him to a scene of his past. Later in the century Vladimir Nabokov exercises a fiercely aestheticized mode of visualizing memory in mnemonic images of the past of his childhood in Russia. His *Speak, Memory: A Memoir* links his fascination with entomology and butterflies to his art of remembering in pictures and words.

As memory researchers from fields as diverse as neuroscience, cognitive psychology, and philosophy have argued, remembering involves a reinterpretation of the past in the present. The process is not a passive one of mere retrieval from a memory bank. Rather, the remembering subject actively creates the meaning of the past in the act of remembering (Rose). Thus, narrated memory is an interpretation of a past that can never be fully recovered. As Daniel L. Schacter has suggested, "memories are records of how we have experienced events, not replicas of the events themselves" (6). He goes on to explore how "we construct our autobiographies from fragments of experience that change over time" (9). That is, we inevitably organize or form fragments of memory into complex constructions that become the changing stories of our lives. Attentive to the role of temporality, Paul John Eakin characterizes memory as "a revisionist faculty" and autobiographical texts as "fictions of a special, memory-based kind; they are fictions about what is itself a fiction, the self" ("Autobiography as Cosmogram," 94). Addressing the role of memory work in the autobiographical act, he stresses "memory's orientation to the future" as people rehearse self-narrations of their experience that have potential to change that experience in the process of telling (95).

According to researchers in developmental psychology, we learn early in childhood what people around us and, by extension, our culture expect us to remember (K. Nelson, 12). We learn techniques for remembering. We learn something about who is charged with remembering and what kinds of memories they are charged with keeping. And we learn the cultural uses of remembering, how certain ways of remembering are elicited, acknowledged, and valued. For instance, in the United States public rituals of remembering include such occasions as Memorial Day parades, Veterans Day marches, and religious holidays. Private rituals include the preservation of objects such as heirlooms and family Bibles, and the continuation of family reunions where people gather to remember, reenact, and reaffirm the family's collective past. Such rituals may be

Autobiographical Subjects

part of the texture of memory evoked in life narrative, but narrators may also struggle with or resist collective forms of cultural remembering, as they find other meanings in these moments and activities.

Memory and History

In the early twenty-first century, some versions of memory are organized digitally in such artifacts as scrapbooks, archives of selfies, and Facebook ledgers. But at other historical moments, cultures have used different means or "technologies" of memory. Early Romans carried the *lares,* urns filled with ancestral remains, to their new homes to be honored as household deities and sites of remembering. During the early modern period "memory theaters" became mnemonic devices. As Frances A. Yates has explored, the memory theater enabled subjects to mentally organize large amounts of material as a set of rooms to move through and remember items by their place in them.

James Olney has distinguished two models of memory at work in Augustine's fourth-century *Confessions,* the archaeological and the processual. The archaeological model of memory is spatial, "a site where . . . [he] can dig down through layer after layer of deposits to recover what he seeks"; memories so recovered will be unchanged, if decaying over time (*Memory and Narrative,* 19). In contrast, the processual model for memory is temporal, "bring[ing] forth ever different memorial configurations and an ever newly shaped self." This kind of remembering is imagined as a process of weaving that makes new forms from memorial strands that are also in flux (20–21).

As these examples indicate, techniques and practices of remembering change. How people remember, what they remember, and who does the remembering are historically specific. A culture's understanding of memory at a particular moment of its history shapes the life narrator's process of remembering. Often a historical moment itself comprises multiple, competing practices of remembering. Narrators at the crossroads of conflicting understandings of memory, such as contemporary Native American writer Leslie Marmon Silko, may explore these competing practices of memory and interrogate the cultural stakes of remembering by juxtaposing a dominant-culture mode and an alternative Indigenous mode. In *Storyteller,* Silko interweaves personal narratives with stories not strictly her own, photographs, and the poems and traditional stories of the Laguna Pueblo. Through joining the personal and the social, she

The Contextual Politics of Remembering

If remembering is a historically inflected practice, it is also contextual. Acts of remembering take place at particular sites and in particular circumstances. We remember the history of a relationship in the context of sexual intimacy or when we celebrate anniversaries. We remember our history as national citizens in the context of parades and national holidays. Similarly, the memory invoked in autobiographical narrative is specific to the time of writing and the contexts of telling. It is never isolatable fact; rather, it is situated association. In *Family Secrets: Acts of Memory and Imagination*, for example, Annette Kuhn explores her past identity as a working-class child in Britain by rereading her family album and reconstructing the secrets hidden in the camera's official snapshots of familiality. She also rereads public documents of the 1953 coronation of Queen Elizabeth II as forms of remembering that create for the nation a "family drama" generating desire for belonging in that larger "family" of Britain.

What is remembered and what is forgotten, and why, changes over time. Inescapably, remembering has a politics. There are struggles over who is authorized to remember and what they are authorized to remember, struggles over what is forgotten, both personally and collectively. For instance, under National Socialism, Germans in the 1930s were schooled (literally and figuratively) to remember the past of the nation as an Aryan past. After World War II the two Germanys were taught to remember different and competing versions of the war and the Holocaust and highly selective versions of the national past, depending on whether they lived in the socialist East or the liberal-democratic West. Since 1989, German autobiographical writing has been negotiating these different versions of national memory and the consequences they had for individual lives, as former East German writers do in such slightly fictionalized works as Christa Wolf's *What Remains (Was Bleibt)*, Marion Brasch's *After This, Silence (Ab Jetzt Ist Ruhe)*, and Jenny Erpenbeck's *Kairos*.

During the past two decades in the United States, we have seen fierce struggles over how the American past is to be remembered at such crucial junctures as the Civil War, the civil rights movement, the

Autobiographical Subjects

Vietnam War era, the 9/11 attacks, and the Trump presidency. Those who celebrate the nineteenth century as the era of America's Manifest Destiny have strongly differing versions of the meanings of westward expansion from those of Native American descendants displaced along the Trail of Tears and across the western plains. For example, Sherman Alexie, a member of the Interior Salish of eastern Washington state and a prolific writer of fictionalized autobiographical texts, compellingly remembers and reinterprets reservation life. His memoir *You Don't Have to Say You Love Me,* focused on the year in which his mother, Lillian, died and he had brain surgery to remove a large tumor, fuses an enduring rage at his abusive mother that challenges the trope of reconciliation in the grief memoir, with moments of wild humor. Similarly, his young adult novel, *The Absolutely True Diary of a Part-Time Indian,* narrates growing up on the Spokane Indian Reservation in ways that challenge stereotypes of the stoic, noble native.

Multiple personal narratives may contribute to revising public memory and contesting official "history." A century after one of the worst racial attacks in U.S. history, the 1921 "Black Wall Street" massacre that destroyed the Greenwood section of Tulsa, Oklahoma, resulting in the murder of up to three hundred and displacing the area's inhabitants, several survivors attested to the event's traumatic circumstances by telling personal stories that had never been included in histories of the state or the country. Insisting on national recognition of this erased past in public demonstrations, in news media, and in three televised documentaries, they lodged claims to reparations for the property and capital of which the original inhabitants and their descendants had been violently deprived. While most of the many books published in recent years are reportage, and only a few are novelized personal narratives (such as *Magic City,* by Jewell Parker Rhodes), gathering personal testimonies has created an archive of dissenting voices.

These examples suggest how the politics of remembering—what is recollected and what is obscured—is central to the cultural production of knowledge about the past, and thus to the terms of individual self-knowledge and its cultural contexts. They point out how, as we learn to read against the ideological grain, autobiographical narratives invite situated readings that reference larger cultural issues and activate archives of long-forgotten knowledge.

Collective Remembering

If we think about remembering not as an entirely privatized activity but as an activity situated in cultural politics, we can appreciate to what degree remembering is a collective activity. On a daily basis we move in and out of various communities of memory—religious, racial, ethnic, gendered, familial. Communities develop their own occasions, rituals, archives, and practices of remembering. They establish specific sites for remembering. Furthermore, particular communities are aided in their acts of remembering by different technologies: the memory theaters of the early modern period, writing, movable type, the digital code of online networks. These become systems of "artificial" memory—not in the sense that the memories are fabricated or false but in the sense that the technologies, as aids to preserving and passing on memories, shape the memories conveyed and the selves those memories construct. For example, the 1954 brutal murder of fourteen-year-old African American Emmett Till in Mississippi by two white men—allegedly for "flirting" with a white girl—has become a focal point of rewriting American history to emphasize the structured centrality of violence toward Black citizens. While there have been many narratives of this killing, such recent sites of collective memory as the Emmett Till Project website and *The Murder of Emmett Till: A Graphic History,* by scholar Karlos K. Hill and artist David Dodson, are concerned with the question of Till's agency. Accordingly, they revise earlier treatments of the story to highlight the denial of the social protections of childhood to Black male youth (see Whitted, 71).[1]

As we have observed, frequently, life narrators incorporate multiple modes and archives of remembering in their narratives. Some of these sources are personal (dreams, family albums, photos, objects, family stories, genealogy). Some are public (documents, historical events, collective rituals). One way of accessing memory may dominate because it is critical to a narrator's project, his sense of the audience for the narrative, or her purpose for making the story public. For example, in his two books of graphic memoir, *Maus: A Survivor's Tale,* Art Spiegelman includes many forms of documentary evidence from the death camps to authenticate his father's story of deportation to Auschwitz before his own birth and understand his family experience differently than he did as a child. Similarly, in her incantatory book-length poem, *Citizen: An American Lyric,* poet Claudia Rankine blends allusions to several forms

Autobiographical Subjects

of lyric poetry and media to make a collage speaking the polyvocality of a collectivized American subject.

In a different vein, food memoirs—gastrography—can become a site of preserving and reactivating collective memory. The memoir of Padma Lakshmi, a popular host on the televised Food Network show *Top Chef* who immigrated from India to the United States as a teen, incorporates, in *Love, Loss, and What We Ate,* many ingredients and techniques from her grandmother's cooking to identify food as a path to greater cultural openness and a way to undercut the media hegemony of dominant-culture food. For such life narrators, using various autobiographical genres to share collective memories may serve to reconstitute fragmented communities, even as they mark and sometimes mourn their loss.

Acts of remembering extend beyond the acknowledgment of collective sites of memory, historical documents, and oral traditions because they engage motives for remembering and question on whose behalf one remembers. Precisely because acts of remembering are relational, they are implicated in how people understand the past and make claims about their versions of it. Memory is inescapably intersubjective, as W. J. T. Mitchell observes: "Memory is an intersubjective phenomenon, a practice not only of recollection of a past *by* a subject, but of recollection *for* another subject" (193 n. 17). Memory is a means of "passing on," of sharing a social past that may have been obscured, thereby activating its potential for reshaping a future of and for other subjects. In sum, however personal, acts of remembering are fundamentally social and collective.

The concept of collective memory helps explain how societies develop notions of shared national history and even how individuals acquire their own memories related to the social frameworks of family, religion, and social class, according to Maurice Halbwachs (cited in Landsberg, 7). Pierre Nora, in his monumental study *Between Memory and History (Les Lieux de mémoire),* theorized that in the nineteenth century a new form of collective public memory developed that was related to national feeling attached to particular places or sites. Alison Landsberg extends earlier theorizing of collective memory by arguing that because of its mass technologies and massive historical events, modernity requires a different concept of collective memory, which she calls "prosthetic memory." Forms of mass culture, such as film, television,

46 Autobiographical Subjects

and the Internet, make specific memories available to large groups, creating "imagined communities" across differences of nation, ethnicity, and geography (8) that share memories to which the people in them have no experiential connection.

But what of questions of collective responsibility for violence and domination? Michael Rothberg proposes the concept of the "implicated subject" as a figure for describing how people "have inherited and benefited from historical injustices" that are often effaced in the processes of collective memory: "Most people deny, look away from, or simply accept the benefits of evil in both its extreme and everyday forms." Employing a framework of implicated subjects, he argues, "can open up a space for new coalitions across identities and groups" and shift issues of accountability from a discourse of guilt to one of responsibility (20). Such figures of implication are "imaginative representations of real but difficult-to-pin-down social forces" that call people to act responsibly, both ethically and politically, and, ideally, to join in collective action (199–200). Thus, collective remembering can activate processes of memory that move beyond a framework of denial or shame to productive intervention.

Memory and Trauma

Life writers often struggle to remember and tell histories of violence and suffering. They do so in narratives of genocide, torture, sexual abuse, AIDS, and disability, among others. In such stories of victimhood and survival the problematic of memory often comes to the fore. For some narrators, the problem of recalling and re-creating a past life involves organizing the inescapable but often disabling force of memory and negotiating its fragmentary intrusions with increasing, if partial, understanding. For some, language fails to capture, or engage, or mediate the horrors of the past and the aftereffects of survival.

In her ten-part autobiographical poem *A Poem without a Hero*, for instance, Russian poet Anna Akhmatova narrates her husband's and son's arrest during 1935–40 (the four years of Stalin's regime of terror) and links her son's imprisonment to the larger tragedy of state-sponsored murder. The subjective "I" breaks down midway through the cycle as she confesses her struggle with the pain of memory and the forgetting offered by madness. Negotiating this break, the narrator moves toward a transpersonal identification with those who suffered. Its testimony to political trauma in both her family and the state makes *A Poem without*

Autobiographical Subjects

a Hero not just an autobiographical poem but also a call to collective Russian conscience.

For Holocaust survivors such as Charlotte Delbo in *Auschwitz and After,* Elie Wiesel in *Night,* and Primo Levi in *Survival in Auschwitz: The Nazi Assault on Humanity,* the struggle with memories of the Holocaust necessitates the return again and again to incomprehensible moments in the past. Levi, for instance, struggles to exorcise memories of a regime of existence whose logic destroyed all the bases of humanity, including the metaphorical and literal dimensions of language itself. And in Spiegelman's doubly autobiographical *Maus,* the distortions and omissions of the father Vladek's memory are a partial amnesia compelling his son Art to narrate the legacies of what Marianne Hirsch calls postmemory, particularly the inaccessible memory of his dead mother.[2]

Narrators suffering from traumatic or obsessional memory may see the act of telling as therapeutic in resolving troubled memories, acknowledging how the process of writing has changed the narrator and the life story itself. In her story of traumatic childhood sexual abuse, *My Father's House: A Memoir of Incest and Healing,* Canadian writer Sylvia Fraser marks the break between the historically situated and the imaginary modes of narrating with different fonts. In this way, the daughter of the father/lover can shuttle between recollection/commentary and fantasy, using writing to engage "the anxiety and rage against a spectral patriarch who is everywhere and nowhere—whose nefarious deeds are hidden in the recesses of the unconscious, and whose authoritarian presence his daughter can never escape" (Henke, 129). The two modes of self-narrating are mutually enabling, as Fraser seeks to capture the multiple modes in which trauma is scripted and exorcised. In other cases, however, narrating a traumatic past becomes a paralyzing form of potential revictimization that is difficult to work through, as Miriam Katin's comics, *We Are on Our Own* and *Letting It Go,* dramatize.

Some narrators engage traumatic remembering around a world-historical event, such as the Holocaust, the Rwandan genocide, the Argentinian "dirty" war, the terrorist attack on 9/11/2001, or the Russian war on Ukraine. Other narrators shift attention to effects in everyday life of inequality and suffering. They tell stories of self, family, or community that illuminate the legacies of larger historical formations, such as processes of racialization, which emerged out of and secured specific conditions of oppression, colonialism, and neocolonialism. Registering the effects of racialization as lived historical legacy in the present, they relocate trauma in everyday life and relations. Such narratives of legacy, lived both as personal history and collective history, often encompass multigenerational family history. Sally Morgan's *My Place* tracks the story of her mother and grandmother back two generations in order to comprehend the costs of brutal family policies of the Australian state such as separation of mixed-race children from their mothers and communities and the sexual and economic exploitation of Aboriginal women. Morgan's attempt to recover the past that was erased in official policies designed to assimilate and "disappear" Aboriginality and in personal refusals of Indigenous identification becomes a way to understand the untold stories of Australian nationalism and the counternarratives of Indigenous Australians.

Several generations of Indigenous Australians told their stories of the Stolen Generations in the late twentieth century, in print, in as-told-to narratives, before the Australian Human Rights Commission, and in film. *Rabbit-Proof Fence,* by Doris Pilkington (Nugi Garimara), is the story of Pilkington's mother and aunt, who with another child in the 1930s escaped from the Moore River Settlement in Perth where they had been forcibly relocated for education and training and trekked a thousand miles to their communities in northwest Australia. Reimagining the achievement of that trek, the daughter/niece registers the struggles of that earlier generation, emphasizes their survival skills, and honors their reconstitution of community in the midst of policies of forced assimilation. Intergenerational life writing of this kind captures the ways in which generations carry different histories and explores those histories of everyday trauma that are embodied in the next generations. It also offers stories that position those who have suffered not only as victims of violent events but as survivors with imagination, energy, and resilience. The traumas of everyday life are thus remembered as collective and systemic.

Reading for Memory

When we read, view, or hear an autobiographical narrative, then, we listen for and attend to the role of remembering—and conscious forgetting—in the act of making meaning out of the past and the present. We may notice an emphasis on particular acts of remembering or particular moods and voices identified with certain memories. We may glimpse the

Autobiographical Subjects

triggering devices that stimulate certain memories. Then, too, narrators themselves may make the act of remembering a significant theme within the narrative. That is, they may be self-reflexive about the problem of remembering and the value of particular kinds of remembering, as are, for example, Saint Augustine in *The Confessions,* Mary McCarthy at the beginning of *Memories of a Catholic Girlhood,* Richard Rodriguez in *Hunger of Memory: The Education of Richard Rodriguez, an Autobiography,* and Alison Bechdel in *Fun Home: A Family Tragicomic, Are You My Mother? A Comic Drama,* and *The Secret to Superhuman Strength.* They may call attention to things forgotten, times irretrievable, and to the personal, familial, and communal stakes of that forgetting.

In *The Autobiography of W. E. B. Du Bois: A Soliloquy on Viewing My Life from the Last Decade of Its First Century,* Du Bois acknowledges both the role and the limits of memory when he observes that "autobiographies do not form indisputable authorities" (12). This insight motivates him to reflect on the failures of remembering and the difficulties of telling his story "frank and fair":

> Memory fails especially in small details, so that it becomes finally but a theory of my life, with much forgotten and misconceived, with valuable testimony but often less than absolutely true, despite my intention. . . . This book then is the Soliloquy of an old man on what he dreams his life has been as he sees it slowly drifting away; and what he would like others to believe. (12–13)

By refiguring his narrative as a "soliloquy" addressed to "others," Du Bois accepts the impossibility of recording only factual truth. Rather, he turns to the possibility of an intersubjective truth informed by acts of remembering—partly dream, partly promissory belief—that invites readers to confirm his interpretation. His text exemplifies how life narratives, through the memories they construct and the meditations on remembering they record, are acts of interpretation by subjects inescapably in historical time and in relation to their own ever-moving pasts.

Narrators, then, may employ rhetorical and visual means that make the act of remembering itself a significant theme. In *Charlotte Salomon and the Theatre of Memory,* a study of Salomon's extensive painted and textual work, *Life? or Theater?,* Griselda Pollock explores how Salomon composed a "theater of memory" as "a fantasia on subjectivity itself," an act of creation and staging that transforms its innovator into the artistic persona "CS" who narrates her story (407). Pollock argues that with its nonchronological and involuted processes, "the entire work seems to have been undertaken to arrive at the inception of its own memory work" (470). Reading for memory, then, attends not just to the contents of memory but to its workings as a metanarrative process.

Finally, the unreliability of memory is thematized as central to some storytelling. Russian writer Maria Stepanova's autobiographical novel *In Memory of Memory* (originally published in Russian in 2017) is acclaimed for the narrator's stylistic experiments with life writing. In it she assembles essays, documents, and literary critique about the inadequacy of her family archive. For Stepanova's narrator, her deceased aunt's diaries are a flat kind of witnessing that lacks emotional authenticity. Her mother's fragmented collections of photos, letters, and objects expose gaps in the family history that render her narrator unable tell a linear or coherent story. But they also produce a different kind of reflexive narrative of frustration with the vagaries of memory that generates acute fragments of autobiographical storytelling.

In reading for memory, then, we also read for the gaps and fissures that may draw us more deeply into what is never a simple or single story.

RELATIONALITY

Concepts of the subject, discussed below, are entangled with the concept of relationality; but as many diverse aspects of relationality have been theorized, we treat them sequentially here.

Relationality in Linguistic and Rhetorical Address

Relationality inheres in the very utterance of an "I," the linguistic and rhetorical marker that projects a fantasy of presence for the singularity of a body. To say "I" is to address an other. "In the light of a unique and unrepeatable identity—irremediably exposed and contingent," Adriana Cavarero argues, "the other is therefore a necessary presence" (89). In the necessary presence of a "you," whether a real or imagined interlocutor, the subject becomes what Cavarero terms a "narratable self." She goes on to observe that the "unique existent" is "an identity which, from beginning to end, is intertwined with other lives—with reciprocal exposures and innumerable gazes—and needs the other's tale" (88). On a fundamental level, then, the subject is a subject of rhetorical relationality, seeking the recognition of an other. Some theorists of this fundamental

Autobiographical Subjects

relationality invoke Mikhail Bakhtin's concept of dialogic subjectivity as explanatory: subjects become conscious through language; social groups maintain social dialects through which subjects become conscious; yet language itself is heteroglossic and infused with multiple meanings. In other words, otherness crosses the tongue or fingers whenever words are spoken, written, or signed, a kind of glottal relationality, since the very words the "I" says come to the subject spoken by others (292).

Relationality and Psychodynamic Processes

Another perspective on theorizing relationality informs psychoanalysis. In versions of Lacanian psychoanalytical theory of the subject, an other is multivalent, including the other of the symbolic system—of what is sayable, of the signifying system that slides across tongues or fingers; the other of primary relations; the other of the unconscious, that is, the other within. Jacques Lacan argues in *The Language of the Self: The Function of Language in Psychoanalysis,* for instance, that the illusion of a whole self, acquired in the mirror stage, is an identification taking place in "the imaginary." The infant is both captivated by and trapped in an image of self, an alienation through which the ego constituted at this stage maintains a false appearance of coherence and integrity. Various French feminists intervened in Lacan's tripartite psychic structure to delineate different versions of relationality: Julia Kristeva elaborated a presymbolic realm of infancy by employing the concept of an instinctual semiotic associated with the Mother, and described the psychodynamic process of abjection through which the threatening unruliness and disturbances of order and orderliness are repressed to achieve the Oedipal resolution of the boy's entry into the symbolic (*Desire* and *Power*). In the Anglo-American field of ego psychology Nancy Chodorow differentiated the fluid relationality of the girl child from the boundedness that defines the impact of the boy child's necessary separation from the Mother (44). She thereby articulated a gendered relationality of permeable ego boundaries.

Relationality and Difference

In response to early theorizing of the liberal subject in the West as an autonomous, rational individual, scholars of marginalized literatures and subjects, beginning in the 1980s and early 1990s, employed and theorized a concept of relationality to capture the "difference" of marginalized forms of writing and subjectivity. In discussions of women's life writing, feminist scholars adapted Chodorow's sexual-difference theory to argue that women's life writing, mimetic of their lives, unfolded through what Susan Stanford Friedman termed the "fluid boundaries" of relationality rather than through clear-cut ego differentiation. They then incorporated this relationality/individuality binary in analyses of life writing by women and men, observing how sexual difference marked the themes, forms, and aesthetics of women's autobiographical practices. Scholars of Native American autobiography in the 1990s brought this binary differentiation to reading Native American narratives as a kind of relationality born of communal social organization and a long history of kinship networks. Some distinguished the thematics, aesthetics, and rhetorics of Native American writing from its more individualistic Anglo-European/American counterpart. However, Hertha D. Sweet Wong, a scholar of Native American literature, critiqued the oversimplification of binary theorizations of relationality and difference, such as man/woman, Indigenous/European colonizer (168–69). Such theorizations are now regarded as too rigid to account for the polyvocality of autobiographical narration.

Relationality and Subjectivation

Theorists uncomfortable with "difference" feminism, as well as those influenced by Michel Foucault and Louis Althusser, located relationality in the dynamics of a subject's subjectivation. For Judith Butler, "The 'I' who cannot come into being without a 'you' is also fundamentally dependent on a set of norms of recognition that originated neither with the 'I' nor with the 'you'" (*Precarious Life*, 45). Such a model of psychic relationality is an effect of two things: the small-"p" power of Foucauldian subjection that informs the relationality of the regulatory norms into which we enter; and interpellation, in Althusser's version of subject formation. Elsewhere Butler writes that gender and sexuality are "*modes of being dispossessed,* ways of being for another, or, indeed by virtue of another" (*Undoing Gender,* 19). Norms inhabit subjects and impel them to certain conditions of performativity through which they secure the norms as their own; sometimes they expose the instability of a norm through their failure to conform. In the case of interpellation, relationality involves the dynamic through which the subject is positioned within the naturalized social locations of institutions such as schools and bureaucracies, ideological agendas, and geopolitical formations.

Autobiographical Subjects

The exercise of brute power in dehumanizing epistemological regimes means that some groups of people are differentially positioned vis-à-vis social norms of intelligibility, discursive regimes, and material conditions of discovery, invasion, colonization, slavery, or the civilizing mission. These formations comprise the historical conditions of the relationality of subordinated others. Constrained life scripts have been written of them and for them by others through slow and eruptive violence. As a consequence, the value of their storytelling, testimony, knowledge-making, and political claims goes unacknowledged or unrecognized; the uniqueness of their narratability is not solicited; and the possibility of their recognition is forestalled. The othering effects of this kind of relationality become an experiential history of being spoken for, that is, being represented as a less-than-human, unmarked, unintelligible other (Weheliye, 13). Approaching the question of relationality and ethics from the histories of those experiencing radical dehumanization and violence for their "otherness," Weheliye implicitly points to an ethics of relational alterity. Relationalities of the present, he argues, are "existent hierarchies"; to counter this dehumanizing relationality, people have to "design novel assemblages of relation" (13) from models of "alternative critical, political, and poetic assemblages" (12). That is, our reading practices need to become attentive to textual lacunae and to what may be unmarked or subordinated.

Relationality, Vulnerability, and Ethical Response

Relationality has also been invoked in explorations of how the ethics of self-narration relates to the vulnerability of the subject. Invoking the late writings of Foucault, Butler argues that the self's founding condition is a vulnerability rooted in its embeddedness in its social conditions and its engagement with others: "The 'I' cannot knowingly fully recover what impels it, since its formation remains prior to its elaboration as reflexive self-knowledge. . . . Conscious experience is only one dimension of psychic life and . . . we cannot achieve by consciousness or language a full mastery over those primary relations of dependency and impressionability that form and constitute us in persistent and obscure ways" (*Giving an Account*, 58). Subjects are opaque to themselves, an opacity that is an effect of several things: the self has only fitful access to the psychic life before and beyond self-consciousness; it is imbricated in the constant self–other interactions of social worlds; and it must employ storytelling modes, tropes, and self-positionings to tell about itself.

Butler observes that in telling a story of itself, the "I" enters a scene of narration that externalizes the self: "The 'I' who begins to tell its story can tell it only according to recognizable norms of life narration. . . . To the extent that the 'I' agrees, from the start, to narrate itself through those norms, it agrees to circuit its narration through an externality, and so to disorient itself in the telling through modes of speech that have an impersonal nature" (*Giving an Account*, 52). To enter into autobiographical acts, the "I" who "agrees" to tell its story enters, negotiates, and adapts to externalities that are "the recognizable norms of life narration." Thus, experiential history and subjectivity are routed through cultural "modes of speech" that produce defamiliarization (52). Such storytelling effects a disorienting instability in self-knowing and introduces difference, unease, and inscrutability. For Butler, recognizing the self's founding vulnerability is precisely what grounds the ethics of self-accounting (64). To the degree that the self eschews the fantasy of interpretive control and relinquishes its project of self-knowing, the lure of "egoic mastery," it opens itself to the opacity of the other as well as the other in itself (58). From this point of view, the relationality of subjects is neither disabling nor escapable. Rather, relationality is a founding condition of our psychic life, our narrative accounts, and our humanity.

Autobiographical subjects, then, are multiply vulnerable: to their own opaqueness, to their relationality to others, and to the norms through which they tell of themselves. Yet Butler situates ethical agency in the willingness of the "I" to give an account of itself as opaque and vulnerable to the other. In such an offering of narration, "nonviolence may well follow from living the persistent challenge to egoic mastery that our obligations to others induce and require" (*Giving an Account*, 64). Agency, then, might be said to derive from our willingness to narrate our opacity, our fragmentation, our limits of knowability, to narrate, that is, "the way in which we are constituted in relationality: implicated, beholden, derived, sustained by a social world that is beyond us and before us" (64). Here Butler undoes the idea that subjects exercise agentic control over the interpretations of their lives in order to become willing to acknowledge the self's opacity and its ethical obligation to the other.

Further, the rhetorical figures, narrative strategies, modes of address, and generic forms tapped in personal storytelling are all res-

Autobiographical Subjects

ervoirs of antecedent others, conduits of a relationality of the "social world that is beyond us and before us," as Butler observes (*Giving an Account,* 64). In this way, the personal storytelling of subjects, which both rehearses and exemplifies relationality, invites a response; and the nature of that response and responsibility opens onto questions of ethical relationality. Cavarero approaches the question of personal storytelling by calling for an ethics that does not privilege responses of empathy and identification, feeling for or feeling as another; for her, "an altruistic ethics of relation does not support empathy, identification, or confusions. Rather this ethic desires a *you* that is truly an *other,* in her uniqueness and distinction. No matter how much you are similar and consonant, says this ethics, your story is never my story" (92). In other words, an ethics of relationality is an ethics that recognizes incommensurability. By contrast, Butler approaches the question of ethical relationality by invoking the subject's primary vulnerability and the need to "vacate the self-sufficient 'I' as a kind of possession": to risk such evacuation requires a "willingness to become undone in relation to others" as "our chance of becoming human" (*Giving an Account,* 136).

These reorientations of the dynamics of relationality resonate with Simone de Beauvoir's concept of an ethics of ambiguity articulated in the mid-twentieth century. Recognizing the importance of de Beauvoir's *Ethics of Ambiguity* to later theorizing of relationality, Françoise Lionnet explores how de Beauvoir refused to reify the self-enclosed ego and its disembodiment of thought persistent in the history of Western philosophy; instead, she proposes an ethics of nurturance and intersubjectivity, an acknowledged otherness that is not a projection of the self-contained ego but an exchange with other "existents." This "nurturing," Lionnet argued "is thus a *relation* that seeks, not to abolish difference or make all relation into self-relation, but to establish the difference of another, the nurtured one" ("Consciousness," 116). Despite the different inflections of these three theorists, their emphases foreground the incommensurability of subjects and the difference of an other as foundational to self-presentation.

Relationality as Assemblage

During the last decade theorists have explored another dimension of the subject's relationality by postulating dynamic webs of assemblages in which human subjects are but one node. In their views, relationality occurs not just between subjects and the forces of subjection, or between individual subjects and the addressee of their narration. Instead, the force fields and networks of relationality vibrate along flows, currents, and myriad interactions that join subjects to environments as well as processes internal and external to them, forms of matter, and other species. Drawing on the groundbreaking theorizing of Karen Barad on assemblages, Anna Poletti reads the autobiographical as an activity in which what she terms "self-life-inscription" occurs as "a materialization of an assemblage": "a set of actions that occur in a situation where humans, nonhumans, machines, objects, and matter are interacting" (*Stories of the Self,* 57). She argues that "thinking of identity and sociality as relational" needs to be extended beyond human subjects to actants in the material world, as "the human is but one of many active, material forces" and urges critics to "turn our attention to 'practices, doings, and actions' rather than representations" (58). In *Bodily Natures: Science, Environment, and the Material Self,* Stacy Alaimo proposed an ecological relationality as transcorporeality. Elaborating how "the human is always intermeshed with the more-than-human world," she argues that this "thinking across bodies may catalyze the recognition that the environment, which is too often imagined as inert, empty space or as a resource for human use, is, in fact, a world of fleshy beings with their own needs, claims, and actions"; with this recognition, she insists, may come acknowledgment of "the often unpredictable and unwanted actions of human bodies, nonhuman creatures, ecological systems, chemical agents, and other actors" (2). Positing and investigating extrahuman relations thus becomes a crucial standpoint for theorizing ecobiographical writing in this age of the Anthropocene.

Reading for Relationality

The concept of relationality has become central to theorizing autobiographical acts and practices. In the late 1990s both Nancy K. Miller (in "Representing Others") and Paul John Eakin (in "Relational Selves, Relational Lives") employed versions of relationality to argue that much autobiographical narrative is relational, that it is often "the other's story" (Eakin, *How Our Lives,* 56). Both critics have pointed out that the notion of autobiographical relationality, which was taken to characterize the difference of women's autobiography in early feminist scholarship, in fact characterizes modes of relationship in much life

Autobiographical Subjects

writing by both men and women. Miller, Eakin, and Susanna Egan in *Mirror Talk* approach autobiography as not a solitary but an interactive story. In Eakin's words, relationality offers not only "the autobiography of the self but the biography *and* the autobiography of the other" (*How Our Lives*, 58). That is, the narrator's story is often refracted through the stories of others, as in the autoethnographic constitution of a community of identification, or in confessional dramas of familiality and familiarity. Indeed, Eakin analyzes familial, community, and ethnic relational narratives as autoethnographic in how they extend the *autos* to a collectivity. For instance, Chinese-born artist Ai Weiwei's memoir *1000 Years of Joys and Sorrows* traces the overlap of his life with that of his father Ai Qing, a renowned poet who was purged and consigned as a "rightist" intellectual to internal exile in 1957, the year his son was born; and the memoir is refracted through twelve-year-old Ai Lao, of the third generation. Living in exile in Europe, Ai Weiwei links their life experiences generationally: "The whirlpool that swallowed up my father upended my life too, leaving a mark on me that I carry to this day" (5). That is, their stories implicate one another's not just as familial history but as lives entwined with what he regards as the repressive political ideology of the Chinese Communist Party.

As we have seen, for other theorists of life writing, relationality is narratively incorporated through Bakhtin's concept of heteroglossic dialogism, that is, the multiplicity of "tongues" or the polyvocality through which subjectivity is enunciated. (See also "Voice in Autobiographical Narration and Presentation" in chapter 3.) As we observed above, the subject is always a subject of the other, constituting and constituted by heterogeneous social discourses. The very words through which a story is "spoken" or written are the language of the other. Williams L. Andrews has effectively employed a Bakhtinian model to read how narratives of the enslaved enact the telling of "free" stories through dialogical shifts. Lionnet, in *Autobiographical Voices,* turns to Edouard Glissant's concept of creolization to propose a theory of autobiographical textuality as a *métissage* of disparate voices in subjects whose cultural origins and allegiances are multiple and conflicting. And Mae Gwendolyn Henderson draws on heteroglossia and glossolalia, the practice of speaking in tongues in some churches, to account for the polyvocality of first-person narrative in African American women's writing. Further, relationality is rhetorically implicated in the addressee(s) posited by the narrator as both the narratee within a text and the ideal reader to whom the narrative is directed and through whom it is imagined and circulated. Relationality, then, indicates how the subject is always in process and thus involved with others.

Finally, by definition, life narrators cannot address the subject other that in a sense "speaks" them. But critics can perform Lacanian readings of the fissures and gaps of texts, as, for example, Shari Benstock does with Virginia Woolf's *Moments of Being*. They can also read such gaps in the tensions of narrative strategies. In *The Lover*, for instance, Marguerite Duras's narrator shifts between the confessional mode of first-person narrative and the novelistic mode of third-person narrative. Duras, according to Suzanne Chester, "undermines the objectification to which she was subjected . . . [and] appropriates the masculine position of the observer" (445). Here the narrator exploits the otherness of her identity as a young white woman in colonial Indochina to undermine the stability of the "I"s of colonizer and colonized.

In sum, relationality is multidimensional, at once self-locating and self-dispossessing. Through its mechanisms of connection, the subject is materialized and undone, possessed and dispossessed. It both comes to know itself and to confront its own opacity, again and again. As we have traced, there are different kinds of relationality that connect the subject: to the social; to psychic otherness within and the pulses of affective response to others coursing through bodies; to subjection before collections of proxy others who enforce regulatory norms and reproduce othering processes that render some subjects insignificant, threatening, or unintelligible; to linguistic dialogism and narratability; to ethical response and responsibility; to a materiality involving that of other species, technologies, and agglomerations of assemblages. Theorizing relationality thus unsettles and questions the notion that self-narration is the monologic utterance of a solitary, introspective subject knowable to itself. Demonstrably, subjects are entangled in multiple, overlapping, and conflicting webs of relationality.

EXPERIENCE

Experience. We have it. It is ours. The intimacy, immediacy, and palpability of our memories tell us so. But what does it mean to say we have an experience? While the experience represented in an autobiographical narrative seems merely personal, it is anything but that. Mediated

Autobiographical Subjects

through memory and language, "experience" is already an interpretation of the past and of our place in a culturally and historically specific present.

Experience as Constitutive of the Subject

A provocative exploration of the phenomenon we call experience can be found in Joan W. Scott's essay "Experience." Scott challenges the foundational status of experience as a ground of analysis and a ground of knowledge about the world and ourselves. She cautions that talking about experience as either internal to an individual (expressive of an individual's consciousness—what we have inside us) or external to the individual ("the material upon which consciousness works"—what happens to us from outside) "leads us to take the existence of individuals for granted" (27). This taken-for-grantedness of the relationship between individual experience and the claim to unique individuality is what Scott calls into question because it obscures how our notion of meaningful experience is socially produced. How do we know what we know about ourselves? How do we know who we are?

Taking the analysis of Teresa de Lauretis as a point of departure, Scott defines "experience" as "a process . . . by which subjectivity is constructed" (27). "Through that process," de Lauretis writes, "one places oneself or is placed in social reality and so perceives and comprehends as subjective (referring to, originating in oneself) those relations—material, economic, and interpersonal—which are in fact social, and, in a larger perspective, historical" (*Alice Doesn't,* 159). Experience, then, is the very process through which a person becomes a certain kind of subject owning certain identities in the social realm, identities constituted through material, cultural, economic, and psychic relations. "It is not individuals who have experience," Scott claims, "but subjects who are constituted through experience." Autobiographical subjects do not predate experience. In effect, autobiographical subjects know themselves as subjects of particular kinds of experience attached to their social statuses and identities. They know themselves to be a "woman" or "child" or "heterosexual" or "worker" or "indigenous" because these identity categories come to seem natural, "given characteristics of persons" (27).

Experience as Discursive

Subjects know themselves in language because experience is discursive, embedded in the languages of everyday life and the knowledge produced at everyday sites. For instance, through the "discourse" of medical institutions (the language, images, metaphors, and acts through which medical institutions produce and circulate knowledge about persons) people learn to understand themselves—"experience" themselves—as "patients" in need of healing or as "diseased" or "insufficient" bodies in need of surgical intervention and repair. This medical discourse also becomes the language through which doctors understand themselves as "scientists" or "healers." Of course, this is only one example of how we understand what has happened or is happening to us, and thus how we know ourselves through what Michel Foucault analyzed as discursive regimes. Every day we know ourselves, or experience ourselves, through multiple domains of discourse, domains that serve as cultural registers for what counts as experience and who counts as an experiencing subject. But since discourses are historically specific, what counts as experience changes over time with broader cultural transformations of collective history.

At the same time that we say that experience is discursive, we recognize that there are human experiences outside discursive frames—affects, bodily conditions and alignments, feelings of spirituality, powerful sensory memories of events and images. Every day, all day long, the materiality of the body affects us, literally as well as discursively. Bodies bleed. They manifest illnesses. They get hurt. They feel hunger, thirst, desire. They turn away, shuddering in shame. These are among the material events in our lives. But in making meaning of these events, we make that meaning, or the "experience" of those events, discursively, in language or image, often as narrative. Thus, we retrospectively make experience and convey a sense of it to others through storytelling; and as we tell our stories, discursive patterns both guide and compel us to tell stories about ourselves in particular ways.

Experience as Interpretation

The discursive nature of experience requires us to be self-reflexive about what we understand as "our experience" or what we think we mean when we say things like "That's just my experience!" or "I'm a man." That is, what seems "ours" or "mine" has been formed and has changed over time, and we can investigate this process of change. This thing called "experience is," as Scott cautions, "at once always already an interpretation *and* is in need of interpretation" (37).

In autobiographical acts, narrators become readers of their experi-

Autobiographical Subjects

ential histories, bringing discursive schema that are culturally available to them to bear on what has happened. The multiple autobiographical narratives of Giacomo Casanova, Frederick Douglass, Marguerite Duras, Buchi Emecheta, Maya Angelou, Maggie Nelson, and Karl Ove Knausgaard, for example, offer fascinating glimpses into life narrators' successive interpretations or revisions of the past. These versions, written at different points in their lives and, in Douglass's case, retelling the "same" story divergently in two subsequent narratives, invite readers to raise a question: Do different readings of an experience signal stages of, or changes in, the overall pattern of beliefs encoded in the autobiographical story? Or do changes from one text to its "sequel" or "prequel" signal larger cultural transformations affecting how people know themselves through the stories that are tellable (and discourses available) to them at particular historical moments?

Experience and Authority

It is important to theorize what we call experience because the narrator's lived experience is the primary kind of evidence asserted in autobiographical acts, the basis on which readers are invited to consider the narrator a uniquely qualified authority. Thus, a narrator's investment in the "authority" of experience serves a variety of rhetorical purposes. It invites or compels the reader's belief in the story and the veracity of the narrator; it persuades the reader of the narrative's authenticity; it validates certain claims as truthful; and it justifies writing and publicizing the life story.

In their autobiographical acts, narrators claim the "authority of experience" both explicitly and implicitly. Implicit claims can be as unobtrusive as the appearance of the autobiographer's name on the title page. This is the case for people who publish what G. Thomas Couser, drawing on Lorraine Adams's essay "Almost Famous," calls "somebody" narratives (*Signifying Bodies,* 1)—public figures and celebrities whose names on the front cover announce their credibility: Nelson Mandela or Mumia Abu-Jamal or Hillary Rodham Clinton or Patti Smith or Keith Richards. The name itself—well known or notorious—is a kind of guarantee. It assures the reader of the authority of the writer to tell his, her, or their story and aims to make the story a credible disclosure to its audience.

By contrast, persons outside the dominant culture who are unknown and marginalized by virtue of their lack of public status writing "nobody memoirs" may make explicit appeals to the authority of experience that confers on them "some body" status (Couser, *Signifying Bodies*, 1). Such appeals can be made on the basis of sexual, or ethnic, or racial, or religious, or national identity claims. In other words, identity confers political and communal credibility. In such cases, a previously "voiceless" narrator from a community not culturally authorized to speak— for instance, an enslaved person, a nonliterate, a child, an inmate of a mental hospital, a formerly colonized person—finds in identification the means and the impetus to speak publicly. Richard Wright, for example, in narrating his autobiography *Black Boy (American Hunger: A Record of Childhood and Youth)*, explicitly situates himself vis-à-vis racialized communities, both Black and white, inviting his reader to accept his narrative as authoritatively representative of the life script of an African American "boy." Similarly, James Baldwin negotiates the ambiguities of being a "native son" in *Notes of a Native Son*.

As the cases of Wright and Baldwin suggest, not all "experience" is accorded social and cultural recognition or legitimacy. Whereas the names of the celebrities cited above bestow the "authority" of experience on "somebody" narrators (even in cases where the narratives are ghostwritten), in "nobody" narratives the authority to narrate is hard-won in a constant engagement with readers posited as skeptical, unbelieving, resistant, and even hostile. Thus, the instability of something called the authority of experience suggests how the category of experience itself is socially, culturally, historically, and politically negotiated.

Reading for the Authority of Experience

Because issues of authority can be crucial to autobiographical acts, life writers have much at stake in gaining the reader's belief in the experiences they narrate and thus having the "truth" of the narrative validated. Persuasion to belief is fundamental to the intersubjective exchange of narrator and reader. Appeals to the authority of experience bring to the fore issues of trust in autobiographical narrating, since the autobiographical relationship depends on the narrator's winning and keeping the reader's trust in the plausibility of the narrated experience and the credibility of the narrator. In some life writing this makes for a complex relationship between narrator and reader.

Consider the case of *Incidents in the Life of a Slave Girl: Written by Herself* by Harriet A. Jacobs, published in 1861. Defenders of slavery were

Autobiographical Subjects

fiercely invested in debunking the authenticity of narratives about life in the slave system. And certain conventions of ex-slave narratives provided grounds for alleging that these stories were fictionalized. Fugitive or formerly enslaved people often gave fictional names to the people in their narratives to maintain secrecy about escapes and to protect people left behind. Often the narratives were "edited," and in the process rearranged and changed, by Northern abolitionists, many of whom helped fugitives to write their narratives and get them published. Given such circumstances, Southern pro-slavery apologists found grounds on which to challenge the credibility and veracity of the narratives and thus the whole enterprise of abolitionism. Jacobs's *Incidents* was drawn into this maelstrom of debatable authenticity and authorship. Jacobs fictionalized the names of people in her narrative, including her own, and depended on the editorial help of abolitionist Lydia Maria Child in revising her text. Soon after publication the narrative was dismissed as a fraud and a fiction. More than a century later, scholar Jean Fagan Yellin documented its historical veracity, which helped move *Incidents* from the status of forgotten fiction to exemplary ex-slave narrative. It became evident that its narrative of brutalization, attempted rape, and imprisonment has a truth value beyond the accuracy of particular facts. The example of *Incidents,* therefore, suggests how narratives, and the authority of experience asserted in them, enter a public arena where issues of verifiability and authenticity are fiercely contested by interested groups and where changing norms of the "truth" of experience lead to reevaluation.

Readers have expectations about who possesses the cultural authority to tell a particular kind of life story. They also have expectations about what stories derived from direct, personal knowledge should assert. For instance, readers expect the ex-slave narrative to be written by a formerly enslaved person, or the Holocaust narrative to be written by a survivor or survivor-descendant, or the narrative of nationalization or exile to be written by an immigrant or refugee. Readers also accept the authority of the near-and-dear to entwine the biography of a loved one with an autobiographical reflection that is mediated through the account of the loved one. In *The Woman Warrior: Memoirs of a Girlhood among Ghosts,* Maxine Hong Kingston braids her stories with the stories of her ancestor No-Name Woman, her mother Brave Orchid, and her aunt Moon Orchid. And Barack Obama juxtaposes stories of growing up with his Kansas-born white mother and her family in Hawai'i to the Kenyan

64 Autobiographical Subjects

father he seeks and Kenyan extended family he recounts discovering in *Dreams from My Father.*

The case of Gertrude Stein's *The Autobiography of Alice B. Toklas* offers a more extreme case of the issue of who claims the authority to tell the story of a loved one. Stein, writing in the voice of her lifelong partner and friend Alice, primarily celebrates the brilliance and accomplishments of Stein and their expatriate circle in Paris of the 1920s and 1930s. Is this, as critics have suggested, fraudulent, an act of ventriloquism in Alice's voice? Is it parasitic, an act of appropriating Alice's experience? Or is it an act of dedicated speaking through the other that commingles the boundaries of separate identities into a shared subject? For Stein, whose response to publishers' requests for her autobiography was "Not possibly," writing "that autobiography" in which "I" and "you," "eye" and "other" become indistinguishable, seems to authorize a subject that is irreducible to either "Gertrude" or "Alice."

IDENTITY

Autobiographical acts involve narrators in "identifying" themselves to the reader. That is, writers make themselves known by acts of identification and, by implication, differentiation.

Identity as Difference and Commonality

Identities materialize within collectivities and out of the culturally marked differences that permeate symbolic interactions within and between collectivities. One is a "woman" in relation to a "man." One is a "disabled" person in relation to someone who is seen as "able." Identities are marked in terms of many categories: gender, race, ethnicity, sexuality, nationality, class, generation, family genealogy, religious belief, and political ideologies, to list the most obvious. These are differences that, at least for now, have meaning in the material and symbolic structures that organize human societies. But identity as difference implies also identity as likeness. As Susan Stanford Friedman notes, "an identity affirms some form of commonality, some shared ground" (*Mappings,* 19). In *The Sweeter the Juice: A Family Memoir in Black and White,* for instance, Shirlee Taylor Haizlip explores how "Black" and "white" identities in the United States are far more fluid than many suspect as she traces a family history that includes the passing of certain aunts and uncles as "white." Reconstructing family trees, Haizlip reconsiders the

Autobiographical Subjects

basis on which racial identities are founded and flounder and exposes the "dark secrets people have in their white souls" (238). She thereby links identity to genealogy in ways that subsequent authors such as Sarah M. Broom, in *The Yellow House: A Memoir,* incorporate to narrate African American identities as complexly structured.

But social organizations and symbolic interactions are always in flux; therefore, identities are necessarily provisional. What may be a meaningful identity on one day or in one context may not be culturally and personally meaningful at another moment or in another context. Think, for instance, of how many identities you cycle through in the course of a day, identities linked to gender, national citizenship, work status, sexuality, class location, generational location, ethnicity, and family constellation. And notice the potential for conflict between or among these different identities. Because of this constant placement and displacement of "who" we are, we can think of identities as multiple and as "contextual, contested, and contingent" (Scott, 36).

Identity, Positionality, and Performativity

As Scott argued for experience, so for identities. They are constructed. They are in language. They are discursive. They are not essential— born, inherited, or natural—though much in social organization leads us to regard identity as given and fixed. Similarly to language, Bakhtin argued that consciousness—which also implies identity as a category of consciousness—is dialogical. That is, it is always implicated in the processes of social exchange. Since social groups have their languages, each member of the group becomes conscious in and through that language. Thus, autobiographical narrators come to consciousness of who they are, of what identifications and differences they are assigned, or what identities they might adopt through the discourses that surround them. And because of what Bakhtin calls "heteroglossia" in the social realm, the multiplicity of languages, words, and meanings that "mutually supplement one another, contradict one another and [are] interrelated dialogically" (292), the subject comes to consciousness through multiple identities and multiple voices. This is why, as Stuart Hall argues, identity is "a 'production' which is never complete, always in process, and always constituted within, not outside, representation" (392).

Identity is voiced in self-presentation. The theoretical concept of *positionality* or "subject position" designates how speaking subjects take up, inhabit, and speak through discourses of identity that are culturally salient and available to them at a particular historical moment. These "subject positions"—for they are always multiple and often contradictory—are effects of social relations whose power is distributed unevenly and asymmetrically across differences. Subject positions thus form at the intersections of multiple discursive trajectories. Foucault established a vocabulary for specifying subject positions in his analysis of "technologies of the self" in confessional practices as imperatives for constituting the "disciplined" subject. Leigh Gilmore has employed his methodology in nuanced readings of the "autobiographics" of a range of women's life writing by focusing on the subject positions that narrators negotiate within the constraints of discursive regimes as they engage with genres of self-presentation that prohibit that speaking *(Autobiographics)*.

Kelly Oliver makes a helpful distinction between subject position and subjectivity: "Subject positions, although mobile, are constituted in our social interactions and our positions within our culture and context. They are determined by history and circumstance. . . . Subjectivity, on the other hand, is experienced as the sense of agency and response-ability that are constituted in the infinite encounter with otherness, which is fundamentally ethical" (17). Thus, while historical situatedness underlies subject positioning, subjectivity is psychoanalytically driven in familial relations by the subject's original separation and alienation, which some view as traumatic (65). Our experience of subjectivity, however, resides in the tension between subject position and the subjectivity that, although prior to position, is interconnected with it.

A second theoretical concept, *performativity*, illuminates how autobiographical occasions serve as dynamic sites for the performance of identities that become constitutive of subjectivity. This concept postulates that identities are not fixed or essentialized attributes of autobiographical subjects; rather, they are enacted and reiterated through cultural norms and discourses, and thus remain provisional and unstable. Much contemporary discussion of life narrative as performative is informed by Butler's deconstruction of a binary gender system and her assertion that gender is performative. For Butler, performativity "must be understood not as a singular or deliberate 'act,' but, rather, as the reiterative and citational practice by which discourse produces the effects that it names" (*Bodies That Matter*, 20).

Theories of performativity have offered critics of life narrative a

Autobiographical Subjects

vocabulary for describing the complexities of how regulatory discourses of identity are related to material bodies, as well as to autobiographical agency. Sidonie Smith reads autobiographical narration as performative because it enacts the "self" it claims has given rise to the "I." Responding to Butler's assertion that "the 'I' neither precedes nor follows the process of . . . gendering, but emerges only within and as the matrix of gender relations themselves," Smith explores how "the interiority or self that is said to be prior to the autobiographical expression or reflection is an *effect* of autobiographical storytelling" ("Performativity," 18).

In a somewhat contrasting view, Eakin locates the performativity of life narrative in what he terms a "shift from a documentary view of autobiography as a record of referential fact to a performative view of autobiography centered on the act of composition" (*Touching the World,* 143). Eakin, however, emphasizes that life writing is a process of constructing a "narratively constituted identity," not an instantiation of an autobiographical subject that, in Barthes's terms, is "merely . . . an effect of language" (*How Our Lives,* 139). As all these theorists imply, identity is not a "solid self" but is productively, as Edward Said's epigraph to this chapter suggests, in contrapuntal movement and without a central theme.

Identity as Historically Specific Model

Cultural identities, according to Stuart Hall, are "the unstable points of identification or suture, which are made, within the discourses of history and culture" (395). Thus they are marked by time and place. There are models of identity culturally available to life narrators at any particular historical moment that influence what is included and what is excluded from an autobiographical narrative. Some models of identity culturally available in the United States over the past three hundred years have included the sinful Puritan seeking the signs of salvation, the self-made man, the struggling and suffering soul, the innocent seeker, the "bad" girl or boy, the adventurer, and the trickster.

Life writers incorporate and reproduce models of identity in their narratives as ways to represent themselves to readers. Consider the single identities announced in the titles of the following life narratives: *Kaffir Boy: The True Story of a Black Youth's Coming of Age in Apartheid South Africa* by Mark Mathabane, *Autobiography of a Face* by Lucy Grealy, *When I Was Puerto Rican* by Esmeralda Santiago. The titles announce a limit of identity that the narratives explore, exploit, and explode. In *Rivethead: Tales from the Assembly Line,* for instance, Ben Hamper reimagines himself as Rivethead, a figure of renegade agency in the monotonous assembly-line life of General Motors. The Rivethead speaks Hamper's fears of fading into the emasculated catatonia of alcohol and mechanized routine and his desire to resist the orders of faceless bureaucrats. As the narrator writes of his alter ego, Rivethead is the "thoroughbred of all thoroughbreds, the quickest triggerman this side of the River Rouge" (119).

Autobiographers often incorporate several models of identity in succession or in alternation to tell a story of serial development. In *Confessions,* Jean-Jacques Rousseau presents himself as an eager schoolboy, "a man of very strong passions" (33), a wicked sensualist, a thief, a true philosopher, and "an old dotard" (9). In *The Autobiography of Malcolm X* the narrator presents himself in successive chapters as "Mascot," "Homeboy," "Harlemite," "Detroit Red," "Hustler," "Satan," "Minister Malcolm X," "Icarus," and "El-Hajj Malik El-Shabazz." These apprenticeships in different models of identity are put on for particular occasions but, when cast off, leave traces that may conflict with other models.

Issues around historically salient models of identity are especially complex in autobiographical narratives of decolonization, immigration, displacement, and exile. For example, Chicanx writer Norma Cantú characterizes her *Canícula* (1995) as a "fictional autobioethnography," many of whose events are "completely fictional" although "true in a historical context" (xi). Provocatively, while Cantú includes photographs of family members and friends, she describes from memory other photos that may not even exist. Further, she refuses to identify her protagonist, called "Nena" and "Azucena," with herself. Thus, locating her protagonist within multiple, conflicting markers of Texan and Mexican ethnic identities, Cantú problematizes readers' expectation that *Canícula* will present her as an embodied Western subject by historicizing the colonial domination experienced by the protagonist's family.

In another colonial context, J. M. Coetzee in *Boyhood: Scenes from Provincial Life* narrates in the third person a memoir of his childhood in the apartheid nation of South Africa in the late 1940s. Refusing his Afrikaner heritage, identifying as English, aligned ideologically with Soviet Russia, and erotically drawn to the "Coloured boys" marginalized by the official identity assigned them by the state, Coetzee's adult narrator explores the vectors of his younger identity as multiply con-

Autobiographical Subjects

structed, in tension, and shifting with political conditions. While boyhood was a fixed period in his life, it was also a time that the narrator reads retrospectively as one when he both tried out possible identities and experienced how their realization was undermined in the repressive apartheid state. In Coetzee's sequel, *Youth: Scenes from Provincial Life II*, situated primarily in England, his narrator revises the contours of that provisional young identity in London, the metropolis of empire, as he becomes uncomfortably aware of his marginal status as an exilic outsider, aspiring poet-writer, and awkward lover there. And in *Summertime*, the third volume of his nonconsecutive life narrative, "John" Coetzee, now asserted as dead, is viewed candidly and critically by five others. Readers of Coetzee's trilogy might well conclude that in them identity is a construct in motion to be interrogated and troubled rather than the formation of a "solid self."

Postcolonial theorists have defined and deployed new terms to characterize colonial and postcolonial subjects as in process that mark the historical, sociocultural, and psychic traces of their displacements and disidentifications with diverse histories of oppression. These critics deploy terms for subject positions such as *hybrid, border, diasporic, mestiza, nomadic, migratory, minoritized*, terms that gloss an "in-between" location for the dynamic oscillations of subjects often uprooted and in motion.

Identities as Intersectional

The effects of this multiplicity of identities are not, however, additive—one identity cannot just be added to another to understand the position from which someone speaks. Rather, various vectors of identity interpenetrate; they are intersectional. To speak autobiographically as a Black woman is not to speak as a "woman" and as a "Black." It is to speak as a Black woman. To speak as an Australian Indigenous man is not to speak as a "man" plus as an "Australian" plus as an "Aboriginal." There is no universal identity of "man" or "woman" outside specificities of historical and cultural location.

The South Asian Canadian writer Michael Ondaatje captures this amorphous intersectionality when he maps his return to the familial and now postcolonial geography of the "Ceylon" of his childhood. *Running in the Family* traces the return home of the migrant writer to a realm of family and myth. Shuttling across identities—Ceylonese, migrant Sri

Lankan, Canadian, Commonwealth expatriate—Ondaatje mixes time past and time present to conjure up the past he describes as a "frozen opera" (22) in order to understand his identity as multiply positioned and continuously mobile.

In her "biomythography," *Zami: A New Spelling of My Name*, Audre Lorde captures this intersectional aspect of identity and difference when she writes of herself and her friends in Greenwich Village in the 1950s:

> Being women together was not enough. We were different. Being gay-girls together was not enough. We were different. Being Black together was not enough. We were different. Being Black women together was not enough. We were different. Being Black dykes together was not enough. We were different. . . . It was awhile before we came to realize our place was the very house of difference rather than the security of any one particular difference. (226)

As no particular distinction can define them, identity becomes a project of continuous self-making and self-unmaking, not just individually but collectively as "les amies," lesbians. Like Lorde in *Zami*, Gloria Anzaldúa in *Borderlands/La Frontera: The New Mestiza* traces the hybridity of her own identity in a way that suggests how multiple and intersectional identities can be. The very title of her autobiographical essays both differentiates English from Spanish and joins them at the border of the slash. The "I"/eye moves back and forth across the border, just as Anzaldúa writes of navigating the intersections of sexuality, ethnicity, gender, and nationality at a historically imposed borderland of Texas and Mexico. Similarly, Barack Obama's *Dreams* shuttles between his racialized identities as both Black and white and neither solely Black nor white. His narrative of becoming a man is traced in his shifting locations as a citizen of Hawai'i, Indonesia, and Kenya, a student in California and in New York, a political organizer in Chicago, and an aspirant to a global citizenship of the future. The many different terms that postcolonial writers have coined to characterize their inextricably mixed identities such as *mixed-race, diasporic,* and *nomadic* indicate the fluidity of identities in movement across political and geographical spaces.

Intersectionality as an analytic emerged from the work of scholars of color during the 1980s and 1990s to adequately capture and tease out the nuances of this interlocking multiplicity of what social scientists

Autobiographical Subjects

would term demographic variables of race, class, gender, and sex. But the limits and problematics of intersectionality as an analytic quickly became the subject of debate: identity is understood as a feature of persons; it is an ontological phenomenon; and given the multiplicity of identities of individual persons, the effects of an increasingly dense concatenation of identifications became hard to handle in analyses of intersectional effects. Theorists found difficulty in containing the ampersand chain (class and race and gender and sexuality and ethnicity and disability and religion, and on and on). The variables proliferated; the methodology for analysis floundered; sociological categories could no longer be contained, giving way to the infinitely complex singularity of the person, of differences within differences. This challenge of intersectional analysis has led to alternate approaches to identity.

Identity, "Doing," and Assemblage Theory

Some recent theorists of the subject have conceptualized identities as projects of "doing," of praxis; they are actions that attempt to have an impact. In this view identities become epistemological grounds or standpoints from which to produce knowledge and self-knowledge. They are conduits that illumine privilege and power to some degree. Identities are used in making claims of solidarity, what Angela Y. Davis regards as a collective consciousness of victimization registered in historical location and material conditions (190). Identities serve as a mode of speaking for and representing through an "I" what Robyn Wiegman describes as "the complexities—historical, economic, political—that identity has tried to speak for" ("Our America," 433). In these ways identities trigger acts of remembering what has been lost to violence. They can be mobilized to register and reanimate occluded histories, establish lineages, or constitute tradition. They become platforms for political demands such as a call for recognition or a claim for rights. Such activities may be mobilized through what Gayatri Chakravorty Spivak terms "strategic essentialism," investing in and claiming a stable and coherent identity in the face of its impossibility (see "Subaltern Studies"). Such practices of identity, however, can be "minefields," as Shuddhabrata Sengupta argues, "and the mines have been lain by armies that have forgotten the map" (634).[3]

The myriad forces and relations implicated in these operations of identity formation and deformation—material, subjective, historical, and sociocultural—suggest how identity in the singular and identities in the plural collect as assemblages; they are taken up, fused or decoupled, arranged. Assemblage theory regards individuals as assemblages of identities in that their experiential histories are lived as a concatenation of several components: identities that are ascribed to them or claimed by them; subject positions that may be multiple, conflictual, intersectional; the grounds of recognition that they seek or refuse; the fantasies that they project; the surveillance, intense or minimal, that disciplines and re-forms them; and the psychic, affective, rational, and embodied networks of relation that join them to others. Autobiographical projects, in this sense, are modes of self-inscription entangled in intersecting assemblages that affect the cultural production, circulation, and reception of identity.[4]

In the last decade, assemblage theory has provocatively approached the complexities of identity by extending the integuments of identity formation beyond the agency of a singular human being. In "Becoming-Intersectional in Assemblage Theory," Jasbir K. Puar argues that the complexities of identity cannot be fully elaborated through the now-pervasive concept of intersectionality as a mutually constitutive process. She observes: "No matter how intersectional our models of subjectivity, no matter how attuned to locational politics of space, place, and scale, these formulations—these fine tunings of intersectionality, as it were, that continue to be demanded—may still limit us if they presume the automatic primacy and singularity of the disciplinary subject and its identitarian interpellation" (62). For Puar, situating "identity" through a concept of assemblage is more productive because it "de-exceptionaliz[es]" the human body and accounts more fully for how "multiple forms of matter can be bodies" that are drawn into relationships with human bodies, human actors (57). By using assemblage theory, Puar shifts the concept of identity from one of ontology to one of action. In assemblage theory, she observes, "categories—race, gender, sexuality—are considered events, actions, and encounters between bodies rather than simply entities and attributes of subjects" (58).

From this theoretical perspective, identities involve encounters rather than attributes. Further, they involve a constellation of agencies—human, technological, phenomenal, material, expressive, linguistic. Identity assemblages, never stable, catalyze and distribute agencies of difference-making, identification, and disidentification across networks of intersecting flows. The concept of identity assemblage, then, expands

Autobiographical Subjects

the repertoire of forces of identity formation. Instead of centering the human being as solely the agency-bearing subject intent on inscribing identity, it expands the object of inquiry to the ways in which identities become imaginable, coalesce, find their medium of communication, unfold, travel outward along publication and reception circuits, and get taken up by diverse audiences. And it addresses histories of both genre formation and global formations such as settler colonialism, as well as communication technologies.

Identity and Virtuality

In the expanding array of platforms and protocols in virtual environments, issues related to the notion of identity become acute for understanding the relationship of subjectivity to autobiographical acts and practices. In online activities, identities are increasingly manipulable and, for some commentators, virtual in ways that seem unbounded, purely a matter of choice and invention among avatars, roles, and subject positions. Paul Longley Arthur, for instance, observes that "online identities are easily manipulated at any time by the individual subject or by others" and this "ability to 'manage' online content at will is changing the way we see ourselves and each other" (76).

The malleability and interchangeability of identities online, however, is qualified offline in several ways by the complexity of identity performance and the situatedness of subjects. Considering the performance of identity, sociolinguist Ruth E. Page distinguishes between those aspects that are "transportable identities," traveling across several kinds of discursive situations, and those aspects that are "discourse- and situated-specific, . . . locally occasioned roles adopted in relation to a particular speech situation" (*Stories and Social Media*, 18). In RealLife (RL) social settings as well, Page observes that not all aspects of identity are intrinsic to a person's performed characteristics; some may be provisionally adopted for a particular occasion or context. While the origins and correlatives of virtual identities are not embodied, as are those presented in RL social settings, distinguishing between transportable and role-based or assumed aspects of identity may enable more nuanced theorizing.

Furthermore, not all valences of identity are equalized and sharable online. New media scholars such as Lisa Nakamura, Helen Kennedy, and Mary L. Gray caution that the utopian vision of the Internet as a site where the free play of identity is unbounded obscures the persistent asymmetries of power and access associated with marginalized and normative identity positions on and offline, and to the labor of producing, circulating, and consuming lives in Web 2.0. Nakamura, for instance, asserts that "the 'larger flows of labor, culture and power' that surround and shape digital media travel along unevenly distributed racial, gendered, and class channels" (1678).[5]

Some artists engaging the representation of identity in and across online platforms and environments have created metadiscursive projects that reformulate identity as contingent and arbitrarily networked, at once fluid and inflected by asymmetrical power relations. Australian painter Jennifer Mills, for example, developed *What's in a Name?* Googling her own name, she found 325 women around the globe, in the United States, Australia, Canada, New Zealand, and elsewhere, who shared it. She used their websites or Facebook pages to make candid watercolor images of her avatars as intimate "secret sharers." Exhibited at the Queensland Art Gallery, *What's in a Name?* illustrates how self-representation through online avatars is an increasingly prominent aspect of contemporary self-identity, yet one that may fracture social identity. One of Mills's "Googlegängers" observes the compelling but dislocated intimacy of the Internet: "The idea that in the mass of difference and differentiation you might have something in common with a stranger has a kind of dizziness about it. These Jennifers have traveled through the hyperreality of the network, and come back home." But while the Internet may enable hitherto unknown identifications across nations and cultures, in reading for identity in online environments it is important to keep in mind how bonds and identifications with others located elsewhere can also be illusory or deceptive. Examples of misrepresentation and fakery abound worldwide. As ever, the enticing promise of claiming a secured, stable identity is vulnerable, and increasingly so on digital platforms.

Reading for Identity

The stuff of autobiographical storytelling is drawn from multiple, disparate, and discontinuous experiences and the multiple identities that are constructed from and constitute those experiences in identity templates. While these models of identity may conflict, as in the case of Rousseau or Malcolm X, not all life writers are aware of the conflicts and contradictions implicit in the identities they present. Some autobiographical

Autobiographical Subjects

narrators thematize the conflictual nature of identity in their narratives, while others do not. Some narrators explicitly resist certain identities; others obsessively work to conform their self-representation to a particular identity frame. Readers can productively attend to such tensions and contradictions, which may be signaled by gaps, inconsistencies, or boundaries breached within autobiographical narratives.

Reading life narrative through the lens of assemblage theory foregrounds how identity statuses, identity discourses, identity attachments, and identity discontents are all in play in the acts, the practices, and the afterlives of self-referential projects. Assuredly, the story of identity is often embedded in narrative plots and unfoldings but also emerges in a life narrative's multiplication of "I"s; in the affective, sensory, haunting surrounds of life storytelling; and in the aesthetic charge and cultural resonance of certain words or phrases, as well as the incoherence and silences of gaps and fragments. The kinds and terms of identification and disidentification—both internal and external to any text—are also inflected by material, social, historical, and ideological components or agencies that swirl around a narrative, erupt out of it, or cling to it as they constitute assemblages of autobiographical inscription.

The processes of composing, publishing, and circulating life stories, with their multiplicity of "I"s, generate heterogeneous agencies that are distributed across dispersed networks of people, materials, and institutions of production and circulation. The coproducers of these narratives, such as ghostwriters, activists, journalists, editors, and translators, can contribute to the desire or compulsion to tell a personal story, both influencing and reframing the kind of story that is told. Furthermore, publishers, marketers, computer engineers, booksellers, and gallery curators participate in bringing life-writing texts and acts to their publics. Online sites, digital platforms, print formats, library registration systems, and archiving protocols influence how accessible those productions may be. Finally, surveillance technologies, censors, and codes of censorship can interrupt and sometimes prevent life-writing texts from circulating.

SPATIALITY

We are bodies inhabiting space; but more importantly, we are both located in and have a sense of belonging to particular places. Emplacement, as the site of self-articulation, engages notions of location and subject position, concepts that are inescapably spatial. The concept of location emphasizes geographical situatedness; but it is not just a collection of geographical sites. It includes the national, ethnic, racial, gendered, sexual, social, and life-cycle coordinates in which narrators are embedded by virtue of their experiential histories and from which they speak. Location expands to include what Susan Stanford Friedman terms "the geopolitics of identity within differing communal spaces of being and becoming" (*Mappings*, 3). She asserts that "a locational approach to feminism incorporates diverse formations because its positional analysis requires a kind of geopolitical literacy built out of a recognition of how different times and places produce different and changing gender systems as these intersect with other different and changing societal stratifications and movements for social justice" (5). Thus, situating a narrator's *location* and *position* is fundamental in reading life writing.

Space as a concept is used in life writing not only as the literal surround, scene of narration, or sense of place. It also has geopolitical resonance for transnational subjects and delineates the psychic terrain of reflection for writers shuttling between social and private worlds or present-day locations and erased pasts. We may even think of life writing, with its paratextual surrounds, as a location in the interactive spaces of publication and circulation.

Space as Material Surround or Place

Although we think of *place* geographically as region or immediate material surround, the sense of place is, as Lawrence Buell argues, necessarily always a social product, not simply an unmarked, unmediated space (*Environmental Imagination*, 21). The natural environment cannot be articulated on its own terms, outside the history of cartographies that have assigned it place-names and boundary markers (77). Thus "felt space" is "space humanized, rather than the material world taken on its own terms" (253). Space becomes place, according to Buell, when one is conscious of where one lives and develops a "sense of place" as a subject inhabiting a specific locale.

Some places are particularly influential. For example, Kathleen A. Boardman and Gioia Woods assert that "one marker of autobiography produced in and about the North American West is a preoccupation with place, along with a focus on identity issues directly related to place: rootedness, anxiety, nostalgia, restlessness" (3). They observe the performance of identity at the intersection of three kinds of location—physical,

Autobiographical Subjects

rhetorical, and political—vectors not reducible simply to geography (19). The location of life writing may be a space as vast as the American West, where landscape becomes a horizon against and through which subjectivity is defined. It may also be a small, even minuscule space. Consider the centrality to the scene of narration of such domestic spaces as the writing desk or word processor, the intimate space of the bedroom or bath, the sociality of the dining room table, of gendered spaces such as the kitchen and the garage/workroom, and that prized space of postmodern self-reflection, the automobile. Or it may be interstitial spaces. Indeed, much modern travel writing turns on the encounter with material space by way of a mode of transportation—train, plane, or an earlier form of conveyance. Sidonie Smith has observed that "the travel narrator negotiates the dynamics of and contradictions in the drift of identity and reveals the ways in which modes of mobility—engines of temporality, spatiality, progression, and destination—are (un)defining" (*Moving Lives,* 27).

Spaces of Sociality

Autobiographical narratives are also organized around *spaces of sociality,* that is, relationships and actions that are formalized in communicative interaction and ritualized or identified by gesture and bodily positioning, as Erving Goffman has suggested *(Gender Advertisements).* In life writing, actors may be situated discursively vis-à-vis others who are present explicitly, as is the host to the guest or traveler, or implicitly, as is the warden in a prison or a divinity to the religious. In such narratives, negotiations occur across boundaries—differences of status, nation, ethnicity, religion, and gender—that are both constructed and redefined in such encounters. As critics attend to these spaces of the self, their dynamics, and the fluctuating positions actors take up within them, they may assign more specific coordinates to relationality in life writing. That is, they can explore how a subject's narration of her or his life is implicated in and impinges on the lives of local others.

Art historian Jennifer González has argued that some contemporary visual life narrative is "autotopography" (see González). Glossing González, cultural critic Mieke Bal defined autotopography as "a spatial, local and situational 'writing' of the self's life in visual art" involving an artist's self-presentation within a surround of cultural objects that reference specific times, places, and networks of the past (163). In visual

78 Autobiographical Subjects

media such as installations, space becomes a three-dimensional field that adds depth and complexity to artistic self-presentation. While this topic is too vast to discuss at length here, consider an example. In the installation *Cornered* African American autobiographical artist Adrian Piper uses spatial positioning strategically to create an in-between space that suggests the impossibility of her social location. Several rows of empty chairs and an overturned table face a corner in which a video screen of her is placed. In it she speaks to the audience about her father's two birth certificates, one identifying him as "white" and the other as "octoroon," referencing the history of miscegenation in the United States, and invites people to consider fictions of their own ancestry. Confronting the audience with these contradictory identifications of her as white and as Black, a space of antagonistic difference, Piper visualizes social relations as an arbitrary practice of racialization that has implications for both artists and viewers. That is, she "corners" viewers in uncomfortable self-reflection about their own sociocultural locations (see Drake).[6]

The sociality of space, then, is not necessarily hospitable; but it is inescapably interactive with audiences.

Geopolitical Space and Spatial Rhetorics

While social relations are situated within geographic spaces, they are sometimes explicitly entangled in *geopolitical space*. For subjects located in complex spaces between citizenship and statelessness, or in motion within or across nations in the throes of violent conflict, questions of migration and the negotiation of borders or points of transition reveal contradictions of geopolitical space.

For example, Esmeralda Santiago's *When I Was Puerto Rican* not only contrasts her experience of coming of age in 1950s San Juan and the countryside with her teenaged years as an immigrant in working-class Brooklyn. The narrative also situates her family story as emblematic of the ambiguous status in the United States of Puerto Ricans, who are citizens for the purpose of military service and the rule of law but who cannot vote. Its coded spaces, especially in scenes of encounter with American government officials, expose how Puerto Ricans are racialized as a Spanglish-speaking, impoverished minority and stereotyped as an ethnic other in the dominant American narrative. Interrogating the space of the watery border between the island of Puerto Rico and the continental United States, as well as the less palpable internal borders of

Autobiographical Subjects

79

its New York neighborhoods, Santiago emphasizes the shifting valences of particular locations and the irreducibility of these heterogeneous sites to a monolithic place called "America." North American theorizing of geographic borders also employs spatial terms to signal location and dislocation. Gloria Anzaldúa proposes the concept of *la frontera* or borderlands as a site of encounter between different cultures that configures local inhabitants as "aliens" in both. Acts of crossing, translating, and inventing new hybrid languages and practices, seen as "linguistic terrorism," are strategies for navigating a geopolitical space that can never be "home" (58–59). In the aftermath of September 11, 2001, the focus on policing national borders as a means of signaling ideological contests has marked historical contestations about citizenship. Heightened border tensions, particularly in the southern states, since the 2010s, have exposed brutal realities about the inadequate and injurious sites of detention in which migrants have been held and the forced relocations that have severed families.

While Anglo-American and Australian theorists of settler colonialism have emphasized encounters across borders, postcolonial theorists have importantly emphasized another sense of the location of colonized subjects as a "third space," in Homi Bhabha's term. For Bhabha the third space is a zone or "place of hybridity" produced at the moment of colonial encounter, a site at which communication, negotiation, and cross-translation may occur; in the third space, "the construction of a political object that is new, *neither the one nor the other*," produces a changed form of recognition (25). Both colonizer and colonized are implicated in the dynamics of this encounter, which may enable the colonized to claim a new political identity through mimicry and innovation, if not always to produce change, at the location of in-between spaces. The concept of situatedness in a third space becomes crucial in theorizing postcolonial life narratives by such writer-critics as Jamaica Kincaid, Maryse Condé, Wole Soyinka, Manthia Diawara, and many others. In such stories an "I" often represents a larger group's experience at powerful moments of social change and articulates the desire for transformation as a social group. Similarly, diasporic locations around the globe can be read as shifting political spaces, as Michael Keith and Steve Pile observe: "Spatiality needs to be seen as the modality through which contradictions are normalized, naturalized and neutralized. . . . Spatialities represent both the spaces between multiple identities and the contradictions within identities" (224–25). That is, the geopolitical may become a space both of negotiation and of erasure.

In thinking about geopolitical space, Wendy S. Hesford has employed the concept of "spatial rhetorics" to discuss how some human rights documentaries about rape in the Balkan conflicts of the 1990s created "a rhetorical space of intersubjectivity" that filmmakers used to engage visual narratives that bear witness to violence and violation, and to elicit a situation of "transnational rhetorical witnessing" ("Documenting Violations," 121). Similarly, Theresa Kulbaga has employed the notion of "spatial rhetorics of memory" to discuss tropes of "memory as both temporally (historically) and geographically (politically) located" (33). For example, Eva Hoffman employs such a spatial rhetoric in the treatment of her Jewish family's post-Holocaust migratory locations in *Lost in Translation*, first to Canada and then to the United States (33). In a different way, German filmmaker Ursula Biemann's documentary film *Performing the Border* represents the United States–Mexico border as a performative space, the site of embodied acts of crossing by women workers. These unstable, conflictual spatial surrounds are vulnerable to manipulation by nations, by transnational corporations, and by violent outlaw practices, as the hundreds of unsolved murders of young women around Ciudad Juárez, Mexico, make clear. These examples suggest how spatial rhetorics are deployed to present autobiographical subjects as migratory and transnationally situated, rather than defined by a stable national identity. Reading for the narrative foregrounding of spatial dynamics across geographic borders that forge new alliances and create hybrid identities enables us to view the spaces of life writing as sites at which global practices may be transacted or contested in geopolitical surrounds.

Spatial Tropes and Topoi of Interiority

We may also think about how space is invoked in life writing through tropes and topoi that metaphorically represent self-relationship. In his *Essays,* Montaigne, for example, often uses tropes of dynamic space to characterize his self-experience. In "Of Presumption" (II, 17) the phrase *je me contreroulle* (653) ("I roll around in myself," trans. Frame, 499) spatially describes the capaciousness and intensity of his self-study. In "Of Solitude" (I, 39) Montaigne asserts that his creative process occurs in the *arriereboutique* (241) or back room of his mind (trans. Frame, 177),

Autobiographical Subjects

a solitary space that he opens to the reader.[7] In a different way Virginia Woolf in "A Sketch of the Past" characterizes the prelinguistic dimension of the relationship to her infant self through spatial metaphor. She says she has "the feeling, as I describe it sometimes to myself, of lying in a grape and seeing through a film of semi-transparent yellow" (65). And later she writes, "I am hardly aware of myself, but only of the sensation. I am only the container of the feeling of ecstasy, of the feeling of rapture" (67). In the fluidity of this "grape" subjectivity, the pre-egoic body becomes a locus of sensation in immediate contact with the world, coexisting as undemarcated (see Smith, *Subjectivity,* 95–96).

An entire autobiographical genre may be established around a spatial metaphor, as with the "interior landscape" that spiritual life narrators from Teresa of Avila to Thomas Merton, from Christians to Buddhists, draw on. Such narratives conduct self-examination according to varied protocols of mystic practice for developing a space of interior life. The spiritual autobiographer often retreats from a hostile external world to create a verbal and imagistic landscape as a site for expressing devotion to an otherworldly being or idea. Another kind of life writing, the apology, often uses the courtroom as a spatial metaphor, imagining the setting of a trial at which arguments for and against the speaker are rehearsed and the reader is invited to act as a jury rendering the verdict. Spatial contexts are similarly implied in the confessional narratives of Augustine and Rousseau, which juxtapose sites of self-exposure and contrition with scenes of flagrant sinning in intimate back rooms.

Reading for Spatiality

Life narratives, as we discussed in the section on memory, may serve as repositories for preserving memory against the erosion of time and the revisions of new generations of historians. Consider how, in places such as Germany, Ireland, Palestine, and South Africa over the past century struggles over geopolitical space have been linked to national self-definition. In Jana Hensel's *After the Wall: Confessions from an East German Childhood and the Life that Came Next* (2008; translation of *Zonenkinder,* 2002), for example, the new Western world that East Germans were exposed to after the demise of the German Democratic Republic was a self-relocation not physically but ideologically. Thirteen when the Wall came down in 1989, Hensel's childhood experiential world was erased except in memory. Artifacts of her youth such as the

82 Autobiographical Subjects

Pioneer photos and membership cards included as photographs, and her recollections of "Ossie" clothing, holidays, and education, artifacts of material life in the East "Zone," become only a zone of memory in the personal archive she shares with her generation. This space of memory is already unavailable to the following generation, who will be "Wessie" subjects. Her generation, Hensel suggests, is stuck in a liminal space of irreconcilable conflict between the former East and a merged nation that has occluded their collective past, making it a space of nowhere.

Autobiographical narratives of lost childhood places in times of political upheaval, migration, or displacement abound. Miriam Katin's graphic memoir *We Are on Our Own* depicts the cataclysmic World War II years in the Hungary she was too young to remember. Both Edward Said's *Out of Place: A Memoir* and Manthia Diawara's *In Search of Africa* are self-theorizing narratives of childhood worlds in the global South they left and the search for what those remembered places have become, by writers whose careers were spent in the global North. Defining themselves across the conflicting ideologies, landscapes, and "weather," in every sense, of such disparate locations may turn "home" into a contradictory or irretrievable place.

Spatiality connotes not just location or shelter but sites of psychic reflection, as well as the spaces of crisis and flow that both structure and disrupt daily life. To think identities, particularly diasporan ones, we now must acknowledge the impact of globalized spaces and such new formations as what Patricia Yaeger calls "the tragic mobility of space" in places marked by conflict, violence, and migration (10).

EMBODIMENT

Life narrative is a site of embodied knowledge, a textual surface on which personal experience is inscribed. While a Cartesian concept of the subject was as a bounded, individual fixity to be governed by the thinking mind, there have always been competing versions in written and visual representation. Now, many theorists regard life narrators as multiply embodied: in the body as a neurochemical system; in the anatomical body; in, as Elizabeth Grosz notes, the "imaginary anatomy" that "reflects social and familial beliefs about the body more than it does the body's organic nature" (39–40). There is also the sociopolitical body, a set of cultural attitudes and discourses encoding the public meanings of bodies that have for centuries underwritten relationships of power.

Autobiographical Subjects

In effect, the body has always been imbricated in life narrative as the source and site of autobiographical utterance and performance, and critical readings can tease out the encoded forms in which it is presented.

The Visible Body

Cultural discourses determine which aspects of bodies become meaningful, when the body becomes visible, how it becomes visible, and what that visibility means. In *Loving in the War Years: Lo que nunca pasó por sus labios* Chicana writer and activist Cherríe Moraga directs attention to the very materiality of her skin as a source of her political consciousness. In this way she joins skin to the body politic, observing the different significations of "light" and "dark" in different communities. Taking her body as a narrative point of departure, she elaborates, through multiple modes of address, her complex cultural position as lesbian, biracial Chicana, and daughter of working-class parents. A very different kind of body is narrated into shape in Annie Dillard's *An American Childhood.* Repeatedly invoking the specificities of "skin" to mark the meeting point of the internal and external worlds, Dillard explores the way in which she learned to fit (and sometimes failed to fit) the skin of her white middle-class identity to the urban location of Pittsburgh. In contrast, Richard Rodriguez meditates on his failure to fit into the skin of Americanized masculinity in *Hunger of Memory.* Figuring himself as an upwardly mobile "scholarship boy," Rodriguez exposes the cost of the politics of skin color that associates darkness with poverty and silence at the same time that he uses this dynamic of marginalization to mask his own homosexual desire. In his embrace of middle-class intellectual masculinity, he writes eloquently of his failure to find acceptance from the Mexican *braceros*/manual workers with whom he works one summer. By shifting modes of masculinity, the younger Rodriguez shifts the skins of his identity. In all these examples, the body—its skin, anatomy, chemistry—resonates as both a locus of identity and a register of the similarities and differences that inflect social identities. As Paul John Eakin argues in *How Our Lives Become Stories: Making Selves,* "our lives in and as bodies profoundly shape our sense of identity" (xi).

Written life narrative, however, omits visible representation of the material body, as G. Thomas Couser observes: "Autobiographical comics artists are of necessity also self-portraitists. Graphic narrative, then, promises to fill in a lacuna that is striking even in written autosomatography: the absence of (the image of) the affected body" (*The Work of Life Writing*, 37).[8] And Elisabeth El Refaie emphasizes, "Graphic memoirists are in the unusual position of having to visually portray themselves over and over again, often at different ages and stages of development, and in many different situations. Thus, *all* autobiographical comics artists are, in the course of their work, constantly being compelled to engage with their physical identities" (62). From Ellen Forney in *Marbles: Mania, Depression, Michelangelo, and Me* representing her manic states in images of her body erupting from cartoon boxes in "sprawling lines and disorganized boxes" to the bodily breakdowns depicted in David B's *Epileptic* or David Small's *Stitches*, viewers observe the centrality of drawing embodied experience to graphic memoirs (Smith and Watson, "Contrapuntal Reading"). A similar point could be made for autobiographical performance and installation art, photographic life narrative, film, and video.

Embodied Memory

Life narrative inextricably links memory and the materiality of the body as components of subjectivity. The ability to recover memories, in fact, depends on the somatic body that perceives and internalizes images, sensations, and experiences of the external world. Subjectivity is impossible unless the subject recognizes her location in the materiality of an everpresent body (Damasio, 239). Moreover, the embodied materiality of memory and consciousness is grounded in neurological, physiological, and biochemical systems, as we discuss below.

For those with Alzheimer's or dementia, memory slips away bit by bit, and others sense that the person is increasingly remote from and lost to them. Coping with such afflictions as Alzheimer's and dementia has generated a large literature by caregivers such as family members and friends of those stricken. In *Elegy for Iris*, John Bayley chronicles how his wife, British writer and philosopher Iris Murdoch, was changed by the onset of the disease and offers a relational portrait of the couple. Numerous narratives by family members such as *Finding Life in the Land of Alzheimer's: One Daughter's Hopeful Story* by Lauren Kessler emphasize how a younger generation might cope with impending loss. By contrast, in *Can't We Talk about Something More Pleasant? New Yorker* cartoonist Roz Chast creates a graphic memoir incorporating family photographs and reproductions of her mother's poems to chart

Autobiographical Subjects

the inevitable loss of her aged parents. The comic narrator's responses to her father's dementia and her mother's increasing physical incapacity as both are institutionalized mix frustration, anger, grief, guilt, and bursts of wild humor that tie their decline and deaths to her own childhood memories.

Narrators may also tell their own stories of losing bodily control, as Thomas DeBaggio does in *Losing My Mind: An Intimate Look at Life with Alzheimer's,* narrating how the progression of the disease enters his everyday life and recording his memories as they are threatened with extinction. Similarly, Wendy Mitchell, with Anna Wharton, narrates the progress of her own early-onset Alzheimer's disease in *Somebody I Used to Know,* as well as *What I Wish People Knew about Dementia.* Her story moves from recognizing her own decline to regarding it as a kind of gift and educating caregivers, doctors, and others with a similar affliction. Her creation of a "memory room" of labeled photographs as a calm place to recover fading associations touchingly suggests the role that life writing may play in supplementing the failing body.

Embodiment, Trauma, Somatic Practices

Approaches to engaging traumatic events and histories are now attending not just to the dynamics and reparative effects of talk therapy but to the potential of somatic practices for strengthening resources toward self-recovery. In *The Body Keeps the Score: Brain, Mind, and Body in the Healing of Trauma,* Bessel Van der Kolk reviews the medical history of trauma and recovery during the long twentieth century. In his narrative of the evolution of his approach to the diagnosis and treatment of survivors, he incorporates insights from neuroscience into understanding post–traumatic stress syndrome of many kinds and describes a broad array of treatment methods now used in clinical practices that focus on those suffering from post–traumatic stress disorder or from horrific experiences of childhood sexual, physical, and emotional abuse. Van der Kolk postulates that for those whose lives are upended and damaged from the experience of trauma, the fear—a fight-flight-or-freeze reflex—generated by the brain's amygdala at moments of fright and terror produces negative emotions that affect the neurochemistry of the brain and interrupt the normal regulating process of messages sent to it from the gut, skin, and muscles (97). In other words, traumatizing assaults activate the reptilian brain underlying consciousness with the result that "people's lives will be held hostage to fear until that visceral experience changes" (99). The path to healing, Van der Kolk argues, needs to be routed through attention to bodily responses and the healing potential the body makes available to sufferers.

A wide array of embodied activities such as yoga, dramatic performance, and artmaking can facilitate the path to healing. In *My Grandmother's Hands: Racialized Trauma and the Pathway to Mending Our Hearts and Bodies,* Van der Kolk's associate Resmaa Menakem applies wisdom about bodily responses learned from his grandmother to analyze the persistence of embodied trauma as it is passed down genetically through the long history of racist violence and white-body supremacy in the United States. Instilled in white bodies as well as Black bodies, trauma has consequences for both those who benefit from its persistence and those who suffer its injustices. He observes: "Trauma always happens *in the body.* It is a spontaneous protective mechanism used by the body to stop or thwart further (or future) potential damage" (7). For Menakem, the social ecology of racism and its structural sedimentation constitute "a collective agony," materialized in his grandmother's hands, that compels collective recognition and healing through body-centered practices, which are incorporated throughout his analysis as a form of racial reckoning.

Other contemporary modes of life writing also attend to somatic practices. In *Black Women's Yoga History: Memoirs of Inner Peace,* historian Stephanie Y. Evans blends multiple genres to engage the history of trauma, somatic healing, and autobiographical stories by American Black women. She offers her personal narrative not in a confessional vein but as an "exposure of truths we have been conditioned to keep secret and hidden" (42). It models "applied intellectual history" by presenting the long history of Africana yoga practice of peaceful healing in the United States that Evans finds in an archive of Black women's life writing recounting the rich healing traditions of Black communities and what she calls "Black women's tradition of inner peace practice" (13). Aiming to bequeath an archive for knowing oneself differently to Black women of the future, she observes, "Memoirs are mentors" (43). Both new narratives and rereadings of past ones focused on somatic practice—in, for example, *The Cancer Journals* of Audre Lorde—encourage readers to observe how healing is enacted through the body.

Autobiographical Subjects

Embodiment and Affect

Bodies are riven with and riveted by eruptive pulsions, often associated with emotions, that materialize as feelings and bodily dispositions of positive, neutral, or negative response. Affects expose the feltness of lived experience as matrices of biological processes and social norms, operations of power, and the circulation of what Sarah Ahmed terms "the rippling effect of emotion" (44). In *The Cultural Politics of Emotion*, Ahmed elaborates a theory of "affective economies" such as hate: "My model of hate as an affective economy suggests that emotions do not positively inhabit *anybody* or *anything*, meaning that 'the subject' is simply one nodal point in the economy, rather than its origin and destination" (46). Thus, Ahmed shifts the locus of affect from individuals to the conditions of encounters. Economies of negative affects and emotions can result in the exclusion of some people from the category of the fully human and their consignment to the category of less-than-human.

Embodiment, Sexuality, and Desire

The cultural meanings assigned to particular bodies affect the kinds of stories people can tell. This aspect of life writing is sometimes neglected by critics who misleadingly assert that the body did not figure in life writing in the West until relatively recently. For instance, it is widely accepted that throughout the nineteenth century, respectable middle-class women could not, and would not, tell explicitly sexual stories about their bodies because the cultural meanings assigned to them concerned myths about the corrupt nature of female sexuality. To speak of sex was to shame or pollute oneself. Some women who wrote confessional narratives about sexual adventures, such as religious women's life stories of shameful desire and a quest for absolution in a spiritual bridegroom, usually gave their narratives to their male confessors, who often edited or did not publish them. The autobiographical writings of Teresa of Avila and Sor Juana Inés de la Cruz, with their earthy metaphors, were notable exceptions. The sensual candor of writers such as Charlotte Charke and Laetitia Pilkington, who published memoirs in the eighteenth century, incited condemnation of both their narratives and their lives. Interestingly, in their "scandalous" narratives, such female narrators mapped their own topography of sexuality, "relegat[ing] unlicensed sexuality to the lower classes," as Felicity A. Nussbaum has noted (179). Thus, even as they spoke of sexual desire, these life narrators echoed the identification of sexual license with lower-class status. While seeming to violate the norms of female self-disclosure, they paradoxically reproduced prevailing norms.

Well into the nineteenth century, many male life writers, though not all, also remained silent, self-censoring the representation of their bodies and male embodiment generally; in so doing, they reproduced the identification of the male autobiographer with rationality, objectivity, and the mind.[9] But the generations of critics who have approached autobiographical narration from this Cartesian mindset overlook the prominence of the body in the life writing of Rousseau, Casanova, Goethe, Gide, and others. Montaigne, at one point characterizing his *Essays* as "some excrements of an aged mind, now hard, now loose, and always undigested" (III, 9, "Of Vanity," *Complete Essays*, 721), suggests how the mind-body binary fails to attend to the "consubstantial" embodiment of language and materiality that drives his *Essays.*

At this contemporary moment, the prolific publication of lesbian, gay, and trans* life writing has transformed both consciousness and social practice. Many coming-out life narratives of gay men indict enforced social norms of heteronormative masculinity and reflect the project of situating male embodiment at a nexus of categories of identity. From renowned writers such as Oscar Wilde, Tennessee Williams, James Baldwin, and David Sedaris to more recent writers, including Reinaldo Arenas in *Before Night Falls,* Kenny Fries in *Body, Remember: A Memoir,* and David Jackson in *Unmasking Masculinity: A Critical Autobiography,* a growing canon of gay life narratives performs the dual labor of critiquing forms of masculinity and chronicling personal discoveries of the social construction of gendered, racial, and sexual identity. Trans* narratives, in particular, unsettle the embodied conditions of heteronormativity, undermine the naturalness of gender binarism, and complicate the politics of narrating the trans* experience itself.

Before the advent of social media and the #MeToo movement, the nineties memoir boom generated a global stream of narratives by women confessing secrets of sexual desire, transgression, or victimization. These narratives publicized both the recognition of bodily desires and the prevalence of sexual abuse, while serving as, in Leigh Gilmore's phrase, "alternative jurisdictions" for indicting abusers (see "Jurisdictions"). Kathryn Harrison in *The Kiss: A Secret Life* and Michael Ryan in *Secret*

Autobiographical Subjects

Life: An Autobiography went public with autobiographical narratives of sexual abuse inflicted on them in childhood. In *Shame,* Annie Ernaux narrates her witnessing, at age twelve, a violent encounter between her parents as a primal scene that replaced a Freudian sexual imaginary with rape and violence as the stain that marked her childhood. In much of the developing world, writing about sexual experience, especially by women, is still prohibited and punished. For some this has come at the cost of incarceration, persecution, and exile. Feminists such as Nawal El Saadawi in Egypt and Ken Bugul in Senegal have defied prohibition by publishing narratives of sexed and gendered bodies. Stories of the body, then, can be deployed in struggles around the politics of sexuality and heteronormativity, the noncongruity of biological sex and gender identity, and the systemic dynamics of predation. (For an extended discussion of LGBTQI life writing, see "Sex and Gender Narrative" in chapter 6.)

Embodiment and Able-Bodiedness

With the rise of activism around differently-abled bodies, discourses of multiple corporealities have arisen to address and critique the notion of able-bodiedness as normative. These include the social meanings of "disability" as stigmatizing and degrading the differently-abled; chronicles of journeys through illness, diagnosis, treatment, and accommodation; the differential treatment of gendered and racialized bodies in medical and epidemiological institutions; and the valuing of neurodiversity.

In the wake of the disability, women's, and gay rights movements in the past quarter century, life writing on the ill, impaired, or "different" body has generated considerable life writing. In *Autobiography of a Face,* for example, Lucy Grealy concentrates on how both she and others see her face differently as it changes over the course of many reconstructive surgeries. Similarly, in *Rearranged: An Opera Singer's Facial Cancer and Life Transposed,* Kathleen Watt narrates how medical treatments for bone cancer devastated her life but eventually brought her survival and strength. In successive essays Nancy Mairs tracks the physical and psychological losses of/in a body becoming increasingly disabled by multiple sclerosis and writes candidly about her sexual desires in order to claim full humanity for herself and others with disabilities.

In memoirs of living and dying with AIDS, David Wojnarowicz, Harold Brodkey, and Paul Monette explore the conjunction of desire, danger, and disease in the male body at a moment of moral panic about the AIDS pandemic. In *Close to the Knives: A Memoir of Disintegration,* Wojnarowicz refuses the fixed cultural identities of "queer" or "gay man" as he writes "close" to the body and its desires. Immersed in the visuality of memory, Wojnarowicz re-creates the specificity of desire and embodiedness as an "I" who has always "lived with the sensations of being an observer of my own life as it occurs" (149) to counter cultural practices that render invisible "any kind of sexual imagery other than straight white male erotic fantasies" (119). The COVID pandemic has also generated a literature of how bodies were disrupted by people's experiences of the virus or the illness or death of others from the disease and its disabling effects.

Another dimension of the relationship of the subject and some bodies involves new engagements with normative able-bodiedness as theorized by scholars and activists in disability studies, often triangulated with queer theory. In *Authoring Autism,* Melanie Yergeau, a neuro-queer scholar of rhetoric, exposes "the ways in which diagnosis of the non-rhetoricity of autism denies autistic people not only agency, but their very humanity" (160). Yergeau both develops the argument "that autistic people and their neuro-circuitry queer the lines of rhetoric, humanity, and agency" (60) and writes as an autistic subject. The issue of normative body size is also probingly pursued in such memoirs as Roxane Gay's *Hunger* and Kiese Laymon's *Heavy,* where the question of "size" is linked to racial marginalization and moralistic stereotypes of certain bodies.

Some recent memoirs also provocatively examine the relation of normative bodies to repressed emotions. For example, Alison Bechdel, in her graphic memoir *The Secret to Superhuman Strength,* explores the range of fitness programs she undertook over decades of her life not only to enhance her strength and mobility but to "numb emotions that her mind deems too dangerous" (Waldman, 60). Transposing pain, anxiety, and grief into sheerly physical sensations in purposeful exercise regimes—running, karate, yoga—"I could feel them not as 'pain' but as a flux of tinglings, pulses, and vibrations" in a kind of egolessness (Bechdel, *Secret,* 116). Narrating, visually and verbally, through the body, Bechdel invites readers to rethink their habitual practices of self-regulation.

Embodiment and the Autobiography of Things

We think of bodies as human or mammalian, but the materiality of nonliving things can also be imprinted with traces of human histories that have autobiographical resonance. Consider, for example, Edmund

Autobiographical Subjects

de Waal's *The Hare with Amber Eyes,* a bestselling memoir in which de Waal traces the history of the Ephrussi, his prominent central European family, from the middle of the nineteenth century to the aftermath of the Holocaust, during which many of its members lost their lives in death camps. From a surviving uncle, de Waal inherited 264 objects, tiny Japanese netsuke, sculptures of animals or spirits often attached to the obi sash of male clothing and other domestic items. De Waal approaches his narrative as a history of touch because, as a sculptor living in England, he holds the netsuke and traces their migration through the hands and houses of earlier family members to retrieve their histories. Using the objects he handles as documentary evidence, de Waal transforms sensual touch into a medium of witnessing.

Similarly, the scraps of things that desperate migrants have carried with them in escaping, sometimes to land in detention camps, are mute things that nonetheless "speak" of a person's experience, as Gillian Whitlock discusses in her analysis of the "embridry" made by refugees held on Nauru Island by the Australian government and sent to activists in Australia. The relationship of refugee to activist is established as an exchange of material objects whose handwork bears autobiographical resonance. As with de Waal's life narrative, these things mutely attest to the violence of forced incarceration and efforts to survive (see Whitlock, "Embridry" and "Objects and Things in Life Narrative").

Embodiment as Assemblage

In the last two decades theorists have elaborated further dimensions of the relationship of body and subject. Assemblage theory informs the "nomadic thought" of Rosi Braidotti who describes the body as "an assemblage of forces, or flows, intensities and passions that solidify in space, and consolidate in time, within the singular configuration commonly known as an 'individual' self" (201). With the technological revolution the body's fluxes of transformation migrate through different channels to a networked and digital sociality of virtual and literal embodiments. Online lives are lived via the virtual embodiments of avatars and surrogate selves in gaming. Human bodies join robotic prostheses in the body's networks of materialization.

Subjects and subjectivity migrate to digital ecologies in which software, fleshware, hardware, network, silicon, and carbon constitute being in the fluid movements across virtual worlds and real life, a transformation of subjectivity and embodiment in the time of computation N. Katherine Hayles explores in *My Mother Was a Computer*: "Encountering intelligent machines from this perspective enables me to see that they are neither objects to dominate nor subjects threatening to dominate me. Rather, they are embodied entities instantiating processes that interact with the processes that I instantiate as an embodied human subject. The experience of interacting with them changes me incrementally, so the person who emerges from the encounter is not exactly the same person who began it" (243). Just as Hayles views herself as changed by these digital encounters, Donna Haraway's forays into transspecies relationality radiate affect outward from a human-centric circulation to relationality with companionate species, the touch of animal to animal: "Through their reaching into each other, through their 'prehensions' or graspings, beings constitute each other and themselves. Beings do not preexist their relating" (6). Thus attentive human subjects are implicated in and changed by the encounters, both technological and animal, they engage with in interactive processes.

Mel Chen turns to the presumed dominance of human subjects to critique their "corporal exceptionalism" as he ponders the significance of toxins and toxicity in his queer body and its relationship to the racialization of lead toxicity in toys imported into the United States from Asia. Joining object-oriented ontology to disability and queer theory, Chen conceptualizes a queer subject of human/object attachment. Living in a toxic environment in which the body is always under assault and through which he moves as a masked man, Chen finds in an affective relationship with his couch a safe space, a partner offering respite from discomfort and pain. "The couch and I are interabsorbent, interporous, and not only because the couch is made of mammalian skin," he writes (203). While this assemblage subject may be less responsive, it is nonetheless an intimate interaction.

Embodiment and Quantification

In our essay "Virtually Me," we noted the rise of the quantified self movement begun in Boston among people who digitally self-monitor their bodily processes—intake and outgo—and activities such as walking and eating. Gary Wolf terms this model of the computational self "the data-driven life." Wolf recognizes that the quantified self, as an assemblage of data driven by the body and by habits, will reorient us to ourselves,

Autobiographical Subjects

even if the impetus to quantify remains attached to a self-developmental imaginary. Paradoxically, the quantified self is at once located as a singularity and anonymized as numeric code.

Life narrators are experimenting with the ways in which digital implants, readouts, and monitoring devices shift the site of self-engagement ever deeper into the materiality of embodied processes. American artist Laurie Frick, with a background in engineering and technology, both engages and "mines" self-quantifying data for a kind of algorithmic art joining online and offline modes of self-portraiture through self-surveilling gadgets such as the "Frickbit," an open access phone app through which people can make their own artworks from Big Data. She observes: "Your sense of who you are is based on the recollection of recent events, and what you are doing and intend to do. It's your basic orientation in the world." Taking the data of her daily life—sleeping, walking, food intake, mood swings, etc.—she also uses algorithmic patterns to make large textured and patterned paintings and multicanvas installations that turn "life's most basic patterns" into "color coded charts" as a patterned vocabulary and grammar for daily self-tracking (*Quantify Me*).

But the quantified self is also qualified by some. In "A Half-Moon on My Skin: A Memoir on Life with an Activity Tracker," Elpida Prasopoulou explores the role of embodiment and "its affective propulsions as the locus of human experience" as an instance of Jane Bennett's "enchanted materialism" (287). Using the form of memoir to present her research on everyday uses of wearables as an example of the Internet of Things, she employs thick description of how people interact with digital devices in experiential computing to problematize current optimistic visions of the data-driven life.

Reading for Embodiment

By exploring the body and embodiment as sites of knowledge production, affect, and desire, life writers do several things. They negotiate cultural norms determining the proper uses of bodies. They engage, contest, and revise laws and norms determining the relationship of bodies to specific sites, behaviors, and destinies. As they do so, they expose, and sometimes queer, the workings of compulsory heterosexuality and of what philosopher Namita Goswami describes as compulsory heteroimperial masculinity (344). The result of this process is to reproduce, mix, or interrogate cultural discourses that, at particular moments, define and distinguish the cultural norms of embodiment.

AGENCY

We like to think of human beings as agents of or actors in their own lives rather than pawns of social structures or unconscious transmitters of cultural scripts and models of identity. As Bessel Van der Kolk observes, agency is a "technical term for the feeling of being in charge of your life . . . knowing where you stand, knowing that you have a say in what happens to you, knowing that you have some ability to shape your circumstances" (95). Consequently, we tend to read autobiographical narratives as acts and thus proofs of human agency. They are seen as sites of agentic narration where people control the interpretation of their lives and stories, telling of individual destinies and expressing "true" selves. In fact, traditional forms of autobiography have often been read as narratives of agency, evidence that people can live and interpret their lives freely as transcendental, universal subjects. But we must recognize that the issue of how subjects claim, exercise, and narrate agency is far from a simple matter of free will and individual autonomy.

The subject conceptualized by the philosophers and writers of the Enlightenment and Romantic periods was the subject as an embodiment and expression of "agency in action" (see Brodsky and LaBrada). Agency for those influenced by liberal thought is understood as the power of human beings to think, transform consciousness, make claims in and on the world, act, and resist assaults on their sovereignty. This is the premier modality of what it means to be human and to be recognized as bearing the identity of universal Man, constituted by rationality, autonomy, self-possession, and free will as grounds for that action. This liberal notion of human agency has been challenged from many perspectives. Women were not included in the category of universal Man; nor were subjugated peoples around the world under conditions of slavery and colonization; nor were the mentally ill and severely disabled. All these categories of people were represented as not fully rational, autonomous, in control of their willpower, and therefore not fully human as agentic subjects. Unable to lodge claims to knowledge-making power, subjected to slow and eruptive violence, those represented as less-than-human were stripped literally and figuratively of their agency. The urgent question becomes, how does one resist?

Over the last half century philosophers and theorists, feminists, formerly colonized peoples, the marginalized and differently-abled have voiced critiques of the liberal notion of agency. A Freudian or psychoanalytic approach foregrounded the uncontrollable workings of the unconscious and desire. Poststructuralist theorists, such as French philosopher Jacques Derrida, argued that meanings in language are never fixed, but are in process, deferred. Foucauldian scholars assert that discursive systems and social structures shape the operations of memory, experience, identity, space, and embodiment, as we have seen above. Postcolonial theory questions the assumption of a universalized Western subject with agency. These critiques are now contributing to multipronged overviews. For example, in *Habeas Viscus,* Alexander Weheliye muses that "if racialization is understood not as a biological or cultural descriptor but as a conglomerate of sociopolitical relations that discipline humanity into full humans, not-quite-humans, and nonhumans, then blackness designates a changing system of unequal power structures that apportion and delimit which humans can lay claims to full human status and which humans cannot" (3). The question of whether a concept of human agency is possible in the face of implacable regulatory norms and interpellation is thus an urgent one, particularly for feminists of color and poststructuralist, postcolonial, postmodernist, and posthumanist scholars.

In the wake of these foundational analyses, the concept of agency is being retheorized, in order to better understand several issues: What are the grounds of oppositional resistance to coercive states and institutions? What routes to self-empowerment and social visibility might be available? How might consciousness and social location be productively transformed? Which activist tactics and strategies could be effective in changing the tenor of one's social relations? To probe these questions of agency, we turn to investigations by a sampling of theorists who have redefined its possibilities and practices.

Agency, Ideology, and Power

Theorists of agency have found the work of Louis Althusser helpful in thinking through ideological contradictions of an Enlightenment notion of human agency. Althusser argues that the subject is a subject of ideology—not in the narrow sense of propaganda but in the broad sense of the pervasive cultural formations of the dominant class. Althusser recognizes the power of coercive state institutions such as the military and the police to conform subjects to particular behaviors, beliefs, and identities. He also recognizes that there are less overtly coercive institutions—social services, educational institutions, the family, literary and artistic production—that "hail" subjects who enter them. By *hailing,* Althusser means the process through which subjects become interpellated, become what institutional discourses and practices make of them. They are "subjected." Most importantly, individuals understand themselves as "naturally" self-produced because the power of ideology to hail the subject is obscured by the very practices of the institution. In this way, people are invested in and mystified by their own production as subjects. That is, they have "false consciousness": they collude in their own lack of agency by believing that they have it. It is not enough, then, to say that people exercise free will because the concept of "free will" is embedded in a historically specific discourse about the Enlightenment individual, through which subjects understand themselves as intellectually mature and free to make their own choices. To claim that all humans have something called "free will" in this way is to misunderstand an ideological concept as a "natural" aspect of existence. The Enlightenment "individual" is itself an effect of ideology.

The theories of Michel Foucault also challenge the Enlightenment concept of the agentic liberal subject as free, rational, and autonomous. Where Althusser emphasizes power that is centripetally concentrated in official and unofficial institutions interpellating subjects, Foucault argues that there is no "outside" to power, that power is capillary, pervasive, inescapable, centrifugally dispersed across microlocations. Power activates through discourses, the languages of everyday life through which knowledge and regimes of truth are produced and distributed. It is through discursive "technologies of self" that subjects come to know themselves, and to surveil themselves. Thus, autobiographical narration functions as a technology of self that constitutes the cultural meanings of experience, as we have seen Joan W. Scott argue. Discursive regimes determine who can tell their stories, what kinds of stories they can tell, and the forms those stories will take. People tell stories of their lives through the cultural scripts available to them, and they are governed by cultural strictures about self-presentation in public. In this sense, then, there is no autonomous, agentic subject outside of discourse, and no freely interpreted or fully controlled self-narration. Given these critiques,

Autobiographical Subjects

can self-representation in life narrative be other than a self-deluding process?

Subsequent theorists have taken these challenges to the liberal notion of human agency, however, as starting points from which to rethink its possibilities. The recurrent themes of these redefinitions circle around several terms: *creativity, heterogeneity, multiplicity, dynamic reconfiguration, excess,* and *ethics.* Political theorist Elizabeth Wingrove rereads Althusser, arguing that "agents change, and change their world, by virtue of the systemic operation of multiple ideologies." Key here is the multiplicity of ideologies through which the subject is hailed. These multiple ideologies "expose both the subject and the system to perpetual reconfiguration" (871). Reconfiguration allows new possibilities to emerge for knowing oneself as a subject and for understanding a system. Such reconfigurations can gain momentum and intensity in times of great mobility. Changes in social, economic, and political formations, for instance, disrupt the traditional social arrangements of identities and behaviors. As a result, new interpretations of experiential history and self-understandings may emerge and be revalued in new locations.

Agency, Tactics, and Strategies

French sociologist and theorist Michel de Certeau, in *The Practice of Everyday Life,* locates agency in what he terms "transverse tactics." Individuals and groups deploy such tactics to manipulate the spaces in which they are constrained, such as the workplace or the home space. For instance, a factory worker may superimpose another system of language or culture onto the system imposed on him in the factory. Combining systems, he can create "a space in which he can find ways of using the constraining order of the place or of the language" to establish "a degree of plurality and creativity." Such modes of "re-use," then, are interventions that open a space of agency within constrained systems (29–30). Another way of understanding reuse is to think of the ways that people living in conditions of extremity—in revolutionary times or times of radical violence and trauma—redefine or resituate the symbolic valences of material, behavioral, or linguistic markers of identification.

Anthropologist Sherry B. Ortner, in contrast, situates agency in the capacities people bring when they play the "games" of culture—with their rules and structures. For Ortner, because sociocultural structures are always partial rather than total, there is always the possibility of changing the rules—although not of escaping rules altogether. An individual's wit and intelligence influence his, her, or their potential for pressuring the rules of the games. In yet another view, French theorist Jean-François Lyotard situates struggles with locating agency in the flexible and uncontrollable networks of language from which people construct their worlds and the ruses those networks spawn through unexpected moves and countermoves. As a result language itself holds strategic potential for the formation of new sociopolitical subjects.

Agency and Disidentification

Feminist theorist Teresa de Lauretis turns to the unconscious as a potential source of agency. The unconscious is a psychic domain of disidentification, a repository of all the experiences and desires that have to be repressed in order for the subject to conform to socially enforced norms ("Eccentric Subjects," 125–27). As such, it lies at the intersection of the psychic and the social. As a repository of the repressed, the unconscious is also a potential site of agency; its excess is a source of resistance to socially enforced calls to fixed identities. In the early work of Judith Butler, resistance to compulsory heteronormativity is located in the agentic effects of what she calls the performativity of subjectivity. According to Butler, identity is enacted daily through socially enforced norms that surround us. Thus, it is through our reenactment of the norms of, say, masculinity or femininity that we know ourselves to be "a heterosexual man" or "a woman." But this enforcement of norms is never totally effective. Individuals fail to conform fully to them because of the multiple, conflicting norms we are called on to reenact in our everyday lives. The failure to conform signals the "possibility of a variation" of "the rules that govern intelligible identity." With that failure reconfigurations or changes of identity may emerge (*Gender Trouble,* 145).

Agency and Social Practices

More recently, Jacques Rancière has focused on how agency is distributed within social situations and critiques forms of subjectivation that characterize humans in theatrical terms as performers in acts of "representing" themselves as an artificial construct. That is, he argues that we need to read the distribution of agency differently. His antifoundationalism, like that of Gilles Deleuze, critiques the notion of a universe of preconstructed individualities and argues for notions of personhood

Autobiographical Subjects

and action that arise out of the materiality of situations. Rancière's shift from a focus on individual agents has intensified in the last decade in response to various materialist theories of agency that decenter human actors and resituate them as assemblages of other humans as well as other species, materials, and systems, in ever-shifting flows.

Postcolonial theorist Arjun Appadurai approaches the concept of agency in this historical moment of global capitalism from another point of view—as residing in the imagination, mobilized as "an organized field of social practices" (327). Imagination negotiates between "sites of agency," namely, the imagined communities in which people participate, and "globally defined fields of possibility" (327). Situated amid multiple forms of imagined worlds, individuals as sites of agency deploy their imaginations as both a social fact and a kind of work to navigate the disjunctures of global flows that create radically different self-understandings. Appadurai's discussion of imagination suggests that agency takes distinct historical forms and operates in distinct geopolitical and geographical contexts. Similarly, Weheliye elaborates on the question of creativity: "What different modalities of the human come to light if we do not take the liberal humanist figure of Man as the master-subject but focus on how humanity has been imagined and lived by those subjects excluded from this domain?" (8). For these theorists, agency is necessarily situated within—and against—social worlds, the surrounds that inform life narratives but are often subordinated or forgotten if we divorce their protagonists from the contexts of communal interactions.

The Distribution of Agencies

In the early twenty-first century, materialist and posthumanist theories of agency have dislodged the human actor as the center of operation as they respond to the question of whether agency is exercised solely by human beings. Agency is relocated in assemblages—of humans, materials, systems of distribution, aspects of political economies, technological affordances—as nodes in an ever-shifting confluence of actors. Setting aside notions of the agency of human will and intentionality, Bennett argues for a concept of distributed agency. Taking up a postmodernist theory of subjection, she advances the concept of "an agency *of* the assemblage" as a collective in which "each member and protomember of the assemblage has a certain vital force. . . . And because each member-actant maintains an energetic pulse slightly 'off' from that of the assemblage, an assemblage is never a solid block"; rather, it is "an open-ended collective, a 'non-totalizing sum'" (24). Conceiving of human agents in this way both decenters and extends the exercise of human agency, even as it calls on life narrators to reconfigure the speaking subject as entangled within fluid assemblages.

Reading for the Politics of Agency

These heterogeneous approaches to the concept of agency offer critical frameworks for considering how people, in the act of narrating their lives, might understand their addressees, frame the stories they tell or draw or otherwise craft, change those stories, gain access to other cultural scripts, come to understand themselves differently, and make claims on others based on their counternarratives. Life narrators might, that is, exercise not something called free will or autonomy, but agency or agentic actions in encounters.

For those inheriting the legacies of a colonial history that rendered their ancestors less than fully human and who are affected by its neocolonial aftereffects, autobiographical narration is both an inviting form and a vexed discourse through which to give an account of oneself. It implicitly claims to be a mode of empowering voices and registering experiential histories of violence and oppression that attest to forms of resistance in the face of damage; but this claim is undermined by its history as a discourse of domination. That is, traditional autobiography has too often functioned as a master narrative of Western hegemony celebrating the sovereign individual and the terms of its agency. As such, it has been a genre inhospitable to people whose cultural modes of expression and terms of self-understanding did, and continue to, value oral and collective forms. And yet, as Gillian Whitlock argues, there is a long textual history of life narratives from former colonial subjects who maneuvered within, and wrestled with, legal and literary constraints on life writing to produce narratives that "gave witness to the previously unseen, and in turn called upon the reader to bear witness to unknown and scarcely imaginable scenes from the 'New World,'" as did the narrative of the formerly enslaved Olaudah Equiano (*Postcolonial Life Narratives,* 16).

Bearing witness and asserting cultural agency by intervening in representations of oneself as the object of the colonial gaze—the "exotic" native other of anthropology or the racialized laborer or enslaved subject

Autobiographical Subjects

of colonialism or the subaltern of imperialism and neocolonialism—depends on taking up the language and media of autobiographical discourse. One strategy for postcolonial subjects in many parts of Africa, Asia, and the Americas to assert cultural agency has been deploying a range of what Caren Kaplan terms "out-law genres," such as autoethnography, *testimonio,* and prison memoir. Kaplan asserts that out-law genres "mix two conventionally 'unmixable' elements—autobiography criticism and autobiography as thing itself." Such mixing can produce a textual "politics of location," a specific context in which the text is produced and the self-narrator situated (119). In such postcolonial life narrative, the combination of out-law genres may both present and withhold the autobiographical by employing forms of autobiographical discourse to assert the cultural difference of a subjectivity that both engages and challenges the Western tradition of individualist life narrative. Senegalese writer Ken Bugul (Mariétou M'baye), for example, in *The Abandoned Baobab: The Autobiography of a Senegalese Woman,* draws on Frantz Fanon's theoretical framework to narrate how she came to consciousness of her identity as a subject of the French empire and critiques the ground of knowing on which she refuses the terms of Western agency.

Some postcolonial critics, however, strongly challenge the notion of postcolonial agency in autobiographical writing as an oxymoron. In a trenchant critique of the genre as incompatible with postcolonial narrative, Spivak makes a crucial distinction between "the generic or structural impossibility of autobiography being narrativized through the agency of colonialism" and "postcolonialist autobiography" in which storytelling as "trying myself out, as ephemeral teller, to you . . . a subaltern, a gendered subaltern" may depend on the withholding of one's autobiography, as conventionally defined ("Three Women's Texts and Circumfession," 11). *I, Rigoberta Menchú: An Indian Woman in Guatemala,* Menchú's narrative as told to Elisabeth Burgos-Debray, is an example of withholding. It interweaves multiple discourses of identity: ethnographic ritual, parody, political manifesto, familial chronicle, and a tragic personal narrative of loss and renunciation. Throughout, Menchú shuttles between cultures (Quiché, Ladino, and Western European), languages (Spanish and Quiché), and positionings (teacher, political activist, daughter, Catholic acolyte, worker, woman) to communicate an urgent testimony of the suffering of her people and the injustice done to them. At the same time, she vows to keep some aspects of her identity secret, thereby resisting readers' desire to possess the truth about the survival of this Indigenous culture and the assumption that readers can "know" a life narrator by reading the narrative. In her testimony Menchú thus illuminates the process of exercising agency both in telling and in withholding cultural stories.

This exploration of how subjectivity and concepts of the subject encompass the many dimensions and dynamics that attach to the assumed agentive "I" or narrator in autobiographical acts and practices invites readers to rethink some assumptions about what happens in life writing. While we may conceive of autobiographical narrators or composers as telling unified stories of their lives and creating or discovering coherent selves, it may be more helpful to approach the unified story and the coherent self as myths of identity. For there is no coherent "self" that predates stories about identity, about "who" one is. Nor could such a unified, stable, immutable self remember and embody everything that has happened in the past. Autobiographical subjects are always fragmented in time, taking a particular or provisional perspective on the moving target of the past, and addressing multiple, disparate audiences.

In theorizing memory, relationality, experience, identity, space, embodiment, and agency we begin to understand the complexities of acts and practices of telling one's story or a community's story through heterogeneous modes of narrating, presenting, performing, and materializing a "life," that is, the process of enacting subjectivity. In order to think more deeply about what happens at the intersection of text and context, we turn next to the rhetorical and communicative features of autobiographical acts.

3
Autobiographical Acts

We are never really the cause of our life, but we can have the illusion of becoming its author by writing it.

—Philippe Lejeune, "The Autobiography of Those Who Do Not Write"

All these people—producers, coaxers, consumers—are engaged in assembling life story actions around lives, events, and happenings—although they cannot grasp the actual life. . . . These congeal or freeze already preconstituted moments of a life from the story teller and the coaxer and await the handling of a reader or consumer.

—Ken Plummer, *Telling Sexual Stories*

Let's situate the autobiographical act in a story, a story in time and place. This situatedness is especially crucial since life narratives are always symbolic interactions in the world. They are culturally and historically specific. They are rhetorical; that is, they are addressed to an audience/reader. They are implicitly involved in negotiations of identity; and they are inevitably fractured by the play of meaning (see Leith and Myerson). Autobiographical acts, then, are anything but simple and transparent.

In *Telling Sexual Stories,* sociologist Ken Plummer, considering autobiographical stories through the lens of a "pragmatic symbolic interactionist ethnography," differentiates three kinds of people who contribute to every story action (xi). There is the producer or teller of the story—what we call the autobiographical narrator. There is the coaxer—the persons or institutions that elicit stories from speakers. There are the consumers, readers, or audiences who interpret stories (20–21). While we take Plummer's tripartite schema as a starting point in the following discussion, we complicate it by introducing other situational and interactional features of autobiographical acts.

103

COAXERS, COACHES, AND COERCERS

Everyday occasions invite the narration of our life stories. Think of autobiographical acts, then, as occasions when people are coaxed or coerced into "getting a life." The coaxer or coercer, in Plummer's terms, is any person or institution or set of cultural imperatives that solicits or provokes people to tell their stories (21). Telling may occur in intimate situations when someone solicits a personal narrative—for example, the intimate exchange between lovers who seek to enhance desire by giving the gift of their memories to one another. Requests for personal narratives may come in letters or e-mail messages from friends and family members: "Tell me what's been happening to you. I haven't heard from you for so long." Compulsions to confess may be coaxed by internalized religious values and practices—voiced confession in the Catholic Church, prayerful silent confession in Protestantism or repentance in Islam, atonement on Yom Kippur. The compulsion to confession may also be of a commercial kind, commodified in talk shows and podcasts or online platforms that package the interests of popular culture in features on "loving too much" or "secret eating." Publishers may invite celebrity figures and influencers to tell or post life narratives to a public hungry for vicarious fame. Friends and colleagues of distinguished people may urge them to tell stories that exemplify the public and professional dimensions of their lives.

Coaxers and coercers are everywhere. Think of these everyday situations in which they solicit people's stories about themselves in the contexts of social institutions:[1]

- In political speeches candidates are expected to tell personal narratives that may project "character" and "values" or situate them in the major wars and movements of the moment or reference specific religious, ethnic, or vocational communities.
- In the communal recitations of self-help groups, participants conform their life stories to the available narrative models offered for making progress in recovery, for example, the Alcoholics Anonymous twelve-step model.
- In family gatherings, individuals participate in the shared recollection of the family's stories as rituals that reinforce family history and the idea of family itself.
- In hospital waiting rooms, people fill out forms requesting

Autobiographical Acts

stories of their bodies. Other versions of body narratives emerge in mammography, ultrasonography, or MRI scans. Digital devices to track bodily information elicit data-driven narratives of the self, as in the quantified self movement.

- People fill out standardized forms for housing vouchers, driver's licenses, or passports. In each of these institutional settings, personal narratives are conformed to bureaucratic imperatives and identities appropriate to the occasion.
- Online dating platforms require people to catalog their histories and desires.
- For employment applications and online services, such as LinkedIn, people prepare résumés requiring conventionalized credentials, condensing varied experiences into specific skills for career advancement.
- When joining groups such as neighborhood associations, churches, veterans' organizations, and fraternities or sororities, people may be called on to tell their stories before the membership.
- Swearing in court to "tell the truth," people before the bar are implicated in competing truth claims for adjudication.

This list could go on and on, through cultural institutions, state bureaucracies, nonstate organizations, friendships, cross-cultural encounters, and other analog and digital communities.

Although the autobiographical narratives of published writers may, in their highly crafted aesthetics, seem far removed from such everyday sites, the coaxing to which they respond shares a number of concerns and features with the kinds of autobiographical presentations that people engage in when telling parts of their stories. Some coaxing is explicit. In his *Confessions* Augustine projects a God needful of his confession. In the section of his autobiography begun in 1788, Benjamin Franklin includes several letters from friends setting out various reasons all Americans would benefit from reading his life story. The "Benjamin Franklin" friends want to elicit from him is, of course, a particular version of Franklin, the statesman, social benefactor, and moral guide. Nineteenth-century narrators of enslavement were urged to recite their stories of its degradations in the halls of abolitionist meetings and for the abolitionist press.

But coaxing is also more broadly diffused throughout a culture. Successive generations of immigrants to the United States, for example, have responded to the need to affirm for other Americans their legitimate membership in the nation by telling stories of assimilation. In the United States as well, public figures such as politicians frequently present their version of past actions in order to defend or justify their choices and to "set the record straight." In writing his apologia, *In Retrospect: The Tragedy and Lessons of Vietnam,* Robert S. McNamara responded to the continuing widespread debate in the United States about the Vietnam War and the role of government officials in waging it.

Coaxing is an integral part of the life-writing process when more than one person is directly involved in producing the story. It can take several forms. In doubled autobiographical narratives, two (or more) people offer their versions of shared events or experiences, as do journalists David Sheff in *Beautiful Boy* and his son Nic Sheff in *Tweak* on their divergent stories of a son's methamphetamine addiction. In as-told-to or ghostwritten narratives, multiple levels of coaxing take place, including those of the ghostwriter or cowriter, whose interview questions, translations of the autobiographer's oral speech, and revisions are often invisible in the final text. This is the case with Alex Haley in *The Autobiography of Malcolm X* and Ida Pruitt in *A Daughter of Han: The Autobiography of a Chinese Working Woman,* based on the narrative of Ning Lao T'ai-t'ai. Yet another case of invisible intervention is that of the publisher who requires that a celebrity, recovery, or trauma narrative be shaped for special audiences.

In collaborative life writing, at least two people are involved in producing the story: one is the investigator, who does the interviewing and assembles a narrative from the primary materials given; the second is the informant, who tells a story through interviews or informal conversations. But with many collaborative narratives, for example "as-told-to" narratives by Native Americans and Indigenous peoples, the situation may be triangulated among three or more parties: ethnographer, subject, and translator. This complex nexus of telling, translating, and editing introduces a set of issues about the process of appropriating and over-writing the original oral narrative, as in the case of *Black Elk Speaks: Being the Life Story of a Holy Man of the Oglala Sioux as Told to John G. Neihardt* (see Couser, "Black Elk"). The publication history of *I, Rigoberta Menchú* reveals a third kind of complexity. Menchú has protested that

Autobiographical Acts

the intervention of its editor, Elisabeth Burgos-Debray, overwrote the versions suggested by its translators, thereby changing the emphases of the narrative (see Canby). The politics of coproduction may be mediated differently when life narrators who are deaf or otherwise prevented from directly recording their life stories depend on someone to transcribe their stories from American Sign Language into a standard language such as English (Bauman, "'Voicing' Deaf Identity" and *Open Your Eyes*).

Lastly, editorial exercise of censorship is an example of coercion in the name of coproduction at the point of publishing the life narrative. When Zora Neale Hurston's *Dust Tracks on a Road: An Autobiography* was being edited for publication, the publisher, concerned about literary propriety for a 1940s white reading public, excised certain phrases and folkloric turns of speech from the manuscript and omitted altogether some "sexy" stories Hurston had included (see Raynaud). These cases suggest that collaborative life writing is a multilingual, transcultural process that often involves coercion and editorial control in the name of preserving the voice, the experience, and the culture of the life narrator.

As we see, the role of coaxers in life narrative can be more coercive than collaborative. Complicated ethical issues arise when one or more people exercise cultural authority over assembling and organizing a life narrative (Couser, "Making, Taking, and Faking Lives"). In giving thematic shape to life writing by virtue of decisions about what is included or excluded, a coaxer can subordinate the narrator's modes and choices of storytelling to another idea of how a life story should read and how its subject should speak appropriately. Although the role of an editorial coaxer is often obscured when the narrative is published, a preface "describing" the working relationship between editor/transcriber and narrating subject may be added to direct the audience's reading.

What is a critical reader to do in engaging the complexities of collaborative texts? All of the examples discussed here argue, first, for specifying the roles of various coaxers in making the autobiographical text and, second, for relinquishing the widespread notion that some texts by vulnerable subjects, such as those with disabilities or indigenous people, produce a kind of unmediated authenticity. The stimulating debates of anthropologists about participant observation, of historians about the authority of primary documents, and of cultural studies theorists about autoethnography offer life-writing scholars sites and tools for situating collaborative life writing as a mode of cultural production in which various voices and versions contest, and contend for, authority.

A related question arises. How do we understand the role of algorithms and protocols on social media as coaxers and coercers of virtual versions of the user? Online sites gather, authorize, and conserve the version of self a user is assembling. Various kinds of documents solicited by the site become evidence capturing varied aspects of the presenter's life, habits, desires, and the like. That is, a site incorporates and organizes documents about a self as a personal archive, and that personal archive may become incorporated into other archives, official or unofficial, designed or accidental. Moreover, the algorithmic data generated by the site directs information about the user into online databases. The prodigious capacities of online archives have therefore shifted how we understand the power of archives and databases to drive and constrainself-presentation.

Neither the archive nor the database has a fail-safe delete button. Code may break down, and the service industry of reputation management may delete substantial data archives. Despite all this, online users continue to contribute user-generated content, which can return as digital afterlife. The search engine as disembodied coaxer is a complication of digital life narrative that can exploit and change the data of our lives in ways needing further investigation.

SITES OF STORYTELLING

Think of sites as both occasional, that is, specific to an occasion, and locational, that is, emergent in a specific mise-en-scène or context of narration. The site is, first, a literal place, a social media platform, a talk show, perhaps, or a social service agency, an airplane, or, as in the case of Carolina Maria de Jesus in *Child of the Dark: The Diary of Carolina Maria de Jesus,* the impoverished *favelas* (slums) of São Paolo, Brazil. But the site of narration is also a moment in history, a sociopolitical space, which affects what kinds of narratives seem "credible" and "real" and what kind of cultural work they do at a given moment. Furthermore, sites have protocols that establish expectations about what kinds of stories are told and are intelligible to others. An autobiographical presentation made on a website, for example, would not be appropriate in a legal setting, where it might cause real problems. That is, the needs, practices,

Autobiographical Acts

and purposes of institutions that effectively manage some aspects of daily life are different from the needs and intentions of storytellers in intimate settings, as well as the ideal self-images narrators would like to project.

Occasional and locational, sites of storytelling in which coaxing and narrating take place are also multidimensional. They may be predominantly personal, institutional, or geographical, though to some extent these three levels often overlap. If we return to the example of a family gathering, autobiographical acts at a reunion might depend on a specific coaxer—say, an uncle asking a niece to recall what it was like to spend time with her grandmother. But this occasion also contributes to supporting or questioning larger notions about the family, such as the role of family reunions in family life, the ways in which storytelling within an extended family binds a group of disparate individuals together, the kinds of stories shared at such occasions, and the kinds that might violate codes of familiality.

Sites of involuntary detainment establish different expectations. If the location is a prison cell, with its monotonous and deindividuating daily routine, autobiographical narrative that imagines forms of resistance, alternative locations, and imaginary futures can enable self-reconstruction and self-determination. For example, Eldridge Cleaver writes *Soul on Ice* in prison as a manifesto aimed at self-liberation, as does Jacobo Timerman in penning *Prisoner without a Name, Cell without a Number*. Similarly, Albertine Sarrazin, a young French vagabond, in "Journal de prison, 1959," writes against the cultural construction of the defeminized female prisoner by imagining and momentarily freeing herself in libidinal stories of heterosexual love and desire.

In many narratives, the geographical location strongly inflects the story being told. Jane Addams's Hull House is both a social institution and a location for intervening in impoverished immigrant Chicago in the early twentieth century. Autobiographies as diverse as Edward William Bok's *The Americanization of Edward Bok: The Autobiography of a Dutch Boy Fifty Years After,* Audre Lorde's *Zami: A New Spelling of My Name,* Vivian Gornick's *Fierce Attachments: A Memoir,* and Patti Smith's *Just Kids,* all situated in New York City, establish richly textured portrayals of its streets, bars, apartments, and urban scene. In the vast and heterogeneous space of the city, stories of lives engage its particular locations as well as the complexity of urban life for various kinds of subjects to produce not "New York City" but diverse stories of the highly charged, sensorily saturated, and often jarring and hostile world of the city. This aspect of life narrative, as yet rarely studied by critics who tend to see the site as a backdrop, shapes the contexts of both autobiographical subjectivity and the kinds of stories that can be told. Conversely, narratives steeped in the specifics of rural place or wilderness—Kathleen Norris's *Dakota: A Spiritual Geography*, Terry Tempest Williams's *Refuge: An Unnatural History of Family and Place*, Michael Ondaatje's *Running in the Family*, Robert Macfarlane's *Underland: A Deep Time Journey*, and Catherine Colman Flowers's *Waste: One Woman's Fight against America's Dirty Secret*—are also sociocultural sites in which struggles about environmental, familial, national, and cultural politics intersect as "layers" of narrative location. The concept of site as space, place, location, both geographical and virtual, emphasizes the situatedness of autobiographical narration.

The Internet offers an apparently singular virtual site of life writing and a heterogeneous array of websites through which the dynamics of space, place, and location affect the possibilities for life narrative and self-presentation. That is, the reality of platforms and protocols shifts the meanings of "sites." *Protocol-driven sites* have elaborate formats, driven by algorithms that dictate how users organize what they tell or present of themselves. The protocols of Facebook, for example, require that users enumerate themselves in established formats, which may suppress some aspects of individual difference. Other site formats that seem constricting or incomplete, however, can be modified or disrupted in order to create more nuanced and complex self-presentations. Users might add photographs or mention distinctive features or tastes to customize a self-presentation, or they might add a link to another site of self that complicates or expands the limits of the protocol template.

While *user-authored sites* observe some protocols, they may be minimal. For example, personal websites, such as LiveJournal and collaborative diary sites, permit blogging of unspecified length without a narrowly scripted protocol and invite interactive comments from others. Users may choose to encode themselves through fantasies of being someone or something else, as avatars or alternative identities. The play of "bricolage," assembling a profile from disparate data and allowing other users to recombine it differently, is also a feature of some online sites.

Autobiographical Acts

Clearly, however, users must conform their stories to the norms and rules of a site and attend to what kind of "life" the site's format solicits. That is, templates shape the user's projection of identity and communal affiliations. They may have formats that constrict or typicalize a subject into a general social type, excluding or deforming a life into a ready-made version. Still, users can intervene in or innovate upon site protocols in ways that keep evolving.

AUTOBIOGRAPHICAL "I"S: HISTORICAL, NARRATING, NARRATED, IDEOLOGICAL

The producer of the story is the autobiographical "I." As chapter 2 asserts, this "I" is not a flesh-and-blood author, an entity that remains unknowable, but a speaker or narrator who refers to him-, her-, or themself. While the speaker, a mark of self-referentiality, has one name, the "I" who seems to be speaking—sometimes through a published text or an intimate letter, sometimes in person or on screen—is composed of multiple "I"s.

Often critics analyzing autobiographical acts distinguish between the "I"-now and the "I"-then, the narrating "I" who speaks and the narrated "I" who is spoken about. This differentiation assumes that the "I"-now inhabits a stable present in reading the "I"-then. It also assumes a normative notion of life narrative as a retrospective narrative about a separable and isolatable past that is fully past. But, as our discussion of processes of autobiographical subjectivity revealed, this limited understanding of life narrative does not account for the complexities of self-narrating or the heterogeneous array of autobiographical modes. Nor does it adequately capture the complexity of the "I" in even the most traditional of autobiographies.

We propose complicating this autobiographical "I" beyond the "I"-then and the "I"-now framework by attending to the multiple "I"-thens, to the ideologies spoken through the "I," to the multiple "I"-nows, and to the flesh-and-blood author.

The "Real" or Historical "I"

Obviously an authorial "I" is assumed from the signature on the title page—the person producing the autobiographical "I"—whose life is far more diverse and dispersed than the story that is being told of it. This is the "I" as historical person, a flesh-and-blood entity located in a particular time and place. This "I," as Chantal Mouffe notes, can be understood as "the articulation of an ensemble of subject positions, corresponding to the multiplicity of social relations in which it is inscribed" (376). This "I" lives or lived in the world, going about the business of everyday life.

Because there are traces of this historical person in various records in the archives of government bureaucracies, churches, family albums, and the memories of others, "I" is verifiable. Her voice, if she is still alive, is audible. But this "I" is unknown and unknowable to readers and is not the "I" accessible in an autobiographical narrative.

The Narrating "I"

The "I" available to readers is the "I" who tells or composes the autobiographical narrative, the narrator or the narrating "I." This is a persona of the historical person who wants to tell, or is coerced into telling, a story about the self. While the historical "I" has a broad experiential history extending a lifetime back into the past, the narrating "I" calls forth only that part of the experiential history linked to the story they are telling. This narrating "I" usually, though not universally, uses the first-person referent in this act.

The Narrated "I"

It is crucial to observe that, and how, the narrating "I" is distinguished from the narrated "I." In the terms of narrative theory, the narrated "I" is the subject of history and the narrating "I" is the agent of discourse. The narrated "I" is the object "I," the protagonist of the narrative, the version of the self that the narrating "I" chooses to constitute through recollection for the reader.

For example, narrators may begin their narratives with memories of childhood, conjuring themselves at the age of five or eight or ten and setting that child version in the world as remembered. That younger "I" may even be given a remembered or reimagined consciousness of the experience of being five or eight or ten as voiced through dialogue or interior monologue. That child, however, is an objectified and remembered "I," the memory of a younger version of a self. The child is not doing the remembering or the narrating of the story. Nor is that narrated "I" directly experiencing that past at the time of writing the narrative or its telling. The narrating "I" confronting the blank page or the computer screen or a live audience is the remembering agent who creates the story.

Autobiographical Acts

And, as we explored in chapter 2, that narrating "I" occupies multiple, sometimes contradictory, subject positions.

Complicating the Narrating "I"–Narrated "I" Distinction

This schematic framework for distinguishing the narrating "I" and the narrated "I" of autobiographical narration and self-presentation, however, is not sufficient when reading a particular autobiographical work. Its neat, binaristic logic needs to be complicated and understood as a starting point from which to explore how the "I" is encoded, represented, and engaged. To that end, the following considerations that qualify the "I" suggest its inherent mobility.

First, there are times when the narrating "I" is situated in the second or third person or first-person plural instead of the more common singular pronoun. Narratives as disparate as those of Edward William Bok, Henry Adams, and J. M. Coetzee are presented through the third-person pronoun. African American artist Faith Ringgold uses the second-person "you" of self-reference in *The Change Series: Faith Ringgold's 100-Pound Weight-Loss Quilt*, where she writes of herself as the "you" of disorderly eating habits. Christa Wolf often uses the second person in *Patterns of Childhood* to distance a past "I" of the Hitler years. The effect of deploying the third-person pronoun is often to disrupt the expectation of first-person intimacy, to create a sense of self-alienation through objectification, and to open a gap between the narrating "I" and an implicit narrating "he" or "she" or "they." By contrast, the effect of using the second-person pronoun is to reroute the expected address between narrator and reader to an unexpected intimacy of exchange between the narrating "I" and narrated "I." In either case, readers become aware of the elastic effect of conventions of distance and intimacy in life writing.

Second, the narrating "I" is neither unified nor stable. It is split, fragmented, provisional, multiple, a subject always in the process of coming together or dispersing. That is, the narrating "I" is an effect composed of multiple voices, a heteroglossia attached to multiple and mobile subject positions. This fragmentation is audible in the multiple voices through which the narrator speaks in the text. (See the section on "Voice in Autobiographical Narration and Presentation," below.) These voices might include the voice of publicly acknowledged authority, the voice of innocence and wonder, the voice of cynicism, the voice of postconversion certainty, the voice of suffering and victimization, and

114   Autobiographical Acts

so on. For instance, the narrating "I" of *The Autobiography of Malcolm X* speaks in several voices: as an angry Black man challenging the racism of the United States, a religious devotee of Islam, a husband and father, a person betrayed, a prophet of hope, among others. (See further discussion of voice in this chapter.)

Third, the narrated "I" can be conspicuously fractured and fragmented thematically in a narrative. In *How I Grew*, Mary McCarthy writes of posing for a poor artist whom she met in Seattle. "Canvas cost a lot," she writes. "So I, who was not yet 'I,' had been painted over or given a coat of whitewash, maybe two or three times, till I was only a bumpiness, an extra thickness of canvas" (161). Here McCarthy differentiates her earlier girl selves from the writer she would become, "I." But those old selves are visible as a palimpsest, a bumpy textual surface that leaves its trace in the layers of covering wash. McCarthy's narrative is a good instance of how a single pronominal "I" may be used to refer to the multiple versions of autobiographical speakers over time. That is, not only the narrated "I" of earlier times but also the narrating "I" in the temporal present can be mobile, fragmented, and heterogeneous.

Fourth, the existence of serial autobiography, either as chapters within a single volume or as multiple texts, challenges any simplistic dichotomy between narrating and narrated "I"s. As one narrative moment and occasion displaces another, stories from the past may be rerouted through different narrating "I"s, who assign different meanings, affective valences, and effects to events, stages in life, conflicts, and traumas. The narrated "I" returns, to be put under a new definition, given new identities, set in a new relation to history. Serializing the "I," then, asserts the condition of mobility, as one version follows another.

Fifth, there are certain narratives in which the narrating "I" produces a narrated "I" that then becomes his, her, or their agent of narration. This narrating "I" can, for instance, be cast as the voice of a younger version of the writer. In such narratives, it remains the case that the older narrator with greater knowledge, narrative experience, and linguistic competence controls the recourse to simplistic vocabulary, truncated phrases, and sensory description, all associated with the youthful narrating "I." The child narrating "I" of the storytelling is an "I" constructed by the experienced narrating "I" to represent the meaning of that narrated child's experience. For example, in his best-selling memoir *Angela's*

Autobiographical Acts

Ashes, Frank McCourt deploys the narrative voice of his younger self to tell a story of growing up in the rough streets and violent homes of Limerick, Ireland, and in New York City. The intimacy of the narrating I's voice breaks through McCourt's attempt to imagine and capture a sense of what that experience might have been like.[2]

Sixth, there may be instances in which the narrated "I" is presented as an imaginary "I," a possible earlier self, composed through the mining of limited archival materials and through historical records of the lived experience of conditions and events. The effect of an imaginary "I" is a "this is what my experiences might have felt like" quality; what I might have been like at the time, what I might have done.

The Ideological "I"

Thus far, we have discussed the "I" as a site of self-relation but not as grounded in any historical location or belief system. But, of course, the "I" is neither a transparent subject nor a free agent. Rather, it is, as Louis Althusser insists, steeped in ideology, in all the institutional discourses through which people come to understand themselves and to place themselves in the world, or as Althusser terms it, through which people are interpellated as certain kinds of subjects. Through discourses people come to know themselves and their experiences in ways that seem normal and natural, although that dismissal of agency has been qualified, as discussed in chapter 2.[3]

The concept of ideological interpellation also illuminates the importance of cultural notions of "I"-ness. The ideological "I" is the concept of personhood culturally available to the narrator when he tells his story (Paul Smith, 105). Historical and ideological notions of the person provide cultural ways of understanding several things: the material location of subjectivity; the relationship of the person to particular others and to a collectivity of others; the nature of time and life course; the importance of social location; the motivations for human actions; the presence of evil, violent, and self-destructive forces and acts; even the metaphysical meaning of the universe. Because every autobiographical narrator is historically and culturally situated, each is a product of his, her, or their particular time and place. A narrator, then, needs to be situated in the historical notion of personhood and the meaning of lives at the time of writing.

The ideological "I" is at once everywhere and nowhere in autobiographical acts, in the sense that the notion of personhood and the ideologies of identity that constitute it are so internalized (personally and culturally) that they seem "natural" and "universal" characteristics of persons. Yet changing notions of personhood affect autobiographical acts and practices; so do the competing ideological notions of personhood coexisting at any historical moment. For the ideological "I" is also multiple and thus potentially conflictual. At any historical moment, there are heterogeneous identities culturally available to a narrator, identities marked through embodiment and through culture: gender, ethnicity, generation, family, sexuality, religion, among others. Some narrators emphasize their ideological complexity (Gloria Anzaldúa, Jean-Jacques Rousseau), while others may bend aspects of the story in depicting a conflict of ideologies and the triumph of one, as in narratives of religious conversion.

For instance, in *A True History of the Captivity and Restoration of Mrs. Mary Rowlandson*, the seventeenth-century Puritan Mary Rowlandson remembers her captivity by the Narragansett Indians. Rowlandson is at a "remove" from her sustaining Puritan belief system and subjected to unfamiliar practices and values that seem incoherent to her. But her experience among the Narragansett also subtly shakes the foundations of that Puritan ideology as she comes to identify with its unsaved, savage other. Despite her return to the community, she now sees its beliefs as one set of values rather than how the world "is" and hence struggles with reoccupying the ideological "I" from which she was forcibly removed. Conversely, in the early twentieth century the Russian revolutionary Alexandra Kollontai negotiates, in her 1926 *Autobiography of a Sexually Emancipated Communist Woman*, the call for a revolutionary "new womanhood" and the cultural force of what she calls "the given model" of normative femininity. Throughout her narrative the residual imprint of the given model persists even as she insists on the transformation to a new ideological model. Thus, the ground of the ideological "I" is only apparently stable, and the possibilities for tension, adjustment, refixing, and unfixing are ever present.

The ideological "I" occupies a different and complex location in Gloria Anzaldúa's *Borderlands/La Frontera*. The narrator is critical of a political ideology of American expansionism that has appropriated Mexican lands and oppressed its people. To counter that prevailing

Autobiographical Acts

ideology, in which she has been schooled and which has judged her as marginal, she counterposes an Indigenous mythology of Mexican figures as a foundation for reorienting Chicanas ideologically toward the "new Mestiza." This figure of hybridity also contests ideologies of the gendered subordination of women and of heteronormativity. Anzaldúa wages her critique across multiple borders, including the linguistic frontier of Spanish-English. In so extensively mapping pressure points of resistance to an imposed ideological "I," she defamiliarizes its naturalness. Her juxtaposing of Mexican goddess figures, queer identification, and activist woman-of-color feminism gives these countervailing beliefs new ideological force.

Ideological "I"s, then, are possible positions for autobiographical narrators to occupy, contest, revise, and mobilize against one another at specific historical moments. Only apparently a "choice," they are nonetheless multiple, mobile, and mutating.

Reading the "I"

With life narratives, readers need to attend to these four "I"s or, rather, to the three that are available in autobiographical acts—the narrating, the narrated, and the ideological. They can look for places where the narrator addresses readers directly or where he calls attention to the act of narrating itself, to problems of remembering and forgetting, to a sense of the inadequacy of any narrative to get at the truth of his life as he is defining it. Readers can also watch how the narrator organizes the times of past, present, and future in the telling of the story as a way of teasing out narrated versions of the "I" presented and the ideological stakes of those representations in the present of narration.

Sometimes narrating "I"s produce an apparently continuous chronology from birth to adolescence to adulthood. Sometimes they produce an explicitly discontinuous narrative, beginning "in the middle" and using flashbacks or flash-forwards. Sometimes exactness of chronology is of little importance to the narrator. Always there are moments in the text when that impression of narrative coherence breaks down, in digressions, omissions, gaps, and silences about certain things, in contradictions. While the narrator's recitation may read as one long, continuous narrative, the text signals discontinuities that will not corroborate readers' fictions of coherence.

As one example, consider how Henry Adams omits the story of

his wife Clover's suicide in *The Education of Henry Adams.* Just at the chronological moment of her suicide, the narrative breaks into two parts. Noting this gap, readers can explore how knowledge of the silence resonates with the story's split structure, undermining the illusion of narrative coherence Adams's narrator seems to project. Readers can construct a coherent "Henry Adams," or other ideologically coherent "I"s, by underreading the ways in which the narrative calls attention to its own fissures.

"I" VARIATIONS: GRAPHIC, WITNESS, ONLINE, AND QUANTIFIED "I"S

With the explosion over the last three decades of life narratives across heterogeneous modes and media of self-presentation, fascinating variations of narrating and narrated "I"s have emerged in four contemporary kinds of life writing: graphic memoir and autographical comics with their vivid visual/verbal dynamics; platforms of online gaming and fantasy worlds where avatars are assembled and deployed; testimonial or witness narratives written, produced, and circulated within the context of human rights activism; and quantified self-data.

The "I"s of Autographics

Several features of autographics—graphic memoirs or autobiographical comics—distinguish the form. Graphic memoir is a hybrid, "cross-discursive form," as Hillary Chute and Marianne DeKoven emphasize, "composed of verbal and visual narratives that do not simply blend together, creating a unified whole, but rather remain distinct" (769). Mixing verbal and visual materials, autographics often present conflicting stories and oscillate between different planes of representation. Readers may observe stories in the visual plane that are not explicitly signaled by the verbal plane, and vice versa, thus engaging contesting stories and interpretations of autobiographical memory and meaning. Marianne Hirsch observes how this mixed visual and textual mode of life narrative foregrounds for the reader what she terms visual–verbal "biocularity." Adopting the term from Peggy Phelan's observations of transmedial effects of words and images in Samuel Beckett's *Waiting for Godot,*[4] Hirsch writes: "With words always already functioning as images and images asking to be read as much as seen, comics are biocular texts par excellence. Asking us to read back and forth between images and

Autobiographical Acts

words, comics reveal the visuality and thus the materiality of words and the discursivity and narrativity of images" ("Editor's Column," 1213).

The complex visual and textual dynamics of autographics achieve various effects. They intensify the entanglements of multiple "I"s across pages of the text. In addition to the frequent evidence of the hand of the author/artist who draws, there is an embodied, drawing "I" that is mostly inferred through its distinctive graphic style of line, visual palette, flow of images, repertoire of repeated images, design of page layout, and abstracted features for representing the protagonist or narrated "I." Paradoxically, this invisible "I" is materialized through aesthetic form and characterological visualization. Occasionally, the implied hand of the "I" is literally imaged on the page in disjunctive scenes referencing the author/artist subject in the act of remembering and composing, as occurs in the opening pages of Spiegelman's *Maus II* or in Bechdel's *Fun Home: A Family Tragicomedy*.

Additionally, the narration and reflection of the narrating "I" unfold in spaces such as text boxes above, across, or outside frames, and occasionally inside frames in visually distinct subsections. The narrated "I" is represented in dialogue bubbles or other conventional kinds of speech spaces attached to the imaged protagonist. Both narrating and narrated "I"s are voiced and visualized as "I"s simplified through abstracted features. This visualized "I" is sometimes referred to as an autobiographical avatar, a term generally limited to what Andrew J. Kunka defines as "the artist's drawn version of his or her self" (255).[5] Theorist Michael A. Chaney proposes an alternative term "I-con" for artists' self-depictions ("Terrors of the Mirror").

The tensions, dissonances, and convergences of this multiplicity of "I"s play out within frames, in gutters, and dynamically across the distinctive page designs through which the autographic at once advances time and retards time, renders visual images, disrupts the visual plane, and solicits biocular forms of knowing and making meaning on the part of the reader-viewer.

The Witnessing "I"

Narratives of witness and testimony to human rights violations often complicate the notion of the "I." The genre of testimony is commonly understood as centered on the "I"-witness to radical suffering and violence, the subject as victim of a rights violation, a seemingly unified

Autobiographical Acts

speaking position. However, the witness-"I" is often collectively produced by numerous actors positioned across asymmetries of power. These include the witness and the witness's community of affiliation; the intended audience within the narrative; the coaxer or interlocutor such as a reporter or activist, if there is one, usually with another affiliation and access to some means of redress; a group of others including the editor, publisher, and translator of the text; and activist groups, marketers, and the persons, organizations, and forums who have solicited, facilitated, and circulated the act of witnessing. Within this ensemble production, the narrating "I" at once occupies, and is assigned, the subject position of a victim to be rescued. Because this I's apparently coherent narration is often produced by means of collective "manufacture," this "I" might be considered a *composite* I, in both its narrating and narrated mode.

Not all witness narratives, however, claim to create a unified subject. Not all are edited and circulated through comparable processes by their publishers. And indeed, not all collective "I"s seek to insert themselves within existing frameworks of testimony and the asymmetrical social relations it establishes. Some radically revise the norms and templates of testimony to forge new genres and structures of witnessing that configure subject positions and discursive strategies differently. When performing these alternative modes of witnessing, they often harness authenticating practices to other ends: they set up complex texts that challenge the reader's impulse to conduct a "rescue reading," and they invite readers to engage in structural analysis of the larger conditions that underlie violence, oppression, and suffering.

The "I" formation we call "coalitional" navigates a desire for authentication in testimony while moving beyond rescue reading. In this "I" formation, collaborative production is not suppressed but foregrounded, and the multiple voices of the "collaborative I" are both distinguished and, at times, blended, as in the example of *Playing with Fire: Feminist Thought and Activism through Seven Lives in India* by the Sangtin Writers and Richa Nagar. Its multiple voices and narrators displace the singular narrative center of victimization that affectively binds readers in conventional first-person witnessing. Instead, readers encounter a "blended but fractured we" (xxxiv) that with its slippery personal pronouns, textual layers, and discursive disjunctions, unsettles identification.

Another "I" witness variation is seen in Dave Eggers's *What*

Autobiographical Acts

Is the What, in which Eggers constructs a double subject across the autobiography-novel boundary as a "negotiable I" traversing problems and contradictions built into the mode of testimonial discourse itself. For this project of witness, Valentino Achak Deng, a "lost boy of Sudan," collaborated with the American writer to inform the public about the fate of the "walking boys" (21). Eggers presents Deng's story, as told to him over the phone and in person, as a novel with the paradoxical subtitle: *The Autobiography of Valentino Achak Deng, a Novel.* The survivor "I" of Deng in the text is thus at once an autobiographical and a fictive "I." This "I" might be conceptualized as a "negotiated I." Readers are invited to focus on how the project emerged from the back and forth movement between two parallel and relational, but distinct, acts of storytelling. In this ongoing and unfinished collaboration, the two parties are differently situated in the text's mix of autobiographical and fictive discourses. The survivor Deng and the writer Eggers come together across asymmetries of location and access to power, as well as discursive universes of reference, to create a narrative that neither could credibly construct alone. In this negotiated coconstruction of testimony, Deng the survivor assigns the work of storytelling to an author, but neither claims exclusive ownership of the story.

Alternative versions of the witnessing "I," such as these, signal how different relationships can be set up between the subject/s of life narratives and those positioned as professionals such as journalists and publishers who authorize and publicize the traumatic story of victimization to a transnational public.

Online "I"s

Online self-presentation raises provocative questions about the kinds of "I"s materialized through the algorithms, protocols, and ready-made environments of online sites that call the singularity and uniqueness of the authored self into question. While the complexities of online "I" configurations and recombinations are too vast a topic to explore here, two suggestive online scenes of complex "I" formations suggest the kind of "I"s that proliferate across heterogeneous online platforms.

First, users can assemble or distribute multiple kinds of "I"s across platforms. The affordances of platforms enable users to present themselves, tell their stories, and enact their fantasies through assemblages of multiple media. They can juxtapose media in ways that can create new configurations of narrating and narrated "I"s. A site can configure the "I" of the user as, for example, a map, a puzzle, a portrait, an assemblage of tastes and habits, a genealogical chronology, a type or representative of a group, an aficionado of particular celebrities, heroes, or sports figures, an influencer of taste and consumer savvy. They can project "I"s and identities as material for reuse and recombinant collaborative potential "I"s. As Maria Schreiber observes in her ethnography of digital sharing of photographs by teenage girls in Vienna, users exploit the potential of multiple platforms to communicate to different audiences the visualized "I"s they desire to share. In this way "software co-constructs processes of editing, distribution, sharing and affirmation" (143) that secures affective networks and binds them to networked sociality.

Second, while the body is always dematerialized in virtual representation, embodiment in many forms and media is a prominent feature of online self-presentation. Users may choose to encode themselves through fantasies of being someone or something else, as avatars or alternative identities. In video games, the concept of an "avatar" suggests the unfixed visual projection of a player's "I." Thomas Apperley and Justin Clemens observe that in digitally constructed realities, the boundaries of self and reality shift and may blur, as avatars construct new kinds of relationship to others, often in the virtual world ("Flipping Out"). In digital worlds and gaming environments, as Elisabeth El Refaie observes, "the participants . . . [are] freer to choose multiple (ideal) versions of themselves" (229, n. 7). The avatar's features can be an entirely fictive, aspirational, endlessly transformable projection of power that visually manifests a pliable sense of identities and "I" potential. They may be fantasy embodiments, engaged through dreams, rituals, myths, or other projections, and imaginary "I"s of extended bodies and empowerment, of malleability and shape-shifting and transgression, with altruistic or demonic aspirations.

The possibility of configuring oneself as an avatar with nonhuman features and capacities on sites such as Roblox or World of Warcraft offers new dimensions to the performance of the self. Bodily extensions and fantasies (e.g., of animals, cartoon heroes, or machines; enhanced, streamlined, or transformed human capacities) are enabled. Such fantasied "I"s may create an illusion that online "I"s can escape wrestling with the politics of identity. While avatars are assumed to function as the

Autobiographical Acts

erasure of identity markers such as race or ethnicity, gender, sexuality, and age, the choice of an avatar can be a form of what Lisa Nakamura labels "identity tourism." She argues that the Internet is not "a postracial space" where users can "'choose' a race as an identity tourist" or withhold a racial identity (1676), and therefore that choosing an avatar is not a means of escape from the constraints of ethical behavior.

The Quantified I

As discussed in the "Embodiment and Quantification" section of chapter 2, the shift from an alphabetical to a computational self has opened the way for individuals to become their own quantification engines. The "I" in this context becomes a site of time-stamped data. As people increasingly contribute their personal data to large databases, their information may become a source of research in the biomedical sciences through applications such as Foursquare, various weight-tracking programs, and online journals such as myfooddiary.com and weightwatchers online.com. Emily Singer observes that "patient groups formed around specific diseases have been among the first to recognize the benefits to be derived from aggregating such information and sharing it" ("The Measured Life"). The quantified self, then, is more than a practice of self-monitoring the embodied "I"; it signals the shift to configuring the "I" as both an agent of data generation and an anonymous participant in collectivized profiles of groups that serve as authorities on themselves. Gary Wolf recognizes that the quantified self, as an assemblage of data driven by the body and by habits, will reorient us to ourselves, even if the impetus to quantify remains attached to a logic of self-development. "When we quantify ourselves," he observes, "there isn't the imperative to see through our daily existence into a truth buried at a deeper level. Instead, the self of our most trivial thoughts and actions, the self that, without technical help, we might barely notice or recall, is understood as the self we ought to get to know" (44).

Efforts to quantify the self, however, occur not just for the purpose of monitoring bodily functions. Bangladeshi American media artist Hasan Elahi, for example, created an ongoing project called Tracking Transience—The Orwell Project, which for many years recorded his movements in multiple, specific ways on his website. He began in response to being detained by the FBI on September 12, 2001. Elahi, an American citizen with a Muslim name who does not speak Arabic, was repeatedly questioned, nine times over six months, and given lie-detector tests concerning his whereabouts during the terrorist attacks (see Mihm). Despite his protestations, he remained a "person of interest" to the FBI (which has never charged him) and vulnerable to rearrest. As a response, for several years Elahi chose to wear a GPS-positioning device and used Google Earth to track his movements to and from airports and hotels, as well as his meals in restaurants and use of public toilets. He regularly posted his movements, using a red arrow to show his location. Elahi wrote: "You want to watch me? Fine. But I can watch myself better than you can, and I can get a level of detail that you will never have." Elahi's self-tracking suggests that the quantified self concerns not simply measurement but may be employed in self-representations with aesthetic and political implications as an innovative means of intervention in the imperative of Big Data (Siegel, 92).

VOICE IN AUTOBIOGRAPHICAL NARRATION AND PRESENTATION

Autobiographical texts often seem to be "speaking" to readers who "hear" a narrative voice distinctive in its emphasis and tone, its rhythms and syntax, its lexicon and affect. How might we understand our attribution of a particular "voice" to life writing? And how do we theorize the relationship of voice to autobiographical acts? This section considers how voice arises at the conjunction of narrating, narrated, and ideological "I"s and distinguishes it from the spoken voice of the historical "I." Although much life writing appears as words on a page, readers experience those words as the narrator talking to them, to persuade or demand, to confess or confide, to mourn or celebrate. James Phelan suggests that the concept of "voice" can be understood as "a metaphor, in which writing gets treated as speech." But, he observes, voice is more than metaphor; it is "a learnable kind of synesthesia: as we see words on a page we can hear sounds" ("Teaching Voice," 2). Those "sounds" give an impression of a subject's interiority, its intimacy and rhythms of self-reflexivity.[6] Voice as an attribute of the narrating "I," then, is a metaphor for the reader's felt experience of the narrator's character, and a marker of the relationship between narrating "I"s and their experiential histories.

In life writing, as opposed to the novel, readers may uncritically ascribe the voice of the narrative to the author. That is, the metaphor of voice attached to the narrating "I" may influence readers to think of

Autobiographical Acts

life writing as monovocal, told by a single individual who controls the telling of the story and its meanings. The syncopations of self-telling, however, are rarely unitary, for the narrating "I" of an autobiographical text is often polyvocal, an ensemble of voices. As Susan Lanser observes, literary voices are "equi-vocal" and "*rely for their meaning on* complex and ambiguous relationships between the 'I' of the author and any textual voice. The 'I' that characterizes literary discourse, in other words, is always potentially severed from *and* potentially tethered to the author's 'I'" (210–11). Autobiographical narration may shift through a register of voices that are all aspects of the narrating persona. These voices may be attached to particular identities and subject positions that the narrator takes up in telling the story: for example, the voice of the parent or the politician, the survivor or the confessor, the renegade or the celebrity, the subaltern or the conqueror. Although the text unfolds through an ensemble of voices, readers ascribe a distinct voice to that ensemble, with a way of organizing experience, a rhetoric of address, a particular register of affect, and an ideological inflection that is attached to the subject's history.

Autobiographical narrators also incorporate the voices of others within their archives of memory and reference. Most prominent among these others is the narrated "I," the voice attached to that remembered version of an earlier self whose interiority is represented through its distinct syntax, rhetorical address, style, and worldview and re-presented through reconstructed dialogue or internal monologue. In coming-of-age narratives, for instance, the narrating "I" can expand the distance between the now-self at the time of narration and the earlier then-version who struggles toward the present, making the voices of the narrating and narrated "I"s markedly distinct.[7] In other narratives, the distance is contracted and the self-commentary may be less ironic, detached, bemused, or censuring.[8]

Autobiographical narration is also populated with external voices. The voices of literal others may be incorporated through citation of dialogue or the use of free indirect discourse (in which the narrating "I" projects another's subjectivity by imagining an interiority of thought and affect). The narrating "I" can embed, for instance, an imagined interiority in the voice of a parent or sibling, a lover or friend. The voices of literal others may be less individuated or specific than those of loved ones and constitute the voice of a community or other kind of collectivity. The narrating I may draw in a web of voices from the oral life of a culture, voices that may be conflicting, as *polyvocality*, or in relative harmony, as *polyphony*.[9] Finally, the voice of another may enter through the narratee (the imagined addressee of the narrative) or the reader to whom the story is directed.

In addition to the voices attached to the narrating "I," a multitude of voices circulate through texts by the operation of language itself, producing the "internal dialogism of the word," a concept developed by Russian theorist Mikhail Bakhtin (282). For Bakhtin, language is the medium of consciousness. Because language registers play, subjectivity itself is dialogical; it is always an effect of "the process of social interaction" (Voloshinov, 11). People become conscious of themselves through the languages available to them in the social groups to which they belong. An individual's language is thus permeated by other people's words; and those words combine as various discourses in the sociocultural field that are multiple, contradictory, and, in Bakhtin's term, heteroglossic. The voices of the narrating "I" and the narrated "I" are permeated by a dialogism through which heterogeneous discourses of identity are dispersed. These discursive fragments affect the ways the past is narrated and the tropes through which its meanings are routed. Françoise Lionnet observes the braiding of voices that issue from diverse languages and ethnic groups in postcolonial life writing. She attends to how narrators mix indigenous, often oral, dialects with colonial or metropolitan languages: "The search for past connections must be a thorough reinterpretation of the texts of the other 'noisy' voices of history" (*Autobiographical Voices*, 23). This dialogism of the word, to which all are subject, suggests that the autobiographical voice is inevitably inflected by such ideological formations as national and/or regional identity, gender, ethnic origin, class, and age. Mae Gwendolyn Henderson, for example, developed the concept of "glossolalia" to particularize African American women's enunciation of a discourse in dialogue with complex otherness (122).[10]

Consider the example of Irish playwright and politician Sean O'Casey's *I Knock at the Door*, which captures the interplay of interiorized and exteriorized voices. In this narrative the adult narrator represents his childhood as a time of coming to his distinctive artistic voice through hearing and imaginatively rescripting both the language and the interior monologues of others, showing how his voice arose from

Autobiographical Acts

the interplay of theirs. The polyvocal voices populating the narrative capture the heteroglossic texture of Irish everyday life in rooms and on the streets of Dublin in a Joycean incantatory mixture of fragments. O'Casey's musical prose with its onomatopoetic lilt interweaves the cadences of oral speech that are distanced from the overview of the storyteller. Furthermore, the crowd itself becomes a collective voice in the telling of public events. Rather than quoted dialogue, narrative voices, both exterior and interior, texture what O'Casey is narrating as speech and not mere reportage of events. Weaving together snatches of dialogue and song heard on the street, repeated proverbs and clichés, he assembles a pastiche of voices that turn what we think of as written life narrative into a lyrical polyvocal song. Voice is dialogically produced yet is not just the sum of other people's voices, a set of citations, or the dialogue of multiple protagonists in a novel; it is a richly textured interplay of heterogeneous voices.

A uniquely compelling textual voice may emerge in the act of articulating a personally or politically unspeakable event. In Joan Didion's *The Year of Magical Thinking,* much of the narrative employs a dry, flat reportage, attentive to details of medical procedure. Another self-reflexive voice tentatively questions her own mental status and juxtaposes citations from other writers about mortality that she references but does not engage. Throughout her memoir, Didion refuses a voice of grief and mourning, the expected way of telling and "overcoming" a story of loss and shock. The process of coming to "speak" the irreversibility of death to herself emerges tentatively, if at all, in a counterpoint of speech and silence.

In focusing on voice readers grant a different kind of authority to narrators in political struggles where their voices may be multifarious and ambivalent. In Frederick Douglass's 1845 *Narrative of the Life of Frederick Douglass,* the narrative "I" shapes a voice both authoritative and stirring to tell the story of his illiterate, voiceless enslaved life. It is the voice of the public abolitionist that Douglass became, mixing the rhythms of classical oratory with the preacher's exhortation. As each sentence unfolds, its cadence resonates with a critique of slavery, contrasting exemplary stories of the stunted humanity he observed in both master and slave with the rhetorician's command of persuasive, periodic sentences that ring with conviction. Successive generations of African American and immigrant life writers mobilized forms of life narrative employing oracular voices that both denounced widespread oppression and proclaimed their humanity and legitimate human rights.

In the last half century, voice has taken on another meaning as a metaphor for speaking the formerly unspeakable. Second-wave feminists and women-of-color activists, inspired by the slogan "the personal is political," used life writing as a discursive mode of coming to voice genre through which women could find, claim, and deploy voices of liberation. Voice became associated with the political agenda of changing women's lives, bringing them into the public sphere as actors, and calling attention to women's experiential histories, stories, and traditions grounded in a politics of differences.

The voicing of socially unsanctioned critique continues in life writing, literally and metaphorically, by many postcolonial writers such as Assia Djebar. Her narrative voice in "Forbidden Gaze, Severed Sound" (in *Women of Algiers in Their Apartment*) incorporates those of women in the harem under imperialism to enunciate "fragments of ancient murmuring" for a silenced group (342). Similarly, other historical and contemporary witnesses and activists—among them those in abolitionist and antislavery movements in England, Canada, the Caribbean, and the United States in the nineteenth century and anticolonial movements in Africa, Asia, Australia, and Latin America in the past century—have framed their testimonies of oppression through voice, as in Domitila Barrios de Chungara's *Let Me Speak!* Bearing witness publicly thus involves several acts: coming to voice, claiming social space, and insisting on the authority of one's previously unacknowledged experiential history. More recent testimonial narratives continue to be characterized by the call for witnesses to come forward to attest to injustice, oppression, and violations of human rights through voicing their stories, sometimes in interlocutory situations where someone records them, such as truth commissions.

Lest we too easily hail the metaphorics of coming to voice as a self-liberating gesture, we might keep in mind that testimony also involves telling stories that place the narrator in jeopardy because what is told is in some sense publicly "unspeakable" in its political context. That is, the personal experience out of which a narrator "speaks truth to power" can be fraught with risk: public condemnation and ostracism or threats to family members. Acts of witness also risk psychic injury. Acts of telling can trigger retraumatization, invite shaming in public exposure, and bring unsympathetic audiences. Moreover, contexts of witnessing such

Autobiographical Acts

as truth commissions and markets for stories of suffering influence and constrain whose story can be heard and what kind of story can be told.

Finally, how might future theorists conceptualize the modifications of voice and articulated self-presentation introduced on social media sites and online platforms?[11] Issues related to voice, voicing, and voicelessness have an urgency at this time in these online environments. New platforms have intensified the pressure to voice oneself, and to project that voice in both intimate and impersonal communicative exchanges. The career of social-media influencer offers opportunities to hone not just an online persona and style but to record one's voice and address an audience of followers. In online environments X's (formerly Twitter's) short messages have an aural quality; and audio-only X Spaces markets itself as "a small experiment focused on the intimacy of the human voice" with chat capability. The "chat" option on many online sites invites users to write as if in conversation with a helper on the other end writing back to them. The ever-expanding possibilities of voiced self-presentation online will surely both change and amplify notions of voice in ways that may reshape life narrative.

RELATIONALITY AND THE OTHERS OF AUTOBIOGRAPHICAL SUBJECTS

As noted in chapter 2, autobiographical acts and practices are relational, routed through others; that is, one's story is bound up with those of others, rendering the boundaries of the "I" shifting and permeable. This narrative relationality invites readers to think about the different kinds of textual others—contingent, historical and mythical, significant, absent idealized, transspecies, and subject other—through which an "I" narrates the formation or deformation of subjectivity and collectivity. Contingent others populate the text as actors in the narrator's script of meaning but are not deeply reflected on. Some others, however, become salient, often intimate others in and of the texts.

Historical others are the identifiable figures of a collective past such as political leaders. Some life narrators engage historical others who serve as generic models of identity culturally available to them. For example, the idea of American presidents, as well as his contact with actual former presidents, drives Edward Bok's *The Americanization of Edward Bok,* a narrative of self-formation as an ambitiously assimilating American. In Maxine Hong Kingston's autobiographical narrative

The Woman Warrior historical and mythical stories of empowered women transmitted through the generations become a means to combat her family's histories of devalued women and enable her to deal with her mother's ambivalent influence. In this text multiple kinds of others inhabit a single life narrative.

Kingston's mother is an example of the third category, a significant other who is deeply implicated in the narrator's own story and contributes to the understanding of her self-formation. Some are the intimate other of everyday life, the family member, lover, mentor, as, for example, in Edmund Gosse's *Father and Son: A Study of Two Temperaments* and John Edgar Wideman's *Brothers and Keepers*. Wideman's story of his brother Robby, who as a youth was convicted of murder on the streets of Pittsburgh and imprisoned for life, is refracted through his own career trajectory as a writer. This relational blending of their vastly different adult experiences creates what Wideman calls a "mix of memory, imagination, feeling, and fact" that characterizes the life experience of many African American men (1). In this relationality the boundary between the biographical and autobiographical starts to blur. Such blurring is intensified in Paul Monette's life narrative *Borrowed Time: An AIDS Memoir*. The partner of Roger Horwitz, a gay man who died of AIDS, Monette narrates several stories simultaneously—a chronological journal of illness and death, a romantic love story that contests popular representations of gay men, an AIDS story of cultural crisis in that community, a narrative of rereading and revising a crisis in the gay community, and a narrative of rereading and revising a journal's gaps and emotions (Couser, *Recovering Bodies*, 155–60).

Another form of significant other to whom a narrative may be addressed and in whom it may invest special meaning is the idealized absent other, whether secular or divine. Such narratives cannot "tell" the other because of the profundity and inextricability of the relationship, but allusions to it as central to self-understanding resonate throughout the narrator's telling of a narrated "I." In his *Confessions,* for example, Augustine rereads his experience before conversion through a language transformed by conversion and his implicit dialogue with God. For Montaigne, his friend La Boétie, who died young, is the significant other whose absence underwrites the *Essays*. While Montaigne praises La Boétie as a "brother" and has La Boétie's essay "Of Voluntary Servitude" published posthumously, he does not embed this "brother's" biography in his own narrative. Rather, in "Of Friendship" Montaigne asserts the

Autobiographical Acts

impossibility of differentiating his friend from himself: "Our souls mingle and blend with each other so completely that they efface the seam that joined them" (I, 28, 139). Similarly, in his collaborative narrative *Black Elk Speaks*, the Lakota shaman incorporates the voices of multiple others as he tells his story through the dreams, visions, and voices of other spiritual leaders. Doing so, Black Elk secures the authority of his own visions by situating himself in a genealogy of visionaries.

Finally, there is a mode of internal or subject Other suggested by postcolonial theory's focus on practices, suppressed by colonial domination, of "talking back" to Western tropes of representation. In *The Autobiography of My Mother*, for example, Jamaica Kincaid performs a daring, sustained dialogue with autobiographical representation that mines paradoxes of subjectivity by voicing the story of a mother her daughter-narrator never knew. Exploiting the tautology that autobiography can only relate the life of the narrating "I," Kincaid insists on the inseparability of the relational mother–daughter bond in the narrative of a mother, suggestively named "Xuela." Inverting Western hierarchies of the solitary, transcendent self, Xuela projects an alternative subjectivity distinct from the Other of a Western self and frequently invokes practices of Obeah, an Afro-Caribbean system of spirituality and the supernatural (Paravisini-Gebert, 3). In a visual parallel, a partial portrait of the mother introduces each of the book's eight major chapters, a subject only coming into full view with the last one (203). The narrative thus subverts autobiographical storytelling by foregrounding a transgressive subject aligned with collective oral storytelling. Reordering self-experience as self-love and self-pleasure, *The Autobiography of My Mother* enacts the seemingly impossible self-production of a marginal figure who speaks her subjectivity as a suppressed otherness.

These multiple others—historical, contingent, significant, idealized but absent, and subject others—suggest the range of relational others evoked and mobilized within life writing for the purposes of self-narrating and self-knowing. The routing of a self, known through its relational others, undermines the understanding of life narrative as a bounded story of the unique, individuated narrating subject. What these examples suggest is that no "I" speaks except as and through its others.

ADDRESSEES

Narrators of necessity tell their stories to someone, meaning that autobiographical acts as communicative exchanges are inherently rhetorical.

132   Autobiographical Acts

That someone might be in the same room, if the narrator's story is told orally. Even in the case of written, posted, drawn, or performed narratives, the narrator addresses an other. As in diaries, that other might be an imagined version of self. Indeed, however "secret" the diary avowedly may be, its "I" is, according to Philippe Lejeune, "motivated by a search for communication, by a will to persuasion" that inevitably postulates a reader ("Practice of the Private Journal," 192). We call this someone "the addressee" or, in narratological terms, "narratee." The narratee, notes narratologist Shlomith Rimmon-Kenan, "is the agent which is at the very least implicitly addressed by the narrator. A narratee of this kind is always implied, even when the narrator becomes his own narratee" (89). That is, even when no other is named as addressee, a reader or listener is implied. Although self-narrators cannot know who their flesh-and-blood readers (or, in Plummer's schema, consumers) will be, an addressee is invariably posited.

The addressees to which self-referential modes are directed vary across time, cultures, and purposes. Some narrators imagine an addressee as an intimate, as Glückel of Hameln does when she addresses her children in her 1690–91 *Memoirs in Seven Little Books* (5). Similarly, English immigrant Frances Anne "Fanny" Kemble addresses her journal entries describing her sojourn in the Georgia Sea Islands in the late 1830s as letters to her friend "Elizabeth," and Ta-Nehisi Coates addresses the letters that compose *Between the World and Me* to his son in response to the succession of Black bodies gunned down by police not held accountable for the deaths.

Other narrators may imagine an addressee at some distance. Spiritual life writers identify a higher power as the implied reader. Others idealize an addressee, as Anne Frank does in constructing the implied reader of her diary as a sympathetic friend whom she names "Kitty." And letter writers who employ the opportunities the form offers to engage in self-reflection, social or political critique, and philosophical speculation in condensed form address their letters to particular persons who are at once specific and universalized, as is the case with the letters of the Indonesian writer and activist Raden Adjeng Kartini, whose *Letters of a Javanese Princess* includes letters written from 1899 to 1904. Sometimes the narrator addresses an anonymous implied reader directly, as Susanna Kaysen does in *Girl, Interrupted*. "Do you believe him or me?" (71–72), she challenges her addressee as she contests the power of the doctor who

Autobiographical Acts

labeled her personality "borderline" and sent her to McLean Hospital as a teenager in the late 1960s. The implied reader can also be a category of people—the white Northerners whom Frederick Douglass addresses in the first of his three autobiographies, or the white Northern "sisters" whom Harriet Jacobs addresses explicitly in her *Incidents in the Life of a Slave Girl.*

Addressees can be imagined and addressed directly in the text or indirectly through the text. Often there are multiple addressees in the narrative, narratees and implied readers addressed simultaneously or in sequence. For instance, when the medieval mystic Margery Kempe dictated her narrative to an amanuensis, she addressed a multiplicity of interlocutors: the God to whom she would manifest her purity of soul; the writer on whom she depended for the preservation of her story; the church fathers who threatened her with excommunication, perhaps even death; the community of Christians before whom she would claim her rightful membership as a true believer and thereby secure her social status. In graphic memoir, the addressee can be visually addressed. In the Auschwitz ("Time Flies") chapter of *Maus II,* the masked mouse artist-narrator directly addresses the reader-viewer about how depressed he has become about the "critical and commercial success" of *Maus I* (Spiegelman, 41). His guilt is visually fantasized as skeletal mouse corpses piled beneath his desk. In online environments addressees can be simultaneously anonymous site visitors, communities of like identities or interests, or specific interlocutors who coconstruct virtual self-presentation by means of platform affordances.

Narrating "I"s and addressees, then, are engaged in a communicative action that is fundamental to autobiographical acts and the kinds of intersubjective truth they construct. Attending to the addressee or implied reader of a life narrative illuminates subtle shifts in narrative intent and the kind of reader the text invites to respond to its rhetoric of intent.

STRUCTURING MODES OF SELF-INQUIRY

Autobiographical acts are investigations into processes of self-knowing. But both the modes of inquiry and the self-knowledge gained or produced vary over time and with cultural locations. Thus, presentations of self-knowledge have histories. How one knows oneself today is very different from how one would have known oneself in a Socratic dialogue. Or in the *Imitatio Christi* of Thomas à Kempis in the early modern period. Or in the ritual Dreaming through which contemporary Indigenous Australians in traditional communities understand their place within a system of totem and kinship and through which they enact their values, beliefs, and relationships.

Some life narrators formalize schemes of self-investigation through a method—and these have varied dramatically. In *The Autobiography of Benjamin Franklin*, Franklin produces self-knowledge through his "Project of Arriving at Moral Perfection." John Donne produces his through relentlessly self-questioning sermons; Montaigne through the self-tryouts of his *Essays*; William Butler Yeats through the mythical system of *A Vision*; Saint Teresa through the topography of "interior landscape"; Robert Burton through the anatomy as a physiological and systemic metaphor. Each narrator developed and improvised on a particular structure of self-investigation.

Some well-known patterns for presenting processes of self-knowing are linked to other genres of literature, such as the novel, and provide templates for autobiographical storytelling. Among them are the bildungsroman or narrative of social development, the *Künstlerroman* or narrative of artistic growth, the confession, memoir, conversion narrative, *testimonio*, and quest for lost identity or a lost homeland or family. The bildungsroman, for instance, unfolds as a narrative of education earned through encounters with mentors, apprenticeship, renunciation of youthful folly, and eventual integration into a dominant social world. The conversion narrative develops through a linear pattern— descent into darkness, struggle, moment of crisis, conversion to new beliefs and world view, and consolidation of a new communal identity, however tentative. In the quest or adventure narrative, a potentially heroic figure alienated from family or home or birthright sets forth on a mission to achieve elsewhere an integration of self that is impossible within the constraints (political, sexual, emotional, economic) imposed in a repressive world. The *testimonio* unfolds through the fashioning of an exemplary protagonist whose narrative bears witness to collective suffering, politicized struggle, and communal survival.

Conventions that are culturally and historically specific govern storytelling options, narrative plotting, and the uses of remembering. Those conventions have histories: that is, at certain historical moments and in specific milieus, certain stories become intelligible and normative. Over time, such stories stretch and change, gain cultural prominence or lose

Autobiographical Acts

their hold. Think, for instance, of how the genre of self-help narratives that has become dominant in contemporary cultural life is modified by the needs and crises of particular social groups and moments. Conventions can also be displaced by newly emergent ones. For instance, autobiographical narratives published in the last four decades—those by women, people of color, and migratory subjects—radically alter the inherited conventions of life narrative in reworking the trajectory of the bildungsroman to account for the oppressive lived realities of formerly subordinated subjects.

And so, in reading or listening to autobiographical narratives, we may attend to methods of self-examination, introspection, and remembering encoded in them through generic conventions. Sometimes narrators turn their method upon particular kinds of experiences, such as dreams, and particular kinds of knowledge, such as intuitive, irrational, supernatural, mystical, or symbolic knowledge. Sometimes they interrogate cultural forms of knowledge valued at the historical moment of writing. Sometimes they establish complex linkages between knowledge of the world/others and self-knowledge. Sometimes they imagine alternative knowledges. And sometimes they refuse the very possibility of self-knowing, as is the case with the narrators of reflexive works by Michel Leiris and Roland Barthes.

As discussed earlier in the section on "Sites of Storytelling," platform design, affordances, and protocols contribute to shaping the content of users' self-presentations. Protocol-driven social media platforms may tightly structure the content users enter, while some user-driven platforms provide more flexibility for longer forms of presenting fragments of a life story or self-portraits. In those contexts, user content may unfold through some of the modes and genres of self-inquiry introduced above, such as the bildungsroman, confession, or testimony. Depending on the platforms used to create content, users may generate and circulate new hybrid modes of inquiry. At the same time the content distributed across various platforms may create multiple, competing versions of self, networked through links or revised versions, some controlled by users to a degree and some outside their knowledge and control.

PATTERNS OF EMPLOTMENT

Our expanded concept of autobiographical acts leads us to review narrative plots or patterns from the perspective of a theory centered in narrative modalities. These are of two kinds, in practice always mixed: temporally based patterns, which concern the organization of narrative times; and spatially based patterns, the "geographics" of narrative subjectivity (Friedman, *Mappings*).[12]

We are subjects in time: the time of bodily rhythms and cycles; the time of everyday lives as unfolding, the sense of one moment successively turning into another; the accumulation of a subjective past; the historical time of an era situating us in a larger narrative. In telling autobiographical stories, these temporalities are refracted through the time of writing, the moment in life when the story is being told.

While there may seem to be a strict division between time-past and time-now, time in narration is always elastic. There are temporal patterns both *of* the narrator's telling and *in* the telling. The past being narrated may be long or short, expanded or condensed. The time of writing may extend over a long duration and its historical moment change radically. Many narratives are written from a relatively fixed moment of time, as is, for instance, Isak Dinesen's *Out of Africa*. In this haunting memorial return, Dinesen reflects, after returning to Denmark, on her years in Kenya as irretrievably past. Some narratives, however, seem to have been written over an expanse of time. Franklin's *Autobiography,* for example, identifies the narrator at different ages and in various professions rereading his past. His autobiographical "I"s are serial, multiple, and heterogeneous, in part because of the long lifespan over which he narrated his life.

Autobiographical narratives are often plotted strictly by chronology, with the narrator looking back on the life course and organizing the segments of telling according to a succession of historical moments. But chronology is only one way to organize the temporality of telling. Time can be scrambled; it can be rendered cyclical or discontinuous, as in postmodern narratives where linear organization may be displaced by achronological modes of emplotment. Narrators may employ schemes of associational, or digressive, or fragmented remembering told through multiple flashbacks and flash-forwards, as does Térèse Marie Mailhot in *Heart Berries: A Memoir*. Such patterns are multidirectional rather than progressive.

Ultimately, time unfolds through no stipulated measure (see Brockmeier). The time-past of the autobiographical subject can be expanded. It can also be compressed, fragmented, or repetitive. It can be belated,

Autobiographical Acts

as it may be for those surviving traumatic events and their aftereffects. And the time of narration can expand when autobiographical narrators reflect on the process of writing their stories. Moreover, time-now and time-past can interpenetrate in ways that confuse the relationship of one time to another, as our discussion of Rowlandson's captivity narrative noted. Because a narrative cannot recount all time of experience, its gaps as well as its articulated times produce meaning. Since autobiographical narration gestures toward the future, the time of the past and the present of writing are also triangulated with time future, as imagined and projected by the narrator.

Temporality intersects as well with the spatiality of autobiographical narration. In invoking a "geographics" of subjectivity, Friedman suggests that the spatial mapping of identities and differences is distinct from the chronological tracking of identity. "The new geographics," she suggests, "figures identity as a historically embedded site, a positionality, a location, a standpoint, a terrain, an intersection, a network, a crossroads of multiply situated knowledges" (*Mappings,* 19). In *The Words to Say It: An Autobiographical Novel,* for instance, Marie Cardinal locates the struggle with her female body in the context of the Algerian struggle for liberation from colonialism. Mapping the intersections of political oppression and psychological repression of colonialism and sexism, the agony of Algeria and the agony of her mother, Cardinal enacts the revolutionary potential of a psychoanalysis that links the psychological to the sociopolitical. Similarly, in Australia, narratives such as Elsie Roughsey Labumore's *An Aboriginal Mother Tells of the Old and the New* and Ruby Langford Ginibi's *Don't Take Your Love to Town* map the diverse geographies of individual struggles within collective histories of physical displacement, cultural dislocation, and state forms of oppression affecting Indigenous peoples.

A pastiche of textual memories may layer the narrative by incorporating multiple forms of self-inquiry, borrowed from such genres as the lyric sequence, fable, essay, diary, meditation, or public testimony. Life narrative may also incorporate multiple media—comics, e-mails, graphic images, photographs, tables, or charts—that juxtapose other geographic sites to that of the verbal story. Narratives composed of heterogeneous modes and media of self-inquiry and organized achronologically enable us to see more clearly how narrated "I"s are indeed multiple.

The conscious diffraction of times of telling and the fragmentation of chronological sequence are narrative means of emphasizing that a subject is not unified or coherent. That is, different modes of emplotment and different media of self-presentation offer possibilities for and constraints on the kind of "I" that can be narrated. Let us briefly consider some narrative genres that have provided occasions for autobiographical acts. The fable presents the narrated "I" as an allegorical type enacting human aspiration, as in, for example, John Bunyan's *Grace Abounding to the Chief of Sinners*. The meditation presents the stages of a narrated "I"'s reflections, with increasing understanding or momentary glimpses of the meaning of a spiritual history, as occurs in *The Shewings of Julian of Norwich*, Teresa of Avila's *Interior Castle*, and Thomas Merton's *The Seven-Storey Mountain*. A secular narrative, such as Robert Burton's *Anatomy of Melancholy* or Loren C. Eiseley's *The Star Thrower*, also can perform a meditative exploration occasioned by situating a life within the context of a system of thought. The lyric sequence may present the narrating "I" as a subject charting its own moments of intense emotion and rereading the narrated "I"'s of previous poems as an increasingly complex structure of self-reflection, as do the sonnet sequences of French Renaissance poet Louise Labé and, in quite different ways, American poets Robert Lowell in *Notebook 1967–68* and *Life Studies* and Claudia Rankine in *Citizen*. The sketch presents the narrated "I" as a subject enmeshed in a way of life that may be recalled precisely because it is a time now past, as happens in Mark Twain's *Life on the Mississippi*.

The emplotment of autobiographical narratives is a dense and multilayered intersection of the temporal and the geographic. By teasing out the complex ways in which life narratives are organized, readers may discover how the cultural, historic, or generic specificities of these emplotments inflect the scope, shape, and social meanings of the story being told.

MEDIA AND AUTOMEDIALITY

The autobiographical is commonly regarded as an extended narrative in written form; but, increasingly, self-presentation is enacted in multiple media, a practice that has given rise to the concept of automediality.[13] The concept, as theorized by Christian Moser and Jörg Dünne, among others, redresses a tendency to consider media as "tools" for rendering a preexistent self. Theorists of automediality emphasize that the choice of medium is determined by the desires and constraints of

Autobiographical Acts

self-expression, and the materiality of a medium is constitutive of the subjectivity rendered. Media technologies do not simplify or undermine the interiority of the subject but, on the contrary, expand the field of self-representation.[14] Automedial narratives engage and mix media such as comics, installations, performance, music, dance, and monologue; the painted or sculpted self-portrait; quilts, collages, and mosaics; body art; murals; photography, film, and video. Further, the platforms and affordances of digital media have greatly expanded the repertoire of modes of self-representation incorporating interactivity and seriality.

The specific visual and verbal media of automedial genres have distinctive conventions with which reader-viewers need to become fluent. In comics or graphic memoirs conventions come into play such as frames, gutters, and many techniques for representing actions and emotions, including the artist's hand to signify self-referential comments. Similarly, documentary film has an extensive repertoire of editing techniques for embedding a narrated life in multiperspectival contexts.

Since the Renaissance, artists' self-portraits have powerfully imaged the social milieu, virtuosity, and cultural myths of mastery through which artists claim the authority of their professional status. In the last half century, the uses of material, visual, and performance media for projects of autobiographical telling have proliferated. In such story quilts as *The French Collection* series, Faith Ringgold chronicles, as a *Künstlerroman*, the life of a black woman artist in Paris and in America. Quilt, painting, text on cloth, the story quilts present, through a fictionalized narrative of African American woman artist Willia Marie, Ringgold's struggle to find her place "in the picture" of Western art history and to make a place in that history for the aesthetics of her African American quilting heritage. The performance pieces of such artists as Laurie Anderson, Alina Troyano (Carmelita Tropicana), Bob Flanagan, Guillermo Gómez-Peña, Marina Abramović, Vaginal Davis, and Dave Chapelle become occasions for staging ethnically, racially, and sexually marked bodies, and for remembering and dismembering the psychic costs of identity, cultural visibility, and the social construction of difference.

The medium that comes most readily to mind in self-representation is photography. Because photos individually or in family albums seem literally to memorialize identity, they often accompany written life narratives, as in those of Mark Twain and August Strindberg. Yet photographs are never only illustrative. Each photo contributes to a separate indexical system of meaning. While they may support or speak to a verbal text, they may also be in tension with or conflict with its claims. The photo-text relationship is theoretically problematized in memoirs such as Roland Barthes's *Camera Lucida,* Norma Elia Cantú's *Canícula: Snapshots of a Girlhood en la Frontera,* Sally Mann's *Hold Still,* and Teju Cole's *Golden Apple of the Sun.* In photographer Joanne Leonard's *Being in Pictures,* experiments with images as a mode of feminist consciousness are prominent, and the retrospective narrative of her professional development as an artist and her experience of motherhood are supplemental to the image. This power of the photograph to image a story of subjectivity has become a fascinating focus of theorizing about life writing, as studies by Teresa Brus *(Face Forms in Life-Writing of the Interwar Years),* Marianne Hirsch *(Family Frames),* Linda Haverty Rugg *(Picturing Ourselves: Photography and Autobiography),* and Timothy Dow Adams *(Light Writing and Life Writing),* suggest.

Finally, media may be assembled into what might be described as an ensemble text of life narrative. This is the case with Kate Bornstein's *Gender Outlaw: On Men, Women, and the Rest of Us.* Bornstein takes their experience as a male-to-female transsexual as a starting point for critiquing the binary social construction of gender and gendered desire. Their strategy of engaging the reader in actively interpreting gendered experience produces a hybrid text, composed of photographs, a play, interviews, the analyses of social critics and scholars, and a dispersed, nonchronological personal narrative. No one medium or generic mode suffices for this ensemble narration, and their cut-and-pasted text suggests both the suturing of body parts and social networks, and the subversion of the system of gender identity that its collage method achieves. As the example of Bornstein's narrative suggests, the media for self-narrating are and have always been multiple, although critics until recently have not often emphasized the autobiographical dimension of genres other than published texts.

Automediality (or autobiomediality) saturates digital self-presentation, providing a theoretical framework for conceptualizing the way subjectivity is constructed online across visual and verbal forms in new media. Brian Rotman locates the concept of autobiomediality in the long history of encounters between diverse oral, written, and ges-

Autobiographical Acts

tural modes of self-enunciation and regards the present moment as "a radically altered regime of space-time" in which there is "an emerging co-presence of mobile, networked selves with identities . . . 'in perpetual formation and reformation at the moment of use'" ("Automedial Ghosts," 121). Ruth E. Page refers to transmediality and multimodality as forms of electronic literature that are gaining attention in narrative studies (see "Stories of the Self"). Automediality implies an aesthetics of collage, mosaic, pastiche through which subjectivity is figured as a bricolage or set of disparate fragments, rather than a coherent, inborn unit of self. Automedial practices of digital life writing impact the prosthetic extension of self in networks, the reorientation of bodies in virtual space, the perspectival positioning of subjects, and alternative embodiments.

Anna Poletti calls for attending to "the role of media and materiality in cultural practices that utilize 'self-life-inscription' in order to make lived experience consequential" and urges life narrative theorists to more strongly recognize "media forms and their material properties as agential forces in the process of citation through which ideas about why life matters are made tangible, available, and portable into other scenes" (*Stories of the Self,* 171). Her comparative media studies approach to "self-life-inscription" as transmedial brings a range of digital practices such as the selfie and Instagram into conversations about how life narrative now occurs and circulates.

ARCHIVES

We may think of archives as reliable institutional sites for storing the defining documents of lives. Yet in *Archive Fever* Derrida cautions against regarding archives as objective sites of authoritative evidence because, as conventionally conceived in the West, archives have been both produced by and implicated in the historical formations of colonialism and imperialism and the rise of nation states over the last five hundred years.

We propose a different concept of the life-narrative archive as one that draws on many kinds of personal effects and experiences. Such spaces as the journal, the attic, and the blog accumulate as personal archives over the lifetime of narrators, who may periodically turn to them for information, documentation, or inspiration. While an archive is not, of itself, an autobiographical act, the curation, selection, and preservation of life materials provide rich sources for self-presentation. For example, *Specimen Days* is a kind of published archive for Walt Whitman. Late in his life (1881), he pieces together fragments of published and unpublished personal writing—sketches, notes, essays, excerpts from a book—to compose a five-part autobiographical narrative that situates his life story within the larger, collective narrative of American modernization over the course of his lifetime. Clearly, constructing an autobiographical narrative is not a transparent rendering of past materials, but a complex process of self-reflection and interpretation. In this sense, life narrators may be understood as curators who combine and entwine documentary sources from official and nonofficial archives with their personal and idiosyncratic sources. Writers turning to their accumulated personal archives may stir up memories, find forgotten voices, and recover traces of past "I"s. Some of that material can serve as evidence within a life narrative, for instance, photos, documents, and historical references to events, places, and people. A writer's history of self-experience may also be recovered in such material artifacts as diaries and letters. Other nonmaterial impressions expressed in language, such as dreams and fantasies, may also be recovered, as well as traces of the nonverbal past of emotions and bodily sensations. This broad sense of "sources" can constitute a personal archive.

Life narrators may use items in their personal archive to trouble earlier understandings of themselves. Some narrators who include personal photographs, for instance, may be moved to reread and resituate their personal pasts differently. Others may trouble the value of their own archival sources, such as a diary. In *Fun Home,* Alison Bechdel's narrator disputes the value of her early diary as authentic archival evidence of her experiential life by metacritically reading it for gaps and overwritten moments. Recognizing "the implicit lie of the blank page," her persona Alison narrates how, as a teenager, she abandoned diary-keeping altogether (186).

Of course, not everyone has access to a robust personal archive, despite retaining memories of the past. Refugees and migrants may have left their archival artifacts behind or had them destroyed. Others may have censored themselves due to the conditions of their lives and come to think of themselves as a nobody whose self-archive has little significance. French scholar Philippe Lejeune has made a sustained study of methods of archival research and the contexts they provide for thinking

Autobiographical Acts 143

about historical shifts in self-conception. For one study, he read ninety-six young girls' diaries of the nineteenth century, most unpublished and archived in libraries or other public or family collections, some solicited through calls to radio stations and ads in newspapers. Assembling this archive enabled Lejeune to raise probing questions about the subjectivity of young women diarists at a time when they "were censored both ideologically and aesthetically" (*Le Moi des Demoiselles,* 131).

Another example involves descendants of formerly enslaved people, who cannot locate official archives to discover records of their dehumanizing capture, export, and enslavement because they were not kept. In such conditions of historical silence, life narrators may confront directly the personal impact of a lack of archival sources and pursue another strategy for reimagining the past. Saidiya Hartman's *Lose Your Mother: A Journey along the Atlantic Slave Route,* narrates an account of her journey to Ghana in search of a genealogical legacy. She observes that in the context of inadequate archives, her quest to "bring the past closer" and "cross the boundary that separated kin from stranger" is foreclosed by the imperatives of historical and geopolitical interests and practices (17). Yet this recognition marks Hartman's point of departure. For over two hundred pages in *Lose Your Mother,* she combines an autobiographical narrative of the journey with a careful, skeptical exploration of the historical records and sites of Ghana's slave trade. Acknowledging her position as a stranger in the archive, her meditative narrative finds an alternative practice for investigating sites of the slave trade by probing the paradox between the lack of archival documentation and her feeling of painful connection and fraught descent.

Similarly, alternative versions of archives can be referenced in postcolonial narratives on memory and subjectivity, such as those of Assia Djebar or Norma Cantú, that mix traces of personal memory and unrecorded histories with imagined alternative pasts. For example, novelist Doris Lessing's memoir, *Alfred and Emily,* tells the story of her parents as British colonists in Southern Rhodesia twice—first, in a novella, as the lives she wished for them; then, as a memoir of the grim realities of their existence. In so doing she juxtaposes documentary and alternative archives to create a fuller version of her parents' potential lives, had they not experienced the impact of World War I.

Other scholars propose expanding the notion of the archive by incorporating embodied experiences and affective traces from the past.

Diana Taylor extends the concept in *The Archive and the Repertoire: Performing Cultural Memory in the Americas* by theorizing how archives may incorporate alternative repertoires. Interested in the distinction "between the *archive* of supposedly enduring materials (i.e., texts, documents, buildings, bones) and the so-called ephemeral *repertoire* of embodied practice/knowledge (i.e., spoken language, dance, sports, ritual)," Taylor argues that "the repertoire . . . enacts embodied memory . . . performances, gestures, orality, movement, dance, singing . . . acts usually thought of as ephemeral, nonreproducible knowledge" (20). And Ann Cvetkovich postulates an "archive of feelings" in turning to personal archives of memory and sensory impressions as kinds of material evidence for unarchived gay and lesbian lives, particularly in documentary films and everyday "oral history, personal photographs and letters, and ephemera" (269).

The twenty-first-century explosion in digital archiving and the rise of Big Data projects have brought materials previously sequestered in less accessible official archives, institutions, and storage facilities into a digital ecology of what Andrew Hoskins calls the "continuously networked present" (cited in Cardell, "Modern Memory-Making," 506). When offline documentary materials are archived online, however, their status is changed by the architecture and degree of interactivity of the platforms and coding systems used, as well as the metadata configurations of software and hardware. This transfer process contributes to what we might call algorithmic curation, which may be more, or less, discriminating in its protocols of collection.

There are also born-digital archives, enabled and sustained by algorithmic logics that feed into repositories of Big Data with massive amounts of information swept from social media sites and data accumulated by governments and other security businesses, as well as hackers. These online archives house digital clutter, the overabundance of available documents. Yet researchers increasingly depend on coders and Web architects to develop metadata and display architecture through which to find and visualize the materials of an experiential history. As pieces of data, and the self-inscription from which they derived, are propelled along networks and through platforms, however, they may undergo "context collapse"—the collapse of earlier contexts of content traveling across the Web as it is republished and repurposed for other audiences (see boyd and Marwick, 13). In online environments, self-curators can-

Autobiographical Acts

not control where all the pieces of their online lives may be taken up, circulated, and stored, or abandoned in the cloud.

As life writing enters the public world and circulates through various routes, it may be taken up in other kinds of projects with archival implications. That is, it may undergo an afterlife as the subject is reframed, the story recontextualized, and its effects changed in subsequent editions or in translation into other media. For example, when women's life narratives are collected in an archival project attesting to human rights abuse, a homogenizing effect can occur. As Kay Schaffer and Sidonie Smith observe, if individuals' stories are situated in new contexts informed by the larger story an anthology is shaped to tell or truncated to fit a volume's requirements for affective appeal, the stories may be undercut in ways that commodify suffering. This is often the result of editorial reshaping of them to fit legal parameters and narrative templates that can distort the original testimony and witness claims.

An archival afterlife may also radically revise the interpretation of a narrative through remediation. German-Jewish artist Charlotte Salomon (1917–43) created a vast autobiographical painted-and-lettered project, *Life? or Theater? (Leben? oder Theater?)*, of her family's and friends' lives near the start of World War II and her own quest to redeem her life from the suicidal ends of so many women in her family by becoming a visual artist. Aspects of the story narrated in *Life? or Theater?* have been dramatized in many media—film, novel, theater, opera—and the remediations present diverse versions of Charlotte as victim, victor, struggling artist, or inheritor of a dark legacy. Dutch filmmaker Frans Weisz's biopic (*Leven? of Theater? [Life? or Theater?]*, 2012), which revisited Salomon's life and work, stages the narrating "I" as making a shocking confession that she murdered the eighty-one-year-old grandfather who continually harassed and upset her. The film allegation that the historical Salomon committed the deed is new, and disputed, material in the archive that has opened her work and life to controversy and reexamination.

Even when all the "evidence" seems to have been found, a life writer's archive may be open-ended. Thus, archives are not fixed and dead repositories of evidentiary documents, but dynamic and shifting sites that draw on stories, tropes, and ready-made genres, as well as feelings, impressions, and imagined narratives. And new information may generate alternative versions of these subjects and interpretations of their projects. Life writers negotiating their relationship to diverse archives inevitably confront thorny questions that can entangle them in the forces and flows of transnational production, circulation, reception, and remediation.

CONSUMERS/AUDIENCES

Life writing is avowedly addressed to one or more narratees and the implied or imagined reader. But there are also actual readers, listeners, and viewers of personal stories, communities Plummer calls "consumers" in the tripartite symbolic interaction that is personal storytelling. Literary critics usually refer to these individuals and groups as audiences or flesh-and-blood readers.

Sometimes audiences are immediate, present. When people tell their life stories before a live audience or on an interactive online site, an audience is palpably there, accessing, soliciting, judging, even contributing to adjusting the story being told. Such audiences may solicit the inclusion of certain identity contents and the silencing of others. And they may persuade a narrator to adopt certain autobiographical voices and mute others. Reading audiences, however, are anonymous, mediated, heterogeneous collectives. Actual readers, unlike imagined readers, may respond in diverse and unpredictable ways. They come to texts from different experiential histories and geopolitical spaces that can produce radically different readings. And because readers "consume" narratives along with other stories from popular as well as literary culture, their responses to life writing are influenced by other kinds of stories in general circulation—in families, communities, regions, nations, diasporas.

Distances of both space and time further complicate our understanding of the responses of audiences to life writing. Scholars of the history of the book try to discover, through research into the material conditions of publication, who constituted "reading publics," the historical consumers of life narratives at various times. They analyze what meanings reading publics assigned a given text in order to understand the cultural meanings it acquired at and since its first publication. And they assess the investments that religious, juridical, political, and cultural institutions may have had in the reproduction—or suppression—of genres of life writing or of a particular personal narrative.

How published narratives are produced and circulated among reading publics and what routes they take through various institutions before they get into people's hands are issues that affect the ways in which life

Autobiographical Acts

writing achieves its ongoing effects. Consider two examples of popular American life writing that circulated among reading publics throughout, and beyond, the nineteenth century: Barbary Coast pirate narratives and Mary Jemison's captivity narrative. A fascinating subgenre, the Barbary Coast captivity narratives (both English and American, authored by Anglo and African writers) were usually told by mariners captured by pirates and held in North Africa. These tales were widely read as popular exploration and adventure stories. But in the United States in the nineteenth century they were also read as cautionary tales, warning of the vulnerability of the new nation to its European trading partners, all of whom sought wealth in Africa (Baepler, 25). These tales mobilized divisions in American discourses of race at a key moment in the early nineteenth century when the slave trade had greatly intensified and slave narratives had begun to circulate. A captive such as African American Robert Adams, who told his story to a white editor in 1816, was read as "white," "Arab," or "negro" by readers whose interpretations of his narrative varied wildly according to their locations and politics (21). A female Barbary Coast captive, Eliza Bradley, wrote "An Authentic Narrative," published in 1820 as the true and harrowing tale of a white English woman who, in captivity, was sheltered and never the victim of sexual advances (247). This narrative, borrowing large parts of its story from a best-selling adventure narrative of its time, captivated readers with its contradictory notions of fragile and independent white womanhood. Barbary Coast narratives traded on exoticizing Africa as a land of extremes in bizarre stories of grotesque spectacles. Both rationalizing and critiquing slavery in the United States, they inaugurated a public taste for Barbary Coast captivity narratives that continues into the present in print and on stage and screen (50–51).

A different aspect of reading publics is evident in the changing responses to the narrative of Mary Jemison, popularly known as "the white woman of the Genesee," told to James E. Seaver. Jemison was captured in 1755 by the Seneca Indians in what is now upstate New York and stayed voluntarily for life with her captors, raising a large family. Her narrative, first published in 1824, was so popular it went through twenty-seven printings and twenty-three editions that ranged in size from 32 to 483 pages. In these editions the story was reshaped as, at various moments, an ethnographic record of life among the Seneca and Iroquois; a "true history" of captive experience; a document attesting

148   Autobiographical Acts

to settler stamina; a nostalgic mourning for the decline of Indian life; a site for displaying photos of the new sites and monuments of western New York; and a popular children's book (Namias, 4–6). In examining its successive editions, we can trace shifts in reading tastes by observing the modifications of content and presentation of the versions over time. Umberto Eco aptly captures the dynamism of public reception for autobiographical narrative by entitling a section of his 1979 book, *The Role of the Reader: Explorations in the Semiotics of Texts*, "How to Produce Texts by Reading Them" (3). Narratives are riddled with the play of meaning beyond any fixed referentiality as reading publics—or consumers—become cocreators of the text by remaking the story through the social codes, psychic needs, and cultural politics of their historical moment.

Stories are also remade through translation across languages, as Bella Brodzki explores in *Can These Bones Live?* Translation, never a transparent process, is a complex transnational mediation of meaning that shifts with social moments and audiences. Brodzki emphasizes how acts of translation inform cultural transactions that convey acts of remembering and mourning across cultural barriers. Even within a single language, it can play a critical role in the history of such genres as enslavement narratives, especially in aiding processes of intergenerational transmission.

PARATEXTUAL APPARATUSES

An additional consideration about autobiographical acts and texts is their situatedness in *paratextual surrounds,* what we might think of as the framing produced by their publication, reception, and circulation. The concept of the paratext is identified with Gérard Genette, who coined the word *paratext* as a combination of *peritext* (all the materials inside the book) and *epitext* (elements outside it such as interviews and reviews) (5). Genette distinguishes paratextual apparatuses from the literary work per se, which is constituted "entirely or essentially, of a text, defined (very minimally) as a more or less long sequence of verbal statements that are more or less endowed with significance" (1). Peritexts are the materials added in the publishing process that accompany the text in some way, including such elements as cover designs, the author's name, the dedication, titles, prefaces, introductions, chapter breaks, and endnotes. Paratextual materials—peritexts and epitexts—may appear to be

Autobiographical Acts

"neutral" aspects of the presentation of a text, but Genette argues that they comprise a threshold that can dramatically affect its interpretation and reception by variously situated reading communities.

Extending Genette's study of paratexts to focus on the autobiographical, Gillian Whitlock observes that life writing circulates as a material object that takes up space on a shelf or in a display addressed to the public, whether or not individuals become its readers (*Soft Weapons*, 56–61). She argues that marketing departments produce a "look" for a book, organizing it not only by its cover but by its epitextual surround, how it is displayed in stores or advertised online, as a commodity for consumption. Examining the production of life narratives of Islamic women published after the September 11, 2001, attacks, she traces how "veiled bestsellers," such as *My Forbidden Face* by Latifa, explicitly promote images of Middle Eastern women's struggles against a brutal patriarchy: the "images, the titles, and the subtitles," she observes, "are designed to grab the Western eye with a glimpse of absolute difference, of the exotic" (59). The effect of this paratextual apparatus is to offer Western readers a fantasy of Islamic desires and rituals for voyeuristic consumption (61–62). Thus, paratexts concern not only who reads whom, when, to what effect, and in what venue or surround, but also the kinds of audience solicited for a text at a given historical moment.

What of the peritextual process? Publishers, editors, compilers, ghostwriters, and translators often reframe a narrative through different kinds of mediations. Editorial choices involve conforming the story to publishing conventions and normalizing the plot by assigning titles, selecting typeface and page layout, organizing the chapters and rearranging their sequence, excising passages, correcting grammar and syntax, and regularizing idioms to make the narrative intelligible to a broad audience. Reframing might involve enhancing the truth claims of the narrative, as when James Frey's editor persuaded him to recast *A Million Little Pieces* as a memoir rather than a novel. Publishers and editors often add footnotes as verification and insert supplementary materials, such as photographs, as documentation of people and events for general readers. Publishers incorporate prefaces that attest to the character of the author. Nineteenth-century slave narratives and twenty-first-century witness narratives are often introduced and situated by an "expert" whose authority lends credibility to the veracity of the life narrative. These peritexts establish the bona fides of the person whose story is told, attaching authenticity to tellers who may lack narrative authority and to stories that contest dominant narratives.

The peritextual packaging of autobiographical writing shapes and situates the narrative by constructing the audience and inviting a particular politics of reading. Compilers and editors sometimes produce collections that place conflicting life stories in dialogue or tension, as did the compilers of hagiographies, medieval saints' lives. Similarly, in our times, there are contemporary collections of witness narratives by, for example, survivors of childhood sexual abuse or the "comfort women" who were forced into sexual servitude by the Japanese military during World War II. Packaging several heterogeneous stories as a collection can blur their differing contexts and truth claims, giving the misleading effect of a single, shared story.

In online environments, in addition to the kinds of paratexts associated with written texts, the screen content may include the visible features of the formal template, blog commentaries, hyperlinks, pop-up ads, associated inventories in sidebar suggestions, "I-like-this" options, and other algorithmically generated matter that mediates acts of self-presentation. Constantly changing frames, driven by behind-the-scenes algorithms, contextualize self-presentation relationally and in ever-changing juxtapositions, affecting how site visitors and reading publics view, read, understand, and respond to the self-presented. For instance, the paratextual box registering the constantly changing number of site visitors on a particular site informs viewers about its popularity and can boost celebrity value. The sources, purposes, and effects of paratextual apparatuses are thus radically altered in online media. Most critically, online paratexts are not only part of author- and/or publisher-generated content; they are also effects of online environments, including site architectures and algorithms, and the economic transactions and business models based on Big Data.

There are also new and striking parasitical aspects of online paratexts. In online environments, paratexts may have no intrinsic relationship to the autobiographical project of the user/author's values, beliefs, and intentions. Indeed, as uninvited occupiers of the screen, paratexts can establish symbiotic relationships with sites: the sites provide advertising space and Big Data for businesses while the paratexts net resources to support site owners. An effect of this symbiotic relationship is that paratexts also project readings of the life and self of site users by imput-

Autobiographical Acts

ing habits, values, and identifications to them. They make linkages unanticipated and unintended by site authors that can inflect, in dramatic and subtle ways, how the presenter is interpreted. They produce "digital character" and project imagined desires, interests, and affiliations. As parasites, online paratexts mobilize the transport of identities to unanticipated locations and stimulate surprising cohabitations.

Because paratexts can be modified over time, online authors can find their self-presentations framed differently whenever they return to their sites. For example, "thinspirational" songs and photos of stick-thin models might change the interpretation of disclosures on a site where users monitor their eating habits. Self-presentations surrounded by pornographic or political-advocacy paratexts might influence how visitors interpret the self-presenter's motives and beliefs. Then, too, because fragments of self-presentations can be, and often are, copied without user authorization, online lives can be resituated on another site and reinterpreted through new paratextual juxtapositions. The circulation and recombination of paratexts open any online life to multiple framings, some of which are chosen by the author, some of which are algorithmic and impersonal, and some of which are effects of ceaselessly shifting placement and juxtaposition.

In sum, paratexts direct the habits of reading publics and may constellate new publics. By understanding that autobiographical narratives are situated in the paratextual materials and practices that surround them, and in the spaces they come to occupy in our daily lives over time, we can more carefully observe how readerly audiences are shaped and changed both historically and in this moment of global capitalism.

"The meanings of stories are never fixed," concludes Plummer, "but emerge out of a ceaselessly changing stream of interaction between producers and readers in shifting contexts. They may, of course, become habitualised and stable; but always and everywhere the meanings of stories shift and sway in the contexts to which they are linked" (21–22). This instability and periodic revision of meaning account for the ever-shifting effects of the autobiographical, and for the joint action of life narrator, coaxer, reader, publishing industry, and online platforms in constructing the narrative.

Getting a life means getting a narrative, and vice versa. In his influential essay "Life as Narrative," Jerome Bruner powerfully articulates the complex interconnections between lives lived and the narratives of lives:

> Eventually the culturally shaped cognitive and linguistic processes that guide the self-telling of life narratives achieve the power to structure perceptual experience, to organize memory, to segment and purpose-build the very "events" of a life. In the end, we become the autobiographical narratives by which we "tell about" our lives. And given the cultural shaping to which I referred, we also become variants of the culture's canonical forms. (15)

The contextual, provisional, and performative aspects of the components of autobiographical acts give shape to and remake life writers' engagements with memory, relationality, experience, identity, spatiality, embodiment, and agency. Understanding the profound complexities of these acts enables us to better understand what is at stake in composing and consuming life narrative in the international autobiographical cultures of the twenty-first century.

4

What about Autobiographical Truth?

I modify facts to such a degree that they resemble truth more than reality.

—André Gide

Much of our scholarly effort over four decades, individually and collaboratively, has been dedicated to challenging the hegemony of autobiography as a cornerstone of Western epistemologies—settler, colonialist, and imperialist—and questioning concepts of the self as any kind of fixed entity. Along with many feminist, queer, and of-color scholars, we disputed the authority of modernist canons and worked to retrieve acts of life narrative—oral, written, performed, and visualized—that had either remained unpublished, inaccessible, or illegible, or had been dismissed as somehow "marginal" to the concept of a canon. We celebrated the profusion of autobiographical writing that emerged with "the personal is political" movements, campaigns of decolonization, and human rights activism. And we pursued theoretical challenges to literary studies within the academy waged by critiques of essentialism, intentionality, transparency, and simplistic notions of truth. We moved from using the term *autobiography* to the more capacious term *life narrative,* recognizing that retrospective autobiography is only one historical mode of the autobiographical. For us the term *life narrative* better captures the breadth and elasticity of the myriad forms of experiential self-storytelling in which people have long engaged.

With each new edition of *Reading Autobiography,* we have reckoned with our understanding of the vast heterogeneity of autobiographical acts and practices across time and around the globe. We have reckoned as well with the challenges of forging theoretical frameworks adequate to the heterogeneity of texts across multiple media and, more recently,

153

digital media. In this third version, we acknowledge a certain perversity in our thinking as we contemplate a fundamental question: How is it possible to continue engaging with self-referential writing and its automedial enactments at a moment when the humanist subject has been unmasked as always already self-interested and self-aggrandizing, a subject of consumption, exploitation, and dispersal across multiple platforms and locations?

In response, we argue that this is precisely the moment for intensified engagement with both earlier acts and texts and the current outpouring of self-explorations that populate best-seller lists, visual and graphic media, and public performance. Neither straightforward confession nor only calculated self-advertising, these efforts to make sense and meaning of a life, while acknowledging the slippery, transient nature of subjectivity, can be seen as democratic expressions that call for continued attention. Remaining stubbornly outside the sanctuary of "high literature," they are registers of what it means to be human in dehumanizing, all-too-human times. If the "self" always was illusory, a fantasized gap between the thinking "I" and what quantum theorist Karen Barad calls "the stranger within," the issues that life narratives raise—of memory, relationality, experience, identity, spatiality, embodiment, and agency—remain timely and compelling. As does the question of autobiographical truth.

Indeed, we thought this chapter would be an extended reckoning with what, after decades of scholarly theorizing and analysis of life narrative, constitutes the "truth" of autobiographical acts and practices. In an era of acknowledged hoaxes, the question seems urgent. But our outline of how to conduct an extended discussion of autobiographical truth was prohibitively long, and drafts of the chapter were uninspiring. This may well be a post-truth age, a time Stephen Colbert termed "truthiness," when Kellyanne Conway's "alternative facts" and the allegations of Donald Trump and other conspiracy theorists about "stolen elections" and "fake news" have gained traction with many. Are George Costanza's words on *Seinfeld* ("Just remember: It's not a lie—if *you* believe it") the hallmark of autobiographical truth now?

Certainly, the stakes for life narrative are high. Allegedly "authentic" narratives of experience, such as Forrest Carter's *The Education of Little Tree,* James Frey's *A Million Little Pieces,* Binjamin Wilkomirski's (real name Bruno Dösseker) claim to be a Holocaust survivor in *Fragments: Memories of a Wartime Childhood,* and the lonelygirl15 video series

What about Autobiographical Truth? 155

are among many recent examples revealed by critics to be conscious misrepresentations.[1] In response, readers have developed a healthy suspicion about the truth of self-proclaimed "autobiographical" narratives, especially narratives of violence, suffering, and ultimate triumph. For example, in response to Norma Khouri's popular memoir, *Forbidden Love: A Harrowing True Story of Love and Revenge in Jordan,* Australian filmmaker Anna Broinowski produced a myth-busting documentary, *Forbidden Lie$.* In the case of *Burned Alive: A Victim of the Law of Men* by the pseudonymous Souad, vigorous controversy about alleged attempts at honor killing ensued that questioned both the narrator's validity and the motives of her French advocacy publishing house (see Smith and Watson, "Witness or False Witness?," 601–4). Such self-invention is by no means only a twenty-first-century phenomenon. Timothy Dow Adams, in *Telling Lies in Modern American Autobiography,* traced allegations brought against prominent life writers such as Lillian Hellman and Malcolm X (in Alex Haley's publication of his autobiography) in mid-twentieth-century America and examined to what extent they were warranted. Casanova's voluminous eighteenth-century memoirs suggest that claims to exaggerated virility, conquest, and success have long accompanied life narrative. Ann Fabian notes the pervasiveness of hoaxing in early American printed texts, and Laura Browder traces the instrumentality of life narrative for those eager to remake their inherited ethnic, class, or gender status in print as particularly a feature of settler colonialism. Even teenaged Benjamin Franklin wrote essays as Mrs. Silence Dogood to advance his journalism career.

Mindful of readers' sensitivity to issues of truth-telling, we nonetheless wonder if it may be more acute in the "age of memoir" because the stakes for our collective well-being seem higher, as political races make clear. The persuasive force of autobiographical writing has long seeded political ambitions and fueled outcomes, as the enormous success of Hitler's manifesto *Mein Kampf* made clear. Now, the affordances of the Internet enable fantasized self-representation as never before, and suspicions about deception are endemic on social media sites. At this juncture, when we recognize that authenticity is a trope and, for some, all life writing is autofiction, *can* life narrative retain its currency as a form distinct from fictional ones such as the novel? Can its claims about the validity of subjective experience still be valued? Or is the criterion of validity in life narrative only what a friend said of Frey's narrative and many support online: "It worked for me"? On what basis may readers decide whether a narrative is reliably drawn from a writer's personal examination of experience and beliefs? Or are all life narratives vulnerable to the suspicion of being manufactured from whole cloth? In the words of a Motown song, should one only "believe half of what you see . . . and none of what you hear"? That is, has the claim to "truth" become so tainted, manipulated, and ideologically driven that any genre staking its value on validity is per se not only suspect but likely unethical?

These thorny questions sent us down a rabbit hole until we decided that we had neither world enough and time for such an inquiry, nor the patience to trace the intricacies of historically diverse regimes of truth-telling and specify the complexity of the question "truth to what?" Reckoning with such questions requires its own book—not one we want to write. But we remain committed to the project of defining life narrative as distinct from fictional forms, despite the use of various fictional strategies in autobiographical works. We subscribe to the view of life narrative announced in Paul John Eakin's title, *Touching the World*, and succinctly summed up in G. Thomas Couser's assertion: "As non-fiction, life writing . . . exerts a kind of leverage, or traction, on the world that fiction lacks" ("Prologue," 8). Making this claim in our post-truth era, however, suggests the need for both new ways of narrating lives and new critical strategies for attending to them.

Recent critical responses suggest the range of positions. Judith Shulevitz cogently sums up a commonsense approach to assessing life narratives: "We judge memoirists the way we judge anyone else: by the quality of their insights; by their tone; by whether they lie for advantage or profit, or offer their stories in good faith" (15). But this norm of judgment, which implies an ethic of truth-telling, may no longer be sufficient in post-truth times. Although readers want to "trust their gut," the variations and alterations of self-presentation enabled by digital media introduce new challenges. Leigh Gilmore has written eloquently of the need to locate alternative jurisdictions for reading autobiographical disclosures and demonstrated in her recent books how illuminating such contextualizations can be. David Shields suggests that negotiating "the lure and blur of the real," in a time when simulacra of reality exceed even what Jean Baudrillard hypothesized, should acknowledge this is the inevitable situation of nonfictional texts (5). His *Reality Hunger: A Manifesto* consists of hundreds of writers' citations on various top-

What about Autobiographical Truth? 157

ics that are unattributed except in an index he urges readers to ignore. Shields observes that appropriation and plagiarism were, throughout history, practiced by many great writers and are inescapable because "reality cannot be copyrighted" (209). Yet readers still seek some form of assurance that we are not being duped or conned when we engage with life narratives.

To what extent does narrative theory offer tools for assessing the truth claims of life narrative? While many narratologists focus on a factual-fictional binary that tends to gravitate to either/ors, James Phelan argues that "a rhetorical ethics of factual narrative" would acknowledge the ethical dimension of such communications while moving beyond a simple ethic of truth-telling. It would focus on both "an ethics of the told (moral values relevant to characters, situation, and events) and an ethics of the telling (moral values relevant to author-narrator-audience relationships)," two aspects that are often intertwined ("Ethics of Factual Narrative," 544). Phelan observes an ethical dimension in the three kinds of telling they take up: reporting, interpreting, and evaluating. Importantly, whether a narrative is predominantly factual or fictional strongly informs its ethical dimension. Using Tobias Wolff's *In Pharaoh's Army: Memories of the Lost War* as an example, Phelan observes that a narrative can be both "ethically powerful and partially flawed," and makes a case for how analyzing the ethics of the telling indicates that "getting the baseline right is necessary but not sufficient." Indeed, "the ethics of the told provides an important baseline, a condition of fundamentally accurate reporting, plausible interpreting, and sensible evaluating upon which the ethics of the whole narrative depends" (553). This dual approach, evaluating the ethics of both the discourse of telling and the truth status of the told, offers a productive dual approach to engaging life narratives.

How have writers themselves addressed issues of truth-telling and the challenge of—and desire to—harness "reality" in writing? We turn to the work of French author Annie Ernaux, 2022 Nobel Laureate in Literature, as exemplary of how nonfictional narrative can situate itself and ask to be read as an act of not just intersubjective exchange but access to shared experiential truth. Notably, in its press release the Swedish Academy acclaimed her work for "the courage and clinical acuity with which she uncovers the roots, estrangements and collective restraints of personal memory" ("Nobel Prize in Literature 2022"). Let us engage in the pleasure of some close reading, the process that first drew us to autobiography studies.

Ernaux has long been a popular, widely read author in France. The style she practices, "l'écriture plate," is a "flat" or plain style of prose, accessible to a wide readership, including the working class of the small town in Normandy where she grew up (Schwartz, 16). While education, marriage, and decades of teaching vaulted her into the middle class, Ernaux remains dedicated to her working-class origins and to left-wing and feminist politics. Each of her books, with the exception of her celebrated *The Years,* is brief and focused on a particular event that occurred in her family or personal past. In significant ways, all of her narratives draw on the diaries she has kept since she was sixteen (though several years of them were destroyed). Her later works sustain a dialogue with this archive of life writing as well as with the versions of experience in her earlier narratives.

Readers and scholars often refer to Ernaux's books as autobiographical novels or autofiction, but both designations are inadequate. Rather, they are a new mode of narrating a life that stands in an interesting and complex relationship to the autobiographical. Indeed, Philippe Lejeune has suggested that they comprise a new genre of self-writing in which her diary entries of various kinds punctuate reflexive narration to stage an ongoing, open-ended process: "They are almost like an installation which exceeds the notion of a closed work or text" (c'est presque comme une "installation" qui dépasse la notion d'œuvre fermée ou de texte; Thumerel, 255). As such, Ernaux's open-ended narratives raise provocative issues for the future of our field and invite readers to rethink the challenges and stakes of autobiographical truth-telling.

Significantly, the cover of each book (in the English translations) bears an unidentified photo of someone who appears to be Ernaux or one of her parents; inside or on the back cover of each is a photograph of the author Ernaux. This paratextual dynamic captures an important aspect of Ernaux's narrative projects. Her narrators are nameless, lacking what Lejeune terms a "signature" as evidence of their autobiographical status. Yet the narratives both mediate and meditate on an image or event from a specific moment in past time, even as they question the vagaries and unreliability of memory, and set it in relation to Ernaux's documented identity as a subject in the world.

Consider how Ernaux strategically uses ethnographic categories

What about Autobiographical Truth? 159

to embed personal trauma in a sociohistorical context. In *Shame,* her childhood memory of the primal scene of her father's attempt to kill her mother is situated within an extended ethnographic recollection of the contexts of her childhood: "I have . . . to explore the laws, rites, beliefs and references that defined the circles in which I was caught up—school, family, small-town life . . . (and) expose the different languages that made up my personality. . . . I shall process (those images) like documents. . . . I shall carry out an ethnological study of myself" (32–33). Autoethnographic documentation thus becomes a means of recasting her narrative against a psychoanalytic reading of personal trauma. By drawing explicitly from both objective records and persistent subjective images in her personal history, she embeds the study of herself in the context of both intimate others and the documentable past they inhabited.

Similarly, *Happening,* written from February to October 1999 and published in 2000, centers on Ernaux's struggle to obtain an abortion in 1963, when the procedure was illegal in France. Its story of an unnamed young woman who discovers she is pregnant after an affair with another college student is counterpointed throughout with the narrator's metacommentary about how she intends to tell the story. "I believe that any experience, whatever its nature, has the inalienable right to be chronicled," the unnamed narrator asserts. "There is no such thing as a lesser truth. Moreover, if I failed to go through with this undertaking, I would be guilty of silencing the lives of women and condoning a world governed by male supremacy" (44). Here her personal story is constitutively related to the political—those who can speak about controversial issues from the perspective of their experiential histories are obliged to do so.

In the initial chapter, the narrator observes that the story of her efforts to obtain an abortion is "one way of measuring [life], possibly the most reliable one of all" (11). In this view, past events are not separable entities; they extend across time, unfolding in ongoing moments, happening.[2] Ernaux's narration strives to represent that sense of duration, of living in time, rather than isolating a moment in the past as a focus. In this, her writing introduces a different criterion of truth-telling, not only in its commitment to narrate the past in its fullness, but in its emphasis on the duration of its unfolding. The guarantor of Ernaux's intersubjective truth is not just a profession of sincerity and ethical commitment but a presentation of, and engagement with, objective markers of her claims that can be recalled and validated by her readers.

At another point in *Happening,* the narrating "I" remarks on the notes scribbled in her address book in 1963: "Because of their physical, imperishable nature, these material traces may be more apt to convey reality than the subjective approach provided by memory or writing" (31). What a challenge to theories of autobiographical writing such a passage poses! "Material traces" as archival evidence of the past attest to "reality"—rather than an interpretation of it—in a way that personal recollection cannot achieve. Claiming the "reality" of the past implicitly prevents assigning *Happening* to the category of autofiction because it offers an apparatus of verification. And yet, such traces must be enclosed in narration; they are not accessible, unmediated, to readers. We might, therefore, think of Ernaux's as a materialist ethic of documentation that insists there is no unmediated access to memory and no truth that is sheerly personal; it must be judged on the archival evidence of the "real" that it offers access to.

Elsewhere in *Happening* the narrator observes, "When I write, I must guard against lyrical outbursts such as anger or pain. . . . the distress I experience on recalling certain images and on hearing certain words is beyond comparison with what I felt at the time: these are merely literary emotions; in other words, they generate the act of writing and justify its veracity" (71). "Merely literary"—Ernaux is after something different from, and more than, a coherent and compelling verbal story distilled from events in the past. What is involved in representing experience, to the extent possible, as it was in the moment of its occurrence? Such unmediated narration is not of course possible—the past is irretrievable in that, as Louis Renza argued decades ago, one cannot reexperience past emotions unfiltered by the writing present; narrators "presentify" (10). But Ernaux attempts to present the past as salient by creating a personal ethic that relies not on assurances of truth-telling but on documented material reality in precisely layered and documented sites of evidence that she references.

Ernaux's meticulous focus on the detail and the emotions of a past moment is accompanied by minimizing her own subjective associations and questioning the reliability of her memory's sedimentations. As an interrogatory stance to her own past experience, this commits her to writing as a project of reality-capture that eschews fictional embellishment; it is rooted in and resonates through the body as it is grounded in collective communal experience. As such, her work is also mistrustful

What about Autobiographical Truth?

of much autobiographical writing as too impressionistic. Strikingly, the next-to-last chapter of *Happening* is a reflection on abortion as "what I consider to be an extreme human experience, bearing on life and death, time, law, ethics and taboo—an experience that sweeps through the body." She concludes, "These things happened to me so that I might recount them. Maybe the true purpose of my life is for my body, my sensations and my thoughts to become writing, in other words, something intelligible and universal, causing my existence to merge into the lives and heads of other people" (91–92). For Ernaux, embodied and felt experience, as represented in language, drives personal narrative, moving it from the solely personal to the sharable. In her understanding of the work that life narrative can do, the truth of the past is imbricated in a larger social truth distilled in writing, a writing necessarily tied to the factual places, events, and persons that underwrite the "real."

Ernaux's other mature works are similarly framed in terms of their concern to narrate reliably and objectively, acknowledging the unreliability and incompleteness of memory. In *The Years* she traces a new, uncharted direction in autobiographical writing by linking her personal past to a collective story that proceeds chronologically, year by year from just after her birth in 1940 to 2007. This schema merges her distanced personal experience with its sociopolitical context, in a mixture of subjective and reportorial narrative voices. In resisting the filter of retrospection, it attempts to replace the condensations of memory with a verbal record of how the past moment was viscerally experienced. That is, the narrative voice seeks to represent time in and as process. For this, Ernaux draws in part on her diaries; but, intriguingly, she almost always distances her personal story into observations of a third-person figure (*elle*). By contrast, collective events are narrated as "we" (*nous*) or "one" (*on*, an impersonal pronoun more frequently used in French), a nonindividuating tactic. Through these narrative strategies the truth of the autobiographical is subtly depersonalized even as it gains energy from her earlier autobiographical writing. Some critics have described this mode of narration as "ethnological"; but the relationship of the personal impressions of "her" to the larger social fabric, as related by a seemingly "neutral" narrator, is more complicated than that term implies. Ernaux's reality takes, as a species of truth-telling, are located in neither the wholly personal nor the wholly social but in the liminal space of their ever-shifting relationship in time.

While we cannot offer an extended discussion of *The Years*, we turn briefly to its conclusion, where Ernaux's narrator reflects, in the third person, on the form she sought to craft by capturing the sensation of "replicating herself and physically existing in several places she's known over her life, and thus attaining a palimpsest time" (226). "Palimpsest time" is a striking phrase for the multiple overlays of temporal moments that form in memory and both enter into and defy representation. Seizing the time of her life as a "sweeping," "indistinct" set of unfolding moments that extend into years leads her toward "a kind of vast collective sensation that takes her consciousness, her entire being, into itself" (227). The effect of "her complete immersion in the images from her memory" is that she is "*taken into* the indefinable whole of the world of now" (227–28). Ultimately "by retrieving the memory of collective memory in an individual memory, she strives to capture the lived dimension of History"; she has reflected on her experience "only to retrieve the world" in a continuous tense that moves through ever-changing time (228). Truth-telling here is expressed in efforts to capture the dynamism of time as continuous and ever-moving.

It is a commonplace of life-narrative theory to say that its texts are both positioned in and mediated by their situatedness in time and in the tension and slippage between the time of the telling and the time of the told. But Ernaux's work, in its commitment to a documentary ethic of narration deeply embedded in material reality, calls the easy narrator-narrated dyad into question. Her example suggests that a more complex retheorizing of how the subject of life writing exists in the time of both her previous experience and her previous writing of it is required for readers to participate in her linkage of personal experience and the material world.

In an intriguing challenge to focusing on the individual in autobiographical narrative as a source or site of "truth," Ernaux's narrator in *The Years* asserts: "There is no 'I' in what she views as a sort of impersonal autobiography. There is only 'one' and 'we,' as if now it were her turn to tell the story of the time-before" (229). Concluding the text with a list of specific past places that correspond to unique personal sensations, Ernaux leaves open a space for the reader—and perhaps larger collectives—to fuse intensely personal affects with constellations of being alive in the ever-shifting here-and-now. Thus, the truth of writing experiential history to which Ernaux aspires is tied to historical and geographic specifics. If "language" is less universal than she acknowledges, so is any collectivity; the heteroglossic capturing of shared experience is irreducibly filtered through a national imaginary, one that in *The Years* is inescapably French. (That is, each language represents and configures experience differently, and existences are shaped by the particulars and limits of their linguistic medium and its social meanings.)

In narratives drawing repeatedly and intricately on the documented materials of her archive of diaries and earlier works, Ernaux offers a new way to engage the theoretical, aesthetic, cultural, and personal stakes and quagmires of ethically telling one's story. One effect of her serial engagements with the autobiographical is to reframe how we situate claims to truth and grounding in "reality" in personal narrative, an urgent question in this fractured moment. Few life writers are likely to emulate Ernaux's rigorous method of precisely specifying the material details and time of an event, and interrogating the relationship of her own location to each unfolding year. But her impulse to shift from the "merely personal" of individual memory to a context that draws on the larger collective experience of her readership offers a multidimensional matrix in which the acts and practices of telling a life are open to verification.

In sum, Ernaux's practice invites us to begin to *read* life narrative differently, attentive to how it documents the material traces grounding the radically personal in sociopolitical contexts that both drive and characterize the tenor and texture of ever-shifting times. While Ernaux's self-reflexive critique of her memories and her juxtaposition of them with the archival documentation of both her diaries and the data of the material world is a compelling response to this twenty-first-century challenge, her documentary ethic of narration deeply embedded in material reality is one writer's way to address a crisis of truth-telling.

For other writers and artists, personal truths may emerge as particular, contingent, and shifting with place and time. There are socially negotiated truths as collective belief, consolidated in regimes of official knowledges or accumulated through practices of producing alternative knowledges. There are dynamic, collaborative truths that emerge from the ongoing interactivity of subjects and interlocutors, increasingly across social media platforms. There are truths embodied in sedimented histories of violence, abuse, and trauma. And there are subjective truths, including personal, experientially based truth, affective truth, the persuasive feltness of memory, and the truth of intimate dreams. While people experience *their* subjective truth in many ways—as personal, social or communal, political, relational, material, historical, ideological, or spiritual—perceived truths are related to the struggle of narrating itself.

Insofar as we acknowledge multiple, shifting kinds of experiential truth, there are also significant ethical considerations concerning the production, circulation, and reception of life writing. With regard to production, we might ask questions about ethical intent in relation to aesthetic effect: How does the ethics of following a particular mode of self-narration or its converse, disrupting generic norms and expectations, affect its credibility? How does an ethic of bearing witness or, conversely, an ethic of appropriating the voice of an other contribute to the salience of a narrative for a particular audience? To what extent are the ethics of disclosure versus the ethics of discretion operative in a work, particularly with deceased or vulnerable subjects? Where is an ethic of hard-won authenticity at work, and where is its performance a calculated act, and on what basis? With regard to circulation, we might ask questions about the ethics of publicity, the ethics of paratextual framing, the ethics of accessibility, the status of translation, as well as observing whether an ethics of promotion is practiced. With regard to reception, we might consider the ethical orientation at play—or absent—in interpreting a life narrative. If the life narrative is being taken up for particular educational, social, political, economic, or spiritual objectives, what ethic implicitly informs its use? (See also the "Ethics" section of the Tool Kit.)

There is no single formula for assessing the ethical validity of a narrative. Exploring the dynamic relationship of ethics and nonfictionality, Julie Rak notes the tension between "being" ethical ("What is it good to be?") and doing the ethical thing ("What is it right to do?"). She enjoins readers to consider how acts of writing and reading can be implicated in either the perpetuation or the correction of historical, social, and personal wrongs ("Roundtable"). That is, applying the interpretive lens of a single concept of truth-telling and a single notion of the ethical is inadequate for engaging the complexity, heterogeneity, and often indeterminate status of subjective discourse as it interacts with experiential history. In James Phelan's terms, as set forth above, readers are challenged to observe both the ethics of the telling and the ethics of the told, to evaluate the authorial accuracy of the story told as well as the teller's moral conviction. For, when readers implicitly invite a narrator to

What about Autobiographical Truth?

"Tell me your life story," it is not just a bid for entertaining distraction. Rather, readers seek insight, affective intensity, inspiration to action, and the possibility of gaining wisdom from both the recognition of another's folly and the complexity of another's truths. At this cultural moment there is a demand for narrators willing not just to confess spectacular transgressions or harms but to reflect on, interrogate, and recognize what is gained in ethically evaluating the material of the rapidly changing everyday world and the myriad "lives" we all perform.

Commitment to self-narration as an epistemological act of examining what one as a subject knows to be or not to be the case remains a basis of both writerly tact and readerly trust. While that does not rule out the use of found, fabricated, strategic, or consciously invented detail, it asks that "my experiments with truth," Mahatma Gandhi's fine title for his autobiography, serve a larger project than personal fantasy or justification. If a kind of intersubjective truth, always tentative and provisional, is to emerge in autobiographical acts, both readers and writers must bring their generous attention and active engagement to the process, even as they recognize that such engagements are performative, situational, relational, and ultimately never complete, epistemologically or ethically.

II

A GUIDE TO READING LIFE NARRATIVE

5

Reading Life Narratives
A Tool Kit of Strategies

I haven't read any of the autobiographies about me.

— Elizabeth Taylor

You pick up a memoir in your local bookstore that looks interesting and read the opening page. Or you come upon a personal narrative in an archive you're perusing for a history project. Or you find yourself a captive listener at a family gathering during which people regale one another with stories of the past. Or you peruse a website where people present stories about their lives and users offer comments in response. Given the complexity of autobiographical acts that we charted in chapters 2 and 3, what kinds of questions come up in engaging these autobiographical narratives? How, exactly, might you approach them?

In this chapter we offer you a tool kit for addressing self-referential texts. The topics, in alphabetical order, provide points of entry and strategies for reading the burgeoning array of life narratives available today. The tool kit may seem daunting in multiplying the questions you can ask of any life narrative. Certainly, some questions are better suited to some texts or some readers. But if you habitually read in terms of, say, reader response, you may find it illuminating to take up the question of embodiment or agency in life narrative. In the multiple patterns, separate voices, divergent memories, and diverse audiences of even apparently uncomplicated life narratives, a world of stories and interpretations may emerge. These questions might also generate points of departure for writing your own autobiographical narrative in the future.

AGENCY

People tell stories of their lives through the cultural scripts available to them, and they are governed by social norms about self-presentation

169

in public. Given constraints, how do people change the narratives or write back to the cultural stories that have scripted them as particular kinds of subjects or denied their subjectivity? What strategies for this "writing back" might enable changing the terms of one's representation in order to gain more agency? What life-writing practices have potential to intervene in existing social and political formations? Where is the narrator self-reflexive about reproducing or interrupting cultural scripts?

Similarly, how do narrators negotiate the expectations about who can tell certain kinds of stories? How, for instance, do particular women write around cultural strictures about female duty, virtue, and modesty when they are engaged in telling their life stories for publication? How do postcolonial subjects write back to the empire that formerly colonized them as childlike or less than human? That is, what strategic means of writing against the myths, narratives, and characterizations that have historically fixed colonial subjects enable them to imagine new or revised narratives of possibility? Where do such narrators speak in multiple voices, employ diverse strategies, or alternate among several audiences to negotiate their stories of de/colonization? How is the political significance of language thematized in the text? What language(s) and strategies of translation do narrators employ in telling their stories?

Agency can also derive from acknowledging the limits of knowing ourselves. Where and how do narrators reflect on the limits of their self-knowing or ability to interpret their lives?

ARCHIVES

In the process of composition and publication, narrators act as readers, interpreters, and curators of archival material, both that which comes from external institutional archives and that which comes from their personal archive of artifacts and materials, including those kept by others and the narrator's own. While archives may seem to be objective sites of authoritative evidence, they are qualified by the historical formations of colonialism and imperialism in which they arose; therefore, such "evidence" can be questioned and subjective sites of knowledge validated as aspects of personal archives.

Where do you find the introduction of or allusion to a personal archive? Does the narrative include personal artifacts, in various media, that it either supports, contradicts, or juxtaposes as alternative versions of a story? Are there implicit tensions or conflicts among different kinds of archival artifacts introduced, for example, between personal documents and photographs? Does the narrating "I" refer to methods of self-curation and to what effect? If means of gaining access to materials stored in family or personal archives are mentioned, how might the narrator's reference be understood, either as an invitation to readers to validate the story with external evidence or as a challenge to its authority?

Where do you observe the inclusion of or allusion to external documentary sources in the life narrative? If there is a discussion of preserving or selecting this archival material, how does it contribute to the narrative's emplotment and persuasiveness? Where does the narrative signal the recovery of earlier documents, artifacts, or other material that attests to the credibility of the narrative? If the narrative has been remediated, how do versions of it in other media retrospectively serve as an archival "afterlife" that may affect readers? If new archival information has been introduced or earlier contexts suppressed, to what effect?

When the narrating "I" is confronting lives and subjective histories erased from official records, are there fragments in marginalia or ledgers that readers can consult to imagine alternative possibilities for storytelling? Are there what Diana Taylor terms "alternative repertoires" of ephemera, such as embodied practices of spoken language, dance, sports, and ritual, invoked by the narrating "I" to contextualize a self-presentation? Is there some version of an "archive of feelings" that makes available impressions, emotions, and sensations that are not documentable as artifacts? Are there ways in which the inaccessible material body of a subject—the compilation of histories, sensations, and affects—can be traced in archival fragments?

When online archives are referenced, many additional issues that are related to the reliability of archival sources arise. If offline documentary materials are archived online, have they been modified by the interactivity of platforms and coding systems used in producing metadata? Have they been affected by the collapse of earlier contexts of content as it is republished and repurposed for other audiences? In online self-curation of a personal archive, how do life narrators negotiate the distribution of fragments of a life and the multiplicity of identities across platforms and timeframes?

AUDIENCES AND ADDRESSEES

An autobiographical narrative may address multiple audiences. Is there a person to whom this text is explicitly addressed, perhaps in the dedication or at a crucial moment in the narrative? Why might the narrator explicitly name and address a specific reader as narratee? Is there another audience, an affiliated community, implicitly addressed? What kind of general reader does the text seem to be addressing? Another way of framing this question is to ask, what kind of reader or ideal audience does the text ask you to be? For instance, are you posited as a sympathetic and forgiving reader, a celebrity maker, a secret sharer, a confessor or therapist, a student? Where does the text instruct you to be that kind of reader? Are there instructions for reading encoded in a preface or embedded in the narrative?

AUTHENTICITY

While authenticity is regarded as a guarantor of a life narrator's integrity, it may be calculated, a pose of "manufactured" sincerity. How we define what is "authentic"—that is, believable, compelling, persuasive, truthful—in a life narrative powerfully affects how we engage it and whether we trust its claims. Many questions can be posed: How do you assess the sincerity of the narrative voice addressing the reader? The narrated I's self-characterization and/or credentials as a historical person? The reliability of the narrative genre? The narrative's coherence or fragmentation? The narrator's self-reflexivity about truth claims made? Paratextual attestations to the truth of the story? The publisher's marketing of it?

Conversely, if you feel a narrative is inauthentic, on what basis is that judgment made? Is it difficult to identify with the narrating "I"? Are the narrative conventions of the genre unfamiliar or discomforting to you? Are there conflicting or troubling details internal to the story? If the investigative work of journalists has made a case against it, what evidence supports that case?

In online self-presentation, issues of "realness" can be challenging to resolve. On sites where the authenticity of self-presentation matters, such as coming-out sites, weight sites, illness sites, or grief sites, what strategies for winning belief are deployed? What guarantors of authenticity are identified, and what kinds of evidence offered? If it is an autobiographical performance using a webcam, is "surveillance realism" manufactured by a crew, which could include a camera person, sound

Reading Life Narratives

person, director, and scriptwriter? Is it a kind of site where users expect and correct for some degree of fabrication or exaggeration? For instance, on dating sites users may expect idealized representations of others, and adjust for vanity-driven profiles.

More complexly, the larger politics of authenticity plays a role in the global circulation of narratives of suffering. If the site is one where users are not identified, how might an aura of authenticity be attached to "anonymity"? If the online identity is fabricated, is a different kind of "truth" posed in order to correct a social harm or inequity to victims who cannot risk speaking out publicly? How might readers adjust for such fabrications, and when and where is it ethical to do so?

AUTHORITY

We expect particular kinds of stories to be told by those who have a direct and personal knowledge of that experience. We also have notions about whose life is important, whose life might be of interest to a broader public, and what experiences "count" as significant. These expectations imply certain questions about life narratives.

Does the narrator address the issue of authority, that is, the "right" to tell this story, directly in the narrative? Where does the narrator seem reticent or troubled in the act of telling the story? Upon what grounds does the narrator assert, imply, or claim the authority to tell the story? Does the narrator have recourse to an authority figure who introduces the text or is prominently cited in it as a source of authorization? If the narrator incorporates reference to or the biography of an authorizing figure into the text, what is the effect of this addition? By the end of the narrative, in what ways have the tactics of telling served to shore up the credibility of the teller and the tale told?

AUTOBIOGRAPHICAL "I"S

It is important to make distinctions among the historical, narrating, narrated, and ideological "I"s of the text (see chapter 3). How is the historical person writing the autobiography situated within a cultural world—as, for instance, outsider, celebrity, immigrant or exile, child? If an outsider or refugee, of what sort and under what conditions? What identity characteristics of the historical person—gender, race or ethnicity, class, sexuality, occupation, religious affiliation, legal status—become salient in the narrative that is told?

What qualities distinguish the narrating "I"? To what extent can its narrative voice be characterized as apologetic, defensive, ironic, romantic, self-important, self-critical, transgressive, et cetera? What is the nature of the gap between the narrating "I" (or narrator) and the narrated "I"? For instance, is the narrated "I" in the text a less sophisticated figure than the narrator? What kind of attention does the narrator pay to the younger, or more naive or successful, personas or versions of self? Are there multiple narrated "I"s? When an author has published a series of life narratives, do multiple narrating "I"s situated in different temporalities arise, and in what relation to one another do they stand?

Historical understandings of what it means to be human and to live a life inform acts of self-narration, constituting the ideological surround from which the narrative "I" emerges. Disparate notions of "I"-ness or personhood often clash and can effect shifts in concepts of human hierarchies, life cycles, public roles, and the relationship of an individual both to various communities and to historical time. Where in the life narrative are markers of an ideological concept of the "I" or of conflicts among contesting notions visible?

AUTOMEDIALITY

Self-presentation can occur in various media, or across multiple media with different conventions and limits. These media are not "tools" for presenting a preexistent self; rather, the materiality of a medium shapes the subject represented. Through what media is a life narrative presented? Writing, comics, installations, performance, music, dance, painted or sculpted self-portrait, collages, photography, film, video? If the media used are drawn or photographed representations of other media, what difference does this re-presentation make? For example, if a photograph is included, how does it support the verbal text, and how is it in tension or conflict with the text's claims? Does one medium dominate and to what effect? If multiple media are extensively employed to produce a hybrid self-presentation, where are you actively invited to interpret this collage method? Are there written descriptions of absent medial representations such as photographs or documents, and if so, to what effect?

Automediality saturates the presentation of digital subjectivity. How is a self extended into, and modified by, online networks? To what extent,

Reading Life Narratives

and where, is a user's presentation rendered as disparate fragments, rather than a unified and coherent entity?

BODY AND EMBODIMENT

Several questions can be posed of a life narrative that bring *embodiment* into focus. Precisely when and where does the body become visible in the narrative? Which part, or functions, or feelings of the body? How does it become visible? What does that visibility mean? How are the narrator's body and its visibility tied to the communities from which the narrator comes?

What cultural meanings outside the text are attached to the narrator's body? Do particular bodily processes take on significance? Does the body, or parts of it, vanish from the narrative at some point? Are there bodies other than the narrator's that the narrator encounters, or labels, or acts on, or assigns meaning to in the course of the narrative? Is the body fetishized, ritualized, or eroticized? Is the body a locus of desire, or an impediment to the circulation of desire? What is the relationship between the material body of a narrating "I" and the body politic? How is the body represented as a site of sensuality and emotion? As a site of knowledge and knowledge production? As a site of labor, disease, disability? Does writing the life narrative seem to have a therapeutic function?

If the body is performed as an autobiographical act, which aspects of it are foregrounded? Which bodily processes enacted? Are other bodies brought into proximity and to what effect? How is the viewer addressed as another body in the relationship?

COAXERS, COACHES, AND COERCERS

Autobiographical acts of writing, speaking, or acting usually do not occur unprompted; they are solicited by real or internalized or imagined others, to whom they are often addressed. As you engage a life narrative, it is important to consider what kind of person or occasion has elicited it. If it is a self-help group, is there a format or model to which the story is expected to conform? If it is responding to an institution that uses standardized forms, which specific kinds of information are solicited, which discouraged? If it involves interpersonal relationships, how is a degree of intimacy invited or controlled? If a form such as a curriculum vitae or résumé is solicited for employment, housing, or membership, how should the personal narrative be tailored to the requirements of the group? If it is one in a series of personal presentations and there are conflicting versions, how might these tensions be navigated?

If the life narrative is by a professional writer or emerges in a literary context and responds to a series of possibly competing expectations, what kinds of coaxing are alluded to? If a specific coach is identified as an inspiration or questioner, how does that person contribute to shaping it? How would you assess the power relationship between the narrator and the identified coach? If the coach is an internalized or fantasized voice—for instance, "Kitty" in Anne Frank's *Diary*—in what ways does it advocate for or against particular disclosures or narrative strategies? Where are there specific linguistic issues of translation, transcription, or generational idioms to be negotiated?

If there is a suggestion that the life narrative was coerced, what are the conditions or situations that occasioned it, and what silences or gaps should be marked? (If it involves a situation of collaboration, such as cowriting or ghostwriting, see chapter 6, "Collaborative and Collective Life Narrative.") Also consider the paratexts surrounding the life narrative; often, they allude to the conditions of coauthoring, coaxing, or coercing. "Behind the scenes" is there an editorial policy, particular audience, or narrative norms and limits that seem to predetermine the kind of story that can be told? Is the story told within a legal institution or during an official hearing and to what effect?

COHERENCE AND CLOSURE

Consider what claims the narrating "I" makes to a coherent story. Does the narrator explicitly assert the coherence of the story? Are there moments when that impression of narrative coherence breaks down in the text? Consider digressions, omissions, contradictions, gaps, and silences about certain things. How does noting a silence or gap affect your reading of the narrative of the historical person? How does a gap affect your understanding of the kind of "I" the narrator wants to project? Consider as well where multiple and conflicting voices emerge in the narrative (see "Voice" at the end of this chapter). If there is a shift in voices at some point, what might occasion it and what is its effect?

How a narrative concludes is also significant. Life narratives can end at any point in the life, when writers feel the story is concluded. And writers may also riff on autobiographical storytelling by projecting beyond their lives and imagining others' responses. Does the narrative ending seem to bring the narrative to a tidy closure and, if so, how? Does this closure seem permanent or is the narrative open to future possibilities? Is it one text in a serial life narrative? (See "Serial Life Narrative" in chapter 6.) What alternative possibilities for closure might other threads of the narrative suggest?

COLLABORATIVE LIFE NARRATIVE

While questions about the psychodynamics or the politics of collaborative life writing cannot easily be resolved, important questions arise about the terms of collaboration. Is the narrative a product of more than one person? What kind of collaborative involvement has there been? Is this an as-told-to or ghostwritten narrative? Has there been an editor, transcriber, amanuensis, interviewer, or translator involved in the project? What role has each person played in the making of the narrative, and what are your sources for knowing this? Who is presented as speaking in the narrative? To put it another way, who says "I," whose voice is heard in the narrative? How has an editor or transcriber made their presence felt or tried to efface their role in producing the narrative? Has the life narrative been translated, and if so, for what kind of audience; and how might linguistic changes affect the story? Is there a glossary or notes on untranslatable terms or phrases? Is there a preface, framing story, or notes that address the relationships among the narrator, informant, editor, and other parties producing the text? What is at stake politically for each of them? Does the plotting or presentational format of the narrative indicate problems or inequities in the collaboration? Who has benefited socially or financially from the telling of the story?

COLLECTIVE AUTOBIOGRAPHICAL PROJECTS

Collective life writing involves the engagement of a group of people in a life-narrative project of communal self-representation. Family, religious, ethnic, and other kinds of identity-based groups may describe the qualities that have defined their shared experience historically, with various participants contributing details of their own experience to build up a larger portrait. In reading such narratives, which aspects of the collective are emphasized as defining, which downplayed? Which characteristics are presented as typical, which as exemplary or aspirational, and which as misrepresentations to be refuted or debunked? What kind of bonds link the collective, and are they long-lasting or formulated for a particular occasion or purpose?

A form of collective life writing that has become politically influential is shared witnessing to individual experiences of human rights violations or mass migration brought on by war, regime change, or climate change. In such narratives of witnessing, whether in print or online, how is the dynamic between an individual history and the recognition of a collective experience represented? Where does a collective "we" tell a shared story? Or, if there is a set of individual narratives in which distinct "I"s speak, what characteristics do the stories share? What are the terms of collectivized self-understanding? What aspects of contributors' stories seem downplayed or minimized? Are there paratexts or passages within the text, or an introduction, that directly address the process of assembling the collective narrative? How do contributors specify the project's ethical concerns? Do you observe any ways in which social inequities or hierarchies influenced the process of gathering, composing, and circulating the collective life-writing project?

ETHICS

The ethical issues of writing life narrative are many and diverse; that is, real consequences for the writer's or other people's lives may ensue from publishing a narrative. For writers, there are issues in the very telling of a life story. This is particularly the case for those G. Thomas Couser calls "vulnerable subjects," who have experienced radical suffering, illness, violence, or precarity and may be retraumatized in narrating it. Audiences may also be aware of real-life consequences that have ensued from going public with such a narrative. How has the narrative been received in various media, and what material and psychic effects may the narrator subsequently have experienced? The ethical stakes may well be complicated by the relationships among collaborators or collective storytellers producing a narrative, as discussed above.

There are, as well, ethical concerns when intimate, even scandalous, details involving others are exposed. Are there revelations in the narrative that might be hurtful or embarrassing to living people—the writer's family, friends, colleagues—or that might compromise other people's reputations? Such issues are heightened in narratives that involve the dead, who cannot respond, or in representing large numbers of the dead through a few exemplary subjects. Where does the narrator signal

Reading Life Narratives

that something that has been divulged is potentially compromising or transgressive? What justifications does the narrator give for publicizing such intimate and potentially compromising details of personal life or the lives of others? What are the cultural conventions in the historical moment of writing that set established limits to self-revelation and the exposure of others? What purposes or motives might the narrating "I" have in violating those norms? Where and how do ethical considerations arise explicitly in the narrative and/or in paratextual features of the text?

There is also an ethics of readership. As readers, we may feel uneasy about reading the narratives of vulnerable subjects. What is ethically involved for a reader in engaging, for example, a narrative of profound suffering? How is your own ethical sense differently addressed in such a life narrative than it would be in a novel? What difference is there in the kind of story that is told? In your assessment of the narrator? And if the narrative circulates among readers around the globe, what different ethical standards of judgment might clash in its reception and its social and political uses? (See also chapter 4.)

EVIDENCE

How does the narrator win the reader's belief and seek to have the "truth" of the narrative validated? What kinds of evidence does the narrator incorporate into the text to persuade the reader of the narrative's claims to truth? How does the narrator authenticate certain truth claims or justify writing and publicizing a personal story? What kinds of authority does that evidence carry? That of personal memory? Dreams? Religious visitations? The testimony of others? What about "objective" evidence, such as photos and documents? References to historical events or places? The authority of other narratives? Note where particular kinds of evidence are introduced into the text. Why and with what effects might evidence from an authority be placed strategically at one point and not another?

Try to be attentive to how you respond to the narrating I's bids for your attention. Is your trust in this story or the storyteller ever undermined? Where and how does that occur? Are there statements or ellipses in the text that conflict with other parts of the narrative, causing you to doubt it? What's at stake for the narrator in persuading you of the truth of the story? What's at stake historically (in the larger society) in having this text accepted as a "truthful" account of a life? What difference would it make to learn that the narrative is a fabrication, in part or all?

If the life narrative is online, how do you assess the reliability of the site or platform? Given the versions of people's lives that may be distributed across online sites, and the algorithms that retrieve vast amounts of self-data, how does the surfacing of earlier or alternative evidence about a person haunt, qualify, or undermine the evidence presented in any particular iteration of a life?

EXPERIENCE

How and when is an appeal to the authority of experience made in the text? Is that appeal to authority gendered? Is it made on the basis of sexual, or ethnic, or racial, or religious, or national identity claims? Are there any indications that the narrator doubts what claims can be made, based on the authority of experience?

Can you identify passages where narrators reflect on the very act of "reading" their own past? Or where they adjust the interpretive lens through which they examine or interrogate their experience? Does the narrator critique the ability to understand the experiences of the past at any points in the text?

Do the different interpretations of an experience in narratives written at different times by the same person signal stages of, or changes in, the overall pattern and beliefs of the autobiographical story? Do the changes from one text to a "prequel" or "sequel" signal that the interpretation of experience is specific to a particular historical moment? Do such changes signal a shift in thinking about the narrator's belief system, or the nature of memory, or a cultural shift in the stories tellable at that historical moment?

The narrator is not the only one engaged in interpreting what constitutes experience. We as readers are also historically embedded, our understanding of what counts as experience historically and geographically situated. How does your historical situation as a reader affect the legibility or readability of the experiential history in the text?

GRAPHIC "I"S

The medium of the comic book shapes the telling of a life story in the biocularity of autographics. When a life is also—and often primarily—narrated visually, reader-viewers have to consider the relationship of the narrating I's comments above the frame or panel to the drawn figures, scenes, and speech bubbles within it. The segmentation of the story into frames, panels, and gutters, as well as the varying sizes and arrangements of boxed or unboxed frames on the page, has rhetorical and affective impacts. To consider how the visual elements of this cross-discursive form shape an autobiographical story, try to describe its style of drawing. What kinds of visual details are emphasized? What are the effects of segmentation through gutters, if used? Where do they reinforce the narrative, where disrupt it? Where does the autographic reference or borrow from other comic book styles? Are other visual media—for instance, photographs, maps, print media, schematic drawings—reproduced in line drawings and to what effect?

Where do images and verbal text echo or support each other? Where does each supply information or a perspective not shown in the other? Where do the visual and verbal stories differ, conflict, or complicate the narrative? If the graphics and the writing were not done by the same person, how do these distinct authorships interface with or interrupt each other?

How does the introduction of a visualized "I" complicate the dynamic of the narrating and narrated "I"s? Are there places where the maker is explicitly self-referential, through showing a hand drawing the image (life-size or not), using a mirror or self-portrait, or incorporating references to an earlier comic or narrative work? To what extent is a coherent or a fragmented, multireferential subjectivity produced?

How does the biocular, graphic mode of life writing enlist the participation of the reader-viewer in completing and interpreting the narrative? Is the implied reader-viewer for the autographic represented within it and to what effect? More broadly, what visual, cultural, and political knowledge does the autographic assume or require? How might it interact with other automedial forms, such as a film version of the narrative?

HISTORY AND AUTHORSHIP

What kinds of historical knowledge can be brought to bear when reading a life narrative?

First, there is the history of the cultural meaning of "authorship." What did it mean to be an "author" at the historical moment in which the narrative was written, published, and circulated? For example, in the fourteenth century, when medieval mystic Margery Kempe dictated her narrative to an amanuensis, she didn't understand herself as an "author" with ownership rights in her story. She was, rather, a Christian supplicant before God and the Church's earthly authorities. Later, the notion of authorship changed radically when copyright, asserting that authors hold a proprietary interest in their own stories, became legally binding in the early nineteenth century.

Second, what cultural meanings were attached to the narrative at the time it was written or published? Were there religious, juridical, political, and/or other cultural institutions invested in particular kinds of life narratives at that historical moment? At that moment, what kind of investments might writers have had in their own personal narratives and in other people's personal narratives? Why might it have been important to narrate to oneself or one's intimates a personal story, or to make it public? Who else might have had an investment in this particular story or in this kind of story?

Third, how do larger historical and cultural conjunctions and shifts influence the composing and publication of a particular narrative? That is, in what ways does the narrative reproduce or interrogate dominant historical narratives of the time? For instance, narratives by Indigenous Australians of the so-called Stolen Generations have exposed the history of state policies through which Aboriginal children were "stolen" from their families and communities in order to enforce assimilationist priorities, and they have issued the call for apologies and reparations.

Finally, we can historicize present practices by asking what kinds of narratives get published or circulated in online sites today. That is, whose stories "go viral" and why? How do political, social, cultural, linguistic, and economic forces inflect user stories and their international circulation? In this age of anonymous and pseudonymous online posting of personal stories, what strategies have emerged for evaluating the validity and authority of such narratives?

HISTORY OF READING PUBLICS

The reading public is not a static entity but a collectivity with sharply differing competencies, interests, and needs. We may ask, who made up the reading public or publics, the consumers, of the life narrative at the time it was written? Who might have heard the story recounted? Who would have been literate and what would the cultural meaning of

Reading Life Narratives

literacy have been? Think of the reading public in expansive terms. Who would have purchased or borrowed the book? Who heard the story as it circulated by word of mouth? What roles might groups such as clubs, libraries, or talk shows have played in the circulation of the narrative? What evidence is available about the kinds of books people were reading at this time or what the author was reading while writing? Or, if there is little evidence about the text, are there other books or kinds of books you might hypothesize that the writer was reading? These can be difficult questions to answer because of the kinds of research required, but they can yield fascinating discoveries.

Books with an extended printing history may suggest changing cultural responses to a narrative that materialize in different editions. The captivity narrative of Mary Rowlandson, originally published in 1682, for example, has a long history of editions, spanning more than three hundred years. Comparing several editions of Rowlandson's narrative reveals changes to the text, inclusion of illustrations, and changes to prefaces and afterwords. In looking at the history of publication, you might ask the following questions. What differences are noticeable in successive editions of the narrative—changes in book size, typeface, use of illustrations, design, quality of paper, cover page, exact title, and so on? Have there been changes in the content or the addition of introductions, prefaces, appendices? How has the narrative been edited at the micro- or macrolevel? Who issued the various editions? Where were they published? What historical factors might account for these changes? What distinguishes the different historical moments of the multiple editions? Can you discern shifting audiences for, and cultural uses of, life narrative through the history of this book? Finally, how did this narrative come into your hands? Where might it go after leaving your hands?

Given the proliferation of online environments in which life narratives now circulate and are repurposed by others, it is difficult to historicize with any precision the emergence and consolidation of users as reading publics. Here, the work of scholars in digital media can significantly inform the field of life narrative.

IDENTITY

What models of identity were culturally salient and intelligible to the narrator at the moment of writing? What models of identity are deployed in the narrative or performance to represent the subject (recall the distinction between the person writing, the narrating "I," and the narrated "I")? What are the features or characteristics of the models of identity included in this self-representation? What qualities or experiences might have been excluded in conforming the narrator's experiential history to a particular model of identity? Are there multiple identities that gain attention throughout the narrative? If so, do they emerge serially or contrapuntally within the text?

How does the narrator negotiate fictions of identity and resistances to the constraints of a given identity in presenting a self fashioned as a gendered, racialized, ethnic, or other kind of subject? Does one difference dominate or structure the narrative at all times? Or is there a multiplication of intersectional identities? Where do you find evidence of conflicting models of identity and to what effects? Does the narrator seem to be aware of the conflicts? If identity is seen as conflictual, is this thematized in the narrative? If the narrator identifies as having multiply marked identities, what holds these differences in some kind of dynamic tension? How can this multiplicity of identities be productively rather than reductively described?

MEMORY

Sites, sources, and affects related to personal memory are central to autobiographical acts. In the work you are engaging, how do particular memories and/or reflections on remembering shape the narrative? What kinds of remembering are emphasized—childhood, courting, "firsts," repressed moments, communal transmissions? What seems to trigger remembering in general, and specific memories? What feelings or affects are attached to various kinds of memories? Does the narrator allude to forgotten things, irretrievable times? Does the narrator make the act of remembering a significant theme within the narrative? That is, how self-reflexive is the narrator about remembering?

What archival storehouses of memory are incorporated in the text? Try to identify and distinguish sources of memory in the text. Are they personal (dreams, family albums, photos, objects, family stories, genealogy)? Are they public (documents, historical events, collective rituals)? What is the relationship of personal to public forms of remembrance in the narrative? If one or the other predominates, how is it related to the life narrative's audiences and purposes?

ONLINE SELF-PRESENTATION

Forms of self-narration, self-presentation, and self-imagination, such as podcasts, blogs, journals, and social networking sites, raise provocative questions: How do online autobiographical "I"s present themselves? Is there a close correlation to the flesh-and-blood historical "I" or is identity fantasized through an avatar or special attributes? Is the assumed or impersonated online "I" personalized, or a typical or exemplary "everyperson"? What coordinates of identity formation—race, gender, sexuality, class, religious belief—are legible or illegible in the self-presentation? If claims are made about the historical life of the narrator, what media for authentication and verification are introduced—photographs, videos, statistics, documents, testimony by others? What kinds of experiences are referenced, and in what forms and media are they presented? Do they correspond to recognized autobiographical genres or discourse, such as testimony to addiction, the tropes of survival and recovery narrative, an *in memoriam* eulogy? For instance, how are the cultural protocols of confession rerouted through virtual worlds?

What aspects of individual subjectivity are solicited or permitted by the protocols and affordances of the site? Can additional personal and subjective details of a life or autobiographical performances be introduced, perhaps as counterimages? If the "I" is performing as an avatar online, is the autobiographical content allowed to disrupt site norms? With regard to the affordances of author-user exchange, what effects are observable as others modify the autobiographical utterances and discourses presented? How might they make the subject a collective and collaborative one?

Online lives are vulnerable to technological obsolescence. They may disappear because they are overwritten or become unreliable, if not regularly updated; moreover, digital code itself breaks down. How is the online archive of self modified by such temporal shifts or by the interactive possibilities of online sites? Since algorithms do the work of registering, archiving, and reaccessing the data of individuals' information and acts of self-presentation, discarded pieces of life stories and presentations can pop up to undercut the portrayal a user is seeking to maintain. What effects on an author-user, as well as site visitors, of difficulties in managing self-curation can be observed? Given the speed of online messaging and the vulnerability of user sites to outing, doxing, gaslighting, identity theft, and cyberstalking, what cautions might readers apply in engaging others' self-presentations?

PARATEXTS

The term *paratext* encompasses *peritexts* (material inside the book) and *epitexts* (material contexts outside the book). These extranarrative components of books and narratives in other media not only frame and contextualize the narrative but target certain reading publics and encourage specific kinds of audience responses and reading practices. What peritextual material is included in the book or performance context beyond the narrative—preface, foreword, introductory remarks, online site-framing, notes, index, photographs or drawings, et cetera? How do the cover illustration, font and lettering, and page design present the life narrative? In print publication, does the cover change with various editions? What epitexts have accompanied the marketing of the printed or e-book, in stores, online, and in newspapers and journals? Where has the text been reviewed and how have those reviews characterized the narrative? For books that include formulated questions for use by readers or activist groups, how do these questions direct the reading of the text? Is it in regular classroom use? Has it been translated, and how is it presented for audiences elsewhere? Is there an audiobook, and how has it been vocally interpreted? Is there any history of recalling, renaming, or reclassifying the book and to what effect?

While narratologist Gérard Genette, who developed the concept of paratexts, did not address how they function in other media—a complex question in the case of documentary film—it is worth considering the kinds of paratexts that are attached to and situate an online self-presentation within a larger surround. Where does the screen content include comments, hyperlinks to blogs, pop-up ads, algorithms in sidebars, "like" options, and number of visits? How do these features contextualize the content differently when they shift? The incorporation of individual posts into larger sites may inflect users' understanding. For example, sites that gather oral histories into an archive often organize individual stories according to an interpretive apparatus that shapes them as a collective overview; sometimes, such rubrics create conflicting or counterhistories. When you consider the different paratextual frames together, to what extent do they set in motion contradictory or competing narratives? Where does the paratextual frame call into

Reading Life Narratives

question the reliability or accuracy of a self-presentation? Can you distinguish between paratextual frames that impose a brand and those that are intentional self-branding? Are there paratexts that serve not to commodify the subject but to project values or explore ethical issues, such as a commitment to social justice or human rights activism?

PATTERNS OF EMPLOTMENT

What generic patterns or templates are used to structure the self-narrative? Is its generic pattern that of the bildungsroman, a story of personal development and education into the social world? A confessional self-examination? A coming to artistic self-consciousness? A story of conversion through fall and enlightenment? A story of individual self-making? A call to action? A narrative of how the individual is embedded in a community? Are there multiple patterns in the text or does one pattern dominate? Where are the shifts in plotting and what are the effects of those shifts?

What are the histories of the generic patterns available to the self-narrator? Where, culturally and historically, do the narrative patterns employed come from? Which come from the dominant culture and which from alternative, diverse, or minoritized cultural sources? Consider the social locations of these stories—schools, religious faiths, political beliefs and practices, family history, work or apprenticeship, cultural stereotypes, histories of radical injury and harm. What are the relationships between narrative patterns and models of identity? For example, a narrative of self-making requires plotting that takes the narrative subject first through an apprenticeship and then through successive stages of public accomplishment and validation.

Options for narrating a life story are drawn from and may incorporate a variety of fixed forms and media. What genres are employed—for instance, lyric poem, fable, letter, essay, meditation, or testimony? Are visual images such as photographs and illustrations embedded in the narrative to tell the story and involve the reader? What are the effects of these images? What possibilities and constraints do each of these forms enable or disable? The fable, for instance, allows the individual "I" to be understood as an allegorical type of human aspiration. The meditation turns the attention away from what an "I" has done in the world and toward the meaning of a precise moment in a larger spiritual history of the individual. The photo at once gives flesh to narrators, embodying

them for the reader, and creates phantom narrators, thereby demateri-
alizing them.

RELATIONALITY

Routing autobiographical acts and practices through a range of relational others—historical, contingent, significant, idealized but absent,
transspecies, and subject others—is integral to an I's narration of the
formation or deformation of subjectivity and collectivity. Is there a significant other posited in the text through whom, to whom, or about
whom the life story is narrated? Who or what is that other—a family
member, friend, mentor, lover, or a divine force? To what extent is the
knowledge of that relation made apparent to the reader? Do we hear
the voices of multiple others explicitly in the text, or implicitly? Where
do the voices of these others emerge? What kind of investment does
the narrator seem to have in someone or something and how does that
investment affect the interpretation that the narrator makes of the life?
What is the impact of this kind of relationality on your understanding
of the rhetorical "I" or of the narrator's subjectivity?

SELF-KNOWLEDGE AND MODES OF INQUIRY

It is helpful to delineate processes or methods of knowledge production in
life narrative. Where does the narrative take up formal self-investigation,
for example, a formal "examination of conscience"? Does the narrator
have a method for interpreting dreams or particular experiences? Does
the narrative give space to multiple kinds of knowledge—intuitive, aesthetic, embodied, irrational, supernatural, mystical, symbolic, communal? Does the narrative incorporate other media, such as photographs,
that introduce different kinds of information and project alternative
modes of knowing? How does the narrative interrogate cultural forms of
knowledge valued at the historical moment of writing? What relationship
does the narrating "I" establish between knowledge of the world or of
others and self-knowledge? Does the narrative itself generate alternative sources of knowledge? Does the act of narrating the life bring the
autobiographical narrator to different ways of knowing that life? What
kind of knowledge could the reading of the life narrative produce for
readers? What kind of knowledge-making does the narrator project for
the reader?

SITES OF STORYTELLING

Sites of personal narration are both historical and occasional; they are dynamically personal yet communal; they are institutional as well as geographical; they are technologically mediated, as in the case of online self-representation. How is the site of a particular narrative historically located? What are its sociopolitical dynamics? What kinds of stories are—or are not—appropriate and legible to tell at this site? How does the site inspire, inform, compel, or impede the shape, rhetoric, and thematics of self-presentation? If aspects of a narrative seem incoherent or resistant to interpretation, are there aspects of the site, such as the stance and ethos of the coaxer soliciting the story, that clash with its avowed purpose?

How might the site affect the way the narrator is seen by, or is invisible to, others—in, for instance, a prison or a refugee camp? In what ways is the narrative invested in engaging the specifics of a site? Are there places in the narrative where the site itself is thematized? In a narrative composed of multimedial material, how is the impact of the site refracted differently across the various media?

With regard to online sites, what differentiates self-presentation on user-driven and protocol-driven platforms? How do the site and its affordances impact the norms of personal narration and the kinds of "I"s that can speak? How do different online platforms affect the kind of person one projects, or the identities one foregrounds?

SPACE AND PLACE

Self-representation involves emplacement of multiple kinds. In what ways is the scene of writing spatialized? How do its coordinates position the narrator in social, geographic, and geopolitical locations? In ideological subject positions? What geographic spaces—for instance, urban, domestic, "foreign"—become legible in the narrative? Where does a myth of self attach to geographic location? This may occur, for example, in ecobiography, which joins the subject and a specific place (such as the American South or West, the Australian outback). How does the narrator negotiate boundaries—of rank, national, ethnic, religious, and gendered difference—that are both constructed and redefined in acts of self-representation and in communicative exchange with the imagined addressee(s)?

What border zones of encounter between self and other (national, ethnic, gendered, etc.) are projected in the narrative? What psychic terrains of remembrance and reflection emerge as the narrator shuttles between social and private worlds or present-day locations and erased pasts? What histories are attached to the spaces of sociality in the text? What thematics of insider and outsider status play out in the narrative? What thematic mobilities inform the narrative, for instance, mobilities of migration, diasporic transit, touristic travel, or refugee statelessness?

Are there ways in which the chosen genre of life writing shapes the story, emplacing the narrator vis-á-vis others, the past, and the meaning accorded the life? What stories—of possession, dispossession, invasion, displacement, erasure, forgetting—are told of geographic and cultural spaces? Is there a trope of spatiality that dominates the narrative? How do the material spaces of life writing—the printed page, the bookstore, the online platform—situate the narrative paratextually?

TEMPORALITY

As readers, we may helpfully distinguish the time of composing the text from the timespan covered in the text and its temporal organization. At what stage in life does the narrator compose the text? Publish it? Perform it? Release it online? Does the narrator speak directly about the act of telling the story, that is, situate the moment of narration? Is the story told at one fixed moment, or are there two or more moments of telling? What characterizes these moments of telling? How are they different from or similar to one another? How do narrative tone and narrative intention shift with the shifts in historical moments or times in the narrator's life cycle? If the narrator has written, visualized, performed, or made public on social media iterations of an autobiographical story, are the same events and life experiences narrated from different, perhaps conflicting, perspectives? Or are stages of the life chronicled in succession?

Within the text, how are the times of past, present, and future organized? Does the narrative relate a continuous chronology from birth to adolescence to adulthood? Does the narrative begin "in the middle" and use flashbacks and flash-forwards? Is the narrative discontinuous, and if so, what effects do these gaps have on the story produced? Why might the narrator have played with or manipulated chronological or historical time in these ways?

Reading Life Narratives

191

TRAUMA AND SCRIPTOTHERAPY

Does the narrative engage issues involved in traumatic or obsessive memory to find ways of telling about events and sufferings that defy language and understanding? Does the narrator struggle to find words to speak something unspeakable? Are those traumatic memories of a personal and/or political sort, or of cumulative or eruptive violence? Consider how the narrator deals with trauma and the resultant obsessional memory or its inaccessibility. Does it come to the fore fragmentarily, or repeatedly, throughout the narrative? Does it seem to be, indeed, can it be, resolved in any way? What kind of understanding through resolution, or lack of resolution, is achieved? Are there significant gaps in the narrative through which the reader can glimpse the unspoken, what cannot be told?

Some therapists and critics have extolled writing about personal traumatic experience as "scriptotherapy." Does the narrator discuss the therapeutic effects of writing or other expression in the text? Is the therapeutic value of writing itself a major theme? Does the expressive process of writing seem to have changed the narrating "I" and the life story itself? Does the narrator present the text as potentially therapeutic for the reader?

VOICE

While there is typically one narrator (narrating "I"), the voices of the narrator may be many. Is the text monovocal or polyvocal? That is, is there one voice dominating the narrative or do multiple and conflicting voices emerge? If one voice dominates throughout the narrative, where and how do other voices emerge? How does the narrating "I" contain or curtail them? If there are multiple voices, when do they emerge and when disappear? Why? Is there a blending or an unresolved tension of voices in the narrative? Is a relationship posited between the individual narrator's voice and the collective voice of some larger community? What values and discourses are identified with that larger collectivity? Is more than one group or collectivity invoked in the text, each with distinct values and languages? What form does that incorporation take, for instance, reported dialogue or explicit memories?

Consider also how voice itself is thematized. Does the narrator explicitly call attention to issues of voice in the text? Are speech and/or silence thematized? What happens at the end of the narrative to multiple voices? Is there a closure to these multiple voices?

In the case of online autobiographical narration, how do other users, when they engage in interactive exchanges, inflect or change the narrating voice? How do such interactive exchanges modify earlier iterations of a personal story or the social uses and meanings of kinds of stories at particular historical moments?

Kinds of Life Narratives
A Compendium of Key Concepts and Genres

> Critical attention to the questions posed by the autobiographical act has become the principal preoccupation of theorists across the entire critical spectrum.
> —James Olney, "Autobiography and the Cultural Moment"

The history of the field of life-writing studies (often referred to as autobiography studies) stretches in the West back to the late nineteenth and early twentieth centuries and, according to William C. Spengemann, to three phenomena: the increasing number of life narratives reaching an interested public; the increasing number of critical essays focused on such narratives; and the influence of German historian Wilhelm Dilthey, who defined the genre of autobiography as "the highest and most instructive form in which the understanding of life comes before us" (*Pattern and Meaning*, 85–86) and called for its use in the writing of history (see Spengemann). Dilthey's student and son-in-law, German philologist Georg Misch, inaugurated the first wave of modern criticism of the field with his vast, multivolume *A History of Autobiography in Antiquity*. He argued that the progressive unfolding of Western history can be read in the representative lives of the leaders who participated in this achievement of civilization, and he discovered particular types of Western man in the self-representational strategies of each generation of autobiographers (12). Both Dilthey and Misch provided a working definition of the genre and its controlling trope—the life of the "great man." They situated that man and his actions in specific historical and cultural contexts and assessed how he and his deeds were "representative" of the times.

This German tradition of *Geistesgeschichte* (intellectual history) excluded other kinds of life narrative practiced for much of human history: letters, diaries, journals, memoirs, and other autobiographical modes of everyday and private life. It also excluded other kinds of subjects. Unmentioned are the nonpublic figures such as women, the formerly enslaved, and colonized peoples whose assertion of human status and exercise of rights as social subjects were systematically restricted and often brutally repressed and whose acts of self-narrating were either silenced, repressed, or ignored. Further, only rarely did they turn to forms of self-representation outside the West in the great biographical traditions of China, Japan, India, and Persia, and they omitted the North African ancestry of an immigrant such as Augustine. Nor did they recognize the significance of oral, nonalphabetic traditions of collective self-inscription in indigenous cultures throughout the world.

In the decades of the 1940s, 1950s, and 1960s, the ascendant New Critics and their acolytes in literature departments championed the concept of the literary text as an aesthetic object and work of value, most fully achieved when irresolvably ambiguous, and eschewed autobiographical works as an inferior, nonliterary mode. But once interest in autobiography began to awaken in a few corners of the academy in the late 1950s, Misch's work was invoked in definitions of *autobiography*. Scholars of autobiographical writing focused their interpretations and built their theories around key life narratives of the "great men of letters," establishing chosen texts as canonical in scholarly discussion and debate. This literary canon, representing what were considered the best and most timeless works produced by Western cultures, served to legitimate autobiography studies as a field worthy of study. Life narratives that emerged as landmarks in the critical study of self-exploration, confession, and self-discovery are familiar; for example, Saint Augustine's *Confessions*, Cellini's *Life*, Rousseau's *Confessions*, Fox's *Journal*, Franklin's *Autobiography*, Goethe's *Truth and Poetry*, Mill's *Autobiography*, Cardinal Newman's *Apologia Pro Vita Sua*, Thoreau's *Walden*. These autobiographies were regarded as high culture, unlike the life narratives of celebrities, military leaders, religious figures, and politicians that ordinary readers sought out with pleasure.

A second phase of autobiography criticism emerging in the period between 1956 and 1970 involved two significant turns. The first turn concerned the application of rigorous critical analysis to autobiographical narration to parallel the intent and seriousness of analysis of the novel,

Kinds of Life Narratives

poetry, and drama. The second turn directed critical focus to the act of self-narrating as the distinctive hallmark of autobiography. First-phase critics, preoccupied with the *bios* of the autobiographer, understood autobiography as a subcategory of the biographies of great men and evaluated the quality of the life lived and the narrator's telling of that truth. Second-phase critics challenged the notion of autobiographical narration as transparent and the underlying assumption that, as James Olney astutely notes, "there was nothing problematical about the *autos,* no agonizing questions of identity, self-definition, self-existence, or self-deception—at least none the reader need attend to—and therefore the fact that the individual was himself narrating the story of himself had no troubling philosophical, psychological, literary, or historical implications" ("Autobiography and the Cultural Moment," 20). By contrast, then, second-phase critics called attention to the complex creative aspects of the autobiographical as an interpretive reading of the writer's experiential history and advanced new understandings of the autobiographical subject.

From the 1970s on, scholars of life writing, increasingly influenced by postmodern theorizing, staged a succession of interventions that shifted attention away from the concept of a universal, individualist "self" who achieved self-discovery, self-creation, and self-knowledge. Instead, they elaborated a new concept of a "subject" riven by self-estrangement and self-fragmentation and observed the problematic relationship of the subject to language and to systems of power. The Lacanian revision of Freudian psychoanalysis challenged the notion of an autonomous self and proposed a split subject always constituted in language. The Derridean notion of *différance* captured the way in which "language, whose meanings are produced by differences . . . tries to set up distinctions necessary for there to be meaning." That is, meanings, always emergent in the system "as a whole," are never fixed, but rely on other signifiers that "lie in waiting, negatively supporting the signifier that has been uttered or written" (Pollock, *Differencing the Canon,* 30). Consequently, meaning is always in process, continuously put off or deferred. Derridean and Lyotardian critiques of universalized or "master" narratives contributed to the deconstruction of "Truth" with a capital T and challenged generic boundaries between fact and fiction. Althusserian approaches argued that ideology constitutes not only socioeconomic relations but subjectivity itself. Social subjects are subjects of ideology, "interpellated" or "hailed" as a particular kind of subject by the very institutions through which those ideologies are reproduced. Foucault's emphasis on discourses of identity and his critique of power analyzed the multiple, dispersed, local technologies of selfhood through which subjects come to self-knowledge in historically specific regimes of truth. Bakhtin's concept of the dialogism of the word and the consequent heteroglossia of utterances replaced the unitary "I" with multiple dialogic voices spoken as the autobiographical "I" speaks in language that has "a multitude of concrete worlds, a multitude of bounded verbal-ideological and social belief-systems" (288).

These theoretical reframings suggest a paradigm shift in understandings of subjectivity, as explored in chapter 2. The project of self-representation could no longer be read as providing direct access to the truth of the self, for truthfulness becomes a more complex phenomenon of narrators struggling to shape an identity out of an amorphous subjectivity. Engaging the challenges posed by postmodernism's deconstruction of any solid ground of selfhood and truth outside of discourse and by postcolonial theory's troubling of established hierarchies of authority, tradition, and influence, by the late 1990s theorists of autobiographical acts and practices accomplished several things. They drew on and adapted aspects of postmodern and postcolonial theory, which are themselves heterogeneous rather than unified fields. They considered generic instability, regimes of truth telling, referentiality, relationality, and embodiment as issues that contest the earlier critical period's assumptions about canonical autobiography. And they expanded the range of life writing and the kinds of stories critics engage in rethinking the field of life narrative.

Feminist theories of representation problematized "experience" as a transparent category of meaning, examined the political dynamics of the "personal," focused on the body as a site of cultural inscription and practices of embodiment, and critiqued the notion of a universalized "woman" by exploring differences among women. Frantz Fanon's and other postcolonial scholars' critiques of the specularity of the colonial gaze reconceptualized relations of domination and subordination in formerly colonized regions and linked the subjection of colonial peoples to international racism at a moment when national liberation movements were disrupting the interdependencies of identity in colonial relationships between the West and its Others. Scholars in postcolonial, ethnic,

Kinds of Life Narratives

and intersectional feminist studies analyzed the effects of discourses of identity and cultural practices on minoritized and/or de/colonized subjects and proposed enabling models of margins and centers. Scholars of gay, lesbian, queer, and, more recently, trans* studies resituated subjectivity as performative and criticized binary models of the organization of gender and sexuality. When cultural studies approaches, long dominant in Great Britain, took hold in the United States, scholars turned a lens on popular, public, and everyday forms of textuality, including everyday practices of self-narration in verbal, visual, and mixed media.

Over the past two decades, scholarly work in life narrative studies has extended in many cross-disciplinary directions: to trauma studies, disability studies, posthumanist studies, studies in cognition and neuroscience, personal narratives and human rights, multimedia studies, social media and online technologies studies, to name only a few. No overview of the generations of critical writing that culminate in the current phase of autobiography criticism could capture the richness, complexity, and heterogeneity of debates now occurring within literary and cultural studies, exemplified in the collections of essays addressing multiple, targeted aspects of life narrative that appeared over the past two decades. But a spate of recent encyclopedic publications signal the canonization of autobiography studies as a literary field. Some of them focus on how the field has expanded to include both autobiographical and biographical works, as the slash between "auto" and "biography" suggests for *The Palgrave Handbook of Auto/Biography*; some link autobiography to autofiction, as does the three-volume *Handbook of Autobiography/ Autofiction*. Others such as *The Cambridge Companion to Autobiography* chart the field's historical development from early foundational works such as those of Augustine and Rousseau to the modern period, with an emphasis on English-language texts. The multivolume *Oxford History of Life-Writing* has to date issued three volumes, addressing life writing in *The Middle Ages* (ed. Winstead), the *Early Modern* period (ed. Stewart), and the *Postwar to Contemporary* era (ed. Hayes). All were initially issued as Kindle books and in hardback. Volumes on *Eighteenth Century, Romantic, Nineteenth Century,* and *Modernist* life writing are to come. Some of these references may be used as online resources; all are hefty volumes with multiple authors.

We elected in this concluding chapter to offer, in alphabetical order, mini essays on concepts and genres that collectively convey the

198 Kinds of Life Narratives

heterogeneity, dynamism, and capaciousness of autobiographical acts and practices in the past and now. We did not include three recent formations of the autobiographical here—autoethnography, autofiction, and autotheory—because they were discussed in chapter 1.

ACADEMIC MEMOIR

Is academic life writing a separate subgenre, or a metadiscursive form for academics who become intrigued with writing a memoir in the process of writing about memoir? In recent decades the academic memoirs that have proliferated in Great Britain, the United States, Canada, France, Australia, and elsewhere offer nuanced versions of this genre.

Many literary critics have ventured into life writing. British academic memoirists Terry Eagleton in *The Gatekeeper: A Memoir* and Lorna Sage in *Bad Blood* write themselves into their adult vocation of English studies by observing how they internalized its norms. Michael Awkward calls his memoir *Scenes of Instruction* a "self-reflexive, self-consciously academic act" that accounts for the "individual, social, and institutional conditions that help to produce a scholar and, hence, his or her professional concerns" (7). Annette Kuhn, in *Family Secrets: Acts of Memory and Imagination,* and Gillian Rose, in *Love's Work,* interrogate the process of making a subject and expose how disciplinary ideologies can enforce conformity and traditional roles (Whitlock, "Disciplining," 51, 55).

Some academic critics of life narrative have told their stories relationally by focusing on the lives of family members. The serial memoirs of Nancy K. Miller, including *Bequest and Betrayal: Memoirs of a Parent's Death, What They Saved: Pieces of a Jewish Past,* and *But Enough about Me: Why We Read Other People's Lives,* as well as her recent autographic cartoon sequences about living with cancer on her website (Miller, "My Multifocal Life"), interweave stories of her family's origins with reflections on how her genealogical and experiential past has shaped her subjectivity. G. Thomas Couser's memoir, *Letter to My Father: A Memoir,* focuses on narrating parts of his father's life hidden from his son through a group of letters, using an account of a hurtful letter that he, at twenty-five, sent to his father as a lens to reinterpret family relationships.

For others, academic memoirs may be embedded relationally in larger social or ethnographical contexts. Carolyn Kay Steedman, in *Landscape for a Good Woman,* takes her own family as a case history to refute the claims of social historians about the subordinate place

Kinds of Life Narratives

of women and children in the rural class structure. Sociologist Laurel Richardson, in *Fields of Play: Constructing an Academic Life* and other memoirs, alternates traditional and experimental writing to connect life to work and explore the circumstances that shape the academic self she became. Similarly, in *Colored People* Henry Louis Gates Jr. embeds his academic aspirations and achievements in a narrative of growing up in rural West Virginia at a mid-twentieth-century moment when processes of racial integration were uneasily underway and "colored" families, while segregated, maintained rich and sustaining cultural rituals.

Academic life narrative can be a vehicle for narrating the prelude to an academic life or a turn away from it, or a means to contest others' versions of one's academic story. Edward Said, in *Out of Place: A Memoir,* focuses on his early life and downplays his academic eminence. Kiese Laymon, in *Heavy: An American Memoir,* traces his journey from Jackson, Mississippi, to New York, where he is a college professor, by charting "his complex relationship with his mother, grandmother, anorexia, obesity, sex, writing, and ultimately gambling" and naming "secrets and lies he and his mother spent a lifetime avoiding" (Laymon, "Heavy"). Academics can also remake themselves, as Nell Irvin Painter does in *Old in Art School: A Memoir of Starting Over.* She narrates how after retiring from Princeton she began a new course of study to remake herself as an artist, shifting her focus from history to the relative invisibility of the women artists she admired and emulated. Conversely, in *Feminist Accused of Sexual Harassment,* Jane Gallop uses life narrative to mount a defense of her position and address those who had accused her. Valerie Lee, in *Sisterlocking Discoarse: Race, Gender, and the Twenty-First-Century Academy,* provocatively links several kinds of memoir writing to narratives of her career as an administrator, teacher, and literary scholar whose story is not of "overcoming" but of being both metaphorically and literally embodied in her "locks" as she negotiates the microaggressions in the contemporary university. The sixteen short personal essays by life narrative scholars in *Career Narratives and Academic Womanhood* (ed. Ortiz-Vilarelle) reflect on career engagements with academic documents that have shaped their lives and self-construction as women professionals. Life narrative may also encapsulate the labor, creativity, and pleasures of classroom teaching. The pages of cartoonist Lynda Barry's *Syllabus: Notes from an Accidental Professor,* for example, are a pastiche of images and handwritten texts, poems, and lessons using color and graphic design to present a term's worth of the innovative assignments she devised for her undergraduate writing workshops.

When historians study *their* own histories as exemplary, they may alter their concept of historical objectivity to foreground personal experience, as Pierre Nora demonstrates in his collection of *Ego-histoires* by French academics, arguing that the self can be used as a "device to claim more authentic and relevant styles of knowledge and scholarship" (quoted in Whitlock, "Disciplining," 47). Along parallel lines Jeremy Popkin's study of historians' life narratives observes the interplay between the context of public events and the texture of personal life. Conversely, in *French Lessons* Alice Kaplan reflects on how her immersion as a student in French history led her to view history paradoxically, particularly in graduate school where she focused on French antisemitic intellectuals, notably Paul de Man, who cooperated with the persecution of the Jews and other groups during World War II.

Some academic life writers explore how a disability or chronic condition has affected their academic life, as do Simi Linton in *My Body Politic* and Mary Felstiner in *Out of Joint.* Or they narrate the stories of differently-abled family members, as does Michael Bérubé in *Life as We Know It: A Father, a Family, and an Exceptional Child* and its sequel *Life as Jamie Knows It: An Exceptional Child Grows Up.*

Cynthia G. Franklin regards academic memoirs as both a form affording insights into how the academy functions and potential sites for reinvigorating humanism and human rights struggles. She explores how they expose challenges to the humanities, such as the corporatization of universities and the creation of a star system for a privileged few (*Academic Lives,* 1–4). Franklin's analysis expands the field of academic memoir to include many kinds of memoir writing that intersect with such areas as postcolonial and disability studies. To the extent that academic memoirs are self-reflexive and attentive to the norms and contradictions of their strategic self-presentations, they might be termed "autocritography" or autocritique, as discussed in chapter 1, in their situating of individual stories in the institutional and social surrounds that shaped and inform them.

ADDICTION NARRATIVE

A kind of conversion narrative in which the reformed subject narrates his, her, or their degeneration through addiction to something—alcohol,

Kinds of Life Narratives

drugs, sex, food, the Internet. Some of the tropes and hallmarks of addiction narrative are the use of confessional discourse, narration of the fall into a state of craving often regarded as a disease, a cry for help as a step toward rehabilitation, and conversion to sobriety as recovery. Life writing chronicling addiction and recovery is not new, as Thomas De Quincey's classic *Confessions of an English Opium Eater* reminds us. But changes in public life over the past three decades have influenced the stories being told now, when self-help movements proliferate. With the increase of drug and alcohol addiction among the middle class, psychopharmacology has also become prominent as social workers view addiction less as a moral condition than a medical one.

Alcohol addiction has inspired a long list of remarkable memoirs. Riveting titles about alcohol addiction such as *Blackout: Remembering the Things I Drank to Forget* by Sarah Hepola, *Wishful Drinking* by Carrie Fisher, and *Lit* by Mary Karr lure readers to the vicarious pleasure of reading about lives wrecked by journeys into oblivion, then in part recovered. Celebrity Matthew Perry's memoir, *Friends, Lovers, and the Big Terrible Thing: A Memoir,* is an explicit "tell-all" about his extreme addiction to alcohol and opiates. His dedication—"For all of the sufferers out there. You know who you are."—suggests why addiction resonates with readers as a vicarious experience. Narratives of health and well-being concerned with addiction to drugs, particularly opiates, are increasingly in demand as addiction to fentanyl-laced drugs reaches epidemic levels. The widely read *Hillbilly Elegy: A Memoir of a Family and Culture in Crisis* by J. D. Vance, and its subsequent film version, exposed widespread addiction within poor white families in Appalachia, including his mother's addiction to opiates and heroin. Prescription-drug abuse memoirs such as *How to Murder Your Life* by Cat Marnell explore possible causes of addiction. Elizabeth Wurtzel's *Prozac Nation* privatizes addiction as an individualized fable of being lost and then found, though not all these narratives end in salvation.

One dominant model of recovery is Alcoholics Anonymous (AA), which ultimately relies on the spiritual intervention of a higher power.[1] Alex Williams describes the template derived from the AA Twelve-Step Program designating the three stages of addiction memoirs as, typically, "Hitting Bottom," "Getting Clean," and "Making Amends," with the degree of emphasis on each part varying with the author's stage of life, degree of success in recovering, and endorsement of, or skepticism about, the addiction-and-recovery process. But life writing about alcoholism can be ambivalent. Caroline Knapp's *Drinking: A Love Story* renders alcoholism in a seductive and intoxicating prose that the book's second half, about finding support in an AA group, cannot sustain. Similarly, the first half of David Carr's *The Night of the Gun* is a rhapsodic rant, while his narration of being sober after joining AA is flat.

While the model of AA recovery has been dominant, there are other models of recovery from addiction. The multiphase recovery model is exemplified in Leslie Jamison's *Make It Scream, Make It Burn*, which recounts how the narrator identified states of intoxication with success as a writer by constructing her narrative in relation to the lives of other alcoholic writers such as John Cheever and Jean Rhys. Alcoholism may be situated within the structural inequalities of economic, social, political, and cultural disenfranchisement, as in Augusten Burroughs's *Dry: A Memoir*, which mingles his story of alcoholism from his position as a gay writer-editor with a critique of both AA and heterosexism.

Alternatively, some life narratives propose the dislocation model as a competing version of addiction, focusing on the social and emotional disconnection experienced by addicted individuals who have lost their connection to community. For example, in the memoir *In My Own Moccasins: A Memoir of Resilience*, Canadian Indigenous writer Helen Knott connects her experience as a Canadian First Nation's writer sent to a Canadian residential school with intergenerational trauma and the experience of sexual violence while emphasizing her resilience through the healing practices of her First Nations culture.

A fourth model, the brain-disease model of addiction, addresses the genetics and biochemistry of the human body in terms of the medicalization of hard drugs now used to combat pain after personal injury. Travis Rieder's *In Pain: A Bioethicist's Personal Struggle with Opioids* offers readers his hard-earned advice and urges them to avoid addiction by resisting their doctors' overprescription of pain medication after injury and advocating for people to control their addictions in order to recover. In another variation, the narrative of addiction is combined with a narrative of filiation, as in the twin memoirs by father David Sheff in *Beautiful Boy: A Father's Journey through His Son's Addiction*, and son Nic Sheff's *Tweak: Growing Up on Methamphetamines*.

In the United States, best-sellers frequently dramatize both addic-

Kinds of Life Narratives 203

tive states and the process of "cure." Publishers solicit addiction narratives for their best-seller potential and market them to self-help audiences. Some tell exaggerated or fabricated stories of degradation and redemption, such as James Frey's infamous addiction narrative, *A Million Little Pieces* (subsequently revealed as a hoax), which unwary readers responded to empathically. It was published as a memoir and touted on *Oprah*, then exposed as a hoax and reissued as a novel. For some readers, it did not matter whether its story of addiction and recovery was in fact "true," because they found the narrative compelling and convincing. (See "Self-Help Narrative.")

For addicts seeking recovery, diary keeping or journaling may serve as a form of testimony like that given at meetings, making such life writing a form of what Suzette Henke terms "scriptotherapy." But the use of diary or journal writing as part of addiction therapy can also enforce a Foucauldian self-surveillance that conforms the writing subject to prescriptive norms. Like other narrative genres of suffering, addiction narratives have become commodified as conversion stories that are circulated broadly to readers eager for vicarious reading about abasement and recovery. They seek the intimacy of a one-on-one reading experience, imagining a personal connection with a narrator whose story of addiction resonates with their own struggles to find wholeness, meaning, and close engagement with the addicted subject, as well as the hope that recovery is possible.

In these politically polarized times, increasingly demarcated ideological notions of identity themselves have become addictive, fueled by mis- and disinformation on social media. For example, alt-right sites may target particular demographics, such as unaffiliated young people or disenfranchised rural Americans, for membership in groups that increasingly reveal their white-supremacist orientation and call for rebellious action, as in the January 6, 2021, insurrection at the Washington, D.C., Capitol. From such centers of grievance, another kind of "recovery" narrative has also emerged in the memoirs of those who participated in white nationalist movements, then narrated their struggle to disengage. Such examples as Michaelis Arno's *My Life after Hate* and Christian Picciolini's *White American Youth: My Descent into America's Most Violent Hate Movement—and How I Got Out* suggest the intensity of efforts to come to terms with hate-driven movements.

For food addiction, see "Food Memoir (Gastrography)."

ADOPTION NARRATIVE

Some critics regard adoption memoir as a coherent genre distinct from other forms of family life narrative because in it personal identity is mediated by a primary rupture, separation from the biological family, whose "ghost-trace . . . lingers in the expression of the individual and resonates culturally because it challenges normative social patterns" (Hipchen and Deans, 163). The scope of adoption memoir spans all members of the triad—birth parent(s), adoptive parent(s), and adoptee—but most narratives have focused on patterns of relinquishing the child and the adoptive narrating I's efforts either to reconstruct the family of origin or to dispute its claims. The contemporary adoption story is typically narrated as a quest that tries to "restore the lost origins of the adoptee" and "forge meaningful connections despite the indeterminacy of one's identity" (Deans, 239, 256). In its focus on "ghost remnants, a road not taken, shadowy traces of memory mixed with desire," adoption memoir valorizes origins and contests the primacy of social construction in constituting the family (Hipchen and Deans, 167).

Adoption narratives explore how experiential histories of adoption for birth mothers, adopting families, and adoptees are affected by sociocultural and political attitudes, nationalist and religious ideologies, and norms surrounding motherhood, female sexuality, and the appropriate future for the child. Some are written from the point of view of a parent. Birth mother Janet Mason Ellerby's adoption memoir, *Following the Tambourine Man,* narrates the act of giving up her baby at sixteen and the decades of loss that ensued as values about adoption culture shifted in mid-twentieth-century America. In Ireland, unwed mothers were often treated as outcasts and coerced to withdraw into such places as Magdalen laundries or abbeys, where they were pressured to relinquish their babies for placement with "respectable" couples. In *I Called Her Mary: A Memoir,* Margaret M. O'Hagan narrates how the unwed pregnancy she spent at Sean Ross Abbey, in 1950s Ireland, set in motion an emotional life steeped in shame and secrecy. Eventually, when the adult daughter Mary, whom she had given up in infancy, found her, "Peg" came to revalue her life.

Other adoption narratives are written from the point of view of the adopted child who undertakes a search for parents. These stories,

Kinds of Life Narratives

some of transnational or transracial adoption, focus on the search for birth mothers and the family secrets or socioeconomic events that may underlie giving up a baby. They often embed explicit or implicit allusions to who is able to become adoptive parents and the political and social policies, exigencies, and calculations that underlie adoption procedures. Over the last half century several narratives of American children searching for a birth parent in parts of Asia have been published. Catherine Ceniza Choy's study, *Global Families: A History of Asian International Adoption in America,* explores how mixed-race children, born of Japanese, Korean, or Vietnamese women and U.S. servicemen, who were adopted in the United States made up an early group of adoptees who formed "global families" that may have contributed to reinforcing racial and cultural hierarchies. For example, in *All You Can Ever Know: A Memoir,* Nicole Chung, born in Seattle and raised in rural Oregon in a white Catholic family, exposes in luminous prose the complexities of searching for her birth family and meeting her birth sister as well as coming to understand the silences around racialized identities and abusive relationships in her family of origin. More generally, transracial adoption narratives offer a prism for probing social inequities among different ethnic communities and classes of people. As, in life writing, all identities are constructed, transracial adoption narratives often highlight the negotiation of racialized boundaries by foregrounding "the literal social construction of families" (Patton, 274).

AGING AND LIFE CYCLE NARRATIVE

Autobiographical narratives are often written in later life and construct a retrospective story line that extends from childhood to the present moment of narration. Some narratives of self-made men, for instance, present the process of aging as teleological, climbing the rungs of the ladder to a pinnacle of success from whence the rest of life may be contemplated in its afterglow. Memoirs of aging—about desires to revamp the body, revive memory, and bewail the finitude of mortality—abound. Novelist Richard Ford in *Between Them: Remembering My Parents* dubbed one's sixties the "permanent period"; and Philip Roth in *Exit Ghost* meditates on the aged, deteriorating male body. Similarly, in memoir form, Nora Ephron in *I Feel Bad about My Neck* bemoans her recalcitrant body's sagging betrayal. As Simone de Beauvoir explored at length in *The Coming of Age*, aging is not only a process of biological decline; most societies structurally devalue their eldest through ageist discrimination.

But not all memoir writers focused on the process of aging and the later-life cycle view aging as unmitigated loss. Much women's life writing on aging emphasizes some benefits of aging with the shift in family position from child to elder, while observing how cultural discourses about the aging female body constrain and distort perceptions of it. In *My Life So Far*, for example, Jane Fonda divides her life into three periods and names her last section, on living consciously in the future, "Beginnings." Serial autobiographies or collections of essays may also track a sequence of lived conditions, as do Maya Angelou's seven books of life writing over four decades, Audre Lorde's later essays, and May Sarton's volumes of journals about later life.

While, with longer lifespans, many writers shift the story of coming of age to the crystallization of consciousness in maturity, others approach the individual's story as the fulfillment of previous generations' histories and aspirations. Edmund Gosse's *Father and Son: A Study of Two Temperaments* and Henry Adams's *The Education of Henry Adams* are narratives of conscious aging that project selves outward and engage contexts larger than family and inherited class position. Increasingly, longevity generates stories in the fullness of time. Harry Bernstein wrote *The Invisible Wall* at the age of ninety-six. "If I had not lived until I was 90," quipped Bernstein, "I would not have been able to write this book" (cited in M. Rich). And in *Having Our Say: The Delany Sisters' First 100 Years*, sisters Sarah and A. Elizabeth recount to interviewer Amy Hill Hearth a chronicle of their life together, embedded within a genealogy of how their family moved from being "colored" in the South to professionals in the North who pursued accomplished careers. Diana Athill, a long-time British editor of famous writers, offers a wise and witty assessment of living toward one's death in *Somewhere towards the End*. With increased longevity, however, and an increase in degenerative diseases such as Alzheimer's, narratives also address the struggle of lovers and caretakers to come to terms with the changes in a beloved partner.

Writing one's later life as a story of conscious aging may indeed motivate cultural rewriting of the life cycle and "age theory" itself. Both Kathleen Woodward and Margaret Morganroth Gullette observe how narratives of aging reorient cultural discourses away from tropes of degeneration and decay. As Gullette suggests in *Declining to Decline*, "I am proposing an active concept of aging as self-narrated experience, the conscious, ongoing story of one's age identity. Once we can firmly distinguish between the culture's aging narrative and our own versions . . . we learn that its threats to being and becoming are resistible" (220). In a different register, Woodward, in "Ageing in the Anthropocene: The View From and Beyond Margaret Drabble's *The Dark Flood Rises*," explores how notions of risk in the context of globalization and climate crises contribute to reshaping processes of aging. She asks, "what are the implications for ageing—and future generations—in the epoch of the Anthropocene?" and opines that "one of the losses we may very well have to anticipate and bear is the loss of years as older adults—of age" (59–60).

APOLOGY

A form of self-presentation as self-defense against the allegations or attacks of others, an apology justifies one's own deeds, beliefs, and way of life. Typically, the formal genre of the apology admits wrongdoing or expresses regret primarily to excuse its speaker. The mode is famously employed by Socrates in Plato's *Apology* and by Montaigne in the "Apology for Raimond Sebond." Apology is both a genre in itself and, as Francis Hart notes, a major stance of self-presentation in personal narratives, often in the autobiographical writings of statesmen. Former secretary of defense Robert S. McNamara, for instance, wrote a justification of his positions and role during the Vietnam War in his 1995 *In Retrospect: The Tragedy and Lessons of Vietnam*. Women writing in the mode of apology may mount a defense of women's intellectual and moral equality, as did Mary Wollstonecraft in *A Vindication of the Rights of Women* and Sor Juana Inés de la Cruz in *The Response*.

AUTIE-BIOGRAPHY

G. Thomas Couser uses this term to signal a first-person life story written by a person diagnosed with autism, as opposed to earlier narratives that were written by a relative or clinician (*Signifying Bodies*, 5). Examples include Donna Williams's *Nobody Nowhere: The Extraordinary Autobiography of an Autistic* and *Somebody Somewhere: Breaking Free from the World of Autism* and Temple Grandin's *The Way I See It: A Personal Look at Autism and Asperger's* (see Sidonie Smith, "Taking It to the Limit").

More recently, autism rights activist Amanda Baggs has used YouTube to critique notions of the autistic as incommunicative in "In My Language," exploring as well the available "shapes of personhood" and critiques of the language of self-described "normals." And in *Authoring Autism* neuro-queer scholar of rhetoric Melanie Yergeau confronts the "clinicalization of rhetoric" (114) about autism by turning nouns into verbs to capture the "motioning" of the embodied rhetor as an autistic subject. She also observes the pleasures of repetition as a communicative idiom to "neuro queer" the discourse on autism and speak an embodied "autistic experiential" (155).

AUTOBIOGRAPHY IN THE SECOND PERSON

In this style of address the narrating "I" replaces the narrated "I" with the second-person "you" and conflates or confounds that "you" with the reader, though it is also understood as the subject's self-address. For example, in *Patterns of Childhood*, Christa Wolf often uses the second person to address both her childhood memories and those of Germans during the Hitler years. In *Wasted*, Marya Hornbacher shifts into "you" to insist on her reader's identification with her descent into the dark night of the anorexic's self-erasure, personalizing the generalized pattern of the anorexic's struggle with her diminishing body and absorbing hungers.

AUTOBIOGRAPHY IN THE THIRD PERSON

In this case the narrating "I" refers to the narrated "I" in the third person, as "he," "she," or "they." Philippe Lejeune observes that "the first person always conceals, then, a secret third person, and in this sense all autobiography is by definition indirect" ("Autobiography in the Third Person," 35). It is, as he observes elsewhere, a situation in which one narrator "pretends to be two" ("The Autobiography of Those Who Do Not Write," 264, n. 10). Another way to describe this style is to understand the "I" as an implied narrator speaking as a ventriloquist through "he," or "she," or "they." But why have recourse to autobiography in the third person? Jean Starobinski suggests that "though seemingly a modest form, autobiographical narrative in the third person accumulates and makes compatible events glorifying the hero who refuses to speak in his own name" (77). In this style, the narrator seems to take on "the impersonal role of historian" (77), presenting the protagonist in the third person. But

Kinds of Life Narratives

the covert identification of the author and third-person pronoun belies this apparent objectivity. And as the third-person self-presentation of Henry Adams in *The Education of Henry Adams* suggests, the role of an apparent self-historian may be ironic and self-deprecating rather than heroic. Aleister Crowley, whose *The Confessions of Aleister Crowley: An Autohagiography* is written in third and then first person, ironically, in his "saintly" send-up of the genre, comments on the impact of writing in the third person: "Previous to the death of Edward Crowley [Aleister's father], the recollections of his son, however vivid or detailed, appeared to him strangely impersonal. In throwing back his mind to that period, he feels, although attention constantly elicits new facts, that he is investigating the behavior of somebody else" (53). Salman Rushdie's *Joseph Anton: A Memoir* is narrated in the third person under the pseudonym "Joseph Anton," in honor of authors Joseph Conrad and Anton Chekhov, whom he reveres. It reflects on literary and personal details of the years he spent in hiding after a 1989 *fatwa* calling for his death, issued by the Supreme Leader of Iran, Ayatollah Khomeini, precipitated ongoing threats to his life. In reflecting on the implications of pronouns in third-person autobiographical narration, Lejeune has coined the term *heterobiography* to describe collaborative or as-told-to life narratives as the inverse of what occurs in autobiography in the third person. While in third-person narrative there is a narrator who pretends to be another, in heterobiography there are "two who pretend to be only one" ("The Autobiography of Those Who Do Not Write," 264 n. 10).

AUTOBIOGRAPHY, VARIANTS

Many critics enjoy punning on the etymologies and referential possibilities of the three Greek words that compose autobiography *(autos, bios, graphe)*. As a result, coinages have abounded for the last four decades, many of which have been noted in various chapters. Among them are alterbiography, autie-biography, autoethnography, autofiction, autographics, autohagiography, autopathography, autosomatography, autothanatography, autotopography, autrebiography, biomythography, ecobiography, erratography, gastrography, heterobiography, jockography, otobiography, periautography, prosopography. Some feminist critics have varied or removed the "life" that was understood to be a masculinist universal: Domna Stanton theorized *autogynography*; Jeanne Perrault writes of women's *autography*; Leigh Gilmore finds the difference of women's life writing in acts of *autobiographics*; Jana Evans Braziel emphasizes the different positioning of diasporan women life writers in their *alter-biographies*. Memoirists and novelists have also troped on the term. J. M. Coetzee uses the term *autrebiography* and practices it in his *Diary of a Bad Year*, a work of autobiographical fiction interweaving three narrative voices for its personas in "a kind of metaphysics of the self" among analytical reason, emotional need, and the body (Deresiewicz). Derrida famously used the term *otobiography* to suggest that autobiography happens "in the ear of the other," asserting that it "says me to me and constitutes the *autos* of my autobiography" for the addressee (*Ear of the Other*, 50–51). Cartoonist Lynda Barry uses the term *autobiofictionalography* to characterize *One Hundred Demons*, a graphic narrative based on her experience but with some fictionalizing "to make myself look as cool as possible" ("Interview"). Putting a posthuman twist on life writing, Louis Van den Hengel proposes the term *zoegraphy* as "a mode of writing life that is not indexed on the traditional notion of *bios*—the discursive, social, and political life appropriate to human beings—but which centers on the generative vitality of *zoë*, an inhuman, impersonal, and inorganic force which . . . is not specific to human lifeworlds, but cuts across humans, animals, technologies, and things" (2). Working along similar lines, Cynthia Huff and Joel Haefner extend this observation to argue that *animalographies* or the life narratives of animals voiced by human companions are "a species of posthuman life writing" in which species become entangled and subjectivities are transformed in the process (155).

While some would argue that all life writing is inescapably Franklinesque *erratography* (a cataloguing of one's mistakes and moral lapses) or, conversely, an *oughtabiography* of regret about the things one should have done, in Chon Noriega's phrase, critics continue to encapsulate theoretical positions in witty phrases about the complexities of self-writing (personal communication, July 28, 2002). Arturo Arias makes an intriguing distinction between *testimonio* and what he terms *autorepresentation* as a practice of gaining agency through distancing in Victor Montejo's *Testimony*. Deena Rymhs proposes the genre of *automobiography* for Indigenous art installations that perform a counternarrative of innovation while reflecting on state curtailment of mobility. Pramod K. Nayar identifies *autobiogenography* as a new formation focused on the human genome, and what Couser dubbed the human *scriptome*, that pressures

Kinds of Life Narratives

subjects to compose *autobiological* narratives. Couser also coins the term *euthanography* for life narratives advocating a merciful end to life. Some European theorists are adopting the term *autosociobiography*, coined by the French writer and Nobel Laureate Annie Ernaux, to characterize texts that systematically combine life writing with sociological analysis, reflecting the dynamics of class relations in the early twenty-first century.

AUTOGRAPHICS

See "Graphic Memoir."

AUTOHAGIOGRAPHY

Hagiography is biographical writing praising the life as exemplary, making the person a "saint." Autohagiography can be used playfully for life writing in which subjects celebrate themselves as "saintly," often ironically, as in Crowley's third-person narrative.

AUTOTHANATOGRAPHY

This term has been applied to autobiographical texts that confront illness and death by performing a life at a limit of its own, or another's, undoing. Nancy K. Miller suggests that "autobiography—identity through alterity—is also writing against death twice: the other's and one's own." For Miller, in a sense "every autobiography, we might say, is also an autothanatography," since the prospect of nonexistence looms inescapably ("Representing Others," 12). Couser characterizes autothanatography as definitive of his focus in scholarly and memoir-writing in *The Work of Life Writing*. Susanna Egan, in an extended treatment of autothanatography, focuses on how the attention of recent life narrators to issues of terminal illness "intensifies the rendition of lived experience, the immediacy of crisis, and the revealing processes of self-understanding" in the process of dying (200). AIDS-related autothanatography, Egan notes, confronts death head on: "Death writing becomes preeminently life writing, and a bid to take charge of how that life writing is read" (207). It is "part of a complex claiming of agency" that attempts to connect the organic to the symbolic (208). At the zero-degree of both life and autobiography, with the death of the writing, or visual, or filmic life narrator, "the subject becomes an object entirely exposed to being read, entirely dependent on its reader for constructions of meaning" (212). A case in point is Harold Brodkey's *This Wild Darkness*. Indeed, the narrative may be completed by another after the subject's death, as was Tom Joslin's film *Silverlake Life: The View from Here* (214). Egan suggests that even in monologic autothanatographies, such as Audre Lorde's *The Cancer Journals* and *A Burst of Light*, the text is dialogic, the voice polyphonic, in integrating the anticipation of death into living (215). Making a record of living in a text that outlives the life, autothanatographies intensively "focus on illness, pain, and imminent death as crucial to the processes of that life" (224). (See also "Grief Narrative.")

It may seem that life narratives centered on death and dying are inescapably somber. But in *I Am, I Am, I Am: Seventeen Brushes with Death*, Irish-Scottish writer Maggie O'Farrell narrates her life in seventeen dated, nonchronological chapters, each named for a body part, that exhilaratingly recount her narrow escapes from certain demise. These range from the opening chapter, "Neck," concerned with how at eighteen she escaped a murderous rapist while hiking, to ones concerned with her obstreperous refusal, as a reckless child, of the bounds of safety. The narrating I's reflections on precarious moments in her life suggest both the difficulty and appeal of this approach: "There seemed no way to translate what had happened into grammar and syntax" (20). Unspeakable though such encounters may be, they also underlie the affirmation of living that her title suggests and that life narrative paradoxically enables.

AUTOTOPOGRAPHY

This term was coined by Jennifer A. González to define how a person's integral objects become, over time, so imprinted with the "psychic body" that they serve as autobiographical objects. The personal objects may be serviceable, such as clothing or furniture. But they may also be physical extensions of the mind—photographs, heirlooms, souvenirs, icons, and so forth: "These personal objects can be seen to form a syntagmatic array of physical signs in a spatial representation of identity" (133). Organized into collections, such material memory landscapes might be as elaborate as a home altar or as informal as a display of memorabilia. Autotopographies are invested with multiple and shifting associative meanings; they are idiosyncratic and flexible, although their materiality prevents free-floating signification (144). The autotopography may act either as a revelation or as a kind of screen memory to aid the forgetting

Kinds of Life Narratives 213

of a traumatic moment. An autotopography can also be a space of utopian identification and mythic history, idealizing the subjectivity that is re-created through the material evidence of artifacts (145). Finally, an autotopography may be thought of as a "countersite" to both resist and converse with mass-media images. It draws from life events and cultural identity to build a self-representation as a material and tactical act of personal reflection (147). For example, Mieke Bal has characterized Louise Bourgeois's *Spider* sculpture as autotopography.

BILDUNGSROMAN, AUTOBIOGRAPHICAL
See "Coming-of-Age Life Narrative."

BIOMYTHOGRAPHY
This term was coined by Audre Lorde to signal how the re-creation of meaning in one's life is invested in writing that renegotiates cultural invisibility. Lorde redefines life writing as a biography of the mythic self (see Raynaud), a self she discovers in imaginatively affiliating with a mythic community of other lesbian women. In *Zami: A New Spelling of My Name,* Lorde uses the term to refer to an affiliation with her mother's place of origin and a sisterhood of lesbian friends *(les amies).* In *The Cancer Journals,* she exemplifies biomythography by combining journal entries and analytical essays to reconstitute herself as an empowered Amazon, a one-breasted warrior/survivor of cancer.

BREAKDOWN AND BREAKTHROUGH NARRATIVE
Although mind and body interact across a permeable border, it is important to distinguish narratives of mental breakdown or psychological vulnerability from those of physical impairment and illness because of different challenges in narrating the story as well as in the discourses around and treatment of such illnesses. Rachel Aviv observes that we invest in reductive theories about the origins of mental illness because "the reality—that mental illness is caused by an interplay between biological, genetic, psychological and environmental factors—is more difficult to conceptualize" (193). Those narrating stories of breakdown and breakthrough resist such reductive theorizing by adding complexity, intimate density, and distinctive critiques to stories of mental struggle.

As shown in narratives of "talking back" to the authority of medical doctors, from Charlotte Perkins Gilman's *The Yellow Wallpaper* to

Freud's patient the Wolf Man (Sergei Pankejeff) and his 1971 response to being pathologized, titled *The Wolf-Man,* there are powerful motives for writing narratives of mental breakdown and breakthrough to some form of recovery. Such narratives may serve as critiques of the gendered, racialized, and often dehumanizing treatment accorded by institutions to vulnerable people, the ways that case studies medicalize body and mind, and the orthodoxy of treatment regimes. This critique is the crux of Susanna Kaysen's *Girl, Interrupted,* in which the adult narrating "I" returns to the scene of her early institutionalization in the late 1960s, juxtaposing her narrated I's version of a two-year stay in her late teens at McLean Hospital with the implicit narrative created by the succession of interspersed documents from the case file obtained by the older narrator. As both the putatively recovered or "sane" narrating "I" and the institutionalized, "crazy," experiencing "I," she holds two socially constructed categories—normalcy and abnormality—in tension. Although Kaysen's narrating "I" works to establish a rapport with readers that will persuade us that her documented diagnosis is erroneous, at key points she shifts her narrative position to an edgy one at the border of sanity, enacting a move that figures borderline personality itself. Even as the narrator asks readers to accord her legitimacy as a fully confessing narrative subject, she both produces and undermines the truth effect of her narrative, marking the instability of a fixed boundary between the fantasized and the objectively documented.

The chronicling of mental breakdown from an asserted position of (partial) recovery raises complex issues related to what Timothy Dow Adams describes as "instabilities [of diagnosis, treatment, and side effects], plus the stigma attached to mental illness" that create "uncertainties on every level" ("Borderline Personality," 108). The paradoxes of narrating how breakdown may generate a breakthrough about oneself and a critique of treatment regimes have been explored in Kay Redfield Jamison's *An Unquiet Mind* and William Styron's *Darkness Visible: A Memoir of Madness.* Lauren Slater's *Lying,* which narrates the physical and psychic effects of her enduring bouts of epilepsy, deliberately blurs the boundary between what is viewed as physical disability and mental illness, but also foregrounds challenges to telling a credible story.

In graphic memoirs of breakdown as a mode of breaking through a troubled state, artists can craft a visual vocabulary and style that convey to readers the felt experience of a disturbed mind. Ellen Forney's

Marbles: Mania, Depression, Michelangelo, and Me uses three visual registers to chronicle her emergence from a diagnosis of bipolarity to her management of it through medication and therapy (Smith and Watson, "Contrapuntal Reading"). In Forney's early pages sprawling lines and disorganized boxes create visual and lexical axes that do not align, projecting an affect of manic highs and euphoric creation similar to what she depicts in artists such as Vincent van Gogh, who ultimately committed suicide. Later, her visual style shifts to diary drawings of a blob-like woman withdrawn into depression and self-loathing. Her third visual register represents therapy sessions in which two actors, herself as a patient and her therapist, confront each another within orderly boxes and panels of reciprocal action and words. Forney offers her narrative as a model to help reader-viewers manage cycles of mania and depression or other mental instability (90). Yet a question lingers in her narrative, whether breaking through manic states and maintaining stability through therapy and medication will undermine an artist's creative energy and vision.

A further kind of uncertainty, related to the powerful "call" of the pleasures of a condition, occurs in some narratives of anorexia and bulimia, such as Marya Hornbacher's *Wasted* and online anorexia blogs. Here, the etiology of the disease is transformed into mental pathology, a compulsive need to fill oneself and to discipline the aberrant body. This compulsion sometimes returns as the repressed desire to fall back into potentially life-threatening habits: the scenes describing bingeing and vomiting in *Wasted* convey the seduction of the condition for the narrating "I," potentially undermining the reader's confidence in the breakthrough to healing that she narrates.

Narratives of mental illness are now shifting from stories by or for medical practitioners and therapists in ways that generate new and insightful encounters. Particularly in graphic memoirs, Erin La Cour and Anna Poletti observe, these narratives are increasingly directed to "reader-patient-people-artist-thinkers reflect[ing] on the diverse and dynamic forms of reading that the patient as 'ordinary reader' of graphic medicine brings to the illness and disability narratives of others" (19).

CAPTIVITY NARRATIVE

An overarching term for any narrative told by someone who is being, or has been, held captive by some capturing group. This category includes

Indian captivity narratives, ex-slave and piracy narratives, spiritual autobiographies, UFO stories, convent captivity stories, and narratives of seduction. Indian captivity narratives, the stories of non-Indians captured by Indigenous people such as Mary Jemison's as-told-to *A Narrative of the Life of Mrs. Mary Jemison,* have since the sixteenth century numbered in the thousands, many written by or about women. They were produced predominantly in what is now the United States, though some were produced in Canada, Australia, and by Africans who escaped from slaveholders, and some published in languages other than English. According to Kathryn Zabelle Derounian-Stodola, "the Indian captivity narrative concerns the capture of an individual or several family members . . . and its plot is most commonly resolved with the captive's escape, ransom, transculturation, or death" (xi). Archival and interpretive work in the paradoxes of identification and reconversion in captivity narrative as a genre of public testimony is likely to rewrite the field of autobiography studies in many modern languages as literary scholars and historians jointly recover more of these narratives.

Contemporary victims of human trafficking narrate a version of captivity stories about their exploitation and that of millions of women, men, and children around the world who have been held by traffickers and their clients for the sex trade and the labor and marriage markets. These stories are gathered on websites mounted by NGOs active in advocating for victims, such as "The Exodus Road."

CASE STUDY

In medical parlance, this term designates a life narrative that is gathered into a dossier in order to identify and diagnose a disease or disorder. Susan Wells tracks the history of the case report, which "was written retrospectively, usually included references to the literature, and articulated the specific case within the context of the ongoing conversation among professionals about issues of diagnosis and treatment." She points to the exigent nature of the case report and its hybridity as an amalgam of "adjacent genres" such as social science discourse, the medical case study, and fiction (355). This mode of life reporting is often associated with Freud's extended analyses of various patients with symptoms such as hysteria and gender-identity disorder. The treatment begins with the patient's production of a story of unhappiness and illness. The unsatisfactory nature of this first narrative usually lets the analyst

Kinds of Life Narratives 217

"see his way about the case" (Freud, 66) in gaps, hesitations, inconclusiveness, and changes in dates, times, and places. That is, narrating patients present clues to another story they are unable to tell. Freud's emphasis is on making, with patients, a new and coherent narrative that, in giving them possession of a past life, enables them to become agents in their stories. Another sense of the case study is discussed in *Landscape for a Good Woman* by Steedman, who critiques its ability to embed gendered social history in the story of rural working-class British mothers (130–31).

CELEBRITY LIFE NARRATIVE

Annually, hundreds of autobiographies of celebrities are published, many with the aid of acknowledged or unacknowledged ghostwriters, by sports figures, musicians, movie stars, military heroes, politicians, online influencers, and other public figures. In the twenty-first century, a flood of narratives by musicians who earned fame in the 1960s, 1970s, and 1980s has hit the bookstores. Such pop singers as The Notorious B.I.G., Bob Dylan, Keith Richards, Barbra Streisand, Eric Clapton, Patti Smith, Jay-Z, and Bruce Springsteen have produced impressive best-selling autobiographical stories in which self-reflection figures prominently and has revived their music. Celebrity sports life writers—from Lisa Leslie and Kareem Abdul-Jabbar in basketball to Jim Bouton in baseball and Abby Wambach and Megan Rapinoe in soccer—narrate their ascendancy in ways that often project positive role models for young people, particularly boys and girls of color. Many celebrity memoirs, however, are formulaic narratives that capitalize on fleeting fame by immersing readers in industry gossip and the vicarious pleasures of a fantasy world of sex, drugs, and rock 'n' roll. Indeed, some celebrity memoirs are stories of people who are famous for being famous, with life and story a recursive formation, as in the case of Paris Hilton, Kim Kardashian, and other recent influencers. Their memoirs are both fertilized by and drawn from their blogs and tweets, as well as fanzines devoted to their words, dress, and doings.

Celebrity narratives can, however, be genuinely innovative life writing. Dylan's *Chronicles* resists linearity in narrating his rise to fame. He employs different voices in successive chapters and focuses on particulars—a friend's bookshelves in the East Village, surreal encounters during a motorcycle trip—to shape, possibly with a ghostwriter, a personal story as engagingly poetic and open-ended as his song lyrics and as shifting in personae as Todd Haynes's biopic, *I'm Not There,* in which six actors play him. Patti Smith's *Just Kids,* with its moving double portrait of her own and photographer Robert Mapplethorpe's rise from destitution to artistic fame, interspersed with her narration of bohemian New York in the 1970s, deservedly won the nonfiction National Book Award in the United States in 2010. She has followed it with three more memoirs mixing personal reflection on writing and photography with stories of other artists, ranging from Arthur Rimbaud to Sam Shepard, that share features of autotheory memoirs of our times.

Celebrity sports life writers often link their own experience in overcoming obstacles with reflections on sports culture stardom, defining a code of ethics for their subsequent careers. Bryan Curtis, who has referred to these narratives as "jockography" and "ludicrous performance art," has described the formula of many: A sports memoir begins with an account of the athlete's most memorable play, chronicles how sports got him, her, or them through an unhappy childhood, and tracks the rise to major league stardom. Of course, most sports memoirs are ghostwritten, but Curtis maintains that some, like *Man in the Middle* by John Amaechi, the NBA player who detailed the trials of being gay in the homophobic Utah Jazz basketball locker room, intervene in larger contemporary discussions. Sports memoir, then, is a hybrid form of life writing combining generic templates such as the conversion, coming-of-age, overcoming-of-origins, and physical limitations stories with the trajectory of early hope, achievement, disillusionment, and distilled wisdom.

Some celebrity memoirs serve larger purposes. In *Life on the Run,* his classic journal of twenty days in a basketball season, Bill Bradley launched his political career. In *Days of Grace,* Arthur Ashe, with the help of biographer Arnold Rampersad, reflected on his career as a Black tennis star, cut short by HIV/AIDS he contracted from blood transfusions for heart surgery, and linked his reflections to a critique of political struggles ranging from gay rights to apartheid and American racism. Many sports memoirs, however, are likely to stress the importance of "the team" as a collectivity with a shared aspiration to transcend individual limits in pursuit of recognition and triumph. As Michael W. Young and Noel Stanley point out, an emphasis on competitive achievement in sports memoirs has "tended to encapsulate, in a brutally simple way,

Kinds of Life Narratives

the success/failure fulcrum of public lives" (839). For some prominent athletes, as for movie stars and musicians, narration of involvement in the cult of celebrity focuses on an inability to live the "star" life that turns dream into nightmare and reflects ambivalence about stardom.

Celebrity life writing may be the literary equivalent of handprints in the sidewalk of Grauman's Chinese Theatre in Los Angeles, a desire to leave a permanent trace of body and moment. It may seem the titillating fare of a culture enamored with larger-than-life, flamboyant bad boys and wild girls. But recent fandom interest in the outpouring of celebrity lives around the world makes clear that it has become a lens for studies of personhood, everyday life, and public fantasy. Along with that outpouring come thorny issues related to what Hannah Yelin terms the "wider celebrity machine," the assemblage of celebrities and ghostwriters, marketers and platform affordances, market forces and readers' desires for revelations, story templates and gender politics *(Celebrity Memoir)*.

See also "Political Life Narrative."

COLLABORATIVE AND COLLECTIVE LIFE WRITING

These terms indicate the production of an autobiographical text by more than one person through one of the following processes: the as-told-to narrative in which an informant tells an interviewer the story of his, her, or their life, as in *Black Elk Speaks*; the ghostwritten narrative recorded, edited, and perhaps expanded by an interviewer, as in many political and celebrity autobiographies; a coproduced or collectively produced narrative in which individual speakers are not specified or in which one speaker is identified as representative of the group; the pooled personal stories that shape and assemble a storytelling community, now often through the affordances of online platforms.

Collaborative narratives are multiply mediated by the interviewer and editor, and often two or more parties are included in the production of the published story, particularly when translation is required. In collaborations, despite assurances of coproduction, power relations between the teller and recorder/editor are often asymmetrical, with the literarily skilled editor controlling the disposition of the informant's narrative material. (See also chapter 3.)

But some collaborations in human rights projects are developing new modes. *Playing with Fire: Feminist Thought and Activism through Seven Lives in India,* for example, initially circulated in Hindi but has reached an international audience in English translation. It was collectively authored by a group of Indian women in Uttar Pradesh, India, called the Sangtin Writers, together with a group leader and with feminist scholar Richa Nagar. Over three years, they developed a collaborative life narrative with a "we" voice that both distinguished individual experiences and blended common experiences into a reflective critical voice. *Playing with Fire* narrates the group's journey or *yatra* to understand their lives through extensive memory work, writing, discussion-based revision, and theoretical analysis. By situating their personal life histories collectively, the nine women address the forms of domination of an NGO that, in their view, spoke as the voice of Indian women in the region yet erased their experience and in some cases the complexities of their caste positions. This experience-based collective method aimed not, as ethnographic projects typically did, to leave them vulnerable to overwriting or appropriation as voiceless subalterns. Rather, the group's personal journals and Nagar's extended postscript reflect on the problematics of who can produce knowledge in a postcolonial context and what methods enable this process. *Playing with Fire* maps multiple stages of the process by which the "memory work" of writing or telling personal stories may contribute not just to individual transformation but to a collectivized self-understanding with potential to intervene in a repressive public sphere.

Collective narratives emerging from mass movements may employ varied methods to collect stories or data and shape a community with potential for narrative activism. As Helga Lenart-Cheng observes in tracking "story revolutions" from the Enlightenment to the present, assembling large numbers of personal stories as textual anthologies has long been a means of activating political consciousness among individuals and forming communities of solidarity across differences. Now, online collections of narratives are ubiquitous on and across platforms that assemble individuals' experiential histories through processes that are interactive and iterative, employing online versioning to create new, evolving communities.

COMING-OF-AGE LIFE NARRATIVE (SOMETIMES CALLED AUTOBIOGRAPHICAL BILDUNGSROMAN)

Life narratives of childhood and education are linked to the genre of the bildungsroman, which emerged in the late eighteenth and early

Kinds of Life Narratives

nineteenth centuries in such autobiographical novels as Dickens's *Great Expectations* and Goethe's *Wilhelm Meister's Apprenticeship*. It is often regarded as an "apprenticeship novel" narrating the development and social formation of a young person who, after extensive travels and encounters, learns to be integrated in a socially acceptable manner. Its plot involves escape from a repressive family and schooling to a journey through the wider world, where encounters with a series of mentors, romantic involvements, and entrepreneurial ventures lead the protagonist to reevaluate assumptions and accept a more constrained role in the bourgeois social order, often by renouncing an ideal or passion and embracing heteronormative social arrangements. Childhood memoirs may focus on lessons learned in the formation of consciousness, such as Russell Baker's *Growing Up*, Jean-Paul Sartre's *The Words*, Simone de Beauvoir's *Memoirs of a Dutiful Daughter*, Maya Angelou's *I Know Why the Caged Bird Sings*, and Richard Wright's *Black Boy*. Many writers narrate their formation as artists (in the related mode of the *Künstlerroman* or novel of artistic development), as does James Joyce in his autobiographical novel, *Portrait of the Artist as a Young Man*, or a memoir modeled in part on it, such as Edna O'Brien's *Country Girl: A Memoir*.

Many coming-of-age narratives trace journeys originating in working-class families that track the dynamics of socioeconomic status and mobility. In his trilogy, *Autobiography of Maxim Gorky: My Childhood, In the World, My Universities*, Maxim Gorky narrates a wide range of jobs and encounters that were formative for himself and exemplary of Russia's move toward socialism. Since the mid-nineteenth century, in both the United States and England, the industrial revolution and the rise of union movements, as well as increasing literacy, led working-class men and women to begin telling their stories, sometimes collectively. In *A New England Girlhood* (1889), Lucy Larcom details a typical story: poverty due to family indebtedness; childhood and young adulthood years working in the Lowell Mills, where her identity and class affiliation began to shift significantly; and her early writing career under the mentorship of poet John Greenleaf Whittier. She eventually became a poet, teacher, and founder of a literary magazine. In her preface, she poignantly recalls her childhood narrated "I": "I can see very distinctly the child that I was, and I know how the world looked to her, far off as she is now. . . . I have enjoyed bringing her back, and letting her tell her story, almost as if she were somebody else. I like her better than I did when I was really a child" (3).

American narratives of working-class Copenhagen immigrants began emerging early in the twentieth century. Jacob Riis, in *The Making of an American,* writes and photographs his growing up as a Danish immigrant on the streets of New York from the perspective of an assimilated American, as does Dutch immigrant Edward William Bok in his Franklinesque *The Americanization of Edward Bok.* However, as Regenia Gagnier observes, many women's working-class autobiographies adapted a middle-class autobiographical model, with its norms of familial, romantic, and financial success, at great psychic cost to the writer. In her view, the clash of enfranchised middle-class norms with disenfranchised working-class circumstances produced "narratives of disintegrated personality" whose buried counternarrative was the cost of individualist ideology for those positioned at the margins (52).

Some autobiographical writers, many of working-class origin, resist viewing childhood as an uplifting education; conversely, they represent the experience as a painful struggle that yields, at best, tales of survival. Although in *Educated,* Tara Westover escapes her childhood experience, such a struggle characterizes her early years. Similarly, Harry Crews's *A Childhood: The Biography of a Place,* rereleased as a Penguin Classic and acclaimed as "flawless, one of the finest ever written by an American," is a tough tale of growing up with tenant-farmer parents in hardscrabble rural Georgia, where the youngster suffered severe physical afflictions in his first eight years, as well as routine family violence and struggles with unrelenting poverty (Cep, 71–75). Crews observed about writing the memoir, "It almost killed me, but it purged nothing" (cited in Cep, 75). Tove Ditlefson's linked memoir trilogy, *Childhood, Youth, Dependency,* narrates her coming of age, mostly in present-tense prose detailing encounters in a mid-century working-class Copenhagen.

Narratives of education may also explore the psychic landscapes of a lost past (see Coe; Rooke) and of repressed childhood trauma, abuse, and patriarchal oppression, as, for example, in nineteenth-century narratives by formerly enslaved African Americans, a popular form in the United States and Europe. Unquestionably, the most widely read enslavement narratives now are *Narrative of the Life of Frederick Douglass* and

Kinds of Life Narratives

Incidents in the Life of a Slave Girl by Harriet Jacobs.[2] Both authors made powerful rhetorical interventions in the repressive institution of slavery by writing stories of emerging from enslavement through self-education and efforts to enter the society of free American citizens—sometimes failed, as in Jacobs's case—while exposing the structural violence of the slavery economy and Christian practices. Often, narratives of enslavement were told to an amanuensis or published with the help of someone in an abolitionist society. Some, such as Olaudah Equiano's *Interesting Narrative* and the *Narrative of Sojourner Truth,* were written in installments and sold during reading tours, in Sojourner Truth's case netting her enough to purchase a home in Michigan.

Theorist Joseph Slaughter argues that the "realist" novel form of the bildungsroman not only projects and naturalizes its protagonist as a self-determining individual with rights, but also incorporates its readers into the social sphere of the nation-state; thus, the form itself "becomes both a plot imposed by force and a potential space of refuge from and redress of state violence against the individual" (347). Contemporary postcolonial writers employing the form typically reshape the story of education as one of becoming alienated subjects of double legacies in ways that interrogate the form's ideology of development, self-determination, and incorporation into the new nation. In the last half century, the narrative of development has been taken up by women and other minoritized or marginalized persons whose life narratives consolidate a sense of emerging identity and an increased role in public life, as in Esmeralda Santiago's *When I Was Puerto Rican* or Frank McCourt's *Angela's Ashes.* That education may be predominantly negative, however, in that assimilation into a dominant culture may remain unattainable or produce alienation from the home community, as in Richard Rodriguez's *Hunger of Memory.*

In some women's writing, the plot of development culminates not in integration but in awakening to gender-based limitations (see Fuderer, 1–6), as occurs in Ken Bugul's *The Abandoned Baobab: The Autobiography of a Senegalese Woman,* set at the cultural crossroads of metropole and postcolony, where conflicting concepts of education and social value collide. Yet, in other narratives of the developing world, the awakening may be to how constraints on gender-based education may be overcome. The title of *I Am Malala: The Story of the Girl Who Stood Up for Education and Was Shot by the Taliban* by Nobel Prize Laureate Malala Yousafzai tells of her experience with repressive state violence and her support by a father who championed his courageous daughter. Its narrative arc concludes with her call, while completing her schooling in Britain, to strengthen girls' education worldwide. The book-club discussions on which Azar Nafisi based *Reading Lolita in Tehran* brought several classics of Western literature to Iranian women. Its prequel/sequel *The Republic of Imagination: America in Three Books,* similarly invites American women to explore specific classic works of literature in order to enter the republic of "free minds." In *Things I've Been Silent About: Memories of a Prodigal Daughter,* her 2008 memoir of growing up in a prominent but argumentative Iranian family during the revolution, Nafisi relates diverse stories of how she learned to negotiate their conflicting stories of education and women's place. Exploring Iranian women's diasporic life writing, including memoirs, documentary films, prison testimonials, and graphic novels, Nima Naghibi observes that such works, yoking remembering to claims of human rights, do the work of "*righting,* or of setting right, historical injustice through the act of writing life narratives" (15).

Gayatri Spivak has discussed the case of postcolonial women writers for whom traditional autobiography has not been a congenial genre for self-reflexivity, given its association with universal individualism and possessive masculinity. Alternatively, women may turn to the form of first-person fiction in writing personal stories that make them less vulnerable to exoticization by metropolitan readers or to shaming within their own cultures. Michelle Cliff's *Abeng* and *No Telephone to Heaven,* Maryse Condé's *I, Tituba, Black Witch of Salem,* Nawal El Saadawi's *Woman at Point Zero,* Mariama Bâ's *So Long a Letter,* Assia Djebar's *Women of Algiers in Their Apartment,* and Calixthe Beyala's *Your Name Shall Be Tanga* are coming-of-age novels by postcolonial women writers who tactically use first- or third-person narrative to both displace and engage personal experience. Françoise Lionnet, in reading these novels autobiographically, observes the permeable boundary they set up between life narrative and the novel (*Autobiographical Voices,* 92–93). American Dave Eggers's writing of Valentino Achak Deng's autobiographical story as a Sudanese "lost boy" in the novel *What Is the What* also encodes layers of personal reference in ways that both incorporate the bildungsroman form and deflect its traditional norms.

Kinds of Life Narratives

There is, then, no simple or unitary way to gloss the myriad narrative trajectories that autobiographical stories of childhood and education may take.

CONFESSION

An oral or written narrative, the confession is addressed to an interlocutor who listens, judges, and has the power to absolve. Confession was originally doubly addressed, to a higher power and to a confessor. In Augustine's narrative, the double address of the confession has been directed to God and the human reader who needs a narrative explanation of sinfulness and redemption. As Stephen Spender argues in "Confessions and Autobiography," the penitent's "purpose is to tell the exact truth about the person whom he knows most intimately . . . himself. His only criterion is naked truth: and usually his truth is naked without being altogether true" (118). Further, he adds, "all confessions are from subject to object, from the individual to the community or creed. Even the most shamelessly revealed inner life pleads its cause before the moral system of an outer, objective life" (120). Confessional life narrative may be a record of some kind of error transformed; it may also be the narrator's attempt to reaffirm communal values or justify their absence (121).

Daniel B. Shea's *Spiritual Autobiography in Early America* explores the uses of confession in Puritan narrative, particularly the conversion experience, and suggests how it is a foundational discourse of American public culture. Rita Felski, in a chapter titled "On Confession" in her book *Beyond Feminist Aesthetics: Feminist Literature and Social Change,* understands feminist confession as a public mode of self-presentation that constitutes feminist community and a counter-knowledge founded on the authority of experience. Michel Foucault extensively explores how confession in the West has served to discipline subjects by managing illegitimate desire and producing knowledge about sexuality (*History of Sexuality,* 58). His analysis has been productively applied to contemporary modes of the confessional such as talk shows, where people's obsessive confessing ritually enacts disorderly desires and behaviors, as well as their containment by the format of the talk show itself (see J. Peck). Now, scholars from a variety of disciplines, including communications, media studies, cultural studies, and literary studies, focus on social networks as diverse platforms for confession and the Internet more broadly as a confessionally oriented environment.

CONVERSION NARRATIVE

This narrative mode is structured around a radical transformation from a faulty or debased "before" self to an enlightened "after" self. The typical pattern involves a fall into a troubled and sensorily confused "dark night of the soul," followed by a "call for help," a process of transformation, and a journey to a "new Jerusalem" or place of membership in an enlightened community of like believers. Conversion experiences as varied as those recounted in John Bunyan's *Grace Abounding*, Frederick Douglass's *Narrative*, Cardinal John Henry Newman's *Apologia Pro Vita Sua: Being a History of His Religious Opinions*, Malcolm X's *Autobiography*, e. e. cummings's *The Enormous Room*, Elizabeth Gilbert's *Eat, Pray, Love* (which she calls "a religious *conversation*" [16]), Ayaan Hirsi Ali's *Infidel* and *Heretic*, and Alcoholics Anonymous narratives share these paradigmatic features. Conversion may be neither definitive nor final, as Malcolm X's chronicling of his multiple conversions suggests.

In the United States, another kind of conversion narrative has emerged as people recovering from addiction to white nationalist hatred of others seek to extract themselves from the movement. As noted above under Addiction Narrative, such examples as Arno in *My Life after Hate* and Picciolini in *White American Youth: My Descent into America's Most Violent Hate Movement—and How I Got Out* trace efforts to come to terms with hate-driven movements through critiquing their immersion in them. Internationally, narratives that chart a movement from infatuation with the intoxicating calls of such extremist movements as ISIS to disillusionment with its brutality and repressiveness also suggest a mode of ideological conversion. In politically polarized times, these memoirs not only suggest paths toward individual recovery and rehabilitation, but pose the possibility of new kinds of community.

DIARY

A form of periodic life writing, the diary is a daily or regular recording of events and impressions, incorporating the writer's or artist's responses to them. Exploring the contemporary uses of diaries, Kylie Cardell characterizes diary writing as "a regularly scheduled block of 'creative' time" (*De@r World*, 31). While some diaries may seem incoher-

Kinds of Life Narratives

ent or haphazard, they "gather force by accretion of experience, always chronological" (Roorbach, 163). Through the force of that accretion, the diarist's voice, suggests Margot Culley, acquires a recognizable narrative persona (12), from Samuel Pepys to Virginia Woolf to Salam Pax in *The Clandestine Diary of an Ordinary Iraqi*, taken from his blogs, and Phoebe Gloeckner in *The Diary of a Teenage Girl: An Account in Words and Pictures*. Culley observes that the diary form is fragmented, revisionary, and ever in process, although the self-constructions in the pages of a written diary are available to the diarist for later viewing, comment, and emendation (20). The actual or perceived immediacy of the genre derives from diarists' lack of foreknowledge about the outcome of the plot of their lives, which creates a "series of surprises to writer and reader alike" (21). As Suzanne L. Bunkers and Cynthia A. Huff observe in their extended and informative overview, diaries incorporate a mode of reflexive critical discourse into the practices of diary keeping.

Critics sometimes distinguish the diary from the journal, arguing that the journal as a form tends to be more a public record, less intimate and confessional than the diary. But Lejeune, in many books and essays of recent decades on the diary form—among them the French diaries of ordinary people, of girls in the nineteenth century, of Anne Frank, and online diaries, which he began studying in 1999—does not make a distinction between the diary and the journal. Regarding diary writing as "an immense field, as yet largely unexplored" and "a social outcast, of no fixed theoretical address," Lejeune asserts it is fundamentally different from autobiography in its orientation toward futurity and the moment, a difference that does not make the form less complex ("Practice of the Private Journal," 202). For Lejeune "the private diary is a *practice*" (187, our emphasis) with a wide range of functions and forms, which may incorporate many kinds of writing, drawing, documents, and objects (191). Fundamentally, every diary postulates a reader, an other to whom it is addressed. Thus, perhaps never truly "sincere" or secret, the diary is "motivated by a search for communication, by a will to persuasion" (192). Lejeune urges future research on several topics: who keeps diaries and their attitudes about them; how one reads another's and one's own journals; and the rights and duties of the diarist (190–200).

The practice of diary writing has a variety of efficacies for the diarist. Annie Ernaux's diary-keeping throughout her life has created a personal archive that she regularly draws on as a more reliable means than memory to document events in her own past, and that of France, that are precisely recounted in her life narratives. Indeed, many graphic memoirs depict diary and comic frames in a kind of dialogical interaction, suggesting that the diary is not just a "source" but a primary form of self-presentation. British graphic and performance artist Bobby Baker described to an interviewer how her diary art was a "defiant personal way of coping" and "became a 'raison d'être'" when she was struggling with mental distress (Kellaway). And Lejeune quips, "It was up to me to show myself some hospitality. I sought refuge in paper" ("Lucullus Dines with Lucullus," 331).

Momentous or life-shattering events may stimulate a spate of diary writing by ordinary people that becomes a kind of collective testimonial to a world event and forms a corpus of first-person responses. For instance, large numbers of refugees seeking asylum around the globe may be moved to communicate their circumstances and struggles in smartphone messages sent from boundary zones, boats, or detention camps. Kurdish-Iranian journalist and Manus Island detainee Behrouz Boochani kept his "Diary of a Disaster" as dated entries on his phone in 2019; in English translation, it was published in *The Guardian* online. Gillian Whitlock observes that "'Diary of a Disaster' is several things: a chronicle of the occupation; a performative space where the diary narrative enables a visceral and intimate account" of the resistance of the men detained on the island ("Disaster," 179); and a demonstration of how "the transformative possibilities of the almost simultaneous act of diary writing online and the act of reading" catalyze "a practice of communicative ethics, creating a polemical and tactical intervention into debates about the war on terror and the invasion of Iraq" (178).

Similarly, during the COVID pandemic, diaries recording the progress of the epidemic included many written or drawn chronicles of symptoms experienced by sufferers and their relatives, some of which were published in newspapers, journals, or blogs. Among them are Jeff Holland's droll "Dear Diary 2020"; Alison Bechdel's daily cartoon drawings "now that all the days are really blurring into one another" (quoted in Loos F-8); autographic artist Lynda Barry's drawings "Documenting All the Small Things That Are Easily Lost"; and the drawn or written expressions of ordinary people posted online that Amelia Nierenberg discusses as "The Quarantine Diaries" of a worldwide "emergent moment." Teju

Kinds of Life Narratives

Cole kept a periodic photo-diary of his kitchen counter from March until early November of 2020 that juxtaposed photographs to written reflections about the precarity of life, anxiety about the upcoming election, memories of his childhood in Nigeria and early years in the United States, and critiques of Western colonialism, as well as pages from the late eighteenth-century cookbook of a slaveholding family in Cambridge, Massachusetts, where he was living, that was published as *Golden Apple of the Sun.*

Another aspect of the diary form is engaged by Liz Stanley and Helen Dampier, who use the term "simulacrum diary" to characterize diaristic texts in which "the moment of writing" is not synonymous with "the scene of what is written about" (25). Applying Jean Baudrillard's concept of the simulacrum, their focus is on texts that "dispute notions of the real" as neither un/real nor a mis/representation but "a replication of the thing itself" in ways that disrupt the polarity of original/copy or real/fake (40). Their example is the case of Boer-activist Johanna Brandt-Van Warmelo, who, in *The Petticoat Commando,* reproduces and arranges passages from a diary she had written as a caseworker in a concentration camp during the South African war in 1901. Despite its belated writing, *The Petticoat Commando* effectively "mimics . . . the 'present-ness' and temporal immediacy of diaries written at the time of the events they describe" (41), making it difficult to differentiate the "real" (a private manuscript) from the "copy" (a public book) and blurring the categories of the authentic and inauthentic, the true and the fictive.

In sum, diary, once regarded as a transparent site of diurnal chronicling, is now theorized as a complex practice of life writing, as Cardell, Lejeune, Rebecca Hogan, Suzanne Bunkers, Cynthia Huff, Helen M. Buss, and others have argued. Recovering and reading often-unpublished life writing requires sophisticated interpretive strategies to explore the contexts of composition and circulation. And the outpouring of online diaries, in visual and written modes, is radically changing the conditions, terms, and theorizing of the diary as a form.

DISABILITY, ILLNESS, AND DIVERSELY EMBODIED NARRATIVES

The body, with its senses and materiality, has long been a central site for remembering the past and envisioning a future. But, as G. Thomas

Couser observes, in the latter decades of the twentieth century some conditions of disease or disability have generated an extensive corpus of life narratives: on breast cancer, HIV/AIDS, deafness, paralysis (*Recovering Bodies*).[3] He points out that blindness, depression, autism, and, arguably, addiction, considered as an illness or disability, could be added to the list, as well as some that seem resistant to verbal representation, such as early-stage Alzheimer's.

Before the disability rights movement became active and successful, many life writers tended to portray themselves as victims and figure disability as a personal illness or tragedy to be overcome by extraordinary effort. Those chronicling their journeys through illness, diagnosis, treatment, and survival shaped their experiences as stories of self-reinvention, as does Carolyn Gold in *When I Died: Rx for Traumatic Brain Injury*, about her long and difficult recovery from West Nile encephalitis. Couser suggests that such narratives of recovery offering hope and inspiration often situate bodies as recovered and revalued, even if the impairment or illness persists.

Recent generations of rights activists now assert that impaired individuals could be accommodated in society if cultural and infrastructural conditions were changed. They insist that the social ascription of "disability" is stigmatizing and degrading to those with impairments because discourses of disability reproduce ableist norms that encode the differences of those with various forms and degrees of ability as abnormative (Gerschick, 1264). As a shift in disability life writing ensued, the body was repositioned in the context of ableist norms. Susannah B. Mintz observes in *Unruly Bodies* that narratives now refuse the familiar scripts of inspiration and triumph-over-adversity to address "the simultaneous fact of the flesh and scriptedness of subjectivity . . . crafting embodied selves through the revisionary properties of language" (212). Now, many telling stories of illness, disability, and neurodiversity incorporate their critiques of regimes of normative embodiment, medical discourse, and diagnostic categorization into their narratives; and they situate individual cases within a critique of how structural racism puts certain populations at a disadvantage for treatment and resources. In "writing back" to the conventional victim narrative of wounded suffering, their narratives call for social change.

The narratives and performances of gay and transgender activists often engage how gendered and racialized bodies receive differential

Kinds of Life Narratives

treatment within both medical and larger cultural discourses as they claim an increasingly vocal and complex communal identity and public presence. The memoirs of HIV/AIDS sufferers are a case in point. Their narratives, entwining memories of caring and loving with arguments for destigmatizing the disease, also became an intervention in national and international debates about how to signify and respond to the HIV pandemic.

Writers living with cancer or other degenerative diseases, such as multiple sclerosis, may address cultural representations of the injured or modified female body as desexualized and enact or perform alternative subjectivities that claim the possibility of a fully sexual body distinct from its conventional representations. Examples include Audre Lorde in *The Cancer Journals* and *A Burst of Light,* Joyce Brabner and Harvey Pekar in the graphic memoir *Our Cancer Year,* Jo Spence in her photographic series *Putting Myself in the Picture,* Hannah Wilke in her installation project *Intra-Venus,* and Nancy Mairs in her collections of personal essays describing the experience of living with multiple sclerosis, and many other narratives. Narrators may serially track the writer's changing condition, as does actor and advocate Michael J. Fox in *No Time Like the Future: An Optimist Considers Mortality,* his third memoir, on aging and approaching mortality with progressively debilitating Parkinson's disease. Similarly, life narrators may narrate their experience of diseases that will foreclose their ability to continue the story, as Wendy Mitchell does in charting the progress of her own early-onset Alzheimer's disease in two narratives coauthored with Anna Wharton, *Somebody I Used to Know* and *What I Wish People Knew about Dementia.*

Activist narratives of illness and disability combine stories of loss and recovery with a call for increased funding for research, new modes of treatment, and more visibility for those on whom the cultural status of being unwhole, grotesque, or uncanny has been conferred. Simi Linton, in *My Body Politic,* observes how forming activist collectivities in disability studies aids people to resist being identified as pathological or abject. By acting collectively, they refuse a marginal location as outsiders and critique "how disability is represented in all kinds of texts—in literature, film, the annals of history" (Dorn). As Rosalia Baena observes, both she and Mary Felstiner in *Out of Joint* use an alternative discourse of disability to "consciously connect their private lives to the social history of disability in the last decades of the twentieth century" ("Disability

Memoirs," 135). In *Squint: My Journey with Leprosy,* for instance, social worker and activist José P. Ramirez Jr. chronicles his early struggles to find an adequate diagnosis for its increasingly severe symptoms and explores the cultural construction of the "leper" as a subject of God's punishment, rather than a person living with Hansen's disease. Such narrative acts of reclaiming a body stigmatized or objectified by medical science often resist naming the body as abnormative and critique notions of the damaged body as a social construction of Western medicine. Thus, writers with disabilities, when positioning themselves as subjects addressing the history of their own marginalization, can reframe their impairment by refusing the diagnosis of disability or stigmatized abnormality, although in this self-presentation one may risk making a spectacle of oneself. But as Norwegian writer Jan Grue, who has a debilitating form of spinal muscular atrophy that confines him to a wheelchair, remarks in *I Live a Life Like Yours: A Memoir* (trans. 2021): "At some point or other I stopped thinking about myself as someone who needed repairing" (quoted in Fox, "Thoughtful Memoir").

Post–traumatic stress disorder (PTSD) as a diagnostic category and lived experience is central to much contemporary life writing about recent wars, and often focused on the consequences of injury, including impairment to body or mind, adjustment to prostheses, and devastated personal lives. For example, the memoir by Bob and Lee Woodruff, *In an Instant: A Family's Journey of Love and Healing,* links the story of the severe head wound Bob Woodruff suffered while working as a foreign correspondent in Iraq and its aftermath to a critique of both medical intervention and American intervention in Iraq.

Some memoirists effectively convey the felt experience of living within the constraints and opportunities of a disabling condition. While Jean-Dominique Bauby's posthumously published memoir *The Diving Bell and the Butterfly* did not become the sensation in the Anglophone world that it became in France, Julian Schnabel's 2007 film of the book brought it to an international public. Because Bauby became a victim of "locked-in" syndrome after an auto accident left only his left eye unparalyzed, transcribing the memoir was a feat; he had to blink a code for the letters of each word of his story to an amanuensis. The narrative itself is a fierce effort not just to remember but to reinhabit moments of his past, impelled by the metaphor of self in his title, and to register some agency in a condition of seeming impossibility. Similarly, such life narratives

Kinds of Life Narratives

of dying as Harold Brodkey's *This Wild Darkness* and Anatole Broyard's *Thanatography: Intoxicated by My Illness* are vigorous narrations of the process of dying.

The subfield of graphic memoirs on illness and disability has become so large that a dedicated website on "graphic medicine," a term coined by Dr. Ian Williams, has been established as "a site that explores the interaction between the medium of comics and the discourse of healthcare" and advocates for "some sort of therapeutic potential" in using comics with patients; it is managed by an international collective including "academics, health carers, authors, artists, and fans of comics and medicine" ("Graphic Medicine"). Both comics and critical studies now abound. La Cour and Poletti observe that "graphic medicine discourse promotes comics as an important medium to depict interactions between individuals, their loved ones, a wide array of healthcare workers, and the health care system as scenes of intercultural, interdiscursive, and intergenerational encounter" (2). As Couser observes, the focus of graphic medicine is on "*taking* back the experience of somatic dysfunction from medical authority and *talking* back to medical discourse" ("Is There a Body?," 348). The boxes, panels, dialogue bubbles, and collages of the comics page offer visual affordances that engage readers in multiple ways with the body of the artist-author-patient and situate these viewers as witnesses to struggles that are materialized and personalized. For artist-authors with physical or psychic illnesses, making a graphic memoir can be cathartic. As comics artist Miriam Katin's persona quips: "if you are in . . . that situation and it hurts and say you can draw, then you must try and draw yourself out of it" (*Letting It Go,* 9). But recovery from illness is not always possible, as Jared Gardner observes in stressing the unique ability of graphic medicine: "with fragments, with fits and starts, with gaps and elisions" comics capture the experience of chronic illness as "one marked not by progress but by recurrence, repetition, and ellipses" ("Out of Sync," 41). And Nancy K. Miller notes their collective importance: "In picturing illness, graphic comics bring individual narratives, stories of pain—often hidden, embarrassing, silent—and chronic suffering into the public imagination, into the domain of social visibility" ("'Is This Recovery?,'" 55).

The Human Genome Project stimulated a new kind of illness narrative focused on the issue of life scripting, that is, the relationship of lived experience to the coding of the gene and genetic inheritance. Alice

Wexler's *Mapping Fate: A Memoir of Family, Risk, and Genetic Research* was one of the first memoirs to link living with Huntington's chorea to questions of how to live when one's life is predetermined beyond human agency. Expanding narrative possibilities into a hybrid memoir form, sociologist Jennifer Natalya Fink, in *All Our Families: Disability Lineage and the Future of Kinship*, entwines stories of her family members, some erased from the collective family story, with her study of the devastating effects of the Nazi selection system, founded in antisemitic, racist, and sexist ideology, of distinguishing the healthy from the "damaged" and "expendable." Observing the persistence of racist and sexist dynamics in the contemporary care system, she proposes a new ethic of care in which kinship and narratives of family lineage become more inclusive and mutually sustaining.

While some theorists have employed the term "autopathography" to characterize personal narratives about illness or disability that contest cultural discourses stigmatizing the writer as abnormal, aberrant, or in some sense pathological (see Hawkins on "pathography"), Couser proposes that such narratives be seen instead as "antipathological." His term *autosomatography* characterizes first-person illness narratives that critique social constructions of the disabled body and incorporate a counternarrative of survival and empowerment to reclaim the individual's or a loved one's body from the social stigmatization and depersonalization of medical discourse (personal correspondence with Julia Watson, June 20, 2000). The burgeoning field of disability and illness studies, from explorations of embodiment in medieval and early modern life writing to contemporary postcolonial memoirs, has been fueled by the work of such scholars as Couser and Susannah Mintz, notably in *Disability Experiences: Memoirs, Autobiographies, and Other Personal Narratives*, their collection of essays on two hundred narrative works written by persons with disabilities from 1470 to 2018. Other scholars of note, including Rosalia Baena, Tobin Siebers, Rosemarie Garland Thomson, Brenda Brueggemann, Lennard Davis, David D. Mitchell and Sharon Snyder, and Jina Kim, critique the disability/impairment distinction of earlier theorists and refine new approaches that engage forms of structural disadvantage such as precarity, dependency, and eco-destruction and contamination. Kim, for example, wages a "crip-of-color critique" at the intersection of "anti-racist, anti-capitalist, and feminist disability politics" and shifts the terms of analysis from disability to dependency

Kinds of Life Narratives

to illuminate the experience of living in the body at this contemporary moment when political, social, and administrative management and infrastructural distribution of help and health differentially value or devalue bodies. For Kim, crip-of-color critique "positions dependency as a node of critical departure, a horizon of potentiality, rather than a transparently pathological condition" (5).

Finally, leading medical schools have begun to develop curricula in what is now called narrative medicine that focus on doctor–patient relationships and equipping professionals to listen to and for patients' stories (see Charon). Narrative medicine asserts that empathic listening can facilitate a more informed and nuanced ethical response to patients and their conditions, and situate individual stories within emerging bioethical concerns.

See also "Addiction Narrative," "Autie-biography," and "Breakdown and Breakthrough Narrative."

ECOBIOGRAPHY, ECOCRITICISM, AND THE ANTHROPOCENE

Ecobiography, or *eco-autobiography,* as Peter F. Perreten terms it, charts human encounters with the specificity of place, its fortunes, conditions, geography, and ecology. It is not a new form. American naturalists John Muir and Edward Abbey in very different ways linked their life writing to stories of place and expressed what Lawrence Buell calls "the environmental imagination." In the autobiographical essays of *Desert Solitaire* and *The Monkey Wrench Gang,* for instance, Abbey represents nature as at times a congenial site from which to critique "civilized society" as wasteful, routinized, and bereft of imagination. He explores how being in places like the Grand Canyon generates bonds of affinity that enable his "gang" to awaken to new political possibilities about themselves as agents protective of a natural world who share an interest in disrupting "civilized" living. His *autotopography,* a concept usually linked to such visual modes as installation art, may be a useful way to think about acts of reading the "I" and its location through each other.

Ecobiographical writers link immersion in nature to expanded human possibility and emotional growth. In *Refuge,* for instance, Terry Tempest Williams suggests that the "wild" of natural place can reawaken the quiescent "wild" in humans. Writers also mine the connection of place to genealogical, communal, and national histories. Like many

Western life writers, Mary Clearman Blew reads herself as "bone deep in landscape" in *All but the Waltz: Essays on a Montana Family* (7). For William Kittredge the place of self-definition is eastern Oregon; for N. Scott Momaday, the West of Arizona's Indigenous territory. Much life writing by Indigenous Americans registers the deep connection of tribal identity to the land. In Australia and Canada, ecobiographers inhabit the space of the outback or reservation, marked with histories and permeated by Indigenous imagination, as a surround that signifies and offers sustaining identifications. For Indigenous Australian life writing the outback can be a source of cultural belonging offering an alternative history to the national story of assimilation produced by an official policy separating Indigenous children from their communities and families.

Life writing in dialogue with place also encompasses urban environments. The city as a space of history and memory that stirs life writing is celebrated in *Istanbul: Memories and the City* by Turkish Nobel Prize–winning writer Orhan Pamuk. Rescripting the shape of memoir through individual, historical, and photographic memories, Pamuk assembles an archive of the city drawn from its collective history during and after the Ottoman Empire, a familial memoir, and his story of coming of age as an artist. Capturing the shifting contours of the great city, he refracts the personal through the collective, the "I" through its spaces and places, to make a dense, textured, urban surround, and juxtaposes his prose with more than a hundred quarter-page black-and-white photographs embedded in the text. Haunted by both the city's mirroring and his sense of a doubled self, "another Orhan," Pamuk tracks how one recognizes oneself through a spatial other and asserts that what we think of as personal identity is already "the myths we tell about our first lives" (8). This chiasmic structure of reflection encapsulates the dialogical relation that life writers trace as autogeographers living in the world.

In the last decades, the vast scope of environmental crises has required radical reorientation to the fragility, precarity, and interconnectedness of the natural world in order to mobilize humanity around the work of eco-survival. At the beginning of the twenty-first century, former U.S. vice president Albert Gore's *An Inconvenient Truth: The Planetary Emergency of Global Warming and What We Can Do about It*, in both the best-selling book and the subsequent documentary, gravely marked the depth of the crisis for a broad public. Since then, ecobiography is often related to travel writing, as in Rory Stewart's *The Places*

Kinds of Life Narratives   237

in Between, which chronicles his experience of walking through a war-ravaged Afghanistan, where eco-destruction makes survival challenging. In *Desert Notebooks: A Road Map for the End of Time,* Ben Ehrenreich combines essay, travel narrative, reportage, and shamanic citation, invoking along the way "Mayan creation myths, anthropological accounts of the decimated Sioux, and Presidential tweets" in order "to chronicle humankind's destructive nature" and thereby situate himself both in the present and in a historical genealogy (quoted in "Briefly Noted"). Ecobiography may also focus on agricultural sustainability, as in Barbara Kingsolver's chronicle of her family's effort to live off the food produced on its and neighbors' farms for a year in *Animal, Vegetable, Miracle.* In *The Shepherd's Life* and *Pastoral Song: A Farmer's Journey* by James Rebanks, a third-generation farmer writes lyrically of the everyday struggles of small farmers to nurture nature and animals in a radically changing environment of global economic and climate change that threatens to render living an ethic of sustainability unsustainable.

Other narratives have emerged out of the paradox of living in and thinking beyond the Anthropocene in life narratives that adopt the attitude of "Ghomanidad": "a reframing of humanity from being, and viewing itself as, a force that is extractive to one that is regenerative and energizing" (Quante and Escott, "Ghomanidad").[4] In the posthumanist vision of *Finding the Mother Tree: Discovering the Wisdom of the Forest,* Suzanne Simard infuses her narrative of profession with an ethic of care that "begins by recognizing that trees and plants have agency. . . . By noting how trees, animals, and even fungi—any and all nonhuman species—have this agency, we can acknowledge that they deserve as much regard as we accord ourselves" (294).

Another mode of autobiographical narrative of ecocrisis analyzes how governments have disadvantaged poor and minority communities by inequitably calculating water and waste resources and allocating healthy and contaminated lands in ways that reflect racialized structures and policies. Mona Hanna-Attisha, a pediatric physician and the director of the pediatric residency program at a teaching hospital affiliated with Michigan State University, published a compelling memoir, *What the Eyes Don't See: The Story of Crisis, Resistance and Hope in an American City,* in which she links her struggle to protect babies from lead poisoning released into the water pipes of Flint, Michigan, to a recognition that "the very people responsible for keeping us safe care more about money and power than they care about us, or our children" (13). Similarly, in *Waste: One Woman's Fight against America's Dirty Secret,* Catherine Colman Flowers exposes the environmental degradation of Lowndes County, Alabama, where she grew up and narrates her process of becoming educated as an activist.

For fuller explorations of ecology and narrative, see Phillips; Buell, *The Environmental Imagination*; and Glotfelty and Fromm.

ETHNIC AND POSTETHNIC LIFE NARRATIVE

A mode of autobiographical narrative that emerged in ethnic communities within or across nations, this kind negotiates ethnic identification around multiple pasts and "multiple, provisional axes of organization" (S. Wong, 160). Within this larger category critics have differentiated immigrant from exile narratives. William Boelhower, following Werner Sollors, presents a transethnic schema of descent and consent through which to read immigrant narratives ("Making of Ethnic Autobiography"). But Sau-Ling Cynthia Wong, critiquing Boelhower's universal ascription of these patterns across ethnic and generational lines, suggests that such a scheme telescopes the experience of different generations into one universal pattern of transindividual ethnic subjectivity and fails to account for generational differences in the mediations of memory and "the historical particularities of various ethnic groups" (160). Narratives of exile inscribe a nomadic subject, set in motion for a variety of reasons and now inhabiting cultural borderlands, who may or may not return "home" but who necessarily negotiates cultural spaces of the in-between where "hybrid, unstable identities" are rendered palpable through the negotiation "between conflicting traditions—linguistic, social, ideological" (Woodhull, 100).

Immigrant narratives and narratives of exile are genres enabling formerly marginal or displaced ethnic and racialized subjects to explore the terms of their cultural identities and their diasporic and transnational allegiances, as Alfred Hornung's work in transnational American studies explores.[5] They aim to reform ethnic subjects, sometimes through assimilation, as in the life narratives of Mary Antin and Edward Bok, and sometimes to revolution, as in Emma Goldman's *Living My Life.* Recently, new kinds of narratives explore a postethnic notion of identity that challenges the assumption of ethnic identity as fixed in place, history, and culture. Postethnicity narratives shift the ground of reference for identity

Kinds of Life Narratives 239

in several ways. They unhinge the relationship of individual memory to the master narrative of a particular community. They question notions of inherent belonging and posit communities that are multiracial. Some of these narratives, like Barack Obama's *Dreams from My Father,* explore biracial heritage, parentage, and identity. Similar trajectories are traced in Gregory Howard Williams's *Life on the Color Line: The True Story of a White Boy Who Discovered He Was Black*; Faith Adielé's *Meeting Faith*; James McBride's *The Color of Water: A Black Man's Tribute to His White Mother*; and Rebecca Walker's *Black, White, and Jewish: Autobiography of a Shifting Self.* Natasha Trethewey's Pulitzer Prize–winning *Native Guard* is a book of poems engaging her heritage as a biracial woman whose Black mother was murdered by her white stepfather when she was a young girl. This narrative is extensively developed in her *Memorial Drive: A Daughter's Memoir.* Other postethnicity narratives explore the shifting meanings of whiteness in changing ethnic communities. In Paul Clemens's *Made in Detroit,* the meanings of being white in Detroit undergo a radical shift after 1970 that requires Clemens to rethink his status as "minority."

See "Geographies of Life Narrative."

FAMILY NARRATIVES: GENEALOGICAL, FILIAL, AND GENERATIONAL

Historically, autobiographical narratives of family and filiation have assumed the centrality of the family as the bedrock of social organization. Over the last half century and certainly in the West, however, a growing cultural sense has arisen that "the family" as an institution is under pressure because of smaller family size, women's increasing participation in work and public life, greater mobility producing immigrant and diasporic formations, and, more recently, the rise of gay marriage and assertions of gender and sexual fluidity. New kinds and configurations of families are taking shape, prompting new models of family narrative responsive to readers' interests. Thus, narratives of family may trace complex genealogies linking one generation of the family to another. Moreover, in an era of confessional memoir, readers are attracted to stories focused on the intimate domain of family life, in all its dysfunctional variations, and relish their exposure of family secrets.[6]

Narratives of family can emerge from burgeoning genealogical research, enabled by access to vast archives of documents available online and the aggregating speed and power of search engines. As a method for charting family history, genealogy locates, authenticates, and organizes personal identity by constructing a family tree of descent. It thereby reinforces the coherence of the family unit as a powerful form of social and relational identity. Its key concept is the pedigree of ancestral evidence based on documents and generational history and verified through fixed protocols, such as trees and charts. Genealogical projects recover the recorded past, which they can verify as official. They focus on the objective documentation of relationship, not on the subjective stories family members remember and recite.[7]

While genealogical research enables family members to reconstruct a collective history of their ancestors and their movement across lands and centuries, its projects can also invite a critique, implicit or explicit, of the concept of genealogy itself. Shirlee Taylor Haizlip includes a genealogical chart in her family memoir *The Sweeter the Juice* but also speculates on those who disaffiliated themselves from their African origins by passing as white. In *One Drop: My Father's Hidden Life—a Story of Race and Family Secrets,* Bliss Broyard, who was raised as white, exposes the secret her father, Anatole Broyard, withheld from his family about their maternal Haitian ancestors; at the cost of abandoning his Black relatives, he chose to construct a professional life as a white writer and "hipster" critic. Raising the question "What am I?" after her father's death, Broyard addresses her own ingrained assumptions about the racial inferiority of African Americans, detailing her quest for her now-scattered Black relatives from New Orleans and her discovery of the cultural meanings of being Creole in the United States. Margo Jefferson has also responded to the perception that African Americans are inevitably working-class people lacking "culture" in *Negroland: A Memoir.* She narrates coming of age in an upper-crust Black family in Chicago that enjoyed status and privilege, while citing systemic efforts and everyday microaggressions aimed at denigrating them.

Many narratives of family seek to memorialize relationships to a parent, sibling, or child, someone with whom the author has had a long-standing affiliation. Couser observes that the vast majority of narratives of affiliation, from Edmund Gosse's *Father and Son* to Paul Auster's *The Invention of Solitude,* are written by sons and daughters about their fathers—imposing, absent, tyrannical, indifferent, duplicitous (see Couser, "Genre Matters"). Paternal absence is part of the story Barack

Kinds of Life Narratives   241

Obama tells in *Dreams from My Father,* of his African father who abandoned his American family to return to Kenya when Barack was two years old. In his autobiographical series, *A Child Called "It," The Lost Boy,* and *A Man Named Dave,* Dave Pelzer chronicles a childhood of abuse at the hands of his mother and his long years of recovery and learning to forgive that followed.

There are of course memoirs by daughters and sons who seek to recover a relationship with a lost mother, as does Michelle Zauner in *Crying in H Mart* or Mary Gordon in *Circling My Mother.* But memoirs of maternal filiation may also critique and disavow mothers, as do Ruth Reichl in *Not Becoming My Mother: And Other Things She Taught Me along the Way,* Rebecca Walker in *Black, White, and Jewish: Autobiography of a Shifting Self,* Kim Chernin in *In My Mother's House,* and Roy Kiyooka in *Mothertalk.* Narratives of filiation may also become a familial affair co-constructed by siblings, as in Sheila Ortiz Taylor and Sandra Ortiz Taylor's memoir of family, *Imaginary Parents.* David Parker observes that in intergenerational life narrative, there is an interplay between autonomy and relationality; that is, "a complex sense of moral obligation" about recasting the dominant family narrative as an ethical imperative (both "self-constituting" and "other-regarding") drives such storytelling (150).

Sometimes the narrative of filiation is a story of detection in which the son or daughter conducts a journey to reconstruct the life story of a lost or abandoning parent. For example, in Mary Gordon's *The Shadow Man: A Daughter's Search for Her Father,* she as daughter discovers through archival research and dogged pursuit of her father's past that he was not the man of family fantasy but an imposter and liar. Sometimes the motivation of narratives of affiliation is to seek imaginative reaffiliation, pursuing a desire to know and gain closeness to a parent who was unavailable in life. Sometimes the narrative is a struggle with grief that may provide consolation for loss. Paul Auster, in *The Invention of Solitude,* details his extended research into his deceased father's "other life," supplementing in writing the father who was largely unavailable to him.[7]

Other narratives of disaffiliation, however, are motivated by scandal, outing, and revenge on a parent for the failure of love, as Couser observes. They may seek to compose an objective and unsentimental record, as Annie Ernaux does in autoethnographical narratives of her childhood and family such as *A Man's Place, A Woman's Story,* and *Shame,* in which she discloses the complexity of her parental relationships and the unease and confusion she experienced as a child around the violence of her family's intimate encounters. Ernaux's relational narratives negotiate both the "stain" of traumatic memories, as Nancy K. Miller has explored, and the remaking of a personal archive of documents and stories as an autoethnographic project to distance the narrator from the entanglements of her past. In other family life narratives, issues of autobiographical ethics come to the fore, as children reveal family secrets in stories that may disturb living parents or siblings. Bechdel, for example, has alluded in interviews to the discomfort that her probing of her father's secret homosexual liaisons with boys and his putative suicide in her graphic memoir *Fun Home* caused her mother and brothers; her second autographic, *Are You My Mother? A Comic Drama,* attempts to contextualize and resolve this tension. For readers and reviewers, questions arise about the conflicting obligation memoirists have in preserving the privacy of family secrets versus pursuing an exploration of their own fraught pasts.

Another category of affiliation narrative has been labeled the "Motherhood Memoir," as in Anne Roiphe's *Fruitful: Living the Contradictions. A Memoir of Modern Motherhood,* in which women write about how becoming mothers has affected their working lives, sexuality, and writing lives. Some fathers, too, particularly in gay couples, write about parenting adopted children, as does Dan Savage in *The Kid: What Happened after My Boyfriend and I Decided to Go Get Pregnant.*

Adoption narratives, a special case of filiation stories, may reflect on ruptured birth parentage and conflicted parent–child affiliations as sons and daughters seek to reunite with a birth parent and recover an originary disrupted filiation through conscious quest (see "Adoption Narrative").[9]

Finally, familial narratives engaging the histories of oppressed and formerly colonized peoples may explore the rich matrix of family history, as in Lorna G. Goodison's lush evocation of family connections to one another and the land of Jamaica in *From Harvey River: A Memoir of My Mother and Her Island* or Edwidge Danticat's *Brother, I'm Dying,* focused on the difficult experiences of her father in the United States and her brother in Haiti. They may also link such connections to conditions in which family relations were violently sundered, as happened in Australia, Canada, and the United States, among other nations, when

Kinds of Life Narratives 243

official government policy separated Indigenous children from their families and traditional communities and relocated them in orphanages, residential schools, or white homes. In North America, such narratives span a century, from the "Sketches" of Lakota Sioux writer Zitkala-Ša at the turn of the twentieth century to Canadian narratives, such as Joseph Auguste (Augie) Merasty's *The Education of Augie Merasty: A Residential School Memoir* and Nicola I. Campbell's *Spíləxm: A Weaving of Recovery, Resilience, and Resurgence* in the early twenty-first century. In response to human rights activism and the United Nations International Decade of the World's Indigenous People, Australian stories of Stolen Generations of such children, now adults, became part of public life through the official collection of oral life stories and commission hearings and reports. For instance, Sally Morgan's widely read hybrid narrative *My Place* narrates her discovery that her mother and grandmother had passed as white, thereby obscuring the story of their aboriginal families and the grandmother's sexual exploitation by a white station owner. While she reconstructs the narrative of her mixed-race mother and her Indigenous grandmother, the identification of the grandfather and father remains hidden from history, even though implications of a white father and grandfather haunt the narrative. The film *Rabbit-Proof Fence* also brought to a worldwide audience the family narrative of Doris Pilkington (Nugi Garimara) who in *Follow the Rabbit-Proof Fence* narrated the history of the escape and long trek of three young Indigenous girls, one of them her mother, who struggle to return to their community in Western Australia after being forcibly taken away from family by the state. These family histories thus rewrite national narratives of settlement, colonization, and Indigenous erasure.

FILMIC AND VIDEO AUTOBIOGRAPHICAL WORKS

The field of cinematic self-representation now encompasses a vast terrain. Defining what constitutes the autobiographical in film, however, is complex, not least because filmmaking is usually a collaborative process. Some might argue that the dense filmic signature of an auteur can be read as autobiographical, as it calls attention to the distinctive qualities of a filmmaker's visual style and historical consciousness. Filmmakers from Federico Fellini, François Truffaut, Jean-Luc Godard, Akira Kurosawa, and Satyajit Ray to Spike Lee, Chantal Akerman, and Jane Campion inscribe their artistic subjectivity in an auteurist aesthetic. Similarly,

244   Kinds of Life Narratives

the films of Werner Herzog are sustained acts of autobiographical film-making, even in an apparent biopic such as *Grizzly Man*.[10] In it Herzog constructs a biographical portrait of bear enthusiast Timothy Tread-well, who was savagely killed by Alaskan grizzlies in 2003, and embeds Treadwell's story in interviews with several people who knew him but offer conflicting views of his fanatical dedication as either egomania or a death wish. In voiceover reflections Herzog inserts himself into the film as a witness at one remove and frames it with a metanarrative on his own career and artistic choices, what Paul John Eakin terms "the story of the story" ("Relational Selves, Relational Lives").

A more explicit mode of the autobiographical in film and video occurs in documentary projects that reference autobiographical evidence.[11] A well-known American self-documenting film is Morgan Spurlock's *Super Size Me,* which follows Spurlock as he endures thirty days of eating only McDonald's fast food for every meal. In effect, Spurlock turns himself into a social experiment and his body into a visual specimen for his audience in order to raise political consciousness about the American phenomenon of overeating and the elastic boundaries of the embodied self. While autobiographical film relies on the tropes and set-ups of the documentary, it can also use them strategically to explore the nature of "fact." Canadian director Sarah Polley's *Stories We Tell* probes her family's secrets, including one centrally concerned with her own identity, by incorporating faux home video footage that appears authentic to interrogate the claims of memory.

Self-documenting films can also be shot and produced by the subjects themselves, as in Jonathan Caouette's *Tarnation,* composed on a Mac computer and self-distributed for the cost of a million dollars. It uses home video to construct a relational portrait of the filmmaker's experience of growing up queer in a poor family in Texas and caring, as an adult, for his mentally ill mother. Caouette interweaves answering machine messages, family photographs, 1980s pop culture fragments, and reenactments of scenes with family members in his narrated coming-of-age and coming-out narrative to make a fragmentary but highly personal film. Anna Poletti provocatively observes, "The film is constructed using collage to produce a text characterized by juxtaposition, ventriloquism, and remediation" that "draw[s] our attention to the citational function of the discourse by speaking in a voice and from a subject position that is clearly not that of the author," enabling Caouette

Kinds of Life Narratives 245

to occupy "a *periperformative* relationship with the performative force of memoir" ("Periperformative Life Narrative," 362). Thus, Caouette both engages with and distances himself from what viewers expect of autobiographical film.

Perhaps the most prominent American autobiographical filmmaker is Michael Moore, an inveterate, wry raconteur of his own experience. Since his memorable debut film, *Roger & Me*, he has written, produced, and starred in autobiographical documentaries presenting himself as a Midwestern working-class man-on-the-street who investigates the dominant institutions of late capitalism, including General Motors, prisons, U.S. gun culture, healthcare, and, in *Where to Invade Next*, a comparative encounter with quality-of-life issues in several European countries. With their humorous confrontations, his self-ironizing autodocs use autobiographical means to mount a defense of public activism as the obligation of every citizen: "Democracy is not a spectator sport, it's a participatory event. If we don't participate in it, it ceases to be a democracy" (quoted in Collett-White).

Autodocumentary filmmaking may also be intriguingly collective in documentaries of a group of lives that function as filmic prosopography. For instance, *Twitch and Shout*, directed by Laurel Chiten, profiles about half a dozen people with Tourette's syndrome who are presented as sharing bodily commonality.

Many published life narratives have been made into films that might be termed *autopics*. These include film adaptations of such life narratives as *Angela's Ashes*; *Country of My Skull*; *Girl, Interrupted*; *Jarhead*; *Malcolm X*; *Rabbit-Proof Fence*; and earlier films such as *The Miracle Worker* (about Helen Keller) and *Three Faces of Eve*. Such adaptations of life writing into film invite our theorizing of representational and storytelling choices in cinematic interpretation of what constitutes adapted filmic autobiography. And they raise the question of whether, in cinematic technology's translations to the screen, the narrative shifts to an autobiographical hybrid or, instead, becomes a biopic.

Indeed, most memoirs are rendered cinematically as versions of the biopic. For example, Reinaldo Arenas's memoir, translated from Spanish as *Before Night Falls*, was filmed by Julian Schnabel in sweeping panoramas that artistically embody the writer's vision. Javier Bardem sensitively portrays the dissident Cuban artist's life of artistic achievement, political struggle to smuggle out his writing, multifarious erotic encounters in the gay underworlds of Havana and New York, and grim death from AIDS. But the film remakes his narrative as a biopic interpreting Arenas's words and images rather than an autobiographical film that he participated in making. Examples of filmic autobiography certainly exist, as in Italian writer-director Nanni Moretti's ongoing series of films wittily and provocatively charting moments of his personal and political life in which he also stars; or the filmic version of Cyril Collard's *Savage Nights (Les Nuits Fauves)*, which he wrote, directed, and acted in.

More typical of mass-market film is Steven Spielberg's *The Fabelmans*, a narrative of a young man's coming-of-age in New Jersey and falling in love with and beginning to make movies. Although semi-autobiographical, it makes no documentary claims and has a cast of actors, though Spielberg cowrote (with Tony Kushner), directed, and produced it. A similar set of semi-autobiographical references in a film with actors informs Paul Thomas Anderson's autobiographical comedy-drama *Licorice Pizza*.

If recent independent filmmaking in the United States and Europe has brought diverse kinds of personal stories and innovative modes of visual self-representation to the fore, avant-garde film and video have had a much longer history. Avant-garde practices of autobiographical film have abounded since at least the 1920s. Some highlights include Maya Deren's *Meshes of the Afternoon*, an experimental film oscillating between objective and subjective shots or points of view; Jerome Hill's autobiographical collage of his life, *Film Portrait*; and the experimental autobiographical films of Stan Brakhage. Idiosyncratic, visionary, and political, such avant-garde films intensify the traces of autobiographical consciousness behind the camera and at the editing table (see Sitney; McHugh; Lewis). In South Africa, William Kentridge's brilliant cartoon sequences in films and photographs, obliquely referencing his personal life, capture the racialized polarities that sustained the apartheid system and influenced the shaping of personal identities. Whether explicitly or only implicitly self-referential, they document practices of racialization that inflect both the contours and the performance of identities. Now, generations of younger scholars are investigating similar histories of filmic self-representation in Australia, France, Germany, India, Poland, Russia, Spain, and throughout Africa and Latin America.

Kinds of Life Narratives

FOOD MEMOIR (GASTROGRAPHY)

The food memoir intersects with food writing generally, spanning writing from the Bible and antiquity to the cultural tales, practices, and politics of the present, as the anthology *Eating Words,* edited by Sandra Gilbert and Roger Porter, suggests. Food memoirs often resituate stories of family and nation, ethnic heritage, and diaspora within the materiality of food cultivation, preparation, and distribution. Rosalia Baena proposed the term *gastrography* to designate life writing in which the story of the self is closely linked to the production, preparation, and/or consumption of food.

Some memoirs, such as renowned chef Julia Child's *My Life in France,* mix the preparation and consumption of food with the specificities of place and the mastery of a vocation. Food critic Ruth Reichl, in *Tender at the Bone* and her subsequent memoirs, chronicles how growing up in a dysfunctional home in the 1950s was mitigated by the pleasures of eating and becoming an accomplished cook. Reichl supplements her narrative with recipes for gastronomic self-improvement, such as a vegetarian casserole recipe from her Berkeley commune days, that enable readers to enter her past. The inimitable Anthony Bourdain, whose *Kitchen Confidential* combined stories of becoming a cook with hair-raising accounts of the kitchens in which he worked, launched a food-memoir boom. His four subsequent series of food-travel television combined travelogues to many countries and observations on their cuisine and food practices with wry self-reflections on his own past, tastes, and desires that suggest how accounts ostensibly about food may incorporate aspects of life narrative.

Memoirs linking ethnicity and food can register difference and specify the coordinates of a writer's cultural identity, as happens in "soul food memoirs." Nikki Giovanni, in *Quilting the Black-Eyed Pea,* for example, describes her grandmother's meatloaf as a metaphor for her family's story over generations. Austin Clarke in *Pig Tails 'n Breadfruit: A Culinary Memoir* incorporates ethnic food into a critique of how economic poverty and cultural richness blended during his childhood in Jamaica. Vertamae Smart-Grosvenor in *Vibration Cooking; or, The Travel Notes of a Geechee Girl,* links recipes from the social contexts of her soul food dishes to stories of African Americans who passed through her life. And Esmeralda Santiago in *When I Was Puerto Rican* includes extended descriptions of Puerto Rican food and recipes, as well as instructions for eating a guava, to contrast the sensuousness of her childhood with the "apple" world of the United States. In *The Language of Baklava*, Diana Abu-Jaber interweaves the pleasures of smelling and eating the flavors of her father's Jordanian past with the family's negotiation of ethnic Los Angeles. In her *Life without a Recipe* food becomes a metaphor for how to reinvent inherited cultural practices as traditional foods are incorporated into folklore about reviving and revaluing communities of origin through gastronomic stories of what is occluded in urban life.

Food memoirs may link cultivation to political critique, as does Barbara Kingsolver's *Animal, Vegetable, Miracle: A Year of Food Life*, which narrates her family's effort to sustain themselves on the food they grow for a year as a means of reorienting themselves to nature. Similarly, in *The Art of the Commonplace* Wendell Berry's essays connect his life as an organic farmer to the seasonal cycle. Gastrographic storytelling can also be used as an index to cultural dysfunction. Morgan Spurlock's autobiographical documentary film, *Super Size Me,* chronicles the internal damage done to his system when he consumes a diet exclusively of McDonald's fast food for one month. The politics of food is directly addressed by renowned nutritionist Marion Nestle in *Slow Cooked: An Unexpected Life in Food Politics.* Her critique urges readers to "consider how food relates to hunger and chronic disease, environmental pollution, or climate change; to systems of agricultural production and distribution; to the ways foods are sold, prepared, and consumed; or to how societies deal with such matters as immigration, racial and gender discrimination, and incarceration," problems she regards as directly related to neoliberal politics (236). Her call for more regulation of food industry practices and less consumption of processed foods now resonates.

Much life writing on food addresses addictive behaviors such as anorexia and bulimia. Marya Hornbacher's *Wasted* tracks how bingeing and purging became a psychic struggle with starvation when food takes on a metaphoric status for her as repulsive materiality. (See the discussion of anorexia and bulimia blogs in "Breakdown and Breakthrough Narrative.") Roxane Gay's *Hunger* and Kim Krans's graphic memoir *Blossoms and Bones: Drawing a Life Back Together* are among many narratives attesting to the power that food addiction exerts on some who have suffered violence or loss, particularly when linked with addictions to sex or substances. (See "Addiction Narrative.") And the

Kinds of Life Narratives 249

rise of quantitative-self life blogs emphasizes the importance of when, what, and how much one consumes for composing a self.

Gastrographic life narratives suggest that "you are what you eat" and imply that they can "cook up" for readers both menus of composing a self and recipes for reshaping subjectivities.

GEOGRAPHIES OF LIFE NARRATIVE

As explored in chapter 2, space, place, and location are central aspects of autobiographical situatedness. Critical geographies thus include both historical contexts and global locations. They examine how subjects are embedded in national imaginaries and in transnational and global circuits of exchange and identification. In retrospect, it is clear that movements to recover groups of noncanonical texts from obscurity contested the prevailing notion of autobiography as a single coherent genre and productively fractured the subject by specifying its diverse historical and geographic difference. In the United States, for example, scholars reclaimed diverse kinds of life writing by African Americans, including escapees from slavery, Latinx and Chicanx, Asian Americans, and Native Americans. Elsewhere, scholars explored the terms of subjectivity across linguistic, cultural, and national divides in response to histories of exploration, conquest, settlement, and liberatory movements in colonial settings. Their reclamation and incorporation of a range of texts countered the prevailing canon, effectively introducing heterogeneous genres, including indigenous codices, life narratives of the religious, ex-slave narratives, and narratives of exploration and displacement.

Now, the cumulative effect of such interventions is evident in the articulation of fields and genres of autobiography studies. For example, in African American life writing, scholars have traced the lines of a tradition from colonial through antebellum, Harlem Renaissance, and Black Power movements to contemporary explorations of racialization. For Latinx and Chicanx life writing, the connections among narratives of exploration, diverse kinds of folkloric writing, missionary journals, and contemporary narratives of coming of age as bi- or multicultural subjects have consolidated rich traditions of self-fashioning in relation to cross-border communities. The complex field of Asian American life writing has been both formed and fractured by its diversity of geographic heritages and affiliations that access different histories and by new trends in transnational, oceanic, and archipelagic studies. The study of the Indigenous and mestizo peoples of the Americas, initially the province of ethnographers in as-told-to narratives, has been reclaimed by a new generation of scholars who differently inflect these histories of encounter, resistance, assimilation, and sovereignty.

Life writing around the world is no longer dominated by studies of the United States and England. In particular national locales, scholars are tracing, for example, the rise of a distinctive Canadian autobiographical writing of settlement, westward displacement, cultural conflict, bilingualism, and contemporary political culture. In Australia, critics have explored how autobiographical writing has reproduced central myths of Australian national identity such as the myth of mateship. They have also tracked how personal narrative became a venue for Indigenous Australians to rewrite the history of encounter and state oppression as well as laying claim to alternative modes of collective identification. Studies of life writing in China explore the intersection of autobiographical discourse and the discourses of modernization in the early part of the twentieth century, during the period of revolutionary consolidation, and now, with the radical transformations of a globalizing China.

In Africa, scholars are attending to the relationship of oral narratives of identity and lineage to first-person life writing; examining the weave of indigenous and colonial languages and discourses in narration; linking testimonial stories of war and enslavement, such as child soldier narratives, to larger struggles for national liberation; and posing questions about Pan-African identity. While life writing from the Middle East is as yet sporadically translated—and often only when it addresses the concerns of the West, as in the narratives of Nafisi, Marjane Satrapi, El Saadawi, and Edward Said—a rich historical heritage of autobiographical writing in Arabic and Farsi exists. As western and eastern European nations renegotiate their histories, borders, and increasingly multinational citizenships, the terms and focus of life writing are changing, not only for contemporary texts but also in how early national literatures are framed and investigated. As scholars define new sets of theoretical terms for investigating the geographical locations, itineraries, and trajectories of autobiographical texts, and engage in international conversations about these questions, the field has become genuinely global.

Now, as autobiographical texts foreground differences in language, culture, tradition, and history, life narratives across dispersed geographical and geopolitical terrains have become autotheoretical in

Kinds of Life Narratives

productive ways. For example, Shirley Geok-lin Lim in *Among the White Moon Faces* contrasts growing up in Malaysia and coming of age as an academic in the eastern United States, and Eva Hoffman in *Lost in Translation* engages her multiple displacements across the Polish and English languages, locations, and remembering selves. In the wake of Said's influential *Culture and Imperialism,* studies in historical perspective on the formation and dissolution of empire have also turned to life writing as an important site of critical cultural inscription. Attentive to how autobiographical acts engage questions and practices of subjects in transition, critics employ Said's critique in examining the legacies of the past in the present for postcolonial subjects and the dispersal across the globe of diasporan subjects or subjects in exile. Comparative investigations of Anglophone autobiographical practices in the British Empire—in Africa, India, and around the world—and similar studies for other former colonial powers promise to contribute important insights about the dynamic relays between metropolitan center and colonial locations of writing and self-imagining. Questions of translation, of "minor literatures," of citizenship and transnational belonging resituate the story of life writing from national locations to sites marked by global flows and mobility.

See "Ethnic and Postethnic Life Narrative," "Indigenous Life Narrative," and "Migrant and Refugee Life Narrative."

GRAPHIC MEMOIR (AUTOGRAPHICS)

Graphic memoir, what Gillian Whitlock terms *autographics,* is a rich site of self-representation reaching large audiences around the world. Drawing on Hirsch's notion of "biocularity" to emphasize the distinctiveness of the verbal–visual conjunction that occurs in comics ("Editor's Column," 1213), Whitlock stresses its potential for a unique response to the historical moment by mediating across cultures and prompting new imaginings ("Autographics," 973). In Japan, France, Belgium, Canada, Italy, the United States, South Africa, and elsewhere, the telling of autobiographical narratives through what are popularly called comics has produced multimodal stories with the potential to intervene directly in social and political debates, not least because they link the cartoon form of popular culture to the narrative practices and theoretical critique of contemporary life writing.

Several features of autobiographical comics distinguish them from other media of self-representation. First, because of the dynamic entanglement of verbal and visual materials, graphic memoirs can project multiple, often conflicting stories rendered in different media. As readers negotiate stories implicit in the visual plane that seem distinct from the narrated story of the written material, for instance, they may uncover interpretive possibilities and complex questions about the nature of autobiographical memory and meaning.

Second, graphic memoirs present the reader with overlapping layers of self-presentation, as explored in chapter 3. There are: the invisible hand of the author-artist that draws the image; the narrating architect of the story whose voice runs above the frame, sometimes in boxes; the narrated "I" as autobiographical avatar who is both imaged and voiced; the characters, including the narrated "I," speaking in dialogue bubbles; the audience, including the addressee within the comic, as well as flesh-and-blood readers; and, often, the artist's hand depicted within one or more frames as a metalevel aesthetic autograph.

Third, with its syncopation of frames and gutters, a graphic memoir plays with time, shifting temporalities, juxtaposing temporal frames, and slowing or speeding up the time of reading itself. That syncopation also introduces disruptions in the visual plane. As a result, observes Jared Gardner, "all comics are necessarily collaborative texts between the imagination of the author/artist and the imagination of the reader who must complete the narrative" that the cartoon's segmented boxes and gutters both initiate and interrupt ("Archives," 800).

Finally, the distinctive character of graphic style, an effect at once of amplification and simplification, enhances what Whitlock notes is "its power to capture character, history and place in an economy of pictures and words" (*Soft Weapons,* 198). "What charges life narrative in comics," she concludes, "is the particular tension and dissonance it generates by mixing codes from juvenilia into autobiographical narratives of history and trauma" (198).

Historically, graphic memoir as a distinct genre gained wide recognition in the United States and beyond with the publication in 1986 of Art Spiegelman's *Maus I: A Survivor Tale. My Father Bleeds History,* although Justin Green's *Binky Brown Meets the Holy Virgin Mary* is credited as the first American graphic memoir, and the form's roots go back to comic strips in various lands. Through *Maus,* Spiegelman joined the comic strip's codes of experimental and renegade juvenilia to a searing

Kinds of Life Narratives 253

autobiographical engagement with his father's traumatic memory and his own postmemory of the Holocaust's effects on his family and community. "Art" is not a fictional character but a figure embodying his creator's experience as a child of survivors growing up in the United States after World War II. In narrating and drawing a tale of his parents' Auschwitz experiences interwoven with a frame narrative involving his interviews with his father, Spiegelman constructs stories within stories entwined in multiple temporalities. Art is both the angry, bereft son and, in *Maus II: A Survivor's Tale. And Here My Troubles Began* (published five years later), the increasingly celebrated, guilt-ridden author of a "comic book" about a horrific event. Such paradoxical narrative locations are foundational to the graphic memoir's recursivity.

Other autographics suggest the potential to address potent issues of gender, sexuality, disability, and nation, and to circulate new multimodal stories about the personal and historical stakes of representation. Marjane Satrapi's two books of autographics about revolutionary-era Iran, *Persepolis* and *Persepolis 2* (published in French and made into a 2007 film), link the coming-of-age story of an only child in a Marxist-leaning, multigenerational bourgeois family, reputedly descended from the kings of Persia, to events in Iran between the late 1970s and the early 1990s. Through starkly abstracted black-and-white cartooning, Satrapi visualizes the psychic life of her childhood and early adulthood selves, the communal struggle of the family against and in the midst of the Iranian revolutionary masses, and the complexities of Iran's struggle to forge an Islamic national imaginary at the sites of its martyred opposition and war dead.

Different autographical possibilities are mobilized in Bechdel's *Fun Home: A Family Tragicomic.* A provocative exploration of sexuality, gendered relations in the American family, and modernist versions of what Bechdel calls "erotic truth," this graphic memoir entwines the story of Alison's family's efforts to form her as feminine, despite her own transgressive desire, with the private trauma of her father's double life as a homosexual and early, violent death. Queering the narrative of genealogical recovery, it routes both his and her stories through references to and images of several kinds of print texts: Modernist literature; lesbian feminist manifestos; letters between her parents during their courtship and in her teenage years; newspaper pages; and her own childhood diaries. Graphic memoir thus becomes a space of collage and counterpoint.[12]

In foregrounding her father's biography, Bechdel counters second-wave feminism's injunction to women to think back through their mothers, by crafting an alternative story of how thinking back through her father's story both affirmed her desire—then coded as transgressive—and struggled with the reality of him as the prime agent of repressing it.

A vast and diverse number of graphic memoirists are now experimenting with distinctive visual aesthetics and thematic complexities. The subfield of graphic medicine has a massive website (www.graphic medicine.org), which lists them by illness. Someone diagnosed with Parkinson's might, for example, turn not to such well-known illness graphic memoirs as David Small's *Stitches* or David B's *Epileptic,* but to one such as *My Degeneration* by Peter Dunlap-Shohl for a wittily depicted account of his symptoms that become manifest over a decade, helpful advice on their management, and wildly funny drawings of specific anxieties. As La Cour and Poletti observe, "the study and production of graphic medicine aims to explore and expose the subjective experiences of health and healthcare systems that may be difficult for both practitioners and patients to understand or explain in either verbal or visual language alone" (1).

Graphic memoirs of refugees' and their descendants' struggles to relocate and make a life abound, from GB Tran's narrative of American resettlement in *Vietnamerica: A Family's Journey* and Gene Luen Yang's *American Born Chinese* to Kate Evans's *Threads: From the Refugee Crisis,* centered on the refugee city, "the Jungle," in Calais, France, which advocates for compassion and resettlement across borders. Comics visualizing such mass movements through the eyes and pens of narrator-participants can be a potent means of intervention in political struggles, as Sidonie Smith observed in discussing "crisis comics" ("Human Rights and Comics"). Joe Sacco's long career as a comics journalist documenting political struggles from Palestine to Bosnia is also subtly autographical in his self-depictions as an observer on the ground. Over fifty years, feminist comics have offered a rich vein of storytelling about issues, from critiquing the urban scene, as does Montreal cartoonist Julie Doucet, to raising controversial issues of incest, as does Phoebe Gloeckner in *The Diary of a Teenage Girl,* and chronicling bipolar illness, as does Ellen Forney in *Marbles: Mania, Depression, Michelangelo, and Me.* Graphic memoirs may serve to depict and preserve memories of sociopolitical

Kinds of Life Narratives 255

struggle, as does John Lewis's *March Trilogy* centered on the American civil rights movement in the sixties. They can explore personal obsession as public confession, as does Hillary Fitzgerald Campbell in *Murder Book: A Graphic Memoir of a True Crime Obsession*; or capture the tenor of a particular social moment, as Kristen Radtke does in *Seek You: A Journey through American Loneliness*.

In the classroom, instructors are using comic narratives of historical struggles, sometimes with autobiographical testimony embedded in them. For example *Abina and the Important Men,* by historian Trevor R. Getz and artist Liz Clarke, is one of a series of comic-book-format texts exploring such forces as colonial imperialism "from below" by focusing in student-friendly ways on archival evidence from forgotten figures such as a nineteenth-century Ghanaian woman, Abina. Alternatively, autobiographical discourse by a philosopher as influential as Bertrand Russell may be embedded in a comic irreverently probing the ir/rationality of the Western world from Athenian democracy to the present, as does the extraordinary *Logicomix*.[13]

Now, book-length critical studies of the field of graphic memoirs and novels abound. Rebecca Wanzo focuses on representations of African Americans in comics by addressing the revisioning of racist cartoon images in *The Content of Our Caricature: African American Comic Art and Political Belonging,* and the liberatory potential of such acknowledgement. Candida Rifkind and Dominic Davies foreground both personal and collective global struggles in *Documenting Trauma in Comics: Traumatic Pasts, Embodied Histories, and Graphic Reportage.* Hillary L. Chute extends her groundbreaking scholarship on theorizing comics, notably graphic memoirs, by analyzing the work comics do in *Why Comics? From Underground to Everywhere.* And, in *Disaster Drawn: Visual Witness, Comics, and Documentary Form,* she asserts that "comics texts give shape to lost histories and bodies," thereby offering "a new seeing" (38) that marks the probing range of graphic memoir now.

As the global reach of graphic memoirs expands, this now-popular form of witnessing to histories of trauma that mark and document the need to remember raises provocative questions for scholars of life narrative to explore. How do graphic memoirs call us to know and see otherwise? How do they produce us as different kinds of readers? How do they witness to public cataclysms and private crises, and to what effect? And how do they circulate and get taken up in larger projects of remembering?

GRIEF NARRATIVE

The successes as a memoir and a play on Broadway of Joan Didion's *The Year of Magical Thinking* and of Richard McCann's *Just a Boy: The True Story of a Stolen Childhood* in London indicate the growing audience for life writing focused on grief and mourning. Didion, to whose memoir we will return, recounts her inability to register her husband's sudden death; McCann narrates his memory of the wrenching loss of his mother in a murder. Such narratives of loss are by no means new. James Ellroy's *My Dark Places,* which details with clinical exactitude his boyhood memory of learning that his mother was violated and strangled in late 1950s Los Angeles and the ensuing police procedures that found no killer, is a cult classic.

In an era of pervasive communication when private emotions ceaselessly circulate online, however, new modes of memorialization and vulnerability to loss register transience and grief in more public forms than did the traditional family album. Memoirs of grief are often passed from hand to hand as how-to guidebooks for those who have suffered a loss, serving as contemporary books of consolation. When the bereaved write memoirs of those lost to them as a form of grief work, they may seek repair or emotional compensation (see H. Nelson). In storytelling, parents mourn the loss of a child to war or accident or illness and the shock of outliving one's own progeny. In writing of deep grief about such a loss, parents, siblings, extended family members, partners, and friends also grieve their own impending mortality and express anxiety about life-threatening illness. And the one who is dying may also seek the consolation of enduring in another medium while recording his own transience, as does filmmaker Tom Joslin in *Silverlake Life,* which intersperses excerpts from his films with footage of his weakening condition.

Yet in some memoirs, narration acts ambivalently as both memorialization of mourning and its melancholic refusal. Didion begins *The Year of Magical Thinking* by recounting the sudden death, one night at dinner, of writer John Gregory Dunne, her husband of nearly forty years. Over several months, the narrator observes her own nonrational responses to the event, as she undertakes efforts aimed at bringing him back or denying that his death really happened. This process is com-

Kinds of Life Narratives

plicated by the sudden and ultimately fatal illness of their thirty-eight-year-old daughter, Quintana Roo, who falls ill and requires extensive hospitalization. Crafting a raw prose to evoke her feelings of pain and rage, Didion resists conventional frames for understanding how this uncharted experience redefines being a "partner" and "mother." Refusing the comfort that writing such a story—as "scriptotherapy"—is supposed to bring, Didion insists on the writing of grief as a fragmentary process and articulates a vulnerability rendered in, but not contained or resolved by, life writing.

Julian Barnes's *Levels of Life,* published five years after the death in 2008 of his wife of thirty years from a brain tumor, also registers the depth of pain and the struggle to find words and a literary form adequate to remembering a loved one and exploring the loss. Indeed, mindful of his wife's discomfort with public attention and intrusion, he rejects the confessional mode of chronicling grief and opens his spare memoir with: "You put together two things that have not been put together before and the world is changed." To capture the qualities of depthless grief, Barnes juxtaposes fragments of narration, a biographical vignette, and meditation in three essays on flight, leveling, and descent. He then turns to his fascination with ballooning and nineteenth-century balloon fanatics who soared high above the earth, confronting the pleasures of ascent and flight, and the dangers of accident and descent, often photographing aerial views along the way. In the third essay, Barnes's descent into grief acknowledges the inadequacy of gestures of sympathy to console, as the stumbling logic of his struggle to remember and bear the pain of forgetting takes over.

Grief about the loss of a family member is a recurrent focus of life narrative. Chimamanda Ngozi Adichie, in her wrenching *Notes on Grief,* probes the emotions that wracked her with the loss of her father from kidney failure at a time when she could not see him during the COVID pandemic in 2020. She reflects on how this experience of personal grief expanded around the world during the epidemic with the loss of family members and friends experienced by millions. In linking these reflections to a biographical sketch of her father's survival during the Biafran war and subsequent success as a professor, she reflects on the precarious nature of life, a feature of many grief life narratives and one expressed in the outpouring of COVID obituaries.

By contrast, the memoir *Brother, I'm Dying* by Haitian American author Edwidge Danticat, is a generational narrative explicitly linking political and personal stories. Danticat, who left Haiti to join her immigrant parents in New York before the Tonton ravaged the country, focuses on the deaths of her father and uncle within months of each other as a way to tell the larger story of a family riven by inequities in two nations. Connecting her extended family to centuries of national history, Danticat foregrounds the intersection of personal, communal, national, and transnational histories of colonial violence and immigrant relocation as she refuses the comfort that expressing one's grief in writing supposedly brings and underscores the vulnerability of refugees in North America.

Indeed, many life narratives of grief and mourning address larger social, cultural, and political issues. In *The Return*, Libyan exile and writer Hisham Matar invites readers to accompany his years-long journey to discover how, when, and under what conditions his father, a noted Libyan dissident and exile, was murdered in one of dictator Muammar Gaddafi's notorious prisons after being abducted at home in Cairo by Egyptian authorities. His quest to find his dead father situates his own story as the son/detective within a story of the nation, while as narrator and tutor he educates readers on the last forty years of Libyan history. Despite his persistent detection, Matar fails on his returns to Egypt and Libya to find either the body or the final story of his father. Narratively, *The Return* is recursive, returning again and again to a few moments: his father being taken from the family in Cairo, the man in the prison cell, and his own failure to discover when and how his father actually died. Thwarted, he finds consolation in writing itself and the literary works he has loved and taught, which guide and inform his struggle to find words adequate to the liminal space of grief he inhabits. Movingly, he writes, "my father is both dead and alive. I do not have a grammar for him. He is in the past, present and future. . . . I suspect that many men who have buried their fathers feel the same. I am no different. I live, as we all live, in the aftermath" (145).

In the United States during the HIV/AIDS crisis, narratives of the loss of loved ones projected not only grief but outrage about the conditions under which people succumbed to HIV/AIDS. For instance, life writer Paul Monette narrated a history of coming out as "always already" gay that was linked to the romance of partnership, the story of struggle against social prejudice and economic disparity, and the diaristic chron-

Kinds of Life Narratives 259

icle of his lover's decline. Monette's three memoirs (*Borrowed Time: An AIDS Memoir*; *Becoming a Man: Half a Life Story*; and *Last Watch of the Night: Essays Too Personal and Otherwise*), like many others, both confront and counter social intolerance of homosexuals and the reactionary linkage of gay sexuality to a culture of drug addiction and perversity. In such examples, constructing a memoir becomes an act of mourning not only personal loss but collective vulnerability.

The numerous online sites of collective mourning that have sprung up also produce new formations of mourning. Online communities now memorialize and grieve the death of celebrities or the victims of much-publicized events that resonate with the public, such as the World Trade Center attacks, terrorist bombings, mass shootings, and wars. Other large-scale public events, such as Hurricane Katrina in New Orleans and environs, the Sandy Hook Elementary School shootings in Connecticut, and the police killing of George Floyd, become occasions for creating online communities that share their grief and loss by posting blogs, photographs, poems, and memorabilia. Because they are interactive, these sites serve not just those close to deceased loved ones but also a network of strangers who express vicarious grief by participating in an extended community of mourners.

For younger generations seeking to reflect on their situatedness in a world in climate crisis, the automedial aspects of life narrative make it both an expressive outlet for voicing grief over the loss and radical transformation of the natural world and an acute call for social justice—in bold, often collectivized multimedia forms such as social media, comics, blogs, public art, flash mobs, and performance art.

See also "Autothanatography."

HUMAN RIGHTS NARRATIVE

Life stories, and the scenes of witness they convey, are involved in campaigns for human rights. Theorists of the human rights regime have assayed its multivalent meanings: as an intricate formation of discourses, protocols, practices, and institutions for dealing with radical suffering; as a lingua franca for activism both nationally and transnationally; as a politicized regime, invoked and deployed in geopolitics; as a contested liberal regime identified with the West and its neoimperial politics; and as a contemporary global formation always in motion and transition.

Scholars theorizing the implications of human rights for life-writing practices have achieved several things. They have situated narratives witnessing to radical injury and suffering in alternative jurisdictions outside courts of law (see Gilmore, "Jurisdictions"). They have critiqued the commodification of narratives of suffering in the production, circulation, and reception of witness narratives in global circuits of human rights movements. They have called attention to the constraints that institutional settings, protocols, and political contexts have exerted on the terms of witnessing and the oppressive aspects of scenes of witnessing, as does Allen Feldman in analyzing the South African Truth and Reconciliation Commission. They have noted the unpredictable and heterogeneous affective responses readers bring to narratives of suffering.

Narratives attesting to human rights violations shape life writing to particular ends, raising complex questions about the invisibility and lack of power of those who suffer. They engage in dialogue about what constitutes a rights violation, as well as what contributes to suffering and trauma. They register the efficacy of witnessing, for witnesses and for organized networks of activists, at this political moment. They expose the operations of the United Nations and nation-based commissions that use protocols and terms of reference to solicit stories, yet constrain the kinds of stories that can be told.

Human rights narratives are also cautionary, suggesting that witnesses who find a sympathetic audience may also be subject to retraumatization and continuing violence. Moreover, audience reactions to stories of profound suffering and harm cannot be predicted. While some may respond to an ethical call for recognition, others may experience compassion fatigue. And, as recent allegations of hoaxing imply, there are inevitably interested parties who seek to discredit the narrative told, as well as the witness. Thus, the reception of narratives of human rights witness may introduce trouble—about who can tell the story and speak for others, and what kinds of stories are likely to gain an audience and readership.

Yet the willingness to come forward to testify, however problematic in the context of human rights protocols and institutions, has produced critical interventions that bring to public attention the erasure of many diverse kinds of violence suffered by various groups in contexts of radical harm. Marie Béatrice Umutesi's *Surviving the Slaughter: The Ordeal of a Rwandan Refugee in Zaire* is a case in point. Her narrative of genocide

Kinds of Life Narratives

and survival combines the survivor's tale of violence, displacement, and vulnerability with the professional sociologist's vantage point of analytical objectivity. Umutesi's experience as a refugee of the Rwandan genocide displaced to a camp in Zaire motivates her journey through the recollected madness of unleashed violence and sanctioned human abandonment as she attempts to answer the question, "What led us to this extremity?" Her standpoint as a professional sociologist enables her to distance herself in contemplating that time of horrific events.

In South Africa some alternative witness narratives probe the relationship of the perpetrator and beneficiary of rights violations, as well as perpetrator and victim. Antjie Krog, who covered the Truth and Reconciliation Commission (TRC) as a journalist for the South African Broadcasting Company, reproduced witness testimonies in *Country of My Skull* as her own act of witness to the suffering and pain of people who appeared before the TRC. A South African of Boer heritage, Krog weaves stories of the TRC through her personal narrative of incomprehension and disintegration, and acknowledges her position as a beneficiary of apartheid as she makes a visionary call for a new future. Michael Rothberg observes that the figure of the beneficiary is one subject position within a constellation of positions "that sit uncomfortably in our familiar conceptual space of victims, perpetrators, and bystanders" (13); his "umbrella" term for this ensemble of positions is that of "implicated subjects," defined as those who "occupy positions aligned with power and privilege without being themselves direct agents of harm; they contribute to, inhabit, inherit, or benefit from regimes of domination but do not originate or control such regimes" (1). By placing testimonies, analysis, and memoir side by side, Krog composes an autocritical collage in which political and personal discourses interrogate one another. Although Krog was challenged for using the voices of Black witnesses in her narrative and for including fictionalized scenes, her effort to ponder the ambiguities and affective complexities of her identity as a South African of Boer ancestry offers a model for a transcultural ethics of care and citizenship (see Schaffer and Smith, "Human Rights, Storytelling").

Taking a different approach, the narrative of Pumla Gobodo-Madikizela, a TRC commissioner and psychologist, offers both a portrait of a perpetrator and her own struggle as a victim of racial apartheid to find a means of personal reconciliation. Her *A Human Being Died That Night* chronicles a series of meetings she had with Eugene De Kock, one of the most reviled perpetrators of the TRC, after he was imprisoned for his crimes. Gobodo-Madikizela's narrative quest culminates in both the discovery of the other in herself and a meditation on reconciliation. The process of narrating a life may itself be drawn into debates about human rights. In a 2000 U.S. court decision in California, motel handyman Cary Stayner, a convicted murderer, was sentenced to life in prison without parole rather than the death penalty, with one provision: he must take the story of his crime to the grave to spare the victim's family any further media attention (see Hanley). That is, publication of his life story was treated as part of his personal rights, subject to being legally revoked in extreme circumstances. (Stayner, who later confessed to additional murders, was retried and sentenced to death in 2003.) Struggles over who has the right to use forms of life narrative, such as enslavement narratives or women saints' chronicles, suggest that the ownership of one's story has historically been less an intrinsic right than a site of contestation, especially for those whose status as citizens was denied or revoked under law.

In the next decades, as climate crises intensify amid political upheavals and renegade viruses, the potential effects of world-threatening forces to longevity will generate an increase in climate and economic refugees seeking relief in receiving countries and antidemocratic attacks on democratic institutions. Organizations such as the United Nations will be tasked with addressing emergent definitions, discourses, and politics of human rights as new kinds and patterns of violence impact the movement of individuals and populations across the globe. Sufferers of such global crises will find means to tell their stories through print and digital media even as drones hover overhead to track and surveil impacted populations, ecological disasters, and geopolitical responses.

See also "Testimonio," "Trauma Narrative," "Witnessing, Acts of."

INDIGENOUS LIFE NARRATIVE

The oral performance of self-narrative existed in many Indigenous cultures prior to literacy—in, for example, the naming songs of Native American cultures and the communal self-locating of the "song lines" of Indigenous Australians. These uses of self-representation in both preliterate and literate non-Western cultures contradict the assertion of an earlier generation of literary critics that the autobiographical is a

Kinds of Life Narratives   263

uniquely Western form and a specific achievement of Western culture at a moment of individuation in the wake of the Enlightenment.

Read postcolonially, the life narratives of Indigenous people tell stories of displacement, mobility, and migration from a perspective of loss and expropriation that is often intermingled with other discourses of identity. Crucial to reading these narratives is the distinction that Arnold Krupat makes about the production of life writing in Indigenous cultures that had not emphasized either the "auto" of the isolate individual or the "graph" or alphabetic writing of lives prior to contact with Europeans. One kind, Krupat argues, is Indian autobiographies, which are "not actually self-written, but . . . of original, bicultural composite composition" and often composed by a trio—a white editor-amanuensis, an Indigenous "subject" who orally presents a life, and a mixed-blood interpreter or translator—in a process of unequal collaboration. Often such narratives are considered to be "as-told-to" narratives, projects that sustain the asymmetrical relations of settler colonialism. (See "Collaborative and Collective Life Writing.")

A second kind of Indigenous life writing is comprised of autobiographical narrative by Indians as "individually composed texts . . . written by those whose lives they chronicle" (Krupat, "Introduction," 3). For example, in 1831, William Apess, in "A Son of the Forest," considered to be the first Native American life narrative in the writer's own words, mixes a narrative of exile from both his birth and adoptive families in his travel adventures with an account of his conversion to evangelical Christianity; at the same time he negotiates his Indigenous identity in an Anglo-American discourse that lacks language for it. Zitkala-Ša in "Impressions of an Indian Childhood," however, contrasts her experience of growing up in an Indigenous culture on a Lakota Sioux reservation with her relocation to a missionary school that, in the name of its civilizing and Christianizing mission, is brutally repressive. Her "sketches" in the early twentieth century reflect on how an education intended to form her as a docile citizen in fact motivated her to reclaim her Indian cultural heritage at a time of its erasure by forced assimilation and to narrate her personal history as a collective story of loss and a quest for dignity.

Within settler nations, narratives of childhood removal continue to chronicle the ravages of racist policies designed to remake Indigenous children as dutiful national subjects. In Canada, *Heart Berries* by Seabird

Island Reserve writer Terèse Marie Mailhot offers a fragmented yet searing narrative that reckons with how the legacy of settler colonialism and forced separation of children from their Indigenous communities created conditions for childhood sexual abuse, even as she grieves the loss of her first child in divorce. Gilmore argues that Mailhot's memoir, "written from breakage and representing a fierce aesthetic achievement," emerges "as matriarchal Indigenous practice, as survival skill, and as literary art" ("#MeToo and the Memoir Boom," 164). As these encounters with history suggest, Indigenous writers and artists are narrating new stories that call for care of self and community in troubled times.

Some Indigenous victims of violence cannot tell their stories or speak their truth—for example, the Indigenous girls and young women who are murdered or go missing in and around Indian country. The 2020 documentary film *Somebody's Daughter,* directed by Rain and realized by an all-Indigenous team, seeks to recover such stories by focusing on missing and murdered women and girls of the Blackfeet Nation and the Confederated Salish-Kootenai Tribes of Montana (see Mabie). The documentary opens with an imaginary autobiographical claim: "I am a full-blooded Native American woman. Being that, I am the most stalked, raped, murdered, sexually assaulted, and abused of any woman of any ethnic group." In saying the names of the girls and women, the film situates personal stories within the contexts of colonialism, genocide, and systemic racism and sexism, articulating from within the deep silence around Native women's experience.

Finally, acknowledging the land claims of Indigenous peoples and the interconnectedness of humans and the land has become an increasingly common practice at academic and activist gatherings in land acknowledgments that situate speakers' identity in relationship to the location and history of the site from which they speak. These acknowledgments serve as secondary witnessing to the territorial history of Indigenous kinship and embodiment. Hawaiian, Canadian, Australian, and some Western American colleagues have taken up this practice common to Indigenous ceremonies for centuries, while noting, as Tarren Andrews observes, that "gatherings . . . take place on stolen land—which in the Americas and the Pacific is every gathering." Andrews goes on to observe that "at their best . . . land acknowledgements give us an opportunity to be unsettled and uncomfortable" (5). Robin Wall Kimmerer's *Braiding Sweetgrass: Indigenous Wisdom, Scientific Knowledge, and the*

Kinds of Life Narratives 265

Teachings of Plants exemplifies an Indigenous response to land acknowledgment in which she narrates multiple stories: of becoming an environmental biologist and of mourning lands threatened with annihilation, praising the efficacy of sweetgrass, and calling for justice to the earth.

We might group these narratives under a term proposed by Krupat, "ethnocriticism," a focus on studying Native American and other Indigenous cultural productions, particularly life narratives, that methodologically fuse a mixture of anthropology, history, and critical theory to create a relativist mode of analytic discourse positioned at multiple "frontiers" of historical and cultural encounter and to pursue a form of strategic essentialism (*Ethnocriticism*, 6–8).

See "Geographies of Life Narrative."

INTERVIEW

While the interview has, until recently, rarely been theorized in literary studies as more than a vehicle for data collection, it is also a mode of performing life narrative, and therefore an autobiographical practice across writing, the visual arts, and digital media. Anneleen Masschelein and Rebecca Roach assert that "the interview [is] an encounter . . . an assemblage of heterogeneous elements [that] promises access to an interior but . . . reveals things other than what it may promise" (173). They raise provocative questions concerning the form's purpose and scope, who maintains editorial control, when an interview is literary, how it should be read, and whether it is "a method, genre, or object" (169).

While the interviewee seems to be the subject of a targeted conversation solicited by an interlocutor who serves as the coaxer, the interviewer's point of view may strongly shape the subjectivity that emerges, as occurs in some qualitative sociology and biographical writing. Sometimes, the participants may construct an extended interview that becomes a book, as do musician Nick Cave and writer Sean O'Hagan, from over forty hours of conversation, in *Faith, Hope, and Carnage*. Or, an extended interview may become a marketing strategy used to boost the outreach and sales of an autobiographical narrative, as occurred when Stephen Colbert interviewed Prince Harry, Duke of Sussex, about episodes and claims in his book *Spare* on his U.S. late-night comedy show (January 10, 2023). And, as theorist Sylvère Lotringer provocatively demonstrated in his 1986 deconstructive performance, "Confessions of a Ventriloquist," it is possible to construct a self-interview, as many French writers

266   Kinds of Life Narratives

have done. It becomes a means to both "give a language to all those voices that speak through us" (Lotringer, 211) and demonstrate how self-presentation may become disappearance, as occurs in the dialogic process through which Lotringer switches positions with his interviewer, one of his pseudonyms, to "achiev[e] such a degree of invisibility" (221).

JOURNAL

The journal is a form of life writing that records events and occurrences, as in Daniel Defoe's *A Journal of the Plague Year*. Some critics distinguish diary from journal by characterizing the journal as a chronicle of public record that is less intimate than the diary. (Philippe Lejeune does not distinguish between them but uses the terms interchangeably.)

The act of journal writing is now used as a verb, journaling, the practice of regular, free life writing. For example, the journal-writing workshops that Ira Progoff has organized and written about make a practice of it through regular writing, as well as medial forms such as drawing, photography, and collaging of scraps of life. Increasingly, users are journaling online through e-books, blogs, and other platforms. (See also Lejeune, "Practice of the Private Journal," "Diary," "Photo-Memoir and Photography in Life Narrative.")

KÜNSTLERROMAN

The *Künstlerroman* is a narrative of artistic education and encounters that lead to growth. In story-quilts such as *The French Collection* series, Faith Ringgold chronicles the life of a Black woman artist in Paris and the United States. Through painting and text on cloth, her fictionalized woman-artist Willia Marie struggles to find her place "in the picture" of Western art history and to make a place in that history for the aesthetics of her African American quilting heritage. Other examples include Goethe's *Truth and Poetry,* George Sand's *Story of My Life: The Autobiography of George Sand,* Sean O'Casey's six-volume life narrative, Nabokov's *Speak, Memory,* and Sartre's *The Words.* In thinly fictionalized form James Joyce's *Portrait of the Artist* and Virginia Woolf's *Moments of Being* trace journeys of coming to artistic consciousness. Several contemporary artists stage their development and emergence as artists in performance venues, as do Laurie Anderson, Alina Troyano (Carmelita Tropicana), Rachel Rosenthal, Guillermo Gómez-Peña, Coco Fusco, and Valie Export. Tove Ditlevsen's trilogy, *Childhood, Youth, Dependency,* is

Kinds of Life Narratives 267

comparably harsh and unromantic in narrating her artistic coming of age, mostly in riveting present-tense prose that details her encounters in a mid-century working-class Copenhagen that was repressive for women and defined by casual brutality at home and work. Her determination to write is an act of both defiance and sustenance, typical of the *Künstlerroman* without its celebratory conclusion. While the memoir concludes with her apparent rehabilitation, its resolution is thrown into question by her later-life struggle with drugs and eventual suicide.

LETTERS

The letter is a mode of directed and often dated correspondence with a specific addressee and signatory, a seemingly private form of writing. But the letter as a public form is an ancient genre that was widely practiced by such writers as Cicero, Seneca, and Pliny. It is the form of the epistles of Paul the Apostle, Augustine, and Saint Jerome, all circulated to their faith communities as manuscripts. At the dawn of the Renaissance, Petrarch's *Familiar Letters* began to use the epistolary form for autobiographical disclosure. Since the eighteenth-century poet Alexander Pope published essays from his own letters during his lifetime, they have begun to be understood as both private correspondence expressing the inner feelings and thoughts of the writing subject and as public documents to be shared within a literary circle. Bernhard Siegert argues that at that moment "every self thus became the subject of its own discourse a priori," and the subject was presumed to precede its representation, circulating as its property in the mail (44). Letters became vehicles through which information is circulated, social roles enacted, and relationships secured, often in a paradoxical mix of intimacy and formality.

Letters are a highly stylized form, employing conventions of politeness and modes of conveying information that are implicated in ideologies of gender, ethnicity, class, and nationality. Although letters often remain unpublished, some famous correspondences, such as those of Abelard and Héloïse, Lady Mary Wortley Montagu to friends, Hester Lynch Piozzi (Thrale) and Samuel Johnson, Marie de Sévigné, and Lydia H. Sigourney have been published and critically studied for their interactional modes of self-presentation. In the twentieth century, the imprisonment of political activists and resistance fighters around the globe often motivated them to write powerful letters from prison to be circulated in the outside world. In Germany during World War II, for example, theologian Dietrich Bonhoeffer's personal and theological letters from Tegel prison while awaiting execution for collusion in the attempt to assassinate Hitler were moving indictments that have become classics of political critique and spiritual consolation. Others whose letters from prison have been widely circulated include Martin Luther King Jr. in the open *Letter from Birmingham Jail,* Eldridge Cleaver in *Soul on Ice,* and Nelson Mandela in his collected prison letters.

The ongoing commentary on self and place by a lifelong letter writer may be read as a kind of memoir, as some have done with the correspondence in *Letters from Tove* of Tove Jansson, the Finnish creator of the Moomin stories and comics. Thus letters are not only historical evidence but rhetorical ego-documents to be theorized. In *In Love and Struggle: Letters in Contemporary Feminism,* Margaretta Jolly explores women's contemporary use of epistolary forms to foreground both a politics of the personal and a means of creating intimacy. Theorizing the formal properties of letters, Liz Stanley has proposed the concept of the *epistolarium* as, in different ways, an epistolary record, a collection of surviving correspondence, and the "ur-letters" created in work on actual letters (218).

Now many letters are sent with near-instantaneous transmission as e-mail, raising complex issues about security, privacy, surveillance, unpredictable sharing, and self-versioning.

MANIFESTO

The manifesto has been variously defined as a declaration or proclamation that may do several things: contest sovereignty; bring something to light or make it manifest in the light of day; announce and/or perform an action publicly; speak as, or for, a group in acts of testimony; or address a desired future. It usually addresses a specific audience whom it aims to galvanize into action around a declared commitment. Manifestos were originally used by authorities to communicate their intentions and rulings. But resistance movements have long adopted the form to assert authority, sometimes ironically, while calling for changes to existing laws and practices. Opposition groups, for example, may make a call for change that incorporates the experience and voices of movement members to urge structural change. Antislavery, feminist, ethnic, and LGBTQI manifestos have adopted this strategy, particularly in moments of social change. From the speech "Ain't I a Woman?," long attributed to Sojourner Truth,[14] to Martin Luther King Jr.'s "I Have a Dream" speech,

Kinds of Life Narratives 269

such calls resound with the need to recognize the rights of politically and economically disenfranchised groups such as African Americans.

Manifestos, as calls to activism in a collective voice, can be impolite or confrontational, as are the "SCUM Manifesto" by Valerie Solanas, "Dyke Manifesto" by the Lesbian Avengers, Simone de Beauvoir's pro-abortion "Manifesto of the 343," and "Riot Grrrl Manifesto" by Bikini Kill. Some that address political issues may use individual experience to inform a structural analysis, as do "The Straight Mind" by Monique Wittig, "Anarchy and the Sex Question" by Emma Goldman, and "What Is to Be Done" by V. I. Lenin. The hundreds of printed sheets of artist Jenny Holzer in "Truisms" (1978–87), which gather lists of popular pronouncements as in-your-face declarations, situate personal points of view ironically—for example, "A lot of professionals are crackpots." Similarly, artist Barbara Kruger's visual–verbal placards, such as "Your body is a battlefield" emblazoned beneath a woman's bifurcated face, serve as visual calls to feminist action. And the anonymous Guerrilla Girls made a career of posting rude, witty posters such as "Do women have to be naked to get into the Met. Museum?" that functioned as manifestos critiquing inequities in the art world.

Among the most significant American life narrative manifestos of recent decades are Gloria Anzaldúa's *Borderlands,* Cherríe Moraga's *Loving in the War Years,* and various essays in the collection *This Bridge Called My Back.* Ta-Nehisi Coates's *Between the World and Me* may be read as a book-length manifesto in the form of a letter to his son that cautions him about the risks of growing up and living while Black. Roxane Gay's 2012 manifesto "Feminism (Plural)," which became the first essay of her *Bad Feminist: Essays* collection, sends up popular culture stereotypes and provides searing takes on what constitutes a "bad feminist" or "good feminist." Manifestos as calls for social reckoning may be embedded in personal stories of awakening to social injustice, as in some narratives of the Black Lives Matter movement. Ecocritical narratives have also embedded manifesto-style pronouncements in their stories. In *Finding the Mother Tree: Discovering the Wisdom of the Forest,* Suzanne Simard, a Canadian professor of forestry, joins a memoir of her education in scientific training, method, and publication practice to both thick description of scientific notebooks and a manifesto for recognition of the "wood wide web" (165) of trees and mycorrhizal fungi that connect mother trees, shrubs, and younger trees in a cooperative network.

Online platforms often serve implicitly as calls to collective action and link their direct addresses to users with recruitment efforts to enlist them by inviting them to share their stories, a new mode of mobilizing autobiographical stories for collective ends. Leigh Gilmore, for example, tracks how Tarana Burke's MeToo movement went viral with the hashtag #MeToo and has served since 2019 as a site of narrative activism through personal storytelling aimed at social change that Gilmore links to the lineage of Harriet Jacobs' ex-slave narrative (see *The #MeToo Effect*).

MEDITATION

The meditation as a literary mode can be traced back to the twelve books of notes to self on personal betterment and explorations of Stoic philosophy as a system of thought written by Roman emperor Marcus Aurelius, who ruled from 161 to 180 CE. Eventually his writings came to be known as *The Meditations of Marcus Aurelius*. Meditation became a prominent mode of writing during the Protestant Reformation of the sixteenth and seventeenth centuries and with the rise of secular humanism. The form is composed of reflections, projecting stages of self-understanding and illuminations with respect to a spiritual or philosophical self-history. According to Louis Lohr Martz, the "meditation" is a rigorous exercise in self-contemplation whose aim "is the state of devotion" (15). When the meditation is put into literary form, its emphasis is on "a process of the mind rather than a particular subject-matter" (324) as the narrator seeks "the work of special grace" (16). The history of self-reflexive meditation in nonfictional prose can be traced through Montaigne's *Essays,* John Donne's sermons, Thomas Browne's *Religio Medici,* Blaise Pascal's *Pensées,* Francis de Sales's *The Introduction to a Devout Life,* Teresa of Avila's *The Interior Castle,* and, more recently, Henry David Thoreau's *Walden* and William Butler Yeats's *A Vision.* Poetry as well offers occasions for meditation, as in the poetry of Gerard Manley Hopkins, Emily Dickinson, Paul Valéry, Rainer Maria Rilke, Wallace Stevens, and T. S. Eliot. The meditative poem, writes Martz, "is a work that creates an interior drama of the mind; this dramatic action is usually (though not always) created by some form of self-address, in which the mind grasps firmly a problem or situation deliberately evoked by the memory, brings it forward toward the full light of consciousness, and concludes with a moment of illumination, where the speaker's self has, for a time, found an answer to its conflicts" (330). Meditative discourse is interwoven in

Kinds of Life Narratives

many life narratives and is prominent in such texts as Thomas Merton's *The Seven-Storey Mountain,* Dorothy Day's *The Long Loneliness,* and Elizabeth Gilbert's *Eat, Pray, Love.*

See "Spiritual Life Narrative."

MEMOIR

Historically, memoirs were a genre of life narrative that situated the subject in a social environment, as either observer or participant, and directed attention more toward the lives and actions of others than the narrator's experience. Secular memoirs, written by public figures such as diplomats and soldiers, emphasized life in the public sphere, chronicling professional careers and activities of historical import. In contemporary parlance, although the terms *autobiography* and *memoir* are used interchangeably, distinctions are relevant. As Lee Quinby notes, "whereas autobiography promotes an 'I' that shares with confessional discourse an assumed interiority and an ethical mandate to examine that interiority, memoirs promote an 'I' that is explicitly constituted in the reports of the utterances and proceedings of others. The 'I' or subjectivity produced in memoirs is externalized and . . . dialogical" (299). Currently, the term, in the singular, has shifted to denote life writing that takes a segment of a life, not its entirety, and focuses on interconnected experiences. Memoirs have been published in many contexts. Domestic memoirs, written as private narratives, focus on accounts of family life, as in Jonathan Franzen's memoir of his father's descent into Alzheimer's, *My Father's Brain.*

Tracing the treatment of the memoir form in the history of autobiography criticism, Julie Rak notes that memoir, in Derridean terms, has been positioned as a *supplement* to autobiography: "Very much like the relationship of 'writing' to plenitude in spoken language . . , in autobiography criticism memoir presents itself as a threat to autobiography because it points out that there is lack in the genre in the first place. Then, like writing, memoir offers itself as a substitute, or sublimation to what should be complete without it" ("Are Memoirs Autobiography?," 317). Efforts to position memoir in a subordinate status vis-à-vis its more august sibling autobiography have failed; and its contemporary popularity and attraction to "ordinary readers," according to Rak, suggest that the social practice of writing and reading memoirs "could contribute to understanding the changing relationship between ideas of selfhood and the role of public and private spheres in late capitalism" (324). For Nancy K. Miller "memoir is fashionably postmodern, since it hesitates to define the boundaries between private and public, subject and object." Central for Miller is the etymological root of the word in the double act of recalling and recording: "To record means literally to call to mind, to call up from the heart. At the same time, record means to set down in writing, to make official. What resides in the province of the heart is also what is exhibited in the public space of the world" (*Bequest and Betrayal*, 43).

The memoir boom has been accompanied by a boom in theoretical studies on the expansiveness, varied discursive modes, routes of circulation, and audiences of the form. Cultural critic Ben Yagoda's *Memoir: A History* is a vertiginous "biography" of it from Augustine's *Confessions* to Augusten Burroughs' life narratives. Using "memoir" interchangeably with "autobiography," Yagoda offers a copious catalogue, from pet memoirs to memoirs of child abuse, sexual abuse, addiction, celebrity, food, family, and the Holocaust, including O. J. Simpson's conditional memoir, *If I Did It*. Probing what might link all of these, he observes how the nagging question of truthfulness emerged with the advent of journalism itself.

In *Memoir: An Introduction,* Couser challenges Yagoda's breezy bromide by giving a precise, succinct overview of the form and its subgenres, its fictional origins and early American roots, and the ethical conundrums raised by some contemporary hoaxes and testimonies. His expansion of the form to film, with "documemoir," and to graphic memoir points toward the automedial dimensions of this evolving mode as "a powerful expression of democracy" (181).

Memoirist Mary Karr, whose edgy life narratives of coming-of-age and addiction are contemporary classics, combines her observations about reading and teaching memoir with writing it in *The Art of Memoir*. Acknowledging that "most memoirists know the past can be a swamp" (89), she includes a list of the "liberties" she's taken with the form (24–26) and writes in a lively, candid voice about developing a voice in each of her memoirs, observations that are richly informative for creative nonfiction writers.

In *BOOM! Manufacturing Memoir for the Popular Market,* Julie Rak turns to how the publishing industry facilitated and profited from the advent of the memoir boom in the United Kingdom and the United

Kinds of Life Narratives

States. Focusing on bookstores, distribution networks, and case studies of two presses and two memoirs, she asserts that memoir has become "a medium of exchange . . . because of its long association with the market and with the liberal democratic ideal of sharing one's life in the public sphere" (208) as "a genre by, for, and about citizenship of specific kind" (209).

Leigh Gilmore argues that markets and jurisdictions of life narrative worked to promote some kinds of life stories and repress others in ways that have tainted the memoir boom. Focusing on how memoir became what she calls a mode of "tainted witness," Gilmore observes that the "neoliberal life narrative" focused on "an 'I' who overcomes hardship and recasts historical and systemic harm as something an individual alone can, should, manage through pluck, perseverance, and enterprise" to promote personal responsibility. In this iteration, it displaced a lineage of feminist memoirs whose political aim was to expose violence. In Gilmore's view, "the radical potential of memoir consists in the public platform it offers to newly visible writers and the social and literary transformations they seek," which "had to be absorbed into neoliberalism by emptying the form of its challenging and politicized content and replacing its aesthetic challenges with the closure of the redemption narrative" (*Tainted Witness*, 89). For Gilmore, the impulse to speak truth to power has shifted to testimony in public forums even as "insufficiently redeemed narrators [are] denigrated" and driven to seek other sites of witnessing (94).

Clearly, tracing the scope and mission of memoir is an ongoing process. While these examples of recent theorizing emphasize its prominence as a form of democratic public utterance, how to evaluate its potency has become increasingly contested.

MIGRANT AND REFUGEE LIFE NARRATIVE

Narratives by immigrants, refugees, and those in exile have long been sites at which formerly marginal, displaced, or threatened subjects explore the terms of their former cultural identities and communities of belonging and assess their newer, provisionally ethnicized and racialized identities and their diasporic transnational affiliations. Some immigrant life narratives, from those of Mary Antin to Esmeralda Santiago and Shirley Geok-lin Lim in the United States and from Sui Sin Far (Edith Maude Eaton) to Michael Ondaatje in Canada, might productively be

274 Kinds of Life Narratives

read as autoethnographic struggles with "self-translation." Many of these narratives serve as a call, sometimes revolutionary, to confront and reform the marginal position of ethnic subjects. Some life writers ply the fiction-nonfiction border of immigrant stories, as does Norma Cantú in characterizing *Canícula* as "fictional autobioethnography," "a collage of stories gleaned from photographs randomly picked . . . with our past and our present juxtaposed and bleeding, seeping back and forth . . . in a recursive dance" (xi–xii).

Refugee narratives enact a complex politics of narrating witness to violence, radical suffering, and displacement from places of origin. They may become entangled in and constrained by the varied protocols, policies, and politics of the receiving nations, with the result that the kinds of stories that can be told for successful acceptance by immigration authorities are continually being modified. As Gillian Whitlock observes, the "agency of testimony is contingent; it responds to changing parameters in law and public policy, new technologies and the communities they engender, changing values in the affective economy, eruptions of violence, and negotiations for social justice in global networks of peace and justice" ("Embridry," 95).[15] Another important issue is raised by Clare Brant, Tobias Heinrich, and Monica Soeting: "What languages, literal and figurative, accompany their transition from one life to another?" (625).

For many immigrants and refugees, the experience of settling in North America generates contemporary versions of the narrative of disillusionment and cynicism that critique the myth of American exceptionalism and the United States as a place of promise and dreams fulfilled. Elizabeth Rodrigues adopts the term "refugee temporality" to capture how, "by insisting that the story is unfinished because the histories underlying the terms of a refugee's arrival are ongoing," refugees writing their temporality offer "a form of knowledge through which the refugee refutes the nation-state's claim of redemption" (119). In her memoir *Beautiful Country,* Qian Julie Wang "endeavor[s] to document my family's undocumented years as authentically and intimately as possible" (3) to narrate the transit of her seven-year-old self in 1994, and her years of underground or "shadow" survival living as undocumented. Adopting the voice and language of a child and young girl who comes of age in the time and space of "gei," she scripts a migration narrative that renders visible and palpable the experiences and fortitude of those who

Kinds of Life Narratives 275

negotiate the state of "undocumentation" in the United States as well as those who perpetuate or challenge the struggles of the undocumented. In recent decades, automedial genres have increasingly been mobilized to tell stories of traumatic flight, transit, migration, and tangled citizenship, especially powerful for capturing the visceral history of communities of refugees. For example, GB Tran recovers his family's history of transit in the graphic memoir *Vietnamerica: A Family's Journey*, which chronicles two stories: that of the parents' struggle to survive the war and escape Vietnam as refugees; and that of the son's Gen X apathy and indifference toward that traumatic past. Tran organizes the points of memory, from divergent historical moments and locations, syncopating chapters that move the parents' story forward and his own backward in time until they merge in the final frames and gutters.

Graphic journalism is also a multimedial mode for telling refugee stories. Rifkind observes that refugee and migrant comics comprise "a subfield of graphic life narratives that uses sequential hand-drawn comics, often produced collaboratively, to intervene in the photographic regime of the migrant as Other that has emerged as the dominant visual record of what T.J. Demos terms 'crisis globalization' [xiii]" ("Refugee Comics," 649). Notably, Joe Sacco's meticulous book-length comics documenting past struggles in contested Palestinian and Bosnian territories put his own avatar into the picture as a witness. Other examples are visual journalist Olivier Kugler's *Escaping Wars and Waves: Encounters with Syrian Refugees*; author-illustrator Don Brown's *The Unwanted: Stories of Syrian Refugees*; and British cartoonist-artist-activist Kate Evans's *Threads: From the Refugee Crisis*. Evans situates the narrative strands of *Threads* in the "Calais Jungle" of France's refugee camps, using lacemaking as a visual leitmotif to represent and embed relationships that develop within them, and trace the factors that led to refugee migration and the social stigmas that their stateless dilemma evokes. These comics of secondary witness interweave the stories refugees tell of their struggles to keep themselves and others afloat and alive while held in what Rifkind terms the "carceral infrastructures of trauma" ("Migrant Detention Comics," 298). They have multiple aims: to educate people in receiving countries, to enlist political and personal support, and to affect financial and policy interventions.

Film also provides an automedial site for narrating refugee lives in transit, particularly as smart phones and video cameras enable refugees to record precarious journeys from African and Asian shores and document the hostile treatment they endure. Films incorporating or referencing this footage, such as Senegalese Moussa Touré's *La Pirogue/ The Boat* and Italian Gianfranco Rosi's acclaimed *Fire at Sea*, embed the personal stories of some interviewees into larger stories of mass migration generated by displacement due to climate-induced and economic inequity. In *Human Flow* Ai Weiwei films fragments of refugee conversations that resonate as collectivized experience of the massive displacement of people around the world. In the meditative, multimedia film *An Opera of the World*, Manthia Diawara juxtaposes his own narrative as an earlier migrant with those of precarious voyagers now. Danish filmmaker Jonas Poher Rasmussen's graphic autodocumentary on the refugee narrative of his high school friend Amin Nawabi (pseudonym) in *Flee*, nominated for three Academy Awards, brings several themes of displacement and dispossession together. The voices of Rasmussen and Amin, a refugee from Afghanistan, blend in an interview as Rasmussen solicits and questions his friend's memories of early childhood, statelessness, and resettlement in Denmark; interwoven in it is Amin's sexual narrative of being gay and becoming protective of his secret, but seeking love and acceptance as a boy and man. As his narrative unfolds in compelling story segments, Amin, reclining on a couch as he looks up and out at the viewer, becomes his earlier self, remembering scenes from his past that are visualized in multiple comics styles. Occasionally, the enactment shifts to live action, a reminder of the "realness" of this lived experience that reinforces a sense of the story's reality as Rasmussen and Amin argue about how the refugee's story should be told.

In coming decades, autobiographical stories of bearing witness to the dispossession and migration occasioned by Russia's war on Ukraine and other continuing conflicts will generate moving accounts by refugees dispersed around the globe. Such life narratives will likely adapt new features as the profound effects of global warming intensify and the numbers of people displaced by climate crises increase exponentially. Those who bear the brunt of environmental racism—in the United States, disproportionately people of color—may tell stories of radical displacement in their struggles to survive, as occurred with Black victims of Hurricane Katrina in New Orleans. We may see new vehicles, media, story forms, and strategies developed by survivors and activists as they join stories of the lived experience of displacement and survival to recognition and analysis of structural racism, white supremacy, and extractive capitalism.

See "Ethnic and Postethnic Life Narrative" and "Geographies of Life Narrative."

NOBODY MEMOIR

The term *nobody memoir* was first used in a review essay, "Almost Famous: The Rise of the 'Nobody Memoir,'" by Lorraine Adams in the *Washington Post*. It was then introduced in life-writing circles by Couser, among others *(Signifying Bodies)*. As he points out, the classification of a memoir depends on whether its author was known before its publication, like Hillary Clinton, or becomes known through its publication, like Lucy Grealy. Adams's taxonomy of the "nobody" memoir includes childhood memoirs of growing up marked by some kind of disadvantage, trauma, or addiction; memoirs of catastrophic physical circumstance; and memoirs of mentally extreme states. Couser extends Adams's distinction by discussing the "some body memoir," that is, the narrative that explores the limits of and circumstances particular to one's embodiment.

ORAL HISTORY

A method of gathering a story in which an interviewer listens to, records, shapes, and edits the life story of another. In what we might call auto-oral history the one who speaks is not the one who writes, and the one who writes is often an absent presence in the text who nonetheless controls its narrative. Oral history is, then, a mediated form of personal narrative that depends on an interviewer who intervenes to collect and assemble a version of stories that are situated and changing. Sherna Berger Gluck and Daphne Patai, in addition to publishing oral histories, have given suggestions on how to conduct them. In its focus on the gatherer and the gathering of the story, oral history is distinct from collaborative autobiography.

In addition to the solo oral history, there are autoethnographic projects that combine first-person oral testimonies with scholarly critique and multimodal glosses on the stories. In *Troubling the Angels: Women Living with HIV/AIDS*, for instance, Patti Lather and Chris Smithies incorporate multiple modes of knowing about HIV/AIDS. They present oral histories of women living with HIV/AIDS through which they weave critical analysis, poetic engagement with metaphors of history, and factoids, to explore how telling one's story and hearing others' stories involve an ethic of knowing and caring in the time of the epidemic.

Collective oral histories, drawn from multiple people's experience of everyday life, use various methods to assemble archives on "The Science of Us." Scholars and researchers from many disciplines have investigated how individuals tell their life stories by borrowing from and innovating upon culturally available models of life writing. In Great Britain the Mass Observation Project, founded in 1937 by sociologist Charles Madge, anthropologist Tom Harrisson, and documentary filmmaker Humphrey Jennings, began an extended investigation of the lives of ordinary people to preserve multiple histories of twentieth-century Britain as embedded in personal narratives. Mass Observation used hundreds of untrained volunteers who kept diaries, as well as anonymous investigators who recorded conversations and actions in a variety of settings, to take the tenor of the times and use their findings to influence public policy. Although Mass Observation was superseded in the mid-1960s by formal market research, it was revived in 1981 at the University of Sussex, which continues to use questionnaires to collect the impressions of its panel of writers and generate changing profiles of the lives of everyday Britons. Similarly, Michael Apted's *Up!* television series interviewed fourteen subjects throughout their lives and embedded their oral histories in documentaries aired every seven years.

Life storytelling in the United States has been stimulated by National Public Radio. Their collections of personal stories, such as "StoryCorps," "This I Believe," and Ira Glass's "Chicago Project," are ongoing projects pursuing National Public Radio's mission "to honor and celebrate one another's lives through listening" (StoryCorps.org). The StoryCorps project, a vast collective oral auto-history that claims to be the largest archive of its kind, invites people in cities across the nation to visit traveling booths and record a story. Since 2003, over half a million ordinary people have recorded aspects of their life stories with family and friends. StoryCorps organizes the stories around themes and preserves them in the Library of Congress. Stories memorialize a dead person, or celebrate love, or recall traumatic events from the past. There are also initiatives to target specific populations, such as stories by people with significant memory loss. And a StoryCorps project "Griot" solicits stories of African Americans.

These digitized oral history projects reach out to ordinary citizens

Kinds of Life Narratives

by projecting common values that build community and memorialize the past. With the ever-expanding storage capacity of the Web, oral history collections are easily accessed by the public. Projects of collective storytelling, whether published as books, films, recordings, or in digital media, situate the individual's oral story in the larger metanarrative of a nation's social history in ways that bind tellers and listeners in an imagined national community.

Digitalization of life narratives, using the storage and communication capacities of the Web, has led to massive archiving of people's stories. Some archive projects capture worldwide attention, such as the Six-Word Life project, begun in 2006 by the online storytelling magazine *Smith,* which drolly invited users to compress their life stories into just six words. Other sites use a targeted outreach to focus their agendas around common experiences, identities, or historical roles in order to preserve past memories or, sometimes, assemble instructive stories for future generations. For example, mentoring sites offer young people information about how earlier generations have used a particular degree in their professional life. Some collections pursue comparative prosopography, as does the Rutgers University History Department's Oral History Project, which collects the stories of alums who served "on the home front and overseas during World War II, the Korean War, the Vietnam War and the Cold War." Some compile transnational collectivities, for example, the Transnational Feminism archive of stories housed at the Institute for Research on Women and Gender at the University of Michigan.

Many prominent archival projects seek to capture and preserve the life stories of survivors, members of groups who have been the victims of mass violence. Two major collections of recorded Holocaust survivor narratives, at the Holocaust Museum in Washington, D.C., and the Fortunoff Video Archive of Holocaust Testimonies at Yale University, have amassed substantial archives as a basis for developing theoretical perspectives on modes, audiences for, and mediation in oral testimony. The survivor archive project of the Urban School of San Francisco's Oral History Archives collects the oral histories of Japanese American men, women, and children held for years in detainment camps during World War II. As Internet technologies make such projects possible at the community level, the documentation of survivors and commemoration of victims of mass violence will likely be enhanced around the world.

Many families create their own oral auto-histories, using autobiographical storytelling to record the lived experience of their members and preserve them along with photographs and memorabilia in automedial scrapbooks. Literary versions of such projects are widespread. In *Maus I and II,* Spiegelman positions the figure of his father Vladek on an exercycle as he narrates his experiences in Poland before, during, and after the Holocaust to his son: panels depicting Vladek's increasingly desperate cycling capture the anxiety of telling his traumatic past and emphasize the viscerally embodied aspects of Spiegelman's graphic memoir.

OTOBIOGRAPHY

In *The Ear of the Other: Otobiography, Transference, Translation,* Jacques Derrida, in discussing Nietzsche and the politics of the proper name, proposed this term to deconstruct the "problematic of the biographical within philosophy" by recuperating the signature in the discourse of Hegel, where it is apparently subordinated, and by asserting its deferral in Nietzsche, where it seems writ large (56–57). Derrida notes, of Nietzsche, "When he writes himself to himself, he writes himself to the other who is infinitely far away and who is supposed to send his signature back to him." His self-relation is inescapably deferred by "the necessity of this detour through the other in the form of the eternal return" (88). Ultimately, the autobiographical is the *fort-da* of self-relation, "the effect of a process of ex-appropriation which produces only perspectives, readings without truth, differences, intersections of affect, a whole 'history' whose very possibility has to be disinscribed and reinscribed" (74).

PERFORMANCE AND THEATER AS AUTOBIOGRAPHICAL

Autobiographical theater, performance, and installation exhibitions comprise a vast sphere of life narrative activity, often using multiple media to construct automedial projects.[16] As artists around the world devise multiple media installations and sculptural experiments in surfaces and depths, they experiment with the limits and elasticity of subjectivity, identity, and embodiment. They thereby redefine the terms of legibility to challenge cultural regimes of hypervisibility and invisibility. Often, their autobiographical performances interrogate cultural norms that have projected on them a subjectivity, an identity, and a life script—

Kinds of Life Narratives

a biography of sorts—of a different order from their own self-experience. In confronting their "subordination in difference," such artists engage with codes of representation that have situated them as objects of representation (Mouffe, 382). Their performances, exhibits, and theatrical works become complex sites of negotiation, appropriation, adaptation, resistance, and re-formation of subjects-in-process engaging the terms, limits, and paradoxes of embodied self-representation.

Several contemporary Anglophone playwrights have mined their experience to construct dramas with arresting personal content. For example, Sir Tom Stoppard, at the end of a long theatrical career in which his work usually avoided autobiographical content, composed *Leopoldstadt,* a play about four generations of his Jewish family; notably, all four of his grandparents were interned and killed during the Holocaust. Stoppard observes, with his typical ambivalence, "Quite a lot of it is personal to me, but I made it about a Viennese family so that it wouldn't seem to be about me" (M. Brown).

Other dramatists are more frankly autobiographical. Throughout her life, African American playwright Adrienne Kennedy has created semi-autobiographical, multimedia pieces concerned with exploring the intersection of race, class, and gender in plays that were often received as "too political"—antiwhite for some, anti-Black for others—in their depictions of the violence of racism and misogyny. For example, *A Movie Star Has to Star in Black and White* articulates the lead character's life through and against the white movie stars she admired while growing up. Although Kennedy's *Funnyhouse of a Negro* was produced off-Broadway by Edward Albee in 1964, her work was largely ignored and first produced on Broadway in her nineties with *The Ohio State Murders.* Typically in Kennedy's plays, "the self is ever-shifting, an identity dispersed across multiple personages, who emerge out of the past" (T. Beard), such as her son in *Sleep Deprivation Chamber.*

Other recent dramatists, including Suzan-Lori Parks, Maria Irene Fornes, Sarah Kane, Caryl Churchill, and Anna Deavere Smith as well as earlier dramatists such as Alice Childress, Susan Glaspell, and Tennessee Williams, also incorporate nonnaturalist autobiographical content, to a greater or lesser extent, into their engagements with sexual and racial politics. Contemporary American playwright Clare Barron, in an interview with Alexis Soloski, acknowledges the autobiographical impulse of her plays, which draw deeply on felt personal experience. She states that her play *I'll Never Love Again* "is literally my diary. It's not even hidden. . . . I feel like I'm exposing myself over and over again, hoping to have some kind of like [*sic*] clarity" (AR4).

Some artists use visual media to locate the autobiographical in the interior of the body, and thereby foreground its absent presence as a central paradox of autobiographical performance. For example, in Mona Hatoum's two-hour video performance *Pull,* the artist placed herself in an exhibition area hidden from the visitor; only her long ponytail, hanging in a niche in the wall, was visible. Visitors confronting the "real" ponytail, and above it a video of the artist who seemed to be hanging upside down, were invited to pull the ponytail and could watch the effect of that on the artist. While viewers assumed the video was recorded and no connection existed between their pulling and Hatoum's facial expression, they were in fact pulling the hair of the artist present behind the wall. As Guy Brett observed, "at a certain moment the spectacle suddenly ceases to be a spectacle" (74) as visitors confronted their role in causing pain to a flesh-and-blood person. In such installations Hatoum attaches the processes of representing subjectivity to the materiality of her body, forcing viewers to confront the conundrum of her presence in apparent absence.

Similarly, contemporary artist Janine Antoni visualizes the psychic interior of drives such as hunger and sexual desire. Her installation *Gnaw* presents the viewer with two three-hundred-pound cubes, one made of chocolate, the other of lard, that the artist has eaten during off-hours in the gallery; out of the regurgitated gnawings she has fashioned new consumer products—lipsticks and chocolate hearts—identified with the social construction of heterosexual femininity. Here the autobiographical body, though absent, is present in its traces: the teeth marks left on massive cubes of chocolate and lard, the chewings that re-form into lipstick and hearts, bodily marks that insert Antoni's autobiographical traces into the picture.

Artists may also work ethnographically to create a performance or exhibit that commemorates or revalues past remembered scenes of collective memory, linking the personal, communal, and ethnic. For example, the massive installation *A Subtlety* by Kara Walker was a white "sugar baby" in the shape of a sphinx, with African American features and a bandanna on her head, mounted outside the Domino Sugar Factory in Brooklyn. It expresses the absent artist's stinging critique of the

Kinds of Life Narratives 283

colonial origins of anti-Black racism in commodities mined by the sweat and tears of enslaved people expropriated from Africa. Collage artist Aminah Robinson produced more than twenty thousand works in her career, many of which combine her self-representation with the oral history of her African American family and community in Columbus, Ohio. Executed in painting, drawing, button-beading, fabric, stitching, and other media, these autoethnographic images connect the tradition and lore of midwestern African America to her own experiential history in a communal visual ethnography of a lost past (see Myers).

Many postcolonial and multicultural artists explore the relationship of a racialized identity to a national identity that has historically dominated and effaced it, and visually recontextualize received autobiographical history to generate new stories that evoke the power of images to stir memory. For example, African American artist Glenn Ligon probes paradoxes about racial identification in works such as *Some Changes* by assembling pieces from two decades that situate his autobiographical narrative within multiply mediated discourses of racialization, "question[ing] the relations between self and shadow, master and slave—how he experiences them internally and with respect to others" (Wexner Center). In sum, all of these theatrical and visual performances enact how artists yoke their autobiographical histories to the materiality of their bodies and their socially conflicted or devalued identities.

PERSONAL ESSAY

A mode of writing that is literally a self-tryout, the personal essay is a testing ("assay") of one's own intellectual, emotional, political, and physiological responses to a given topic. Since its development by Montaigne as a form of self-exploration engaging with the received wisdom of antiquity, the essay has been a site of self-creation, often refracted through reflections on the thoughts of others. The personal essay can be strongly self-referential, as in several essay collections by Nancy Mairs and bell hooks. Prominent practitioners of the personal essay now include Zadie Smith (most recently *Intimations: Six Essays*), Wendell Berry (*What I Stand On: The Collected Essays of Wendell Berry, 1969–2017*), Anne Lamott (*Dusk, Night, Dawn: On Revival and Courage*), David Sedaris (*Calypso* and *Happy-Go-Lucky*), and André Aciman (*Alibis: Essays on Elsewhere*).

PHOTO-MEMOIR AND PHOTOGRAPHY IN LIFE NARRATIVE

Photo-memoirs are life narratives that unfold in part through photographic images introduced as turning points that generate related stories, capture memories, or reveal secrets probed by the writer; yet the photograph, as a distinct medium, may depict a dissonant story that asks to be read against the narrated story. As Arnaud Schmitt observes, "While autobiographers use photographs primarily for their illustrative or referential function, photographers have a much more complex interaction with pictures in their autobiographical accounts" (*Photographer as Autobiographer,* 1). For example, Sally Mann's remarkable *Hold Still: A Memoir with Photographs* juxtaposes her own photographs on nearly every page with those of over three dozen others to create her coming-of-age story. It draws on papers and photographs, discovered in the family attic, that disclose family scandals, to shape a story of growing up in rural Virginia and breaking free from its confines to become a brilliantly controversial photographer of the private lives of families—controversial because of the possibly transgressive photographs she takes of her children. Patti Smith's *Just Kids* parallels her narration of Robert Mapplethorpe's and her own coming-of-age stories with thirty photographs by Mapplethorpe, other artists, and herself that depict memorable moments of their private and emergent public lives, though their celebrity status makes even their youthful images iconic. And singer Bret Michaels of the rock band Poison titles his photo-driven memoir *Auto-scrap-ography,* Volume 1: *My Life in Pictures & Stories,* arranging photographs and handwritten stories to narrate his "roses-and-thorns" journey through adversity and celebrity in a career of more than thirty-five years. His neologism for a memoir foregrounding photographs that mark turning points in one's life story suggests how scrapbooks arrange photographs and memorabilia to commemorate life highlights.

Photo-memoir is by no means a new genre and has often been a mode used by photojournalists. *Let Us Now Praise Famous Men,* for example, is a collective biography on which American writer James Agee collaborated with photographer Walker Evans to document the struggles of poor tenant farmers during the Great Depression in the United States. Photo-memoir is also a vehicle for journalists' life narratives such as *It's What I Do: A Photographer's Life of Love and War* by Pulitzer Prize–

Kinds of Life Narratives 285

winning photojournalist Lynsey Addario. In harrowing detail, it narrates her years as a war correspondent over the past two decades in conflicts in Afghanistan, Iraq, Libya, Darfur, and other places and chronicles her experiences of being kidnapped, fusing personal experience with a political critique of "the war on terror." When photographs do more than illustrate, when they seek to authenticate a text, Schmitt argues, reader-viewers are called on to ask, "how does the text/image hybridity function in an autobiographical context"? (3). Susan Sontag's *On Photography* argued that readers engaging with photo-memoirs need to consider to what extent the photographs "document" and substantiate the written story and to what extent they present counternarratives challenging or complicating its verbal "truth." As Adams trenchantly observed in *Light Writing and Life Writing: Photography in Autobiography,* photographic self-portraits "call into question the idea of likeness" (230). Yet "all photographic portraits are memoirs in that they always include an interaction between photographer and photographed" (232). Even where photographs are withheld in a life narrative referencing them, such as Roland Barthes's famous example of not including the "Winter Garden" photograph in his *Camera Lucida,* they mark alternative storytelling possibilities. The "mysterious, illusive quality" between "the dossier of fact" and "the invitation of fiction" in the oscillations of both photography and autobiography is a provocation, rather than fully a verification, that invites our continuing reflection (Adams, 242).

Artists have pursued photographic experiments that reconceptualize the very notion of self-portraiture during the past several decades. A photograph (or photographs) may accompany an autobiographical narrative, be alluded to but absent, or stand in the place of an absent but suggested narrative, in a photographic series. In such series, that is, multiple self-portraits expose an autobiographical subject to view as they engage the illusory and unstable nature of the exposed subject. The photograph presents the "I" in the photograph as at once a flesh-and-blood subject and a dematerialized phantom of an invisible photographer. The uncanny self-portraits of such self-photographers as Claude Cahun, Francesca Woodman, and Cindy Sherman interrogate self-identity as they double "I"s, unfix genders, and unmask conventions of self-portraiture by their impersonation of popular or artistic images. Photographic self-representation, then, shares the troubled relationship of a represented subject to its flesh-and-blood maker that we have observed in verbal autobiographical texts; and it also engages viewers intersubjectively in acts of seeing differently.

Sequential photographic self-presentation has enabled some artists to represent subjectivity as processual rather than static and to emphasize that identity is performative, not intrinsic. Eleanor Antin's series of self-photographs on weight loss, titled *Carving: A Traditional Sculpture,* presents a set of photographed poses that playfully reiterate, with variation, the artist's shedding of weight as a gradual displacement of female embodiment by negative space on the photograph's surface. No single pose or frame of the sequence is the "definitive" or "truthful" self-portrait. In sequential self-portraiture, such artists may engage stages of the life cycle: for instance, performing the childhood past or enacting daughterhood, maternity, professional roles, bodily illness and disability, and aging. In a reflective vein, Joanne Leonard composes *Being in Pictures,* in images and text, as a magisterial yet intimate evocation of her photographic "life." She juxtaposes a narrative of her professional development as an artist and her personal experience of motherhood with a retrospective exhibition of her photographic experiments to render feminist consciousness in action as a series of visible images. In serial self-representation, viewers witness the artist's body multiply—in parts, at angles, inside out, upside down, three-dimensionally, perspectivally—as part of a larger story about women's relation to historical representations of woman and gendered sexuality.

Artists also mobilize photographic images to intervene in experiential histories marked by racial and sexual politics, as does Renee Cox in her *Yo Mama* series of photographic self-portraits. Through this photographic series Cox, performing the *Yo Mama* figure of Black street talk, places her own body at various cultural locations and in art-historical and ethnographic cultural intertexts. In *Yo Mama's Last Supper,* Cox assumes the central space of the da Vinci painting, displacing the Christ figure with her own photographed naked self-portrait to intervene in its tableau of white masculinity. In *Venus Hottentot 2000,* she assumes the place of the "Hottentot Venus," the fetishized African woman of nineteenth-century ethnography, to critique a history of cultural representations in which the Black female body is absent or caricatured. As Cox "looks" out from sites of representation not created for her, she asserts autobiographical agency for the gendered and racially marked body (Myers, 27). As African American painter and photographer

Kinds of Life Narratives

Mickalene Thomas observed of her own work, "exploring self-portraiture prepared me to think honestly about what it means to be the subject of the image without being reduced to the object of the viewer" (Rosen).

Joanne Leonard has recently noted that one of her students referred to a photo essay with herself as the main character as an *autoimaginography*. This suggestive term underscores how fluid, complex, and heterogeneous the connections between the photographic and the autobiographic are.

POETIC AUTOBIOGRAPHY

A mode of the lyric distinguished, according to James Olney, not by content but by "the formal device of recapitulation and recall" ("Some Versions of Memory," 252). It may appear that all lyric poetry is life writing in that the speaker of the lyric inscribes a subjective self to explore emotions, vision, and intellectual states. We need, however, to distinguish certain kinds of lyrics that announce themselves as "autobiography" from *lyric* as an umbrella term for many forms of poetic self-inscription. Exploring texts he calls *poetic autobiographies,* such as T. S. Eliot's *Four Quartets* and Paul Valéry's *The Young Fate,* Olney argues that what characterizes the lyric as autobiographical includes extended engagement with the uses of memory and qualities of internal states of consciousness. Since the early nineteenth century, he notes, poetic autobiography has centered on a sustained exploration of "the growth of a poet's mind," as in William Wordsworth's subtitle to *The Prelude, Growth of a Poet's Mind.* In other instances, the lyric projects introspective seekers immersing themselves in the landscapes, both rural and urban, of the American Republic in crisis and transformation, as in Walt Whitman's "Song of Myself" and *Specimen Days.* The broader scope of lyrical life narrative needs further study but is suggested in later twentieth-century works such as the twelve books of autobiographical poetry of Nobel Prize winner Louise Glück, Robert Lowell's *Life Studies,* Adrienne Rich's *Diving into the Wreck,* A. R. Ammons's *Tape for the Turn of the Year,* John Ashbery's *Self-Portrait in a Convex Mirror,* Anne Sexton's *Live or Die.* Recent poets have entwined personal narratives with critiques of racialized citizenship and migration in works such as Claudia Rankine's *Citizen: An American Lyric,* Javier Zamora's *Unaccompanied,* Natasha Trethewey's Pulitzer Prize–winning *Native Guard,* and Alora Young's *Walking Gentry Home: A Memoir of My Foremothers in Verse.*

POLITICAL LIFE NARRATIVE

Politicians and political leaders have long written life narratives in the wake of their public service. In the political life of the United States, the personal story has often been central to projecting myths of origin, fables of character, ledgers of leadership, and visions for national aspirations. American presidents penned autobiographies for several purposes: to offer their analyses, complaints, and justifications for their actions; to detail challenges and achievements in office; and to set forth their version of their legacy. But in the last thirty years something different is occurring in the United States and elsewhere. Many candidates now publish life narratives prior to their presidential campaigns as necessary performances of identity and scripts of identification, as well as fare for their fan bases.[17]

In 2008, Barack Obama's memoir *Dreams from My Father* was reissued in the aftermath of his Whitmanesque invocation of the heterogeneity of "America" in 2004 and his subsequent rise to celebrity status. In Obama's unique case, the narrated life, deftly deploying the autobiographical discourses of journey and of double-consciousness, enabled this first-term senator to run for president in 2008. A second book in 2006 resituated his personal story as a message of "hope" and ideas. At the same time, remediations of Obama's 1995 narrative, leading up to the primary and general elections, took his claims out of context and often tainted them to reinterpret his narrative as one of threatening radicalism.

Democratic senator Hillary Rodham Clinton's *Living History* was conceived as a prologue to her first presidential campaign in 2008 and a narrative enabling readers to imagine a woman as president. Through it, Clinton confronted the bias against women in high office, exposed the workings of gender ideology, affirmed her long struggle to change the terms of women's participation in public life, and claimed her career as a breakthrough story of overcoming the gendered barriers to presidential leadership. In advance of her 2016 campaign she published *Hard Choices* to reinforce her earlier memoir with the perspectives she had gained and accomplishments she had achieved as Obama's secretary of state. Yet she was twice unsuccessful in her bid for the presidency, raising a question about the extent to which public media discourses counteracted the stirring self-assertions of her memoirs.

In another variant of the political life narrative, Republican sena-

Kinds of Life Narratives

tor John McCain, in five coauthored autobiographical narratives written before throwing his hat into the presidential ring in 2008, linked the autobiographical discourses of family genealogy, profession, and generation—his as a wounded and captured Vietnam War veteran—to project his identity as the maverick son of a military family and situate his origins in a family history of military service to the nation. When he swept through the United States on his "Service to America" "biography tour," in March 2008, he revisited states, towns, and schools that had been formative in his young life, rousing voters with the intimacy of a sentimental reunion story centered on a younger version of himself. Thus, in the 2008 election published life narratives and their oral performances played a pivotal role.

But the role of memoir was challenged and in part supplanted in the 2016 election by Donald Trump's strategic use of Twitter as a rapid-fire means to communicate his takes on daily events and his critiques of the current administration and other candidates. It became a mode of up-to-the-minute self-presentation without an apparatus for fact-checking. True, Trump had also collaborated with Tony Schwartz on *Trump: The Art of the Deal,* a memoir and advice book about his purported rise to wealth and power that again became a best-seller during his campaign, and contributed to the image of him constructed by the television show *The Apprentice* as a savvy, decisive businessman. If social media made Donald Trump a hypervisible candidate, it also offered those in his administration a mouthpiece for supporting or contesting his claims. Ultimately many of them would publish memoirs upon leaving—or being fired from—his controversial administration and reap publicity and profits. Some, like his vice president Mike Pence and secretary of state Mike Pompeo, were clearly positioning themselves for their own future candidacies; others aired their versions of why they were fired to redress perceived harm to their reputations and to share insider gossip. And the candidate who lost to him—Hillary Rodham Clinton—went on the record in *What Happened* with her account of the surprising Trump victory. After those tumultuous years it is unclear how decisive a role memoir will play in future elections. But it will remain a vehicle for past presidents, as well as their wives and cabinets, to narrate their versions of their years as, or around, the head of state.

Elsewhere in the world, life narrative has served to secure the role of revolutionary leaders in the wake of movements of liberation and decolonization. As Philip Holden explores in *Autobiography and Decolonization: Modernity, Masculinity, and the Nation-State,* modernist autobiographies recounting stories of education, heroism, progress, and incorporation have been written by generations of anticolonial leaders who became "fathers" of their nations, among them, Jawaharlal Nehru, Kwame Nkrumah, and Kenneth Kaunda, as well as an occasional "mother" such as Benazir Bhutto and Golda Meir. Such narratives effectively parallel the autobiographical trope of "the growth of the individual" to "the growth of a national consciousness and, frequently proleptically, the achievement of an independent nation-state" (5). Holden observes that such autobiographies serve two functions: "They demonstrate to an international audience, through the life of a representative individual who is paradoxically also an exceptional leader, the nation's entry into modernity. At the same time, they function within the nation as documents of—and indeed, by being read, as incitements to—the production of citizens of the new nation-state" (5). From distinct geographical locations, by recounting stories of specific struggles for independence and national identity, these narratives produce and claim in the international public sphere an "indigenizing modernity" (17).

Inspiring political life narratives have also been written on what South African writer Bessie Head's memoir called *A Question of Power* by rebels and revolutionary leaders who never held the office of president, such as suffragette E. Sylvia Pankhurst, Rosa Luxemburg, Leon Trotsky, Mother Jones, Mahatma Gandhi, Elizabeth Gurley Flynn, Che Guevara, and Head. In *Américanas, Autocracy, and Autobiographical Innovation: Overwriting the Dictator,* Lisa Ortiz-Vilarelle considers the relationship of life writing and dictatorship in the Americas by focusing on the cases of five women who wrote back to the leaders of their twentieth-century autocratic governments in the Dominican Republic of Rafael Trujillo, the Somoza dynasty in Nicaragua, the charismatic Perons in Argentina, Castro's Cuba, and Pinochet's Chile. The women writers formally experiment with self-representations in producing counternarratives that depict them as self-aware, resisting subjects rewriting gendered narratives of national identity. The Nobel Peace Prize has also recognized the accomplishments of many activists who subsequently published life narratives that recount how they learned to intervene in

Kinds of Life Narratives 291

national or international situations, sometimes endangering themselves in the process of becoming resisters and leaders. Maria Ressa, Wangari Maathai, Shirin Ebadi, Malala Yousefzai, Leymah Gbowee, Ellen Johnson Sirleaf, and Mother Teresa are among recent winners whose memoirs of becoming activists and leaders have circulated widely and influentially.

The life narratives of "fathers" and "mothers" of the nation do the social work of constituting the subjects of the nation, while reading such life writing becomes a self-constituting act of citizenship-formation. That is, readers attach themselves affectively to the story, life, and body of the leader and thus to the nation. Aspects of a leader's individual story authenticate for the reader-citizen how the nation itself is embodied. And readerly acts collectively produce a common story that joins people to, and in, the national imaginary. As these performances of autobiographical narrative project a vision of collective desires, beliefs, and character, they educate successive generations of readers—for better or for worse.

Politicians' narratives raise issues about the kinds of stories inscribed in published life narratives, the performative identities they sanction and circulate, the national and international arenas of politics through which they circulate, and the kinds of citizens they project as readers. They also raise issues about the constructed networks and intricate meshworks of political organizations and the narrated lives such organizations underwrite and construct. They illuminate the liberal, neoliberal, or conservative inflections underlying much life writing. And they illustrate how the circuits of autobiographical discourses of constituent, citizen, and netizen interact in forming—or undermining— global citizenship.

PRISON NARRATIVE

A mode of captivity narrative written during or after incarceration, life writing from prison may become an occasion for prisoners to inscribe themselves as fully human in the midst of carceral systems designed to dehumanize them by rendering them anonymous, passive, and fearful. Prison narratives also offer occasions for prisoners to forge or preserve identity under duress. Jensen observes that prisoners held in Guantánamo focus on external communication, not just to the outside world but "to fellow detainees, jailers, and indeed, Allah" (169). She observes the importance for detainees of writing autobiographically about their circumstances and condition: "Like prisoners in the Gulag, the men held without charge and tortured at Guantánamo" in their own words "turned to writing poetry as a way to maintain their sanity, to memorialize their suffering and to preserve their humanity through acts of creation" (170, and citing *Poems from: The Detainees Speak*). Additionally, H. Bruce Franklin suggests, "most current autobiographical writing from prison intends to show the readers that the author's individual experience is not unique or even extraordinary" (250). Indeed, Eleanor March explores prisoner writing as an act of translation that describes prison life to other prisoners and the nonprisoner reader and probes how they establish their credibility as translators of prison life, proposing a typology of "the carceral authorial process" (573).

Prison narratives critique state repression in particular national contexts. While Barbara Harlow distinguishes two categories of prisoners—common-law and political detainees—she insists that they cannot be sharply distinguished ("From the Women's Prison"). In the case of prisoners identifying themselves as detainees, she notes, "their personal itineraries, which have taken them through struggle, interrogation, incarceration, and, in many cases, physical torture, are attested to in their own narratives as part of a historical agenda, a collective enterprise" (506). Prison narratives also expose the contradictions of democratic nations such as the United States, as do Assata Shakur in *Assata: An Autobiography* and Eldridge Cleaver in *Soul on Ice.* They register the dangers of dissidence in new postcolonial nations, as in Ngũgĩ wa Thiongo's *Detained: A Writer's Prison Diary* and Nawal El Saadawi's *Memoirs from the Women's Prison.* They bear witness to the brutality of particular political regimes: to South African apartheid in Ruth First's *117 Days: An Account of Confinement and Interrogation under the South African 90-Day Detention Law,* Breyten Breytenbach's *The True Confessions of an Albino Terrorist,* and Nelson Mandela's *Long Walk to Freedom: The Autobiography of Nelson Mandela*; and to the Argentine military junta in Jacobo Timerman's *Prisoner without a Name, Cell without a Number.*

Prison narratives are centrally concerned with narrating the shifts in consciousness occasioned by imprisonment and by activist agendas of educating the outside world about the lived realities of incarceration and its politics. Stories of surviving incarceration project agency, resilience, and resistance in ways that sometimes catapult the author/survivor to

Kinds of Life Narratives

celebrity status. While readers in the West often interpret such stories as reinforcing the heroism of the single individual saying "no" to power and resisting a regime with integrity and purpose, prison narratives often involve a collective dimension. They may become a mode of memorialization, as in Argentinian American Alicia Partnoy's *The Little School,* a set of fictionalized "tales" capturing the lived experience of being incarcerated by the Argentinian junta. Partnoy powerfully combines the representation of incarceration as physical and mental torture with a testimonial call on behalf of the collectivity of those who perished in detention.

In other contexts, individual witnesses are encouraged to tell their stories as a way to join collective actions aimed at bringing a particular rights violation to public attention. For example, former World War II sex prisoners in Korea and the Philippines who had been brutally exploited by the Japanese military occupation were sought by feminist activists in the early 1990s to enable the former sex prisoners to redefine their experience as violent rape and rights violation. While some of these stories have been collected in anthologies and individual witnesses have spoken on college campuses in Australia and the United States, activist anthologies of the stories of such witnesses to suffering and harm may conform individual narratives to a "master" script in ways that erase their particular differences (see Schaffer and Smith, *Human Rights,* 123–52).

PROSOPOGRAPHY

A practice of making a collective study of the characteristics shared by a group whose members' biographies often cannot be referenced, in order to discover relationships and patterns among their lives at a particular historical moment. While Quintilian, in classical rhetoric, related it to prosopopoeia, the figurative evocation of an absent or imagined person, prosopography has become an important form for analyzing the structure and changing roles of groups for historians using data of various kinds.

SCRIPTOTHERAPY

A term coined by Suzette Henke to signal the ways in which autobiographical writing functions as a mode of self-healing, scriptotherapy includes the processes of both "writing out and writing through traumatic experience in the mode of therapeutic reenactment" (xii).

Henke attends to several twentieth-century women's life narratives that focus on such childhood trauma as incest and abuse, which adult narrators—for example, Anaïs Nin and Sylvia Fraser—record in order to both heal themselves and reconfigure selves deformed by earlier abuse.

Meg Jensen asserts that the key functions in using forms of writing narratives of trauma are "the ability to express what Coleridge termed 'woeful agony'" and the need "to protect the self from overwhelming emotion associated with such expression" (185). She observes, "while the first step toward healing from traumatic experience is finding a way to communicate suffering without retraumatizing oneself in the process, the key to *recovery* is the collaborative exchange of interest, emotion, and understanding that arises when that story is *heard*" in writing or oral or visual testimony through intentional listening (278). In Jensen's view, what matters is not just the ways in which such genres as "a war memoir, an autobiographical novel, a prison poem, an autography, or a public memorial" narrate the details of an event, "but also . . . the ways in which those narratives express their anger, hurt, frustration and bitterness toward the unanswerable question: 'why'?" (278).

SELF-HELP NARRATIVE

There are many varieties of self-help narratives, how-tos based on the author's personal experience of regulating daily life—the size and shape of one's body, the raising of children and pets, recovery from or accommodation to illness, the cultivation of education, hobbies, or virtue, and so on. Books on self-care, such as Eckhart Tolle's *Practicing the Power of Now: Essential Teachings, Meditations, and Exercises,* offer guides to therapeutic self-reflection or to spiritual counsel and spur readers to find a voice and construct their stories of questing, questioning, discovery, and renewed interior life through such practices as journaling, blogging, or writing about photographs of themselves. A prominent form for the last several decades has been the self-help narrative for those addicted to drugs or alcohol. Typically, the narrative follows a pattern that includes a fall into dissolution; alienation from a community; employment and financial loss; recognition of the need for help; renunciation of the substance or behavior; and often trust in a higher power and recovery of a truer postaddiction self. Such distinguished writers as Augusten Burroughs *(Dry: A Memoir),* David Carr *(The Night of the Gun),* Mary Karr *(Lit: A Memoir),* Caroline Knapp *(Drinking: A Love Story),* and Leslie

Kinds of Life Narratives 295

Jamison (*The Recovering: Intoxication and Its Aftermath*) have incorporated features of this pattern in memoirs of recovery from addiction. (See "Addiction Narrative.")

Another contemporary mode of self-help narrative concerns migrants and refugees fleeing violence or poverty and seeking new lives elsewhere. They narrate "how-to" stories that document details of survival and relocation and instruct others on how to successfully manage transit and entry. Some small presses promote these life stories as guidebooks to help those trying to settle in an unfamiliar country and find support, community resources, safe housing, and employment while seeking legitimacy. For example, Bay Mademba, in *Il mio viaggio della speranza (My Voyage of Hope)*, narrates, in conjunction with his editor, his voyage from North Africa to Florence in quest of Italian refugee status and new employment, with some details obscured to protect those who helped him.

Web platforms accumulate all kinds of self-help narratives, long and short, fragmentary and sometimes interactive. These combine to generate small data and Big Data for self-understanding and self-diversion. A feature of some platforms involves protocols through which users monitor their bodily processes, weight, intake, outgo, and activities. Participation in such self-studies and the narratives of the body they register for users can be understood as quantitative self-help.

SELF-PORTRAIT (IN FRENCH, *AUTOPORTRAIT*)

In modernity and postmodernity, autobiographical inscription inheres in a variety of media, including performance, installation, visual/verbal diary, collage, quilting, sculpture, and so forth. Primarily the term *self-portrait* is used for artists' painted, photographed, drawn, or printed portraits of themselves. But in literary studies, *self-portrait* has been used to distinguish the present-oriented from the retrospectively oriented autobiographical narrative. William L. Howarth argued that "an autobiography is a self-portrait" (85) and explored analogies between Renaissance self-portraits and autobiographies throughout Western history. But later theorist Michel Beaujour challenges this analogy between visual and written self-portraiture. Beaujour distinguishes the literary self-portrait from the autobiography as a "polymorphous formation, a much more heterogeneous and complex literary type than is autobiographical narration" (25). Self-portraiture is not self-description but "the mirror whose reflecting function is mimicked in the symmetrical statement: me by me" (31). Insisting that the literary self-portrait as an act of "painting" oneself is inescapably metaphorical, not literal, Beaujour defines verbal self-portraiture as "focused on the present of writing rather than the remembrance of the past and referring all things to the speaking subject and his perceptions" (340). In the self-portrait, according to Beaujour, the intent is not as much to reconstitute the subject of history in a remembered past as to meditate on the processes of self-writing itself. Here the narrating "I" as the agent of discourse is concentrated in a present in which the self can never be fixed. In French studies, Candace Lang has argued that the literary self-portrait is not a memoir but a genre of postmodern autobiography, with Roland Barthes its best-known practitioner ("Autobiography").

See our introduction in *Interfaces* for a fuller account of self-portraiture.

SERIAL LIFE NARRATIVE

A term for autobiographical work published in multiple volumes (or films, videos, artworks). Although some writers consider these as "chapters" in an ongoing life story, many significantly revise their narratives from the perspectives of different times of writing that change their interpretations of experience. When Mary McCarthy and Frederick Douglass, for example, published their narratives at different stages of their lives, the emphasis fell on dramatically different moments. Maya Angelou published seven autobiographical narratives that move from her great coming-of-age work, *I Know Why the Caged Bird Sings*, to multifarious reflections on experiences and journeys throughout her long life. As Nicole Stamant observes, Angelou's volumes are episodic, collecting different stories to form a mosaic in which each becomes an archive for its successors. Collectively, they create a "composite reflection" of her memories (54) that "highlights the social collectivity of African Americans" in the "hyper-relationality of subjectivity" (56). In different ways, the interwoven life narratives of writers as distinct as Karl Ove Knausgaard, Dave Pelzer, Augusten Burroughs, Paul Monette, Isabel Allende, and many others are resonantly serial works, with later installments commenting on, revisioning, and extending earlier iterations and, in cases such as those of Michelle Cliff, J. M. Coetzee, and Emmanuel Carrère, troping on the notion of serial memoir itself.

Kinds of Life Narratives

Graphic memoirs also provide rich occasions for serially narrating the events and foibles of a particular family's life as exemplary of archived collective memory that references larger historical forces, notably in the comics of Spiegelman, Marjane Satrapi, and Bechdel. As Stamant observes, drawing on the example of *Maus,* the episodic presentation of self and related others in such graphic memoirs "challenges traditional concepts of sequential or continuous history" because "memory, collection, archivization, and recollection" are serial, recursive, and self-reflexive processes (89).

Consider the project of novelist, playwright, and poet Deborah Levy, who spent her childhood in South Africa but resides in London. Her memoir trilogy "Living Autobiography," includes three volumes, *Things I Don't Want to Know, The Cost of Living,* and *Real Estate,* that explore gendered asymmetry in her gradual dismantling of the state of conventional motherhood with which her adult life began. As one critic observes, her focus is on "women striving to align their possession by the chaos of motherhood with their immense creative ambition" (Denker). In the trilogy, Levy's quest is both artistic and spatial, moving from discontent with her conventional family life; to initial disorder in the "Corridors of Love," a crumbling flat; to eventual recognition as a Booker Prize–nominated writer that enables her to, in many senses, establish her "real" home as an artist. Like many serial autobiographers, Levy changes the story as her circumstances change. As she told an interviewer, her three life narratives are "hopefully not being written at the end, with hindsight, but in the storm of life" (Nicol). Seriality, in Levy's work, becomes a mode for experimental storytelling with an "I" who relishes her own dynamic instability.

In an expanded view of seriality, a writer's previous autobiographical writing may serve as a personal archive for reworking the past. This occurs in complex ways with Annie Ernaux's narratives about her mother's and father's relationship and the death of each, as well as her own abortion narrative *Happening,* as the relationship of prequel and sequel becomes recursive.

The proliferation of serial memoirs in various media invites further theorizing that might center on exploring such questions as: How is the notion of a writer's identity changed or reinterpreted across multiple narratives? How does the use of varied life narrative genres in different installments inflect a serial project? If a text serves as a sociopolitical

298 Kinds of Life Narratives

intervention at the time of its writing, how do its marketing and circulation affect its readership in later volumes as readers respond interactively through book tours and blogs?

SEX AND GENDER NARRATIVE

Narratives of gender foregrounding identity, performance, expression, or life course and sexuality, including sexual orientation, sexual transformation, and sexual violence, now constitute a distinct autobiographical subgenre. And there are precursor narratives in earlier centuries that chronicle experiential histories of gender performance and transvestism, such as Catalina de Erauso's early seventeenth-century *The Lieutenant Nun: Memoir of a Basque Transvestite in the New World* and cross-dressing English actress Charlotte Charke's eighteenth-century *A Narrative of the Life of Mrs. Charlotte Charke.* The modern coming-out narrative emerged in the last third of the twentieth century, with life narratives such as Audre Lorde's *Zami: A New Spelling of My Name,* a "biomythography" about escaping repression against lesbians to a fantasized island where they can live collectively as friends and lovers, and the circulation of post-Stonewall lesbian and gay histories, though earlier versions abound.[18] Coming-out narratives inscribe stories of the nascent sense of same-sex desire, the psychic costs of passing as heteronormative, the turning point of proclaiming one's sexual orientation, and the aftereffects of that act, as well as struggles to embody and validate chosen sexual identities. Betty Berzon, in *Surviving Madness,* for instance, links her recovery from a mental breakdown and suicide attempts to coming out as a lesbian at forty and working as a gay therapist.

Often these stories insist on the intersection of sexual and gender identities with other identities. For women of color, feminist anthologies published by small presses, such as *This Bridge Called My Back,* edited by Cherríe Moraga and Gloria Anzaldúa, and *Making Face, Making Soul = Haciendo Caras,* edited by Anzaldúa, have for decades served as an intersectional archive of lesbian life writing. Gay memoirs often unfold at an intersection of identities as well: Kenny Fries's *Body, Remember* negotiates his identifications as disabled, Jewish, and gay; and Jaime Manrique in *Eminent Maricones: Arenas, Lorca, Puig, and Me* tells his story of living as a gay Latinx artist through its intersections with the lives of three eminent Hispanic writers.

Contemporary LGBTQI life writing also explores a diversity of

Kinds of Life Narratives

experiential histories, eschewing an earlier emphasis on victimization and stigmatization, to tell stories of living in committed relationships, building a reconfigured family, and wielding power and authority in sociopolitical life. Bechdel's graphic memoir *Fun Home: A Family Tragicomic* tracks the different valences of being gay for her father's and her own generation. Augusten Burroughs's *Running with Scissors* explores his ambivalent relationship to family and his childhood performance of alternative sexual roles. Dan Savage's *The Kid* focuses on his and his partner's adoption of a baby boy; and his *The Commitment: Love, Sex, Marriage, and My Family* uses his experience of family life to engage issues of gay marriage. Maggie Nelson's life narrative *The Argonauts* proposes a reckoning with gender, sexuality, pregnancy, motherhood, and queerness in the hybrid form of autotheory. Nelson's provocative language inaugurates a journey that both exposes the risks of and celebrates desire and caring.

Queer and trans* narratives challenge prevailing discursive configurations of the lesbian and the gay man and complicate directions of desire by unfixing the alignment of body, desire, and the performance of identity. Jay Prosser in *Second Skins: The Body Narratives of Transsexuality* emphasizes the physicality of embodiment. Discussing Leslie Feinberg's *Stone Butch Blues,* Prosser observes, "the transgendered subject's role is that of a debunker"; in queer gender narratives "sex and gender appear not as distinctive and substantial characters but as evanescent, nonreferential, and overlapping codes" (485). That is, trans* embodiment undermines the expectation of either being or becoming a fixed gender identity. Queer narratives, as illuminated through Prosser's trans* perspective, disrupt and expose the linear narrative of consolidating a sexual identity, gay or straight, that underlay an earlier generation of gay memoir.

Trans* writers now use an asterisk as "a reminder that gender identity is always also inflected by affective, cultural, racial, socioeconomic and environmental factors" (Horvat et al., 2–3). Trans* life writing joins acts of self-narrating and self-performance to the theoretical analysis of sexualized identities. Such narratives as Jan Morris's *Conundrum,* Kate Bornstein's *Gender Outlaw: On Men, Women, and the Rest of Us,* Jennifer Finney Boylan's *She's Not There: A Life in Two Genders* and *Good Boy: My Life in Seven Dogs,* Julia Serano's *Whipping Girl: A Transsexual Woman on Sexism and the Scapegoating of Femininity,* Juliet Jacques's

Trans: A Memoir, and the edited collection (from Joan Nestle, Clare Howell, and Riki Anne Wilchins) *GenderQueer: Voices from Beyond the Sexual Binary* capture the instabilities of gendered identities. That is, they register the lack of a "natural" alignment of bodies, sexualities, and gender assignments. Combining personal history with analysis that theorizes the dispersal of a fixed point of reference and identification around normative masculinities and femininities, these narratives are simultaneously several things: life stories, manifestos about the instability of gender identities, invitations to readers to reimagine their own embodied identities as unfixed from gender norms, and witness narratives to the heterogeneity of trans* experiential histories. Other trans* writing exposes the risks of unintelligibility that conventions of trans* memoir itself threaten (see Vipond). Many younger writers mine the affordances of various online platforms to present fragments of their lives and communicate about "salient political issues that impact trans lives and self-representations" (see Horvat et al., 5). Collectively, trans* memoirs, performances, and virtual activity enjoin readers to resist what Chimamanda Ngozi Adichie refers to as "The Danger of a Single Story."

But tensions surround the circulation of some memoirs by trans* life narrators. Nonbinary artist Maia Kobabe created a graphic memoir, *GenderQueer: A Memoir,* for young adults on issues of gender identity and coming out as gender-nonconforming. Using the pronouns *e, em, eir,* Kobabe narrates the stages of eir coming out and sources of support e encountered. Kobabe states: "In many ways, I wrote this book as a letter to my parents and my extended family, hoping that they would finally understand what I was trying to say and really know me at a deeper level" (PEN America). After the comic was adopted by many American schools and public libraries, in the current polarized climate around race and sexuality it became so controversial that it was challenged by school boards, pulled from many school and public libraries, and is now one of the most frequently banned books in the United States.

Life writing centered on heterosexuality and normative gender identities also takes intriguing turns, as in Gina Frangello's eloquent and searing narrative of failing marriage, adultery, and the divagations of desire in *Blow Your House Down: A Story of Family, Feminism, and Treason.* Chris Kraus's slightly fictionalized memoir, *I Love Dick,* narrates in provocative detail her sexual obsession with British media scholar Dick

Kinds of Life Narratives 301

Hebdige, composed as an autotheoretical foray in dozens of diaristic letters; it later became a popular television series of the same name. Artistic and literary projects, such as the performance art of Alina Troyano as Carmelita Tropicana, collected in *I, Carmelita Tropicana: Performing between Cultures*, probe performative femininity as a script imposed on diverse desires. Jane Juska's *A Round-Heeled Woman: My Late-Life Adventures in Sex and Romance* explores sexuality as an option in conscious aging, detailing sexual encounters arranged long distance around the United States that reflect the political consciousness she developed while teaching reading in a prison. By contrast, in the best-selling *The Sexual Life of Catherine M.*, French art dealer Catherine Millet invites readers to join her in "the quest for the sexual grail," detailing explicit encounters that attempt to demystify the erotic.

Finally, life narratives about gender and sexuality often engage the sexual abuse and exploitation of women, men, and children. The women's movement created preconditions and provided discourse and motivation for women and men to tell stories of childhood sexual violence and incest; memoirs of violation continue to narrate compelling stories. Alice Sebold's *Lucky* details her rape as a college freshman and her subsequent prosecution of her attacker. Kathy O'Beirne's *Don't Ever Tell: Kathy's Story. A True Tale of a Childhood Destroyed by Neglect and Fear* charts her extensive childhood abuse, rape, and incarceration in a laundry run by the Catholic Magdalens in Ireland.[19] Chanel Miller, a Stanford University student who had been raped by another student, Brock Turner, in 2015, went to trial as "Emily Doe." Turner was charged with three counts of felony sexual assault and given a very lenient sentence by judge Aaron Persky after Miller had read her victim statement. When her powerful statement was published by BuzzFeed, she was sought out by the editor in chief of Viking Press to write a memoir, subsequently published in 2019 as *Know My Name*; it won a National Book Critics Circle Award. Subsequently Jerry Brown, then governor of California, approved a law mandating minimum sentences for sexual assault cases. As Leigh Gilmore observes in her 2023 book on the topic, Chanel Miller's memoir is another example of inspirational narrative activism.

Some writers have shifted the terms of the story from victimization, humiliation, violent abuse, and a legacy of self-loathing and vulnerability to exploring the erotics of encounter, the recoding of the body, and the agency that writing one's life may provide in the act of claiming a past. Since Kathryn Harrison's 1997 *The Kiss* broke new ground about the complexities of memory and desire in incest narratives, sexual stories can no longer be characterized simply as narratives of lost innocence or polarized tales of conquest and victimhood; the conflicting pulls of desire and fantasy complicate the "authority" of experience. Michael Ryan's *Secret Life* interweaves a narrative of being sexually abused as a boy with the compulsion to be a sexual seducer that he developed as a young man. In the powerfully innovative *In the Dream House: A Memoir,* Carmen Maria Machado employs a kaleidoscopic succession of tropes and metaphors to make fragmented forays into her remembered past—a history of lesbian desire, relationship, and community—as she explores the paradoxes of an emotionally abusive lesbian relationship and her struggle to extract herself from it.

"SLAVE" NARRATIVE

What have historically been defined as narratives of the enslaved comprise a mode of life narrative written by a fugitive or freed ex-slave about captivity, oppression—physical, economic, and emotional—and escape from bondage into some form of freedom, exemplified in the earliest widely read narrative by Olaudah Equiano, *The Interesting Narrative of the Life of Olaudah Equiano, or Gustavus Vassa the African.* In the United States the first narrative of an enslaved man, *The Life of William Grimes, the Runaway Slave, Written by Himself,* was published in 1825 to raise money for Grimes to buy his freedom from his former master under threat of being returned to slavery in the South. Narratives of the enslaved were usually antebellum (published before the Civil War), though narratives of uplift chronicled the experience of some former slaves after emancipation, as did Booker T. Washington's *Up from Slavery.* Of course, the dates of enslavement differ in different nations, and some narratives were published well into the twentieth and twenty-first centuries. For example, *The Autobiography of a Runaway Slave,* the life narrative of Esteban Montéjo, enslaved in Cuba, as told to Miguel Barnet, was first published in Spanish in 1966. Frances Smith Foster notes that U.S. narratives of enslavement were a popular form; hundreds were published, and some went through many editions and sold thousands of copies. The form has also generated a rich critical literature and been influential for the development of later African American narrative

Kinds of Life Narratives 303

forms, as Robert B. Stepto notes in describing four modes of narratives of the enslaved—eclectic, integrated, generic, and authenticating. Olney describes ten conventions characteristic of narratives of enslavement, including, among others, the narrative's engraved, signed portrait; a title page asserting that the narrative was written by the formerly enslaved; testimonials and prefatory material by white abolitionists; a beginning of "I was born"; accounts of whippings by cruel masters and mistresses and the enslaved's resistance to them; an account of the enslaved's difficulties in learning to read and write; denunciations of Christian slaveholders as the cruelest; accounts of successful effort(s) to escape; and the choice of a new last name (Olney, "'I Was Born,'" 152–53). Because the ability of the formerly enslaved to become literate was often contested, several narratives were denounced as inauthentic, for example, Harriet Jacobs's *Incidents in the Life of a Slave Girl* (later shown by Jean Fagan Yellin to have been authored by Jacobs under the pseudonym Linda Brent). The narratives of formerly enslaved persons importantly challenge myths of the slave system promulgated in the plantation culture of Southern literature and history and, according to William L. Andrews, "culminate in texts that weave together multiple autobiographical traditions and voices to produce a sense of collectivized black identity" ("African-American Autobiography Criticism," 206–7). Samira Kawash calls for rethinking concepts of enslavement narrative because the "freedom" promised in emancipation from slavery as a negation of the enslaved as property is interrogated in many of these narratives as incomplete, since the formerly enslaved were unable to claim the property rights of liberal citizen subjects (50).

SPIRITUAL LIFE NARRATIVE

This mode of life writing, with its vast corpus, traces the narrator's emerging consciousness back to "the acquisition of some sort of saving knowledge and to an awakening of an awareness within" regarding a transcendental power, as do Andrews's examples of nineteenth-century African American women preachers (*Sisters of the Spirit,* 1). Spiritual life narrative in the Christian tradition typically unfolds as a journey through sin and damnation to a sense of spiritual fulfillment and arrival in a place of sustaining belief. Sometimes journeying, with its profound moments of solitude, motivates the rededication, intensification, or clarification of spiritual beliefs and values, as John D. Barbour elaborates for the Western tradition through readings of various autobiographical writings by Augustine, Rousseau, Thoreau, and Merton, among others, in *The Value of Solitude: The Ethics and Spirituality of Aloneness in Autobiography*. In considering how the experience of detachment from others may contribute to, or hinder, spiritual searching, he observes that much autobiographical writing, as an ethical or religious reflection on one's life, is itself an exercise in solitude. In other cases, particularly in modern and contemporary life narratives, the quest may be unfulfilled or delusory.

A pattern of conversion and its aftermath are traditionally foregrounded in spiritual life narratives. (See "Conversion Narrative.") The "first" book-length autobiographical narrative in the West is generally acknowledged to be the *Confessions* of Saint Augustine, written around 397 CE. Augustine's "I" retrospectively views his early life from the perspective of his conversion to Christianity. Saved, he looks back to assess the workings of grace in his wayward life and the stages of his spiritual salvation. The postconversion Augustine construes the first half of his life as a chronological narrative of error and self-indulgence, from his youth through his pursuit of education and erotic love. In book 8, he narrates the moment of conversion when he was called by a voice to seek dialogue with an unapproachable God; thereafter, he reflects on the centrality of memory to spiritual salvation.

Over the next thousand years, most autobiographical writing in the West was done by religious men and women as a form of devotion in the service of spiritual examination. These narratives sought the signs of God's grace in the life of Christ and Christian saints and tried to erase the traces of sin by effacing the stubborn self, as occurs in the *Shewings* of Dame Julian of Norwich and the meditations of mystics such as Hildegard of Bingen, Hadewijch, and Angela of Foligno in Italy. In the narrated visions through which they attempted to represent their relationship to an unrepresentable deity, female mystics, according to Laurie Finke, "claimed the power to shape the meaning and form of their experiences" even though they "did not claim to speak in [their] own voice[s]" (44). Later Christian mystics such as Teresa of Avila, John of the Cross, and Sor Juana Inés de la Cruz used autobiographical models to narrate their visionary quests and assert their spiritual authority in the face of challenges by religious superiors. In his 1555 life narrative, *St. Ignatius' Own Story, as Told to Luis González de Cámara*, the founder

Kinds of Life Narratives

of the Jesuit order narrates the history of inward growth and interior transformation differently. Ignatius presents himself as a contemplative in action by alluding to particulars of the world in which he studied, taught, and traveled. Objectifying himself as an actor in the world and recording the externalization of his character, he shows how the religious subject becomes a subject of history. Here the presentation of subjectivity is, as with the medieval mystics, in the service of an external source; that source is now not timeless and transcendent but embedded in the material conditions of history.

Medieval poets, in linking romantic love to a quest for the divine, also created works that structurally and rhetorically were deeply influential for later autobiographical writing. In different ways Dante's journeys in the *Divine Comedy* and the *Vita Nuova* (new life) are models of earthly struggle as his "lost" self on life's path travels from a descent into myriad embodiments of secular error to enlightenment and salvation as his human love for Beatrice leads him to redemptive divine love. Similarly, Petrarch's long letter addressed to Augustine, "The Ascent of Mount Ventoux," narrates his climb as he reflects on the vanity of his earthly love for Laura, his perusal of Augustine's *Confessions* at the apex, and the descent during which he reflects on how the outer journey of climbing life's mountain and the inner world of his own being are related. The arc of these journeys informs much subsequent Western spiritual self-reflection.

While medieval Christian writers deployed a rhetoric of self-reference in their quests for salvation, the challenges and complexities of self-reference and self-study they encounter do not yet present the self-fashioned private individual of later early modern narrative. After the rise of dissenting sects in the Protestant Reformation of the sixteenth century, spiritual autobiography was increasingly employed to defend a community of believers. The Puritan revolution in England engendered John Bunyan's *Grace Abounding to the Chief of Sinners* and George Fox's *Journal*. In his journal, Fox attempts to acquaint readers with his character and religious views. In Bunyan's project of self-biography, an ideal dissenting self is assessed in the terms of Puritan religious prescription. The dissenting subject is at once subservient and free: subservient in being required to choose a path to salvation, but free to choose the path of subservience. Among the Puritans, Quakers, and other dissident religious communities in the New World, writers of spiritual autobiography found themselves in a dilemma: How could they validate narratives of conversion and salvation as authentic and irreversible when the self was "fallen"? In these religious communities, the collective's history and the individual's spiritual life narrative are interdependent and inextricable.

If Augustine's *Confessions* were informed by a confessional narrative of renouncing his wayward past and embracing Christian salvation and a personal relationship to a mystical divine beyond language, that pursuit of self-transformation as salvation is absent in Jean-Jacques Rousseau. His disavowals of a divine power in his *Confessions* shape a narrative quest that is explicitly secular and sensual, as he claims in asserting a unique subjectivity, not made in the model of any god: "I venture to believe that I am not made like any of those who are in existence; if I am not better, at least I am different" (3). The "natural man" he seeks to be, outside bourgeois society, rejects the quest for spiritual salvation. While the later eighteenth century saw several pietistic movements throughout Europe and the early Americas, Romantic individualism replaced the spiritual quest with a social or transcendental one grounded in a concept of an unspecific deity or pantheistic world, reflected in autobiographers as diverse as Franklin, Goethe, and Emerson.

Throughout the twentieth century the quest structure persists in journey narratives by spiritual seekers around the world. The most prominent is Mahatma Gandhi's *An Autobiography; or, The Story of My Experiments with Truth.* Other influential writers such as Paramahansa Yogananda in *The Autobiography of a Yogi* focus on practices of meditation; life narratives by many gurus over the last century chart a similar path. Some writers have relocated their spiritual quests to social activism, as does Dorothy Day in *The Long Loneliness,* while Trappist monk Thomas Merton in *The Seven-Storey Mountain* immerses himself in contemplative solitude.

Contemporary writers may also undertake journeys that become spiritual quests, as does Elizabeth Gilbert in *Eat, Pray, Love: One Woman's Search for Everything across Italy, India, and Indonesia.* Western Buddhist travelers to Tibet and nearby regions have employed the trek as self-transformation, notably in Peter Matthiessen's *The Snow Leopard* and Andrew Harvey's *Journey in Ladakh.* Some journey narratives explore other spiritual systems, such as Asra Nomani's *Tantrika: Traveling the Road of Divine Love.* Memoirs such as Gershom Scholem's *From Berlin to Jerusalem* draw on Jewish mysticism rooted in the *Zohar* of the Kabbalah, while autobiographical poets such as Robert Bly draw on multiple

Kinds of Life Narratives

sources of visionary writing, notably the poet Rumi, to enhance their own meditative voices. Indigenous narratives of spiritual quest relocate spirituality as inextricable from the land, as do N. Scott Momaday in *The Way to Rainy Mountain*, Noe Álvarez in *Spirit Run: A 6,000-Mile Marathon through North America's Stolen Land*, and Joy Harjo in *Crazy Brave: A Memoir* and *Poet Warrior*. Similarly, Kathleen Norris in *Dakota: A Spiritual Geography* and Terry Tempest Williams in *Refuge: An Unnatural History of Family and Place* and subsequent narratives link natural environments with a spiritually informed quest for peace and harmony.

Some narratives by Muslims describe conversions in the process of immigration to Western nations, such as Kaighla Um Dayo's *Things That Shatter*. Others, such as Fatima Mernissi's fictionalized *Dreams of Trespass: Tales of a Harem Girlhood*, critique Islamic strictures on educating and empowering women. Conversely, *The Autobiography of Malcolm X* and Muhammad Ali and Hana Yasmin Ali's *The Soul of a Butterfly: Reflections on Life's Journey* both foreground conversion to the values and beliefs of Islam as integral to their sociopolitical quests.

Throughout the past century, narratives of loss of belief or escape from religious dogma have also become more prevalent, in works as diverse as Edmund Gosse's *Father and Son*, Jeannette Winterson's *Why Be Happy When You Could Be Normal?*, and Emmanuel Carrère's *The Kingdom*.

TESTIMONIO

The term in Spanish literally means "testimony" and connotes an act of testifying or bearing witness legally or religiously. John Beverley defines Latin American *testimonio* as "a novel or novella-length narrative in book or pamphlet . . . form, told in the first person by a narrator who is also the real protagonist or witness of the events he or she recounts, and whose unit of narration is usually a 'life' or a significant life experience" (92–93). In *testimonio*, the narrator intends to communicate the situation of a group's oppression, struggle, or imprisonment; to claim some agency in the act of narrating; and to call on readers to respond actively in judging the crisis. Its primary concern is sincerity of intention, not the text's literariness (94). And its ideological thrust is the "affirmation of the individual self in a collective mode" (97), as in Nobel Peace Prize–winner Rigoberta Menchú's *I, Rigoberta Menchú*. In her introduction to a forum on "Collective Embodiment and Social Praxis," Sarah Brophy

308 Kinds of Life Narratives

notes that "testimonio today responds to the uninhabitability of the present world, insisting that we are never actually alone in these struggles and that there is 'nourishment'" to be found in differently embodied accounts of our multilayered pasts, presents, and futures (Brophy, 440, citing Freeman, 19). Extending the definition of *testimonio*, Laura J. Beard argues in *Acts of Narrative Resistance: Women's Autobiographical Writings in the Americas* that it is one of several "genres of resistance" through which contemporary First Nations women challenge cultural definitions imposed on them by writing narratives that seek to name and claim their own experience.

TRAUMA NARRATIVE

"Trauma," derived from the Greek word for "wound," describes an experience of extreme horror or shock that cannot be incorporated unproblematically within memory. Trauma studies was consolidated as a field in the 1990s, as scholars across the humanistic disciplines theorized the condition and its aftereffects on survivors, including the succeeding generations who may be haunted by *postmemory*. The term was coined by Marianne Hirsch, who enumerates its many dimensions: "mourning for a lost world, the impulse to repair the loss and to heal those who have suffered it, anger about the absence of public recognition, frustration in the face of our own ignorance and impotence . . . [inheriting] a trauma that survives the survivors, overwhelming the present and hijacking the future" ("Debts," 222).

Gilmore notes that "the subject of trauma refers to both a person struggling to make sense of an overwhelming experience in a particular context and the unspeakability of trauma itself, its resistance to representation" (*Limits of Autobiography*, 46). She stresses trauma's self-altering or self-shattering character and the difficulties in attempting to articulate it (6). Gilmore's later study, *Tainted Witness*, observes the intersection of trauma with gender and race, and historicizes a "blank" in responses to it: "that norms of justice and personhood do not fully include women, and their agency, value, and even existence are often denied through this exclusion" (25). Psychoanalytical theorists of trauma, among them Cathy Caruth, Shoshana Felman, and Dori Laub, argue that speaking the unspeakable involves the narrator in a struggle with memory and its belatedness; for, as Caruth argues, "the experience of trauma . . . would thus seem to consist . . . in an inherent latency within the experience

Kinds of Life Narratives

itself" (7–8). This latency of traumatic memory, and the way in which "to be traumatized is precisely to be possessed by an image or event," manifests itself in the psychic delay of memory's temporality and the crisis of its truth (4–5). Caruth asserts that "the fundamental dislocation implied by all traumatic experience" lies in "both its testimony to the event and to the impossibility of its direct access" (9).

Stories of traumatic experience focus on the narrator's reliving of a past event and emphasize a gap that cannot be closed between the narrating present and the narrated past. Thus, while the act of remembering recalls the originary trauma, it does not heal, but rather exposes, the wound. Gilmore points out the central conundrum of such narratives: "although trauma must be spoken in order to heal the survivor and the community, language is inadequate to do this" ("Trauma," 885). With its troubled relationship to processes of memory, trauma is thus not only located in the past event but may be reexperienced in the narrative present of storytelling. Nancy K. Miller characterizes the effects of trauma as "indelible stains in the brain" that writing seeks both to expunge and to preserve ("Memory Stains," 41). Life writing on trauma can elicit an experience of disorder in the reader, as Brodzki observes, by choosing not to represent an experience of horror or trauma explicitly, but to figure it through a text's structure or the use of flashback and repetition ("Trauma," 128–30).

Trauma narratives have become pervasive in contemporary life, as stories of personal experience circulate internationally in ways that reshape the relationship of public and private discursive spheres, and may produce a counterdiscourse aimed at the erasure of individual suffering in official historical memory (Gilmore, "Trauma," 885). The many forms of life writing that transmit traumatic memory are shaped by particular cultural and linguistic contexts, as well as the limits of specific genres. With the intensified recording, archiving, and analysis of traumatic experience during the last four decades, trauma stories of many kinds have come to the fore: of personal experience of violation or abuse; of experience in the Holocaust and other genocidal wars, some told at truth commission hearings or in the memoirs of child soldiers; of dislocation for the children of the Stolen Generations in Australia and Indigenous people in Alaska, Canada, and throughout the Americas; and in the testimonies to atrocity of antiwar activists around the world.

While in the nineties scholars tended to assert that trauma may facilitate self-help and healing (see Henke on "scriptotherapy"), in the past two decades witnessing has been retheorized. Kate Douglas and Gillian Whitlock, in introducing edited volumes of *Life Writing* (2008), observed that "relocated trauma studies" have been integrated "into comparative perspectives that travel South and into various cultural frameworks and traditions" (3). Scholars exploring the effects and impact of the Truth and Reconciliation Commission hearings in South Africa, for instance, have noted that organized scenes of witness to the traumatic past may restage the violence of the perpetrator-victim relationship (see Feldman), spurring retraumatization rather than healing or recovery. In non-Western contexts the critique of a psychoanalytically based talk-therapy model of witnessing to trauma is especially pertinent. Some scholars point to alternative strategies for surviving and healing from violence and harm that may draw on collective healing practices, as in the project of telling, listening, and collaborating undertaken by the Sangtin Writers in *Playing with Fire: Feminist Thought and Activism through Seven Lives in India.* Others note that the notion of trauma needs to be decoupled from psychoanalytic discourses in order to address "concepts of social suffering that address the communal without assuming a uniformity of trauma across a social spectrum" (Kennedy and Whitlock, Conference announcement).

Graphic memoir has also become a mode for artist-authors to explore their own or others' traumatic pasts, harnessing the visual and expressive potential of comics to address readers directly and movingly. Prominent autographics such as *Maus, Fun Home,* and *Persepolis* promoted new conceptualizations of how, and to what ends, trauma may be narrated. *Maus* in particular, with "its spiralling layers of self-reflexivity, its braiding of multiplying and sometimes duplicitous icons, its meshing of forms and genres, and the visceral, embodied response that it continues to elicit from new readers" has generated new theorizations of trauma (Davies, 5). Indeed, comics not only thematize and visualize trauma, but serve as innovative sites for setting out models of ethical witnessing. And as Hillary Chute observes in *Disaster Drawn: Visual Witness, Comics, and Documentary Form,* comics is not just an aesthetic medium but a mode of historical documentation reliant on earlier forms of visual documentation to represent the personal and collective trauma generated by the violence of war.

At this moment, increasing threats to human environments from

Kinds of Life Narratives

the effects of climate change—health, food supplies, and relationship to the natural world and other species—will challenge scholars in trauma studies to develop new understandings of the temporalities of traumatic imagination and histories. A possible feature of life writing by millennial and Gen Z climate activists will be its potential refraction through what the Bureau of Linguistic Reality describes as "Pre-Traumatic-Stress Disorder": "a condition in which a researcher experiences symptoms of trauma as they learn more about the future as it pertains to climate change and watch the world around them not taking necessary precautions." Another potential generic mode of trauma life narrative may be an alignment with horror narratives emerging out of "solastalgia"—"a form of homesickness one gets when one is still at home, but the environment has been altered and feels unfamiliar" (Quante and Escott, "Solastalgia"). In sum, for younger generations coming to reflect on their situatedness in a world in climate crisis, the automedial aspects of life narrative may make it both an expressive outlet for outrage and mourning and a call to social justice—in bold, often collectivized multimedial forms, such as comics, blogs, public art, flash mobs, and performance art.

See also "Grief Narrative," "Human Rights Narrative," "Testimonio," and "Witnessing, Acts of."

TRAVEL NARRATIVE

This broad term encompasses multiple forms of life writing, including travelogue, travel journal, (pseudo)ethnography, adventure narrative, quest, letters home, and narratives of exotic escape. Journey narratives extend back to biblical narratives of enslavement and escape and the wanderings of Gilgamesh. Autobiographical narratives of travel for battle and tourism extend in the West back to the Greeks and Romans and in Arabian and Chinese lands to long before the printing press. Travel narratives are usually written in the first person and focus, progressively or retrospectively, on a journey. Subordinating other aspects of the writer's life, they typically chronicle or reconstruct the narrator's experiences of encounter, displacement, and travail and observations about the unknown, the foreign, the uncanny. In this way they become occasions for both reimagining and misrecognizing identity (Bartkowski, xix), and for resituating the mobile subject in relation to a home and its ideological norms.

The self-exploration of writers in the early modern period through centuries of colonization both motivated and paralleled geographical exploration of the globe as travelers began to record the findings of their journeys. These travel narratives posing an "I" who navigates new worlds through pilgrimage, migration, encounter, conquest, and transformation are exemplified in *The Travels of Marco Polo* of 1271, which inaugurated, over the next four centuries, a plethora of voyage narratives to exotic destinations. European adventurers and explorers returned home with tales of hardships and survival, dangerous transit, and wondrous encounters (Pratt, *Imperial Eyes,* 20). Often presenting themselves as heroic survivors and their project as one of mapping new worlds, these writers used self-referential storytelling to articulate an emergent subjectivity that Mary Louise Pratt characterizes as that of "a European global or planetary subject" (9). This global subject was "male, secular, and lettered" and viewed the world through the lens of "planetary consciousness" (29–30).

In the Americas, narratives of exploration, colonization, captivity, and contested hegemony abounded in the sixteenth and seventeenth centuries. In his 1578 *History of a Voyage to the Land of Brazil, Otherwise Called America,* Jean de Léry provides an eyewitness account that mixes encounters with "exotic" natives, tales of hardships at sea, religious controversy among the Huguenots, and personal reflections on contact with other worlds, a narrative project that comes to inflect his own subjectivity. As in Montaigne's "Of Cannibals," which indicts colonizing Europeans as more barbaric than the "barbarians" of the New World, for Léry, contact with Indigenous people calls "civilizing" practices into question and suggests that an "Indigenous" collectivized subjectivity may be superior to that of the Western "new man." While Captain John Smith's brash fabulations signaled one option for storytelling in North America, captivity narratives in the New World reworked the tropes of conversion narratives in the context of the radical dislocation created by contact in the New World. By contrast, eighteenth-century bourgeois gentlemen, like the explorers and aristocrats before them, who set off on the road and traveled through Europe on what became known as the "grand tour," wrote about their travels as a *peregrinatio academica* (Leed, 184–85; Chard, 1–39). In their travel journals James Boswell, Charles Burney, and Thomas Nugent recorded their observations as educational journeys through successive cultures. Typically, grand tourists followed a prescribed curriculum and set of exercises codified in guidebooks

Kinds of Life Narratives 313

written by their tutors, such as *The Compleat Gentleman; or, Directions for the Education of Youth as to Their Breeding at Home and Travelling Abroad,* written by Jean Gailhard. The bourgeois subject of the tour and its journal imagined himself as the newly enlightened man of broad learning and experience who was preparing to assume "the responsibilities of the well-born male to family, class, and nation" (Porter, 35).

In the nineteenth century, travel narratives adopted an increasingly wide range of writing practices. Romantic travelers penned narratives of encounter with sublime landscapes, as did Wordsworth on his visionary journey through the Alps in *The Prelude.* Naturalists and scientists recorded the details of their immersion in flora and fauna and their recognition of natural processes, as did Charles Darwin in recounting his years of surveying the South American coast in *The Voyage of the Beagle.* Missionary David Livingstone and explorer Henry Morton Stanley composed proto-ethnographic travel accounts while writer-scholar Richard Burton and the poet Arthur Rimbaud wrote of adventurous journeys to lands they found exotic. Many Victorian novelists such as Anthony Trollope and William M. Thackeray and later nineteenth-century authors such as Mark Twain were also prolific travel writers.

Although travel is associated with the cultural logic of masculinity, women have always been in motion and their traveling has been gendered and embodied. Some have penned travel narratives, as did Egeria in her innovative late fourth-century *Peregrinatio.* At least one tourist discovered that the education she received through the grand tour made the return to family responsibilities impossible. Lady Mary Wortley Montagu, traveling with her husband, who was British ambassador to the Sultanate of Turkey, carefully composed and copied her "embassy letters," published after her death, to friends and family in England, using her observant autobiographical eye to compose a detailed revisionist account of women's lives in the Turkish seraglio and refigure its notion of woman as a sign "of liberty and freedom" (Lowe, 45). American women preachers narrated itinerant lives of spiritual quest and ministry, as did Jarena Lee in *The Life and Religious Experience of Jarena Lee* and Zilpha Elaw in *Memoirs of the Life, Religious Experience, and Ministerial Travels and Labours of Mrs. Zilpha Elaw, an American Female of Colour.* Nineteenth-century women also began to undertake extended travels and write about them, as did freeborn Nancy Prince about travels to Russia and Jamaica, Isabella Bird throughout

Asia, Isabelle Eberhardt in her North African "nomad diaries," and Mary Kingsley as an ethnographic and scientific travel writer in West Africa. As increasing means of mobility advanced by the new technologies of motion, trains, automobiles, and planes in the twentieth century arrived with democratization, literacy, education, and industrialization, a host of adventurous women and men too numerous to name traveled extensively and wrote stirring accounts of their adventures. These include twentieth- and twenty-first-century authors Isak Dinesen, Graham Greene, Rebecca West, George Orwell, Beryl Markham, Bruce Chatwin, M. F. K. Fisher, Maya Angelou, Mary Morris, William Least Heat Moon, Jamaica Kincaid, Jan Morris, Pico Iyer, Paul Theroux, Anthony Bourdain, John McPhee, Peter Matthiessen, Saidiya Hartman, and Robert F. Pirsig. Now, while memoirists such as Patti Smith combine travel with tracing the literary past of favorite writers, adventurous travel is the focus of television programs such as Bear Grylls's "explorations" and the digital journals posted and updated by many travel writers, making travel writing a near-ubiquitous form of self-expression.

For other aspects of travel narrative, see "Ecobiography, Ecocriticism, and the Anthropocene."

WAR MEMOIR

What should comprise the parameters of war memoirs and military life writing as a life narrative genre is under discussion, as scholars Alex Vernon, Craig Howes on the oral histories of veterans, and Jon Alexander on POW memoirs observe. Vernon notes that the conventions of the war memoir focus on "what war does to men as well as what men do in war" ("Submission and Resistance," 165). Memoirs may involve a soldier's submission to and acknowledgment of powerlessness, as does Anthony Swofford's *Jarhead,* with its wry humor. But some writers, notably Tim O'Brien in *The Things They Carried,* rework the form of the war memoir in acts of self-construction that change its dynamic. And the memoirs of African child soldiers raise very different issues from those of participants in organized national armies.

Although nations are now increasingly incorporating women in combat positions in their militaries, women's autobiographical writing on war has existed for centuries, and scholarship is just beginning to

Kinds of Life Narratives 315

catch up to it. The online "Gender and War since 1600" site lists hundreds of narratives, most of which tell of women's experiences of wars in the twentieth century. Some of the narratives come from nurses who counter notions of war heroism. For example, in the impressionistic memoir *The Forbidden Zone,* as well as in her poetry, Mary Borden, a British nurse on the French front in World War I, emphasized the lived subjectivity of caring for damaged bodies and the struggle to adequately remember fragmentary impressions of the daily assault of blood, trauma, and destruction. Women in war zones were also both ravaged and at times empowered by their experiences, as their diaries attest. One of them, Marta Hillers's *A Woman in Berlin: Eight Weeks in a Conquered City,* was originally published anonymously and translated into English for an American audience in 1954. In it, Hillers chronicles the serial rape of German women, including herself, by Russian soldiers and women's strategies for survival that ironically included help from Russian soldiers.[20]

Young adults have also written narratives of wartime life. At the end of the twentieth century, *Zlata's Diary: A Child's Life in Sarajevo,* became an international best-seller. For a two-year period from September 1991 to October 1993, young Zlata Filipović kept a diary in which she recorded her observations of everyday life in an increasingly besieged Sarajevo. In summer 1993, Zlata shared her diary with her teacher, who found a publisher in Sarajevo through the sponsorship of the International Centre for Peace. On its publication in French and then in English, Zlata became instantly famous internationally as a young "Anne Frank." The circulation and reception of Zlata's diary effectively commodified a child's-eye view of war, inviting empathetic reading while reducing the complexity of the historical event.

A radically different kind of child war memoir, emerging in human rights campaigns since the 1990s, involves the life narratives of former African child soldiers. Their shocking stories narrate coming of age as gun-toting, brutally violent young men and women captured and reformed by campaigns of organized hypermasculinization that turned them into perpetrators of violence. In the West, the figure of the child soldier exploited by a brutal regime appeals to readers' fantasies of rescuing innocents under assault in wars whose complexity is not fully understood. In *A Long Way Gone,* for instance, Ishmael Beah tells of the coming of internecine war in Sierra Leone that destroyed his community and changed him and the boys with whom he escaped, first, into desperate wanderers and, upon capture, into drugged and brutalized trained killers. Beah's story of surviving his victimization and complicity and ultimately immigrating to the United States, where he was "rehumanized," was long a best-seller and made him a television celebrity.[21]

The geopolitics of violence and the stakes of exposing brutal degradation combined with the thorny issues involved in narrating violent past experience, however, often prompt campaigns to discredit such narratives of war and the credibility of the witness. This occurred both with Beah's narrative and with Ugandan writer and activist China Keitetsi's *Child Soldier: Fighting for My Life*. These challenges to the authenticity of child-soldier accounts may lead readers to interrogate their own expectations about "evidence" and the differing conventions of war memoir around the globe.

As literary scholars increasingly assemble canons of war life writing online, issues of definition such as the "war" on a pandemic or climate change may shift its terms. As the extensive use of digital technologies in combat changes its terms, writers and scholars of gendered difference are revising previously held assumptions about the form of the war memoir. Further, smart phones, with their video capacities, are now enabling citizens and soldiers to regularly report on everyday life in war zones, from the Ukraine to Ethiopia, Yemen to Myanmar, and beyond.

WITNESSING, ACTS OF

As an act of being present to observe or to give testimony on something, witnessing suggests how subjects respond to trauma. The witness can be identified as an "eyewitness," a firsthand observer whose narrative has multiple functions—chronicle, testimony, consciousness raising—or a secondhand witness, who responds to the witness of others. Kelly Oliver notes, "Witnessing has the double sense of testifying to something that you have seen with your own eyes and bearing witness to something that you cannot see" (18). Thus, eyewitnesses are judged by the accuracy of their testimony based on firsthand knowledge, while bearing witness implies a stance toward "something beyond recognition that can't be seen" (16). Oliver emphasizes that witnessing is an act addressed to an other, real or imagined, with the possibility of response. These two senses of witnessing are inevitably in a tension that Oliver argues may

Kinds of Life Narratives 317

be productive for getting beyond retraumatization to a more humane, ethically informed future (17–18).

For traumatic testimony to be heard, a sympathetic listener is needed to serve as a witness and help redress the psychic isolation that traumatic experience produces. The circulation of acts of witnessing may raise issues of "secondary witnessing" if exposure to a narrative of violence evokes a traumatic experience for the hearer (Douglas and Whitlock, 139). Although becoming aware of "the strange and estranging legacy of trauma" is difficult, people often feel an ethical imperative to read and circulate such stories (Brodzki, "Trauma," 129).

Acts of witnessing propel a variety of life narratives. Some embed witness in historical or political events, such as Vladek's testimony in Spiegelman's *Maus* (on the Holocaust), the testimonies Antjie Krog incorporates in *Country of My Skull* (on the Truth and Reconciliation Commission hearings in South Africa), Ishmael Beah's *A Long Way Gone* (as a child soldier in Sierra Leone), Maria Rosa Henson's *Comfort Woman: A Filipina's Story of Prostitution and Slavery under the Japanese Military* (testifying to World War II sex slavery), and Doris Pilkington's *Rabbit-Proof Fence* (on the forced separation of Aboriginal children from their families in Australia). Witnessing to trauma as a performative act in personal contexts occurs in such narratives as Alice Sebold's *Lucky,* Kathryn Harrison's *The Kiss,* Dave Pelzer's *A Child Called "It,"* and Bettina Aptheker's *Intimate Politics.*

Expanding the archive of acts of witnessing essential to projects of social justice, Gilmore argues for reading across multiple genres, finding in the autobiographical fiction of Jamaica Kincaid, for instance, the figure of the "literary witness" who "uses autobiographical fiction in a project of witnessing the impact of colonial violence and decolonization on gendered family relationships" ("'What Was I?,'" 79). Such witnesses to radical injury and violence, Gilmore notes, may resist the norms of personal witnessing that have emerged in the regime of human rights. Among these are the protocols of who tells their story, the story-forms that gain publisher interest, and the appeals to readers' empathetic identification, all of which serve to advance "a thickened discursive context" for "explor[ing] the limits of articulating the human that arise from empire" ("'What Was I?,'" 83).

In a different vein, W. G. Sebald's *Austerlitz* (2001) experiments with "found lives" to present an obliquely personal narrative entwining imagination and memory with archival materials that "reads" a past he did not directly experience. The fabricated life of his character Austerlitz is embedded in a text rich with numbers, documents, photographs, and historical references that seem to verify its autobiographical status. Performing a composite life, Sebald inserts photographs, purportedly of Austerlitz but some in fact of himself, the apparently objective narrator-author born after World War II. The life fabricated as autobiographical is not, however, a hoax in historical fact, but a conflation signaling Sebald's post-memorial sense of responsibility for the Holocaust, rendering it both an impossible and an ethical act of witnessing. Linking disparate times, places, and identities, *Austerlitz* suggests both the implicatedness of subjects in histories of violence that predate them and the transhistorical connections enabled by acts that suture memory and imagination.

The saliency of individual witnessing described above persists, but it is being overtaken by the pervasive presence of online technologies that alert a larger public to radical suffering and grievance, netizen microactivisms, digitally driven surveillance technologies, and user expertise (see Schaffer and Smith, "E-Witnessing"). Social networking, remote sensing, and hacking all extend the possibilities for witnessing events, registering resistance, and mobilizing action. This ensemble of digital technologies, platforms, and assemblages—joining user, story, interface, and device—is transforming notions of who and what does the witnessing, how it circulates, and what its efficacy is in the global arena of human rights activism.

Acknowledgments

About five years ago, we decided to write a streamlined version of this book, which was first published in 2001, then revised and greatly expanded in 2010, for the information-rich times we now live in. It has been a daunting project—like raising a child three times. Examining our own evolving understanding of life writing and questioning some of the assumptions we confidently asserted in earlier editions have been both enlightening and humbling. Retirement has allowed us time for fine-tuning and rich conversations about the evolution of the field over five decades and, while we have not produced a brief manual, we have extensively updated and in places rethought concepts central to life narrative.

We are grateful for the continuing support of the University of Minnesota Press over three decades. Douglas Armato and Leah Pennywark, and before them Richard Morrison and Biodun Iginla, have encouraged our wide-ranging investigation into life narrative and guided its successive stages. Our copy editors (for the first edition, Therese Boyd; second edition, Louisa Castner; and this edition, Deborah A. Oosterhouse) expertly accommodated our editorial needs. Our trusted indexer, Suzanne Aboulfadl, has repeatedly applied her indexing expertise to make this book accessible. We owe a special debt of gratitude to Sidonie's research assistant Catherine Brist, who constructed bibliographies and shared in the research labor and intellectual excitement of revising and expanding this book.

Our conceptual debts are numerous. We are enduringly grateful to Mary Louise Pratt for prodding us to address the exclusionary implications of the term "autobiography" and move to the more encompassing term "life narrative." The comparative theorizing of such postcolonial critics as Barbara Harlow, Philip Holden, Françoise Lionnet, and Gillian Whitlock has been influential in engaging the diverse meanings and consequences of telling a life story. Our dear departed colleague Timothy Dow Adams contributed both his critical acumen and his incomparable wit to our thinking in the first two editions, particularly during the

West Virginia University Summer Seminar in Literature and Cultural Studies that he invited us to lead in 1998. We have appreciated the savvy counsel of William L. Andrews, a consistent supporter of our work. Kay Schaffer, Sidonie's collaborator on *Human Rights and Narrated Lives,* called our attention to the importance of human rights storytelling on issues of trauma, testimony, and acts of witnessing. Gillian Whitlock's enthusiastic support for the teachability of *Reading Autobiography* has been encouraging, and her insights illuminating.

The contributions of several scholars in our field sustained and enriched our own work. Alfred Hornung, an energetic, steadfast leader in autobiography studies since its inception in the 1980s, has, in addition to writing or editing over two dozen books in the field, organized several life writing conferences and workshops and founded the Obama Institute at the Johannes Gutenberg University of Mainz for American and transnational study of life narrative. The theoretical interventions and autocritical forays of Nancy K. Miller, as both critic and practitioner of life writing, have been inspirational for more than three decades. The groundbreaking studies of Paul John Eakin on life writing as a mode of storytelling that intersects with such fields as neuroscience and anthropology have complemented and stimulated our own inquiries. Julie Rak's invigorating questions at conferences, in correspondence, and in her essays and books have often prompted us to reconceptualize the social and material contexts and networks of life narrative. James Phelan's theorizing of voice, intended audience, and the ethics of narration have inspired us to rethink the contexts and consequences of narrating. G. Thomas Couser's shrewd insights and wide-ranging investigations in disability studies have informed our thinking on the vulnerability of subjects. Leigh Gilmore's dazzling forays into the application of life narrative to contemporary issues inspired us to examine the uses and effects of public storytelling. Conversations with a host of European, Australian, and African colleagues, including Clare Brant, Gisela Brinker-Gabler, Fatou Diouf Kandji, Kateryna Olijnyk Longley, Ioana Luca, Anneleen Masschelein, Christian Moser, Griselda Pollock, Arnaud Schmitt, Monica Soeting, Claudia Ulbrich, and Gudrun Wedel, spurred us to think more comparatively.

The extraordinary efforts of Craig Howes, coeditor of the journal *Biography,* director of the Center for Biographical Research at the University of Hawai'i, Manoa, and manager of the International

Acknowledgments 321

Auto/Biography Association listserv, have consistently inspired fresh insights and enhanced scholarly expertise. His intellectual generosity has unflaggingly nurtured and supported our work and that of our colleagues in autobiography studies. The close collaboration of the *Biography* editorial team in surveying and supporting work in life narrative worldwide is evident in its annual "International Year in Review" overviews of work by scholars, now from more than twenty-five countries.

We recognize with gratitude the formative influence on autobiography studies of two foundational scholars. Independently, each of us was sustained by James Olney's generous and thoughtful support of our work at an early stage. James's profound engagement with questions of self-referential discourse as "metaphors of self," his commitment to building the field of autobiography studies, and his generosity to younger scholars remain inspirational long after his death. Philippe Lejeune's extensive and groundbreaking body of work on autobiography and the personal journal and his leadership, for more than three decades, of the Association for Autobiography and Autobiographical Heritage in France exemplify how a scholar may join academic research to life writing publics and apply discoveries to both historical and everyday uses. His dedication to and delight in the work of autobiography studies is a model of passionate engagement.

Closer to home, the advisors from our early careers were formative in the bold choice each of us made to focus on autobiographical writing at a time when it was regarded as a species of the "intentional fallacy." Julia is grateful above all to her early mentors, Max Wei Yeh and Alexander Gelley. Sidonie is grateful to her advisor Roger Salomon, who suggested she explore African American autobiography for her dissertation project and remained a staunch supporter throughout her career.

Our thinking has been informed, shaped, and enriched by ongoing interactions on the International Auto/Biography Association listserv and at its conferences, and in oral and written dialogues with our colleagues. They—and we—are an intrepid band of scholars working to bring academic legitimacy to the field of life narrative; we have challenged, cajoled, and consoled one another for more than three decades. In particular, Jon Alexander, O.P., Laura Beard, William Boelhower, Clare Brant, Bella Brodzki, Ricia Chansky, Robert Folkenflik, Cynthia Franklin, Joseph Hogan, Rebecca Hogan, Margaretta Jolly, Roseanne Kennedy, Valerie Lee, Lisa Ortiz-Vilarelle, Jeremy Popkin, Roger

Porter, and Hertha Dawn Sweet Wong shared their insights, readings, and probing questions with us. In visual and graphic media, as well as performance and self-portraiture, the advice of our colleagues Hillary Chute, Julie Codell, Lesley Ferris, Jared Gardner, Kathleen McHugh, Chon Noriega, and Candida Rifkind informed our discussions of automediality in self-representation. In digital forms, established and emerging scholars probing the proliferating modes of online lives, among them Laurie McNeill, Anna Poletti, Julie Rak, Brian Rotman, and John Zuern, have called our attention to the theoretical implications of digital subjectivity. Finally, the perceptive observations of our undergraduate students and the insights of our graduate students have long inspired us in theorizing life narrative across diverse media.

As our networks expanded over the decades, each of us also worked with other communities on aspects of life writing at several sites: the Ludwig Boltzmann Institute for the History and Theory of Biography in Vienna, Austria; Gabrielle Jancke and the DFG Research Group on Ego-documents in Transcultural Perspective at the Free University, Berlin; Deborah Madsen, University of Geneva, and the Society of Swiss Americanists; Renata Jambresic Kirin and the Institute for Ethnology and Folklore of the University of Zagreb; Max Saunders and Clare Brant of the Centre for Life Writing Research at King's College, London; Volker Depkat at the University of Regensburg and the Leibniz Institute for East and Southeast European Studies; Jasmina Lukic and other faculty of the Central European University, Budapest; the American studies faculty in Istanbul, Turkey, particularly Oya Berk and Sirma Soran at Haliç University and Hülya Adak at Sabanci University; Adelina Sánchez-Espinosa and the GEMMA program at the University of Granada, Spain; Martina Wagner Egelhaaf and the Forum for Life Writing Research at the University of Münster, Germany; Monica Soeting and the Autobiography and Biography Network of the University of Amsterdam; the Women's Archive team of the Institute of Literary Research of the Polish Academy of Sciences, Warsaw, Poland; the Post Human Seminar of the Center for Biographical Research, University of Hawai'i; Klaus Benesch and the Bavarian American-Academy, Munich; Ela Klimek-Dominiak and the Institute of English Studies, University of Wroclaw, Poland; Christian Moser and Regine Strätling of InterArt at the Free University, Berlin; Meg Jensen and the Centre for Life Narrative Studies of Kingston University, England; Margaretta Jolly and the Sussex

Acknowledgments   323

University Centre for Life History and Life Writing Research; Marlene Kadar at York University, Toronto, Canada; Chutima Pragatwutisarn at Chulalongkorn University, Bangkok, Thailand; and Sibghatullah Khan, National University of Modern Languages, Islamabad, Pakistan. The biannual conferences of the International Auto/Biography Association and its branches in Europe, Asia-Pacific, and the Americas remain an invaluable source of insight and inspiration on new developments in our ever-expanding field. Finally, we enthusiastically welcome the surge of activity and interest in several nations: the People's Republic of China, particularly the Center for Life Writing, Shanghai Jiao Tong University; Finland, especially the Centre for the Study of Storytelling, Experientiality, and Memory at the University of Turku; and centers in Brazil, England, Estonia, France, Germany, India, Poland, the Republic of Ireland, and Spain.

Julia is grateful for the resources made available by The Ohio State University and the insights of her colleagues in the Department of Comparative Studies and Project Narrative. Sidonie is appreciative of the generous support made available by the University of Michigan.

Finally, we acknowledge how the wisdom of self-reflexive writers has both schooled and comforted. Studying life narrative is, if nothing else, an enduring lesson in humility. As Montaigne observed in "Of Experience," "There is no use our mounting on stilts, for on stilts we must still walk on our own legs. And on the loftiest throne in the world we are still sitting only on our own rump."

Notes

1. DEFINING AND DISCERNING LIFE NARRATIVE FORMS

1. See Olney, "Some Versions of Memory/Some Versions of Bios," for a parsing of the Greek etymology.

2. See Folkenflik, "Introduction," 13–14 n. 42, for a translation of this passage from Lejeune's *L'Autobiographie en France*, 241.

3. Although Ann Yearsley's preface to the fourth edition of her *Poems, On Several Occasions,* published in 1786, is an extended autobiographical refutation of the charge of ingratitude to her patron, Hannah More, the word *autobiographical* does not appear in its title ("Mrs. Yearsley's Narrative"), as we incorrectly claimed in the first edition, citing Robert Folkenflik. He has since noted this error (private correspondence, December 22, 2009).

4. See, for example, Richard Bowring, "The Female Hand in Heian Japan," on Heian Japan; Tetz Rooke's *In My Childhood,* and Farzaneh Milani's *Veils and Words,* studies of Arab autobiography; and Erwin Panofsky's interesting discussion of tombstone epigraphs in ancient Greece, *Tomb Sculpture.*

5. George Gusdorf makes this assertion explicit when he states, "Autobiography becomes possible only under certain metaphysical preconditions. . . . The curiosity of the individual about himself, the wonder that he feels before the mystery of his own destiny is thus tied to the Copernican Revolution. . . . It asserts itself only in recent centuries and only on a small part of the map of the world. . . . The conscious awareness of the singularity of each individual life is the late product of a specific civilization" ("Conditions and Limits of Autobiography," 29–31). The assumption that writing autobiography is the mark of attaining individuality and the highest achievement of Western civilization is evident in other critics such as Karl Joachim Weintraub, *The Value of the Individual,* and Roy Pascal, *Design and Truth in Autobiography.*

6. James Olney similarly opted, in *Memory and Narrative,* for a term more inclusionary than *autobiography* in discussing the writings of Augustine, Rousseau, and Beckett. Interested in exploring the autobiographical rather than fixing its rules and conventions, Olney employs the term *life-writing* to embrace diverse modes of the autobiographical: "Although I have in the past written frequently about autobiography as a literary genre, I have never been very comfortable doing it. . . . I have never met a definition of autobiography that I

325

could really like. . . . It strikes me that there has been a gradual alteration—an evolution or devolution as one may prefer—in the nature of life-writing or autobiography over the past sixteen centuries, moving from a focus on 'bios,' or the course of a lifetime, to focus on 'autos,' the self writing and being written; and this shift . . . has introduced a number of narrative dilemmas requiring quite different strategies on the writers' part" (xv).

7. We are grateful to G. Thomas Couser for pointing out the usefulness of this distinction and tracking the somewhat inconsistent shift between the two terms in the first edition of this book.

8. In *History, Historians, and Autobiography,* Popkin also notes how history, in reconstructing the "big picture" of the past, is modified in the genre he identifies as historians' autobiographies, the life narratives of scholars becoming historians.

9. At the American Studies Association conference session on biography in 2005, participants used the term *new biography* to describe a series of practices that their own work was incorporating: the relaxing of constraints of evidence, greater use of such storytelling forms as dialogue and setting, and the introduction of uncertainty or speculation.

10. For expanded analyses of the genre of biography and its relationship to other forms of life writing, see Nadel, *Biography,* and Backscheider, *Reflections on Biography.*

11. Saldívar acknowledges that his "biography" is an autoethnographic work that incorporates aspects of his own experience as a young Chicanx man growing up in the Southwest and that Paredes was an intellectual mentor.

12. See the special sections on the biopic in *Biography* (e.g., vol. 23, no. 1, Winter 2000; vol. 26, no. 1, Summer 2011; vol. 41, no. 3, Summer 2018), as well as regular essays and reviews, for overviews of the genre and suggestive essays on its norms and practices in film, television, video, and other media formats.

13. Though he uses the term *autobiography* in his many studies of life narrative, Lejeune expanded the scope of autobiographical texts beyond traditional works of bourgeois subjects in the nineteenth and twentieth centuries to include narratives by those who self-publish their life histories in France and those whose personal stories are dictated because they are not authors. See "The Autobiography of Those Who Do Not Write" and "Practice of the Private Journal."

14. See our discussion of *What Is the What?* in "Witness or False Witness?" and *A Heartbreaking Work* in "The Rumpled Bed of Autobiography."

15. In "Three Women's Texts and Circumfession," Gayatri Spivak discusses how such texts refuse both "autobiography" as the classic genre of "great lives" and the inventions of fiction in carving out alternative narrative spaces.

16. See James Wood's insightful discussion of Knausgaard's *My Struggle,*

Notes to Chapter 2   327

shockingly titled *Min Kamp* in Norwegian, as both a conventional autobiography, "one of those highly personal modern or postmodern works, narrated by a writer, usually having the form if not the veracity of memoir," and a meta-meditation on authorship "concerned with the writing of a book that turns out to be the text we are reading" that is indebted to Proust and the Rilke of *The Notebooks of Malte Laurids Brigge* ("Total Recall").

2. AUTOBIOGRAPHICAL SUBJECTS

1. See Whitted, "Comics and Emmett Till."

2. For a discussion of postmemory, the memory of the child of survivors, see Hirsch, who notes that postmemory is distinguished from memory by generational distance and from history by deep personal connection (*Family Frames*, 22).

3. In a call to "disarm" the mines, Sengupta insists that "there are cross-cutting histories of oppression and violence, that no one is innocent, and that all of us are implicated somewhere in our histories or in the histories of our ancestors as victims and as aggressors" (636).

4. For more elaboration of life narrative and identity assemblages, see Sidonie Smith, "Autobiographical Inscription."

5. Many of our discussions of digital life narratives and self-presentation throughout this edition are adapted from our essay "Virtually Me."

6. See the transcription of Piper's performance in Witzling, *Voicing Today's Visions*, 302–5.

7. The sentence is worth citing: "Il se faut reserver une arriereboutique toute nostre, toute franche, en laquelle nous éstablissons nostre vraye liberté et principale retraicte et solitude" (241), translated as "We must reserve a back shop all our own, entirely free, in which to establish our real liberty and our principal retreat and solitude," in *Complete Essays* (177 n. 50).

8. Material on autosomatography and graphic memoir is adapted in part from Julia Watson, "Drawing Is the Best Medicine."

9. Studying how male embodiment is presented or concealed in life narratives is a rich prospect for future research. Ken Plummer's *Telling Sexual Stories*, Martin A. Danahay's *A Community of One*, Trev Lynn Broughton's *Men of Letters, Writing Lives*, and Philip Holden's *Autobiography and Decolonization* explore texts, tropes, and critical lenses for critiquing models of masculinity.

3. AUTOBIOGRAPHICAL ACTS

1. This catalog of everyday situations is excerpted with permission of the University of Minnesota Press from our introduction to *Getting a Life* (2–3).

2. Narrative theorist James Phelan argues that the narrating in *Angela's Ashes* is filtered through an implied author beyond the narrating "I." The

implied author, for Phelan, is "the knowable agent . . . who determines which voices the narrator adopts on which occasions—and . . . provides some guidance about how we should respond to those voices" (*Living to Tell about It,* 69). In our view, however, it is crucial to insist on the mobility of the narrating and narrated "I"s that makes an implied author possibly superfluous.

3. While Althusser's dismissal of agency in the face of pervasive ideological interpellation may be too hasty, as the occasional, partial, and imperfectly enabling force of testimonial discourse in autobiographical projects indicates, his focus on the many routes of interpellation influence the subsequent theorizing of subject positions, and thus of the mobile positionalities of the "I."

4. The term is derived from Peggy Phelan's concept of "biocularity" (1285).

5. Some other theorists in the field of comics studies question whether the concept of avatar is a useful way of describing the complex "I"s in graphic memoirs. Hillary Chute, whose focus is on word-image relationships and dominant themes and genres of comics, usually employs only "narrator" and "character" *(Why Comics?)* and has expressed unease with the notion of the avatar (personal conversation with Julia Watson, 2015).

6. Twentieth-century modernism is the high point for the association of voice with interiority in such innovations as the interior monologue and stream-of-consciousness techniques identified with Marcel Proust, James Joyce, Virginia Woolf, and F. Scott Fitzgerald, among others. In this central innovation of the modernist novel, voice is rendered not in dialogue but through indirect discourse as textured subjectivity. The reader is invited into an interiority that involves an intimate exchange with a fictional presence.

7. See James Phelan's discussion of Frank McCourt's *Angela's Ashes* for a nuanced reading of how the difference between the narrating and narrated "I"s affects the reader's sense of McCourt's ethical stance in the first book and, by contrast, in his sequel *'Tis (Living to Tell about It).*

8. James Phelan suggests a useful set of differentiations for the kinds of distance that affect the play of voices across narrating and narrated "I"s, including "temporal, intellectual, emotional, physical, psychological, ideological, and ethical" gaps ("Voice," 139).

9. Susanna Egan observes that a text may generate the "polyphonic harmony" of a community of voices, either between dual narrators or between the narrator and the reader. See *Mirror Talk.*

10. See our more extended discussion in the introduction to *Women, Autobiography, Theory* (30–31).

11. As Brian Rotman observes, "Now, at the beginning of the computational era, the default is the lettered self of the alphabetic 'I' which confronts a still forming, embryonic and open-ended virtual 'I'. We, here in the text, still

Notes to Chapter 4   329

lettered denizens of the alphabetic world, confront our virtual manifestations. We not only experience 'everyone to whom we are connected [...] as if they are exactly next to us', but increasingly experience ourselves in this manner: our actual, alphabetic selves are in pervasive proximity—internal and external—to their virtual counterparts" ("Gesture and the I Fold," 78).

12. Friedman is interested in the geographics of identity as a contemporary cultural practice in this time: "Rhetorically speaking, geographics involves a shift from the discourses of romanticism to those of post-modernity" (*Mappings*, 19).

13. The term was developed by Jörg Dünne and Christian Moser, as well as other European scholars of life writing, to expand the definition of how subjectivity is constructed in writing, image, or new media. See also Nadja Gernalzick, *Temporality in American Filmic Autobiography* and Brian Rotman, "Gesture and the I Fold."

14. Scholars in media studies and autobiography studies invoke a set of related terms to illuminate the relationship of technologies and subjectivity: medium, mediation, mediatization, automediality, autobiomediality, and transmediality. Jay David Bolter and Richard Grusin, for instance, describe the relation of medium and mediation in this way: "A medium is that which remediates. It is that which appropriates the techniques, forms, and social significance of other media and attempts to rival or refashion them in the name of the real" (*Remediation*, 65). British cultural studies theorists are concerned to distinguish mediatization generally from mediation. "Mediation," observes Nick Couldry, "emphasize[s] the heterogeneity of the transformations to which media give rise across a complex and divided social space" ("Mediatization or Mediation?," 375). Mediatization, in contrast, "describes the transformation of many disparate social and cultural processes into forms or formats suitable for media representation" (377). His argument is that media cannot simply be conceptualized as "tools" for presenting a preexisting, essential self. Rather, the materiality of the medium constitutes and textures the subjectivity presented. Media technologies, that is, do not just transparently present the self. They constitute and expand it, and imagine new kinds of virtual sociality, which do not depend on direct or corporeal encounter. (This discussion is drawn from Smith and Watson, "Virtually Me," 77.)

4. WHAT ABOUT AUTOBIOGRAPHICAL TRUTH?

1. See our essay "Witness or False Witness?" for an extended discussion of life narratives that misrepresent aspects of the writer's past experience and relate them to what we term "the metrics of authenticity."

2. Ernaux's epigraph for the book is "'I wish for two things: that happening turn to writing. And that writing be happening.'—Michel Leiris" (French

330 Notes to Chapter 4

ethnographer and writer with a four-volume memoir). The title in French is *Evênement,* which may also connote the evanescence of an event in time. *Happening* did not circulate in a U.S. trade paperback edition until 2019; a film based on the narrative was in theaters internationally in 2022.

6. KINDS OF LIFE NARRATIVES

1. Throughout this discussion of alcohol and opiate addiction, we are indebted to Kevin van Egdom's MA thesis, "Re-Constructing the Past," for which Julia Watson was the external reader.

2. See William L. Andrews, in *To Tell a Free Story,* for an overview of the origins and development of the genre. His "African-American Autobiography Criticism" surveys the development of criticism of the ex-slave narrative. James Olney's essay "'I Was Born'" discusses conventions of the genre. Samira Kawash, *Dislocating the Color Line,* critiques the notion of "freedom" attained.

3. Throughout this discussion, we use the term *disability* even as we recognize that recent work has critiqued use of the term as implicated in ableist discourse. We note that some scholars now use the phrase "critical disability studies" to imply the critique of terms such as *the disabled* and *disability* itself. The term *differently-abled* is an awkward alternative.

4. *Anthropocene* is a scientific and cultural term for the current geological era, during which the effects of human activity have dramatically influenced climate and environmental change.

5. Hornung is the coeditor with Nina Morgan and Takayuki Tatsumi of *The Routledge Companion to Transnational American Studies,* and he has been the editor of the *Journal of Transnational American Studies* since 2008.

6. See the special issue on "Life Writing and the Generations," *a/b: Auto/Biography Studies* (19, nos. 1–2). We recommend David Parker's discussion of the interplay of autonomy and relationality in various kinds of intergenerational narratives, in "Narratives of Autonomy and Narratives of Relationality in Auto/Biography."

7. For expanded discussion, see Julia Watson, "Ordering the Family"; and Julie Rak, "Radical Connections."

8. See Timothy Dow Adams, *Light Writing and Life Writing,* chap. 1.

9. See the special issue of *a/b: Auto/Biography Studies* (18, no. 2) on adoption narratives; and Marianne Novy's edited collection, *Imagining Adoption.*

10. We are indebted to Jim Lane's presentation on this film at the 2006 International Auto/Biography Association meeting in Mainz. Herzog's film is indebted to Jon Krakauer's ecobiography of McCandless's journey, *Into the Wild.*

11. Lane has long focused on autobiographical film. In *The Autobiographical Documentary in America from the 1960s to the Present,* he discusses such films as *Roger and Me, Sherman's March,* and *Silverlake Life.* Lane has noted

Notes to Chapter 6

the emergence of new hybrid kinds of autobiographical documentary film in forms of self-documenting and multiplying the subjects of documentation. Susanna Egan also explores a range of "thanatographical" films about death and mourning in *Mirror Talk.* See also Renov, *The Subject of Documentary,* and Gaines and Renov, *Collecting Visible Evidence.*

12. See Julia Watson, "Autographic Disclosures" for an extended discussion of *Fun Home.*

13. For an extended discussion of these different forms of "autobio-pedagogical comics," see our essay "Auto/biographics and Graphic Histories Made for the Classroom," from which some of the discussion in this entry is adapted.

14. Nell Irvin Painter's biography of Sojourner Truth asserts that she did not use the phrase. See Painter, *Sojourner Truth.*

15. For recent work in autobiography studies on refugee narratives, see "Forum: Refugee Narratives" in *a/b: Auto/Biography Studies* 32, no. 3 (2017): 625–81; and *Documenting Trauma in Comics,* edited by Dominic Davies and Candida Rifkind.

16. Women's self-presentations in these media are explored and theorized in our collection *Interfaces: Women, Autobiography, Image, Performance* and in some recent work of life narrative.

17. Material from this entry on "Political Life Narrative" has been in part excerpted from two essays: Sidonie Smith, "Autobiographical Discourse in the Theaters of Politics" and Sidonie Smith, "'America's Exhibit A.'"

18. See Ken Plummer's *Telling Sexual Stories* for an overview of many kinds of coming-out stories, including antecedents of British practices enacting them.

19. The book has sold nearly a half million copies. In 2006, five of her eight siblings told *The Guardian* that much of the book was fantasy, although O'Beirne produced documents to assert the contrary and argues she was vindicated by a lie detector test (see Addley, "Author Accused of Literary Fraud").

20. When published in Germany in 1959, it was critically attacked for its unheroic presentation of women and not republished in Hillers's lifetime, though it has been republished and made into a film since her death.

21. In 2007, Andrew Denton, an Australian interviewer, questioned the accuracy of dates and events in *A Long Way Gone,* suggesting it manifested troubling inconsistencies (Denton, "Ishmael Beah").

Bibliography

LIFE NARRATIVES

Abbey, Edward. *Desert Solitaire: A Season in the Wilderness.* New York: Simon and Schuster, 1968.

———. *The Monkey Wrench Gang.* Philadelphia: Lippincott, 1975.

Abelard, Peter, and Héloïse. *The Letters of Abelard and Héloïse.* Translated by Betty Radice. Harmondsworth: Penguin, 1974.

Abu-Jaber, Diana. *The Language of Baklava.* New York: Pantheon, 2005.

———. *Life without a Recipe.* New York: W. W. Norton, 2016.

Abu-Jamal, Mumia. *Live from Death Row.* New York: Harper Perennial, 1996.

Aciman, André. *Alibis: Essays on Elsewhere.* New York: Farrar, Straus and Giroux, 2011.

Adams, Henry. *The Education of Henry Adams: An Autobiography.* Boston: Houghton Mifflin, 1918.

Addams, Jane. *Twenty Years at Hull-House: With Autobiographical Notes.* New York: Macmillan, 1910.

Addario, Lynsey. *It's What I Do: A Photographer's Life of Love and War.* New York: Penguin, 2015.

Adichie, Chimamanda Ngozi. *Notes on Grief.* New York: Knopf, 2021.

Adielé, Faith. *Meeting Faith: The Forest Journals of a Black Buddhist Nun.* New York: Norton, 2004.

Ai Weiwei. *1000 Years of Joy and Sorrow.* New York: Crown, 2021.

———. *Human Flow: Stories from the Global Refugee Crisis.* Princeton, N.J.: Princeton University Press, 2020.

Akhmatova, Anna. *A Poem without a Hero.* Translated by Carl R. Proffer. Ann Arbor: Ardis, 1973.

Alexander, Jon. *American POW Memoirs from the Revolutionary War through the Vietnam War: The Autobiography Seminar.* Eugene, Ore.: Wipf & Stock, 2007.

Alexie, Sherman. *The Absolutely True Diary of a Part-Time Indian.* New York: Little, Brown, 2007.

———. *First Indian on the Moon.* Brooklyn: Hanging Loose Press, 1993.

———. *You Don't Have to Say You Love Me.* New York: Little, Brown, 2017.

Bibliography

Ali, Muhammed, with Hana Yasmin Ali. *The Soul of a Butterfly: Reflections on Life's Journey.* New York: Simon and Schuster, 2004.

Allen, Paula Gunn. "The Autobiography of a Confluence." In *I Tell You Now: Autobiographical Essays by Native American Writers,* edited by Brian Swann and Arnold Krupat, 143–54. Lincoln: University of Nebraska Press, 1987.

Allende, Isabel. *Paula.* New York: Harper Perennial, 1996.

Álvarez, Noe. *Spirit Run: A 6,000-Mile Marathon through North America's Stolen Land.* New York: Catapult, 2020.

Amaechi, John. *Man in the Middle.* New York: ESPN, 2007.

Ammons, A. R. *Tape for the Turn of the Year.* Ithaca, N.Y.: Cornell University Press, 1965.

Anderson, Laurie. *Stories from the Nerve Bible: A Retrospective, 1972–1992.* New York: Harper Perennial, 1994.

Anderson, Paul Thomas, dir. *Licorice Pizza.* Beverly Hills, Calif.: Metro-Goldwyn-Mayer, 2021.

Andrews, William L., ed. *Sisters of the Spirit: Three Black Women's Autobiographies of the Nineteenth Century.* Bloomington: Indiana University Press, 1986.

Angela of Foligno. *Complete Works.* Translated by Paul Lachance. New York: Paulist Press, 1993.

Angelou, Maya. *The Heart of a Woman.* New York: Random House, 1981.

———. *I Know Why the Caged Bird Sings.* New York: Random House, 1969.

Antin, Eleanor. *Carving: A Traditional Sculpture.* Chicago: Art Institute of Chicago, 1972.

Antin, Mary. *The Promised Land.* Boston: Houghton Mifflin, 1912.

Antoni, Janine. *Gnaw.* London: Saatchi Collection, 1992.

Anzaldúa, Gloria. *Borderlands/La Frontera: The New Mestiza.* San Francisco: Spinsters/Aunt Lute, 1987.

———, ed. *Making Face, Making Soul = Haciendo Caras: Creative and Critical Perspectives by Feminists of Color.* San Francisco: Aunt Lute Foundation, 1990.

Apess, William. "The Experience of Five Christian Indians of the Pequot Tribe." In *On Our Own Ground: The Complete Writings of William Apess, a Pequot,* edited by Barry O'Connell, 117–61. Amherst: University of Massachusetts Press, 1992.

———. "A Son of the Forest." In *On Our Own Ground: The Complete Writings of William Apess, a Pequot,* edited by Barry O'Connell, 1–97. Amherst: University of Massachusetts Press, 1992.

Apted, Michael, dir. *The Up! Series.* New York: First-Run Features, 2004.

Aptheker, Bettina. *Intimate Politics: How I Grew Up Red, Fought for Free Speech, and Became a Feminist Rebel.* Emeryville, Calif.: Seal Press, 2006.

Bibliography

Arenas, Reinaldo. *Before Night Falls: A Memoir.* Translated by Dolores M. Koch. New York: Penguin, 1994.

Arno, Michaelis. *My Life after Hate.* Milwaukee: Authentic Presence Publications, 2012.

"Article 27." Quantified Self: Self-Knowledge through Numbers. https://quantifiedself.com/about/article27.

Ashbery, John. *Self-Portrait in a Convex Mirror.* New York: Viking, 1975.

Ashe, Arthur, and Arnold Rampersad. *Days of Grace: A Memoir.* New York: Knopf, 1993.

Athill, Diana. *Somewhere towards the End: A Memoir.* New York: W. W. Norton, 2009.

Augustine, Saint, Bishop of Hippo. *The Confessions of St. Augustine.* Translated by Rex Warner. New York: New American Library, 1963.

Auster, Paul. *The Invention of Solitude.* New York: Penguin, 1982.

Awkward, Michael. *Scenes of Instruction: A Memoir.* Durham, N.C.: Duke University Press, 1999.

Bâ, Mariama. *So Long a Letter.* London: Virago Press, 1982.

Baepler, Paul, ed. *White Slaves, African Masters: An Anthology of American Barbary Captivity Narratives.* Chicago: University of Chicago Press, 1999.

Baker, Russell. *Growing Up.* New York: Penguin, 1982.

Baldwin, James. *Notes of a Native Son.* Boston: Beacon, 1957.

Barnes, Julian. *Levels of Life.* New York: Knopf, 2013.

Barrios de Chungara, Domitila, and Moema Viezzer. *Let Me Speak! Testimony of Domitila, a Woman of the Bolivian Mines.* New York: Monthly Review Press, 1978.

Barry, Lynda. "Interview with Lynn Neary." *Talk of the Nation.* National Public Radio. Aired October 1, 2002. https://www.npr.org/templates/story/story.php?storyid=1150937.

———. *One Hundred Demons.* Seattle: Sasquatch, 2002.

Barthes, Roland. *Camera Lucida: Reflections on Photography.* Translated by Richard Howard. New York: Hill and Wang, 1981.

———. *Roland Barthes by Roland Barthes.* Translated by Richard Howard. New York: Hill and Wang, 1977.

Bauby, Jean-Dominique. *The Diving Bell and the Butterfly.* Translated by Jeremy Leggatt. New York: Knopf, 1997.

Bayley, John. *Elegy for Iris.* New York: Macmillan, 2000.

Beah, Ishmael. *A Long Way Gone: Memoirs of a Boy Soldier.* New York: Farrar, Straus and Giroux, 2007.

Beauvoir, Simone de. *The Coming of Age.* Translated by Patrick O'Brian. New York: Putnam, 1972.

Bibliography

———. *The Ethics of Ambiguity.* Translated by Bernard Frechtman. New York: Citadel Press, 2000.

———. *Memoirs of a Dutiful Daughter.* Translated by James Kirkup. New York: Harper Perennial, 2005.

Bechdel, Alison. *Are You My Mother? A Comic Drama.* New York: Houghton Mifflin Harcourt, 2012.

———. *Fun Home: A Family Tragicomic.* Boston: Houghton Mifflin, 2006.

———. *The Secret to Superhuman Strength.* New York: Mariner, 2021.

Benjamin, Walter. *Berlin Childhood around 1900.* Translated by Howard Eiland. Cambridge, Mass.: Harvard University Press, 2006.

———. *The "Berlin Chronicle" Notices.* Translated by Carl Skoggard. Portland, Ore.: Pilot Editions, 2015.

———. *Moscow Diary.* Edited by Gary Smith, translated by Richard Sieburth. Cambridge, Mass.: Harvard University Press, 1986.

Bernstein, Harry. *The Invisible Wall: A Love Story That Broke Barriers.* New York: Ballantine, 2007.

Berry, Wendell. *The Art of the Commonplace: The Agrarian Essays of Wendell Berry.* Edited by Norman Wirzba. Washington, D.C.: Counterpoint, 2002.

———. *What I Stand On: The Collected Essays of Wendell Berry, 1969–2017.* New York: Library of America, 2019.

Bérubé, Michael. *Life as Jamie Knows It: An Exceptional Child Grows Up.* Boston: Beacon, 2016.

———. *Life as We Know It: A Father, a Family, and an Exceptional Child.* New York: Vintage, 1998.

Berzon, Betty. *Surviving Madness: A Therapist's Own Story.* Living Out Series. Madison: University of Wisconsin Press, 2002.

Beyala, Calixthe. *Your Name Shall Be Tanga.* Translated by Marjolijn de Jager. Oxford: Heinemann Educational Publishers, 1996.

Bhutto, Benazir. *Benazir Bhutto: Daughter of the East.* London: Hamilton, 1988.

Biemann, Ursula, dir. and prod. *Performing the Border.* Switzerland/Mexico, 1999.

Bird, Isabella. *Collected Travel Writings of Isabella Bird.* Bristol: Ganesha Publications, 1997.

Black Elk. *Black Elk Speaks: Being the Life Story of a Holy Man of the Oglala Sioux as Told to John G. Neihardt.* New York: W. Morrow, 1932.

Blew, Mary Clearman. *All but the Waltz: Essays on a Montana Family.* Norman: University of Oklahoma Press, 1991.

Bok, Edward William. *The Americanization of Edward Bok: The Autobiography of a Dutch Boy Fifty Years After.* New York: Scribner's, 1922.

Boorman, John, dir. *In My Country.* New York: Sony Picture Classics, 2004.

Bibliography

Borden, Mary. *The Forbidden Zone: A Nurse's Impressions of the First World War.* Edited by Hazel Hutchinson. London: Modern Voices, 2008.

Bornstein, Kate. *Gender Outlaw: On Men, Women, and the Rest of Us.* New York: Routledge, 1994.

Boswell, James. *Boswell on the Grand Tour: Germany and Switzerland, 1764.* Edited by Frederick A. Pottle. London: W. Heinemann, 1953.

———. *Boswell on the Grand Tour: Italy, Corsica, and France, 1765–1766.* Edited by Frank Brady and Frederick A. Pottle. London: W. Heinemann, 1955.

Bourdain, Anthony. *Kitchen Confidential: Adventures in the Culinary Underbelly.* New York: Bloomsbury Publishing, 2000.

Boylan, Jennifer Finney. *Good Boy: My Life in Seven Dogs.* New York: Celadon Books, 2020.

———. *She's Not There: A Life in Two Genders.* New York: Broadway Books, 2003.

Brabner, Joyce, Harvey Pekar, and Frank Stack. *Our Cancer Year.* New York: Four Walls Eight Windows, 1994.

Bradley, Bill. *Life on the Run.* New York: Quadrangle/New York Times Books, 1976.

Brasch, Marion. *Ab Jetzt Ist Ruhe: Roman meiner fabelhaften Familie.* Frankfurt am Main: S. Fischer Verlag, 2012.

Breytenbach, Breyten. *The True Confessions of an Albino Terrorist.* London: Faber and Faber, 1984.

Brodkey, Harold. *This Wild Darkness: The Story of My Death.* New York: Henry Holt, 1996.

Broinowski, Anna, dir. *Forbidden Lie$.* San Francisco: Roxie Releasing, 2007.

Brontë, Charlotte. *Jane Eyre.* Edited by Margaret Smith. New York: Oxford University Press, 1998.

Broom, Sarah M. *The Yellow House: A Memoir.* New York: Grove Press, 2019.

Brown, Don. *The Unwanted: Stories of Syrian Refugees.* New York: Houghton Mifflin Harcourt, 2018.

Browne, Thomas. "Religio Medici." In *Selected Writings,* edited by Geoffrey Keynes, 5–89. Chicago: University of Chicago Press, 1968.

Broyard, Anatole. *Thanatography: Intoxicated by My Illness.* New York: Ballantine, 1993.

Broyard, Bliss. *One Drop: My Father's Hidden Life—a Story of Race and Family Secrets.* New York: Little, Brown, 2007.

Bunyan, John. *Grace Abounding to the Chief of Sinners.* Edited by Roger Sharrock. Oxford: Clarendon Press, 1962.

Burroughs, Augusten. *Dry: A Memoir.* New York: St. Martin's, 2003.

———. *Running with Scissors: A Memoir.* New York: Picador, 2002.

Burton, Robert. *Anatomy of Melancholy.* Edited by Holbrook Jackson. London: Dent, 1972.

Cahun, Claude. *Disavowals or Cancelled Confessions*. Translated by Susan de Muth. Cambridge, Mass.: MIT Press, 2008. Originally published as *Aveux non avenus*. Paris: Editions de Carrefour, 1930.

Campbell, Hillary Fitzgerald. *Murder Book: A Graphic Memoir of a True Crime Obsession*. Kansas City, MO: Andrews McMeel Publishing, 2021.

Campbell, Nicola I. *Spíləxm: A Weaving of Recovery, Resilience, and Resurgence*. Winnipeg: HighWater Press, 2021.

Cantú, Norma Elia. *Canícula: Snapshots of a Girlhood en la Frontera*. Albuquerque: University of New Mexico Press, 1995.

Caouette, Jonathan, et al., dirs. *Tarnation*. Wellspring Media, 2003.

Cardano, Girolamo. *The Book of My Life*. Translated by Jean Stoner. New York: Dover, 1962.

Cardinal, Marie. *The Words to Say It: An Autobiographical Novel*. Translated by Pat Goodheart. Cambridge, Mass.: VanVactor and Goodheart, 1983.

Carr, David. *The Night of the Gun*. New York: Simon and Schuster, 2008.

Carrère, Emmanuel. *The Kingdom: A Novel*. Translated by John Lambert. New York: Farrar, Straus and Giroux, 2017.

———. *My Life as a Russian Novel: A Memoir*. Translated by Linda Coverdale. New York: Metropolitan Books, 2010.

Carter, Forrest. *The Education of Little Tree*. New York: Delacorte Press, 1976.

Casanova, Giacomo. *History of My Life*. 12 vols. Translated by Willard R. Trask. New York: Harcourt, Brace and World, 1966–71.

Casas, Bartolomé de Las. *Witness: Writings of Bartolomé de Las Casas*. Edited and translated by George Sanderlin. Maryknoll, N.Y.: Orbis, 1992.

Casserly, Paul, Mark McNeill, and Irena Dol, dirs. *Why Am I? The Science of Us*. New Zealand: Razor Films, 2016.

Cave, Nick, and Sean O'Hagan. *Faith, Hope and Carnage*. New York: Farrar, Straus and Giroux, 2022.

Cavendish, Margaret. *The Life of William Cavendish, Duke of Newcastle, to Which Is Added the True Relation of My Birth, Breeding, and Life*. 2nd ed. Edited by C. H. Firth. London: G. Routledge and Sons, 1903.

Cellini, Benvenuto. *Autobiography of Benvenuto Cellini*. Translated by George Bull. Harmondsworth: Penguin, 1956.

Charke, Charlotte. *A Narrative of the Life of Mrs. Charlotte Charke (Youngest Daughter of Colley Cibber, Esq.), Written by Herself*. Edited by Leonard R. N. Ashley. Gainesville, Fla.: Scholar's Facsimiles and Reprints, 1969.

Chast, Roz. *Can't We Talk about Something More Pleasant?* New York: Bloomsbury Publishing, 2014.

Chernin, Kim. *In My Mother's House: A Daughter's Story*. New York: Harper and Row, 1983.

Child, Julia, Louisette Bertholle, and Simone Beck. *Mastering the Art of French Cooking*. Vol. 1. New York: Knopf, 1961.

Bibliography   **339**

Child, Julia, and Alex Prud'homme. *My Life in France.* New York: Knopf, 2006.

Chiten, Laurel, dir. *Twitch and Shout.* Harriman, N.Y.: New Day Films, 1994.

Chung, Nicole. *All You Can Ever Know: A Memoir.* New York: Catapult, 2018.

Clapton, Eric, and Christopher Simon Sykes. *Eric Clapton: The Autobiography.* London: Century, 2007.

Clarke, Austin. *Pig Tails 'n Breadfruit: A Culinary Memoir.* New York: New Press, 1999.

Cleaver, Eldridge. *Soul on Ice.* New York: McGraw-Hill, 1968.

Clemens, Paul. *Made in Detroit: A South of 8-Mile Memoir.* New York: Doubleday, 2005.

Cliff, Michelle. *Abeng: A Novel.* New York: Crossing Press, 1984.

———. *No Telephone to Heaven.* New York: Vintage Books, 1989.

Clinton, Hillary Rodham. *Hard Choices.* New York: Simon and Schuster, 2014.

———. *Living History.* New York: Simon and Schuster, 2003.

———. *What Happened.* New York: Simon and Schuster, 2017.

Coates, Ta-Nehisi. *Between the World and Me.* New York: Spiegel and Grau, 2015.

Coetzee, J. M. *Boyhood: Scenes from Provincial Life.* New York: Viking, 1997.

———. *Diary of a Bad Year.* London: Harvill Secher, 2007.

———. *Doubling the Point: Essays and Interviews.* Edited by David Attwell. Cambridge, Mass.: Harvard University Press, 1992.

———. *Summertime: Fiction.* New York: Viking, 2009.

———. *Youth: Scenes from Provincial Life II.* New York: Viking, 2002.

Cohen, Leonard. "I Can't Forget." Recorded August–November 1987. Track 7 on *I'm Your Man.* Columbia Records, 1988.

Cole, Teju. *Golden Apple of the Sun.* London: MACK, 2021.

Colette, Sidonie-Gabrielle. *Earthly Paradise: An Autobiography.* Edited by Robert Phelps. New York: Farrar, Straus and Giroux, 1966.

Collard, Cyril, dir. *Les Nuits Fauves* [Savage Nights]. New York: PolyGram Video, 1994.

———. *Savage Nights.* Translated by William Rodarmor. Woodstock, N.Y.: Overlook Press, 1994.

Condé, Maryse. *Hérémakhonon: A Novel.* Translated by Richard Philcox. Washington, D.C.: Three Continents Press, 1982.

———. *I, Tituba, Black Witch of Salem.* Charlottesville: University Press of Virginia, 1992.

Couser, G. Thomas. *Letter to My Father: A Memoir.* Lanham, Md.: Hamilton Books, 2017.

Crews, Harry. *A Childhood: The Biography of a Place.* New York: Penguin, 2022.

Crowley, Aleister. *The Confessions of Aleister Crowley: An Autohagiography.* New York: Penguin, 1989.

cummings, e. e. *The Enormous Room.* New York: Modern Library, 1934.

Bibliography

Dangarembga, Tsitsi. *Nervous Conditions.* London: Women's Press, 1988.

Dante Alighieri. *Dante Alighieri's Divine Comedy.* Translated by Mark Musa. Bloomington: Indiana University Press, 1971.

———. *La Vita Nuova* [The New Life]. Translated by Mark Musa. Bloomington: Indiana University Press, 1962.

Danticat, Edwidge. *Brother, I'm Dying.* New York: Knopf, 2007.

Darwin, Charles. *Voyage of the Beagle.* London: Penguin, 1989.

Davey, Moyra. *Les Goddesses.* Chicago: Art Institute of Chicago, 2011.

David B. *Epileptic.* New York: Pantheon, 2005.

David M. Rubenstein National Institute for Holocaust Documentation. United States Holocaust Memorial Museum, Washington, D.C., 2023.

Day, Dorothy. *The Long Loneliness: The Autobiography of Dorothy Day.* New York: Harper Bros., 1952.

Dayo, Kaighla Um. *Things That Shatter: A Memoir.* Self-published, 2019.

DeBaggio, Thomas. *Losing My Mind: An Intimate Look at Life with Alzheimer's.* New York: Simon and Schuster, 2001.

Defoe, Daniel. *A Journal of the Plague Year* [1722]. New York: Dutton, 1966.

Delbo, Charlotte. *Auschwitz and After.* Translated by Rosette C. Lamont. New Haven, Conn.: Yale University Press, 1995.

De Quincey, Thomas. *Confessions of an English Opium Eater* [1821]. Oxford: Woodstock, 1989.

Deren, Maya, dir. *Maya Deren, Collected Experimental Films.* New York: Mystic Fire Video, 1986.

Derounian-Stodola, Kathryn Zabelle, ed. *Women's Indian Captivity Narratives.* New York: Penguin, 1998.

De Sales, Saint Francis. *The Introduction to a Devout Life.* Ilkley: Scolar Press, 1976.

Descartes, René. *Discourse on Method; and, Meditations on First Philosophy.* Translated by Elizabeth S. Haldane and G. R. T. Ross. Edited by David Weissman. New Haven, Conn.: Yale University Press, 1996.

Diawara, Manthia. *In Search of Africa.* Cambridge, Mass.: Harvard University Press, 1998.

———, dir. *An Opera of the World.* Lisbon: MauMaus/Lumiar Cité, 2017.

———, dir. *Rouch in Reverse.* New York: Third World News Reel, 1995.

Diaz, Junot. *The Brief Wondrous Life of Oscar Wao.* New York: Riverhead Books, 2007.

Dickens, Charles. *David Copperfield.* Edited by Nina Burgis. New York: Oxford University Press, 1981.

———. *Great Expectations.* Oxford: Oxford University Press, 2008.

Dickinson, Emily. *The Poems of Emily Dickinson.* Cambridge, Mass.: Belknap Press of Harvard University Press, 1999.

Didion, Joan. *The Year of Magical Thinking.* New York: Knopf, 2005.

Bibliography 341

Dillard, Annie. *An American Childhood*. New York: Harper and Row, 1987.

Dinesen, Isak. *Out of Africa*. New York: Random House, 1938.

Ditlevsen, Tove. *The Copenhagen Trilogy: Childhood, Youth, Dependency*. Translated by Tiina Nunnally and Michael Favala Goldman. New York: Farrar, Straus and Giroux, 2020.

Djebar, Assia. *Fantasia, an Algerian Cavalcade*. Translated by Dorothy S. Blair. London: Heinemann, 1993.

———. "Forbidden Gaze, Severed Sound." Excerpted in *Women, Autobiography, Theory: A Reader*, edited by Sidonie Smith and Julia Watson, 337–42. Madison: University of Wisconsin Press, 1998.

Donne, John. *Sermons*. New York: Meridian Books, 1958.

Dostoyevsky, Fyodor. *Notes from Underground*. New York: Signet, 1961.

Doucet, Julie. *My New York Diary*. Montreal: Drawn and Quarterly Publications, 1999.

Douglass, Frederick. *Life and Times of Frederick Douglass*. New York: Collier, 1962.

———. *My Bondage and My Freedom*. New York: Dover, 1969.

———. *Narrative of the Life of Frederick Douglass, an American Slave*. New York: Signet, 1968.

Doxiadis, Apostolos, and Christos H. Papadimitriou. *Logicomix: An Epic Search for Truth*. New York: Bloomsbury, 2009.

Du Bois, W. E. B. *The Autobiography of W. E. B. Du Bois: A Soliloquy on Viewing My Life from the Last Decade of Its First Century*. New York: International Publishers, 1968.

Dunlap-Shohl, Peter. *My Degeneration: A Journey through Parkinson's*. University Park: Pennsylvania State University Press, 2015.

Duras, Marguerite. *The Lover*. Translated by Barbara Bray. New York: Pantheon, 1985.

Dylan, Bob. *Chronicles*. New York: Simon and Schuster, 2004.

Eagleton, Terry. *The Gatekeeper: A Memoir*. London: St. Martin's Griffin, 2003.

Ebadi, Shirin, with Azadeh Moaveni. *Iran Awakening: A Memoir of Revolution and Hope*. New York: Random House, 2006.

Eggers, Dave. *A Heartbreaking Work of Staggering Genius*. New York: Vintage, 2000.

———. *What Is the What: The Autobiography of Valentino Achak Deng, a Novel*. San Francisco: McSweeney's, 2006.

Ehrenreich, Ben. *Desert Notebooks: A Road Map for the End of Time*. Berkeley: Counterpoint, 2020.

Eiseley, Loren C. *The Star Thrower*. New York: Times Books, 1978.

El Saadawi, Nawal *A Daughter of Isis: The Autobiography of Nawal El Saadawi*. Translated by Sherif Hetata. London: Zed Books, 1999.

———. *Memoirs from the Women's Prison*. Translated by Marilyn Booth. London: Women's Press, 1986.

———. *Woman at Point Zero*. Translated by Sherif Hetata. London: Zed Books, 1983.

Elahi, Hasan. "Tracking Transience—The Orwell Project." 2005–2014. http://elahi.wayne.edu/track/.

Elaw, Zilpha. "Memoirs of the Life, Religious Experience, Ministerial Travels, and Labors of Mrs. Zilpha Elaw." In Andrews, *Sisters of the Spirit*, 49–160.

Eliot, T. S. *Four Quartets*. New York: Harcourt Brace Jovanovich, 1971.

Ellerby, Janet Mason. *Following the Tambourine Man: A Birthmother's Memoir*. New York: Syracuse University Press, 2007.

Ellison, Ralph. *Invisible Man*. New York: Random House, 1952.

Ellroy, James. *My Dark Places: An L.A. Crime Memoir*. New York: Knopf, 1996.

Emecheta, Buchi. *Head above Water*. Oxford: Fontana, 1986.

Ephron, Nora. *I Feel Bad about My Neck: And Other Thoughts on Being a Woman*. New York: Vintage, 2008.

Equiano, Olaudah. *The Interesting Narrative and Other Writings*. Edited by Vincent Carretta. New York: Penguin, 2003.

Erauso, Catalina de. *The Lieutenant Nun: Memoir of a Basque Transvestite in the New World*. Translated by Michele Stepto and Gabriel Stepto. Boston: Beacon, 1996.

Ernaux, Annie. *Happening*. Translated by Tanya Leslie. New York: Seven Stories Press, 2001.

———. *I Remain in Darkness*. Translated by Tanya Leslie. New York: Seven Stories Press, 1999.

———. *A Man's Place*. Translated by Tanya Leslie. New York: Seven Stories Press, 1992.

———. *Shame*. Translated by Tanya Leslie. New York: Seven Stories Press, 1998.

———. *A Woman's Story*. Translated by Tanya Leslie. New York: Seven Stories Press, 1991.

———. *The Years*. Translated by Alison L. Strayer. New York: Seven Stories Press, 2017.

Erpenbeck, Jenny. *Kairos*. Translated by Michael Hoffman. New York: New Directions, 2023.

Evans, Kate. *Threads: From the Refugee Crisis*. New York: Verso, 2017.

Evans, Stephanie Y. *Black Women's Yoga History: Memoirs of Inner Peace*. Albany: State University of New York Press, 2021.

The Exodus Road. https://theexodusroad.com.

Falkoff, Marc, ed. *Poems from Guantánamo: The Detainees Speak*. Iowa City: University of Iowa Press, 2007.

Bibliography

343

Fanon, Frantz. *Black Skin, White Masks.* Translated by Charles Lam Markmann. New York: Grove Press, 1967.

Feinberg, Leslie. *Stone Butch Blues: A Novel.* Ithaca, N.Y.: Firebrand Books, 1993.

Felstiner, Mary. *Out of Joint: A Private and Public Story of Arthritis.* Lincoln: University of Nebraska Press, 2005.

Fershleiser, Rachel, and Larry Smith, eds. *Not Quite What I Was Planning: Six-Word Memoirs by Writers Famous and Obscure, from Smith Magazine.* New York: HarperPerennial, 2008.

Filipović, Zlata. *Zlata's Diary: A Child's Life in Sarajevo.* New York: Penguin, 1995.

Finger, Anne. *Elegy for a Disease: A Personal and Cultural History of Polio.* New York: St. Martin's Press, 2006.

Fink, Jennifer Natalya. *All Our Families: Disability Lineage and the Future of Kinship.* Boston: Beacon, 2022.

First, Ruth. *117 Days: An Account of Confinement and Interrogation under the South African 90-Day Detention Law.* New York: Stein and Day, 1965.

Fisher, Carrie. *Wishful Drinking.* New York: Simon and Schuster, 2008.

Flanagan, Bob. *Bob Flanagan: Super-Masochist.* Edited by Andrea Juno and V. Vale. San Francisco: Re/Search Publications, 1993.

Flowers, Catherine Coleman. *Waste: One Woman's Fight against America's Dirty Secret.* New York: New Press, 2020.

Flynn, Elizabeth Gurley. *I Speak My Own Piece: Autobiography of "The Rebel Girl."* New York: Masses and Mainstream, 1955.

Fonda, Jane. *My Life So Far.* New York: Random House, 2005.

Ford, Richard. *Between Them: Remembering My Parents.* New York: HarperCollins, 2017.

Forney, Ellen. *Marbles: Mania, Depression, Michelangelo, and Me.* New York: Gotham Books, 2012.

Fox, George. *The Journal of George Fox.* Cambridge: Cambridge University Press, 1952.

Fox, Michael J. *No Time Like the Future: An Optimist Considers Mortality.* New York: Flatiron Books, 2021.

Frangello, Gina. *Blow Your House Down: A Story of Family, Feminism, and Treason.* Berkeley: Counterpoint, 2021.

Frank, Anne. *The Diary of a Young Girl.* Translated by B. M. Mooyaart-Doubleday. Garden City, N.Y.: Doubleday, 1952.

Franklin, Benjamin. *The Autobiography of Benjamin Franklin: A Genetic Text.* Edited by J. A. Leo LeMay and P. M. Zall. Knoxville: University of Tennessee Press, 1981.

Franzen, Jonathan. "My Father's Brain: What Alzheimer's Takes Away." *New*

Yorker, September 2, 2001. https://www.newyorker.com/magazine/2001/09/10/jonathan-franzen-my-fathers-brain.

Fraser, Sylvia. *My Father's House: A Memoir of Incest and Healing.* New York: Harper and Row, 1987.

Frey, James. *A Million Little Pieces.* New York: N. A. Talese/Doubleday, 2003.

Frick, Laurie. *Quantify Me.* Women & Their Work, Austin, January 14 – March 10, 2012. https://do512.com/events/weekly/sat/laurie-frick-quantify-me.

Fries, Kenny. *Body, Remember: A Memoir.* Madison: University of Wisconsin Press, 2003.

Fusco, Coco. *English Is Broken Here.* New York: New Press, 1995.

Gailhard, Jean. *The Compleat Gentleman; or, Directions for the Education of Youth as to Their Breeding at Home and Travelling Abroad.* London: Thomas Newcomb, 1678.

Gallop, Jane. *Feminist Accused of Sexual Harassment.* Durham, N.C.: Duke University Press, 1997.

Gandhi, Mahatma K. *An Autobiography; or, The Story of My Experiments with Truth.* 2 vols. Translated by Mahadev Desai. Ahmedabad: Navajivan Publishing House, 1927–29.

Gates, Henry Louis, Jr. *Colored People: A Memoir.* New York: Knopf, 1994.

Gay, Roxane. *Bad Feminist: Essays.* New York: Harper Perennial, 2014.

———. *Hunger: A Memoir of My Body.* New York: HarperCollins, 2017.

Getz, Trevor R., and Liz Clarke. *Abina and the Important Men: A Graphic History.* New York: Oxford University Press, 2016.

Gibbon, Edward. *Memoirs of My Life.* Edited by Georges A. Bonnard. London: Nelson, 1966.

Gilbert, Elizabeth. *Eat, Pray, Love: One Woman's Search for Everything across Italy, India, and Indonesia.* New York: Viking, 2006.

Gilman, Charlotte Perkins. *The Living of Charlotte Perkins Gilman: An Autobiography.* Madison: University of Wisconsin Press, 1990.

———. *The Yellow Wallpaper.* New York: Feminist Press, 1973.

Ginibi, Ruby Langford. *Don't Take Your Love to Town.* Edited by Susan Hampton. New York: Penguin, 1988.

Giovanni, Nikki. *Quilting the Black-Eyed Pea: Poems and Not Quite Poems.* New York: William Morrow, 2002.

"Global Feminisms Project." University of Michigan Department of Women's and Gender Studies, 2023. https://sites.lsa.umich.edu/globalfeminisms/.

Gloeckner, Phoebe. *The Diary of a Teenage Girl: An Account in Words and Pictures.* Berkeley: Frog, 2002.

Glückel of Hameln. *The Memoirs of Glückel of Hameln.* Translated by Marvin Lowenthal. New York: Schocken, 1977.

Gobodo-Madikizela, Pumla. *A Human Being Died That Night: A South African Story of Forgiveness.* Boston: Houghton Mifflin, 2003.

Bibliography

Goethe, Johann Wolfgang von. *The Auto-Biography of Goethe. Truth and Poetry: From My Own Life.* 2 vols. Translated by John Oxenford. London: Bell and Daldy, 1872.

——. *The Sorrows of Young Werther and Novella.* Translated by Elizabeth Mayer, Louise Brogan, and W. H. Auden. New York: Modern Library, 1993.

——. *Wilhelm Meister's Apprenticeship.* Translated by R. Dillon Boylan. London: G. Bell and Sons, 1898.

Gold, Carolyn. *When I Died: Rx for Traumatic Brain Injury.* Self-published, 2020.

Goldman, Emma. *Living My Life.* Edited by Richard Drinnon and Anna Maria Drinnon. New York: New American Library, 1977.

Gómez-Peña, Guillermo. *A New World Border: Prophecies, Poems, and Loqueras for the End of the Century.* San Francisco: City Lights Books, 1996.

Goodison, Lorna G. *From Harvey River: A Memoir of My Mother and Her Island.* New York: Amistad, 2008.

Gordon, Mary. *Circling My Mother.* New York: Anchor, 2008.

——. *The Shadow Man: A Daughter's Search for Her Father.* New York: Random House, 1996.

Gore, Albert, and Melcher Media. *An Inconvenient Truth: The Planetary Emergency of Global Warming and What We Can Do about It.* Emmaus, Penn.: Rodale Press, 2006.

Gorky, Maxim. *Autobiography of Maxim Gorky: My Childhood, In the World, My Universities.* Translated by Isidor Schneider. New York: Citadel Press, 1949.

Gornick, Vivian. *Fierce Attachments: A Memoir.* Boston: Beacon, 1987.

Gosse, Edmund. *Father and Son: A Study of Two Temperaments.* London: W. Heinemann, 1907.

Grandin, Temple. *The Way I See It: A Personal Look at Autism and Asperger's.* Arlington, Tex.: Future Horizons, 2015.

Grealy, Lucy. *Autobiography of a Face.* Boston: Houghton Mifflin, 1994.

Grimes, William. *Life of William Grimes, the Runaway Slave.* Edited by William L. Andrews and Regina E. Mason. New York: Oxford University Press, 2008.

Grue, Jan. *I Live a Life Like Yours: A Memoir.* Translated by B. L. Crook. New York: Farrar, Straus and Giroux, 2021.

"GWOnline: Bibliography, Filmography and Webography: Gender and War Since 1600." Carolina Gender, War and Culture Series. University of North Carolina at Chapel Hill Department of History, 2023. https://gwonline.unc.edu/.

Hadewijch. *The Complete Works.* Translated by Columba Hart. New York: Paulist Press, 1980.

Haizlip, Shirlee Taylor. *The Sweeter the Juice: A Family Memoir in Black and White.* New York: Simon and Schuster, 1994.

Halkett, Anne. *The Autobiography of Anne, Lady Halkett*. Edited by John Gough Nichols. Westminster: Camden Society, 1875.

Hamper, Ben. *Rivethead: Tales from the Assembly Line*. New York: Warner Books, 1991.

Hanna-Attisha, Mona. *What the Eyes Don't See: The Story of Crisis, Resistance, and Hope in an American City*. New York: One World Books, 2018.

Harjo, Joy. *Crazy Brave: A Memoir*. New York: W. W. Norton, 2012.

Harrison, Kathryn. *The Kiss: A Secret Life*. New York: William Morrow, 1998.

Harry, Duke of Sussex. *Spare*. New York: Random House, 2023.

Hartman, Saidiya V. *Lose Your Mother: A Journey along the Atlantic Slave Route*. New York: Farrar, Straus and Giroux, 2007.

Harvey, Andrew. *A Journey in Ladakh: Encounters with Buddhism*. Boston: Mariner Books, 2000.

Hatoum, Mona. *Mona Hatoum*. London: Phaidon Press, 1997.

———. *Pull*. Live three-day video performance and installation (White Cube, London; Galerie Chantal Crousel, Paris; British School at Rome). 1995.

Haynes, Todd, dir. *I'm Not There*. New York: Weinstein Company, 2008.

Head, Bessie. *A Question of Power*. London: Heinemann Educational, 1974.

Hearth, Amy Hill, A. Elizabeth Delany, and Sarah L. Delany. *Having Our Say: The Delany Sisters' First 100 Years*. New York: Dell, 1993.

Hensel, Jana. *Zonenkinder*. Rowohlt: Reinbek, 2002.

Henson, Maria Rosa. *Comfort Woman: A Filipina's Story of Prostitution and Slavery under the Japanese Military*. Lanham, Md.: Rowman and Littlefield, 1999.

Hepola, Sarah. *Blackout: Remembering the Things I Drank to Forget*. New York: Grand Central Publishing, 2015.

Herzog, Werner, dir. *Grizzly Man*. Santa Monica, Calif.: Lions Gate Home Entertainment, 2005.

Heumann, Judith, with Kristen Joiner. *Being Heumann: An Unrepentant Memoir of a Disability Rights Activist*. Boston: Beacon Press, 2020.

Hildegard of Bingen. *Hildegard of Bingen: The Book of the Rewards of Life*. Translated by Bruce W. Hozeski. New York: Garland, 1994.

Hill, Jerome. *Film Portrait*. Buffalo, N.Y.: SUNY Buffalo Media Library, 1972.

Hill, Karlos K., and David Dodson. *The Murder of Emmett Till: A Graphic History*. New York: Oxford University Press, 2021.

[Hillers, Marta]. *A Woman in Berlin: Eight Weeks in a Conquered City: A Diary*. Translated by Philip Boehm. London: Virago Press, 2005.

Hirsi Ali, Ayaan. *Heretic: Why Islam Needs a Reformation Now*. Toronto: Alfred A. Knopf, 2015.

———. *Infidel*. New York: Simon & Schuster, 2006.

Hoffman, Eva. *Lost in Translation: A Life in a New Language*. Boston: E. P. Dutton, 1989.

Bibliography 347

hooks, bell. *Bone Black: Memories of Girlhood.* New York: Henry Holt, 1996.

Hopkins, Gerard Manley. *The Poems of Gerard Manley Hopkins.* 4th ed. Edited by W. H. Gardner and N. H. MacKenzie. London: Oxford University Press, 1967.

Hornbacher, Marya. *Wasted: A Memoir of Anorexia and Bulimia.* New York: Harper Perennial, 1999.

Hurston, Zora Neale. *Dust Tracks on a Road: An Autobiography.* 2nd ed. Edited by Robert Hemenway. Urbana: University of Illinois Press, 1984.

Ignatius of Loyola, Saint. *St. Ignatius' Own Story, as Told to Luis González de Cámara.* Translated by William J. Young. Chicago: Loyola University Press, 1956.

Isaacson, Walter. *Benjamin Franklin.* Farmington Hills, Mich.: Thorndike Press, 2004.

Isay, Dave, ed. *Listening Is an Act of Love: A Celebration of American Life from the StoryCorps Project.* New York: Penguin, 2007.

Jacobs, Harriet A. *Incidents in the Life of a Slave Girl: Written by Herself.* Edited by Lydia Maria Child and Jean Fagan Yellin. Cambridge, Mass.: Harvard University Press, 1987.

Jacques, Juliet. *Trans: A Memoir.* New York: Verso, 2015.

Jamison, Kay Redfield. *An Unquiet Mind.* New York: Knopf, 1995.

Jamison, Leslie. *Make It Scream, Make It Burn.* New York: Little, Brown, 2019.

———. *The Recovering: Intoxication and Its Aftermath.* London: Granta, 2018.

Jansson, Tove. *Letters from Tove.* Edited by Boel Westin and Helen Svensson. Translated by Sarah Death. Minneapolis: University of Minnesota Press, 2020.

Jefferson, Margo. *Negroland: A Memoir.* New York: Vintage, 2015.

Jemison, Mary. *A Narrative of the Life of Mrs. Mary Jemison.* Edited by James E. Seaver. Norman: University of Oklahoma Press, 1992.

Jesus, Carolina Maria de. *Child of the Dark: The Diary of Carolina Maria de Jesus.* Translated by David St. Clair. New York: E. P. Dutton, 1962.

Johnson, Nunnally, dir. *The Three Faces of Eve.* 20th Century Fox Home Entertainment, 2004.

Johnson, Samuel. *Johnson and Queeney: Letters from Dr. Johnson to Queeney Thrale from the Bowood Papers.* Edited by Marquis of Lansdowne. New York: Random House, 1932.

Johnson, Samuel, and Hester Lynch Piozzi. *The Letters of Samuel Johnson with Mrs. Thrale's Genuine Letters to Him.* Edited by R. W. Chapman. Oxford: Clarendon Press, 1952.

Jorgensen, Christine. *Christine Jorgensen: A Personal Autobiography.* New York: P. S. Eriksson, 1967.

Joslin, Tom, dir. *Silverlake Life: The View from Here.* Zeitgeist Films, 1993.

Joyce, James. *A Portrait of the Artist as a Young Man: Text, Criticism, and Notes.* Edited by Chester G. Anderson. New York: Viking Press, 1968.

Juana Inés de la Cruz, Sor. *A Sor Juana Anthology*. Translated by Alan S. True-blood. Cambridge, Mass.: Harvard University Press, 1988.

Julian of Norwich. *The Shewings of Julian of Norwich*. Edited by Georgia Ronan Crampton. Kalamazoo, Mich.: Medieval Institute Publications, 1994.

Juska, Jane. *A Round-Heeled Woman: My Late-Life Adventures in Sex and Romance*. New York: Villard, 2003.

Kaplan, Alice. *French Lessons: A Memoir*. Chicago: University of Chicago Press, 1993.

Karr, Mary. *Lit: A Memoir*. New York: HarperCollins, 2009.

Kartini, Raden Adjeng. *Letters of a Javanese Princess*. Translated by Agnes Louise Symmers. New York: Norton, 1964.

Kaysen, Susanna. *Girl, Interrupted*. New York: Vintage Books, 1993.

Keitetsi, China. *Child Soldier: Fighting for My Life*. Johannesburg: Jacana Media, 2005.

Keller, Helen, with John Albert Macy and Annie Sullivan. *The Story of My Life*. New York: Doubleday, Page, 1903.

Kemble, Frances Anne. *Journal of a Residence on a Georgian Plantation, 1838–1839*. Edited by John A. Scott. Athens: University of Georgia Press, 1984.

Kempe, Margery. *The Book of Margery Kempe*. Translated by B. A. Windeatt. London: Penguin, 1994.

Kempis, Thomas à. *Imitatio Christi*. Translated by Leo Sherley-Price. Harmondsworth: Penguin, 1952.

Ken Bugul. (Mariétou M'baye). *The Abandoned Baobab: The Autobiography of a Senegalese Woman*. Translated by Marjolijn De Jager. Brooklyn: Lawrence Hill Books, 1991.

Kennedy, Adam P., and Adrienne Kennedy. *Sleep Deprivation Chamber*. New York: Theatre Communications Group, 1996.

Kennedy, Adrienne. *Funnyhouse of a Negro*. New York: Samuel French, 2011.

———. *A Movie Star Has to Star in Black and White*. In *The Adrienne Kennedy Reader*. Minneapolis: University of Minnesota Press, 2001.

———. *The Ohio State Murders*. New York: Samuel French, 2021.

Kessler, Lauren. *Finding Life in the Land of Alzheimer's: One Daughter's Hopeful Story*. New York: Penguin, 2007.

Khaldun, Ibn. *Ibn Khaldun His Life and Works*. Edited by Mohammad Abdullah Enan. Kuala Lumpur: The Other Press, 2007.

Khouri, Norma. *Forbidden Love: A Harrowing True Story of Love and Revenge in Jordan*. London: Doubleday, 2003.

Kimmerer, Robin Wall. *Braiding Sweetgrass: Indigenous Wisdom, Scientific Knowledge, and the Teachings of Plants*. Minneapolis: Milkweed Editions, 2013.

Bibliography 349

Kincaid, Jamaica. *Annie John.* New York: Farrar, Straus and Giroux, 1983.

——. *The Autobiography of My Mother.* New York: Plume, 1997.

Kingsolver, Barbara, Steven L. Hopp, and Camille Kingsolver. *Animal, Vegetable, Miracle: A Year of Food Life.* New York: HarperCollins, 2007.

Kingston, Maxine Hong. *The Woman Warrior: Memoirs of a Girlhood among Ghosts.* New York: Vintage, 1976.

Kittredge, William. *Hole in the Sky: A Memoir.* New York: Knopf, 1992.

Kiyooka, Roy. *Mothertalk: Life Stories of Mary Kiyoshi Kiyooka.* Edmonton: NeWest Press, 1997.

Kleege, Georgina. *Blind Rage: Letters to Helen Keller.* Washington, D.C.: Gallaudet University Press, 2006.

Knapp, Carolyn. *Drinking: A Love Story.* New York: Dell, 1997.

Knausgaard, Karl Ove. *My Struggle.* Translated by Don Bartlett. New York: Farrar, Straus and Giroux, 2012.

Knott, Helen. *In My Own Moccasins: A Memoir of Resilience.* Regina: University of Regina Press, 2019.

Kobabe, Maia. *GenderQueer: A Memoir.* Portland: Oni Press, 2019.

Kobiela, Dorota, and Hugh Welchman, dirs. *Loving Vincent.* Sopot: BreakThru Productions and Trademark Films, 2017.

Kollontai, Alexandra. *The Autobiography of a Sexually Emancipated Communist Woman.* Edited by Irving Fetscher. Translated by Salvator Attanasio. New York: Schocken, 1975.

Krakauer, Jon. *Into the Wild.* New York: Anchor, 2007.

Krans, Kim. *Blossoms and Bones: Drawing a Life Back Together.* San Francisco: HarperOne, 2020.

Kraus, Chris. *I Love Dick.* Los Angeles: Semiotext(e), 1997.

Krog, Antjie. *Country of My Skull: Guilt, Sorrow, and the Limits of Forgiveness in the New South Africa.* New York: Times Books, 1999.

Kuhn, Annette. *Family Secrets: Acts of Memory and Imagination.* London: Verso, 1995.

Kuusisto, Stephen. *Planet of the Blind.* New York: Dell, 1998.

Labé, Louise. *Complete Poetry and Prose.* Translated by Annie Finch et al. Chicago: University of Chicago Press, 2006.

Labumore, Elsie Roughsey. *An Aboriginal Mother Tells of the Old and the New.* Edited by Paul Memmott and Robyn Horsman. Fitzroy, Victoria: McPhee Gribble, 1984.

Lakshmi, Padma. *Love, Loss, and What We Ate: A Memoir.* New York: Ecco, 2016.

Larcom, Lucy. *A New England Girlhood.* Boston: Corinth Books, 1961.

Latifa. *My Forbidden Face.* New York: Miramax Books, 2002.

Latifah, Queen, and Karen Hunter. *Ladies First: Revelations of a Strong Woman.* New York: William Morrow, 1999.

Laye, Camara. *The Dark Child*. Translated by James Kirkup. New York: Noonday Press, 1954.

Laymon, Kiese. "Heavy." https://www.kieselaymon.com/heavy.

———. *Heavy: An American Memoir*. New York: Scribner, 2018.

Lee, Jarena. "Life and Religious Experience of Jarena Lee." In Andrews, *Sisters of the Spirit*, 25–48.

Leiris, Michel. *Manhood: A Journey from Childhood into the Fierce Order of Virility*. Translated by Richard Howard. New York: Grossman, 1963.

———. *Scraps*. Vol. 2 of *Rules of the Game*. Translated by Lydia Davis. Baltimore: Johns Hopkins University Press, 1997.

———. *Scratches*. Vol. 1 of *Rules of the Game*. Translated by Lydia Davis. Baltimore: Johns Hopkins University Press, 1997.

Leonard, Joanne. *Being in Pictures: An Intimate Photo Memoir*. Ann Arbor: University of Michigan Press, 2008.

Léry, Jean de. *History of a Voyage to the Land of Brazil, Otherwise Called America*. Translated by Janet Whatley. Berkeley: University of California Press, 1990.

Lessing, Doris. *Alfred and Emily*. New York: Harper, 2008.

Levi, Primo. *Survival in Auschwitz: The Nazi Assault on Humanity*. Translated by Stuart Woolf. New York: Collier Books, 1993.

Levy, Deborah. *The Cost of Living: A Working Autobiography*. New York: Bloomsbury Publishing, 2018.

———. *Real Estate: A Living Autobiography*. New York: Bloomsbury Publishing, 2021.

———. *Things I Don't Want to Know: On Writing*. New York; Bloomsbury Publishing, 2013.

Lewis, John, Andrew Aydin, and Nate Powell. *March*. Marietta, Ga.: Top Shelf Productions, 2016.

Ligon, Glenn. *Some Changes*. Touring exhibition. Wexner Center for the Arts, The Ohio State University, Columbus, January 26 to April 15, 2007.

Lim, Shirley Geok-lin. *Among the White Moon Faces: An Asian-American Memoir of Homelands*. New York: Feminist Press, 1996.

Linton, Simi. *My Body Politic: A Memoir*. Ann Arbor: University of Michigan Press, 2006.

Lispector, Clarice. *Agua Viva*. Translated by Stefan Tobler. New York: New Directions, 2012.

lonelygirl15. *Lonelygirl15*. YouTube series, June 16, 2006–August 1, 2008. https://www.youtube.com/user/lonelygirl15.

Lorde, Audre. *A Burst of Light*. Toronto: Women's Press, 1988.

———. *The Cancer Journals*. Argyle, N.Y.: Spinsters, 1980.

———. *Zami: A New Spelling of My Name*. Trumansberg, N.Y.: Crossing Press, 1982.

Bibliography

Lowell, Robert. *Life Studies*. New York: Farrar, Straus, and Cudahy, 1959.

———. *Notebook 1967–68*. New York: Farrar, Straus and Giroux, 1969.

Macfarlane, Robert. *Underland: A Deep Time Journey*. New York: W. W. Norton, 2019.

Machado, Carmen Maria. *In the Dream House: A Memoir*. Minneapolis: Graywolf Press, 2019.

Mademba, Bay. *Il mio viaggio della speranza* [My voyage of hope]. Pisa: Giovane Africa Edizioni, 2011.

Mailhot, Térèse Marie. *Heart Berries: A Memoir*. Berkeley: Counterpoint, 2018.

Mairs, Nancy. *Voice Lessons: On Becoming a (Woman) Writer*. Boston: Beacon, 1997.

———. *Waist-High in the World: A Life among the Nondisabled*. Boston: Beacon, 1996.

Malcolm X, with Alex Haley. *The Autobiography of Malcolm X*. New York: Grove, 1965.

Mandela, Nelson. *Long Walk to Freedom: The Autobiography of Nelson Mandela*. Boston: Little, Brown, 1994.

———. *No Easy Walk to Freedom: Articles, Speeches, and Trial Addresses*. London: Heinemann, 1973.

———. *The Struggle Is My Life*. New York: Pathfinder Press, 1986.

Mangold, James, dir. *Girl, Interrupted*. Culver City, Calif.: Columbia Tristar Home Video, 1999.

Mann, Sally. *Hold Still: A Memoir with Photographs*. New York: Little, Brown, 2015.

Mann, Thomas. *Buddenbrooks: The Decline of a Family*. Translated by H. T. Lowe-Porter. New York: Vintage, 1952.

Manrique, Jaime. *Eminent Maricones: Arenas, Lorca, Puig, and Me*. Living Out Series. Madison: University of Wisconsin Press, 1999.

Marnell, Cat. *How to Murder Your Life: A Memoir*. New York: Simon and Schuster, 2017.

Martineau, Harriet. *Harriet Martineau's Autobiography*. Edited by Maria Weston Chapman. Boston: James R. Osgood, 1877.

Mass Observation: Recording Everyday Life in Britain. University of Sussex, 2015. http://www.massobs.org.uk/.

Matar, Hisham. *The Return: Fathers, Sons and the Land in Between*. New York: Random House, 2017.

Mathabane, Mark. *Kaffir Boy: The True Story of a Black Youth's Coming of Age in Apartheid South Africa*. New York: Macmillan, 1986.

Matthiessen, Peter. *The Snow Leopard*. New York: Viking, 1978.

McBride, James. *The Color of Water: A Black Man's Tribute to His White Mother*. New York: Riverhead Books, 1996.

McCann, Richard. *Just a Boy: The True Story of a Stolen Childhood*. London: Ebury Press, 2005.

McCarthy, Mary. *How I Grew*. San Diego: Harcourt, Brace, Jovanovich, 1987.

———. *Memories of a Catholic Girlhood*. New York: Harcourt, Brace, 1957.

McCourt, Frank. *Angela's Ashes: A Memoir*. New York: Scribner, 1996.

McNamara, Robert S. *In Retrospect: The Tragedy and Lessons of Vietnam*. New York: Times Books, 1995.

Meir, Golda. *My Life*. New York: Putnam, 1975.

Menchú, Rigoberta. *I, Rigoberta Menchú: An Indian Woman in Guatemala*. Edited by Elisabeth Burgos-Debray. Translated by Ann Wright. London: Verso, 1984.

Mendes, Sam, dir. *Jarhead*. Universal City, Calif.: Universal Pictures, 2006.

Merasty, Joseph Auguste. *The Education of Augie Merasty: A Residential School Memoir*. Regina: University of Regina Press, 2017.

Mernissi, Fatima. *Dreams of Trespass: Tales of a Harem Girlhood*. Cambridge: Perseus, 1994.

Merton, Thomas. *The Seven-Storey Mountain*. New York: Harcourt, Brace, 1948.

Michaels, Bret. *Auto-scrap-ography*. Vol. 1: *My Life in Pictures & Stories*. Michaels Entertainment Group, 2020.

Mill, John Stuart. *Autobiography*. London: Longmans, Green, Reader, Dyer, 1873.

Miller, Chanel. *Know My Name: A Memoir*. New York: Viking, 2019.

Miller, Nancy K. *Bequest and Betrayal: Memoirs of a Parent's Death*. New York: Oxford University Press, 1996.

———. "My Multifocal Life." 2012–2020. http://nancykmiller.com/my-multifocal-life/.

Millet, Catherine. *The Sexual Life of Catherine M.* Translated by Adriana Hunter. New York: Grove Press, 2001.

Mills, Jennifer. *What's in a Name?* QAGOMA, Brisbane, 2009–11.

Mitchell, Wendy, with Anna Wharton. *Somebody I Used to Know: A Memoir*. New York: Ballantine, 2018.

———. *What I Wish People Knew about Dementia*. London: Bloomsbury Publishing, 2022.

Moaveni, Azadeh. *Honeymoon in Tehran: Two Years of Love and Danger in Iran*. New York: Random House, 2009.

———. *Lipstick Jihad: A Memoir of Growing Up Iranian in America and American in Iran*. New York: Public Affairs, 2005.

Modjeska, Drusilla. *Poppy*. Sydney: Pan Macmillan, 1997.

Momaday, N. Scott. *House Made of Dawn*. New York: New American Library, 1969.

———. *The Names: A Memoir*. New York: Harper and Row, 1976.

Bibliography

———. *The Way to Rainy Mountain*. Albuquerque: University of New Mexico Press, 1969.

Monette, Paul. *Becoming a Man: Half a Life Story*. New York: Harcourt, Brace, Jovanovich, 1992.

———. *Borrowed Time: An AIDS Memoir*. San Diego: Harcourt, Brace, 1998.

———. *Last Watch of the Night: Essays Too Personal and Otherwise*. New York: Harcourt Brace, 1994.

Montagu, Lady Mary Wortley. *The Letters and Works of Lady Mary Wortley Montagu*. Edited by Lord Wharncliffe. New York: AMS Press, 1970.

Montaigne, Michel de. *The Complete Essays of Montaigne*. Translated by Donald M. Frame. Stanford, Calif.: Stanford University Press, 1958.

———. *Les Essais*. 2nd ed. Paris: Presses universitaires de France, 1992.

Montéjo, Esteban. *The Autobiography of a Runaway Slave*. Edited by Miguel Barnet. Translated by Jocasta Innes. New York: Pantheon, 1968.

Montejo, Victor. *Testimony: Death of a Guatemalan Village*. Translated by Victor Perera. Willimantic, Conn.: Curbstone Press, 1987.

Moore, Michael. *Here Comes Trouble: Stories from My Life*. New York: Grand Central Publishing, 2011.

———, dir. *Roger & Me*. New York: Dog Eat Dog Films, 1989.

———, dir. *Where to Invade Next*. New York: Dog Eat Dog Films and IMG Films, 2015.

Moraga, Cherríe. *Loving in the War Years: Lo que nunca pasó por sus labios*. Boston: South End Press, 1983.

Moraga, Cherríe, and Gloria Anzaldúa, eds. *This Bridge Called My Back: Writings by Radical Women of Color*. New York: Kitchen Table Press, 1983.

Morgan, Sally. *My Place*. Freemantle: Freemantle Arts Press, 1987.

Morris, Jan. *Conundrum*. London: Faber, 1974.

Mother Jones. *The Autobiography of Mother Jones*. Edited by Mary Field Parton. Chicago: Charles H. Kerr, 1925.

Muir, John. *The Story of My Boyhood and Youth*. Boston: Houghton Mifflin, 1913.

Musil, Robert. *The Man without Qualities*. Translated by Eithne Wilkins. London: Secker and Warburg, 1953.

Nabokov, Vladimir. *Speak, Memory: An Autobiography Revisited*. New York: G. P. Putnam's Sons, 1966.

Nafisi, Azar. *Reading Lolita in Tehran: A Memoir in Books*. New York: Random House, 2003.

———. *The Republic of Imagination: America in Three Books*. New York: Viking, 2014.

———. *Things I've Been Silent About: Memories of a Prodigal Daughter*. New York: Random House, 2008.

Nelson, Maggie. *The Argonauts*. Minneapolis: Graywolf Press, 2015.

354   **Bibliography**

Nestle, Joan, Clare Howell, and Riki Anne Wilchins. *GenderQueer: Voices from Beyond the Sexual Binary*. Los Angeles: Alyson Books, 2002.

Nestle, Marion. *Slow Cooked: An Unexpected Life in Food Politics*. Oakland: University of California Press, 2022.

Newman, Cardinal John Henry. *Apologia Pro Vita Sua: Being a History of His Religious Opinions*. Edited by Martin J. Svaglic. Oxford: Clarendon Press, 1967.

Nietzsche, Friedrich. *On the Genealogy of Morals and Ecce Homo*. Translated and edited by Walter Kaufmann. New York: Vintage, 1967.

Nin, Anaïs. *Incest: From a Journal of Love. The Unexpurgated Diary of Anaïs Nin, 1932–1934*. New York: Harcourt Brace Jovanovich, 1992.

Nomani, Asra Q. *Tantrika: Traveling the Road of Divine Love*. San Francisco: HarperOne, 2003.

Norris, Kathleen. *Dakota: A Spiritual Geography*. Boston: Houghton Mifflin, 1993.

Noyce, Phillip, dir. *Rabbit-Proof Fence*. Burbank, Calif.: Miramax Home Entertainment, 2003.

Obama, Barack. *Dreams from My Father: A Story of Race and Inheritance*. New York: Times Books, 1995.

O'Beirne, Kathy. *Don't Ever Tell: Kathy's Story. A True Tale of a Childhood Destroyed by Neglect and Fear*. Edinburgh: Mainstream Publishing, 2006.

O'Brien, Edna. *Country Girl: A Memoir*. New York: Little, Brown, 2012.

O'Brien, Tim. *The Things They Carried: A Work of Fiction*. Boston: Houghton Mifflin, 1990.

O'Casey, Sean. *I Knock at the Door: Swift Glances Back at Things That Made Me*. New York: Macmillan, 1950.

O'Farrell, Maggie. *I Am, I Am, I Am: Seventeen Brushes with Death*. London: TinderPress, Headline Publishing Group, 2017.

O'Hagan, Margaret, and Thomas A. Gorman. *I Called Her Mary: A Memoir*. Self-published, 2021.

Olds, Sharon. *The Father*. New York: Knopf, 1992.

Ondaatje, Michael. *Running in the Family*. New York: Norton, 1982.

Painter, Nell. *Old in Art School: A Memoir of Starting Over*. Berkeley: Counterpoint, 2018.

Pamuk, Orhan. *Istanbul: Memories and the City*. Translated by Maureen Freely. New York: Knopf, 2005.

Pankejeff, Sergei. *The Wolf-Man. With the Case of the Wolf-Man, by Sigmund Freud*. Edited by Muriel Gardner. New York: Basic Books, 1971.

Parker, Alan, dir. *Angela's Ashes*. Hollywood: Paramount Pictures, 2000.

Partnoy, Alicia. *The Little School: Tales of Disappearance and Survival in Argentina*. Translated by Lois Athey. Pittsburgh: Cleis Press, 1986.

Bibliography

Pascal, Blaise. *Pensées*. Translated by A. J. Krailsheimer. Harmondsworth: Penguin, 1966.

Pax, Salam. *The Clandestine Diary of an Ordinary Iraqi*. New York: Grove, 2003.

Peck, Raoul, dir. *I Am Not Your Negro*. Rémi Grellety, Hébert Peck, and Raoul Peck, 2017.

———, dir. *Lumumba*. Zeitgeist, 2001.

Pelzer, David J. *A Child Called "It": An Abused Child's Journey from Victim to Victor*. Deerfield Beach, Fla.: Health Communications, 1995.

———. *The Lost Boy: A Foster Child's Search for the Love of a Family*. Deerfield Beach, Fla.: Health Communications, 1997.

———. *A Man Named Dave: A Story of Triumph and Forgiveness*. New York: Plume, 2000.

Penn, Arthur, dir. *The Miracle Worker*. Culver City, Calif.: MGM/UA Home Video, 1992.

Pepys, Samuel. *Diary and Correspondence of Samuel Pepys, Esq*. 6 vols. London: Bickers and Son, 1875–79.

Perec, Georges. *W, Or the Memory of Childhood*. Translated by David Bellos. Boston: David R. Godine, 2003.

Perry, Matthew. *Friends, Lovers, and the Big Terrible Thing: A Memoir*. New York: Flatiron Books, 2022.

Petrarch, Francis. "The Ascent of Mount Ventoux." In *Petrarch: A Humanist among Princes. An Anthology of Petrarch's Letters and of Selections from His Other Works*, edited and translated by David Thompson, 27–36. New York: Harper and Row, 1971.

Picciolini, Christian. *White American Youth: My Descent into America's Most Violent Hate Movement—and How I Got Out*. New York: Hachette, 2017.

Pilkington, Doris. *Rabbit-Proof Fence*. New York: Miramax Books, 2002.

Pilkington, Laetitia. *Memoirs of Mrs. Laetitia Pilkington, 1712–1750, Written by Herself*. London: George Routledge and Sons, 1928.

Piper, Adrian. *Cornered*. New York: New Museum of Contemporary Art, 1988.

Plato. *Apology of Socrates*. Translated by Michael C. Stokes. Warminster: Arris and Phillips, 1997.

Plutarch. *Plutarch: The Lives of the Noble Grecians and Romans, the Dryden Translation*. Chicago: Encyclopedia, 1990.

Polley, Sarah, dir. *Stories We Tell*. Ottawa: National Film Board of Canada, 2012.

Polo, Marco. *The Travels of Marco Polo, the Venetian*. Translated by William Marsden. Edited by Thomas Wright. New York: AMS Press, 1968.

Prasopoulou, Elpida. "A Half-Moon on My Skin: A Memoir on Life with an Activity Tracker." *European Journal of Information Systems* 26, no. 3 (2017): 287–97.

Preciado, Paul B. *Testo Junkie: Sex, Drugs, and Biopolitics in the Pharmacopornographic Era*. Translated by Bruce Benderson. New York: Feminist Press, 2013. Originally published as *Testo Yonqui*. Madrid: Espasa Calpe, 2008.

Prince, Nancy. *A Narrative of the Life and Travels of Mrs. Nancy Prince*. 2nd ed. Boston: Nancy Prince, 1853.

Prosser, Jay. *Second Skins: The Body Narratives of Transsexuality*. Gender and Culture Series. New York: Columbia University Press, 1998.

Proust, Marcel. *The Remembrance of Things Past*. 2 vols. Translated by C. K. Scott Moncrieff. New York: Random House, 1932–34.

Pruitt, Ida. *A Daughter of Han: The Autobiography of a Chinese Working Woman*. Stanford, Calif.: Stanford University Press, 1945.

Radtke, Kristen. *Seek You: A Journey through American Loneliness*. New York: Pantheon Books, 2021.

Rain, dir. *Somebody's Daughter*. Alter-Native Media, 2020.

Ramirez, José. *Squint: My Journey with Leprosy*. Hattiesburg: University of Mississippi Press, 2009.

Rankine, Claudia. *Citizen: An American Lyric*. Minneapolis: Graywolf Press, 2014.

Rasmussen, Jonas Poher, dir. *Flee*. Monica Hellstrom, Signe Byrge Sorensen, and Charlotte de la Gournerie, 2021.

Rebanks, James. *Pastoral Song: A Farmer's Journey*. New York: Custom House, 2020.

———. *The Shepherd's Life: Modern Dispatches from an Ancient Landscape*. New York: Flatiron Books, 2015.

Reichl, Ruth. *Comfort Me with Apples: More Adventures at the Table*. New York: Random House, 2002.

———. *Garlic and Sapphires: The Secret Life of a Critic in Disguise*. New York: Penguin, 2005.

———. *Not Becoming My Mother: And Other Things She Taught Me along the Way*. New York: Penguin, 2009.

———. *Tender at the Bone: Growing Up at the Table*. New York: Broadway Books, 1999.

Rhodes, Jewell Parker. *Magic City: A Novel*. New York: HarperCollins, 1997.

Rich, Adrienne. *Diving into the Wreck: Poems, 1971–72*. New York: Norton, 1973.

Richards, Keith, with James Fox. *Life*. New York: Little, Brown, 2010.

Richardson, Laurel. *Fields of Play: Constructing an Academic Life*. New Brunswick, N.J.: Rutgers University Press, 1997.

Rieder, Travis. *In Pain: A Bioethicist's Personal Struggle with Opioids*. New York: HarperCollins, 2019.

Rilke, Rainer Maria. *Duino Elegies*. Translated by David Young. New York: Norton, 1978.

Bibliography

———. *The Notebooks of Malte Laurids Brigge.* Translated by Stephen Mitchell. New York: Limited Editions Club, 1987.

Ringgold, Faith. *The Change Series: Faith Ringgold's 100-Pound Weight-Loss Quilt.* New York: Bernice Steinbaum Gallery, 1987.

———. *Dancing at the Louvre: Faith Ringgold's French Collection and Other Story Quilts.* Berkeley: University of California Press, 1998.

Rodriguez, Richard. *Hunger of Memory: The Education of Richard Rodriguez, an Autobiography.* Boston: D. R. Godine, 1981.

Roiphe, Anne. *Fruitful: Living the Contradictions. A Memoir of Modern Motherhood.* Boston: Houghton Mifflin, 1996.

Rose, Gillian. *Love's Work: A Reckoning with Life.* London: Chatto and Windus, 1995.

Rosi, Gianfranco, dir. *Fire at Sea.* Gianfranco Rosi, Paolo Del Brocco, Donatella Palermo, 2016.

Roth, Philip. *Exit Ghost.* New York: Vintage International, 2008.

Rousseau, Jean-Jacques. *Confessions.* Translated by Angela Scholar. New York: Oxford University Press, 2000.

Rowlandson, Mary. "A True History of the Captivity and Restoration of Mrs. Mary Rowlandson," edited by Amy Schrager Lang. In *Journeys in New Worlds,* edited by William L. Andrews et al., 27–65. Madison: University of Wisconsin Press, 1990.

Rutgers University Department of History. *The Rutgers Oral History Archives of World War II, the Korean War, the Vietnam War and the Cold War.* Copyright 2022. http://oralhistory.rutgers.edu/.

Ryan, Michael. *Secret Life: An Autobiography.* New York: Pantheon, 1995.

Sage, Lorna. *Bad Blood.* New York: Harper Perennial, 2003.

Said, Edward W. *Out of Place: A Memoir.* New York: Knopf, 1999.

Salinger, J. D. *The Catcher in the Rye.* Boston: Little, Brown, 1951.

Salomon, Charlotte. *Leben? oder Theater? (Life? or Theatre?).* Cologne: Taschen, 2017.

Sand, George (Aurore Dudevant Dupin). *Story of My Life: The Autobiography of George Sand.* Edited by Thelma Jurgrau. Albany: State University Press of New York, 1991.

Sangtin Writers and Richa Nagar. *Playing with Fire: Feminist Thought and Activism through Seven Lives in India.* Minneapolis: University of Minnesota Press, 2006.

Santiago, Esmeralda. *When I Was Puerto Rican.* New York: Vintage, 1993.

Sarrazin, Albertine. "Journal de Prison, 1959." In *Le Passe-Peine: 1949–1967,* 102–68. Paris: Julliard, 1976.

Sarton, May. *At Eighty-Two: A Journal.* New York: Norton, 1996.

———. *Journal of a Solitude.* New York: Norton, 1973.

Sartre, Jean-Paul. *The Words.* Translated by Bernard Frechtman. New York: Vintage, 1981.

Satrapi, Marjane. *Persepolis.* Translated by Mattias Ripa. New York: Pantheon, 2004.

———. *Persepolis 2: The Story of a Return.* Translated by Mattias Ripa. New York: Pantheon, 2004.

Satrapi, Marjane, and Vincent Paronnaud, dirs. *Persepolis.* Sony Pictures Classics, 2007.

Savage, Dan. *The Commitment: Love, Sex, Marriage, and My Family.* New York: Dutton, 2005.

———. *The Kid: What Happened after My Boyfriend and I Decided to Go Get Pregnant. An Adoption Story.* New York: Plume, 2000.

Schnabel, Julian, dir. *At Eternity's Gate.* Los Angeles: Riverstone Pictures, 2018.

———, dir. *Before Night Falls.* Los Angeles: New Line Home Entertainment, 2001.

———, dir. *The Diving Bell and the Butterfly.* Burbank, Calif.: Touchstone Home Entertainment, 2008.

Scholem, Gershom. *From Berlin to Jerusalem: Memories of My Youth.* Translated by Harry Zohn. Philadelphia: Paul Dry Books, 2012.

Sebald, W. G. *Austerlitz.* Translated by Anthea Bell. New York: Random House, 2001.

———. *The Emigrants.* Translated by Michael Hulse. New York: New Directions, 1997.

Sebold, Alice. *Lucky.* New York: Scribner, 1999.

Sedaris, David. *Calypso.* New York: Back Bay Books, 2018.

———. *Happy-Go-Lucky.* New York: Little, Brown, 2022.

———. *Naked.* Boston: Little, Brown, 1997.

Serano, Julia. *Whipping Girl: A Transsexual Woman on Sexism and the Scapegoating of Femininity.* Emeryville, Calif.: Seal Press, 2007.

Sévigné, Marie de, Rabutin Chantal. *Letters of Madame de Sévigné to Her Daughter and Her Friends.* Translated by Leonard Tancock. Harmondsworth: Penguin, 1982.

Sexton, Anne. *Live or Die.* Boston: Houghton Mifflin, 1966.

Shakur, Assata. *Assata: An Autobiography.* Westport, Conn.: L. Hill, 1987.

Sheff, David. *Beautiful Boy: A Father's Journey through His Son's Addiction.* Boston: Houghton Mifflin, 2008.

Sheff, Nic. *Tweak: Growing Up on Methamphetamines.* New York: Atheneum Books for Young Readers, 2007.

Sherman, Cindy. *Cindy Sherman: Retrospective.* New York: Thames and Hudson, 1997.

Bibliography

Shields, David. *Reality Hunger: A Manifesto.* New York: Vintage, Random House, 2010.

Sigourney, Lydia H. *Letters of Life.* New York: D. Appleton, 1866.

Silko, Leslie Marmon. *Storyteller.* New York: Seaver Books/Grove Press, 1981.

Simard, Suzanne. *Finding the Mother Tree: Discovering the Wisdom of the Forest.* New York: Knopf, 2021.

Simpson, O. J., Dominick Dunne, and Pablo F. Fenjves. *If I Did It: Confessions of the Killer.* New York: Beaufort Books, 2006.

Slater, Lauren. *Lying: A Metaphorical Memoir.* New York: Random House, 2000.

Small, David. *Stitches: A Memoir.* New York: W. W. Norton, 2009.

Smart-Grosvenor, Vertamae. *Vibration Cooking; or, The Travel Notes of a Geechee Girl.* New York: Ballantine, 1992.

Smith, John. *The Complete Works of Captain John Smith (1580–1631).* 3 vols. Edited by Philip L. Barbour. Chapel Hill: University of North Carolina Press, 1986.

Smith, Patti. *Just Kids.* New York: Ecco, 2010.

Smith, Zadie. *Intimations: Six Essays.* New York: Penguin, 2020.

Sojourner Truth. *Narrative of Sojourner Truth.* Edited by Margaret Washington. New York: Random House, 1993.

Souad. *Burned Alive: A Victim of the Law of Men.* Translated by Judith Armbruster. New York: Warner Books, 2004.

Soyinka, Wole. *Aké: The Years of a Childhood.* New York: Random House, 1981.

Spence, Jo. *Putting Myself in the Picture: A Political, Personal, and Photographic Autobiography.* London: Camden Press, 1986.

Spiegelman, Art. *Maus I: A Survivor's Tale. My Father Bleeds History.* New York: Pantheon, 1986.

———. *Maus II: A Survivor's Tale. And Here My Troubles Began.* New York: Pantheon, 1991.

Spielberg, Steven, dir. *The Fabelmans.* Universal City, Calif.: Universal Pictures, 2022.

Spurlock, Morgan, dir. *Super Size Me.* Culver City, Calif.: Columbia TriStar Home Entertainment, 2004.

Steedman, Carolyn Kay. *Landscape for a Good Woman.* New Brunswick, N.J.: Rutgers University Press, 1986.

Stein, Gertrude. *The Autobiography of Alice B. Toklas.* New York: Harcourt Brace, 1933.

———. *Everybody's Autobiography.* New York: Random House, 1937.

Stendhal (Marie-Henri Beyle). *The Life of Henry Brulard.* Translated by Jean Stewart and B. C. J. G. Knight. New York: Noonday Press, 1958.

360 Bibliography

Stepanova, Maria. *In Memory of Memory.* Translated by Sasha Dugdale. New York: New Directions, 2021.

Stevens, Wallace. *Collected Poems.* New York: Knopf, 1954.

Stewart, Rory. *The Places in Between.* Orlando, Fla.: Harcourt, 2006.

Strachey, Lytton. *Eminent Victorians: Cardinal Manning, Dr. Arnold, Florence Nightingale, General Gordon.* New York: Modern Library, 1933.

Streisand, Barbra. *My Name is Barbra.* New York: Viking, 2023.

Strindberg, August. *The Son of a Servant.* Translated by Claud Field. New York: Putnam's Sons, 1913.

Styron, William. *Darkness Visible: A Memoir of Madness.* New York: Random House, 1990.

Sui Sin Far. "Leaves from the Mental Portfolio of an Eurasian." *The Independent,* January 21, 1909, 125–32.

———. "Sui Sin Far, the Half Chinese Writer, Tells of Her Career." *Boston Globe,* May 5, 1912 (morning edition), 31.126.

Swofford, Anthony. *Jarhead: A Marine's Chronicle of the Gulf War and Other Battles.* New York: Scribner, 2003.

Taylor, Sheila Ortiz, and Sandra Ortiz Taylor. *Imaginary Parents: A Family Autobiography.* Albuquerque: University of New Mexico Press, 1996.

Teresa of Avila, Saint. *Interior Castle.* Translated and edited by E. Allison Peers. Garden City, N.Y.: Doubleday, 1961.

———. *The Life of Teresa of Jesus: The Autobiography of St. Teresa of Avila.* Translated by E. Allison Peers. Garden City, N.Y.: Doubleday, 1960.

Thiong'o, Ngũgĩ wa. *Detained: A Writer's Prison Diary.* London: Heinemann, 1981.

Thoreau, Henry David. *Walden.* Edited by J. Lyndon Shanley. Princeton, N.J.: Princeton University Press, 1971.

Thrale, Hester. *Thraliana; The Diary of Mrs. Hester Lynch Thrale (Later Mrs. Piozzi), 1776–1809.* 2 vols. Edited by Katharine C. Balderston. Oxford: Clarendon Press, 1942.

Timerman, Jacobo. *Prisoner without a Name, Cell without a Number.* Translated by Toby Talbot. New York: Knopf, 1981.

Tolle, Eckhart. *Practicing the Power of Now: Essential Teachings, Meditations, and Exercises from "The Power of Now."* New York: New World Library 2001.

Touré, Moussa, dir. *La Pirogue/The Boat.* Paris: Rezo Films, 2012.

Towner, Myriah, Ladi'Sasha Jones, and Clarisse Rosaz Shariyf, curators. *Emmett Till Project.* Schomburg Center for Research in Black Culture, New York Public Library, 2015. https://www.emmetttillproject.com/.

Tran, GB. *Vietnamerica: A Family's Journey.* New York: Villard, 2010.

Trethewey, Natasha D. *Memorial Drive: A Daughter's Memoir.* New York: Ecco, 2020.

Bibliography

———. *Native Guard.* Boston: Houghton Mifflin, 2006.

Troyano, Alina, et al. *I, Carmelita Tropicana: Performing between Cultures.* Boston: Beacon, 2000.

Trump, Donald J., with Tony Schwartz. *Trump: The Art of the Deal.* New York: Ballantine Books, 1987.

Twain, Mark. *Life on the Mississippi.* New York: Penguin, 1984.

Umutesi, Marie Béatrice. *Surviving the Slaughter: The Ordeal of a Rwandan Refugee in Zaire.* Women in Africa and the Diaspora. Madison: University of Wisconsin Press, 2004.

Urban School of San Francisco. *Telling Their Stories: Oral History Archives Project.* http://www.tellingstories.org.

Valéry, Paul. *La Jeune Parque* [The young fate]. Translated by Alistair Elliot. Chester Springs, Penn.: Dufour Editions, 1997.

Vance, J. D. *Hillbilly Elegy: A Memoir of a Family and Culture in Crisis.* New York: Harper, 2016.

Vizenor, Gerald. "Crows Written on the Poplars: Autocritical Autobiographies." In *I Tell You Now:* Autobiographical *Essays by Native American Writers,* edited by Brian Swann and Arnold Krupat, 99–109. Lincoln: University of Nebraska Press, 1987.

Walker, Kara. *A Subtlety.* Domino Sugar Refinery, New York, 2014.

Walker, Rebecca. *Black, White, and Jewish: Autobiography of a Shifting Self.* New York: Riverhead Books, 2001.

Wang, Qian Julie. *Beautiful Country: A Memoir of an Undocumented Childhood.* New York: Anchor Books, 2021.

Warner-Vieyra, Myriam. *Juletane.* Translated by Betty Wilson. London: Heinemann, 1987.

Washington, Booker T. *Up from Slavery.* New York: Doubleday, 1998.

Watt, Kathleen. *Rearranged: An Opera Singer's Facial Cancer and Life Transposed.* New York: Heliotrope Books, 2023.

Weisz, Frans, dir. *Leven? of Theater?* [Life? or Theater?]. Amsterdam Homescreen, 2012.

Westover, Tara. *Educated: A Memoir.* New York: Random House, 2018.

Wexler, Alice. *Mapping Fate: A Memoir of Family, Risk, and Genetic Research.* Berkeley: University of California Press, 1996.

Whitman, Walt. "Song of Myself." In *Leaves of Grass.* New York: Heritage Press, 1950.

———. *Specimen Days.* Vol. 1 of *Prose Works, 1892.* Edited by Floyd Stovall. New York: New York University Press, 1963.

Wideman, John Edgar. *Brothers and Keepers.* New York: Holt, Rinehart and Winston, 1984.

Wiesel, Elie. *Night.* Translated by Stella Rodway. New York: Hill and Wang, 1960.

Bibliography

Wilke, Hannah. *Intra-Venus*. Photography. New York: Ronald Feldman Gallery, 1994.

Wilkomirski, Binjamin. *Fragments: Memories of a Wartime Childhood*. Translated by Carol Brown Janeway. New York: Schocken Books, 1996.

Williams, Donna. *Nobody Nowhere: The Extraordinary Autobiography of an Autistic*. New York: Times Books, 1992.

———. *Somebody Somewhere: Breaking Free from the World of Autism*. New York: Times Books, 1994.

Williams, Gregory Howard. *Life on the Color Line: The True Story of a White Boy Who Discovered He Was Black*. New York: Dutton, 1995.

Williams, Terry Tempest. *Refuge: An Unnatural History of Family and Place*. New York: Vintage Books, 1992.

Winterson, Jeanette. *Why Be Happy When You Could Be Normal?* New York: Grove Press, 2012.

Witzling, Mara, ed. *Voicing Today's Visions: Writings by Contemporary Women Artists*. New York: Universe Publishing, 1994.

Wojnarowicz, David. *Close to the Knives: A Memoir of Disintegration*. New York: Vintage Books, 1991.

Wolf, Christa. *Patterns of Childhood*. Translated by Ursula Molinaro and Hedwig Rappolt. New York: Farrar, Straus and Giroux, 1980.

———. *What Remains and Other Stories*. Translated by Heike Schwarzbauer and Rick Takvorian. New York: Farrar, Straus and Giroux, 1993.

Woodman, Francesca. *Francesca Woodman: Photographic Work*. Wellesley, Mass.: Wellesley College Museum, 1986.

Woodruff, Lee, and Bob Woodruff. *In an Instant: A Family's Journey of Love and Healing*. New York: Random House, 2008.

Woolf, Virginia. *Orlando. A Biography*. London: Hogarth Press, 1928.

———. *The Sickle Side of the Moon: The Letters of Virginia Woolf, 1932–1935*. Edited by Nigel Nicolson and Joanne Trautmann. London: Hogarth Press, 1979.

———. "A Sketch of the Past." In *Moments of Being*, edited by Jeanne Schulkind, 2nd ed., 61–137. New York: Harcourt Brace, 1985.

Wordsworth, William. *The Prelude; or, Growth of a Poet's Mind*. Edited by Ernest De Selincourt. Oxford: Clarendon Press, 1959.

Wright, Richard. *Black Boy (American Hunger): A Record of Childhood and Youth*. Restored ed. New York: Harper Collins, 1993.

Wurtzel, Elizabeth. *Prozac Nation: Young and Depressed in America*. Boston: Houghton Mifflin, 1994.

Yale University Library. Fortunoff Video Archive for Holocaust Testimonies. 2005. http://www.library.yale.edu/testimonies/.

Yang, Gene Luen. *American Born Chinese*. New York: First Second Books, 2007.

Bibliography

Yeats, W. B. *Autobiographies: Reveries over Childhood and Youth and the Trembling of the Veil.* New York: Macmillan, 1927.

———. *A Vision.* London: Macmillan, 1937.

Yogananda, Paramahansa. *The Autobiography of a Yogi.* Los Angeles: Self-Realization Fellowship, 1998.

Young, Alora. *Walking Gentry Home: A Memoir of My Foremothers in Verse.* London: Hogarth, 2022.

Yousafzai, Malala. *I Am Malala: The Girl Who Stood Up for Education and Was Shot by the Taliban.* New York: Little, Brown, 2013.

Zamora, Javier. *Unaccompanied.* Port Townsend, Wash.: Copper Canyon Press, 2017.

Zauner, Michelle. *Crying in H Mart: A Memoir.* New York: Knopf, 2022.

Zitkala-Ša. "Impressions of an Indian Childhood." In *Classic American Autobiographies,* edited by William L. Andrews, 414–32. New York: Mentor, 1992.

SECONDARY WORKS

Adams, Lorraine. "Almost Famous: The Rise of the 'Nobody Memoir.'" *Washington Post,* April 10, 2002.

Adams, Timothy Dow. "Borderline Personality: Autobiography and Documentary in Susanna Kaysen's *Girl, Interrupted.*" *Life Writing* 2, no. 2 (2005): 103–21.

———. *Light Writing and Life Writing: Photography in Autobiography.* Chapel Hill: University of North Carolina Press, 1990.

———. *Telling Lies in Modern American Autobiography.* Chapel Hill: University of North Carolina Press, 2000.

Adams, Tony E., Stacy Holman Jones, and Carolyn Ellis, eds. *Handbook of Autoethnography.* 2nd ed. New York: Routledge, 2022.

Addley, Esther. "Author Accused of Literary Fraud Says: 'I Am Not a Liar. And I Am Not Running Any More.'" *Guardian,* September 23, 2006.

Adichie, Chimamanda Ngozi. "The Danger of a Single Story." *TEDGlobal,* 2009. https://www.ted.com/talks/chimamanda_ngozi_adichie_the_danger _of_a_single_story/comments.

Ahmed, Sarah. *The Cultural Politics of Emotion.* New York: Routledge, 2014.

Alaimo, Stacy. *Bodily Natures: Science, Environment, and the Material Self.* Bloomington: Indiana University Press, 2010.

Althusser, Louis. *On Ideology.* London: Verso, 1984.

Andrews, Tarren. "The Role of Land Acknowledgments." *MLA Newsletter* 52, no. 1 (Spring 2020): 5.

Andrews, William L. "African-American Autobiography Criticism: Retrospect and Prospect." In Eakin, *American Autobiography,* 195–215.

———. *To Tell a Free Story: The First Century of Afro-American Autobiography, 1760–1865.* Urbana: University of Illinois Press, 1986.

Appadurai, Arjun. "Disjuncture and Difference in the Global Cultural Economy." In *Colonial Discourse and Post-Colonial Theory: A Reader,* edited by Patrick Williams and Laura Chrisman, 324–39. New York: Columbia University Press, 1994.

Apperley, Thomas, and Justin Clemens. "Flipping Out: Avatars and Identity." In *Boundaries of Self and Reality Online: Implications of Digitally Constructed Realities,* edited by Jayne Gackenback and Johnathan Bown, 41–56. London: Elsevier, 2017.

Arias, Arturo. "Victor Montejo and the Maya Perspective: Framing New Kinds of Indigenous Autorepresentations." *a/b: Auto/Biography Studies* 31, no. 3 (2016): 487–507.

Arthur, Paul Longley. "Digital Biography: Capturing Lives Online." *a/b: Auto/Biography Studies* 24, no. 1 (2009): 74–92.

"Autosociobiography: Global Entanglements of a Literary Phenomenon. Workshop." Organized by Johanna Bundschuh-van Duikeren, Marie Jacquier, and Peter Löffelbein. *EXC 2020: Temporal Communities.* Freie Universität, Berlin, March 23–25, 2023. https://www.temporal-communities.de/events/workshop-autosoziobiographie.html.

Aviv, Rachel. *Strangers to Ourselves: Unsettled Minds and the Stories That Make Us.* New York: Farrar, Straus and Giroux, 2022.

Backscheider, Paula R. *Reflections on Biography.* Oxford: Oxford University Press, 2001.

Baena, Rosalia. "Disability Memoirs in the Academic World: Mary Felstiner's *Out of Joint* and Simi Linton's *My Body Politic.*" *Interdisciplinary Literary Studies* 15, no. 1 (2013): 127–40.

———. "Gastro-Graphy: Food as Metaphor in Fred Wah's *Diamond Grill* and Austin Clarke's *Pig Tails 'n Breadfruit.*" *Canadian Ethnic Studies* 38, no. 1 (Spring 2006): 105–16.

Bakhtin, M. M. *The Dialogic Imagination: Four Essays.* Edited by Michael Holquist. Translated by Caryl Emerson and Michael Holquist. Austin: University of Texas Press, 1981.

Bal, Mieke. "Autotopography: Louise Bourgeois as Builder." In Smith and Watson, *Interfaces,* 163–85.

Barad, Karen. "On Touching the Stranger Within—The Alterity That Therefore I Am." *The Poetry Project.* https://www.poetryproject.org/library/poems-texts/on-touching-the-stranger-within-the-alterity-that-therefore-i-am.

Barbour, John D. *The Value of Solitude: The Ethics and Spirituality of Aloneness in Autobiography.* Charlottesville: University of Virginia Press, 2004.

Bibliography

Barry, Lynda. "Documenting All the Small Things That Are Easily Lost." *New York Times,* May 1, 2020.

———. *Syllabus: Notes from an Accidental Professor.* Montreal: Drawn and Quarterly, 2014.

Bartkowski, Frances. *Travelers, Immigrants, Inmates: Essays in Estrangement.* Minneapolis: University of Minnesota Press, 1995.

Bauman, H.-Dirksen L. *Open Your Eyes: Deaf Studies Talking.* Minneapolis: University of Minnesota Press, 2008.

———. "'Voicing' Deaf Identity: Through the 'I's and Ears of an Other." In Smith and Watson, *Getting a Life,* 47–62.

Baxter, Katherine, and Cat Auburn. "Introduction for Special Issue 'Autotheory in Contemporary Visual Arts Practice.'" *Arts* 12, no. 1 (2023): art. 11. https://doi.org/10.3390/arts12010011.

Beard, Laura J. *Acts of Narrative Resistance: Women's Autobiographical Writings in the Americas.* Charlottesville, University of Virginia Press, 2009.

Beard, Laura J., and Ricia Anne Chansky, eds. *The Divided States: Unraveling National Identities in the Twenty-First Century.* Madison: University of Wisconsin Press, 2023.

Beard, Thomas. "A Romance with the Screen: Theater Legend Adrienne Kennedy Looks Back." *Current,* June 10, 2020.

Beaujour, Michel. *Poetics of the Literary Self-Portrait.* Translated by Yara Milos. New York: New York University Press, 1991.

Bennett, Jane. *Vibrant Matter: A Political Ecology of Things.* Durham, N.C.: Duke University Press, 2010.

Benstock, Shari. "Authorizing the Autobiographical." In *The Private Self: Theory and Practice of Women's Autobiographical Writings,* edited by Shari Benstock, 10–33. Chapel Hill: University of North Carolina Press, 1988.

Beverley, John. "The Margin at the Center: On 'Testimonio' (Testimonial Narrative)." In Smith and Watson, *De/Colonizing the Subject,* 91–114.

Bhabha, Homi K. "Introduction: Locations of Culture." In *The Location of Culture,* 1–27. London: Routledge, 1994.

Boardman, Kathleen A., and Gioia Woods. *Western Subjects: Autobiographical Writing in the North American West.* Salt Lake City: University of Utah Press, 2004.

Boelhower, William. "The Making of Ethnic Autobiography in the United States." In Eakin, *American Autobiography,* 123–41.

Bolter, Jay David, and Richard Grusin. *Remediation: Understanding New Media.* Cambridge, Mass.: Massachusetts Institute of Technology Press, 2000.

Bowring, Richard. "The Female Hand in Heian Japan: A First Reading." In *The*

Female Autograph: Theory and Practice of Autobiography from the Tenth to the Twentieth Century, edited by Domna C. Stanton, 55–62. Chicago: University of Chicago Press, 1987.

boyd, danah, and Elizabeth E. Marwick. "I Tweet Honestly, I Tweet Passionately: Twitter Users, Context Collapse, and the Imagined Audience." *New Media Society* 13, no. 1 (2010): 1–20.

Braidotti, Rosi. "Posthuman, All Too Human: Towards a New Process Ontology." *Theory, Culture & Society* 23, nos. 7–8 (2006): 197–208.

Brant, Clare, Tobias Heinrich, and Monica Soeting. "The Placing of Displaced Lives: Refugee Narratives." *a/b: Auto/Biography Studies* 32, no. 3 (2017): 625–28.

Braziel, Jana Evans. "Alterbiographic Transmutations of Genre in Jamaica Kincaid's 'Biography of a Dress' and *Autobiography of My Mother*." *a/b: Auto/Biography Studies* 18, no. 1 (2003): 85–104.

Brett, Guy. *Mona Hatoum.* Interview by Michael Archer; essays by Guy Brett and Catherine De Zegher. London: Phaidon Press, 1997.

"Briefly Noted." Review of *The Beauty in the Breaking, Desert Notebooks, Heaven and Earth* and *Love After Love. New Yorker,* August 17, 2020. https://www.newyorker.com/magazine/2020/08/17/the-beauty-in-breaking-desert-notebooks-heaven-and-earth-and-love-after-love.

Brockmeier, Jens. "Autobiographical Time." *Narrative Inquiry* 10, no. 1 (2000): 51–73.

Brodkey, Linda. "Writing on the Bias." *College English* 56, no. 5 (September 1994): 524–48.

Brodsky, Claudia, and Eloy LaBrada, eds. *Inventing Agency: Essays on the Literary and Philosophical Production of the Modern Subject.* New York: Bloomsbury Academic, 2017.

Brodzki, Bella. *Can These Bones Live? Translation, Survival, and Cultural Memory.* Stanford, Calif.: Stanford University Press, 2007.

———. "Trauma and Transgression." In *Teaching the Representation of the Holocaust,* edited by Marianne Hirsch and Irene Kacandes, 123–48. New York: Modern Language Association, 2004.

Brophy, Sarah. "On the Times and Places of Embodied Testimony: Remaking the World." *a/b: Auto/Biography Studies* 33, no. 2 (2018): 437–40.

Brostoff, Alex, and Lauren Fournier. "Introduction: Autotheory ASAP! Academia, Decoloniality, and 'I.'" *ASAP/Journal* 6, no. 3 (2021): 489–502.

Broughton, Trev Lynn. *Men of Letters, Writing Lives: Masculinity and Literary Auto/Biography in the Late-Victorian Period.* New York: Routledge, 1999.

Browder, Laura. *Slippery Characters: Ethnic Impersonators and American Identities.* Chapel Hill: University of North Carolina Press, 2000.

Bibliography

Brown, Mark. "Jewish District Inspires Tom Stoppard in 'Personal' New Play." *Guardian,* June 26, 2019.

Brueggemann, Brenda. *Deaf Subjects: Between Identities and Places.* New York: New York University Press, 2009.

Bruner, Jerome. "Life as Narrative." *Social Research* 54 (Spring 1987): 11–32.

Bruś, Teresa. *Face Forms in Life-Writing of the Interwar Years.* London: Palgrave Macmillan, 2023.

Buell, Lawrence. "Autobiography in the American Renaissance." In Eakin, *American Autobiography,* 47–69.

———. *The Environmental Imagination: Thoreau, Nature Writing, and the Formation of America.* Cambridge, Mass.: Harvard University Press, 1995.

Bunkers, Suzanne L., and Cynthia A. Huff. "Issues in Studying Women's Diaries: A Theoretical and Critical Introduction." In *Inscribing the Daily: Critical Essays on Women's Diaries,* edited by Suzanne L. Bunkers and Cynthia A. Huff, 1–22. Amherst: University of Massachusetts Press, 1996.

———. "Midwestern Diaries and Journals: What Women Were (Not) Saying in the Late 1800s." In *Studies in Autobiography,* edited by James Olney, 190–210. New York: Oxford University Press, 1988.

Burt, Raymond L. "The Bildungsroman." In Jolly, *Encyclopedia of Life Writing,* 1:105–7.

Buss, Helen M. *Mapping Ourselves: Canadian Women's Autobiography in English.* Montreal: McGill-Queen's University Press, 1993.

Butler, Judith. *Bodies That Matter: On the Discursive Limits of "Sex."* New York: Routledge, 1993.

———. *Gender Trouble: Feminism and the Subversion of Identity.* New York: Routledge, 1990.

———. *Giving an Account of Oneself.* Bronx: Fordham University Press, 2005.

———. *Precarious Life: The Power of Mourning and Violence.* London: Verso, 2004.

———. *Undoing Gender.* New York: Routledge, 2004.

Canby, Peter. "The Truth about Rigoberta Menchú." *New York Review of Books,* April 8, 1999, 28–33.

Cardell, Kylie. *De@r World: Contemporary Uses of the Diary.* Madison: University of Wisconsin Press, 2014.

———. "Modern Memory-Making: Marie Kondo, Online Journaling, and the Excavation, Curation, and Control of Personal Digital Data." *a/b: Auto/ Biography Studies* 32, no. 3 (2017): 499–517.

Caruth, Cathy, ed. *Trauma: Explorations in Memory.* Baltimore: Johns Hopkins University Press, 1995.

Cavarero, Adriana. *Relating Narratives: Storytelling and Selfhood.* London: Routledge, 2000.

Cep, Casey. "*A Childhood* Is One of the Finest Memoirs Ever Written." *New Yorker,* March 28, 2022, 71–75.

Certeau, Michel de. *The Practice of Everyday Life.* Translated by Steven Rendall. Berkeley: University of California Press, 1984.

Chaney, Michael A. *Fugitive Vision: Slave Image and Black Identity in Antebellum Narrative.* Bloomington: Indiana University Press, 2008.

———. "Terrors of the Mirror and the 'Mise en Abyme' of Graphic Novel Autobiography." *College Literature* 38, no. 3 (Summer 2011): 21–44.

Chard, Chloe. *Pleasure and Guilt on the Grand Tour: Travel Writing and Imaginative Geography, 1600–1830.* Manchester: Manchester University Press, 1999.

Charon, Rita. *Narrative Medicine: Honoring the Stories of Illness.* New York: Oxford University Press, 2006.

Chen, Mel. *Animacies: Biopolitics, Racial Mattering, and Queer Affect.* Durham, N.C.: Duke University Press, 2012.

Chester, Suzanne. "Writing the Subject: Exoticism/Eroticism in Marguerite Duras's *The Lover* and *The Sea Wall.*" In Smith and Watson, *De/Colonizing the Subject,* 436–57.

Chodorow, Nancy. *The Reproduction of Mothering: Psychoanalysis and the Sociology of Gender.* Berkeley, Calif.: University of California Press, 1978.

Choy, Catherine Ceniza. *Global Families: A History of Asian International Adoption in America.* New York: New York University Press, 2013.

Chute, Hillary. *Disaster Drawn: Visual Witness, Comics, and Documentary Form.* Cambridge, Mass.: Harvard University Press, 2016.

———. *Why Comics? From Underground to Everywhere.* New York: Harper, 2017.

Chute, Hillary L., and Marianne DeKoven. "Introduction: Graphic Narrative." *Modern Fiction Studies* 52, no. 4 (Winter 2006): 767–82.

Clare, Stephanie D. *NonBinary: A Feminist Autotheory.* Cambridge: Cambridge University Press, 2023. https://doi.org/10.1017/9781009278645.

Coe, Richard. *When the Grass Was Taller: Autobiography and the Experience of Childhood.* New Haven, Conn.: Yale University Press, 1984.

Collett-White, Mike. "'Capitalism Is Evil,' Says New Michael Moore Film." *Reuters,* September 6, 2009.

Couldry, Nick. "Mediatization or Mediation? Alternative Understandings of the Emergent Space of Digital Storytelling." *New Media and Society* 10, no. 3 (2008): 373–91.

Couser, G. Thomas. "Black Elk Speaks with Forked Tongue." In *Studies in Autobiography,* edited by James Olney, 73–88. New York: Oxford University Press, 1988.

———. "Genre Matters." *Life Writing* 2, no. 2 (2005): 123–40.

———. "Introduction: The Some Body Memoir." In *Signifying Bodies: Disability*

Bibliography

in Contemporary Life Writing, 1–15. Ann Arbor: University of Michigan Press, 2009.

———. "Is There a Body in This Text? Embodiment in Graphic Somatography," *a/b: Auto/Biography Studies* 33, no. 2 (2018): 347–73.

———. "Making, Taking, and Faking Lives: The Ethics of Collaborative Autobiography." In "Literature and Ethical Criticism," special issue, *Style* 32, no. 2 (Summer 1998): 334–50.

———. *Memoir: An Introduction.* Oxford: Oxford University Press, 2012.

———. *Memory and Narrative: The Weave of Life-Writing.* Chicago: University of Chicago Press, 1999.

———. "Prologue. Death and Life Writing: Reflections on My Morbid Career." In *The Work of Life Writing: Essays and Lectures,* 1–9. New York: Routledge, 2021.

———. *Recovering Bodies: Illness, Disability, and Life Writing.* Madison: University of Wisconsin Press, 1997.

———. *Signifying Bodies: Disability in Contemporary Life Writing.* Ann Arbor: University of Michigan Press, 2009.

———. *The Work of Life Writing: Essays and Lectures.* New York: Routledge, 2021.

Couser, G. Thomas, and Susannah Mintz, eds. *Disability Experiences: Memoirs, Autobiographies, and Other Personal Narratives.* Farmington Hills, Mich.: Macmillan Reference USA, 2019.

Culley, Margo. "Introduction." In *A Day at a Time: Diary Literature of American Women from 1764 to the Present,* edited by Margo Culley, 3–26. New York: Feminist Press, 1985.

Curtis, Bryan. "Capote at the Bat." *New York Times Play Magazine,* November 2007, 34, 36.

Cvetkovich, Ann. *An Archive of Feelings: Trauma, Sexuality and Lesbian Public Cultures.* Durham, N.C.: Duke University Press, 2003.

Damasio, Antonio R. *Descartes' Error: Emotion, Reason, and the Human Brain.* New York: Putnam, 1994.

Danahay, Martin. *A Community of One: Masculine Autobiography and Autonomy in Nineteenth-Century Britain.* Albany: State University of New York Press, 1993.

———. "Professional Subjects: Prepackaging the Academic C.V." In Smith and Watson, *Getting a Life,* 351–68.

Davies, Dominic. "Introduction." In Davies and Rifkind, *Documenting Trauma in Comics,* 1–26.

Davies, Dominic, and Candida Rifkind, eds. *Documenting Trauma in Comics: Traumatic Pasts, Embodied Histories, and Graphic Reportage.* London: Palgrave, 2020.

Davis, Angela Y. "Rape, Race, and the Myth of the Black Racist." In *Women, Race, and Class*, 172–201. New York: Vintage, 1983.

Deans, Jill R. "The Birth of Contemporary Adoption Autobiography: Florence Fisher and Betty Jean Lifton." In "Adoption Life Writing: Origins and Other Ghosts," special issue, *a/b: Auto/Biography Studies* 18, no. 2 (2003): 239–58.

Demos, T. J. *The Migrant Image: The Art and Politics of Documentary during Global Crisis*. Durham, N.C.: Duke University Press, 2013.

Denker, Kristen. "Deborah Levy's Luminous Investigation of Female Ambition." *New Republic*, August 31, 2021.

Denton, Andrew. "Ishmael Beah." *Enough Rope with Andrew Denton*. Accessed November 12, 2009. http://www.abc.net.au/tv/enoughrope/transcripts/s19 68333.htm.

Deresiewicz, William. "Foes." *The Nation*. https://www.thenation.com/article/archive/foes/.

Derounian-Stodola, Kathryn Zabelle, and James A. Levernier. *The Indian Captivity Narrative, 1550–1900*. New York: Twayne, 1993.

Derrida, Jacques. *Archive Fever: A Freudian Impression*. Translated by Eric Prenowitz. Chicago: University of Chicago Press, 1995.

———. *The Ear of the Other: Otobiography, Transference, Translation*. Edited by Christie V. McDonald. Translated by Peggy Kamuf. New York: Schocken, 1985.

DiBattista, Maria, ed. *The Cambridge Companion to Autobiography*. Cambridge: Cambridge University Press, 2014.

Dilthey, Wilhelm. *Pattern and Meaning in History: W. Dilthey's Thoughts on History and Society*. Edited by H. P. Rickman. New York: Harper and Row, 1960.

———. *Selected Writings*. Edited and translated by H. P. Rickman. New York: Cambridge University Press, 1976.

Dorn, Mike. "Simi Linton Promotes DS in the *Village Voice*." Disability Studies, Temple University. August 8, 2005. http://disstud.blogspot.com/2005/08/simi-linton-promotes-ds-in-village.html.

Doubrovsky, Serge. "Autofiction." *a/f: Auto/Fiction* 1, no. 1 (2013): 1–3.

Douglas, Kate, and Gillian Whitlock. "Editorial: Trauma in the Twenty-First Century." In "Trauma in the Twenty-First Century," special issue, *Life Writing* 5, no. 1 (2008): 1–9.

Doyle, Rob. "*Yoga* by Emmanuel Carrère Review—the Writer Who Ate Himself." *Observer*, May 29, 2022.

Drake, Jennifer. "Variations of Negation: Breaking the Frame with Lorna Simpson and Adrian Piper." In Smith and Watson, *Interfaces*, 211–39.

Du Bois, W. E. B. *The Souls of Black Folk: Essays and Sketches*. Chicago: A. C. McClurg, 1903.

Bibliography

Dünne, Jörg, and Christian Moser. "Automédialité: Pour un dialogue entre médiologie et critique littéraire." *Revue d'Études Culturelles* 4 (Hiver 2008): 11–20.

Eakin, Paul John, ed. *American Autobiography: Retrospect and Prospect.* Studies in Autobiography. Madison: University of Wisconsin Press, 1991.

———. "Autobiography as Cosmogram." In *Writing Life Writing: Narrative, History, Autobiography,* 90–107. New York: Routledge, 2020.

———. *How Our Lives Become Stories: Making Selves.* Ithaca, N.Y.: Cornell University Press, 1999.

———. *Living Autobiographically: How We Create Identity in Narrative.* Ithaca, N.Y.: Cornell University Press, 2008.

———. "Relational Selves, Relational Lives: Autobiography and the Myth of Autonomy." In *How Our Lives Become Stories,* 43–98.

———. *Touching the World: Reference in Autobiography.* Princeton, N.J.: Princeton University Press, 1992.

———. *Writing Life Writing: Narrative, History, Autobiography.* New York: Routledge, 2020.

Eco, Umberto. *The Role of the Reader: Explorations in the Semiotics of Texts.* Bloomington: Indiana University Press, 1979.

Egan, Susanna. *Mirror Talk: Genres of Crisis in Contemporary Autobiography.* Chapel Hill: University of North Carolina Press, 1999.

Effe, Alexandra, and Hannie Lawlor. "Introduction: From Autofiction to the Autofictional." In *The Autofictional: Approaches, Affordances, Forms,* edited by Alexandra Efee and Hannie Lawlor, 1–18. London: Palgrave, 2022.

Ellis, Carolyn. *The Ethnographic I: A Methodological Novel about Autoethnography.* Walnut Creek, Calif.: AltaMira Press, 2004.

Ellis, Carolyn, Tony E. Adams, and Arthur P. Bochner. "Autoethnography: An Overview." *Forum Qualitative Sozialforschung / Forum: Qualitative Social Research* 12, no. 1 (2010), art. 10, http://nbn-resolving.de/urn:nbn:de:0114 -fqs1101108.

El Refaie, Elisabeth. *Autobiographical Comics: Life Writing in Pictures.* Jackson: University of Mississippi Press, 2012.

Fabian, Ann. *The Unvarnished Truth: Personal Narratives in Nineteenth-Century America.* Berkeley: University of California Press, 2000.

Feldman, Allen. "Memory Theaters, Virtual Witnessing, and the Trauma-Aesthetic." *Biography* 27, no. 1 (Winter 2004): 163–202.

Felman, Shoshana, and Dori Laub. *Testimony: Crises of Witnessing in Literature, Psychoanalysis, and History.* New York: Routledge, 1992.

Felski, Rita. *Beyond Feminist Aesthetics: Feminist Literature and Social Change.* Cambridge, Mass.: Harvard University Press, 1989.

Finke, Laurie. "Mystical Bodies and the Dialogics of Vision." In *Maps of Flesh and Light: The Religious Experience of Medieval Women Mystics*, edited by Ulrike Wiethaus, 28–44. Syracuse, N.Y.: Syracuse University Press, 1993.

Folkenflik, Robert. "Introduction: The Institution of Autobiography." In *The Culture of Autobiography: Constructions of Self-Representation*, edited by Robert Folkenflik, 1–20. Palo Alto, Calif.: Stanford University Press, 1993.

Foster, Frances Smith. *Witnessing Slavery: The Development of Ante-Bellum Slave Narratives*. Westport, Conn.: Greenwood Press, 1979.

Foucault, Michel. *The History of Sexuality*, vol. 1. Translated by Robert Hurley. New York: Pantheon, 1978.

———. "Technologies of the Self." In *Technologies of the Self: A Seminar with Michel Foucault*, edited by Luther H. Martin, Huck Gutman, and Patrick H. Hutton, 16–49. Amherst: University of Massachusetts Press, 1988.

Fournier, Lauren. *Autotheory as Feminist Practice in Art, Writing, and Criticism*. Cambridge, Mass.: MIT Press, 2021.

———. "Call for Papers: 'Autotheory' Special Issue of *ASAP/Journal*." *ASAP/Journal: Association for the Study of the Arts of the Present*, October 8, 2019.

Fox, Michael J. "Michael J. Fox Reviews a Thoughtful Memoir on the Challenges of Living with Disability" [review of Jan Grue, *I Live a Life Like Yours: A Memoir*]. *New York Times*, August 15, 2021.

Franklin, Cynthia G. *Academic Lives: Memoir, Cultural Theory, and the University Today*. Athens: University of Georgia Press, 2009.

———. *Writing Women's Communities: The Politics and Poetics of Contemporary Multi-Genre Anthologies*. Madison: University of Wisconsin Press, 1997.

Franklin, H. Bruce. *Prison Literature in America: The Victim as Criminal and Artist*. Westport, Conn.: L. Hill, 1978.

Freeman, Elizabeth. *Time Binds: Queer Temporalities, Queer Histories*. Durham, N.C.: Duke University Press, 2010.

Freud, Sigmund. "Fragment of an Analysis of a Case of Hysteria." In *The Standard Edition of the Complete Psychological Works of Sigmund Freud*, edited by James Strachey, 7:3–122. London: Hogarth Press, 1953.

Friedman, Susan Stanford. *Mappings: Feminism and the Cultural Geographies of Encounter*. Princeton, N.J.: Princeton University Press, 1998.

———. "Spatial Poetics and Arundhati Roy's *The God of Small Things*." In *A Companion to Narrative Theory*, edited by James Phelan and Peter J. Rabinowitz, 192–205. Malden, Mass.: Blackwell, 2005.

———. "Women's Autobiographical Selves: Theory and Practice." In *The Private Self: Theory and Practice of Women's Autobiographical Writings*, edited by Shari Benstock, 34–62. Chapel Hill: University of North Carolina Press, 1988.

Fuderer, Laura Sue. *The Female Bildungsroman in English*. New York: Modern Language Association of America, 1990.

Bibliography

Gagnier, Regenia. *Subjectivities: A History of Self-Representation in Britain, 1832–1920.* New York: Oxford University Press, 1991.

Gaines, Jane, and Michael Renov. *Collecting Visible Evidence.* Visible Evidence Series. Minneapolis: University of Minnesota Press, 1999.

Gardner, Jared. "Archives, Collectors, and the New Media Work of Comics." *Modern Fiction Studies* 52, no. 4 (Winter 2006): 787–806.

———. "Autography's Biography, 1972–2007." *Biography* 31, no. 1 (Winter 2008): 1–26.

———. "Out of Sync: Chronic Illness, Time, and Comics Memoir." In *Graphic Medicine,* edited by Erin La Cour and Anna Poletti, 39–52. Honolulu: University of Hawai'i Press, 2022.

Genette, Gérard. *Paratexts: Thresholds of Interpretation.* Literature, Culture, Theory Series. Cambridge: Cambridge University Press, 1997.

Gernalzick, Nadja. *Temporality in American Filmic Autobiography: Cinema, Automediality and Grammatology with "Film Portrait" and "Joyce at 34."* Heidelberg: Universitätsverlag Winter, 2018.

Gerschick, Thomas Joseph. "Toward a Theory of Disability and Gender." *Signs: Journal of Women in Culture and Society* 25, no. 4 (Summer 2000): 1263–68.

Gilbert, Sandra M., and Roger J. Porter, eds. *Eating Words: A Norton Anthology of Food Writing.* New York: Norton, 2015.

Gilmore, Leigh. *Autobiographics: A Feminist Theory of Women's Self-Representation.* Ithaca, N.Y.: Cornell University Press, 1994.

———. "Jurisdictions: *I, Rigoberta Menchú, The Kiss,* and Scandalous Self-Representation in the Age of Memoir and Trauma." *Signs: Journal of Women in Culture and Society* 28, no. 2 (Winter 2003): 695–718.

———. *The Limits of Autobiography: Trauma and Testimony.* Ithaca, N.Y.: Cornell University Press, 2001.

———. "#MeToo and the Memoir Boom: The Year in the US." *Biography* 42, no. 1 (2019): 162–67.

———. *The #MeToo Effect: What Happens When We Believe Women?* New York: Columbia University Press, 2023.

———. *Tainted Witness: Why We Doubt What Women Say about Their Lives.* New York: Columbia University Press, 2017.

———. "Trauma and Life Writing." In Jolly, *Encyclopedia of Life Writing,* 2:885–87.

———. "'What Was I?': Literary Witness and the Testimonial Archive." *Profession,* 2011, 77–84.

Glissant, Edouard. *Caribbean Discourse: Selected Essays.* Translated by J. Michael Dash. Charlottesville: University Press of Virginia, 1989.

Glotfelty, Cheryll, and Harold Fromm, eds. *The Ecocriticism Reader: Landmarks in Literary Ecology.* Athens: University of Georgia Press, 1996.

Bibliography

Gluck, Sherna Berger, and Daphne Patai, eds. *Women's Words: The Feminist Practice of Oral History.* New York: Routledge, 1991.

Goffman, Erving. *Gender Advertisements.* New York: Harper and Row, 1979.

———. *The Presentation of Self in Everyday Life.* Garden City, N.Y.: Doubleday, 1959.

González, Jennifer A. "Autotopographies." In *Prosthetic Territories: Politics and Hypertechnologies,* edited by Gabriel Brahm Jr. and Mark Driscoll, 133–50. Boulder, Colo.: Westview Press, 1995.

Goswami, Namita. "Autophagia and Queer Transnationality: Compulsory Heteroimperial Masculinity in Deepa Mehta's *Fire.*" *Signs: Journal of Women in Culture and Society* 33, no. 2 (Spring 2008): 342–69.

"Graphic Medicine." Graphic Medicine International Collective, 2023. https://www.graphicmedicine.org/.

Gray, Mary. "Negotiating Identities/Queering Desires: Coming Out Online and the Remediation of the Coming-Out Story." *Journal of Computer-Mediated Communication* 14, no. 4 (2009): 1162–89.

Gronemann, Claudia. "Autofiction." In Wagner-Egelhaaf, *Handbook of Autobiography/Autofiction,* 2:241–46.

Grosz, Elizabeth. *Volatile Bodies: Toward a Corporeal Feminism.* Bloomington: Indiana University Press, 1994.

Gullette, Margaret Morganroth. *Declining to Decline: Cultural Combat and the Politics of the Midlife.* Charlottesville: University Press of Virginia, 1997.

———. "No Longer Suppressing Grief: Political Trauma in Twentieth Century America." *Life Writing* 5, no. 2 (2008): 253–61.

Gusdorf, Georges. "Conditions and Limits of Autobiography." Translated by James Olney. In Olney, *Autobiography,* 28–48.

Hall, Stuart. "Cultural Identity and Diaspora." In *Colonial Discourse and Post-Colonial Theory: A Reader,* edited by Patrick Williams and Laura Chrisman, 392–403. New York: Columbia University Press, 1994.

Hamilton, Nigel. *Biography: A Brief History.* Cambridge, Mass.: Harvard University Press, 2007.

Hanley, Christine. "Handyman Sentenced to Life in Prison." *Columbus Dispatch,* September 14, 2000, A-10.

Hanscombe, Elisabeth. "Aspects of Trauma: Incest, War and Witness." *Life Writing* 5, no. 1 (2008): 117–24.

Haraway, Donna. *The Companion Species Manifesto: Dogs, People and Significant Otherness.* Edited by Matthew Begelke. Chicago: Prickly Paradigm Press, 2003.

Harlow, Barbara. "From the Women's Prison: Third World Women's Narratives of Prison." *Feminist Studies* 12, no. 3 (Autumn 1986): 501–24.

———. *Resistance Literature.* New York: Methuen, 1987.

Harry, Duke of Sussex. "Prince Harry, The Duke of Sussex Talks #Spare with

Stephen Colbert—EXTENDED INTERVIEW." *The Late Show with Stephen Colbert*, CBS, January 11, 2023. https://www.youtube.com/watch?v=E 6l0ObY2XVM.

———. *Spare*. New York: Random House, 2023.

Hawkins, Anne Hunsaker. *Reconstructing Illness: Studies in Pathography*. West Lafayette, Ind.: Purdue University Press, 1993.

Hayes, Patrick, ed. *The Oxford History of Life-Writing*. Vol. 7: *Postwar to Contemporary, 1945–2020*. Oxford: Oxford University Press, 2022.

Hayles, N. Katherine. *My Mother Was a Computer: Digital Subjects and Literary Texts*. Chicago: University of Chicago Press, 2005.

Henderson, Mae Gwendolyn. "Speaking in Tongues: Dialogics, Dialectics, and the Black Woman Writer's Literary Tradition." In *Changing Our Words: Essays on Criticism, Theory, and Writing by Black Women*, edited by Cheryl A. Wall, 116–42. New Brunswick, N.J.: Rutgers University Press, 1989.

Henke, Suzette. *Shattered Subjects: Trauma and Testimony in Women's Life-Writing*. New York: St. Martin's Press, 1998.

Hesford, Wendy S. "Documenting Violations: Rhetorical Witnessing and the Spectacle of Distant Suffering." *Biography* 27, no. 1 (Winter 2004): 104–44.

———. *Framing Identities: Autobiography and the Politics of Pedagogy*. Minneapolis: University of Minnesota Press, 1999.

Hipchen, Emily, and Jill Deans. "Introduction: Adoption Life Writing: Origins and Other Ghosts." In "Adoption Life Writing: Origins and Other Ghosts," special issue, *a/b: Auto/Biography Studies* 18, no. 2 (2003): 163–70.

Hirsch, Marianne. "Debts." *a/b: Auto/Biography Studies* 32, no. 2 (2017): 221–23.

———. "Editor's Column: Collateral Damage." *PMLA* 119, no. 5 (October 2004): 1209–15.

———. *Family Frames: Photography, Narrative, and Postmemory*. Cambridge, Mass.: Harvard University Press, 1997.

———. "Masking the Subject: Practicing Theory." In *The Point of Theory: Practices in Cultural Analysis*, edited by Mieke Bal and Inge E. Boer, 109–24. New York: Continuum, 1994.

Hogan, Rebecca. "Engendered Autobiographies: The Diary as a Feminine Form." In "Autobiography and Questions of Gender," special issue, *Prose Studies* 14, no. 2 (September 1991): 95–107.

Holden, Philip. *Autobiography and Decolonization: Modernity, Masculinity, and the Nation-State*. Madison: University of Wisconsin Press, 2008.

———. "Other Modernities: National Autobiography and Globalization." *Biography* 28, no. 1 (Winter 2005): 89–103.

Holland, Jeff. "Dear Diary 2020 Edition." *Medium*, July 3, 2020. https://medium.com/@ffejdnalloh21/dear-diary-2020-edition-9406f477d7b7.

Holman, C. Hugh. "Preface." In *A Handbook to Literature*, edited by William Flint Thrall and Addison Hibbard, v–vi. New York: Odyssey Press, 1960.

Hornung, Alfred, and Ernstpeter Ruhe, eds. *Postcolonialism and Autobiography: Michelle Cliff, David Dabydeen, Opal Palmer Adisa*. Amsterdam: Rodopi, 1999.

Hornung, Alfred, Nina Morgan, and Takayuki Tatsumi, eds. *The Routledge Companion to Transnational American Studies*. New York: Routledge, 2019.

Horvat, Ana, Orly Lael Netzer, Sarah McRae, and Julie Rak. "Unfixing the Prefix in Life-Writing Studies: Trans, Transmedia, Transnational." *a/b: Auto/Biography Studies* 34, no. 1 (2019): 1–17.

Howarth, William L. "Some Principles of Autobiography." In Olney, *Autobiography*, 84–114.

Howes, Craig. "Life Writing." *Oxford Research Encyclopedia of Literature Online*, 2020. https://doi.org/10.1093/acrefore/9780190201098.013.1146.

———. *Voices of the Vietnam POWs: Witnesses to Their Fight*. New York: Oxford University Press, 1993.

Huff, Cynthia, and Joel Haefner. "His Master's Voice: Animalographies, Life Writing, and the Posthuman." *Biography* 35, no. 1 (Winter 2012): 153–69.

Iverson, Stefan. "Transgressive Narration: The Case of Autofiction." In *Narrative Factuality: A Handbook,* edited by Monika Fludernik and Marie-Laure Ryan with Hanna Specker, 555–64. Berlin: De Gruyter, 2020.

Jackson, David. *Unmasking Masculinity: A Critical Autobiography*. London: Unwin Hyman, 1990.

Jensen, Meg. *The Art and Science of Trauma and the Autobiographical: Negotiated Truths*. Cham: Palgrave Macmillan, 2019.

Jolly, Margaretta, ed. *Encyclopedia of Life Writing: Autobiographical and Biographical Forms*. 2 vols. London: Fitzroy Dearborn, 2001.

———. *In Love and Struggle: Letters in Contemporary Feminism*. New York: Columbia University Press, 2008.

Jones, E. H. "Autofiction: A Brief History of a Neologism." In *Life Writing: Essays on Autobiography, Biography, and Literature,* edited by Richard Bradford, 174–84. Houndmills: Palgrave Macmillan, 2010.

Kaplan, Caren. "Resisting Autobiography: Out-Law Genres and Transnational Feminist Subjects." In Smith and Watson, *De/Colonizing the Subject*, 115–38.

Karr, Mary. *The Art of Memoir*. New York: Harper Perennial, 2015.

Katin, Miriam. *Letting It Go*. Montreal: Drawn and Quarterly, 2013.

———. *We Are on Our Own*. Montreal: Drawn and Quarterly, 2006.

Kawakami, Akane. "Annie Ernaux, 1989: Diaries, Photographic Writing and Self-Vivisection." *Nottingham French Studies* 53, no. 2 (2014): 232–46.

Kawash, Samira. *Dislocating the Color Line: Identity, Hybridity, and Singularity in African-American Narrative*. Stanford, Calif.: Stanford University Press, 1997.

Keith, Michael, and Steve Pile, eds. *Place and the Politics of Identity*. London: Routledge, 1993.

Bibliography

Kellaway, Kate. "The Interview: Bobby Baker." *Guardian,* June 27, 2009.

Kennedy, Helen. "Beyond Anonymity, or Future Directions for Internet Identity Research." *New Media and Society* 8, no. 6 (2006): 859–76.

Kennedy, Rosanne, and Gillian Whitlock. Conference announcement for "Testimony, Trauma and Social Suffering: New Contexts/New Framings," April 14–16, 2009, Research School of Humanities, Australian National University, Canberra, Australia.

Kermode, Frank. "Fictioneering." *London Review of Books,* October 8, 2009, 9–10.

Kim, Jina B. "Anatomy of the City: Race, Infrastructure, and U.S. Fictions of Dependency." PhD diss., University of Michigan, 2016.

Kjerkegaard, Stefan, and Arnaud Schmitt. "Karl Ove Knausgaard's *My Struggle: A Real Life in a Novel.*" *a/b: Auto/Biography Studies* 31, no. 3 (2016): 553–79.

Krailsheimer, A. J. *Studies in Self-Interest: From Descartes to La Bruyère.* Oxford: Clarendon Press, 1962.

Kristeva, Julia. *Desire in Language: A Semiotic Approach to Literature and Art.* Edited by Leon Roudiez. Translated by Thomas Gora and Alice Jardine. New York: Columbia University Press, 1980.

———. *The Powers of Horror: An Essay on Abjection.* Translated by Leon Roudiez. New York: Columbia University Press, 1982.

Krupat, Arnold. *Ethnocriticism: Ethnography, History, Literature.* Berkeley: University of California Press, 1992.

———. *For Those Who Come After: A Study of Native American Autobiography.* Berkeley: University of California Press, 1985.

———. "Introduction." In *Native American Autobiography: An Anthology,* 3–17. Madison: University of Wisconsin Press, 1994.

Kugler, Olivier. *Escaping Wars and Waves: Encounters with Syrian Refugees.* University Park: Pennsylvania State University Press, 2018.

Kulbaga, Theresa. "Trans/National Feminist Lives." PhD diss., The Ohio State University, 2006.

Kunka, Andrew J. *Autobiographical Comics.* New York: Bloomsbury Academic, 2017.

La Cour, Erin, and Anna Poletti. "Graphic Medicine's Possible Futures: Reconsidering Poetics and Reading." In *Graphic Medicine,* edited by Erin La Cour and Anna Poletti, 1–23. Honolulu: University of Hawai'i Press, 2022.

Lacan, Jacques. *The Language of the Self: The Function of Language in Psychoanalysis.* Translated by Anthony Wilden. Baltimore: Johns Hopkins University Press, 1968.

Lackey, Michael. "Beyond Postmodern Blurring: Epistemic Precision in Writing about a Life." *a/b: Auto/Biography Studies* 36, no. 1 (2021): 1–8.

———. "Locating and Defining the Bio in Biofiction." *a/b: Auto/Biography Studies* 31, no. 1 (2016): 3–10.

Landsberg, Alison. *Prosthetic Memory: The Transformation of American Remembrance in the Age of Mass Culture.* New York: Columbia University Press, 2004.

Lane, Jim. *The Autobiographical Documentary in America from the 1960s to the Present.* Wisconsin Studies in Autobiography. Madison: University of Wisconsin Press, 2002.

Lang, Candace D. "Autobiography in the Aftermath of Romanticism." *Diacritics* 12 (Winter 1982): 2–16.

———. *Irony/Humor: Critical Paradigms.* Baltimore: Johns Hopkins University Press, 1988.

Lanser, Susan S. "The 'I' of the Beholder: Equivocal Attachments and the Limits of Structuralist Narratology." In *A Companion to Narrative Theory,* edited by James Phelan and Peter J. Rabinowitz, 206–19. Malden, Mass.: Blackwell, 2005.

Lather, Patti, and Chris Smithies. *Troubling the Angels: Women Living with HIV/AIDS.* Boulder, Colo.: Westview Press, 1997.

Lauretis, Teresa de. *Alice Doesn't: Feminism, Semiotics, Cinema.* Bloomington: Indiana University Press, 1984.

———. "Eccentric Subjects: Feminist Theory and Historical Consciousness." *Feminist Studies* 16, no. 1 (Spring 1990): 115–50.

Lee, Valerie. *Sisterlocking Discoarse: Race, Gender, and the Twenty-First-Century Academy.* Albany: State University of New York Press, 2021.

Leed, Eric J. *The Mind of the Traveler: From Gilgamesh to Global Tourism.* New York: Basic Books, 1991.

Leith, Dick, and George Myerson. *The Power of Address: Explorations in Rhetoric.* London: Routledge, 1989.

Lejeune, Philippe. "The Autobiographical Pact." In Lejeune, *On Autobiography,* 3–30.

———. "The Autobiographical Pact *(bis)."* In Lejeune, *On Autobiography,* 119–37.

———. *L'Autobiographie en France.* Paris: Colin, 1971.

———. "Autobiography in the Third Person." In Lejeune, *On Autobiography,* 31–51.

———. "The Autobiography of Those Who Do Not Write." In Lejeune, *On Autobiography,* 185–215 and 264–71.

———. "Lucullus Dines with Lucullus." In *On Diary,* edited by Jeremy Popkin and Julie Rak, translated by Katharine Durnin, 329–36. Honolulu: Center for Biographical Research, University of Hawai'i Press, 2009.

———. *Le Moi des Demoiselles: Enquête sur le Journal de Jeune Fille.* Paris: Editions du Seuil, 1993.

———. *On Autobiography.* Edited by Paul John Eakin. Translated by Katherine Leary. Minneapolis: University of Minnesota Press, 1989.

Bibliography

———. *On Diary*. Edited by Jeremy Popkin and Julie Rak. Translated by Katharine Durnin. Honolulu: Center for Biographical Research, University of Hawai'i, 2009.

———. "The Practice of the Private Journal: Chronicle of an Investigation (1986–1998)." Translated by Russell West. In *Marginal Voices, Marginal Forms: Diaries in European Literature and History*, edited by Rachel Langford and Russell West, 185–211. Amsterdam: Rodopi, 1999.

Lenart-Cheng, Helga. *Story Revolutions: Collective Narratives from the Enlightenment to the Digital Age*. Charlottesville: University of Virginia Press, 2022.

Leon, Concepción de. "You Know Emily Doe's Story, Now Learn Her Name." *New York Times*, September 4, 2019. https://www.nytimes.com/2019/09/04/books/chanel-miller-brock-turner-assault-stanford.html.

Lewis, Jon, ed. *The End of Cinema as We Know It: American Film in the Nineties*. New York: New York University Press, 2001.

Lim, Shirley Geok-lin. *Writing S.E./Asia in English: Against the Grain, Focus on Asian English-Language Literature*. London: Skoob Books, 1994.

Lindemann Nelson, Hilde. *Damaged Identities, Narrative Repair*. Ithaca, N.Y.: Cornell University Press, 2001.

Lionnet, Françoise. *Autobiographical Voices: Race, Gender, Self-Portraiture*. Ithaca, N.Y.: Cornell University Press, 1989.

———. "Consciousness and Relationality: Sartre, Lévi-Strauss, Beauvoir, and Glissant." In "Rethinking Claude Lévi-Strauss (1908–2009)," special issue, *Yale French Studies*, no. 123 (2013): 100–117.

———. "Of Mangoes and Maroons: Language, History, and the Multicultural Subject of Michelle Cliff's *Abeng*." In Smith and Watson, *De/Colonizing the Subject*, 321–45.

———. *Postcolonial Representations: Women, Literature, Identity*. Ithaca, N.Y.: Cornell University Press, 1995.

Loos, Ted. "What Has Lockdown Meant for L.G.B.T.Q. Artists and Writers?" *New York Times*, June 16, 2020.

Lotringer, Sylvère. "Confessions of a Ventriloquist." Translated by Catherine Combes. In "Interviewing as Creative Practice," special issue, *Biography* 41, no. 2 (Spring 2018): 199–234.

Lowe, Lisa. *Critical Terrains: French and British Orientalisms*. Ithaca, N.Y.: Cornell University Press, 1992.

Lyotard, Jean-François. *The Postmodern Condition: A Report on Knowledge*. Translated by Geoff Bennington and Brian Massumi. Minneapolis: University of Minnesota Press, 1984.

Mabie, Nora. "New Missing and Murdered Indigenous Woman Documentary Premieres Today." *Great Falls Tribune / Statesman Journal*, January 15, 2020.

March, Eleanor. "Narratives of Translators: The Translational Function of Prisoner Writing." *Life Writing* 19, no. 4 (2022): 573–91.

Martz, Louis Lohr. *The Poetry of Meditation: A Study in English Religious Literature of the Seventeenth Century.* New Haven, Conn.: Yale University Press, 1954.

Mason, Wyatt. "How Emmanuel Carrère Reinvented Nonfiction." *New York Times Magazine,* March 2, 2017.

Masschelein, Anneleen, and Rebecca Roach. "Putting Things Together: Introduction to Interviewing as Creative Practice." In "Interviewing as Creative Practice," special issue, *Biography* 41, no. 2 (Spring 2018): 169–78.

McHugh, Kathleen. "Lourdes Portillo, Rea Tajiri, and Cheryl Dunye: History and Falsehood in Experimental Autobiographies." In *Women and Experimental Filmmaking,* edited by Jean Petrolle and Virginia Wright Wexman, 107–28. Urbana: University of Illinois, 2005.

———. "Where Hollywood Fears to Tread: Autobiography and the Limits of Commercial Cinema." In Lewis, *The End of Cinema as We Know It,* 269–76.

McLaughlin, Becky. "Call for Papers: Autotheory and Its Others." January 4, 2023. https://call-for-papers.sas.upenn.edu/cfp/2023/01/02/autotheory-and -its-others.

Menakem, Resmaa. *My Grandmother's Hands: Racialized Trauma and the Pathway to Mending Our Hearts and Bodies.* Las Vegas: Central Recovery Press, 2017.

Menand, Louis. "Lives of Others." *New Yorker,* August 4, 2007, 64–66.

Meskimmon, Marsha. *The Art of Reflection: Women Artists' Self-Portraiture in the Twentieth Century.* New York: Columbia University Press, 1996.

Mihm, Stephen. "24/7 Alibi, The" *New York Times Magazine,* December 9, 2007.

Milani, Farzaneh. *Veils and Words: The Emerging Voices of Iranian Women Writers.* Syracuse: Syracuse University Press, 1992.

Miller, Nancy K. *But Enough about Me: Why We Read Other People's Lives.* Gender and Culture Series. New York: Columbia University Press, 2002.

———. "Closing Comments." Presented at the International Auto/Biography Association, Life Writing and Translations conference, Honolulu, Hawai'i, 2008.

———. "The Entangled Self: Genre Bondage in the Age of Memoir." *PMLA* 122, no. 2 (March 2007): 537–48.

———. *Getting Personal: Feminist Occasions and Other Autobiographical Acts.* New York: Routledge, 1991.

———. "'Is This Recovery?' Chronicity and Closure in Graphic Illness Memoir." In *Graphic Medicine,* edited by Erin La Cour and Anna Poletti, 53–70. Honolulu: University of Hawai'i Press, 2022.

Bibliography 381

———. "Memory Stains: Annie Ernaux's *Shame.*" *a/b: Auto/Biography Studies* 14, no. 1 (1999): 38–50.

———. "Out of the Family: Generations of Women in Marjane Satrapi's *Persepolis.*" *Life Writing* 4, no. 1 (2007): 13–30.

———. "Representing Others: Gender and the Subjects of Autobiography." *differences* 6, no. 1 (1994): 1–27.

———. "Toward a Dialectics of Difference." In *Women and Language in Literature and Society,* edited by Sally McConnell-Ginet, Ruth Borker, and Nelly Furman, 258–73. New York: Praeger, 1980.

———. "Writing Fictions: Women's Autobiography in France." In *Life/Lines: Theorizing Women's Autobiography,* edited by Bella Brodzki and Celeste Schenck, 45–61. Ithaca, N.Y.: Cornell University Press, 1988.

Mintz, Susannah B. *Unruly Bodies: Life Writing by Women with Disabilities.* Chapel Hill: University of North Carolina Press, 2007.

Misch, Georg. *A History of Autobiography in Antiquity.* 2 vols. Translated by E. W. Dickes. London: Routledge and Paul, 1950.

Mitchell, David D., and Sharon Snyder. *Narrative Prosthesis: Disability and the Dependencies of Discourse.* Ann Arbor: University of Michigan Press, 2001.

Mitchell, W. J. T. *Picture Theory: Essays on Visual and Verbal Representation.* Chicago: University of Chicago Press, 1994.

Moser, Christian. "Autoethnography." In Wagner-Egelhaaf, *Handbook of Autobiography/Autofiction,* 2:232–40.

Mouffe, Chantal. "Feminism, Citizenship, and Radical Democratic Politics." In *Feminists Theorize the Political,* edited by Judith Butler and Joan W. Scott, 369–84. New York: Routledge, 1992.

Myers, Susan. "Precious Moments." Gallery notes. Hammond Harkins Gallery, Columbus, Ohio, 2000.

Nadel, Ira Bruce. *Biography: Fiction, Fact, and Form.* New York: St. Martin's, 1984.

Naghibi, Nima. *Women Write Iran: Nostalgia and Human Rights from the Diaspora.* Minneapolis: University of Minnesota Press, 2016.

Nakamura, Lisa. "Cyberrace." *PMLA* 123, no. 5 (October 2008): 1673–82.

Namias, June. "Introduction." In *A Narrative of the Life of Mrs. Mary Jemison,* edited by James E. Seaver, 3–45. Norman: University of Oklahoma Press, 1992.

Nayar, Pramod K. "Autobiogenography: Genomes and Life Writing." *a/b: Auto/Biography Studies* 31, no. 3 (2016): 509–25.

Nelson, Hilda Lindemann. *Damaged Identities, Narrative Repair.* Ithaca, NY: Cornell University Press, 2001.

Nelson, Katherine. "The Psychological and Social Origins of Autobiographical Memory." *Psychological Science* 4, no. 1 (January 1993): 7–14.

Nicol, Patricia. "Deborah Levy Interview: Why Her Booker-Longlisted Novel 'Began with Glam Rock.'" *Sunday Times* (London), August 25, 2019.

Nierenberg, Amelia. "The Quarantine Diaries." *New York Times,* March 30, 2020.

Nora, Pierre, "Introduction." *Essais d' Ego-histoire.* Translated by Stephen Muecke. Paris: Gallimard, 1984.

———. *Les Lieux de mémoire.* Vols. 1–3. Paris: Gallimard, 1984–92.

Novy, Marianne, ed. *Imagining Adoption: Essays on Literature and Culture.* Ann Arbor: University of Michigan Press, 2001.

Nussbaum, Felicity A. *The Autobiographical Subject.* 2nd ed. Baltimore: Johns Hopkins University Press, 1995.

Oliver, Kelly. *Witnessing: Beyond Recognition.* Minneapolis: University of Minnesota Press, 2001.

Olney, James, ed. *Autobiography: Essays Theoretical and Critical.* Princeton, N.J.: Princeton University Press, 1980.

———. "Autobiography and the Cultural Moment: A Thematic, Historical, and Bibliographical Introduction." In Olney, *Autobiography,* 3–27.

———. "'I Was Born': Slave Narratives, Their Status as Autobiography and as Literature." In *The Slave's Narrative,* edited by Charles T. Davis and Henry Louis Gates Jr., 148–74. New York: Oxford University Press, 1985.

———. *Memory and Narrative: The Weave of Life-Writing.* Chicago: University of Chicago Press, 1998.

———. *Metaphors of Self: The Meaning of Autobiography.* Princeton, N.J.: Princeton University Press, 1972.

———. "Some Versions of Memory/Some Versions of Bios: The Ontology of Autobiography." In Olney, *Autobiography,* 236–67.

Ortiz-Vilarelle, Lisa. *Américanas, Autocracy, and Autobiographical Innovation: Overwriting the Dictator.* New York: Routledge, 2020.

———, ed. *Career Narratives and Academic Womanhood: In the Spaces Provided.* New York: Taylor and Francis, 2023.

Ortner, Sherry B. *Making Gender: The Politics and Erotics of Culture.* Boston: Beacon, 1996.

Page, Ruth E. *Stories and Social Media: Identities and Interaction.* London: Routledge, 2012.

———. "Stories of the Self on and off the Screen." *Electronic Literature: New Horizons for the Literary,* edited by N. Katherine Hayles, https://newhorizons.eliterature.org/essay.php@id=6.html.

Painter, Nell Irvin. *Sojourner Truth: A Life, A Symbol.* New York: W. W. Norton, 1997.

Panofsky, Erwin. *Tomb Sculpture: Four Lectures on Its Changing Aspects from Ancient Egypt to Bernini.* Edited by H. W. Janson. New York: H. N. Abrams, 1964.

Bibliography

Paravisini-Gebert, Lisabeth. *Jamaica Kincaid: A Critical Companion.* Westport, Conn.: Greenwood Press, 1999.

Parker, David. "Narratives of Autonomy and Narratives of Relationality in Auto/Biography." In "Life Writing and the Generations," special issue, *a/b: Auto/Biography Studies* 19, nos. 1–2 (2004): 137–55.

Parsons, J. M., and A. Chappell, eds. *The Palgrave Handbook of Auto/Biography.* London: Palgrave Macmillan, 2020.

Pascal, Roy. *Design and Truth in Autobiography.* Cambridge, Mass.: Harvard University Press, 1960.

Patton, Sandra. "Race/Identity/Culture/Kin: Constructions of African American Identity in Transracial Adoption." In Smith and Watson, *Getting a Life,* 271–96.

Peck, Janice. "The Mediated Talking Cure: Therapeutic Framing of Autobiography on TV Talk Shows." In Smith and Watson, *Getting a Life,* 134–55.

PEN America. "Banned in the USA Spotlight: Maia Kobabe." Interview with Lisa Tolin. https://pen.org/maia-kobabe-gender-queer-interview/.

Perreault, Jeanne. *Writing Selves: Contemporary Feminist Autography.* Minneapolis: University of Minnesota Press, 1995.

Perreten, Peter F. "Eco-Autobiography. Portrait of Place: Self-Portrait." *a/b: Auto/Biography Studies* 18, no. 1 (2003): 1–22.

Phelan, James. "The Ethics of Factual Narrative," in *Narrative Factuality: A Handbook,* edited by Monika Fludernik and Marie-Laure Ryan with Hanna Specker, 543–53. Berlin: De Gruyter, 2020.

———. *Living to Tell about It: A Rhetoric and Ethics of Character Narration.* Ithaca, N.Y.: Cornell University Press, 2004.

———. "Voice; or, Authors, Narrators, and Audiences." In *Teaching Narrative Theory,* edited by James Phelan, Brian McHale, and David Herman, 137–50. New York: Modern Language Association, 2010.

Phelan, Peggy. "Lessons in Blindness from Samuel Beckett." *PMLA* 119, no. 5 (October 2004): 1279–88.

Phillips, Dana. "Ecocriticism, Literary Theory, and the Truth of Ecology." *New Literary History* 30, no. 3 (Summer 1999): 577–602.

Plummer, Ken. *Telling Sexual Stories: Power, Change, and Social Worlds.* London: Routledge, 1995.

Poletti, Anna. "Periperformative Life Narrative: Queer Collages." *GLQ: A Journal of Lesbian and Queer Studies* 22, no. 3 (2016): 359–79.

———. *Stories of the Self: Life Writing after the Book.* New York: New York University Press, 2020.

Pollock, Griselda. *Charlotte Salomon and the Theatre of Memory.* New Haven, Conn.: Yale University Press, 2018.

———. *Differencing the Canon: Feminist Desire and the Writing of Art's Histories*. London: Routledge, 1999.

Popkin, Jeremy D. "Historians on the Autobiographical Frontier." *American Historical Review* 104, no. 3 (June 1999): 725–48.

———. *History, Historians, and Autobiography*. Chicago: University of Chicago Press, 2005.

Porter, Dennis. *Haunted Journeys: Desire and Transgression in European Travel Writing*. Princeton, N.J.: Princeton University Press, 1991.

Pratt, Mary Louise. *Imperial Eyes: Travel Writing and Transculturation*. London: Routledge, 1992.

———. "Mad about Menchú." *Lingua Franca* 9, no. 8 (November 1999): 22.

———. "'Me llamo Rigoberta Menchú': Auto-Ethnography and the Recoding of Citizenship." In *Teaching and Testimony: Rigoberta Menchú and the North American Classroom*, edited by Allen Carey-Webb and Stephen Benz, 57–72. Albany: State University of New York Press, 1996.

Progoff, Ira. *At a Journal Workshop: Writing to Access the Power of the Unconscious and Evoke Creative Ability*. Los Angeles: J. P. Tarcher, 1992.

Prosser, Jay. "No Place Like Home: The Transgendered Narrative of Leslie Feinberg's *Stone Butch Blues*." *Modern Fiction Studies* 41, nos. 3–4 (Fall–Winter 1995): 483–514.

Puar, Jasbir K. "'I Would Rather Be a Cyborg than a Goddess': Becoming-Intersectional in Assemblage Theory." *philoSOPHIA* 2, no. 1 (2012): 49–66.

Quante, Heidi, and Alicia Escott. Bureau of Linguistical Reality. 2014. https:// bureauoflinguisticalreality.com/.

Quinby, Lee. "The Subject of Memoirs: *The Woman Warrior*'s Technology of Ideographic Selfhood." In Smith and Watson, *De/Colonizing the Subject*, 297–320.

Rak, Julie. "Are Memoirs Autobiography? A Consideration of Genre and Public Identity." *Genre: Forms of Discourse and Culture* 37, nos. 3–4 (2004): 306–26.

———. *BOOM! Manufacturing Memoir for the Popular Market*. Waterloo: Wilfrid Laurier University Press, 2013.

———. "The Digital Queer: Weblogs and Internet Identity." *Biography* 28, no. 1 (Winter 2005): 166–82.

———. *Negotiated Memory: Doukhobor Autobiographical Discourse*. Vancouver: University of British Columbia Press, 2004.

———. "Radical Connections: Genealogy, Small Lives, Big Data." *a/b: Auto/ Biography Studies* 32, no. 3 (2017): 479–97.

———. "Roundtable: Imagining the Past, Present and Future of Theory in the Study of Life Writing." Presentation at XII International Auto/Biography Association Conference, 2022, Turku, Finland, June 17, 2022.

Bibliography

Raynaud, Claudine. "'A Nutmeg Nestled Inside Its Covering of Mace': Audre Lorde's *Zami*." In *Life/Lines: Theorizing Women's Autobiography*, edited by Bella Brodzki and Celeste Schenck, 221–42. Ithaca, N.Y.: Cornell University Press, 1988.

Reed-Danahay, Deborah E. *Auto/Ethnography: Rewriting the Self and the Social*. New York: Berg, 1997.

Renov, Michael. *The Subject of Documentary*. Visible Evidence Series. Minneapolis: University of Minnesota Press, 2004.

Renza, Louis A. "The Veto of the Imagination: A Theory of Autobiography." *New Literary History* 9, no. 1 (Autumn 1977): 1–26. Republished in Olney, *Autobiography*, 268–95.

Reynolds, Stephen. "Autobiografiction." *Speaker*, n.s., 15, no. 266 (October 1906): 28–30.

Rich, Motoko. "Successful at 96, Writer Has More to Say." *New York Times*, April 7, 2007, A21.

Richter, Gerhard. *Walter Benjamin and the Corpus of Autobiography*. Detroit: Wayne State University Press, 2000.

Rifkind, Candida. "Migrant Detention Comics and the Aesthetic Technologies of Compassion." In *Documenting Trauma in Comics: Traumatic Pasts, Embodied Histories, and Graphic Reportage*, edited by Dominic Davies and Candida Rifkind, 297–316. London: Palgrave, 2020.

———. "Refugee Comics and Migrant Topographies." *a/b: Auto/Biography Studies* 32, no. 3 (2017): 648–54.

Rimmon-Kenan, Shlomith. *Narrative Fiction: Contemporary Poetics*. London: Routledge, 1983.

Rodrigues, Elizabeth. "We Have Never Been a Nation of Immigrants: Refugee Temporality as American Identity." In Beard and Chansky, *The Divided States*, 116–39.

Rooke, Tetz. *In My Childhood: A Study of Arabic Autobiography*. Stockholm: Stockholm University Press, 1997.

Roorbach, Bill. *Writing Life Stories*. Cincinnati: Writer's Digest, 1999.

Rosen, Sarah. "Artist Mickalene Thomas Makes Portraits to Bring Out Your Inner Foxy Brown." *Dazed*, April 5, 2018.

Rothberg, Michael. *The Implicated Subject: Beyond Victims and Perpetrators*. Stanford: Stanford University Press, 2019.

Rotman, Brian. *Becoming Beside Ourselves: The Alphabet, Ghosts, and Distributed Human Being*. Durham, N.C.: Duke University Press, 2008.

———. "Gesture and the I Fold." *Parallax* 15, no. 4 (2009): 68–82.

———. "Automedial Ghosts." *Profession*, 2011, 118–22.

Rugg, Linda Haverty. *Picturing Ourselves: Photography and Autobiography*. Chicago: University of Chicago Press, 1997.

Rymhs, Deena. "Discursive Delinquency in Leonard Peltier's *Prison Writings.*" *Genre: Forms of Discourse and Culture* 35, nos. 3/4 (2002): 563–74.

Said, Edward. *Culture and Imperialism.* New York: Vintage Books (Random House), 1993.

Saldívar, Ramón. *The Borderlands of Culture: Américo Paredes and the Transnational Imaginary.* Durham, N.C.: Duke University Press, 2006.

———. *Chicano Narrative: The Dialectics of Difference.* Madison: University of Wisconsin Press, 1990.

Saunders, Max. "Autofiction, Autobiografiction, Autofabrication, and Heteronymity: Differentiating Versions of the Autobiographical." *Biography* 43, no. 4 (2020): 763–80.

Schacter, Daniel L. *Searching for Memory: The Brain, the Mind, and the Past.* New York: Basic Books, 1996.

Schaffer, Kay, and Sidonie Smith. "E-Witnessing in the Digital Age." In *We Shall Bear Witness: Life Narratives and Human Rights,* edited by Meg Jensen and Margaretta Jolly, 223–37. Madison: University of Wisconsin Press, 2014.

———. *Human Rights and Narrated Lives: The Ethics of Recognition.* New York: Palgrave Macmillan, 2004.

———. "Human Rights, Storytelling, and the Position of the Beneficiary: Antjie Krog's *Country of My Skull.*" *PMLA* 121, no. 5 (October 2006): 1577–84.

Schmitt, Arnaud. "Avatars as the Raison d'Être of Autofiction." *Life Writing* 19, no. 1 (2022): 15–16.

———. *The Photographer as Autobiographer.* London: Palgrave, 2022.

Schreiber, Maria. "Audiences, Aesthetics and Affordances: Analysing Practices of Visual Communication on Social Media." *Digital Culture & Society* 3, no. 2 (2017): 143–63.

Schwartz, Alexandra. "Memory Serves: How Annie Ernaux Turns the Past into Art." *New Yorker,* November 21, 2022, 16–22.

Scott, Joan W. "Experience." In *Feminists Theorize the Political,* edited by Judith Butler and Joan W. Scott, 22–40. New York: Routledge, 1992.

Sengupta, Shuddhabrata. "I/Me/Mine—Intersectional Identities as Negotiated Minefields." In "New Feminist Theories of Visual Culture," special issue, *Signs*: Journal of Women in Culture and Society 31, no. 3 (2006): 629–39.

Shea, Daniel B. *Spiritual Autobiography in Early America.* Madison: University of Wisconsin Press, 1988.

Sheringham, Michael. *Everyday Life: Theories and Practices from Surrealism to the Present.* Oxford: Oxford University Press, 2009.

———. *French Autobiography: Devices and Desires.* Oxford: Clarendon Press, 1993.

Shulevitz, Judith. "My True Story." Review of Ben Yagoda, *Memoir: A History. New York Times Book Review,* November 22, 2009, 15.

Bibliography

Shumaker, Wayne. *English Autobiography: Its Emergence, Materials, and Forms.* Berkeley: University of California Press, 1954.

Siebers, Tobin. *Disability Theory.* Ann Arbor: University of Michigan Press, 2008.

Siegel, Steffen. "Sich selbst im Auge behalten: Selbstüberwachung und die Bilderpolitik des Indiskreten" [Keeping an eye on oneself: Self-surveillance and the cultural politics of indiscretion]. *KulturPoetik* 12, no. 1 (2012): 92–108.

Siegert, Bernhard. *Relais: Literature as an Epoch of the Postal System.* Translated by Kevin Repp. Stanford, Calif.: Stanford University Press, 1999.

Singer, Emily. "The Measured Life." *MIT Technology Review,* June 21, 2011. https://www.technologyreview.com/2011/06/21/193829/the-measured -life/.

Sitney, P. Adams. *Visionary Film: The American Avant-Garde.* 2nd ed. Oxford: Oxford University Press, 1979.

Slaughter, Joseph R. *Human Rights, Inc.: The World Novel, Narrative Form, and International Law.* New York: Fordham University Press, 2007.

Smith, Paul. *Discerning the Subject.* Minneapolis: University of Minnesota Press, 1988.

Smith, Sidonie. "'America's Exhibit A': Hillary Rodham Clinton's *Living History* and the Genres of Political Authenticity," *American Literary History* 24, no. 3 (Fall 2012): 523–42.

———. "Autobiographical Discourse in the Theaters of Politics," *Biography* 33, no. 1 (Winter 2010): v–xxvi.

———. "Autobiographical Inscription and the Identity Assemblage." In *Inscribed Identities: Writing as Self-Realization,* edited by Joan Ramon Resina, 75–90. London: Routledge, 2019.

———. "Human Rights and Comics: Autobiographical Avatars, Crisis Witnessing, and Transnational Rescue Networks." In *Graphic Subjects: Critical Essays on Autobiography and Graphic Novels,* edited by Michael A. Chaney, 61–72. Madison: University of Wisconsin Press, 2011.

———. *Moving Lives: Twentieth-Century Women's Travel Writing.* Minneapolis: University of Minnesota Press, 2001.

———. "Performativity, Autobiographical Practice, Resistance." *a/b: Auto/Biography Studies* 10, no. 1 (1995): 17–33.

———. *A Poetics of Women's Autobiography: Marginality and the Fictions of Self-Representation.* Bloomington: Indiana University Press, 1987.

———. *Subjectivity, Identity, and the Body: Women's Autobiographical Practices in the Twentieth Century.* Bloomington: Indiana University Press, 1993.

———. "Taking It to the Limit One More Time: Autobiography and Autism." In Smith and Watson, *Getting a Life,* 226–48.

388   Bibliography

———. "Theorizing the Subject." In *Oxford Encyclopedia of Literature*. Oxford: Oxford University Press, 2020. http://dx.doi.org/10.1093/acrefore/978019 0201098.013.1132.

Smith, Sidonie, and Julia Watson. "Auto/biographics and Graphic Histories Made for the Classroom, from *Logicomix* to *Abina and the Important Men*." In *Oxford University Press Handbook of Comic Book Studies,* edited by Frederick Luis Aldama, 268–92. Oxford: Oxford University Press, 2020. Online 2019: https://doi.org/10.1093/oxfordhb/9780190917944.013.28.

———. "Contrapuntal Reading in Women's Comics: Alison Bechdel's *Fun Home* and Ellen Forney's *Marbles*." In *Women's Life Writing and the Practice of Reading: She Reads to Write Herself,* edited by Valérie Baisnée-Keay, Corinne Bigot, Nicoleta Alexoae-Zagni, and Claire Bazin, 21–47. London: Palgrave Macmillan, 2018.

———. "Days of Reckoning: Prospects for Life Narrative 2020." In Beard and Chansky, *The Divided States,* 296–324.

———, eds. *De/Colonizing the Subject: The Politics of Gender in Women's Autobiography.* Minneapolis: University of Minnesota Press, 1992.

———, eds. *Getting a Life: Everyday Uses of Autobiography.* Minneapolis: University of Minnesota Press, 1996.

———. "In the Wake of the Memoir Boom." In *Reading Autobiography: A Guide for Interpreting Life Narratives,* 2nd ed., 127–65. Minneapolis: University of Minnesota Press, 2010.

———, eds. *Interfaces: Women, Autobiography, Image, Performance.* Ann Arbor: University of Michigan Press, 2002.

———. "Introduction: Mapping Women's Self-Representation at Visual/Textual Interfaces." In Smith and Watson, *Interfaces,* 1–46.

———. "Introduction: Situating Subjectivity in Women's Autobiographical Practices." In *Women, Autobiography, Theory: A Reader,* edited by Sidonie Smith and Julia Watson, 3–52. Madison: University of Wisconsin Press, 1998.

———. "New Genres, New Subjects: Women, Gender and Autobiography after 2000." *Revista Canaria de Estudios Ingleses* 58 (April 2009): 13–40.

———. *Reading Autobiography: A Guide for Interpreting Life Narratives,* 2nd ed. Minneapolis: University of Minnesota Press, 2010.

———. "The Rumpled Bed of Autobiography: Extravagant Lives, Extravagant Questions." *Biography* 24, no. 1 (Winter 2001): 1–14.

———. "Say It Isn't So: Autobiographical Hoaxes and the Ethics of Life Narrative." In *Life Writing: Autobiography, Biography, and Travel Writing in Contemporary Literature,* edited by Koray Melikoğlu, 15–34. Stuttgart: Ibidem Verlag, 2007.

———. "Virtually Me: A Toolkit about Online Self-Presentation." In *Identity*

Bibliography

Technologies: Constructing the Self Online, edited by Anna Poletti and Julie Rak, 70–94. Madison: University of Wisconsin Press, 2014.

———. "Witness or False Witness? Metrics of Authenticity, Collective I-Formations, and the Ethic of Verification in First-Person Testimony." *Biography* 35, no. 4 (Fall 2012): 590–626.

Soloski, Alexis. "Her Pain, in Her Own Words." *New York Times,* January 16, 2022, AR4.

Sontag, Susan. *On Photography.* New York: Picador, 1973.

Spender, Stephen. "Confessions and Autobiography." In Olney, *Autobiography,* 115–22.

Spengemann, William C. *The Forms of Autobiography: Episodes in the History of a Literary Genre.* New Haven, Conn.: Yale University Press, 1980.

Spivak, Gayatri Chakravorty. "Lives." In *Confessions of the Critics: North American Critics' Autobiographical Moves,* edited by H. Aram Veeser, 205–18. New York: Routledge, 1996.

———. "Subaltern Studies." In *In Other Worlds: Essays in Cultural Politics,* 270–304. New York: Routledge, 1998.

———. "Three Women's Texts and Circumfession." In *Postcolonialism and Autobiography: Michelle Cliff, David Dabydeen, Opal Palmer Adisa,* edited by Alfred Hornung and Ernstpeter Ruhe, 7–22. Amsterdam: Rodopi, 1998.

Stamant, Nicole. *Serial Memoir: Archiving American Lives.* New York: Palgrave Macmillan, 2014.

Stanley, Liz. "The Epistolarium: On Theorizing Letters and Correspondences." *Auto/Biography* 12, no. 3 (2004): 201–35.

Stanley, Liz, and Helen Dampier. "Simulacrum Diaries: Time, the 'Moment of Writing' and the Diaries of Johanna Brandt-Van Warmelo." *Life Writing* 3, no. 2 (2006): 25–52.

Stanton, Domna C. "Autogynography: Is the Subject Different?" In *The Female Autograph: Theory and Practice of Autobiography from the Tenth to the Twentieth Century,* edited by Domna C. Stanton, 3–20. Chicago: University of Chicago Press, 1987.

Starobinski, Jean. "The Style of Autobiography." In Olney, *Autobiography,* 73–83.

Stepto, Robert B. *From Behind the Veil: A Study of Afro-American Narrative.* Champaign-Urbana: University of Illinois Press, 1979.

Stewart, Alan, ed. *The Oxford History of Life-Writing.* Vol. 2: *Early Modern.* Oxford: Oxford University Press, 2018.

Strayer, Alison L. "Translator's Note." In *The Years,* by Annie Ernaux, 233–37. New York: Seven Stories Press, 2017.

Sturrock, John. "The New Model Autobiographer." *New Literary History* 9, no. 1 (Autumn 1977): 51–63.

Swedish Academy. "The Nobel Prize in Literature 2022." Nobel Prize Outreach AB 2022. Press release, October 6, 2022. https://www.nobelprize.org/prizes /literature/2022/press-release.

Taylor, Diana. *The Archive and the Repertoire: Performing Cultural Memory in the Americas.* Durham, N.C.: Duke University Press, 2003.

Thomson, Rosemarie Garland. *Extraordinary Bodies: Figuring Physical Disability in American Culture and Literature.* New York: Columbia University Press, 1997.

———. *Freakery: Cultural Spectacles of the Extraordinary Body.* New York: New York University Press, 1996.

———. "Integrating Disability, Transforming Feminist Theory." *NWSA Journal* 14, no. 3 (2002): 1–32.

Thumerel, Fabrice. "Entretien d'Annie Ernaux avec Philippe Lejeune." In *Annie Ernaux: Une œuvre de l'entre-deux,* edited by Fabrice Thumerel, 253–58. Arras: Artois Presses Université, 2004.

Van den Hengel, Louis. "'Zoegraphy': Per/forming Posthuman Lives." *Biography* 35, no. 1 (Winter 2012): 1–20.

Van der Kolk, Bessel. *The Body Keeps the Score: Brain, Mind, and Body in the Healing of Trauma.* New York: Penguin, 2014.

Van Egdom, Kevin. "Re-Constructing the Past: A Critical Discourse Analysis of Three Alcohol Memoirs." MA thesis, Royal Roads University, Canada, 2020.

Vernon, Alex. *Arms and the Self: War, the Military, and Autobiographical Writing.* Kent, Ohio: Kent State University Press, 2005.

———. "Submission and Resistance to the Self as Soldier: Tim O'Brien's Vietnam War Memoir." *a/b: Auto/Biography Studies* 17, no. 2 (2002): 161–79.

Vipond, Evan. "Becoming Culturally (Un)intelligible: Exploring the Terrain of Trans Life Writing." *a/b: Auto/Biography Studies* 34, no. 1 (2019): 19–43.

Voloshinov, V. N. *Marxism and the Philosophy of Language.* Translated by Ladislav Matejka and I. R. Titunik. New York: Seminar Press, 1973.

Waal, Edmund de. *The Hare with Amber Eyes: A Hidden Inheritance.* New York: Picador, 2010.

Wagner-Egelhaaf, Martina, ed. *Handbook of Autobiography/Autofiction,* 3 vols. Berlin: De Gruyter, 2019.

Waldman, Katy. "Alison Bechdel's Ultimate Workout." *New Yorker,* May 10, 2021, 59–62.

Wanzo, Rebecca. *The Content of Our Caricature: African American Comic Art and Political Belonging.* New York: New York University Press, 2020.

Watson, Julia. "Autographic Disclosures and Genealogies of Desire in Alison Bechdel's *Fun Home.*" *Biography* 31, no. 1 (Winter 2008): 27–58.

Bibliography

————. "Drawing Is the Best Medicine: Somatic Dis-ease and Graphic Revenge in Miriam Katin's *Letting It Go*." In *Graphic Medicine*, edited by Erin La Cour and Anna Poletti, 147–67. Honolulu: University of Hawai'i Press, 2022.

————. "The Exquisite Ironies of Philippe Lejeune: Nine Auto-Anti-Theses." In "Cher Philippe: A Festschrift for Philippe Lejeune," special issue, *European Journal of Life Writing* 7 (2018): 9–18. https://ejlw.eu/article/view/319 10/29318.

————. "Manthia Diawara's Autoethnographic Forays in Memoir and Film from 'Counter-' to 'Strong' to 'Beyond.'" In "Self/Culture/Writing: Autoethnography in the 21st Century," edited by Lisa Ortiz-Vilarelle, special issue, *Life Writing*, 18, no. 3 (2021): 317–35.

————. "Ordering the Family: Genealogy as Autobiographical Pedigree." In Smith and Watson, *Getting a Life*, 297–323.

————. "Strategic Autoethnography and American Ethnicity Debates: The Metrics of Authenticity in *When I Was Puerto Rican*." In "Women's Life Writing and Diaspora," special issue, *Life Writing* 10, no. 2 (2013): 129–50.

Weheliye, Alexander Ghedi. *Habeas Viscus: Racializing Assemblages, Biopolitics, and Black Feminist Theories of the Human*. Durham, N.C.: Duke University Press, 2014.

Weintraub, Karl Joachim. *The Value of the Individual: Self and Circumstance in Autobiography*. Chicago: University of Chicago Press, 1978.

Wells, Susan. "Freud's Rat Man and the Case Study: Genre in Three Keys." *New Literary History* 34, no. 2 (Spring 2003): 353–66.

Wexner Center. "International Tour of Glenn Ligon's Provocative Works Makes Only Midwestern Stop at the Wexner Center." Press release, January 17, 2007. https://wexarts.org/press/international-tour-glenn-ligon-s-provocative-works-makes-only-midwestern-stop-wexner-center.

White, Hayden. *The Content of the Form: Narrative Discourse and Historical Representation*. Baltimore: Johns Hopkins University Press, 1987.

Whitlock, Gillian. "Autographics: The Seeing 'I' of the Comics." *Modern Fiction Studies* 52, no. 4 (Winter 2006): 965–79.

————. "The Diary of a Disaster: Behrouz Boochani's 'Asylum in Space.'" *European Journal of Life Writing* 7 (2018): 176–82. https://ejlw.eu/article/view/31909.

————. "Disciplining the Child: Recent British Academic Memoir." In "Life Writing and the Generations," special issue, *a/b: Auto/Biography Studies* 19, nos. 1–2 (2004): 46–58.

————. "Embridry." *Profession*, 2011, 85–97.

————. *The Intimate Empire: Reading Women's Autobiography*. New York: Cassell, 2000.

————. "Objects and Things in Life Narrative." In *Research Methodologies for*

Auto/Biography Studies, edited by Kate Douglas and Ashley Barnwell, 34. New York: Routledge, 2019.

———. *Postcolonial Life Narratives: Testimonial Transactions.* Oxford: Oxford University Press, 2015.

———. *Soft Weapons: Autobiography in Transit.* Chicago: University of Chicago Press, 2007.

Whitted, Qiana. "Comics and Emmett Till." In *Picturing Childhood: Youth in Transnational Comics,* edited by Mark Heimermann and Brittany Tullis, 70–91. Austin: University of Texas Press, 2017. Also available at the Emmett Till Project, https://www.emmetttillproject.com/home2.

Wiegman, Robyn. "In the Margins with *The Argonauts.*" *Angelaki* 23, no. 1 (2018): 209–13.

———. "Our America: Nativism, Modernism, and Pluralism." *American Literature* 69, no. 2 (June 1997): 432–33.

Williams, Alex. "Addiction Memoirs Are a Genre in Recovery." *New York Times,* February 13, 2020.

Williams, Raymond. *The Long Revolution.* London: Chatto and Windus, 1961.

Wingrove, Elizabeth. "Interpellating Sex." *Signs: Journal of Women in Culture and Society* 24, no. 4 (Summer 1999): 869–93.

Winstead, Karen A., ed. *The Oxford History of Life-Writing.* Vol. 1: *The Middle Ages.* Oxford: Oxford University Press, 2020.

Winter, Jessica. "Essay: Our Autofiction Fixation." *New York Times Book Review,* March 14, 2021.

Wolf, Gary. "The Data-Driven Life." *New York Times Magazine,* April 28, 2010, 38–45. https://www.nytimes.com/2010/05/02/magazine/02self-measurement-t.html.

Wong, Hertha D. Sweet. "First-Person Plural: Subjectivity and Community in Native American Women's Autobiography." In *Women, Autobiography, Theory: A Reader,* edited by Sidonie Smith and Julia Watson, 168–78. Madison: University of Wisconsin Press, 1998.

———. *Sending My Heart Back across the Years: Tradition and Innovation in Native American Autobiography.* New York: Oxford University Press, 1992.

Wong, Sau-Ling Cynthia. "Immigrant Autobiography: Some Questions of Definition and Approach." In Eakin, *American Autobiography,* 142–70.

Wood, James. "Total Recall: Karl Ove Knausgaard's *My Struggle.*" *New Yorker,* August 6, 2012. http://www.newyorker.com/magazine/2012/08/13/total-recall.

Woodhull, Winifred. *Transfigurations of the Maghreb: Feminism, Decolonization, and Literatures in France.* Minneapolis: University of Minnesota Press, 1993.

Bibliography

Woodward, Kathleen. *Aging and Its Discontents: Freud and Other Fictions.* Bloomington: Indiana University Press, 1991.

———. "Aging in the Anthropocene: The View from and beyond Margaret Drabble's *The Dark Flood Rises.*" In *Literature and Aging,* edited by Elizabeth Barry with Margery Vibe Skagen, 37–64. Cambridge: D.S. Brewer: 2020.

———, ed. *Figuring Age: Women, Bodies, Generations.* Bloomington: Indiana University Press, 1999.

Yaeger, Patricia. "Introduction: Dreaming of Infrastructure." *PMLA* 122, no. 1 (January 2007): 9–26.

Yagoda, Ben. *Memoir: A History.* New York: Riverhead Books, 2009.

Yates, Frances A. *The Art of Memory.* Chicago: University of Chicago Press, 1966.

Yelin, Hannah. *Celebrity Memoir: From Ghostwriting to Gender Politics.* London, Palgrave Macmillan, 2020.

Yellin, Jean Fagan. *Harriet Jacobs: A Life.* New York: Basic Civitas Books, 2004.

Yergeau, Melanie. *Authoring Autism: On Rhetoric and Neurological Queerness.* Durham, N.C.: Duke University Press, 2018.

Young, Michael W., and Noel Stanley. "Sporting Auto/biography." In Jolly, *Encyclopedia of Life Writing,* 2: 837–40.

Publication History

Material in the discussion of autoethnography in chapter 1 is adapted from Julia Watson, "Manthia Diawara's Autoethnographic Forays in Memoir and Film from 'Counter-' to 'Strong' to 'Beyond,'" in "Self/Culture/Writing: Autoethnography in the 21st Century," edited by Lisa Ortiz-Vilarelle, special issue, *Life Writing* 18, no. 3 (2021): 317–35. Copyright 2021 Julia Watson. Courtesy of Informa UK Limited, trading as Taylor and Francis Group 2021; reprinted by permission of Taylor and Francis Ltd, https://www.tandfonline.com/.

The discussion of relationality and other aspects of subjectivity in chapter 2 is adapted in part from Sidonie Smith, "Theorizing the Subject," in *The Oxford Encyclopedia of Literature* (Oxford: Oxford University Press, 2020). http://dx.doi.org/10.1093/acrefore/9780190201098.013.1132.

New material in the section on identity in chapter 2 is adapted from Sidonie Smith, "Autobiographical Inscription and the Identity Assemblage," in *Inscribed Identities: Writing as Self-Realization,* ed. Joan Ramon Resina (London: Routledge, 2019), 75–90. Reprinted by permission of Taylor and Francis Group.

Discussion of autobiographical spaces in chapter 2 is adapted from Julia Watson, "The Spaces of Autobiographical Narrative," in *Räume des Selbst. Selbstzeugnisforschung transkulturell* (Selbstzeugnisse der Neuzeit 19), ed. Andreas Bähr/Peter Burschel/Gabriele Jancke (Köln/Weimar/Wien: Böhlau, 2007), 13–25.

Chapter 6 includes material adapted from Sidonie Smith and Julia Watson, "Autobiographical Reckonings in America's Restless Twenty-First Century," in *The Divided States: Unraveling National Identities in the Twenty-First Century,* ed. Laura J. Beard and Ricia Anne Chansky (Madison: University of Wisconsin Press, 2023), 296–324.

Discussion of visual, performance, pieced, and multimedia art is adapted from Sidonie Smith and Julia Watson, "Introduction: Mapping Women's Self-Representation at Visual/Textual Interfaces," in *Interfaces: Women's Visual and*

Performance Autobiography in the Twentieth Century, ed. Sidonie Smith and Julia Watson (Ann Arbor: University of Michigan Press, 2002), 1–46.

Discussions of digital life writing and self-preservation are adapted from Sidonie Smith and Julia Watson, "Virtually Me: A Toolkit about Online Self-Presentation," in *Identity Technologies: Constructing the Self Online,* ed. Anna Poletti and Julie Rak (Madison: University of Wisconsin Press, 2014), 70–94.

Material on archives in this book has been reprinted and adapted with permission from Sidonie Smith and Julia Watson, "Alternative, Imaginary, and Affective Archives of the Self in Women's Life Writing," *Tulsa Studies in Women's Literature* 40, no. 1 (Spring 2021): 15–43. Copyright 2021 the University of Tulsa.

Material on autofiction is drawn in part from Sidonie Smith and Julia Watson, "A Personal Introduction to *Life Writing in the Long Run,*" in *Life Writing in the Long Run: A Smith and Watson Autobiography Studies Reader* (Ann Arbor: Michigan Publishing, 2016), xix–li.

Material on Philippe Lejeune and diary is adapted from Julia Watson, "The Exquisite Ironies of Philippe Lejeune: Nine Auto-Anti-Theses," in "Cher Philippe: A Festschrift for Philippe Lejeune," special issue, *European Journal of Life Writing* 7 (2018): 9–18. https://ejlw.eu/article/view/31910/29318.

Index

Abandoned Baobab, The: The Autobiography of a Senegalese Woman (Ken Bugul), 101, 223
Abbey, Edward, 235
Abdul-Jabbar, Kareem, 217
Abelard, Peter, 267
Abeng: A Novel (Cliff), 33, 224
Abina and the Important Men (Getz), 255
able-bodiedness, embodiment and, 89–90
ableist norms, 230
Aboriginal Mother Tells of the Old and the New, An (Labumore), 137
Abramović, Marina, 139
Absolutely True Diary of a Part-Time Indian, The (Alexie), 43
Abu-Jaber, Diana, 248
Abu-Jamal, Mumia, 61
academic memoir, 198–200
Acts of Narrative Resistance: Women's Autobiographical Writings in the Americas (Beard), 308
Adams, Clover, 118
Adams, Henry, 12, 117–18, 206, 209, 224
Adams, Lorraine, 61, 277
Adams, Robert, 147
Adams, Timothy Dow, 140, 155, 214
Adams, Tony E., 26
addiction, food writing and, 248
addiction narrative, 200–204; models of, 201–2; self-help, 294
addressees, 131–33
Adichie, Chimamanda Ngozi, 257, 300
Adielé, Faith, 239
adoption narrative, 204–5, 242
affect, embodiment and, 87

affiliation narrative, 240, 242
Africa: life writing from, 33, 250; oral genealogy narratives and, 5; oral narrative in, 250
African American comics, 255
African American identity, 65
African American life writing, 249; voice and, 127–28
African American women preachers, 303
African American women writers, polyvocality and, 57
African child soldiers, war memoirs of, 314–16
After the Wall: Confessions from an East German Childhood and the Life that Came Next (Hensel), 81–82
After This, Silence (Ab Jetzt Ist Ruhe) (Brasch), 42
"Ageing in the Anthropocene: The View From and Beyond" (Woodward), 207
agency(ies), 94–102; defined, 94; disidentification and, 98–99; distribution of, 99–100; evolving concepts of, 94–95; ideology, power, and, 95–97; in life narratives, 169–70; postcolonial, challenges of, 101; postcolonial theory and, 95; reading for politics of, 100–102; redefinitions of, 95–99; social practices and, 98–99; tactics, strategies and, 97–98
aging, narratives of, 205–7
aging and life cycle narrative, 205–7
Água Viva (Lispector), 24
Ahmed, Sarah, 87
Ai Lao, 57
Ai Qing, 57

397

398 Index

Ai Weiwei, 57, 276
AIDS, memoirs of living/dying with, 89–90
AIDS-related autothanatography, 211
"Ain't I a Woman" (Truth), 268
Akerman, Chantal, 243
Akhmatova, Anna, 46–47
Alaimo, Stacy, 56
alcohol addiction: memoirs about, 201–2. *See also* addiction narrative
Alcoholics Anonymous (AA), 201–2
Alcoholics Anonymous narratives, 226
Alexander, Jon, 314
Alexie, Sherman, 43
Alfred and Emily (Lessing), 143
Ali, Hana Yasmin, 307
Ali, Mohammed, 307
All but the Waltz: Essays on a Montana Family (Blew), 236
Allen, Paula Gunn, 3
Allende, Isabel, 296
All Our Families: Disability Lineage and the Future of Kinship (Fink), 234
All You Can Ever Know: A Memoir (Chung), 205
"Almost Famous: The Rise of the 'Nobody' Memoir'" (Adams), 277
alterbiography, 209
Althusser, Louis, 52, 115, 328n3; on agency, 95–96; on subjectivity, 195–96
Álvarez, Noe, 307
Alzheimer's disease, 84–85, 231
Amaechi, John, 218
American Born Chinese (Yang), 254
American Childhood, An (Dillard), 83
Americanization of Edward Bok, The: The Autobiography of a Dutch Boy Fifty Years After (Bok), 109, 129, 222
American past, varying remembrances of, 42–43
Among the White Moon Faces (Lim), 251
"Anarchy and the Sex Question" (Goldman), 269
ancestry, fictions of, 78
Anderson, Laurie, 139, 266

Anderson, Paul Thomas, 246
Andrews, Tarren, 264
Andrews, William L., 57, 303, 330n2
Angela of Foligno, 304
Angela's Ashes (film), 245
Angela's Ashes (McCourt), 114–15, 223, 327n2, 328n7
Angelou, Maya, 11, 61, 206, 221, 296, 314
animalographies, 210
Animal, Vegetable, Miracle: A Year of Food Life (Kingsolver), 237, 248
Anne, Lady Halkett, 12
Anne Frank: The Diary of a Young Girl (Frank), 176
Annie John (Kincaid), 15
anorexia: food writing and, 248; life narrative and, 208, 215
Anthropocene, 235–38; defined, 330n4; in life narratives, 237
anthropology, decolonization and, 25
Antin, Mary, 238, 273
antiracist protest, 22–23
An Unquiet Mind (Jamison), 12
Anzaldúa, Gloria, 21–22, 70, 79, 116–17, 269, 298
Apess, William, 9–10, 263
Apologia Pro Vita Sua: Being a History of His Religious Opinions (Newman), 194, 226
apology, 207; life writing as, 81; McNamara and, 106
Apology (Plato), 207
"Apology for Raimond Sebond" (Montaigne), 207
Appadurai, Arjun, 99
Apperley, Thomas, 122
Apted, Michael, 278
Aptheker, Bettina, 317
Archive and the Repertoire, The: Performing Cultural Memory in the Americas (Taylor), 144
Archive Fever (Derrida), 141
archives, 141–46; alternative versions of, 143–44; Big Data project and, 144; born-digital, 144–45; digital, 144–45;

Index

399

formerly enslaved people and, 143; of
memory, 184; online, 171; reading life
narratives and, 170–71
Arenas, Reinaldo, 88, 245
Are You My Mother? A Comic Drama
(Bechdel), 49, 242
Argentina: "dirty" war in, 47; political life
narratives from, 292
Argonauts, The (Nelson), 24, 299
Arias, Arturo, 210
Art of Memoir, The (Karr), 272
Art of the Commonplace, The (Berry), 248
Arthur, Paul Longley, 73
"Ascent of Mount Ventoux, The"
(Petrarch), 305
Ashe, Arthur, 218
assemblage: agency and, 99; embodiment
as, 91–93; relationality and, 55–56
assemblage theory: "doing" identity and,
71–73; reading life narrative through,
75
assimilation, stories of, 106
At Eternity's Gate (Schnabel), 14
Athill, Diana, 206
Auburn, Cat, 19–20
Augustine, 49, 130, 225, 272, 304–5;
confessional narratives of, 81; letters
of, 267
Auschwitz and After (Delbo), 47
Auster, Paul, 32, 240, 241
Austerlitz (Sebald), 318
Australia, Indigenous stories of, 48
Australians, "song lines" of, 5
authenticity, reading for, 172–73
"Authentic Narrative, An" (Bradley), 147
Authoring Autism (Yergeau), 90
authority: establishing in life narratives,
173; experience and, 61–62
author–reader relationship, Lejeune and,
16
authorship, cultural meaning of, 181
autie-biography, 209
autism, life narratives and, 207–8
autobioethnography, 210, 274
autobiografiction, 32

autobiographical acts, 103–52; addressees
and, 131–33; archives and, 141–46;
autobiographical "I"s and, 111–18 (*see
also* autobiographical "I"s; autobiographical narration; relationality);
coaxers, coaches, and coercers, 104–8;
consumers/audiences and, 146–48;
media and automediality, 138–41;
1990s theorists of, 196; paratextual
apparatuses, 148–52; and patterns of
employment, 135–38; self-inquiry
modes and, 133–35; situatedness of,
103; storytelling sites and, 108–11
autobiographical comics, 331n12; "I"s of,
118–19
*Autobiographical Documentary in
America from the 1960s to the Present*
(Lane), 330n10
autobiographical ethics, 242
autobiographical "I"s, 111–18; absent
other and, 131; distinguishing,
173–74; ideological, 115–17; "I"s
of autographics, 118–19; narrated,
112–13; narrating, 112; narrating
"I"–narrated "I" distinction, 113–15;
negotiated, 121; online, 121–23,
185–86; quantified, 123–24; reading,
117–18; "real" or historical, 111–12;
variations in, 118–24; witnessing,
119–20
autobiographical narration: spatiality of,
137; voice in, 124–29
autobiographical narrators, versus
historians, 9–10
autobiographical subject, 39–102; absent
other and, 130; agency(ies), 95–102;
embodiment, 82–95; experience,
58–64; historical others and, 129–30;
identity, 64–75; memory, 39–50; relationality, 50–58, 129–31; spatiality,
75–82. *See also* agency(ies); embodiment; experience; identity; memory;
relationality; spatiality
autobiographical truth, 153–65; as collaborative, 163–64; criteria for assessing,

156–58; Gandhi and, 165; hoaxing and, 154–56; reading for, 172–73

Autobiographical Voices (Lionnet), 57

autobiography: clarification of terms for, 7–8; Dilthey's definition of, 193; exclusionary aspect of, 6–7; first use of term, 4; "great man" focus of, 193; Greek roots of, 3–4; heteronymic, 32; high culture, 194; versus life narrative, 153; versus memoir, 271–72; in North American West, 76–77; postcolonial theory and, 69; pre-Enlightenment use of, 4; reader expectations for, 36; serial, 114; Western use of term, 6

Autobiography (Martineau), 6

Autobiography (Mill), 6

Autobiography, An; or, The Story of My Experiments with Truth (Gandhi), 306

Autobiography and Decolonization (Holden), 327n9

Autobiography of a Face (Grealy), 67, 89

Autobiography of Alice B. Toklas, The (Stein), 64

Autobiography of a Runaway Slave, The (Montéjo), 302

Autobiography of a Sexually Emancipated Communist Woman (Kollontai), 116

Autobiography of a Yogi, The (Yogananda), 306

Autobiography of Benjamin Franklin, The (Franklin), 134, 136, 194

Autobiography of Malcolm X, The (Haley), 68, 106, 155, 226, 307

Autobiography of Maxim Gorky: My Childhood, In the World, My Universities (Gorky), 221

Autobiography of My Mother, The (Kincaid), 131

"Autobiography of Those Who Do Not Write, The" (Lejeune), 103

Autobiography of W. E. B. Du Bois, The: A Soliloquy on Viewing My Life from the Last Decade of Its First Century (Du Bois), 49

autobiography variants, 209–11

autobiography–biography boundary, blurring of, 130

autobiomediality, digital self-presentation and, 140–41

autocritique, 19. *See also* autotheory

autoethnography, 5, 24–29, 209; colonialism and, 27; emergence of, 24–25; temporality and, 27–28; visual media and, 28–29

autofabrication, 32

autofiction, 29–37, 209; defined, 29; Doubrovsky and, 29–32; European context of, 34–35; versus related terms, 32

autofiction, 32

autographics: "I"s of, 118–19. *See also* graphic memoir

autogynography, 209

autohagiography, 210

auto-heteronymic fiction, 32

automediality, 138–41, 174–75; digital self-presentation and, 140–41

autonomy, versus relationality, 330n4

auto-oral history, 277

autopathography, 234

autopics, examples of, 245

autosomatography, 84, 234

autothanatography, 211–12

autotheory: definitions of, 19–20; life narrative and, 17–24; strands of, 20–23

autotopography, 77, 212–13, 235

autrebiography, 209

avatar, 122–23, 328n5

Aviv, Rachel, 213

Awkward, Michael, 198

Bâ, Mariama, 224

Bad Blood (Sage), 198

Bad Feminist: Essays (Gay), 269

Baena, Rosalia, 231, 234, 247

Baker, Bobby, 228

Baker, Russell, 221

Bakhtin, Mikhail, 51, 57, 65, 126, 196

Bal, Mieke, 77, 213

Index

Baldwin, James, 14, 62, 88
Barad, Karen, 56, 154
Barbary Coast pirate narratives, 147
Barbour, John D., 304
Bardem, Javier, 245–46
Barnes, Julian, 257
Barnet, Miguel, 302
Barrios de Chungara, Domitila, 128
Barry, Lynda, 199, 210, 228
Barthes, Roland, 21, 29, 135
Bauby, Jean-Dominique, 232
Baudrillard, Jean, 156, 229
Baxter, Katherine, 19–20
Bayley, John, 84
Beah, Ishmael, 315–16, 317, 331n20
Beard, Laura J., 308
bearing witness, voice and, 128–29. *See also* witness narrative; witnessing
Beaujour, Michel, 295
Beautiful Boy: A Father's Journey through His Son's Addiction (Sheff), 106, 202
Beautiful Country (Wang), 274–75
Beauvoir, Simone de, 22, 55, 205–6, 269
Bechdel, Alison, 49, 142, 228, 242, 253, 297, 299
Beckett, Samuel, 118–19
Becoming a Man: Half a Life Story (Monette), 259
Before Night Falls (Arenas), 88, 245
Before Night Falls (film/Schnabel), 245
Being Heumann: An Unrepentant Memoir of a Disability Rights Activist (Heumann), 23
Being in Pictures (Leonard), 140
Benjamin, Walter, 20
Bennett, Jane, 93, 99–100
Benstock, Shari, 58, 131
Bequest and Betrayal: Memoirs of a Parent's Death (Miller), 22, 198
Berlin Childhood around 1900 (Benjamin), 20, 27
Berlin Chronicle, A (Benjamin), 20
Bernstein, Harry, 206
Berry, Wendell, 248
Bérubé, Michael, 200

Berzon, Betty, 298
Between Memory and History (Nora), 45
Between the World and Me (Coates), 132, 269
Beverley, John, 307
Beyala, Calixthe, 224
Beyond Feminist Aesthetics: Feminist Literature and Social Change (Felski), 225
Bhabha, Homi, 26–27, 79
bhakti poetry, 5
Biemann, Ursula, 80
Big Data projects, 244, 295
bildungsroman, 224–25; characteristics of, 223; development of, 15, 16; examples of, 134; in postcolonial life writing, 33–34; in twentieth century, 16. *See also* coming-of-age life narrative
binary gender system, Butler and, 66
Binky Brown Meets the Holy Virgin Mary (Green), 252–53
biocularity, 118, 251, 238n4
biofiction, versus novelistic mode, 13–14
biographer, versus self-life narrator, 11–12
biography: life narrative and, 10–15; "new," 13
Biography: A Brief History (Hamilton), 10
biomythography, 27–28, 70, 213
biopic, 14, 326n12
Bird, Isabella, 314
Black Boy: A Record of Childhood and Youth (Wright), 62, 221
Black Elk Speaks: Being the Life Story of a Holy Man of the Oglala Sioux as Told to John G. Neihardt, 106, 131, 219
Blackfeet Nation, 264
Blackout: Remembering the Things I Drank to Forget (Hepola), 201
"Black Wall Street" massacre, 43
Black, White, and Jewish: Autobiography of a Shifting Self (Walker), 239, 241
Black women, inner peace tradition of, 86

Black Women's Yoga History: Memoirs of Inner Peace (Evans), 86

Blew, Mary Clearman, 236

Blind Rage: Letters to Helen Keller, 23

Blossoms and Bones: Drawing a Life Back Together (Krans), 248

Blow Your House Down: A Story of Family, Feminism, and Treason (Frangello), 300

Bly, Robert, 306–7

Boardman, Kathleen A., 76

Bochner, Arthur P., 26

Bodily Natures: Science, Environment, and the Material Self (Alaimo), 56

body/embodiment, questions for, 175

Body Keeps the Score, The: Brain, Mind, and Body in the Healing of Trauma (Van der Kolk), 85–86

body narratives, 104–5

Body, Remember: A Memoir (Fries), 88, 298

Boelhower, William, 238

Bok, Edward William, 109, 129, 222, 238

Bolter, Jay David, 329

Bone Black: Memories of Girlhood (hooks), 22

Bonhoeffer, Dietrich, 267–68

Boochani, Behrouz, 228

Book of My Life, The (Cardano), 5, 18

BOOM! Manufacturing Memoir for the Popular Market (Rak), 272–73

Borden, Mary, 315

borderlands, Anzaldúa's concept of, 79

Borderlands/La Frontera: The New Mestiza (Anzaldúa), 22, 70, 116–17, 269

Borderlands of Culture: Américo Paredes and the Transnational Imaginary (Saldívar), 13

border tensions, 79

Borges, Jorge Luis, 33

Bornstein, Kate, 140, 299

Borrowed Time: An AIDS Memoir (Monette), 130, 259

Boswell, James, 312

Bourdain, Anthony, 247, 314

Bourgeois, Louise, 213

Burroughs, Augusten, 299

Bouton, Jim, 217

Bowring, Richard, 325n4

Boyhood: Scenes from Provincial Life (Coetzee), 68–69

Boylan, Jennifer Finney, 299

Brabner, Joyce, 231

Bradley, Bill, 218

Bradley, Eliza, 147

Braiding Sweetgrass: Indigenous Wisdom, Scientific Knowledge, and the Teachings of Plants (Kimmerer), 264–65

Braidotti, Rosi, 91

Brakhage, Stan, 246

Brandt-Van Warmelo, Johanna, 229

Brant, Clare, 274

Brasch, Marion, 42

Braziel, Jana Evans, 210

breakdown and breakthrough narrative, 213–15

Brent, Linda. *See* Jacobs, Harriet A.

Breytenbach, Breyten, 292

Brief Wondrous Life of Oscar Wao, The (Diaz), 15–16

British Empire, Anglophone autobiographical practices in, 251

Brodkey, Harold, 89–90, 212, 233

Brodzki, Bella, 148, 309

Broinowski, Anna, 155

Brontë, Charlotte, 15

Broom, Sarah M., 65

Brophy, Sarah, 308

Brostoff, Alex, 24

Brother, I'm Dying (Danticat), 242, 257–58

Brothers and Keepers (Wideman), 12, 130

Broughton, Trev Lynn, 327n9

Browder, Laura, 155

Brown, Don, 275

Brown, Jerry, 301

Browne, Thomas, 18, 270

Broyard, Anatole, 233, 240

Broyard, Bliss, 240

Index

Brueggemann, Brenda, 234
Bruś, Teresa, 140
Buell, Lawrence, 76, 235
Bugul, Ken. *See* Ken Bugul
bulimia: food writing and, 248; narratives of, 215
Bunkers, Suzanne L., 227, 229
Bunyan, John, 226, 305
Bunyan, Paul, 138
Burgos-Debray, Elisabeth, 101
Burke, Tarana, 270
Burned Alive: A Victim of the Law of Men (Souad), 155
Burney, Charles, 312
Burroughs, Augusten, 202, 272, 294, 296, 299
Burst of Light, A (Lorde), 212, 231
Burt, Raymond L., 15–16
Burton, Robert, 18, 134
Buss, Helen M., 229
But Enough about Me: Why We Read Other People's Lives (Miller), 198
Butler, Judith, 52, 53–55; on binary gender system, 66; on identity, 98; on relationality, 52–55

Cambridge Companion to Autobiography, The, 197
Camera Lucida (Barthes), 21, 140
Campbell, Hillary Fitzgerald, 255
Campbell, Nicola I., 243
Campion, Jane, 243
Canadian autobiographical writing, 250
Cancer Journals, The (Lorde), 86, 212, 213, 231
Canícula: Snapshots of a Girlhood en la Frontera (Cantú), 140, 274
Can These Bones Live? (Brodzki), 148
Can't We Talk about Something More Pleasant? (Chast), 84–85
Cantú, Norma Elia, 140, 274
Caouette, Jonathan, 244–45
captivity narrative, 147–48, 183, 215–16, 312
Cardano, Girolamo, 5, 18

Cardell, Kylie, 226, 229
Cardinal, Marie, 137
Career Narratives and Academic Womanhood (Ortiz-Vilarelle, ed.), 199
Carmelita Tropicana. *See* Troyano, Alina
Carolina Maria de Jesus, 108
Carr, David, 202, 294
Carrère, Emmanuel, 35, 296, 307
Carter, Forrest, 154
Caruth, Cathy, 308
Casanova, Giacomo, 61, 88
case study, 216–17
Catcher in the Rye, The (Salinger), 15
Cavarero, Adriana, 50
Cave, Nick, 265
Cavendish, Margaret, 12
celebrity life narrative, 217–19
Cellini, Benvenuto, 5, 194
censorship, editorial, 107
Certeau, Michel de, on agency, 97
Chaney, Michael A., 119
Change Series, The: Faith Ringgold's 100-Pound Weight-Loss Quilt (Ringgold), 113
Chapelle, Dave, 139
Charke, Charlotte, 87, 298
Charlotte Salomon and the Theatre of Memory (Pollock), 49–50
Chast, Roz, 84–85
Chatwin, Bruce, 314
Cheever, John, 202
Chekhov, Anton, 209
Chen, Mel, 92
Chernin, Kim, 12, 241
Chester, Suzanne, 58, 131
"Chicago Project" (Glass), 278
Chicanx life writing, 249
Child, Julia, 247
Child, Lydia Maria, 63
Child Called "It," A: The Lost Boy (Pelzer), 241, 317
Child of the Dark: The Diary of Carolina Maria de Jesus, 108
child sexual abuse: settler colonialism and, 264. *See also* sexual abuse

404 Index

Child Soldier: Fighting for My Life (Keitetsi), 316
child soldiers, war memoirs of, 314–16
Childhood, A: The Biography of a Place (Crews), 222
childhood trauma, scriptotherapy and, 294
Childhood, Youth, Dependency (Ditlevsen), 222, 266–67
China: life writing in, 250; self-narrative in, 5
Chitten, Laurel, 245
Chodorow, Nancy, 51
Choy, Catherine Ceniza, 205
Christianity, spiritual autobiography and, 304–6
Christian spirituality, 18
Chronicles, Volume One (Dylan), 217–18
Chung, Nicole, 205
Chute, Hillary L., 118, 255, 310, 328n5
Cicero, 267
Circling My Mother (Gordon), 241
Citizen: An American Lyric (Rankine), 24, 44–45, 138
Clandestine Diary of an Ordinary Iraqi, The (Salam Pax), 227
Clapton, Eric, 217
Clare, Stephanie D., 22–23
Clarke, Austin, 247
Clarke, Liz, 255
Cleaver, Eldridge, 109, 268
Clemens, Justin, 122
Clemens, Paul, 239
Cliff, Michelle, 33, 224, 296
Clifford, James, 25
Clinton, Hillary Rodham, 61, 277
Close to the Knives: A Memoir of Disintegration (Wojnarowicz), 89–90
closure, reading for, 176–77
coach, roles of, 104–8, 175–76
Coates, Ta-Nehisi, 132, 269
coaxer, 104–8; roles of, 103, 107–8, 175–76; social media/algorithms and, 108
coaxing: examples of, 104–6; in ghostwritten narratives, 106

coercer, 104–8; ethical issues and, 107–8; roles of, 175–76
coercing, examples of, 104–5
Coetzee, J. M., 36, 68–69, 113, 210, 296
coherence, reading for, 176–77
Colbert, Stephen, 154, 265
Cole, Teju, 140, 228–29
Coleridge, Samuel Taylor, 17, 294
collaborative life writing, 106–7, 177, 219–20
Collard, Cyril, 246
collective remembering, 44–46
colonial gaze, critiques of, 196–97
colonial imperialism, graphic memoir and, 255
colonialism, agency and, 100–101
colonized subject: autoethnography and, 24–25; narratives of, 242–43; postcolonial theory and, 79
Colored People (Gates), 199
Color of Water, The: A Black Man's Tribute to His White Mother (McBride), 239
Comfort Woman: A Filipina's Story of Prostitution and Slavery under the Japanese Military (Henson), 317
comic books: life narratives as, 180–81. *See also* graphic memoir
Coming of Age, The (Beauvoir), 206
coming-of-age life narrative, 220–25. *See also* bildungsroman
coming-out life narrative, 88, 298
Commitment, The: Love, Sex, Marriage, and My Family (Savage), 299
Community of One, A (Danahay), 327n9
Compleat Gentleman, The: or, Directions for the Education of Youth as to Their Breeding at Home and Traveling Abroad (Gailhard), 313
composite "I," 120
computational self, 92–93
Condé, Maryse, 33, 79, 224
Confederated Salish-Kootenai Tribes, 264
confession, 225–26
confessional narratives, 81. *See also*

Index

405

Confessions (Augustine); *Confessions* (Rousseau)
Confessions (Augustine), 5, 39–40, 49, 105, 194, 225, 272, 304, 305, 306; absent other and, 130; memory in, 41
Confessions (Rousseau), 5, 27, 68, 194
Confessions of Aleister Crowley, The: An Autohagiography (Crowley), 209
Confessions of an English Opium Eater (De Quincey), 17, 201
"Confessions of a Ventriloquist" (Lotringer), 265–66
Conrad, Joseph, 209
Content of Our Caricature, The: African American Comic Art and Political Belonging (Wanzo), 255
Conundrum (Morris), 299
conversion narrative, 226, 312
Conway, Kellyanne, 154
Cornered (Piper), 78
Cost of Living, The (Levy), 297
Costanza, George, 154
Couldry, Nick, 329n14
Country Girl: A Memoir (O'Brien), 221
Country of My Skull (Krog), 245, 261, 317
Couser, G. Thomas, 37, 61–62, 178, 198, 207, 210–11, 326n7; on affiliation narratives, 240; on disability life narratives, 229–30; on disaffiliation narratives, 241; on graphic medicine, 233; on graphic narrative, 83–84; on illness narratives, 234; on leverage of nonfiction, 156; on life writing terminology, 8; nobody memoir and, 277; on overview of memoir, 272
COVID pandemic: bodies disrupted by, 90; diary accounts of, 228
Crazy Brave: A Memoir (Harjo), 307
creolization, Glissant's concept of, 57
Crews, Harry, 222
"crip-of-color critique," 234–35
"crisis comics," 254
critical essays: increasing number of, 193. *See also* New Critics

criticism: postmodern, 195; reframings of, 194–97
Cromwell, Thomas, 13–14
Crowley, Aleister, 209
"Crows Written on the Poplars: Autocritical Autobiographies" (Vizenor), 21
Crying in H Mart (Zauner), 241
Culley, Margot, 227
cultural factors, autobiographical "I" and, 115
cultural identity, 67
cultural otherness, 27
Cultural Politics of Emotion, The (Ahmed), 87
culture, memory and, 40–41
Culture and Imperialism (Said), 251
cummings, e. e., 226
Curtis, Bryan, 218
Cvetkovich, Ann, 144

Dakota: A Spiritual Geography (Norris), 110, 307
Dampier, Helen, 229
Danahay, Martin A., 327n9
Dangarembga, Tsitsi, 33
"Danger of a Single Story, The" (Adichie), 300
Dante Alighieri, 395
Danticat, Edwidge, 242, 258
Dark Child, The (Laye), 33
Darkness Visible: A Memoir of Madness (Styron), 214
Darwin, Charles, 313
Daughter of Han, A: The Autobiography of a Chinese Working Woman (Pruitt), 106
Davey, Moyra, 24
David B, 84, 254
David Copperfield (Dickens), 15
Davies, Dominic, 255
Davis, Angela Y., 71
Davis, Lennard, 234
Davis, Vaginal, 139
Day, Dorothy, 306
Days of Grace (Ashe), 218

death writing, 211–12
DeBaggio, Thomas, 85
Declining to Decline (Gullette), 207
decolonization: anthropology and, 25; subject formation and, 26
Defoe, Daniel, 266
DeKock, Eugene, 261–62
DeKoven, Marianne, 118
Delany, A. Elizabeth, 206
Delany, Sarah, 206
Delbo, Charlotte, 47
Deleuze, Gilles, 98–99
dementia, 84–85
Demos, T. J., 275
Deng, Valentino Achak, 121, 224. See also *What Is the What* (Eggers)
Denton, Andrew, 331n20
De Quincey, Thomas, 17, 201
Deren, Maya, 246
Derounian-Stodola, Kathryn Zabelle, 216
Derrida, Jacques, 95, 141, 195, 210
de Sales, 270
Descartes, René, 6, 18
Desert Notebooks: A Road Map for the End of Time (Ehrenreich), 237
Desert Solitaire (Abbey), 235
Design and Truth in Autobiography (Pascal), 325n5
de Staël, Madame, 5
Detained: A Writer's Prison Diary (Ngũgĩ), 292
dialogism of words, 126
diary, 226–29; addiction and, 203; versus journal, 266; online, 227; simulacrum, 229
Diary of a Bad Year (Coetzee), 210
Diary of a Disaster (Boochani), 228
Diary of a Teenage Girl, The: An Account in Words and Pictures (Gloeckner), 227, 254
diasporas, as political spaces, 79–80
Diawara, Manthia, 28–29, 79, 82, 276
Diaz, Junot, 15–16
Dickens, Charles, 15, 221
Dickinson, Emily, 270

Didion, Joan, 127, 256
"difference," marginalized writing forms and, 51–52
differently-abled bodies, 89–90, 330n3
Dillard, Annie, 83
Dilthey, Wilhelm, 15, 193
Dinesen, Isak, 136
disability: academic life and, 200; critique of term, 330n3; as stigmatizing term, 89, 230, 232
Disability Experiences: Memoirs, Autobiographies, and Other Personal Narratives (Couser and Mintz), 234
disability/illness life narratives, 230–35
disability rights movement, 22–23, 230
Disaster Drawn: Visual Witness, Comics, and Documentary Form (Chute), 255, 310
Discourse on the Method (Descartes), 6
discursive regimes, 60
Dislocating the Color Line (Kawash), 330n2
D'Israeli, Isaac, 4
Ditlevsen, Tove, 222, 266
Divine Comedy (Dante), 305
Diving Bell and the Butterfly, The (Bauby), 232
Djebar, Assia, 33, 128, 224
documemoir, 272
Documenting Trauma in Comics: Traumatic Pasts, Embodied Histories, and Graphic Reportage (Davies and Rifkind), 255
Dodson, David, 44
Donne, John, 134, 270
Don't Ever Tell: Kathy's Story. A True Tale of a Childhood Destroyed by Neglect and Fear (O'Beirne), 301, 331n18
Don't Take Your Love to Town (Ginibi), 137
Dostoyevsky, Fyodor, 15
Doubrovsky, Serge, 29–32; on autobiography versus autofiction, 30–31; autofiction and, 35
Doucet, Julie, 254

Index

407

Douglas, Kate, on trauma narrative, 310
Douglass, Frederick, 61, 127, 133, 222–23, 226, 296
Doyle, Bob, 35
dreaming, ritual, of Indigenous Australians, 134
Dreams from My Father (Obama), 64, 70, 239, 241
Dreams of Trespass: Tales of a Harem Girlhood (Mernissi), 307
Drinking: A Love Story (Knapp), 202, 294–95
Dry: A Memoir (Burroughs), 202, 294
du Bellay, Joachim, 18
Dunlap-Shohl, Peter, 254
Dunne, John Gregory, 256
Dünne, Jörg, 329n13
Duras, Marguerite, 29, 58, 61, 131
Dust Tracks on a Road: An Autobiography (Hurston), 27, 107
"Dyke Manifesto" (Lesbian Avengers), 269
Dylan, Bob, 14, 217

Eagleton, Terry, 198
Eakin, Paul John, 40, 56–57, 67, 83, 156, 244
Eating Words: A Norton Anthology of Food Writing (Gilbert and Porter, eds.), 247
Eaton, Edith Maude, 273
Eat, Pray, Love: One Woman's Search for Everything across Italy, India, and Indonesia (Gilbert), 226, 306
Eberhardt, Isabelle, 314
Ecce Homo (Nietzsche), 19
Eco, Umberto, 148
ecobiography, 235–38
ecocriticism, 235–38
Educated (Westover), 222
education, narratives of, 222–23
Education of Augie Merasty, The: A Residential School Memoir (Merasty), 243
Education of Henry Adams, The (Adams), 12, 118, 206, 209

Education of Little Tree, The (Carter), 154
Effe, Alexandra, 33
Egan, Susanna, 57, 211, 328n9, 330n10
Egdom, Kevin van, 330n1
Eggers, Dave, 32–33, 120–21, 224
Ego-histoires (Nora), 200
Ehrenreich, Ben, 237
Eiseley, Loren C., 138
Elahi, Hasan, 123–24
Elaw, Zilpha, 313
Elegy for a Disease: A Personal and Cultural History of Polio (Finger), 23
Elegy for Iris (Bayley), 84
Eliot, T. S., 270
Ellerby, Janet Mason, 204
Ellis, Carolyn, 26
Ellison, Ralph, 15
Ellroy, James, 256
El Refaie, Elisabeth, 84, 122
embodiment, 82–94; able-bodiedness and, 89–90; affect and, 87; as assemblage, 91–93; autobiography of things and, 90–91; differently-abled bodies and, 89; embodied memory and, 84–85; male, 88; quantification and, 92–93; reading for, 93–94; sexuality and desire and, 87–89; of trauma, 86; trauma, somatic practices, and, 85–87; visible body and, 83–84
"Embridry" (Whitlock), 91
Emecheta, Buchi, 61
Emerson, Ralph Waldo, 306
Emigrants, The (Sebald), 13
Eminent Maricones: Arenas, Lorca, Puig, and Me (Manrique), 298
Eminent Victorians (Strachey), 13
emplotment, patterns of, 187–88
Enlightenment: agency defined by, 94–95; autobiography and, 4–5, 6; and critiques of self-reflexive literature, 18; traditional autobiography and, 20
Enlightenment subject, postmodern challenges to, 6
Enormous Room, The (cummings), 226
enslavement narrative: formerly enslaved

people, archives and, 143; popularity and significance of, 302–3; rethinking, 303. *See also* "slave" narrative

environmental racism, 276–77

environment crisis, trauma narrative and, 310–11

Ephron, Nora, 205

Epileptic (David B), 84, 254

epistolarium, 268

epitext, defined, 186

Equiano, Olaudah, 100, 223, 302

Erasmus, Desiderius, 18

Erauso, Catalina de, 298

Ernaux, Annie, 28–29, 34–35, 89, 211, 227–28, 241–42, 297, 329n2; and reading life narrative differently, 158–59; truth-telling and, 157–63

Erpenbeck, Jenny, 42

erratography, Franklinesque, 210

Escaping Wars and Waves: Encounters with Syrian Refugees (Kugler), 275

Essays (Montaigne), 5, 18, 27, 80–81, 88, 134, 270; absent other and, 130

ethical issues: autobiographical, 242; in collaborative writing, 106–8; in life writing, 156–57, 164, 178–79; relationality and, 53–55

Ethics of Ambiguity (Beauvoir), 55

ethnic/postethnic life narrative, 238–39

ethnocriticism, 265

Evans, Kate, 254, 275

Evans, Stephanie Y., 86

evidence: reading for, 179–80; in self-life-narrative versus biography, 12–13

exile narratives, 238

"Exodus Road, The," 216

experience, 58–64; authority of, 61–62, 180; as constitutive of subject, 59; as discursive, 59–60; as interpretation, 60–61; reading for authority of, 62–64; social nonrecognition of, 62

Export, Valie, 266

ex-slave narrative, 330n2. *See also* "slave" narrative

Fabelmans, The (Spielberg and Kushner), 246

Fabian, Ann, 155

fable, narrative "I" in, 138

Facebook, protocols of, 110

Face Forms in Life-Writing of the Interwar Years (Bruś), 140

Faith, Hope, and Carnage (Cave and O'Hagan), 265

false consciousness, 96

Familiar Letters (Petrarch), 267

Family Frames (Hirsch), 140

family narrative, 239–43; genealogical research and, 239–40

family reunions, as storytelling sites, 109

Family Secrets: Acts of Memory and Imagination (Kuhn), 42, 198

Fanon, Frantz, 101, 196

Fantasia, an Algerian Cavalcade (Djebar), 33

Fate: A Memoir of Family, Risk, and Genetic Research (Wexler), 234

Father and Son: A Study of Two Temperaments (Gosse), 206, 240, 307

Feinberg, Leslie, 299

Fellini, Federico, 243

Felman, Shoshana, 308

Felski, Rita, 225

Felstiner, Mary, 200, 231

"Female Hand in Heian Japan, The" (Bowring), 325n4

"Feminism (Plural)" (Gay), 269

Feminist Accused of Sexual Harassment (Gallop), 199

feminist comics, 254

feminist protest, autotheory and, 22–23

feminist theory, 106–7; autotheory and, 19–20

fictional characters, life stories of, 15

Fields of Play: Constructing an Academic Life (Richardson), 199

Fierce Attachments: A Memoir (Gornick), 109

Index

filmic and video autobiographical works, 243–46

Film Portrait (Hill), 246

Fils (Doubrovsky), 35

Finding Life in the Land of Alzheimer's: One Daughter's Hopeful Story (Kessler), 84

Finding the Mother Tree: Discovering the Wisdom of the Forest (Simard), 237, 269

Finger, Anne, 23

Fink, Jennifer Natalya, 234

Finke, Laurie, 304

Fire at Sea (Rosi), 276

First, Ruth, 292

Fischer, Michael M. J., 25

Fisher, Carrie, 201

Fisher, M. F. K., 314

Fitzgerald, F. Scott, 328n6

Flanagan, Bob, 139

Flee (Rasmussen), 276

Flowers, Catherine Colman, 110, 238

Floyd, George, online mourning and, 259

Folkenflik, Robert, 4, 325n3

Following the Tambourine Man (Ellerby), 204

Fonda, Jane, 206

Food, Loss, and What We Ate (Lakshmi), 45

food memoir (gastrography), 45, 247–49

"Forbidden Gaze, Severed Sound" (Djebar), 128

Forbidden Lie$ (Broinowski), 155

Forbidden Love: A Harrowing True Story of Love and Revenge in Jordan (Khouri), 155

Forbidden Zone, The (Borden), 315

Forney, Ellen, 84, 214–15, 254

Foster, Frances Smith, 302

Foucauldian theory, agency and, 95

Foucault, Michel, 52, 53; on agency and power, 96; on confession in West, 225; on discursive regimes, 60; on identity and power, 196; positionality and, 66

Fournier, Lauren, 19, 23–24

Fox, George, 194, 305

Fox, Michael J., 231

Fragments: Memories of a Wartime Childhood (Wilkomirski), 32, 154

Frangello, Gina, 300

Frank, Anne, 132, 176

Franklin, Benjamin, 105, 134, 136, 194, 306; as Mrs. Silence Dogood, 155

Franklin, Cynthia G., 200

Franklinesque erratography, 210

Franzen, Jonathan, 271

Fraser, Sylvia, 47, 294

French Collection, The, series (Ringgold), 266

French Lessons (Kaplan), 200

Freud, Sigmund, 214, 216

Freudian theory, 195

Frey, James, 32, 149–50, 154, 203

Frick, Laurie, 93

Friedman, Susan Stanford, 52, 64, 76, 137, 329n12

Friends, Lovers, and the Big Terrible Thing: A Memoir (Perry), 201

Fries, Kenny, 88, 298

From Berlin to Jerusalem (Scholem), 306

From Harvey River: A Memoir of My Mother and Her Island (Goodison), 242

frontera, la, Anzaldúa's concept of, 79

Fruitful: Living with Contradictions. A Memoir of Modern Motherhood (Roiphe), 242

Fun Home: A Family Tragicomedy (Bechdel), 49, 119, 141, 242, 253–54, 310, 331n11

Fusco, Coco, 266

Gaddafi, Muammar, 258

Gagnier, Regenia, 222

Gailhard, Jean, 313

Gallop, Jane, 199

Gandhi, Mahatma, 165, 306

Gardner, Jared, 233, 252

Index

Garimara, Nugi. *See* Pilkington, Doris

Gatekeeper, The: A Memoir (Eagleton), 198

Gates, Henry Louis, Jr., 199

Gay, Roxane, 90, 248, 269

gay life narratives, 230–31; gay life writing and transformation of consciousness and practice, 88; gay marriage, life narrative of, 299; gay memoirs, 298. *See also* LGBTQI life writing

Geertz, Clifford, 25

Geistesgeschichte, exclusions of, 193–94

"Gender and War since 1600" website, 315

Gender Outlaw: On Men, Women, and the Rest of Us (Bornstein), 140, 299

GenderQueer: A Memoir (Kobabe), 300

GenderQueer: Voices from Beyond the Sexual Binary (Nestle, Howell, and Wilchins, eds.), 300

genealogical research, family narrative and, 239–40

Genette, Gérard, 29, 148, 186

genocide: Rwandan, 47, 260–61. *See also* Holocaust life writing; Rwandan genocide

genres, 193–318; academic memoir, 198–200; addiction narrative, 200–204; adoption narrative, 204–5; aging and life cycle narrative, 205–7; apology, 207; autie-biography, 207–8; autobiography variants, 209–11; autohagiography, 211; autothanatography, 211–12; autotopography, 212–13; bildungsroman, 224–25; biomythography, 213; breakdown and breakthrough narrative, 213–15; captivity narrative, 215–16; case study, 216–17; celebrity life narrative, 217–19; collaborative and collective life writing, 219–20; coming-of-age life narrative, 220–25; confession, 225–26; conversion narrative, 226; diary, 226–29; disability, illness, diversely embodied narratives, 229–35; ecobiography, ecocriticism,

and Anthropocene, 235–38; ethnic/postethnic life narrative, 238–39; family narratives, 239–43; filmic and video autobiographical works, 243–46; food memoir (gastrography), 247–49; geographies of life narrative, 249–51; graphic memoir, 251–56; grief narrative, 256–59; human rights narrative, 259–62; Indigenous life narrative, 262–65; interview, 265–66; journal, 266; *Künstlerroman,* 266–67; letters, 267–68; manifesto, 268–70; meditation, 270–71; memoir, 271–73; migrant/refugee life narrative, 273–77; nobody memoir, 277; oral history, 277–80; prosopography, 293; scriptotherapy, 293–94; second-person autobiography, 208; self-help narrative, 294–95; self-portrait *(autoportrait),* 295–96; serial life narrative, 296–98; sex and gender narrative, 298–302; "slave" narrative, 302–3; spiritual life narrative, 303–7; testimonio, 307–30; third-person autobiography, 208–9; trauma narrative, 308–11; travel narrative, 311–14; war memoir, 314–16; witnessing, 316–18

geographies of life narrative, 249–51

Germany's past, context of remembering and, 42

Gernalzick, Nadja, 329n13

"Gesture and the 'I' Fold" (Rotman), 329n11

Getz, Trevor R., 255

"Ghomanidad," defined, 237

Gibbon, Edward, 11

Gide, André, 88, 153

Gilbert, Elizabeth, 226, 306

Gilman, Charlotte Perkins, 213–14

Gilmore, Leigh, 6, 88, 156, 209–10; on human right narratives, 260; on Internet manifestos, 270; on Mailhot's narrative, 264; on memoir boom, 273; on narrative activism, 301–2;

Index

on positionality, 66; on trauma narrative, 308–9; on witness narrative, 317
Ginibi, Ruby Langford, 137
Giovanni, Nikki, 247
Girl, Interrupted (film), 245
Girl, Interrupted (Kaysen), 132–33, 214
Glass, Ira, 278
Glissant, Edouard, 57
Global Families: A History of Asian International Adoption in America (Choy), 205
Gloeckner, Phoebe, 227, 254
glossolalia, 126
Gluck, Sherna Berger, 277
Glückel of Hameln, 5, 132
Gobodo-Madikizela, Pumla, 261–62
Godard, Jean-Luc, 243
Goddesses, Les (Davey), 24
Goethe, Johann Wolfgang, von, 15, 18, 88, 194, 221, 266, 306
Goffman, Erving, 77
Gold, Carolyn, 230
Golden Apple of the Sun (Cole), 140, 229
Goldman, Emma, 238, 269
Gómez-Peña, Guillermo, 139, 266
González, Jennifer A., 77, 212
Good Boy: My Life in Seven Dogs (Boylan), 299
Goodison, Lorna G., 242
Gordon, Mary, 241
Gore, Albert, 236
Gorky, Maxim, 221
Gornick, Vivian, 109
Gosse, Edmund, 130, 206, 240, 307
Goswami, Namita, 93–94
Grace Abounding to the Chief of Sinners (Bunyan), 138, 226, 305
Grandin, Temple, 207
graphic "I"s, in life narratives, 180–81
graphic journalism, refugee stories and, 275
graphic medicine, 233, 254
graphic memoir, 84–85, 251–56, 272; distinguishing features of, 251–52; gender identity and, 300; on illness/

disability, 233; impacts of, 255–56; and influence of visual elements, 181; "I"s of, 118–19, 180–81; of mental illness, 215; as serial narratives, 297; sex and gender narrative and, 299; trauma and, 310
Gray, Mary L., 73–74
Grealy, Lucy, 67, 89
Great Expectations (Dickens), 221
"great man" focus, 193
Green, Justin, 252
grief narrative, 256–59
Grimes, William, 302
"Griot," 278
Grizzly Man (Herzog), 244
Grosz, Elizabeth, 82
Growing Up (Baker), 221
Grue, Jan, 232
Grusin, Richard, 329
Grylls, Bear, 314
Guerrilla Girls, 269
Gullette, Margaret Morganroth, 206–7
Gusdorf, Georges, 6, 325n5

Habeas Viscus (Weheliye), 95
Hadewijch, 304
Haefner, Joel, 210
Haizlip, Shirlee Taylor, 64–65, 240
Halbwachs, Maurice, 45
Haley, Alex, 106, 155
"Half-Moon on My Skin, A: A Memoir on Life with an Activity Tracker" (Prasopoulou), 93
Hall, Stuart, 67
Hamilton, Nigel, 10
Hamper, Ben, 68
Handbook of Autobiography/Autofiction (Wagner-Egelhaaf, ed.), 30, 197
Handbook of Autoethnography (Adams, Jones, and Ellis), 26
Hanna-Attisha, Mona, 237
Happening (Ernaux), 159–61, 297
Haraway, Donna, 92
Hare with Amber Eyes, The (Waal), 91
Harjo, Joy, 307

412   Index

Harrison, Kathryn, 88, 302, 317
Harrisson, Tom, 278
Hart, Francis, 207
Hartman, Saidiya, 143, 314
Harvey, Andrew, 306
Having Our Say: The Delany Sisters' First 100 Years (Delany and Delany), 206
Hayles, N. Katherine, 92
Haynes, Todd, 14, 218
Heart Berries: A Memoir (Mailhot), 136, 263–64
Heartbreaking Work of Staggering Genius, A (Eggers), 33
Hearth, Amy Hill, 206
Heavy: An American Memoir (Laymon), 90, 199
Hebdige, Dick, 301
Heinrich, Tobias, 274
Hellman, Lillian, 155
Héloïse, 267
Henderson, Mae Gwendolyn, 57, 126
Henke, Suzette, 203, 293–94
Hensel, Jana, 81
Henson, Maria Rosa, 317
Hepola, Sarah, 201
Hérémakhonon: A Novel (Condé), 33
Herzog, Werner, 35, 244, 330n9
Hesford, Wendy S., 80
heterobiography, 209
heteroglossia: consciousness and, 65; Irish speech and, 127
heteroglossic dialogism, 57, 126
heteronymic autobiography, 32
Hildegard of Bingen, 304
Hill, Jerome, 246
Hill, Karlos K., 44
Hillbilly Elegy: A Memoir of a Family and Culture in Crisis (Vance), 201
Hillers, Marta, 315, 331n19
Hilton, Paris, 217
Hirsch, Marianne, 47, 118, 140, 308
Hirsi Ali, Ayaan, 226; *Heretic*, 226; *Infidel*, 226
historians, versus autobiographical narrators, 9–10

History, Historians, and Autobiography (Popkin), 326n8
history, memory and, 41–42
History of Autobiography in Antiquity, A (Misch), 4–5, 193
History of a Voyage to the Land of Brazil, Otherwise Called America (Léry), 312
Hitler, Adolf, 155
HIV/AIDS sufferers, grief narratives and, 231, 258
hoaxing, autobiographical, 154–56
Hoffman, Eva, 80, 251
Hogan, Rebecca, 229
Holden, Philip, 327n9
Hold Still (Mann), 140
Holland, Jeff, 228
Holocaust life writing, 42, 44, 47, 252–53
Holzer, Jenny, 269
hooks, bell, 22
Hopkins, Gerard Manley, 270
Hornbacher, Marya, 208, 215, 248
Hornung, Alfred, 238, 330n5
Horwitz, Roger, 130
Hoskins, Andrew, 144
Howarth, William L., 295
Howell, Clare, 300
Howes, Craig, 8, 314
How I Grew (McCarthy), 114
How Our Lives Become Stories: Making Selves (Eakin), 83
How to Murder Your Life (Marnell), 201
Huff, Cynthia A., 210, 227, 229
Human Being Died That Night, A (Gobodo-Madikizela), 261
Human Flow (Ai Weiwei), 276
human genome project, illness narratives and, 233–34
Humanism, self-reflective literature and, 18
human rights narrative, 243, 259–62
human rights violations, witnessing "I" and, 119–21
human trafficking, narratives of, 216
Hunger (Gay), 90, 248
Hunger of Memory: The Education of

Index

Richard Rodriguez, an Autobiography (Rodriguez), 49, 83, 223
Hurricane Katrina, online mourning and, 259
Hurston, Zora Neale, 19, 107

I Am, I Am, I Am: Seventeen Brushes with Death (O'Farrell), 212
I Am Malala: The Story of the Girl Who Stood Up for Education and Was Shot by the Taliban (Yousafzai), 223–24
I Am Not Your Negro (Peck), 14
Ibn Khaldûn, 5
I, Carmelita Tropicana: Performing Between Cultures (Troyano), 301
identity, 64–75; cultural, 67; as difference and commonality, 64–65; "doing," 71–73; geopolitics of, 76; as historically specific, 67–69; as intersectional, 69–71; models of, 183–84; myths of, 102; positionality and performativity and, 65–67; as provisional, 65; racial, 64–65; reading for, 74–75; virtuality and, 73–74
ideological "I," 115–17
ideology, concept of agency and, 95–97
I Feel Bad about My Neck (Ephron), 205
If I Did It (Simpson), 272
"I Have a Dream" speech (King), 268–69
I Knock at the Door (O'Casey), 126–27
I Know Why the Caged Bird Sings (Angelou), 221, 296
I Live a Life Like Yours: A Memoir (Grue), 232
illness life narratives. *See* disability/illness life narratives
Il mio viaggio della speranza (My Voyage of Hope) (Mademba), 295
I Love Dick (Kraus), 24, 300–301
imaginary "I," 115
Imaginary Parents (Taylor and Taylor), 241
Imagining Adoption (Novy), 330n8
Imitatio Christi (Thomas à Kempis), 133–34
immigrant narratives, 127–28, 238

immigrants: disillusionment of, 274–75; life stories of, 104
I'm Not There (Haynes), 14, 218
Imperial Eyes: Travel Writing and Transculturation (Pratt), 24–25
"Impressions of an Indian Childhood" (Zitkala-Ša), 263
In an Instant: A Family's Journey of Love and Healing (Woodruff and Woodruff), 232
incest narratives, 302
Incidents in the Life of a Slave Girl: Written by Herself (Jacobs), 62–63, 133, 223, 303
Inconvenient Truth, An: The Planetary Emergency of Global Warming and What We Can Do About It (Gore), 236
Indigenous Australians: Dreaming of, 134; life writing of, 182, 236, 250
Indigenous cultures, self-narrative and, 5
Indigenous life narrative, 262–65
Indigenous/mestizo life writing, 250
Indigenous people, censorship of writing of, 107–8
Indigenous spiritual quests, 307
Indigenous stories, Australian, 48
In Love and Struggle: Letters in Contemporary Feminism (Jolly), 268
In Memory of Memory (Stepanova), 50
In My Mother's House (Chernin), 241
In My Own Moccasins: A Memoir of Resilience (Knott), 202
inner peace, black women's tradition of, 86
In Pain: A Bioethicist's Personal Struggle with Opioids (Rieder), 202
In Pharaoh's Army (Wolff), 157
inquiry, modes of, 188
In Retrospect: The Tragedy and Lessons of Vietnam (McNamara), 105, 207
In Search of Africa (Diawara), 28, 82
intellectual history, exclusions of, 193–94
Interesting Narrative of the Life of Olaudah Equiano or Gustavus Vassa the African, The (Equiano), 223, 302

414 Index

Interfaces: Women, Autobiography, Image, Performance (Smith and Watson), 296, 331n15

Interior Castle, The (Teresa of Avila), 130, 270

Internet: fantasized self-representation and, 155; life writing and, 110–11; utopian vision of, 73–74

interview, 265–66

In the Dream House: A Memoir (Machado), 302

Intimate Politics (Aptheker), 317

Intra-Venus (Wilke), 231

Introduction to the Devout Life (de Sales), 270

Invention of Solitude, The (Auster), 240, 241

Invisible Man (Ellison), 15

Invisible Wall, The (Bernstein), 206

I, Rigoberta Menchú: An Indian Woman in Guatemala (Menchú/Burgos-Debray), 101–2, 106–7, 307

Islamic-Arabic literature, self-narrative in, 5

Istanbul: Memories and the City (Pamuk), 236

I, Tituba, Black Witch of Salem (Condé), 224

Iverson, Stefan, 33

"I Was Born" (Olney), 330n2

Iyer, Pico, 314

Jackson, David, 88

Jacobs, Harriet A., 62–63, 133, 223, 270, 303

Jacques, Juliet, 299–300

Jamaica Kincaid: A Critical Companion (Paravisini-Gebert), 131

Jamison, Kay Redfield, 12, 214

Jamison, Leslie, 202, 295

Jane Eyre (Brontë), 15

Jansson, Tove, 268

Japan: autobiographical forms in, 5; World War II sex prisoners and, 293

Jarhead (film), 245

Jarhead (Swofford), 314

Jay-Z, 217

Jefferson, Margo, 240

Jemison, Mary, 147–48, 216

Jennings, Humphrey, 278

Jensen, Meg, 294

Jerome (Saint), 267

John of the Cross, 304

Johnson, Samuel, 267

Jolly, Margaretta, 268

Joseph Anton: A Memoir (Rushdie), 209

Joslin, Tom, 212, 256

Journal (Fox), 194, 305

journal, versus diary, 266

"Journal de prison, 1959" (Sarrazin), 109

journaling, addiction and, 203

Journal of the Plague Year, A (Defoe), 266

Journey in Ladakh (Harvey), 306

Joyce, James, 16, 29, 221, 266

Juana Inés de la Cruz, 87, 207, 304

Juletane (Warner-Vieyra), 33

Julian of Norwich, 304

Juska, Jane, 301

Just a Boy: The True Story of a Stolen Childhood (McCann), 256

Just Kids (Smith), 109, 218

Kabbalah, 306

Kaffir Boy: The True Story of a Black Youth's Coming of Age in Apartheid South Africa (Mathabane), 67

Kaigla Um Dayo, 307

Kairos (Erpenbeck), 42

Kaplan, Alice, 200

Kaplan, Caren, 101

Kardashian, Kim, 217

Karr, Mary, 201, 272, 294

Kartini, Raden Adjeng, 132

Katin, Miriam, 82, 233

Kawash, Samira, 303, 330n2

Kaysen, Susanna, 132–33, 214

Keitetsi, China, 316

Keller, Helen, 23

Kemble, Frances Anne "Fanny," 132

Kempe, Margery, 133, 181–82

Ken Bugul (Mariétou M'baye), 89, 101, 223

Index

Kennedy, Helen, 73–74
Kentridge, William, 246
Kermode, Frank, 36
Kessler, Lauren, 84
Khomeini, Ayatollah, 209
Khouri, Norma, 154
*Kid, The: What Happened after My
    Boyfriend and I Decided to Go Get
    Pregnant* (Savage), 242, 299
Kim, Jina, 234–35
Kimmerer, Robin Wall, 264–65
Kincaid, Jamaica, 15, 79, 314, 317
King, Martin Luther, Jr., 268–69
Kingdom, The (Carrère), 307
Kingsley, Mary, 314
Kingsolver, Barbara, 237, 248
Kingston, Maxine Hong, 7, 63, 129–30
Kiss, The: A Secret Life (Harrison), 88,
    302, 317
Kitchen Confidential (Bourdain), 247
Kittredge, William, 236
Kiyooka, Roy, 241
Kjerkegaard, Stefan, 34
Kleege, Georgina, 23
Knapp, Caroline, 202, 294–95
Knausgaard, Karl Ove, 33, 34, 61, 296, 326n16
Knott, Helen, 202
knowledge production, modes of, 188
Know My Name (Miller), 301
Kobabe, Maia, 300
Kobiela, Dorota, 14
Kollontai, Alexandra, 116
Krakauer, Jon, 330n9
Krans, Kim, 248
Kraus, Chris, 24, 300–301
Kristeva, Julia, 51
Krog, Antjie, 261, 317
Kruger, Barbara, 269
Krupat, Arnold, 263, 265
Kugler, Olivier, 275
Kuhn, Annette, 42, 198
Kulbaga, Theresa, 80
Kunka, Andrew J., 119
Künstlerroman, 266–67; defined, 221,
    266; examples of, 134

Kurosawa, Akira, 243
Kushner, Tony, 246
Kuusisto, Stephen, 23

Labé, Louise, 18, 138
Labumore, Elsie Roughsey, 137
Lacan, Jacques, 51, 131, 195
Lackey, Michael, 14
La Cour, Erin, 233, 254
Lady Murasaki, 5
Lakshmi, Padma, 45
Lanser, Susan, 125
Landsberg, Alison, 45
Landscape for a Good Woman (Steed-
    man), 13, 198–99, 217
Lane, Jim, 309n10, 330n9
Lang, Candace, 296
*Language of the Self, The: The Function of
    Language in Psychoanalysis* (Lacan),
    51, 131
Larcom, Lucy, 221–22
*Last Watch of the Night: Essays Too
    Personal and Otherwise* (Monette),
    259
Lather, Patti, 277–78
Latifa, 149
Latinx life writing, 249
Laub, Dori, 308
Lauretis, Teresa de, 59, 98
Lawlor, Hannie, 33
Laye, Camara, 33
Laymon, Kiese, 90, 199
Least Heat Moon, William, 314
Lee, Spike, 243
Lee, Valerie, 199
Leiris, Michel, 27, 135
Lejeune, Philippe, 103, 208, 209, 266;
    on addresses, 132; archival research
    and, 142–43; on author–reader
    relationship, 16–17; on autobi-
    ographical pact, 29, 36; autobiogra-
    phy defined by, 3–4; on biography
    versus autobiography, 10; on
    diaries, 227–28, 229; Doubrov-
    sky and, 31; on Ernaux's new

life writing genre, 158; on expanded scope of autobiographical texts, 326n13; on new life writing genre, 158

Lenart-Cheng, Helga, 220

Lenin, V. I., 269

Leonard, Joanne, 140

Léry, Jean de, 312

Lesbian Avengers, 269

lesbian life writing, 88, 298

Lessing, Doris, 143

Let Me Speak! (Barrios de Chungara), 128

Letter from Birmingham Jail (King), 268

letters, 267–68

Letters from Tove (Jansson), 268

Letters of a Javanese Princess (Kartini), 132

Letter to My Father: A Memoir (Couser), 198

Letting It Go (Katin), 47

Levels of Life (Barnes), 257

Leven? Or Theater? (Life? or Theater?) (film), 145

Levi, Primo, 47

Levy, Deborah, 297

Lewis, John, 255

LGBTQI life writing, 22, 89, 268, 298–302

Licorice Pizza (Anderson), 246

Lieutenant Nun, The: Memoir of a Basque Transvestite in the New World (Erauso), 298

Life (Cellini), 194

Life (Teresa of Avila), 5

Life and Religious Experience of Jarena Lee, The (Lee), 313

Life as Jamie Knows It: An Exceptional Child Grows Up (Bérubé), 200

Life as We Know It: A Father, a Family, and an Exceptional Child (Bérubé), 200

life narrative: versus autobiography, 153; autoethnography and, 24–29; autofiction and, 29–37; autotheoret-ical, 250–51; autotheory and, 17–24; biography and, 10–15; criteria for ethics of, 156–57; cross-disciplinary directions in, 197; digitized, 278–79; distinguishing among terms for, 6; embodied knowledge and, 82; history and, 8–10; identity models in, 67–68; increasing numbers of, 193; novel form and, 15–17; postcolonial, 33–34, 79–80; and preservation of memory, 81; rights of use, 262; terms of, 3–8. *See also* life writing; reading life narratives

life-narrative archive: differing concept of, 141–42. *See also* archives

life narrative genres. *See specific genres*

Life of William Grimes, the Runaway Slave, Written by Himself, The (Grimes), 302

Life on the Color Line: The True Story of a White Boy Who Discovered He Was Black (Williams), 239

Life on the Mississippi (Twain), 138

Life on the Run (Bradley), 218

Life? or Theater? (Leben? oder Theater?) (Salomon), 145

life stories, solicitors of, 104–5

Life Studies (Lowell), 138

Life without a Recipe (Abu-Jaber), 248

life writers, spiritual, 132–33

life writing: collaborative, 106; collaborator alterations in, 106–7; consumers/audiences of, 146–48; criticism of (*see* criticism: reframings of; New Critics); male, 88; misrepresentations of, 154–55; place and, 235–38; Western emphasis on, 194

Light Writing and Life Writing (Adams), 140

Lim, Shirley Geok-lin, 251, 273

linguistic address, relationality in, 50–51

Linton, Simi, 200, 231

Lionnet, Françoise, 24–26, 33–34, 224; creolization and, 57; *métissage* and, 126

Index

417

Lispector, Clarice, 24
Lit: A Memoir (Karr), 201, 294
Little School, The (Partnoy), 293
LiveJournal, 110
Lives of the Noble Grecians and Romans (Plutarch), 12
"Living Autobiography" (Levy), 297
Living My Life (Goldman), 238
Livingstone, David, 313
Logicomix, 255
Lonelygirl15 video series, 154
Long Loneliness, The (Day), 306
Long Walk to Freedom: The Autobiography of Nelson Mandela (Mandela), 292
Long Way Gone, A (Beah), 315–16, 317, 331n20
Lorde, Audre, 27–28, 70, 206, 212, 213, 231, 298
Lose Your Mother: A Journey along the Atlantic Slave Route (Hartman), 143
Losing My Mind: An Intimate Look at Life with Alzheimer's (DeBaggio), 85
Lost in Translation (Hoffman), 80, 251
Lotringer, Sylvère, 265–66, 301
Lover, The (Duras), 58, 131
Love's Work (Rose), 198
Loving in the War Years: Lo que nunca pasó por sus labios (Moraga), 21–22, 83, 269
Loving Vincent (Kobiela and Welchman), 14
Lowell, Robert, 138
Lucky (Sebold), 301, 317
Lumumba (Peck), 14
Lying (Slater), 214

Macfarlane, Robert, 110
Machado, Carmen Maria, 302
Madge, Charles, 278
Made in Detroit (Clemens), 239
Mademba, Bay, 295
Magic City (Rhodes), 43
Mailhot, Terèse Marie, 136, 264
Mairs, Nancy, 89, 231

Make It Scream, Make It Burn (Jamison), 202
Making Face, Making Soul = Haciendo Caras (Anzaldúa, ed.), 298
Making of an American, The (Riis), 222
Malcolm X, 74, 155
Malcolm X (film), 245
Man, Paul de, 200
Mandela, Nelson, 61, 292
manifesto, 268–70; defined, 268
"Manifesto of the 343" (Beauvoir), 269
Man in the Middle (Amaechi), 218
Mann, Sally, 140
Mann, Thomas, 16
Man Named Dave, A (Pelzer), 241
Manrique, Jaime, 298
Man's Place, A (Ernaux), 241
Mantel, Hillary, 13–14
Mapplethorpe, Robert, 218
Marbles: Mania, Depression, Michelangelo, and Me (Forney), 84, 215, 254
March Trilogy (Lewis), 255
Marcus Aurelius, 270
Markham, Beryl, 314
Marnell, Cat, 201
Martineau, Harriet, 6
Martz, Louis Lohr, 270
Mary: A Memoir (O'Hagan), 204
Mason, Wyatt, 35
Masschelein, Anneleen, 265
Mass Observation Project, 278
Matar, Hisham, 258
Mathabane, Mark, 67
Matthiessen, Peter, 306, 314
Maus (Spiegelman), 47, 297, 310, 317
Maus I: A Survivor's Tale: My Father Bleeds History (Spiegelman), 44, 252
Maus II: A Survivor's Tale: And Here My Troubles Began (Spiegelman), 119, 133, 253
McBride, James, 239
McCann, Richard, 256
McCarthy, Mary, 49, 114, 296
McCourt, Frank, 114–15, 223, 327n2, 328n7

McNamara, Robert S., 106, 207
McPhee, John, 314
media, 138–41
mediation, versus mediatization, 329n14
medicine, narrative, 235
meditation, 270–71
Meditations of Marcus Aurelius, 270
Meeting Faith (Adielé), 239
Mein Kampf (Hitler), 155
memoir, 271–73; versus autobiography, 271–72; current use of term, 7; historical use of, 4–5; secular, 271
Memoir: A History (Yagoda), 272
Memoir: An Introduction (Couser), 272
Memoirs from the Women's Prison (Saadawi), 292
Memoirs in Seven Little Books (Glückel of Hameln), 132
Memoirs of a Dutiful Daughter (Beauvoir), 221
Memoirs of the Life, Religious Experience, and Ministerial Travels and Labours of Mrs. Zilpha Elaw, an American Female of Colour (Elaw), 313
Memorial Drive: A Daughter's Memoir (Trethewey), 239
Memories of a Catholic Girlhood (McCarthy), 49
memory, 39–50; embodied, 84–85; as evidence, 12; intersubjective nature of, 45; models of, 41–42; reading for, 48–50; sensory, 39–41; spatiality and, 81–82; spatial rhetorics of, 80; technologies of, 41; trauma and, 46–48; unreliability of, 50. *See also* remembering; scriptotherapy; trauma
Memory and Narrative (Olney), 325n6
memory culture and, 40–41
Menakem, Resmaa, 86
Menand, Louis, 10
Menchú, Rigoberta, 101–2, 307
Men of Letters, Writing Lives (Broughton), 327n9
mental illness, stigma of, 214

mental illness treatment, "talking back" to, 214
Mernissi, Fatima, 307
Merton, Thomas, 81, 138, 304, 306
Meshes of the Afternoon (Deren), 246
métissage, 25
#MeToo movement, 88, 270
Michaelis, Arno, 203, 226
Middle East, life writing in, 250
migrant narratives, 27
migrant/refugee life narrative, 273–77
migrants, self-help narrative and, 295
Milani, Farzaneh, 325n4
Mill, John Stuart, 6, 194
Miller, Chanel, 301
Miller, Nancy K., 7, 22, 56–57, 198, 211, 233, 242, 272
Millet, Catherine, 301
Million Little Pieces, A (Frey), 32, 149–50, 154, 155–56, 203
Mills, Jennifer, 74
Min Kamp (Knausgaard), 327n16
Mintz, Susannah B., 230, 234
Miracle Worker (film), 245
Mirror Talk (Egan), 331n10
"Mirror Talk" (Miller, Eakin, Egan), 57
Miscellanies (D'Israeli), 4
Misch, Georg, 4–5, 193–94
missing and murdered Indigenous women, 264
Mitchell, David D., 234
Mitchell, W. J. T., 45
mixed-race children, adoption narratives and, 205
Modjeska, Drusilla, 12
Momaday, N. Scott, 236, 307
Moments of Being (Woolf), 58, 131, 266
Monette, Paul, 89–90, 130, 258–59, 296
Monkey Wrench Gang, The (Abbey), 235
Montagu, Mary Wortley, 267, 313
Montaigne, Michel de, 18, 27, 39, 80–81, 88, 130–31, 134, 207, 270, 312
Montéjo, Esteban, 302
Montéjo, Victor, 210
Moore, Michael, 245

Index

419

Moraga, Cherríe, 21–22, 83, 269, 298
More, Hannah, 325n3
Moretti, Nanni, 246
Morgan, Sally, 48, 243
Morris, Jan, 299, 314
Morris, Mary, 314
Moscow Diary (Benjamin), 20
Moser, Christian, 27, 329n13
"Motherhood Memoir," 242
Mothertalk (Kiyooka), 241
Mouffe, Chantal, 112
Muir, John, 235
Murder Book: A Graphic Memoir of a True Crime Obsession (Campbell), 255
Murder of Emmett Till, The: A Graphic History (Hill and Dodson), 44
Murdoch, Iris, 84
Musil, Robert, 16
My Body Politic (Linton), 200, 231
My Childhood (Rooke), 325n4
My Dark Places (Ellroy), 256
My Degeneration (Dunlap-Shohl), 254
My Father's Brain (Franzen), 271
My Father's House: A Memoir of Incest and Healing (Fraser), 47
My Forbidden Face (Latifa), 149
My Grandmother's Hands: Racialized Trauma and the Pathway to Mending Our Hearts and Bodies (Menakem), 86
My Life after Hate (Michaelis), 203, 226
My Life as a Russian Novel (Carrère), 35
My Life in France (Child), 247
My Life So Far (Fonda), 206
My Mother's House: A Daughter's Story (Chernin), 12
My Mother Was a Computer (Hayles), 92
My Place (Morgan), 48, 243
My Struggle (Knausgaard), 33, 34, 326n16

Nabokov, Vladimir, 40, 266
Nafisi, Azar, 224, 250
Nagar, Richa, 120, 220
Naghibi, Nima, 224

Nakamura, Lisa, 73–74
narrated "I," 112–13
narrating "I," 112; and earlier versus now self, 125; polyvocal, 125
narrative: automedial, 138–41; "somebody" versus "nobody," 62. *See also* genres; reading life narratives
narrative medicine, 235
Narrative of Sojourner Truth (Truth), 223
Narrative of the Life of Frederick Douglass (Douglass), 127–28, 222–23, 226
Narrative of the Life of Mrs. Charlotte Charke, A (Charke), 298
Narrative of the Life of Mrs. Mary Jemison, A (Jemison), 216
narrator: location and position of, 76; role of, 103
National Public Radio, story collections of, 278
Native American autobiography, 52, 243
Native American cultures, oral genealogy narratives and, 5
Native Americans: as-told-to narratives and, 106–7; remembering American past and, 43
Native Guard (Trethewey), 239
Nawabi, Amin, 276
Nayar, Pramod K., 210
Negroland: A Memoir (Jefferson), 240
Neihardt, John G., 106
Nelson, Maggie, 24, 61, 299
Nervous Conditions (Dangarembga), 33
Nestle, Joan, 300
Nestle, Marion, 248
new biography: use of term, 326n9
New Critics, emergence of, 194
New England Girlhood, A (Larcom), 221–22
Newman, Cardinal John Henry, 194, 226
Ngũgĩ wa Thiong'o, 292
Nierenberg, Amelia, 228
Nietzsche, Friedrich, 19
Night (Wiesel), 47
Night of the Gun, The (Carr), 202, 294
Nin, Anaïs, 294

9/11/2001, 47
Ning Lao T'ai-t'ai, 106
"nobody" memoir, 277
"nobody" narratives, 62, 277
Nobody Nowhere: The Extraordinary Autobiography of an Autistic (Williams), 207
Nomani, Asra, 306
Nora, Pierre, 45, 200
Noriega, Chon, 210
Norris, Kathleen, 110, 307
North American West, autobiography set in, 76–77
Not Becoming My Mother: And Other Things She Taught Me along the Way (Reichl), 241
Notebook 1967–68 (Lowell), 138
No Telephone to Heaven (Cliff), 224
Notes from Underground (Dostoyevsky), 15
Notes of a Native Son (Baldwin), 62
Notes on Grief (Adichie), 257
No Time Like the Future: An Optimist Considers Mortality (Fox), 231
Notorious B.I.G., 217
nouvelle Roman, 29
novel form, life narrative and, 15–17
Novy, Marianne, 330n8
Nugent, Thomas, 312
Nussbaum, Felicity A., 87–88

Obama, Barack, 63–64, 70, 239, 241
O'Beirne, Kathy, 301, 331n18
O'Brien, Edna, 221
O'Brien, Tim, 32, 314
O'Casey, Sean, 126, 266
O'Farrell, Maggie, 212
"Of Cannibals" (Montaigne), 312
O'Hagan, Margaret M., 204
O'Hagan, Sean, 265
Old in Art School: A Memoir of Starting (Painter), 199
Oliver, Kelly, 66
Olney, James, 330n2; on Augustine's *Confessions,* 41; on enslavement

narratives, 303; on life writing versus autobiography, 325n6; second-phase criticism and, 195
Ondaatje, Michael, 69–70, 110, 273–74
One Drop: My Father's Hidden Life— a Story of Face and Family Secrets (Broyard), 240
One Hundred Demons (Barry), 210
117 Days: An Account of Confinement and Interrogation under the South African 90-Day Detention Law (First), 292
1000 Years of Joys and Sorrows (Ai Weiwei), 57
online diaries, 227
online "I"s, 121–23
online media, voice and, 129
online narratives: evidence in, 180; questions for, 185–86
Opera of the World, An (Diawara), 28–29, 276
oral history, 277–80; collective, 278; digitized, 278–79
"Ordering the Family" (Watson), 330n6
Orlando (Woolf), 13
Ortiz-Vilarelle, Lisa, 199
Ortner, Sherry B., on agency, 97–98
Orwell, George, 314
otherness, cultural, 27
others: absent, 130; historical, 129–30
oughtabiography, 210
Our Cancer Year (Brabner and Pekar), 231
"outlaw genres," 101
Out of Africa (Dinesen), 136
Out of Joint (Felstiner), 200, 231
Out of Place: A Memoir (Said), 82, 199
Oxford History of Life-Writing, 197
Ozeki, Ruth, 32

Page, Ruth E., 73, 141
Painter, Nell Irvin, 199, 331n13
Palgrave Handbook of Auto/Biography, 197
Pamuk, Orhan, 236
Pankejeff, Sergei, 214

Index

Panofsky, Erwin, 325n4
paratext: defined, 148; online, 150–51; reading for, 176, 185–87
paratextual apparatuses, 148–52
paratextual materials, examples and effects of, 148–49
Paravisini-Gebert, Lisabeth, 131
Parker, David, 241, 330n5
Partnoy, Alicia, 293
Pascal, Blaise, 18, 270
Pascal, Roy, 31, 325n5
Pastoral Song: A Farmer's Journey (Rebanks), 237
Patai, Daphne, 277
Patterns of Childhood (Wolf), 113, 208
Paul the Apostle, 267
Pax, Salam, 227
Peck, Raoul, 14
Pekar, Harvey, 231
Pelzer, Dave, 241, 296, 317
Pensées (Pascal), 270
Pepys, Samuel, 227
Perec, Georges, 17
Peregrinatio (Egeria), 313
performativity, concept of, 66–67
Performing the Border (Biemann), 80
peritext, defined, 186
peritextual process, 149–50
Perrault, Jeanne, 209
Perreten, Peter F., 235
Perry, Matthew, 201
Persepolis (Satrapi), 253, 310
Persepolis 2 (Satrapi), 253
Persky, Aaron, 301
personal archives, allusions to, 170–71
Pessoa, Fernando, 32
Petrarch, 267, 305
Petticoat Commando, The (Brandt-Van Warmelo), 229
Phelan, James, 124, 327n2; on *Angela's Ashes,* 328n7; on autobiographical truth, 157, 164; on narrating versus narrated "I"s, 327n8
Phelan, Peggy, 118, 328n4
photography, 139–40

Picciolini, Christian, 203, 226
Picturing Ourselves: Photography and Autobiography (Rugg), 140
Pig Tails 'n Breadfruit: A Culinary Memoir (Clarke), 247
Pilkington, Doris (Nugi Garimara), 48, 317
Pilkington, Laetitia, 87
Piozzi, Hester Lynch (Thrale), 267
Piper, Adrian, 78
Pirogue, La (The Boat) (Touré), 276
Pirsig, Robert F., 314
Places in Between, The (Stewart), 236–37
Planet of the Blind (Kuusisto), 23
player's "I," 122
Playing with Fire: Feminist Thought and Activism through Seven Lives in India (Sangtin Writers), 120, 219–20, 310
Pliny, 267
Plummer, Ken, 103, 104, 132, 327n9, 331n17
Plutarch, 12
Poems, On Several Occasions (Yearsley), 325n3
Poem without a Hero (Akhmatova), 46–47
Poet Warrior (Harjo), 307
Poletti, Anna, 56, 141, 233, 244, 254
political movements, autotheory and, 22–23
Polley, Sarah, 244
Pope, Alexander, 267
Popkin, Jeremy D., 9, 200, 326n8
Poppy (Modjeska), 12
Portrait of the Artist as a Young Man (Joyce), 221, 266
positionality: concept of, 65–66; postcolonial terms for, 69
postcolonial agency, challenges of, 101
postcolonial narratives, archives and, 143–44
postcolonial theory, 69; autobiography and, 196
postcolonial women's writing, 224–25
postcolonial writing, voice and, 128

422 Index

postethnicity narratives, 238–39
postmemory, 47, 308, 327n2
postmodern theory: autobiography and, 196; Enlightenment subject and, 6; life writing criticism and, 195
post-traumatic stress disorder (PTSD), life narratives and, 232
power, Foucault's concept of, 96
POW memoirs, 314
Practice of Everyday Life, The (Certeau), 97
Practicing the Power of Now: Essential Teachings, Meditations, and Exercises (Tolle), 294
Prasopoulou, Elpida, 93
Pratt, Mary Louise, 24–26, 312
Preciado, Paul B., 24
Prelude, The (Wordsworth), 313
Pre-Traumatic-Stress Disorder, defined, 311
Prince, Nancy, 314
Prince Harry, Duke of Sussex, 265
prison: letters from, 268; as storytelling site, 109
Prisoner without a Name, Cell without a Number (Timerman), 109, 292
Progoff, Ira, 266
pronouns: author uses of, 113; *e, em, eir*, 300
prosopography, defined, 293
Prosser, Jay, 299
protocol-driven sites, 110
Proust, Marcel, 16, 29, 40, 328n6
Prozac Nation (Wurtzel), 201
Pruitt, Ida, 106
psychodynamic processes, relationality and, 51
PTSD, life narratives and, 232
Puar, Jasbir K., 72
Puerto Ricans, racialization of, 78–79

"Quarantine Diaries, The" (Nierenberg), 228
queer life narratives, 299
Quilting the Black-eyed Pea (Giovanni), 247

Quinby, Lee, 271
Quintilian, 293

Rabbit-Proof Fence (film), 245
Rabbit-Proof Fence (Pilkington), 48, 243, 317
racial identity, 64–65
racialization, 48
racism, environmental, 276–77
Radtke, Kristen, 255
Rak, Julie, 6–7, 164, 271, 272–73
Ramirez, José P., Jr., 232
Rampersad, Arnold, 218
Rancière, Jacques, 98
Rankine, Claudia, 24, 44–45, 138
Rapinoe, Megan, 217
Rasmussen, Jonas Poher, 276
Ray, Satyagit, 243
reader/audience, role of, 103
reading life narratives: agency and, 169–70; archives and, 170–71; audiences and addressees, 172; for authenticity, 172–73; and authority of experience, 180; automediality and, 174–75; body and embodiment and, 175; coaxers, coaches, and coercers and, 175–76; coherence and closure and, 176–77; collaborative, 177; collective projects of, 177–78; cultural meanings and, 182; distinguishing autobiographical "I"s and, 173–74; distinguishing narrating "I" and, 174; emplotment patterns and, 187–88; establishing authority in, 173; graphic "I"s and, 180–81; history and authorship of, 181–82; identity and, 183–84; memory and, 184; online, 185–86; for paratexts, 185–87; reading public and, 182–83; relationality and, 188; self-knowledge, modes of inquiry and, 188–89; space and place and, 189–90; storytelling sites and, 189; temporality and, 190; trauma, scriptotherapy and, 191; voice and, 191–92; and who can tell stories, 170

Index

423

reading life writing: ethical issues and, 178–79; for evidence, 179–80
Reading Lolita in Tehran (Nafisi), 224
reading publics, history of, 182–83
Real Estate (Levy), 297
Reality Hunger: A Manifesto (Shields), 156–57
Rebanks, James, 237
"Re-Constructing the Past" (Egdom), 330n1
Recovering, The: Intoxication and Its Aftermath (Jamison), 295
Reed-Danahay, Deborah, 25–26
Refuge: An Unnatural History of Family and Place (Williams), 110, 235, 307
refugee life narratives, 254
refugee narratives, on film, 275–76
refugees: self-help narrative and, 295; from war-torn countries, 276–77
Reichl, Ruth, 241, 247
relationality, 50–58; as assemblage, 55–56; autobiographical subjects and, 129–31; difference and, 51–52; in linguistic and rhetorical address, 50–51; psychodynamic processes and, 51; reading for, 56–58, 188; subjectivation and, 52–53; things and, 92; transspecies, 92; and vulnerability and ethical response, 53–55
"Relational Selves, Relational Lives" (Eakin), 56
Religio Medici (Browne), 270
remembering: contextual politics of, 42–43; kinds of, 184; politics of, 42–43
Renza, Louis, 160
"Representing Others" (Miller), 56
Republic of Imagination, The: America in Three Books (Nafisi), 224
Response, The (Sor Juana), 207
Return, The (Matar), 258
Reynolds, Stephen, 29
rhetorical address, relationality in, 50–51
Rhodes, Jewell Parker, 43
Rhys, Jean, 202

Richards, Keith, 61, 217
Richardson, Laurel, 199
Richter, Gerhard, 20–21
Rieder, Travis, 202
Rifkind, Candida, 255, 275
Riis, Jacob, 222
Rilke, Rainer Maria, 270
Rimbaud, Arthur, 218, 313
Rimmon-Kenan, Shlomith, 132
Ringgold, Faith, 113, 139, 266
"Riot Grrrl Manifesto" (Bikini Kill), 269
Rivethead: Tales from the Assembly Line (Hamper), 68
Roach, Rebecca, 265
Robbe-Grillet, Alain, 29
Rodrigues, Elizabeth, 274
Rodriguez, Richard, 49, 83, 223
Roger & Me (Moore), 245, 330n10
Roiphe, Anne, 242
Roland Barthes by Roland Barthes, 21, 29
Role of the Reader, The: Explorations in the Semiotics of Texts (Eco), 148
Ronsard, 18
Roo, Quintana, 257
Rooke, Tetz, 325n4
Rose, Gillian, 198
Rosenthal, Rachel, 266
Rosi, Gianfranco, 276
Rothberg, Michael, 46, 261
Rotman, Brian, 140–41, 328n11, 329n13
Rouch, Jean, 28
Rouch in Reverse (Diawara), 28–29
Round-Heeled Woman, A: My Late-Life Adventures in Sex and Romance (Juska), 301
Rousseau, Jean-Jacques, 27, 68, 74, 81, 88, 116, 194, 304
Rowlandson, Mary, captivity narrative of, 183
Rugg, Linda Haverty, 140
Rules of the Game, The (Leiris), 27
Running in the Family (Ondaatje), 69–70
Running with Scissors (Burroughs), 299
Rushdie, Salman, 209
Russell, Bertrand, 255

424 Index

Russia, war on Ukraine, 47
Rwandan genocide, 47, 260–61
Ryan, Michael, 89, 302
Rymhs, Deena, 210

Saadawi, Nawal El, 89, 224, 250, 292
Sacco, Joe, 254, 275
Sackville-West, Vita, 13
Sage, Lorna, 198
Said, Edward, 39, 67, 82, 199, 250, 251
Saldívar, Ramón, 13, 326n11
Salinger, J. D., 15
Salomon, Charlotte, 49–50, 145
Sand, George, 266
Sandy Hook Elementary School shootings, online mourning and, 259
Sangtin Writers, 120
Santiago, Esmeralda, 26, 67, 223, 247–48, 273
Sappho of Lesbos, 5
Sarraute, Nathalie, 29
Sarrazin, Albertine, 109
Sarton, May, 206
Sartre, Jean-Paul, 27, 221, 266
Satrapi, Marjane, 250, 253, 297
Saunders, Max, Doubrovsky and, 29, 31–32
Savage, Dan, 242, 299
Savage Nights (Les Nuits Fauves) (film), (Collard), 246
Scenes of Instruction (Awkward), 198
Schacter, Daniel L., 40
Schaffer, Kay, 145
Schmitt, Arnaud, 32, 34
Schnabel, Julian, 14, 232
Scholem, Gershom, 306
Schreiber, Maria, 122
Scott, Joan W., 59, 65, 96–97
scriptotherapy, 191, 203, 293–94
SCUM Manifesto (Solanas), 269
Seaver, James E., 147
Sebald, W. G., 13, 318
Sebold, Alice, 301, 317
Second Skins: The Body Narratives of Transsexuality (Prosser), 299

second-person autobiography, 208
second-wave feminists, life writing of, 128
Secret Life: An Autobiography (Ryan), 89, 302
Secret to Superhuman Strength, The (Bechdel), 49
Sedaris, David, 88
Seek You: A Journey through American Loneliness (Radtke), 255
self: computational, 92–93; questioning concepts of, 153
self-help narrative, 294–95
self-inquiry modes, 133–35
self-life inscription, 56
self-life narrator, versus biographer, 11–12
self-life writing, working definition of, 36–37
self-narrative, Indigenous cultures and, 5
self-portrait, 139, 295–96
self-presentation, Augustinian versus Greco-Roman, 17–18
self-reflexive literature: Humanism and, 18; men's narratives of, 89; women's narratives of, 88
Seneca, 267
Sengupta, Shuddhabrata, 71, 327n3
Serano, Julia, 299
serial life narrative, 296–98
settler colonialism, 79; "as-told-to" narratives and, 263; child sexual abuse and, 264
Seven-Storey Mountain, The (Merton), 138, 306
Sévigné, Marie de, 267
sex and gender narrative, 298–302
sexual abuse: men's narratives of, 89; women's narratives of, 88
sexual abuse narratives, 301
Sexual Life of Catherine M., The (Millet), 301
sexual-difference theory, 52
sexuality, embodiment and, 87–89
Shadow Man, The: A Daughter's Search for Her Father (Gordon), 241

Index

425

Shame (Ernaux), 159, 241–42
Shea, Daniel B., 225
Sheff, David, 106, 202
Sheff, Nic, 202
Shepard, Sam, 218
Sherman's March, 330n10
She's Not There: A Life in Two Genders
(Boylan), 299
Shewings of Julian of Norwich, 138, 304
Shields, David, 156
Shulevitz, Judith, 156
Siebers, Tobin, 234
Siegert, Bernhard, 267
significant others, in narrator's life story,
130
Signifying Bodies (Couser), 62
Sigourney, Lydia H., 267
Silko, Leslie Marmon, 41–42
Silverlake Life: The View from Here
(Joslin), 212, 256, 330n10
Simard, Suzanne, 237, 269
Simpson, O. J., 272
simulacrum diary, 229
Singer, Emily, 123
*Sisterlocking Discoarse: Race, Gender, and
the Twenty-First-Century Academy*
(Lee), 199
"Sketch of the Past, A" (Woolf), 81
"Sketches" (Zitkala-Ša), 242
Slater, Lauren, 214
Slaughter, Joseph, 223
"slave" narrative, 6, 147, 222–23, 302–3;
Bakhtinian model and, 57; challenges
to authenticity of, 62–63. *See also*
enslavement narrative; ex-slave
narrative
*Slow Cooked: An Unexpected Life in Food
Politics* (Nestle), 248
Small, David, 84, 254
Smart-Grosvenor, Vertamae, 247
Smith, John, 312
Smith, Patti, 61, 109, 217, 218
Smith, Sidonie, 145, 254, 331n16; on
performativity, 67; on travel narrative,
77

Smithies, Chris, 277–78
Snow Leopard, The (Matthiessen), 306
Snyder, Sharon, 234
sociality, spaces of, 77–78
social media: coaxers and coercers and,
108; protocol-driven, 135; voice and,
129
social practices, agency and, 98–99
sociopolitical memoir, 255
sociopolitical sites, 110
Socrates, 207
Soeting, Monica, 274
Solanas, Valerie, 269
solastalgia, 311
Sollors, Werner, 238
So Long a Letter (Bâ), 224
somatic practices, trauma and, 85–87
Somebody I Used to Know (Wharton),
231
"somebody memoir," 277
Somebody's Daughter (Rain), 264
*Somebody Somewhere: Breaking Free from
the World of Autism* (Williams), 207
Somewhere towards the End (Athill), 206
"song lines," Australian, 5
"Son of the Forest, A" (Apess), 263
*Soul of a Butterfly, The: Reflections on
Life's Journey* (Ali and Ali), 307
Soul on Ice (Cleaver), 109, 268
South Africa: political life narratives
from, 292; witness narratives and, 261
Southey, Robert, 4
Soyinka, Wole, 79
space(s): geopolitical, 78–80; in life
narratives, 189–90; as material
surround/place, 76–77; of sociality,
77–78
Spare (Prince Harry), 265
spatial rhetorics, 78–80
spatial tropes, 80–81
spatiality, 75–82, 137; broadened
definition of, 82; reading for, 81–82.
See also space(s)
Speak, Memory: A Memoir (Nabokov),
40, 266

426 Index

Specimen Days (Whitman), 141
Spender, Stephen, 3, 10–11
Spengemann, William C., 193
Spider (Bourgeois), 213
Spiegelman, Art, 44, 47, 119, 133, 252, 297, 317
Spiegelman, Vladek, 317
Spielberg, Steven, 246
Spílax̱m: A Weaving of Recovery, Resilience, and Resurgence (Campbell), 243
Spirit Run: A 6,000-Mile Marathon through North America's Stolen Land (Álvarez), 307
Spiritual Autobiography in Early America (Shea), 225
spiritual life narrative, 303–7; Christian, 303–6; Eastern religions, 306; Indigenous, 306–7; Jewish, 306; Muslim, 307
Spivak, Gayatri, 71, 101, 224, 326n15
Springsteen, Bruce, 217
Spurlock, Morgan, 244, 248
Squint: My Journey with Leprosy (Ramirez), 232
Stamant, Nicole, 296, 297
Stanley, Henry Morton, 313
Stanley, Liz, 229, 268
Stanton, Domna, 209
Starobinski, Jean, 208
Star Thrower, The (Eiseley), 138
Stayner, Cary, 262
Steedman, Carolyn, 13, 198, 217
Stein, Gertrude, 19, 64
Stepanova, Maria, 50
Stevens, Wallace, 270
Stewart, Rory, 236–37
St. Ignatius, 304–5
St. Ignatius' Own Story, as Told to Luis González de Cámara, 304–5
Stitches (Small), 84, 254
Stone Butch Blues (Feinberg), 299
Stories We Tell (Polley), 244
story action, roles in, 103
StoryCorps, 278
Story of My Life, The (Keller), 23

Story of My Life: The Autobiography of George Sand (Sand), 266
story quilts, 139, 266
Storyteller (Silko), 41–42
storytelling sites, 104–8, 189
Strachey, Lytton, 13
"Straight Mind, The" (Wittig), 269
Streisand, Barbra, 217
Strindberg, August, 140
Styron, William, 214
subject: Enlightenment concept of, 94; position versus subjectivity of, 66; positionality of, 65–66; postcolonial, 100–101; postmodern concept of, 195
subjectivation, relationality and, 52–53
subjectivity, paradigm shift in concept, 195–96
subject vulnerability, relationality and, 53–55
subordinated others, relationality of, 53
Sui Sin Far (Edith Maude Eaton), 273
Summertime (Coetzee), 36, 69
Super Size Me (Spurlock), 244, 248
Survival in Auschwitz: The Nazi Assault on Humanity (Levi), 47
Surviving Madness (Berzon), 298
Surviving the Slaughter: The Ordeal of a Rwandan Refugee in Zaire (Umutesi), 260–61
Sweeter the Juice, The: A Family Memoir in Black and White (Haizlip), 64–65, 240
Swofford, Anthony, 314
Syllabus (Barry), 199

Tainted Witness (Gilmore), 308
"talking back," 26, 213–14
Tantrika: Traveling the Road of Divine Love (Nomani), 306
Tarnation (Caouette), 244–45
Taylor, Diana, 144, 171
Taylor, Elizabeth, 169
Taylor, Sandra Ortiz, 241
Taylor, Sheila Ortiz, 241
Taylor, William, of Norwich, 4

Index

technology, memory and, 41
Telling Lies in Modern American Autobiography (Adams), 155
Telling Sexual Stories (Plummer), 103, 327n9, 331n17
temporality, 27–28; memory and, 40; reading for, 190
Temporality in American Filmic Autobiography (Gernalzick), 329n13
Tender at the Bone (Reichl), 247
Teresa of Avila, 5, 81, 87, 134, 138, 270, 304
testimonio, 5, 134, 210, 307–8
Testimony (Montejo), 210
Testo Junkie (Preciado), 24
Thackeray, William M., 313
"thanatographical" films, 330n10
Thanatography: Intoxicated by My Illness (Broyard), 233
Theroux, Paul, 314
things, embodiment and, 90–91
Things I Don't Want to Know (Levy), 297
Things I've Been Silent About: Memories of a Prodigal Daughter (Nafisi), 224
Things That Shatter (Kaigla), 307
Things They Carried, The (O'Brien), 32, 314
This Bridge Called My Back (Moraga and Anzaldúa, eds.), 269, 298
This Wild Darkness (Brodkey), 212, 233
Thomas à Kempis, 133–34
Thomson, Rosemarie Garland, 234
Thoreau, Henry David, 194, 270, 304
Threads: From the Refugee Crisis (Evans), 254, 275
Three Faces of Eve (film), 245
Till, Emmett, 44
Timerman, Jacobo, 109, 292
Tolle, Eckhart, 294
Tomb Sculpture (Panofsky), 325n4
topoi of interiority, 80–81
To Tell a Free Story (Andrews), 330n2
Touching the World (Eakin), 156
Touré, Moussa, 276
Tran, GB, 254, 275
Trans: A Memoir (Jacques), 300

transgender life narratives, 230–31
translations, 148
trans* life writing, 88, 299; heterogeneity of, 300; use of asterisk and, 299
transnational aspects of life writing, 13, 25–26, 76, 80, 121, 146, 148, 205
transracial adoptions, 205
trauma: embodiment, somatic practices, and, 85–87; memory and, 46–48; new theorizations of, 310
"Trauma in the Twenty-First Century" (Douglas and Whitlock, eds.), 310, 317
trauma narrative, 191, 293–94, 308–11; retraumatization and, 310; types of, 309
travel narrative, 311–14; characteristics of, 311; by women, 313–14
Travels of Marco Polo, The, 312
Treadwell, Timothy, 244
Trethewey, Natasha, 239
Trollope, Anthony, 313
Troubling the Angels: Women Living with HIV/AIDS (Lather and Smithies), 277–78
Troyano, Alina (Carmelita Tropicana), 139, 266, 301
True Confessions of an Albino Terrorist, The (Breytenbach), 292
True History of the Captivity and Restoration of Mrs. Mary Rowlandson, A (Rowlandson), 116
Truffaut, François, 243
"Truisms" (Holzer), 269
Trump, Donald, 154
Truth, Sojourner, 223, 268, 331n13
Truth and Poetry: From My Own Life (Goethe), 18–19, 194, 266
Truth and Reconciliation Commission, 261–62, 310
Turner, Brock, 301
Twain, Mark, 138, 140, 313
Tweak: Growing Up on Methamphetamines (Sheff), 106, 202
Twitch and Shout (Chitten), 245

Ukraine, Russia's war on, 47, 276
Umutesi, Marie Béatrice, 260
Underland: A Deep Time Journey
(Macfarlane), 110
Undoing Gender (Butler), 52
United States, cultural identity and, 67
*Unmasking Masculinity: A Critical
Autobiography* (Jackson), 88
Unquiet Mind, An (Jamison), 214
Unruly Bodies (Mintz), 230
Unwanted, The: Stories of Syrian Refugees
(Brown), 275
Up! (Apted), 278
Up from Slavery (Washington), 302
user-authored sites, 110–11

Valéry, Paul, 270
*Value of Solitude, The: The Ethics and
Spirituality of Aloneness in Autobiography* (Barbour), 304
Value of the Individual, The (Weintraub),
325n5
Van den Hengel, Louis, 210
Van der Kolk, Bessel, 85–86, 94
Van Gogh, Vincent, 14, 215
Vance, J. D., 201
Veils and Words (Milani), 325n4
Vernon, Alex, 314
*Vibration Cooking; or, The Travel Notes
of a Geechee Girl* (Smart-Grosvenor),
247
Vico, Giambattista, 18
Vietnamerica: A Family's Journey (Tran),
254, 275
Vindication of the Rights of Woman, A
(Wollstonecraft), 207
violence, collective memory and, 46
virtuality, identity and, 73–74
"Virtually Me: A Toolbox about Online
Self-Presentation" (Smith and
Watson), 92
Vision, A (Yeats), 134, 270
visual media, autoethnographic storytelling and, 28–29
Vita Nuova, La (Dante), 305

Vizenor, Gerald, 21
voice, 124–29; and bearing witness, 128;
external, 125–26; fantasized, 176; as
metaphor, 124–25; in polyvocal narration, 125; in postcolonial writing,
128; previously silenced, 62; reading
for, 191–92; unspeakable events and,
127–28
Voyage of the Beagle, The (Darwin), 313
vulnerability, relationality and, 53–55

Waal, Edmund de, 90–91
Wagner-Egelhaaf, Martina, 30
Waiting for Godot (Beckett), 118–19
Walden (Thoreau), 194, 270
Walker, Rebecca, 239, 241
Wambach, Abby, 217
Wang, Qian Julie, 274
Wanzo, Rebecca, 255
war memoir, 314–16
Warner-Vieyra, Myriam, 33
Washington, Booker T., 302
*Waste: One Woman's Fight against
America's Dirty Secret* (Flowers), 110,
238
Wasted (Hornbacher), 208, 248
Watson, Julia, 26, 330n6, 331n11
*Way I See It, The: A Personal Look at
Autism and Asperger's* (Grandin), 207
Way to Rainy Mountain, The (Momaday),
307
We Are on Our Own (Katin), 47, 82
web platforms, self-help, 295
Weheliye, Alexander, 95, 99
Weintraub, Karl Joachim, 6, 325n5
Weisz, Frans, 145
Welchman, Hugh, 14
Wells, Susan, 216
West, Rebecca, 314
Westover, Tara, 222
Wexler, Alice, 233–34
Wharton, Anna, 231
*What Is the What: The Autobiography of
Valentino Achak Deng* (Eggers), 33,
120–21, 224, 326n24

Index

"What Is to Be Done" (Lenin), 269

What I Wish People Knew about Dementia (Wharton), 231

What Remains (Was Bleibt) (Wolf), 42

What's in a Name? (Mills), 74

What the Eyes Don't See: The Story of Crisis, Resistance and Hope in an American City (Hanna-Attisha), 237–38

What They Saved: Pieces of a Jewish Past (Miller), 198

When I Died: Rx for Traumatic Brain Injury (Gold), 230

When I Was Puerto Rican (Santiago), 26, 67, 78, 223, 247–48

Where to Invade Next (Moore), 245

Whipping Girl: A Transexual Woman on Sexism and the Scapegoating of Femininity (Serano), 299

White American Youth: My Descent into America's Most Violent Hate Movement—and How I Got Out (Picciolini), 203, 226

white nationalist movements, conversion narratives of, 203, 226

Whitlock, Gillian, 91, 100, 149, 228, 251, 252, 274, 310

Whitman, Walt, 142

Whittier, John Greenleaf, 221

Why Be Happy When You Could Be Normal? (Winterson), 307

Why Comics? From Underground to Everywhere (Chute), 255

Wideman, Edmund, 130

Wideman, John Edgar, 11, 12

Wiegman, Robyn, 19–20, 71

Wiesel, Elie, 47

Wilchins, Riki Anne, 300

Wilde, Oscar, 88

Wilhelm Meister's Apprenticeship (Goethe), 15, 221

Wilke, Hannah, 231

Wilkomirski, Binjamin (Bruno Dösseker), 32, 154

Williams, Gregory Howard, 239

Williams, Ian, 233

Williams, Tennessee, 88

Williams, Raymond, 29

Williams, Terry Tempest, 110, 235, 307

Wingrove, Elizabeth, 97

Winterson, Jeannette, 307

Wishful Drinking (Fisher), 201

witnessing: in collective life writing, 178; risks of, 128–29

witnessing "I," 119–21

witness narrative, 316–18; paratexts and, 150; South African, 261

Wittig, Monique, 269

Wojnarowicz, David, 89–90

Wolf, Christa, 42, 114, 208

Wolf, Gary, 92–93, 123

Wolff, Tobias, 157

Wolf Man, The (Pankejeff), 214

Wollstonecraft, Mary, 207

Woman at Point Zero (Saadawi), 224

Woman in Berlin, A: Eight Weeks in a Conquered City (Hillers), 315, 331n19

Woman's Story, A (Ernaux), 241

Woman Warrior, The: Memoirs of a Girlhood among Ghosts (Kingston), 7, 63, 129–30

Women of Algiers in Their Apartment (Djebar), 224

women of color: life writing of, 128; sex and gender narrative and, 298

women's domestic lives, 6

women's life writing, 223–24; confessional, 88; postcolonial, 224–25; war memoirs, 314–15. *See also individual writers*

women's movement, sexual violence narratives and, 301

Wong, Hertha D. Sweet, 52

Wood, James, 326n16

Woodruff, Bob, 232

Woodruff, Lee, 232

Woods, Gioia, 76

Woodward, Kathleen, 206–7

Woolf, Virginia, 3, 13, 16, 29, 58, 81, 131, 227, 266, 328n6

430 Index

Words, The (Sartre), 27, 221, 266
Words to Say It: An Autobiographical Novel, The (Cardinal), 137
Wordsworth, William, 313
working-class narratives, 221–22
Work of Life Writing, The (Couser), 211
World War II, sex prisoners in, 293
W, Or the Memory of Childhood (Perec), 17
Wright, Richard, 62, 221
Wurtzel, Elizabeth, 201

Yagoda, Ben, 272
Yang, Gene Luen, 254
Yates, Frances A., 41
Year of Magical Thinking, The (Didion), 127, 256
Years, The (Ernaux), 28, 34, 161–63
Yearsley, Ann, 325n3
Yeats, William Butler, 134, 270
Yelin, Hannah, 219

Yellin, Jean Fagan, 63, 303
Yellow House, The: A Memoir (Broom), 65
Yellow Wallpaper, The (Gilman), 213–14
Yergeau, Melanie, 90
Yoga (Carrère), 35
Yogananda, 306
You Don't Have to Say You Love Me (Alexie), 43
"Your body is a battlefield" (Kruger), 269
Your Name Shall Be Tanga (Beyala), 224
Yousafzai, Malala, 224
Youth: Scenes from Provincial Life II (Coetzee), 69

Zami: A New Spelling of My Name (Lorde), 28, 70, 109, 213, 298
Zauner, Michelle, 241
Zitkala-Ša, 242, 263
Zlata's Diary: A Child's Life in Sarajevo (Filipović), 315

Sidonie Smith is the Lorna G. Goodison Distinguished University Professor Emerita of English and Women's and Gender Studies at the University of Michigan. Her books include *A Poetics of Women's Autobiography: Marginality and the Fictions of Self-Representation; Subjectivity, Identity, and the Body: Women's Autobiographical Practices in the Twentieth Century;* and *Moving Lives: Twentieth-Century Women's Travel Writing* (Minnesota, 2001). She is coauthor of *Human Rights and Narrated Lives: The Ethics of Recognition.*

Julia Watson is Academy Professor Emerita of Comparative Studies, a former associate dean of Arts and Sciences, and a core faculty member of Project Narrative at The Ohio State University.

Together, the authors have also written *Life Writing in the Long Run: A Smith and Watson Autobiography Studies Reader.* They have coedited *De/Colonizing the Subject: The Politics of Gender in Women's Autobiography* (Minnesota, 1992); *Getting a Life: Everyday Uses of Autobiography* (Minnesota, 1996); *Women, Autobiography, Theory: A Reader; Interfaces: Women, Autobiography, Image, Performance*; and *Before They Could Vote: American Women's Autobiographical Writing, 1819–1919.*

Milton Keynes UK
Ingram Content Group UK Ltd.
UKHW042036080724
445192UK00003B/10